Karen Ball

DAVID VON DREHLE is the author of three previous books, including the award-winning *Triangle,* an account of the Triangle shirtwaist factory fire, which *The New York Times* called "social history at its best." An editor at large at *Time* magazine, he and his family live in Kansas City.

ALSO BY DAVID VON DREHLE

Triangle:
The Fire That Changed America

Deadlock:
The Inside Story of America's Closest Election
(with the Political Staff of *The Washington Post*)

Among the Lowest of the Dead:
Inside Death Row

Additional Praise for *Rise to Greatness*

"A compelling, sharply written narrative of the events of 1862, when the odds were against the survival of the Union itself . . . Amid the shelves of Civil War tomes, *Rise to Greatness* stands out as a brisk, compact history of Lincoln's evolution as a leader. Von Drehle persuasively calls 1862 'the hinge of American history.'" —*Miami Herald*

"Riveting . . . Equal parts war story, political intrigue, and character study, the book at times reads as much like a John Grisham page-turner as serious history. . . . For those with an invigorated taste to learn more about Lincoln—the real man, not the icon—*Rise to Greatness* is a must read." —*Omaha World-Herald*

"More has been written and discussed about Abraham Lincoln than about any other U.S. president, and for good reason. . . . The Von Drehle book and the Spielberg film effectively serve as bookends to the story of how Lincoln's personality allowed him to navigate and shape the beginning of the war and the end of it." —*Harvard Business Review*

"Appealingly written and artistically constructed . . . Von Drehle, a first-rank narrator, writes better than most historians. . . . [His] largest contribution lies in his illuminating discussions of Lincoln as a superb leader." —*The Oregonian*

"A marvelous and gripping story, compellingly and beautifully written." —*Commentary Magazine*

"In *Rise to Greatness*, acclaimed author David Von Drehle has created a deeply human portrait of arguably America's greatest president, fueled by a rich, dramatic narrative focusing on our most fateful year." —*The Blaze*

"Brilliant." —*Real Clear Politics*

RISE TO GREATNESS

RISE TO GREATNESS

ABRAHAM LINCOLN *and*

America's Most Perilous Year

DAVID VON DREHLE

Picador   Henry Holt and Company   New York

www.picadorusa.com
www.twitter.com/picadorusa • www.facebook.com/picadorusa
picadorbookroom.tumblr.com

Picador® is a U.S. registered trademark and is used by Henry Holt and Company under license from Pan Books Limited.

For book club information, please visit www.facebook.com/picadorbookclub or e-mail marketing@picadorusa.com.

Designed by Kelly S. Too
Maps by Gene Thorp

The Library of Congress has cataloged the Henry Holt and Company edition as follows:

Von Drehle, David.
    Rise to greatness : Abraham Lincoln and America's most perilous year / David Von Drehle.—1st ed.
        p.   cm.
    Includes bibliographical references and index.
    ISBN 978-0-8050-7970-8
    1. Lincoln, Abraham, 1809–1865.   2. Lincoln, Abraham, 1809–1865—Military leadership.   3. Political leadership—United States—History—19th century.   4. United States—Politics and government—1861–1865.   5. United States—History—Civil War, 1861–1865.   I. Title.   II. Title: Abraham Lincoln and the making of America.
    E457.45.V67 2012
    973.7092—dc23
    [B]   2012013053

Picador ISBN 978-1-250-03780-0

Picador books may be purchased for educational, business, or promotional use. For information on bulk purchases, please contact Macmillan Corporate and Premium Sales Department at 1-800-221-7945, extension 5442, or write specialmarkets@macmillan.com.

First published in the United States by Henry Holt and Company

First Picador Edition: October 2013

10   9   8   7   6   5   4   3   2   1

For Henry, Ella, Addie, and Clara:
Never doubt the power of courage and determination.

CONTENTS

RISE TO GREATNESS

"SO MUCH WAS ALL COMPRESSED"

The year began with a day so warm and fine that only the calendar said January. There would be few pleasant moments in 1862, but New Year's Day in Washington, D.C., was one of them. Everyone was out enjoying the sunshine that morning—women in demure bonnets, men wishing they had left their overcoats at home, children dodging and shouting. The dusty streets of the half-built city were filled with people making their way toward the White House, where, by tradition, the president threw open the doors on the first day of each year.

Never had there been so large a crowd. The capital had doubled in size in the previous six months and was rapidly doubling again, as young men by the tens of thousands poured into Washington to join the Army of the Potomac. In April 1861, when war broke out between North and South, the entire U.S. Army numbered about 16,000 men, spread in little garrisons across the continent. By November, nearly five times that number, some 75,000 troops, could be mustered in a single field outside Washington for a presidential review. The ranking U.S. general planned to lead a column of more than a quarter of a million troops against the rebellious South.

Everywhere one looked in the capital, there were soldiers and more soldiers, brimming with zeal, eager for action, ignorant of war. They filled camps covering miles of hillsides in all directions. By day, the untested warriors marched and drilled, or cut logs and dug trenches to ring the capital with forts and firing pits. By night, some crowded into slapdash saloons and boardinghouse brothels. This instant army, like a great magnet, attracted regiments of merchants, job seekers, journalists, do-gooders, adventurers, spies, thieves, and would-be war contractors. A dull, swampy city was transformed in weeks into an overcrowded hive of patriotism, opportunism, and paranoia.

On the new year's first morning, multitudes packed themselves into the blocks around the Executive Mansion, flowing down wooden sidewalks and dirt streets onto Pennsylvania Avenue, Washington's only paved thoroughfare. There, the clip-clop of horseshoes and clanking of swords signaled the passage of freshly minted officers in full regalia: gold braid, white gloves, yellow sashes, obsidian boots. Carriage wheels rattled and friends called greetings, while somewhere in the distance, a Marine band blared martial music. Directly north of the White House, in the grand town houses around Lafayette Square, servants hurried to finish polishing the silver and laying out refreshments, for it was also tradition that the owners of these houses—cabinet members and sea captains and confidants of presidents past and present—would open their own doors.

The New Year's Day open house was a ritual of democracy in the spirit of Andrew Jackson, whose statue, atop a rearing horse, adorned the center of Lafayette Square. On this one day, everyone was welcome in the halls of power, from statesmen to workingmen, from consuls to clerks, from the Roman-nosed senator Orville Hickman Browning to the scoundrel who picked Browning's pocket. It was "the greatest jam ever witnessed on any similar occasion," one newspaper correspondent observed. The people of Washington, it seemed, had somehow agreed for a few hours to forget their desperate situation and celebrate a new beginning.

Absent the holiday exuberance, however, a cool assessment of the country's present circumstances would show that the American republic was in grave danger. The hope that secession fever would burn itself out was being trampled in the rush to battle stations. Strategies for reviving pro-Union sentiments in the South were stymied by the sheer size of the breakaway Confederate States of America, which covered an expanse larger than the entire European territory conquered by Napoleon. A pocket of loyalists in western Virginia had been liberated the previous summer by Union troops marching eastward from Ohio, but the pro-Union population of the more remote Appalachian Mountains, in eastern Tennessee and western North Carolina, was scarcely reachable down long dirt roads through hostile territory. Elsewhere in Dixie, what Union sentiment survived was scattered and cowed. The Confederacy was in the process of mobilizing a greater percentage of its population as soldiers than any European power had ever achieved. Those troops were led by some of the most experienced military men on the North American continent, starting with Confederate president Jefferson Davis, a West Point graduate, combat veteran, and former U.S. secretary of war.

The Confederacy also wielded a powerful economic weapon: near total control of the global cotton supply, at a time when textiles were driving the industrial revolution and cotton was perhaps the world's most important commodity. The cotton embargo enforced by rebel leaders was a gun to the heads of the British and French governments, putting tremendous pressure on them to support Southern independence. Pressure aside, the idea that the Confederacy—now a powerful country in its own right—could be tamed and forced back into the Union by an army of raw volunteers, led by an unschooled frontier lawyer as commander in chief, struck most European observers as far-fetched, even preposterous. "It is in the highest Degree likely that the North will not be able to subdue the South," the British prime minister, Lord Palmerston, counseled his Foreign Office.

Such skepticism was reinforced by conditions on the ground. Rebel soldiers menaced Washington from nearby Manassas, Virginia, where they had routed a Union army a few months earlier. Jefferson Davis was weighing a campaign into Maryland to stir up secessionists and cut off the capital from the North. Confederate artillery commanded the Potomac River above and below the capital, effectively sealing the waterway. No one in civilian authority had any detailed knowledge of the plans being prepared by the Union's top general, George B. McClellan; worse, McClellan was ill and rumored to be dying.

The federal government, meanwhile, appeared overwhelmed. The president was increasingly seen as feckless and inadequate. Congress was in the hands of a political party that had never governed before. The Treasury Department was broke, yet federal spending was multiplying as never before; in 1862, the government would spend six times as much as in 1861. (Northern banks, fearing a panic by demoralized investors, had closed their exchange windows, refusing to redeem paper money with gold or silver.) The War Department was a corrupt shambles, its chief on the verge of being fired. Despairing State Department envoys to Britain and France believed that the great powers were aligned against their

besieged government; it appeared to be only a matter of time before
Europe would intervene to settle the conflict in favor of the Confederacy. A rebel diplomat crowed from London, "At present there is a prob-
ability that our recognition by her Britannic Majesty's Government will
not be much longer delayed." President Davis considered European
intervention almost inevitable, and he shaped his strategies around that
confidence.

To the east of the White House, at the far end of that lone paved avenue, stood the unfinished U.S. Capitol, darkly crowned by the cast-iron
skeleton of an enormous dome. To the south of the mansion, across a
fetid bog, rose the sad stump of the Washington Monument, abandoned
for lack of funds. These uncompleted projects were silent reminders that
great things had been planned in this city, and large dreams dreamt. The
boldest of all the American dreams was the vision of a great new nation
that would span the continent, dominate the hemisphere, and rival any
country on earth. This dream of one nation indivisible, from sea to shin-
ing sea, was the true prize at stake in the terrible months ahead.

Americans in 1862 understood what later generations have largely forgotten: if secession managed a first success, there would be no logical end
to it. Why would two nations, North and South, neatly divide the space
and resources they once had shared? New and more complex fault lines
would surely open. Already, respectable New Yorkers could be heard suggesting that their city ought to declare itself an independent free port,
like Hamburg in Europe. The bonds holding New England to the old
Northwest—Ohio, Indiana, Illinois, Iowa, Michigan, Wisconsin—were
weak and fraying. And if the Union shattered east of the Mississippi, there
would be little to connect any of the pieces to the treasure lands of the
West. A strong current of independence still ran through the old Republic
of Texas; how could anyone be confident that the Lone Star State would
remain bound to the Confederacy? In Missouri, the celebrated explorer
and politician John C. Frémont was said to be scheming to create an independent nation on the western banks of the Big Muddy. Beside the Pacific,
Californians were talking about striking out on their own—after all, less
than a dozen years of statehood tied them to the faraway Union.

Secession, then, was a tiger that might bite in many directions. As
Andrew Johnson of Tennessee, a leading Southern Unionist, asked, "If
there is one division of the states, will there not be more than one?"
Wouldn't North America soon be as fragmented and war-prone as Europe,

"thirty-three petty governments with a little prince in one, a potentate in another, a little aristocracy in a third, a little democracy in a fourth, and a republic somewhere else; a citizen not being able to pass from one State to another without a passport . . . with quarrelling and warring among the little petty powers, which would result in anarchy?" Johnson argued persuasively that dissolution of the Union would "only be the beginning of endless war."

Nor was territory the only thing at stake. Secession, if allowed to stand, would deliver a fatal blow to the ideal of constitutional government in a diverse nation. If the U.S. Constitution could be dissolved by a dissatisfied minority, then it was unsustainable for the long run. Such a system could solve only easy problems and survive only mild disagreements. If secession prevailed, the Constitution of Madison, Hamilton, Jay, and Washington would fail the test of great governments, which is the ability to endure, even flourish, through crisis. As the president had recently put it in his annual message to Congress, "The insurrection is largely, if not exclusively, a war upon the first principle of popular government—the rights of the people." (Two years later, at Gettysburg, he would put the case more memorably.) Southerners maintained that they were fighting for their own rights, especially the right to their lawful property, namely slaves; and to travel with that property through Northern states; and to live without fear that abolitionists would encourage runaways or incite slave uprisings. But many in the North believed that the integrity of the nation came first, for no rights of any kind could be guaranteed by a powerless government. Union, in fact, was the cornerstone of the Constitution, and it said so with the opening words of the Preamble: "We the People, in order to form a more perfect Union . . ."

In the speeches and posters and banners and newspapers that rallied the soldiers to Washington, the words "Union" and "Freedom" were virtually inseparable. But when the cards of history were still facedown, to believe that the United States would ultimately survive this crisis required a leap of faith, and as the second year of secession began, that leap was increasingly difficult to make. From the days of the Romans to revolutionary France, no republic had ever survived such a calamity. Both experience and history suggested that—with so much at risk and such strong enemies—only a dictatorship could reunite the country.

In the smoke-choked barrooms of Washington's finest hotels, at the dinner tables of senior Union officers, in the drawing rooms of

Washington's leading politicians, the possibility that a military dictator might soon replace the president was endlessly discussed. McClellan, the Union commander, had toyed with the idea that he might become exactly that sort of savior: "I almost think were I to win some small success now, I could become Dictator," he wrote to his wife, and he did nothing to discourage the press from assigning him the nickname "the Young Napoleon." He even posed for official photographs with his hand tucked into his tunic.

Other murmurings around Washington conjured John Frémont delivering the coup d'état. Frémont's wife, the formidable daughter of Missouri's legendary senator Thomas Hart Benton, had threatened something along those lines during an angry meeting with the president. Even Charles Sumner, chairman of the Senate Foreign Relations Committee, found himself pining for a despot. The man in the White House could wield virtually unlimited power in this crisis, Sumner wrote to a friend, "but how vain to have the power of a God, if not to use it God-like." Whatever face it wore, dictatorship seemed at least as plausible to reasonable people as the notion that a constitutional republic of elected leaders could somehow survive a trial as profound as the Civil War.

As thousands of people made their way to the White House on the first day of 1862, the city swirled with talk of conspiracies and coups, swinging wildly from military mania to existential dread and back again. With the nation sundered by war, the stakes were as plain as the morning's blue sky: the American experiment was on the brink of failure, a half-finished dream at risk of becoming as forlorn as the abandoned obelisk, as unrealized as the Capitol dome.

That balmy January day began what would prove the most eventful year in American history, and perhaps the most misunderstood. It was the year in which the Civil War became a cataclysm, the federal government became a colossus, and the Confederacy came nearest to winning its independence, yet suffered the key losses that led to its doom. Eighteen sixty-two sounded the death knell of slavery, and it forged the military leaders who would eventually win the war, men like Grant, Sherman, Sheridan, and Farragut. In indelible ink, it fashioned the astounding blueprint of modern America, an America of continental breadth, rapid communication, networked transportation, widespread education, industrial might, and high finance. At the same time, it revealed the dear cost of entry into that future, payable in blood and misery, on battlefields from Shiloh to Sharpsburg, Pea Ridge to Fredericksburg. Most of all, though, 1862 was the year the sixteenth president of the United States, Abraham Lincoln, rose to greatness.

As the year approached, one U.S. senator presciently observed: "Never has there been a moment in history when so much was all compressed into a little time." And never since the founding of the country had so much depended on the judgment, the cunning, the timing, and the sheer endurance of one man.

I

NEW YEAR'S DAY

Abraham Lincoln stood that morning in sunlight slanting through the tall windows of the Blue Room, taking his place at the head of a receiving line with his wife, Mary. For most Washingtonians, this open house was their first chance to see the new president up close. He cut such a strange figure, all angles and joints and imperfect proportions: giant feet, impossibly long limbs, enormous forehead, pendulous lip. His huge hands were stuffed into white kid gloves—like twin hams, he was liable to joke. Some tall men slouch self-consciously, but not Lincoln. He had always been proud of his physique, and enjoyed challenging other men to contests of strength, which he inevitably won. He used his size subtly to intimidate, even as he used his humor to put people off guard. At fifty-two, Lincoln was 180 pounds of muscle on a six-foot-three-and-three-quarter-inch frame, and he wore his black suit narrowly tailored to fit his sinewy shoulders and thin waist. He would soon be wasting away, losing as much as thirty pounds in three years, but for now Lincoln was still the virile figure of his campaign propaganda, the rail-splitter whose blend of brain and brawn reflected America's favored image of itself: strong, bright, and independent.

His friend and occasional bodyguard Ward Hill Lamon stood close to Lincoln that day. Lamon, too, was a strong and solid man, but in the eyes of the artist Alfred Waud, sketching the scene from the corner of the room, he looked ordinary beside the looming, dominant president. Lincoln had a shambling animal force about him, which some found appealing and others found unsettling. Women were constantly flirting with him; at the same time, some of Washington's leading Democrats referred to him as "the gorilla." Countering this force was his gentle, sorrowful expression, which was, according to a painter who studied him for a portrait, "remarkably pensive and tender, often inexpressibly sad, as if the reservoir of tears lay very near the surface."

Magnetic, keenly sensitive, often able to understand others better than they understood themselves, Lincoln was, nevertheless, profoundly isolated, and this was a source of his sadness. He "never had a confidant," his law partner and biographer William Herndon wrote. "He was the most reticent and mostly secretive man that ever existed." Lincoln usually masked this isolation behind jokes and anecdotes and apparent bursts of candor. But even his brief descriptions of his youth strike a note of profound loneliness; he was, he once wrote, "a strange, friendless, uneducated, penniless boy." His mother died when he was nine; soon afterward, Lincoln's father abandoned him and his sister in the wilderness, to be cared for only by a slightly older cousin. The father returned months later to find the Lincoln children filthy, poorly fed, and in rags. Now, four decades later, Abraham Lincoln was no longer a lonely genius on a raw frontier, but he bore the internal scars of a boy who learned not to let others too close.

As eleven A.M. approached—the hour when Washington's dignitaries would greet the president—a throng of visitors formed into a long line winding down Pennsylvania Avenue. Stationed at intervals, maintaining order, were uniformed officers of the new District of Columbia police department. (The capital had never before been large enough to warrant its own force.) The police opened a path through the crowd for members of Congress, cabinet secretaries, ambassadors, and generals. The carriage of Attorney General Edward Bates rolled up the curved driveway, past a mossy statue of Thomas Jefferson, and came to a stop at the tall doors. A Jovian man with thick gray hair swept back from his stern face, Bates took his place near the head of the line of dignitaries, and soon found himself reaching out to shake the president's hand. The master politician was an ardent hand-shaker, taking a half step forward and leaning into the grip while locking on with his blue-gray eyes. But as Bates felt his hand swallowed up and heard Lincoln greet him in his surprisingly high and reedy voice, he harbored unnerving doubts about this man's ability to meet the crisis.

The previous evening, Bates had been struck by how rudderless the president seemed, his apparent weakness revealing itself as never before during an extraordinary meeting at the White House. Coming at the end of a year of low moments, this was perhaps the lowest. With his cabinet gathered around him, Lincoln was forced to reveal under questioning by an aggressive delegation from Congress—the Joint Congressional Committee on the Conduct of the War—just how little he actually knew about the plans and operations of the Union armies. After the meeting, Bates sat up late into the night, confiding his fears to his diary.

The meeting would have rattled anyone's confidence, even had confidence not already been in such short supply. What happened that evening was simple enough: Congress flexed its muscles. The potential for tension between the legislative and executive branches was built into the Constitution, but that tension was made worse by the timing of the war. Congress was not in session when the Rebels fired on Fort Sumter in April 1861, so the president—who had been in office only a little more than a month—was free to set the country's war machinery in motion, and he promptly issued a flurry of executive orders and called for troops to be mustered. In July, the legislators convened long enough to be told that they needed to raise some $300 million for the war, a staggering amount given that the entire federal budget was less than $80 million. By the time Congress returned in December, the price tag had doubled, to some $50 million per month.

Bristling with pent-up frustration and ambition, the senators and representatives surveyed the war effort and saw only confusion, corruption, failure, and delay. This was a Congress of unusual clarity and appetite: after years of stalemate, of southern lawmakers thwarting northern agendas and vice versa, the South's secession had broken the logjam. The awakening power of the 37th Congress invigorated the members of the newly appointed Joint Committee on the Conduct of the War, and when they marched into Lincoln's workroom on New Year's Eve, they were champing at the bit.

The committee's chairman was Senator Benjamin Wade of Ohio, "Bluff Ben," a fiery abolitionist who believed that Lincoln was too soft on the war because he sympathized with slave owners. Twice in recent months, the president had overruled abolitionists in the military as they rushed to proclaim freedom for slaves. The first to do so was John Frémont, a hero in the president's fledgling Republican Party. When Lincoln voided Frémont's proclamation of freedom for slaves in Missouri, he outraged many of the same people who had worked to elect him just a year earlier. "The President has lost ground amazingly," wrote Senator William P. Fessenden of Maine. Then, in December, Lincoln had instructed government printers to destroy a report issued by Secretary of War Simon Cameron, in which Cameron called for emancipating slaves and arming them as Union troops. Again, the antislavery vanguard howled.

Lincoln endured the outrage because he believed the Union could not be saved without support from loyal slaveholders, especially those in his birthplace, Kentucky. That state was the strategic core of the country: Kentucky controlled the Ohio River and guarded the eastern flank of Missouri, another loyal slave state located on a key waterway. If Kentucky left the Union, and if Missouri followed, the Ohio and Mississippi Rivers would fall under Confederate control, strangling American commerce. "I think to lose Kentucky is nearly the same as to lose the whole game," Lincoln once said.

This sensible view made little impression on Senator Wade, who was neither strategic nor pragmatic. He was a man of passions who drank hard and swore often. To Wade, Lincoln's slow and calculating approach to slavery provided clear evidence of weak character in a man who, as Wade once put it, was "born of 'poor white trash' and educated in a slave state."

Now, in the flickering glow of gas lamps, as the last hours of 1861 ticked away, Wade opened the meeting with a dire accusation. "Mr. President, you are murdering your country by inches in consequence of the inactivity of the military and the want of a distinct policy in regard to slavery." The barrage continued from there. Why, the committee members demanded, had there been no movement of Union forces in the two months since the disastrous battle at Ball's Bluff, where the Rebels drove Union forces into the Potomac River, and bodies washed all the way to the Georgetown waterfront? Why were so many of the Union's leading generals members of the opposition Democratic Party? Was their lack of progress a sign of traitorous sympathy for the Confederates? Most important, what plans existed for attacking the rebels, and when would they be launched?

The interrogation of the president and his cabinet went on for some ninety minutes. Between the committee's hostile questions and the unsatisfying answers from Lincoln and his advisers, a "strange and dangerous" fact dawned, as Edward Bates noted: no one really knew what the generals were up to. "The secretary of war and the President are kept in ignorance of the actual condition of the army and [its] intended movements," the attorney general confided to his diary. Meanwhile, the rest of Lincoln's cabinet, Bates mused, came off as an assortment of chattering, uncooperative men, "each one ignorant of what his colleagues are doing." The blame for these sad truths, he concluded, lay with Abraham Lincoln, "an excellent man, and, in the main wise; but he lacks will and purpose, and, I greatly fear, he has not the power to command."

If Bates was correct, then never in the four score and five years of the nation's existence had such a gap yawned between a president's abilities and his burdens. On January 1, 1862, Lincoln's crises ranged from the fiscal to the global to the military—but they began at home. Mary Todd Lincoln, wearing a dark dress with a contrasting collar, and a flowered headpiece trailing ribbons, looked tiny beside the president as they greeted visitors to the White House. Yet, she too was a formidable person, and she presented her husband with a considerable set of challenges.

Nine years younger than he, Mary was less a soul mate than she was evidence that opposites attract. He was self-confident; she was insecure. He was disciplined; she was impulsive. He was melancholy; she was electrifying. Lincoln was swept away by the force of her personality, her sister recalled: "[He] was charmed with Mary's wit and fascinated with her quick sagacity." But Mary was also volatile, "one day so kindly, so considerate, so generous," the next "so unreasonable, so irritable." Her temper was notorious back home in Springfield, where she had once thrown hot coffee at her husband and another time bloodied his nose with a stick. If anything, her moods had worsened in Washington: the president's secretaries John Nicolay and John Hay complained about her behind her back, calling her "La Reine" when they were being generous and "the Hell-cat" when they weren't. But Mary was her husband's greatest supporter. She believed in him when others lost faith, and she nourished his enormous ambitions.

Unfortunately, Mary Lincoln's judgment was often abysmal. A friend recalled that as president, Lincoln lived "constantly under great apprehension lest his wife should do something which would bring him into disgrace." Her lavish spending and weakness for flattery had already threatened to fester into a scandal. "Flub-dubs for this damned old house!" Lincoln exploded when he learned how much Mary had poured into carpets and draperies and furniture and dishes at a time when Union soldiers were shivering under shoddy blankets. Soon enough the president would discover that she was manipulating White House accounts in an effort to mask her overspending. She was taking bribes from office seekers in exchange for her support. In one case, she was rumored to be having an affair with an unqualified job-hunter.

And there was more: a few weeks earlier an advance copy of the president's message to Congress had somehow turned up in the saucy *New York Herald*. Mary tried to have the White House gardener take the blame for the leak, but it was eventually traced to a disreputable bon vivant named Henry Wikoff—he preferred to be called "Chevalier Henry Wikoff"—who had sweet-talked his way into the first lady's confidence. The "Chevalier" was notorious for a memoir in which he described the time he kidnapped a woman in hopes of winning her love (only to wind up in prison), and his friendship with Mary scandalized the capital. "What does Mrs. Lincoln mean by . . . having anything to do with that world-renowned whoremonger and swindler?" wondered one prominent Republican. General John Wool, a seasoned veteran of the regular army, reported with concern that Mary had called on Wikoff at Willard's Hotel, where she met him in the lobby, helped him don his gloves, and rode off with him in her carriage. "Some very extraordinary storeys are told of this Lady," the general concluded. Evidently, Wikoff had persuaded Mary to give him a look at the text of the president's message, and had passed along the best parts to the *Herald*.

Yet another family scandal involved one of Mary's half-brothers, David Todd, an officer in the Confederate army. Until recently, Todd had served as commandant of the squalid Richmond warehouses hastily converted into prisons to hold Union soldiers captured in the battle of Bull Run. Reports had begun to reach the North of Todd's drunken brutality. His prisons were filthy; he had beaten and even stabbed prisoners. If his captives stood too close to the windows, it was said, he allowed guards to take potshots at them from the streets. Most offensive of all to Northern sensibilities, Lincoln's brother-in-law reportedly kicked the body of a dead Federal soldier into a Richmond street.

Distrust and suspicion were the nitrogen and oxygen of Washington's atmosphere; the city inhaled ordinary disagreements and exhaled charges of treason. A few weeks earlier, for example, General McClellan had accused *The New York Times* of aiding the Confederates by publishing maps of Federal positions. "A case of treasonable action as clear as any that can be found," he fumed, and he "urgently" recommended that Secretary of War Cameron censor the paper. Upon investigating the leak, Cameron quickly determined that the information in the newspaper had been made public by his own War Department. A minor episode, but one that gives a whiff of the poisonous cloud over the capital. In such an environment, it was no small matter to have a notorious traitor in the president's own family, and a first lady who consorted with a spy.

Lincoln's domestic life was impossible to separate from his official duties, not least because his home and his office were all crowded together on the second floor of the White House. Construction of a separate office wing for the president and his staff lay decades into the future. For now, the combination of Lincoln's young family and his rapidly expanding duties meant that space inside the Executive Mansion was taxed as never before. He and Mary shared quarters with their sons Willie and Tad; welcomed their older son, Robert, when he was home from college; made room for various visiting relatives from Mary's side of the family; and hosted their youngest sons' best friends, Bud and Holly Taft, for frequent sleepovers, all while giving over about a third of their square footage for Lincoln's office and cabinet room, plus work space for three clerks (two of whom shared a bedroom in the White House), plus a waiting room for the constant stream of visitors who demanded Lincoln's time. Often, the low grumbling of impatient favor seekers mixed with the stomps and shouts of rambunctious boys: Lincoln's sons were known to burst into their father's office at all hours. The boys didn't even leave for school; Mary had created a makeshift classroom for them and their friends at one end of the State Dining Room.

Fortunately, Lincoln was accustomed to bustle. As a boy, he once shared a one-room cabin with at least seven other people. Faced with the constant distractions of the wartime White House, he made good use of the powers of concentration he had developed in his youth, though to outsiders he often appeared to be lost in a daydream or deep in a trance. Lincoln also took advantage of his insomnia: "While others are asleep, I think," he explained. "Night is the only time I have to think." He often sought refuge beyond the White House walls. Lincoln had a way of suddenly turning up in offices and parlors around the capital, having walked or ridden over without fanfare. His tendency to drop in without warning was an irritant to stuffy characters like McClellan, an endearing quality to many others, and a source of worry among friends who feared for

Lincoln's safety as he strolled the streets or rode around on horseback and in open carriages.

The stifling atmosphere of the White House was made heavier by the blanket of grief spread by the growing conflict. Already, the war had touched Lincoln intimately: in fact, the first Union soldier killed in action was one of his former law clerks, a dashing young man named Elmer Ellsworth. On hearing the news, Lincoln burst into tears. The soldier's body was brought to the White House for a hero's funeral. A few months later, Senator Edward Baker—a friend so close that Lincoln had named his second son for him—was killed in the fiasco at Ball's Bluff. Lincoln "loved him like a brother," and would say that Baker's death was the "keenest blow" he suffered during the war. With his friends dying and his family torn in two (David Todd was one of several Lincoln in-laws fighting for the Confederacy), the president was one of the first Americans to learn just how bitter and painful this war of brothers would be.

As Lincoln welcomed visitors on New Year's Day, he finally had reason to hope that Mary's troubles were in capable hands, thanks to the man standing beside them in the reception line. A veteran bureaucrat of enormous charm and discretion, Benjamin French had mastered Washington protocol and grown wise to its snares. He was an ideal choice to serve as unofficial adviser, confidant, and minder; he would protect the first lady, as much as possible, from her own worst tendencies. French had made a strongly favorable impression on the Lincolns during a memorable evening at the White House a few weeks earlier. The occasion was a performance by "Herr Hermann," a famous sleight-of-hand artist, who consented to do a few of his tricks very slowly, so that the invited audience could see how the magic was accomplished. (At one point, Hermann asked the president for his handkerchief. "You've got me now," Lincoln replied. "I ain't got any!" The well-bred George McClellan, in attendance that night, was appalled by the president's uncouth response.) The Lincolns met French during the reception before the performance; the courtier immediately found much to admire in the first lady. She "looked remarkably well & would be taken for a young lady at a short distance," he thought. "She seemed much at her ease & strove to be very agreeable." French saw Mary as she wished to be seen, and he was the soul of discretion. Though he came to know her uncomfortably well ("I always felt as if the eyes of a hyena were upon me"), French would not list her offenses even in the confessional of his own diary: "It is not proper that I should write down, even here, all that I know!"

After reaching the end of the receiving line, Attorney General Bates turned to watch the arrival of the diplomatic corps—"a gawdy show," he thought of the exotic figures in their varied national costumes. This attitude would undoubtedly have been shared by many of his countrymen. Bates was a practical lawyer from St. Louis, crossroads of the frontier, where minds were trained on the new world, not the old. Lincoln, too, had probably taken a provincial perspective until his duties demanded otherwise; there is scant evidence that he gave much thought to foreign relations before he became president.

But now the world pressed in too powerfully to ignore. As the president's closest staff members, his secretaries Nicolay and Hay, wrote in their history of the Lincoln administration: "The most critical point of the contest on both sides was the possibility of foreign intervention." In his message to Congress in December, Lincoln had explained that securing support from foreign powers was the essential element of the Confederate strategy for victory. Mighty in cotton but weak in manufacturing, the Rebel states intended to lure Europe into the conflict—especially Great Britain, which possessed the naval strength that the Confederacy sorely lacked. British ships could break the Union blockade and open Southern ports, protecting cotton on its way out while allowing weapons and supplies to flow in. Lincoln well understood that the growing armies in Union blue would have little hope of conquering the rebellion unless he could keep the Europeans on the sidelines.

Among the envoys entering the Blue Room that day was a square-faced man with shiny black hair whose arrival sent a current of excitement through the crowd. Richard Bickerton Pemell Lyons, a career diplomat and the first Viscount Lyons, was Great Britain's minister to the United States. The two countries had an unusually complicated relationship; cousins in history, partners in commerce, they were riven by rivalry. Two times in less than a century they had been at war. In recent weeks, they had come dangerously close to a third.

The arrival of Lord Lyons sent a surge through the room because only a short time earlier, in late December, he had received instructions from

London to prepare for a formal withdrawal from Washington. This break in diplomacy would, if it came, almost certainly be followed by war. The crisis stemmed from the arrest of two Confederate officials as they attempted to reach Europe to appeal for support. Until the South's secession, both these men had been important figures at Washington events like this one. James Mason, a wild-haired Virginian, had been president pro tempore of the U.S. Senate. John Slidell of Louisiana had served in the Senate as well. As they embarked on their mission to Europe, yet another distinguished Washingtonian—navy captain Charles Wilkes, famed explorer of Antarctica and the Pacific—learned from his station in the Caribbean that Mason and Slidell could be found aboard the British steamship *Trent*. The idea of such high-ranking U.S. officials touring London and Paris to promote the breakup of the Republic was too much for Wilkes to swallow. He overtook the *Trent*, ordered a warning shot fired across her bow, then sent a boarding party to seize the traitorous former senators.

Wilkes's bold step was entirely unauthorized, and clearly violated Britain's declared neutrality in the North-South conflict. But the captain had shown exactly the sort of spine many Unionists were clamoring for from Washington, and he was glorified in Northern newspapers. Congress passed a resolution extolling his action and ordered a gold medal struck bearing his likeness. Lincoln, however, was put in a terrible spot, because the British were understandably furious. The *Trent* affair threatened to undo months of careful maneuvering to isolate the Confederacy.

Britain's elderly prime minister, Lord Palmerston, summoned his cabinet when the news reached London, flung his hat on the table, and declared: "You may stand for this, but damned if I will!" As he calmed down, though, the shrewd and patient Palmerston saw that the *Trent* crisis presented both an opportunity and a danger. His government was already annoyed with the United States over tariffs and the cotton shortage. And the United States had recently sent packing a British consul, Robert Bunch, because of his sympathy for the Confederacy. These issues aside, Britain had grave reservations about the rapid rise of the young nation. It might not be the worst thing for England if the South were to win its independence and disrupt the American ascent to international power.

In the wake of Captain Wilkes's rash act, the world watched to see whether Britain would use its muscle to break up the United States. Many influential figures hoped the answer would be yes. America's envoy to

France, William Dayton, reported that Europe's "aristocracy [is] bent upon . . . the destruction of our government and the permanent failure of our institutions." Another American diplomat, Cassius M. Clay, declared of England's ruling class, "They [hope] for our ruin! They are jealous of our power."

But Europe was no longer in thrall to its aristocrats. In England, the burgeoning middle class took pride in the British Empire's leading role in fighting the slave trade. The industrial working class felt kinship with the free-labor North against the slave-labor South. Palmerston's public, in other words, was deeply divided; so he moved with characteristic caution. He dispatched British troops to reinforce the Canadian border and instructed Lord Lyons to demand an apology from the American president. When the demand was presented to Queen Victoria for her approval, Her Majesty's husband, Prince Albert, lowered the heat still further, editing the document to give Lincoln more room to save face.

Even so, the prospect of freeing Mason and Slidell was a bitter one. The secretary of state, William Seward, devised an artful response to the British demands, claiming that respect for neutral ships was a "confessedly American" principle, and that therefore the United States would "cheerfully" agree to undo what Wilkes had done. After listening to Seward's draft, Lincoln tried, but failed, to make a logical case in favor of defiance. What he could not support by logic, he would not indulge out of emotion. So he gave Palmerston everything but a formal apology—and, by caving in, further inflamed the critics who judged him to be weak. "People are almost frantic with rage," Lincoln's friend Joseph Gillespie reported from Illinois. "Succumbing to England has ruined the Administration beyond redemption."

Now, the presence of Lord Lyons at the White House and his willingness to shake Lincoln's hand signified that the American response to the crisis was acceptable to Great Britain. The immediate danger was past and, this very morning, Mason and Slidell were walking out of a New York prison, free to resume their voyage. At least for the moment, England would remain a bystander in the Civil War. But Lincoln had seen how quickly the Europeans could rise to the verge of action, and he had discovered how strong pro-Confederate feelings ran in key precincts of Britain and France. He understood that only one thing would keep the foreign powers in check: Union victories. Of which, nine months into the war, there had been almost none.

As the receiving line moved forward, Lincoln greeted the last of the diplomats. According to protocol, they would be followed by members of the
Supreme Court, but justices were in short supply. Of the Court's nine
seats, two were vacant because their occupants had died and a third justice had resigned to join the Confederacy. These departures put Lincoln
in a tricky spot, because in those days Supreme Court justices were
appointed to represent the various federal judicial circuits. Two of the
three missing justices had represented regions that were now in rebellion.
To find loyal Southerners to fill those seats was a difficult proposition; on
the other hand, if Lincoln nominated Northerners, it might be read as a
sign that he was giving up on his effort to restore the Union and accept-
ing the departure of the South. This was the explanation that Lincoln
gave to Congress for his failure to fill the empty seats, and it was no doubt
true as far as it went. But something more was also at work. Of the three
branches of the federal government, only the Supreme Court was led by a
Southern sympathizer. This gave Lincoln reason to want the court to
remain as toothless as possible.

That New Year's morning, Chief Justice Roger B. Taney was not
among those who paid his respects at the White House. After more than
thirty years in the upper reaches of American government—first as attorney general, then as Treasury secretary, and for more than a quarter century as Chief Justice—Taney felt free to spurn the president he had come
to despise. The Chief Justice was oil to Lincoln's water, a well-born
Andrew Jackson Democrat where Lincoln was a self-made Henry Clay
Whig. Yet Taney, as much as any man, had put Lincoln on the road to the
presidency. As the author of the court's *Dred Scott* decision, the infamous
1857 ruling that people of African ancestry could never enjoy the constitutional rights of U.S. citizens, Taney convinced many moderate Northerners that the long-smoldering problem of slavery now threatened their
own freedom and the nation's survival. Taney's radical judgment effectively nullified the Missouri Compromise of 1820 and denied the authority given to residents of U.S. territories by the Kansas-Nebraska Act of
1854 to decide for themselves whether to prohibit slavery. The next step,
many commentators believed, would be a ruling that denied the authority of Northern states to ban slavery.

Lincoln's powerful critiques of the *Dred Scott* holding had helped to lift him from relative obscurity onto the national stage. In his famous "House Divided" speech, in his debates with Stephen A. Douglas, and yet again in the Cooper Union speech that opened his presidential bid, the prairie lawyer relentlessly attacked Taney's opinion, and even indicted Taney himself as part of a conspiracy to spread slavery. In his sly and folksy way, Lincoln eroded Taney's credibility and stature everywhere his speeches were published, for he spoke of the Chief Justice not with awe but with scorn, referring to the venerable jurist by his first name only: "Roger." Though Lincoln and Douglas would be linked forever, in many ways Taney was his true intellectual nemesis.

Now, more than four years after *Dred Scott,* most of the powerful friends of slavery had left the capital. Yet Taney remained. Others in Washington might express sympathy and even affection for the Confederacy, but Taney was still in a position to do something about it—or at least, to try. He had already ordered Lincoln to release suspected Rebel spies and saboteurs being held without charges in Maryland. Lincoln ignored the order, dealing with the prisoners on his own timetable. If given the chance, Taney was prepared to rule that Lincoln's call for volunteer troops, his blockade of Southern ports, and his emerging plans to pay for the war with paper money also violated the Constitution. And Taney would surely try to stop any forced emancipation of slaves. As Lincoln worked through these explosive issues, especially the core question of slavery, he had to avoid placing Taney in a position where he could turn the court's authority against him. In a battle for the Constitution, it would be a priceless propaganda victory for the South to have the Chief Justice denounce Lincoln as a lawless tyrant.

Following the justices came the military men, lushly bearded and vainglorious. There were many more than in past years, reflecting the swelling ranks of generals and colonels and majors and captains leading the Union's overnight armies. Each officer present at the White House stood in for perhaps a thousand more in camps across the country: the untested, largely untrained commanders of green troops from Maine to Missouri. In a matter of months, the Federal armed forces had grown nearly fiftyfold. "I very much doubt whether any other nation ever made such an effort in so short a time," one European observer ventured. And yet, in those vast armies, there was not a single combat-ready man with more than a few months' experience at leading large forces. In the words of one historian: "They knew almost nothing about the history and theory of war or of strategy." They were terribly ill-equipped: to prepare a campaign in the Mississippi River valley, the commanding general had to use maps he found in a bookstore. The Civil War, at this point, was a struggle directed by novice generals in command of amateur troops.

The senior officers from America's last significant war, the invasion of Mexico in 1846, were old men by 1862. Mere lieutenants in Mexico were now sporting stars on their shoulders, and making plans, in some cases, to lead columns of troops ten times the size of the armies that crossed the Rio Grande. Other Union generals had even less experience, or none at all. Volunteer militia were the backbone of the Civil War army, and volunteers elected their own officers. Thus, colonels often gained their rank merely by being the most popular men in the towns where the regiments were assembled. Or the richest: senior officers frequently earned their braid by purchasing uniforms and train tickets for their men. Often conniving, highly political, or—worst of all—incompetent as officers, America's mayors, newspaper editors, lawyers, factory owners, and sons of millionaires were recast in a twinkling as colonels in the grand crusade. Inevitably the colonels wanted to be brigadier generals, and nearly every brigadier a major general.

Lincoln's job was to glean somehow, from these thousands of unproven men, the few with the stuff of true leaders. As he was already discovering, a West Point education or a long stretch in uniform provided no guarantee of military ability. That January morning, in fact, Lincoln shook hands with General William B. Franklin, a fine engineer. (West Point specialized in turning out engineers.) He greeted General Samuel Heintzelman, a seasoned commander of frontier garrisons. He clasped hands with General Silas Casey, author of a soon-to-be-published manual of infantry tactics. These men knew everything that books could teach about war. They looked splendid in dress blue. But time would show that none was a true warrior-general, nor were many others like them.

If any man had seemed to radiate the promise of greatness, it was George McClellan. He had a powerful intellect (he graduated second in his West Point class), he exuded charisma, and he thrived on discipline. Diminutive—his men called him Little Mac—but broad-shouldered and dashingly mustached, McClellan looked born to be cast in bronze and, until he fell sick, he had been ubiquitous in the streets and camps of

Washington. From early morning until long past nightfall, McClellan could be seen striding purposefully from one meeting to the next, or storming impatiently about the capital on horseback. He also seemed to be blessed with the priceless gift of victors everywhere: good timing. Plucked from private life at the outbreak of the war, McClellan was placed in command of Ohio's volunteers. In the summer of 1861, he led a relatively small column of militia through western Virginia and, moving quickly, scattered Rebels and secured a vital railroad on the way. His triumphant little army was nearing Washington when another Union force, led by General Irwin McDowell, was whipped by the Rebels near the railroad junction at Manassas. Because he was close by and had a couple of minor victories to his name, McClellan was the obvious choice to assume command of the demoralized troops in and around the capital.

In that role, he worked something like a miracle, turning a multitude of raw volunteers into a disciplined army. Astride his big black charger, or smartly saluting troops as they paraded past his headquarters, or twirling his cap to acknowledge the cheers of his men, McClellan looked every inch the ideal leader in an age when Napoleon was the measure. Soon enough, the venerable Lieutenant General Winfield Scott decided that he was too old, at seventy-five, to vie with this exceedingly ambitious underling. On November 1, Scott retired as general in chief, and Lincoln promoted McClellan. Still just thirty-four, McClellan was suddenly overall leader of the world's largest armed force and, simultaneously, operational head of the Union's single biggest command, the Army of the Potomac. The job provided enough work for at least two able men, but McClellan assured Lincoln, saying, "I can do it all."

At first, the president believed that he and McClellan could work together. In what John Hay called a "fatherly" talk soon after the promotion, Lincoln told his young general: "Draw on me for all the sense I have, and all the information." But McClellan, a man of military training and eastern refinement, did not value the lessons accrued by the unpolished Lincoln. The more authority McClellan was given, the less respect he accorded the president until, by the beginning of 1862—having received all the favors Lincoln had to give—the general had cut Lincoln out of the loop almost entirely and begun developing his battle plans within a clique of like-minded men. Nor was McClellan's scorn reserved for Lincoln; he had a low opinion of nearly all politicians, believing that they inflamed disputes rather than resolved them. He preferred to think of himself as their opposite: the soul of reason, a master of crisis, the savior of the nation. "By some strange operation of magic I seem to have become *the* power in the land," McClellan exulted to his wife when he was called to the defense of the capital. He enjoyed "letter after letter . . . conversation after conversation . . . alluding to the Presidency, Dictatorship etc." that his supporters saw in his future. And though he disavowed any such goal, his relatives and friends, placed in key staff positions and high commands, weren't always so circumspect.

One evening in November, during one of his forays away from the stifling White House, Lincoln led Hay and Secretary of State Seward on a walk to McClellan's nearby headquarters. For weeks, the president had been trying to lead McClellan to the conviction that the fine brigades drilling in the warm, dry autumn fields around Washington must soon be put to use. Newspapers demanded action. Congress demanded action. Financiers of the nation's skyrocketing debt demanded action. The general's contempt for political pressure was leading to a dangerous blindness, Lincoln believed. But McClellan cared little for Lincoln's counsel, nor did he see the need to keep the president informed. "The Commander-in-Chief . . . has no business to know what is going on," he had declared. That evening, when Lincoln's little group entered the general's house, they were told that McClellan was out. Lincoln took a seat in the parlor. Eventually, the general burst into the house and stormed up the stairs. Lincoln waited another half hour; when at last he asked about the delay, he was informed that McClellan had gone to bed.

Hay was stunned by this "unparalleled insolence," which he read as "a portent" of evils to come. For the first time, the president's young secretary concluded that the loose talk about a military coup might have some basis in fact. Lincoln took the snub in stride, reminding Hay that a national crisis was no time to make points of etiquette. Over the next few days, the president outlined his thoughts for the general in writing. But McClellan was just as dismissive on paper as he was in person; he returned Lincoln's memo with a few unenlightening comments in the margins and a cryptic reference to a secret plan he was cooking up.

Outwardly, Lincoln was unperturbed. Inwardly, he was beginning to suspect that McClellan's personality was all wrong for his vast responsibilities. Wittingly or unwittingly, the president had helped to create the general's enormous power without realizing that the unseasoned young man harbored a dangerous combination of certitude and distrust. McClellan believed that he knew best in all things, and he confused questions with criticism, disagreement with enmity. He indulged a haughty pride that made him unwilling to explain his ideas or defend his actions, yet if others failed to support his unexplained decisions, then the fault was theirs, not his. "It is terrible to stand by & see the cowardice of the Pres[ident], the vileness of Seward, the rascality of Cameron," McClellan had recently written, ticking through his many inferiors in the cabinet. "Welles is an old woman—Bates an old fool. . . . The people think me all powerful. Never was there a greater mistake—I am thwarted & deceived by these incapables at every turn." Volatile and occasionally almost paranoid, McClellan bounced wildly between unfounded overconfidence and hand-wringing worry, so that he could not settle on a clear-eyed assessment of military or political situations.

Lincoln missed the more open communication he had enjoyed with Winfield Scott, who—though he was too old and sick to command troops—was a deeply experienced soldier. Scott was also genuinely respectful of the president and willing to help him gain an understanding of the enormous military task ahead. Now, with Scott gone from the capital and McClellan shutting him out, Lincoln began to seek advice from an informal network of men outside the chain of command, among them Montgomery Meigs, the master organizer who had engineered the Capitol dome project; Gustavus Fox, the can-do assistant navy secretary; and John Dahlgren, another navy man, who shared Lincoln's passion for new inventions, especially those involving guns. These were men more likely to solve a problem than to be one.

The president recognized, though, that he would have to develop and rely on his own judgments about how the war should be fought. Accordingly, the self-taught Lincoln decided to undertake a crash course in military tactics and strategy. Virtually everything he knew well, from prose style to politics, from arithmetic to law, he had learned through solitary reading, personal experience, conversation, and deep thought. He ordered a selection of books on military science from the stacks at the Library of Congress and began to work through them. Though "his reading was laborious and by no means rapid," one associate recalled, the absorbency of his mind made him a quick study. "He needed fewer 'explanations' than any other man I ever knew."

Hovering over everything on this fine January morning, the burden touching all others, was the problem of slavery. Everyone who greeted Lincoln that day had strong opinions about the topic, which in turn fed equally strong disagreements. The passage of a century and a half since 1862 has joined the Civil War and the demise of slavery as tightly as thunder and lightning. But as that year began, only the most zealous believed that the war must settle the future of slavery. Most felt, as the nation's founders had, that the key to holding the Union together was to avoid the issue as much as possible. Lincoln's generation of leaders had grown from childhood to maturity under the constant threat of disunion; they scarcely knew a time when American politics was not entering, enduring, or recuperating from a sectional crisis. Those earlier dramas—over Missouri statehood, nullification, the Mexican War, the Fugitive Slave Act, the Kansas-Nebraska Act—had been resolved short of an all-out war on slavery. Why must this be different?

Lincoln himself would eventually look back on the opening phases of the war and recall just how foggy the role of slavery had been. In his Second Inaugural Address, he said: "All knew that [slavery] was somehow the cause of the war," loading the word "somehow" with mystery. The Confederacy sought to "strengthen, perpetuate, and extend" slavery, he said, "while the Government claimed no right to do more than to restrict the territorial enlargement of it." In other words, the South was fighting to defend the slave system, but it didn't follow that the North was united by a desire to destroy slavery. This distinction, often confusing to later generations of Americans, was second nature to many of Lincoln's visitors. "Neither party expected" a war of great "magnitude," Lincoln continued, and "neither anticipated that the cause of the conflict might cease with or even before the conflict itself should cease." The result we now take for granted—a blood-soaked struggle leading to emancipation—was, at the start of 1862, still an "astounding" notion, as Lincoln put it.

Some of the members of Congress passing through the Blue Room to shake Lincoln's hand that day were drawn to that astounding possibility with all the fervor of crusaders. For men like Zachariah Chandler of Michigan, George Julian of Indiana, Lyman Trumbull of Illinois, and Henry Wilson and Charles Sumner of Massachusetts, abolition was a moral imperative, and the war was its hour of fulfillment. But there were other men, like Orville Browning of Illinois and Charles Wickliffe of Kentucky, for whom that notion was appalling. They were certain that a war to free the slaves was a war most Northerners would reject, and they had sound reasons for that belief. Browning's Illinois, for example, banned free blacks from settling within the state's boundaries. Slaveowners in Wickliffe's Kentucky, meanwhile, held 225,000 blacks in bondage. McClellan's words to an influential political leader land brutally on modern ears, but he was voicing a wish widespread in the early days of the war when he wrote: "Help me dodge the nigger—we want nothing to do with him."

Lincoln faced no greater challenge than that of holding these vastly differing parties together long enough for the war's own nature to reveal itself. To him, human history was an inexorable current that sometimes meandered, sometimes raged, but ultimately found its own course. And although it was his oft-spoken view that history was flowing away from slavery toward freedom, he believed that his most important responsibility was to keep the Union from breaking up short of that destination.

So while abolitionists pressed him for a war on slavery and conservatives pleaded with him to submerge the issue, Lincoln was steering a middle way, guided by two principles. First, his actions must be consistent with the Constitution; this would show Northern conservatives that he was not a radical, and simultaneously protect his flank against Chief Justice Taney. In Lincoln's view, this principle, however sensible, severely limited his options, because the Constitution specifically recognized the existence of slavery and the right of states to maintain it. His second principle was that he would work through his options starting with the most cautious initiatives, because he understood that with each step he took on this volatile issue, there was no going back. Overreach could be fatal, so he would have to make his way forward very carefully, even as the world around him was aflame. Lincoln never claimed to "comprehend the whole of this stupendous crisis," nor to "fully understand and foresee it all," he once said. "And that being the case, I can only go just as fast as I can see how to go."

One small step involved the tiny state of Delaware, in which lived approximately eighteen hundred slaves, most of them in a single county on the Maryland border. Lincoln had recently decided to put the full force of his power and persuasion into the seemingly small initiative of freeing Delaware's slaves. This hardly seemed like a radical idea: Delaware did not share any borders with the Confederacy, and its legislature had once come within a single vote of abolishing slavery. Lincoln believed that if he could coax Delaware to free its slaves, the result would be the snowball that starts the avalanche. Maryland would soon follow suit, and then the other border slave states, Missouri and Kentucky, would do the same. This would sap Confederate morale while galvanizing support for the North among antislavery Europeans. The tide of the war would turn, the Constitution would be preserved, and slavery would be on the path to extinction—all because of Delaware.

The trouble was that Delaware did not care for abolitionists, a fact made perfectly clear in the 1860 election, when the state chose for its senators "two of the most truculent proslavery Democrats on Capitol Hill." But Lincoln was undeterred, and was crafting a tiptoe process of gradual emancipation in which the federal government would pay up to $500 for each slave set free. He planned to propose that Delaware immediately free all slaves over the age of thirty-five and also declare freedom for all children born to slaves henceforth. When every slave in the state had reached the age of thirty-five, the gradual process would be complete, although Lincoln suspected that total emancipation would come more quickly once partial emancipation got under way. "If Congress will pass a law authorizing the issuance of bonds for the payment of the emancipated Negroes in the border states," he told a friend, "Delaware, Maryland, Kentucky, and Missouri will accept the terms." After that, the gradual death of slavery would be inevitable. Delaware, he believed, was "the initiative to hitch the whole thing to."

The plan seemed eminently reasonable to Lincoln. But these were not reasonable times. Many of those who tolerated slavery immediately attacked his proposal as an unprecedented federal intervention in what was properly a state-level issue. Meanwhile, antislavery forces in Congress and the press grew increasingly outraged by what they saw as Lincoln's pussyfooting. "Timid, vacillating, & inefficient" was Senator Chandler's assessment of the president's strategy for dealing with slavery. When Senator Wade told the president on New Year's Eve that he was "murdering [the] country by inches," he was giving voice to the feelings of many.

Lincoln shook the last dignitary's hand; then, precisely at noon, as *The New York Times* reported, "the gates were thrown open to the public, and the immense multitude made a simultaneous rush for the reception room." Scrambling up the mansion driveway, jostling for advantage as they passed through the doors, the crowd slowed near the East Room, where the Lincolns had relocated to greet the general public. Care had been taken to protect Mary's recent purchases. Protective cloths were laid over the East Room carpets, marking a path from the doors, past the president, to a flight of temporary steps through a tall window and down to the lawn.

Attorney General Bates fretted about the crowd "overwhelming the poor fatigued President," and by the end of the reception Lincoln's right hand was indeed numb and trembling. In two hours, the president had shaken hundreds if not thousands of hands. "There certainly never was a man who [shook hands] with the celerity and abandon of President Lincoln," wrote one observer. "He goes it with both hands, and hand over hand, very much as a sailor would climb a rope. What is to the satisfaction of all is, that he gives a good honest, hearty shake, as if he meant it." Lincoln's aides were constantly trying to limit the time he spent meeting office seekers, grieving mothers, delegations of churchmen, and other visitors, but the president understood keenly the value of these encounters. Further, he scoffed at fears for his safety. "Anything that kept the people themselves away from him he disapproved," said Hay.

Lincoln knew that these were the citizens who paid the taxes and sent the soldiers. If there was pain to endure and sacrifice to be made to save the Union, her citizens must carry the cost. And he was confident they would, if only he could explain the need for the war and show them some results. No generals and no strategies would save the Union if these ordinary people did not choose to save it, and so Lincoln tried to help them see that their power—not his—was at stake. Not only did the citizenry have the right to elect a government, they should be able to trust that the losing voters would not destroy the nation in protest. This principle, above all others, was worth fighting for, and it was at the heart of Lincoln's conviction that the Union must not ransom its future to an aristocracy of slave owners.

Having made his own way up from a dirt-floored hovel, Lincoln believed that economic opportunity, the right to rise in the world, was the foundation of political liberty. Slavery, for Lincoln, was the ultimate repudiation of the link between effort and advancement. Owning slaves, he once remarked to a friend, was the sign of "the gentleman of leisure who was above and scorned labour." But in a healthy society, Lincoln believed, nothing was above labor—neither wealth, nor aristocracy, nor dictatorial power. "The prudent, penniless beginner in the world, labors for wages awhile, saves a surplus with which to buy tools or land for himself;

then labors on his own account another while, and at length hires another new beginner to help him," Lincoln said. "This is the just, and generous, and prosperous system which opens the way to all—gives hope to all, and consequent energy, and progress, and improvement of condition to all. No men living are more worthy to be trusted than those who toil up from poverty." These good citizens, the president believed, must never surrender their power.

On that first day of the new year, Abraham Lincoln shook those outstretched hands until his fingers trembled because with the public on his side he might be able to untangle this horrible knot: master the army, hold Europe at bay, tame the Congress, coordinate the government, rescue the Treasury, launch an offensive, hold on to the border states, solve the problem of slavery, and somehow preserve his own sanity. Without public support, the country was finished. Lincoln knew he must move quickly—but never faster than the public could tolerate. He must move boldly—but never more vigorously than the people would sustain. He was driven by a simple theory, one friend summed up: "That but one thing was necessary, and that was a united North."

The president shook the last hand at about two P.M., and then the final visitors descended from the East Room window to the White House lawn. Beyond the gates, the holiday continued long into the night, with parades and cannon fire and barrels of beer. Lincoln's right arm ached, and his thoughts were dark. As he told a trusted friend the next day, he was, for the first time, beginning to consider "the bare possibility of our being two nations." But he had sworn a solemn oath to preserve the Constitution and, as the coming year would prove, he did not give up easily. So Lincoln walked with his ungainly stride down the long central corridor of the White House and climbed the stairs to the second floor. With his boys lost joyfully in the celebration outside, there was nothing to keep him from the office, and though he was exhausted, it was time to go to work.

Lincoln's first task as the year began was to get the army moving. So much hinged on the idea of action. Action would raise the mood of the public. It would create a unifying sense of purpose in the North, and that, in turn, would strengthen congressional support for the administration and unfreeze the market for government bonds. Action would stave off foreign intervention, as the European powers waited to judge the results.

Action would begin to push the front lines southward, out of the border states, and thus would bind Kentucky, Maryland, and Missouri more tightly to the Union.

The question was not what to do, but how to make it happen. At the embarrassing cabinet meeting on New Year's Eve, Bates had urged Lincoln to take charge of the army himself, rather than defer to military men who were just as inexperienced in large-scale warfare as their commander in chief was. "We have no general who has any experience in the handling of large armies—not one who has ever commanded 10,000 under fire," Bates observed. He suggested that the president appoint a personal staff of professional soldiers, "two or three or four," who could translate his thinking into crisp military orders. Anyone who refused to fall in line should be cashiered. "By law, [you] must command," Bates summed up, speaking as one lawyer to another. "The Nation requires it, and History will hold [you] accountable."

As a matter of constitutional theory, Bates was on solid ground. The president was commander in chief. But Bates's prescription ignored important political realities, and therefore his advice was of limited value to a man who ate, slept, and breathed political realities. For Lincoln, the military battlefield was inseparable from the political battlefield; he drilled this idea into his aides until they could channel the president's philosophy. "Every war is begun, dominated, and ended by political considerations," explained John Nicolay and John Hay, Lincoln's faithful secretaries. "Without a nation, without a Government, without money or credit, without popular enthusiasm which furnishes volunteers, or public support which endures conscription, there could be no army and no war. . . . War and politics, campaign and statecraft, are Siamese twins, inseparable and interdependent."

George McClellan was a colossal political reality, built up during the previous months into a hero for millions of Americans. He had created the Army of the Potomac, and now he was his soldiers' idol. The Constitution might say that he was Lincoln's subordinate, but political reality decreed him to be an independent power whose influence rivaled—and perhaps exceeded—Lincoln's own. Elected by the smallest plurality in American history, Lincoln was "a minority president," as he put it himself, while McClellan was "a majority general." And despite Lincoln's insistence on action, his senior commander was determined not to be rushed.

True, McClellan's deliberate pace had begun to tarnish his star, but

Lincoln's popularity was battered as well. He had infuriated ardent
Republicans by removing Frémont, the party's original standard-bearer,
from command in Missouri. Lincoln had outraged bellicose patriots by
apologizing to Great Britain over the *Trent* affair. He was too conservative for radical Republicans and too radical for conservative Democrats.

Worst of all, the country was losing hope. Public pessimism was quickly
eroding the president's power. Congressman Henry L. Dawes, of Massachusetts, writing to his wife as the new year dawned, described the widespread lack of faith in Lincoln's administration: "Times are exceedingly
dark and gloomy—I have never seen a time when they were so much so.
Confidence in everybody is shaken to the very foundation— The credit of
the Country is ruined—its arms impotent, its Cabinet incompetent, its
servants rotten, its ruin inevitable."

In such a weakened condition, Lincoln lacked the leverage necessary
to budge an obstacle as weighty as General McClellan and unstick his
motionless armies. No matter what Bates might believe, two or three or
four presidential aides with West Point credentials would hardly alter that
situation. Even so, fate had offered Lincoln a tiny opening: McClellan's
grave illness.

Disease was rampant in filthy wartime Washington, where churches
were hastily converted into hospitals by laying rough planks across the
pew backs to serve as infirmary floors. Soldiers were dying at a shocking rate: "Forty or fifty per day are carried off," wrote one observer—the
equivalent of a regiment wiped out every three weeks. The capital city
was a cauldron of epidemics. Measles: on that New Year's Day, in a makeshift ward not a mile from the White House, a hundred young men from
a single regiment, the 11th Maine, were near death. Smallpox: "There are
cases of it in almost every Street in the City," wrote a diarist as the disease
leaped from unvaccinated soldiers into the parlors of the city's civilians.
"There is said to be over 400 cases in private families." Typhoid fever: this
was McClellan's scourge, a deadly bacterial infection spread through
drinking water contaminated by human waste. No one was safe from its
ravages in a city where the watershed was crowded with tens of thousands of volunteer soldiers living in unsanitary camps. Even at the White
House, where drinking water poured from modern indoor plumbing, the
pipes that fed the faucets drew straight from the unclean Potomac.

The general's sudden illness caught Lincoln and his cabinet off guard,
and to make matters worse, McClellan's chief of staff (General Randolph

Marcy, who happened to be McClellan's father-in-law) was also down with the fever. If these two men died, McClellan's secret plans might die with them, and the extent of Lincoln's ignorance about military preparations would become obvious not just to his cabinet and the congressional joint committee, but to the whole country. Yet here as well was an opportunity for Lincoln: with his general in chief at death's door, he had an excuse to bypass McClellan and open direct communication with key generals at the next level in the chain of command. It was the only tool the president had, so he grabbed it.

His first attempts were simple enough. Immediately after the New Year's Eve cabinet meeting, Lincoln had sent telegrams to the generals commanding U.S. armies in the west. He opened his message by informing them that "General McClellan is sick." Staff officers at the War Department could easily have delivered this news, but doing so himself let Lincoln assert his authority. He did so briskly in his next sentences, asking whether his generals were cooperating with each other. As he put it to Major General Henry W. Halleck, commanding in St. Louis, referring to Brigadier General Don C. Buell in Louisville: "Are General Buell and yourself in concert?"

Now, working in his office on New Year's Day, Lincoln read their extremely discouraging answers. "There is no arrangement between General Halleck and myself," Buell reported. Halleck's telegram concurred: "I have never received a word from General Buell. I am not ready to cooperate with him. Hope to do so in a few weeks." No communication whatsoever: not a word, not even ready for a word, and this from the two men whose forces were charged with subduing the Confederate heartland. Halleck closed his telegram on a patronizing note. "Too much haste will ruin everything," he cautioned the president.

In the U.S. Army, Henry Wager Halleck—author of treatises on topics ranging from military strategy to international law; distinguished lecturer ("The Elements of Military Art and Science") at the Lowell Institute in Boston—was known as Old Brains. However, Old Brains was completely wrong. Too much caution was far more dangerous than too much haste, for the air was going out of the Union. Lincoln took a clean sheet of his official letterhead and picked up his pen. In short order, he composed replies to the two western generals.

One of Lincoln's most striking talents was his ability to condense large ideas into strong, concise prose. The messages he wrote on January

1, 1862, are textbook examples. Though only a few sentences long, they distilled many months of study and consultation. "My dear General Halleck," he began in his firm, tight script. After advising Halleck that McClellan should not be disturbed, he reached the point of his missive, saying that he was "very anxious" to have the western armies move soon— and not just move, but move together. Lincoln proposed that Halleck send a force down the Mississippi toward Columbus, Kentucky, where Rebel forces under Leonidas Polk had accumulated 143 artillery pieces of various vintages and descriptions at a fortress on the bluffs. Confederates had proclaimed Columbus "the Gibraltar of the West"; it was the left-flank anchor of their long defensive line strung thinly across the crucial Bluegrass State. Further, Lincoln proposed that, while Halleck moved on Columbus, Buell should take his Army of the Cumberland south from Louisville to engage the other end of the Confederate western line. The president wanted very much for Buell's troops to liberate the Union loyalists in the mountains of eastern Tennessee.

Both missions were essential to Lincoln's basic strategy for defeating the Rebels. His ideas had begun to take shape under the influence of McClellan's predecessor, the old warhorse Winfield Scott. When Lincoln arrived in Washington as president, he found Scott elderly, overweight, and creaky, but still in possession of the sharp strategic mind that had once inspired the Duke of Wellington to call him "the greatest living soldier." Lincoln and Scott had much in common: Whigs by temperament, they were both reared in border slave states (Scott was a Virginian). Both were tall and imposing; both were avid readers and sly humorists. Crucially, both men believed that secession lacked popular support in the South. The Confederacy, they felt, had been hatched by wealthy slave owners to advance their interests at the expense of ordinary Southerners. On the basis of this conviction, Scott formulated a strategy for smothering the rebellion by blockading Southern ports and sending an army to open the Mississippi, the vital artery linking North and South. With these objectives achieved, secession fever would burn itself out and Southern loyalty would reemerge. Months after Scott left Washington, the president still had in mind the twin goals of opening the Mississippi River by capturing Columbus, and bolstering Southern Unionists in eastern Tennessee.

But Lincoln's thinking had clearly ripened through his reading and reflection on military strategy, because he also outlined an additional concept that would be essential to Union victory against the sprawling South. The Rebels had a relatively small population and a very long border to defend. The North had far more men, and more guns to arm them, and more farms to feed them. The way to bring these advantages to bear, the president had realized, was to send multiple Union armies to strike simultaneously along the Confederate line, forcing the undermanned Rebels to concentrate against one attack, thus leaving another point undefended. In his letter to Halleck, he suggested that "a real or feigned attack upon Columbus from up-river," in coordination with Buell's march into Tennessee, would compel the Rebels to choose. If the Confederates defended Columbus, they would be strung too thinly to hold Nashville. Conversely, if the Rebels shifted troops from Columbus to strengthen Nashville, they would be "throwing Columbus into our hands." Then he noted, "I sent General Buell a letter similar to this."

Lincoln was walking on thin ice here, and he knew it. As a civilian whose military experience consisted of a few weeks' service in the Illinois state militia, who was he to instruct Old Brains and McClellan's chum Buell in fine points of strategy? So he added a note of deference: "You and he will understand much better than I how to do it." But Lincoln reverted to a commanding note as he closed, showing just what he thought of Halleck's warning about too much haste: "Please do not lose time in this matter. Yours, very truly, A. Lincoln."

The president wrote a third note on New Year's Day, this one to McClellan. Someone had told him, perhaps during the reception in the Blue Room, that the bedridden general was, through the fog of his fever, quite nervous about the congressional joint committee. Eager to get his side of things on the record quickly, McClellan had planned to meet with Senator Wade's inquisitors at the outset of their work. But then he had fallen ill, and now the committee was busy investigating the war effort without him—and not, McClellan feared correctly, with friendly intent. "My dear general," Lincoln began, "I hear that the doings of the Investigating Committee, give you some uneasiness." He continued soothingly: "You may be entirely relieved on this point. The gentlemen . . . were with me last night; and I found them in a perfectly good mood."

This wasn't exactly true, but even Abraham Lincoln would bend the truth when he absolutely needed to. And particularly at this point, he would say almost anything to spur his generals into action.

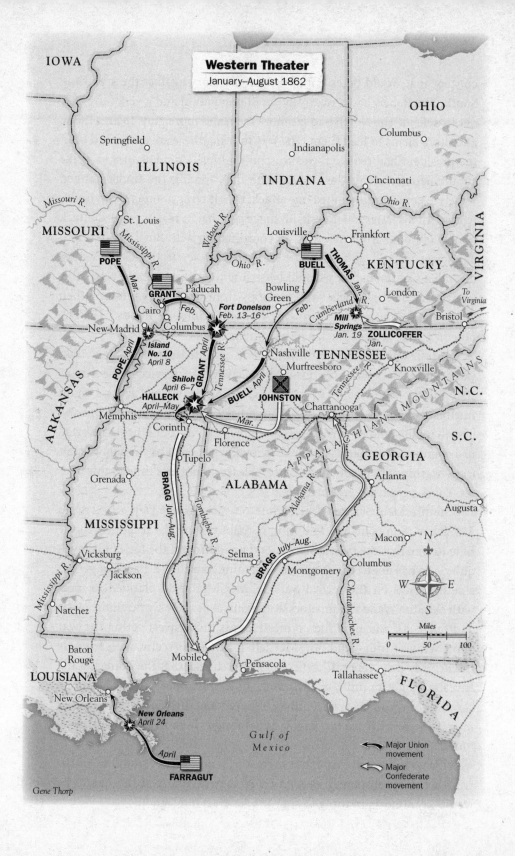

Western Theater
January–August 1862

IOWA

ILLINOIS

Springfield

INDIANA

Indianapolis

OHIO

Columbus

Cincinnati

MISSOURI

Missouri R.

St. Louis

Mississippi R.

POPE

GRANT

Paducah

Cairo

Columbus

New Madrid

Mar.

Feb.

POPE *April*

Island No. 10 April 8

Wabash R.

Ohio R.

Louisville

Frankfort

BUELL

THOMAS *Jan.*

KENTUCKY

Bowling Green

Feb.

London

Cumberland R.

Mill Springs Jan. 19

ZOLLICOFFER
Jan.

VIRGINIA

To Virginia

Bristol

Fort Donelson Feb. 13–16

Tennessee R.

Nashville

Murfreesboro

TENNESSEE

Knoxville

N.C.

Shiloh April 6–7

HALLECK April–May

GRANT *April*

BUELL *April*

JOHNSTON

Memphis

Corinth

Florence

Mar.

Chattanooga

APPALACHIAN

MOUNTAINS

S.C.

ARKANSAS

Tupelo

Tennessee R.

Alabama R.

Atlanta

GEORGIA

Augusta

MISSISSIPPI

Grenada

BRAGG July–Aug.

ALABAMA

Selma

Macon

Columbus

Tombigbee R.

BRAGG July–Aug.

Montgomery

Chattahoochee R.

N

Vicksburg

Jackson

Mississippi R.

Natchez

Mobile

Pensacola

Tallahassee

FLORIDA

Miles

0   50   100

Baton Rouge

LOUISIANA

New Orleans

New Orleans April 24

April

FARRAGUT

Gulf of Mexico

⬅ Major Union movement

⬅ Major Confederate movement

Gene Thorp

2

JANUARY

A cold front swept into Washington on the second day of January. Blustery winds rattled the canvas of the soldiers' tents and raised the dust from dry streets. Behind the winds came freezing temperatures and, intermittently for the next month, every variety of wetness: snow, sleet, rain, fog. Roads around Washington, which seemed always to be in one miserable condition or another, changed from powder to mire, and drivers who had been licking grit from their teeth a few days earlier now found themselves bogged down in a foul, sticky mix of mud and manure. The bad roads were more than just an inconvenience. Mud made it nearly impossible to move the army, with its countless tons of artillery and supplies.

Lincoln braved that day's chill wind to visit McClellan in his big house on Lafayette Park, taking with him the discouraging wire he had received from Halleck. The president was in a low mood; one adviser who spoke to him that day said that Lincoln permitted himself to wonder what it might mean to have the old United States split into "two nations. . . . He did not see how the two could exist so near to each other." Reaching McClellan's house, he was pleased to find that the worst of the typhoid—high fever, blackened tongue, foul breath—was past. His general in chief seemed "very much better."

McClellan did not appear upset that Lincoln was dealing directly with the western commanders. Perhaps he was pleased to have the president "browsing" (as McClellan disdainfully referred to Lincoln's amiable hunts for information) in places other than his own headquarters. For whatever reason, after Lincoln's visit McClellan gathered his strength to dictate a message, the first he had sent in two weeks, endorsing the president's advice to Halleck. "Not a moment's time should be lost," he wrote.

Lincoln's communications with Halleck and Buell deepened over the next week. By chattering telegraph, the president and his western generals went back and forth over issues of how and where and especially when their armies would move. Halleck protested that he needed more men, and his men needed more guns. He criticized Buell's Nashville strategy ("condemned by every military authority I have ever read," he sniffed). For a time, Buell simply disappeared from telegraph range. "Delay is ruining us," Lincoln protested, "and it is indispensable that I have something definite." Exasperated, he ordered the generals to produce a time-table for joint action, but Halleck and Buell ignored him. "It is exceedingly discouraging," Lincoln admitted to his secretary of war, Simon Cameron. "As everywhere else, nothing can be done."

Three days after the president's first visit to McClellan's home, he traveled there again, this time carrying an infuriating telegram from Buell in which the general declared that he "attached little or no importance" to a campaign into eastern Tennessee. A light snow over an earlier crust of sleet covered the ground, and the rutted side streets were frozen. Lincoln did much of his best thinking while walking, and since he resisted all efforts to surround him with bodyguards, he almost certainly made this trip alone or nearly alone. Dressed in his black cloak and hat, stark against the whiteness of the lawn, the president cut a distinctive figure. "When he walked he moved cautiously but firmly; his long arms and giant hands swung down by his side," his law partner William Herndon once wrote. "He put the whole foot flat on the ground at once, not landing on the heel; he likewise lifted his foot all at once, not rising from the toe, and hence there was no spring to his walk. His walk was undulatory—catching and pocketing tire, weariness and pain, all up and down his person, and thus preventing them from locating."

McClellan was still weak from his illness, but after his meeting with Lincoln the general again took up his pen, this time to write a spine-stiffener to his old friend Buell. "The political consequences of the delay . . . will be much more serious than you seem to anticipate," McClellan warned. He had his own reasons for wanting Buell to be more aggressive: if Buell could get far enough into Tennessee to cut the South's main east–west railroad, then McClellan could launch his campaign in Virginia without worrying about Rebel reinforcements pouring in from the west. Nevertheless, the young general's explicit support of Lincoln's efforts might have been a sign that he was awakening to political reality himself.

Yet when it came to his own conduct and his own command, McClellan was as uncooperative as ever. Despite Lincoln's encouragement on New Year's Day, by January 6 the general still had not met with the Joint Committee on the Conduct of the War. When the cabinet convened that day for a discussion with the committee, the radicals from Congress were angrier than before. Ben Wade and the others pressed Lincoln to fire McClellan. They were sure that the general's Democratic, antiabolition views were the root cause of his army's failure to do anything more assertive than dig trenches around Washington and march in parades. "A great deal of discussion took place," Treasury Secretary Chase noted mildly in his diary. Chase, in fact, was one of the most active participants, and he clearly had an agenda of his own.

Lincoln's cabinet was, in the words of Doris Kearns Goodwin, "a team of rivals," comprising Lincoln's vanquished political opponents and leading members of the opposition Democratic Party. It was the embodiment of the clashing fragments of the Union and, like the Union itself, was easily distracted from the crisis of the moment by the chafing of past disputes and by scheming over future rivalries. Others in the cabinet tried to suppress their political ambitions, but Salmon Chase did not. Even while serving in 1862 as one of Lincoln's most important advisers, Chase was obviously angling to run for the presidency in 1864. "He has got the presidential maggot in his head and it will wriggle there as long as it is warm," Lincoln observed. Playing the dual role of key official and leading rival kept Chase quite busy. In fact, he was starting to worry that service to Lincoln was a dead weight dragging him down. "He would rather be on the bench of the Supreme Court, or in the Senate," a confidant reported. "He begins to fear that to reach the presidency, with Seward's opposition and all the contingencies and very great dangers of managing the finances during this very great crisis, is rather a 'hard road to travel.'"

An errand Chase ran on that morning of January 6, before the cabinet meeting, provides a vivid example of his conflicted circumstances. He had been working furiously for months to patch up the government's dire fiscal situation; reluctantly, he had concluded that the United States could no longer afford to tie the value of the dollar to fixed amounts of gold or silver. Until now, U.S. currency had been backed by precious metals, so a person holding a paper dollar could actually trade it at the bank for a dollar's worth of gold. But with the cost of the war rising exponentially, the supply of precious metal was no longer sufficient. In late December 1861, Chase had informed Congress that by July 1 of the next year the federal debt would be more than $500 million, a greater than fourfold increase in a single year. This news had set off a bank panic and frozen the bond market; the only solution, Chase reluctantly concluded, was to switch to fiat money—so-called greenbacks, supported by nothing but the public's faith in the government—which the Treasury could print as needed. The fact that Wall Street seemed willing to go along with such a dangerously inflationary plan was a testament to Chase's reputation and credibility.

A believer in sound money, Chase found the new monetary system unappealing. Even so, once the change was made it dawned on him that people all over the country were about to receive valuable pieces of paper from the government, paper that would feed their families, pay their rent, and appease the tax man. In that case, he thought, why not put his own handsome visage on those pieces of paper, making his face literally the face of prosperity and trustworthiness, putting his picture in the pockets of every American voter? And since design of the new money was his responsibility, he had gone that morning to a photographer's studio for an official portrait. The photographer posed Chase with his arms crossed over his chest and his face slightly turned from the camera—an image that would soon be the most widely distributed in the country.

Lincoln explained to one confidant that he "had determined to shut his eyes to all these performances" of Chase's political ambition because the man "made a good secretary." He well knew what Chase was up to, but could not afford to lose him. "I have all along clearly seen his plan of strengthening himself. Whenever he sees that an important matter is troubling me, if I am compelled to decide it in a way to give offense to a man of some influence, he always ranges himself in opposition to me and persuades the victim . . . that he would have arranged it very differently. . . . I am entirely indifferent as to his success or failure in these schemes, so long as he does his duty as the head of the Treasury Department."

Chase was particularly shifty during the cabinet meeting with the joint committee on January 6. First he defended McClellan as "the best man for the place," who would surely have things moving by now if he hadn't fallen ill. Then he pivoted to undercut McClellan by suggesting that command of the Army of the Potomac be transferred to a Republican favorite, Irwin McDowell. Supreme command and field command were too much for McClellan, or any one man, to handle, Chase argued. This was a reasonable observation, but Chase's solution was wildly impractical. McDowell was the general who had failed at Bull Run. The idea that he could be placed in command of the army McClellan had built, or that McClellan would willingly share power, was absurd. But Chase was eager for the support of the pro-McDowell Republicans on the congressional committee, and his suggestion seemed calibrated to please them.

All the talk by Chase and others that day led nowhere. The committee was sent away with only a promise from Lincoln to speak once more with McClellan. But this time, when the president ambled into the general's house, he was turned away. The general, he was told, was too weak to see him. Whether McClellan had experienced a relapse or was simply fed up with visits from Lincoln is not clear. Little Mac did complain a few days later that "they don't give me time to recover," but he seemed fine when the Lincoln boys, Willie and Tad, roamed over to his headquarters the day after their father was rebuffed. They returned with news that McClellan had been out for a brisk ride in the subfreezing cold.

After his unsuccessful attempt to meet with his general in chief, Lincoln delivered his advice on paper. "You better go before the Congressional Committee the earliest moment your health will permit—to-day if possible," Lincoln counseled McClellan. Still, the general didn't budge.

About this time, an alarming dispatch arrived in Washington from Charles Francis Adams, the American minister in London. Adams warned that the British government would face a wave of pro-Confederate opinion when Parliament convened in January. For months, there had been no official forum outside the British cabinet in which to debate the idea of European intervention. But when the House of Lords met, the matter was likely to be at the top of the agenda, and Adams feared the pressures that would be unleashed. "Nothing but very marked evidences of progress towards success will restrain for any length of time the hostile tendencies" in elite British opinion, Adams warned.

But how and where could Lincoln demonstrate marked evidences of progress? The president pored over the varnished maps that hung on his office wall. Nicolay and Hay, who spent uncounted hours with Lincoln in his office, reported that "no general in the army studied his maps . . . with half the industry" of the president. And few men could get more from a map than he, a former flatboat pilot, surveyor, and title attorney.

Visitors to the White House often came away with stories of Lincoln's animated lectures on aspects of the war, delivered while his long, bony fingers traced lines on those maps. The charts showed an immense Confederate territory: the eleven seceded states covered three quarters of a million square miles and stretched from the Potomac to the Rio Grande, from the southern tip of Florida to the northern border of Tennessee. (In addition, Confederate armies were deployed northward into "neutral" Kentucky.) Secretary of State Seward, Lincoln's frequent companion at the maps, lamented that even sophisticated people underestimated the sheer scope of the Union's task. They failed "to apprehend that the insurrection has disclosed itself over an area of vast extent, and that military operations, to be successful, must be on a scale hitherto practically unknown in the art of war."

But to a man who could read them, the maps suggested how the enormous project might be tackled. Like a slab of marble, the South was veined with lines along which it could be pierced and split. These features fell into three types. The first were the mountains of the Appalachian range, a political fault line separating the eastern Confederacy from the west. Because the terrain was unsuitable for plantation agriculture, the settlers in these mountains had no economic interest in slavery, nor did they relish the idea of living in a new nation run by plantation aristocrats. This explained Lincoln's urgent desire to reach east Tennessee, and do for Unionists there what McClellan had done for the mountain Unionists of western Virginia. "My distress is that our friends in East Tennessee are being hanged and driven to despair, and even now I fear, are thinking of taking rebel arms for the sake of personal protection," he explained.

The rough dirt roads of the South were of little use as invasion routes: a team of mules could haul a wagon only so far before the animals would eat more than the wagon could hold, and long supply lines over poor roads through hostile territory have always been an invitation to military disaster. Railroads, however, offered a second way of piercing the Confederacy. Unfortunately for the Union, relatively few rail lines had been built from north to south, and those that existed were highly vulnerable to rebel cavalry raids and guerrilla operations.

Far more dependable as highways to supply and transport Union forces were the great rivers; thus the Ohio, the Mississippi, and the many navigable waterways flowing into them provided the third means of exploiting the South's terrain. Lincoln knew from deep experience that the American interior was "a frontier of rivers," for he had spent his young manhood all over the waterways of the West. The first dollar he ever earned was for ferrying passengers to a steamboat on the Ohio River; a year later, he steered a flatboat from Rockport, Illinois, on the Ohio, down the Mississippi to New Orleans. At twenty-one, he forded the Wabash River when it was swollen with rain, wrestling his family's oxen through the roiling waters. At twenty-two, he built another flatboat, launched it in the Illinois River, and once more made the long, looping, oxbowed trip down the Mississippi to New Orleans. Attempting to prove that a steamboat could travel the Sangamon River, Lincoln got stuck at the little town of New Salem, Illinois, where he soon began his political career—on a platform of improving rivers for navigation. He even received a patent on an invention for lifting steamboats over shoals.

Lincoln had seen the western rivers in flood and in drought, and he knew their moods and seasons. Now, as president, he saw that the rivers crisscrossing the South could substantially offset the problem of inadequate roads. If "evidences of progress" were needed, the rivers could open the way.

For months, buyers from the army and navy had been bustling around river wharfs from Pittsburgh, Pennsylvania, to Cairo, Illinois, purchasing steamboats to serve as troop transports and cargo ships. Lincoln took particular interest in a frantic construction project in and around St. Louis, where a boatwright and bridge builder named James Eads was creating a fleet of steam-powered, ironclad gunboats designed to navigate in shallow water and carry an array of heavy cannon. The Eads boats, dubbed "turtles," were ungainly things, ugly but tough. By early January there were seven turtles in the water, all nearing completion.

Yet Lincoln was impatient for his "brown water navy" to get moving. The Confederates weren't waiting idly for the attack. They were building forts on the rivers, and they had their own ironclad gunboats under construction in New Orleans.

Fog lay thick in the Washington swamplands on January 10; the streets melted into soupy ooze. Lincoln convened the cabinet again, this time for one of its gloomiest meetings yet, a freewheeling ventilation of fears and frustrations over the fact that nearly two weeks had gone by since the New Year's Eve session and still they knew nothing of McClellan's intentions. Attorney General Bates wondered aloud whether McClellan had any real plans at all; he then repeated his well-worn speech to Lincoln, urging him to trust his judgment and assert his authority, somehow failing to see that this was exactly what Lincoln was trying to do. Secretary of the Navy Gideon Welles echoed the sentiment; like many navy men, he enjoyed thinking that all the army needed was a swift kick. Lincoln replied by explaining that generals are not the sort of men who respond well to scolding and kicking.

The meeting came to a close and again nothing had been accomplished. By now the president was nearly beside himself. It was all meetings and telegrams and hand-wringing, but still no action. Lincoln fled the White House and strode across the lawn to the War Department, where he entered the office of Montgomery Meigs, quartermaster general, one of the most competent staff officers in the country. There, Lincoln expressed his profound frustration. "The people are impatient; Chase has no money and tells me he can raise no more; the General of the Army has typhoid fever. The bottom is out of the tub," Lincoln declared. "What shall I do?" Though prone to his own occasional crises of confidence, Meigs proved sturdy that day, offering the distraught president a concrete plan. It was a variation on the maneuver that Lincoln employed on New Year's Day: skip past McClellan and deal directly with the next level of generals. Meigs told the president he should convene a council of war.

A hand-picked group gathered that evening at the White House. Chase was invited, as was Secretary of State Seward. Two generals from McClellan's Army of the Potomac were summoned, one a friend of the general and one a rival. Meigs was a little late in arriving, along with Postmaster General Montgomery Blair, the only member of Lincoln's cabinet with a West Point education. The secretary of war, Simon Cameron, was conspicuously missing; in his place was a deputy, Peter Watson.

Cameron had become an insufferable obstacle to Union progress, a crucial department head who could not be counted on. His management of the War Department was impotent and widely seen as corrupt. He was so notorious for his habit of leaking vital information that the navy implored Lincoln to exclude him from meetings to plan the recapture of New Orleans. But because Cameron was head of a powerful political machine in the vital state of Pennsylvania, he had to be handled carefully. By this time, Lincoln had decided to fire Cameron as soon as he found a replacement, but he had confided this plan only to Seward.

Lincoln opened the meeting with a soliloquy that proved his patience had worn thin. He offered a detailed recitation of woes, from the collapse of government finances, to the pressure from congressional radicals, to the lack of cooperation between Halleck and Buell. Most of all, there was the problem of McClellan, who once again had refused to see him. Lincoln must talk to someone, and so, he told the two generals, he was turning to them. If McClellan was not going to use the army, Lincoln said tartly, he "would like to borrow it," as long as he "could see how it could be made to do something."

Not surprisingly, the generals—Irwin McDowell and William B. Franklin—provided two very different responses. McDowell, the Republican favorite, proposed a fresh march on Richmond by way of Manassas; in other words, he wanted to pursue the same strategy that had failed so disastrously the previous summer. Franklin, a member of McClellan's clique of senior officers, countered by suggesting that the Army of the Potomac should instead move south by water, taking ships down Chesapeake Bay to flank the Confederates, land to the east of Richmond, and move quickly on the Rebel capital.

Finally the cat was out of the bag: this was the secret plan that McClellan had been hatching. But Franklin was forced to acknowledge that it was far from mature; of the two strategies, only McDowell's could be executed quickly. Lincoln's options, then, were to wait some more, or fight another battle at Bull Run against an enemy that was, for all the war council knew, stronger than ever. Stymied again, he asked the generals to gather more information and return for yet another meeting.

This cannot have felt like a turning point. Hemmed in and oppressed, Lincoln had an overpowering sense that he could afford to take only the smallest, most careful steps. According to Herndon, who paid a visit to Washington around this time, the president cryptically confided: "Traitors are under me, around me, and above me. I do not know whom to trust and must move slowly and cautiously."

Yet the ad hoc council marked a significant shift. Too much pressure for action was building; Lincoln had jostled too many generals and rubbed too many sensitive egos for the situation to remain frozen. Tiny fissures, almost imperceptible, were beginning to appear in the Union position, cracks that would soon widen. For one thing, McClellan's letter to Halleck, dictated from his sickbed, evidently made an impression. Halleck was enough of a professional soldier to understand that when the president and the general in chief were both instructing him to send an expedition southward, he ought to launch some boats and march some troops. McClellan's letter to Buell, meanwhile, had reached Louisville and made a similar impression there.

But Lincoln didn't know that the ice was beginning to break, so he kept chipping away.

January 11 was a fine Saturday, warm and pleasant. The Taft boys were visiting; though the president's sons were notorious for barging in on their father as he held cabinet meetings or pondered state papers, today Willie, Tad, and their two friends thundered up the stairs and clambered out onto the roof, where they put the finishing touches on the quarterdeck of an imaginary warship. Pretending to be sailors in a fleet commanded by Commodore Abraham Lincoln, the four boys took turns scanning the Potomac and its yonder shore through a spyglass, alert for signs of enemy activity.

Thus protected, the president worked at his desk. He had at last found his way out from under the Cameron problem, and now he crafted an artful pair of letters to his secretary of war. One letter fired the man, and the other tried to make him feel good about it.

The U.S. ambassador to Russia, a flamboyant abolitionist named Cassius Marcellus Clay, had asked to return from St. Petersburg to lead troops into battle. The prospect of General Clay excited few people other than the man himself, for he was impulsive and emotional, notorious for brawling and dueling. But the opening in Russia created a suitable post for a former secretary of war. Lincoln's first letter to Cameron, written for public consumption, briskly informed him that he would be nominated for the Russian mission two days hence. This letter would show the public that the president was serious about cleaning up the War Department. But Lincoln knew that Cameron would read the official letter as "a dismissal, and, therefore, discourteous," according to Salmon Chase, and the president understood that an offended Cameron was a dangerous Cameron. So he wrote a second, longer letter, which he marked private. In this one, Lincoln nursed Cameron's wounded pride, assuring the ousted secretary of his esteem and friendship. This deft bit of diplomacy was successful: Cameron resigned without public complaint.

Lincoln's dismissal of Cameron went smoothly because he had found another Pennsylvanian to fill the post. But his outgoing and incoming secretaries of war shared little besides their home state; substituting Edwin M. Stanton for Simon Cameron was like replacing a butter knife with a buzz saw. Warned that the energetic, headstrong lawyer might "run away with the whole concern," Lincoln countered with a story of a preacher whose sermons were so passionate that folks had to put bricks in the preacher's pockets to keep him from flying away. "I may have to do that with Stanton," he said, "but if I do, bricks in his pocket will be better than bricks in his hat."

Yet Stanton was not an obvious choice. At a time when congressional Republicans were complaining about Democrats in key positions, Stanton was one more Democrat, and he was tainted by his service as attorney general in the do-nothing administration of the previous president, James Buchanan. Lincoln's adviser Montgomery Blair warned darkly that Stanton was not to be trusted. And the president's own experience of Stanton would have seemed to rule out any hope of an appointment. Years earlier, Lincoln had been retained as one of several lawyers helping to defend a manufacturer of reaping machines against the powerful McCormick Company in a patent dispute. Stanton was the star of the manufacturer's defense team, and he had gone to great lengths to humiliate Lincoln when the case finally went to trial. Calling him "that damned long armed Ape," Stanton refused to seat Lincoln at counsel's table, or even to let him eat breakfast with the legal team.

But Lincoln had a short memory for slights, especially slights that might hamper his larger aims. His favorite expression, according to John Hay, was "I am in favor of short statutes of limitations in politics." As he once observed: "Perhaps I have too little [resentment], but I never thought it paid. A man has not time to spend half his life in quarrels. If any man ceases to attack me, I never remember the past against him." To Lincoln, a grudge was a waste of resources: if a person could be useful to him, he cared little whether the man was a friend or a foe. Nor did Lincoln much care what individuals thought about him. Hay once scoffed when someone suggested that Lincoln was a modest man. No modest man becomes great, Hay insisted. Lincoln's typical reaction to criticism, the secretary noted, was to brush it aside as ignorance. "I know more about it than them," he would say.

Stanton also had a crucial supporter. During the final months of Buchanan's term, as secession mania spiked across the South and members of Buchanan's cabinet plotted with the Rebels, William Seward had used his seat in the Senate to try to save the Union and stop the rush toward war. This effort to find a compromise left the senator's more radical Republican friends disillusioned, but it gave Seward a behind-the-scenes view of Stanton. He saw a man desperate to snuff the rebellion and furious in his contempt for the Southern rabble-rousers. Stanton was tireless in funneling intelligence from inside Buchanan's cabinet to Seward, and Seward came to trust Stanton's energy, determination, and loyalty. And by now, Lincoln had come to trust Seward.

McClellan, meanwhile, had received reports of Lincoln's war council of the previous evening; characteristically, he immediately suspected a conspiracy to strip him of power. He dispatched one of his most trusted staff officers, Colonel Thomas Key, to seek Chase's help. The Treasury secretary advised Key that McClellan should stop flaunting his personal disrespect for Lincoln and pay the honor due the office of the presidency. The general should make regular reports to Lincoln, in person or through an aide, rather than waiting for the president to come to him. McClellan did not accept advice easily, but this time he tried.

He emerged from his sickroom the next morning, January 12, and appeared unannounced at the White House. For the first time, the general sketched his secret plan for the president. It was much as William Franklin had outlined it at the war council: put the army on boats, steam southward past the rebels at Manassas, and land in the rear of General Joseph E. Johnston's Confederate army. From there, the Federals would march on Richmond. It was a sound strategy in almost every respect, but Lincoln remained skeptical. The Confederates were entrenched just a day's march from Washington, with batteries effectively blockading the Potomac. What if, instead of retreating to defend Richmond, they waited until McClellan set off, and then attacked Washington? The Union could not afford to lose the capital even for a few days, not with European powers itching for a chance to declare Confederate victory.

Instead of thanking McClellan for sharing his plan, Lincoln merely said he would ask his war council about it the next day. He also told McClellan that he was welcome to attend the council. Here was another sign of change: before the general in chief fell sick, Lincoln's goal was to persuade him to share information. Now a grudging peek into McClellan's plans was no longer sufficient. Lincoln intended to probe, prod, and even modify those plans. Their relationship had subtly, but fundamentally, shifted. And if George McClellan was ill-tempered and suspicious on his way into the White House that morning, he was boiling mad on his way out.

With so little real news to process, the Washington rumor mill was running double shifts. Sketchy reports of genuine activity—General Ambrose Burnside sailing from Hampton Roads with a hundred ships carrying a strike force down the Atlantic coast; Halleck ordering some sort of expedition in the West—were quickly blown into dramatic tales of crushing blows about to be landed. "It is thought that at least 400,000 Men, good Union soldiers, will move this week," one man summed up.

The lobbies and bars of the Washington hotels were the mills where gossip was spun into common knowledge. Officers mixed easily with civilians, passing tidbits back and forth over brandy and water. Now and then a Confederate spy would feed a scrap of disinformation into the machine and listen with satisfaction as it was picked up and processed into gospel. One hotel was not enough to contain all the chatter. Fresh rumors were churned out at the National and at Brown's, but the elite mill was Willard's, a great barn of a hotel on Pennsylvania Avenue near the Treasury Department. Though Willard's was arguably even "shabbier and dirtier" than the National, one British journalist reported, it was unquestionably "the house of call for everybody who has business in Washington. From early morning till late at night its lobbies and passages were filled with a motley throng of all classes and all nations." Through clouds of cigar smoke, cabinet secretaries, major generals, senators, and congressmen came and went endlessly across the hotel's spit-stained carpets.

Lincoln's secretaries appeared at Willard's for supper virtually every night. John Nicolay and John Hay were "irresistible personalities"—two young men with nearly unparalleled access to "the Tycoon," as they called Lincoln—and they often found themselves "holding court among the belles." Nicolay was the older of the two, almost thirty, engaged to a girl back home and diligent about writing her almost every day. He was a Bavarian immigrant who had arrived in America with his parents at the age of five. As a teen, he went to work in the print shop of an antislavery newspaper in Illinois, working his way quickly from reporter to editor to owner. His coverage of Republican politics caught Lincoln's eye, and when he moved to Springfield for a job in the state government, Nicolay had a front-row seat on the future president's rise. In 1860, he served as jack-of-all-trades to the presidential nominee.

The clever and cutting Hay also had been known to Lincoln for years; Hay's uncle Milton had a law office next door to Lincoln's. A dandy and a bit of a snob, Hay was raised in Illinois but educated at Brown University, where he was named poet of the class of 1858. When Lincoln won the election, Nicolay recruited Hay as an assistant, and together they moved to Washington, even though the White House budget at the time included only enough money for one presidential assistant. A spot was found for Hay on the payroll of the Pension Office until Congress gave Lincoln a second employee. Baby-faced at twenty-three, Hay was the velvet and Nicolay—irascible and fiercely protective of the president's time—the hammer.

A place like Willard's would have little appeal to Lincoln, who neither drank nor smoked. He preferred to relax through private conversation, and on the evening of January 12, he welcomed his old Illinois colleague Orville Hickman Browning for a long talk after supper. Lincoln had known Browning for years; across more than two decades they had colluded and vied in the quest for influence in Illinois politics. Browning had come to Washington some six weeks earlier to fill the Senate seat vacated by the sudden death of Lincoln's famous rival Stephen A. Douglas. Lincoln knew immediately that Browning could be a useful liaison to the Senate; what he probably didn't anticipate was that the senator would become an almost daily visitor, a sounding board, a friend with whom he could vent his cares, and a comrade in grief. In the early days of the war, both Lincoln and Browning lost young men whom they had loved like sons. Browning's ward William Shipley was killed in the battle of Belmont only a few months after Elmer Ellsworth, Lincoln's former law clerk, was gunned down in Alexandria.

As they sat together that night in the glow of the gas lamps, their talk turned to Lincoln's crash course in military strategy. The president had evidently gained much confidence in his ability to think like a general. In fact, he startled Browning by saying that he was weighing the idea of taking command himself; he'd be a warrior-president, leading troops to the fields of battle. It would be unprecedented, yes, but so was everything else that was happening. Lincoln then reviewed for Browning his still-evolving strategy for winning the war. The North must move aggressively on multiple fronts all at once.

With satisfaction Lincoln also told Browning that the western generals were finally acting on his strategy. Newspapers that morning reported that Halleck had ordered a sizeable force down the Mississippi toward the rebel citadel at Columbus. What they didn't know, Lincoln disclosed, was that this move was just "a feint" in support of a push into Tennessee by Buell. The president spoke with confidence because he had received a telegram from Buell that day, promising Lincoln that he would "devote all of my efforts to your views, and [McClellan's]."

The president was entitled to feel satisfied. Less than two weeks had passed since Halleck and Buell dismissed Lincoln's initial telegrams out of hand. Too much haste would ruin everything, they'd said. Now they were both moving, just as Lincoln had urged them to do. The moves weren't terribly impressive—not in their particulars, anyway. But together they turned out to be the beginning of something decisive to the fate of the Union.

In response to the president's plea for action, Buell sent a force of about 4,000 men under Brigadier General George Thomas to challenge a

Rebel army under the former congressman Felix Zollicoffer. On January 19, Thomas defeated Zollicoffer's force in the battle of Mill Springs, near the entrance to the Cumberland Gap. It was the first significant land-based Union victory of the war.

Meanwhile, the feint ordered by Halleck was a miserable affair, day after day of sloppy marching along muddy roads in snow and sleet to no purpose that the troops could see. One column marched from Cairo, Illinois, down the Mississippi to menace Columbus; these soldiers were accompanied by several of the Eads turtles, which threw shells at the fortress on the bluffs. A second column left nearby Paducah, Kentucky, and headed up the Tennessee River toward a pair of Confederate forts under construction.

As Lincoln predicted, the Rebels were frozen in their places by the movements of these two columns and so unable to combine with Zollicoffer to fight against Thomas. But the ultimate impact of the feint on the future of the Union went well beyond Thomas's morale-boosting victory at Mill Springs. Of far greater importance was the vital intelligence gleaned by the brigadier general who commanded that miserable march. That general—a compactly built man in a scruffy uniform, a distinguished veteran of the Mexican War who somehow had never lived up to his potential—was Ulysses S. Grant.

The outbreak of the Civil War had found Captain Grant behind the counter of his father's leather goods store in Galena, Illinois, making a botch of civilian life. Like many promising young officers of the 1850s, including McClellan, Buell, and Halleck, Grant had grown tired of the dull grind of the peacetime army. Unlike those other men, he left the service under a cloud, amid rumors of excessive drinking as he served lonely garrison duty in California far from his wife, Julia. His reputation was so tarnished that, after Fort Sumter, McClellan rejected Grant's application to join his staff.

Those who knew him better, the men of Galena, felt differently. They turned to Grant to help them organize a regiment of volunteers. "I would rather like a regiment," he allowed, "yet there are few men really competent to command a thousand soldiers, and I doubt whether I'm one of them." He was correct about most men, but wrong about himself. His brisk and uncomplaining efficiency made him a natural leader, and soon he attracted the attention of Illinois politicians, one of whom, Lincoln's friend Representative Elihu Washburne, pressed for Grant's promotion to brigadier general of volunteers. Grant assumed command over the army's operations at Cairo, the strategic point at which the Ohio River flows into the Mississippi.

He had not been there long before he focused on a Confederate position, not far to the southeast, "of immence importance to the enemy, and of course correspondingly important for us," as he later recalled. Just inside the Confederacy, the Cumberland and Tennessee rivers converged until they were only a dozen miles apart. These two waterways pierced the center of the Confederate line in the West and opened the way into deep Dixie. When, in September 1861, the Confederate general Leonidas Polk violated Kentucky's announced neutrality by seizing the town of Columbus, Grant moved swiftly to occupy Paducah and Smithland at the mouths of the two rivers. Astutely, he announced that he was entering Kentucky in peace, solely to protect the citizens from Polk's invasion. Thus, the young general placed the blame on the Rebels and grabbed two vital prizes, all without firing a shot. In retrospect, this strategic masterstroke marked him from the start as something special.

Now Rebel troops were at work building forts not far from Paducah to protect this natural gateway, and Grant was eager to strike before the defenses were made impregnable. Using Halleck's feint toward Columbus as a chance to collect information on the condition of the forts, Grant sent a detachment led by Brigadier General C. F. Smith to have a look around. Smith reported that the two forts guarding the Tennessee were extremely vulnerable to attack. Fort Henry, on the eastern riverbank, was set on such low ground that some of its guns were flooded. A replacement for Fort Henry, called Fort Heiman, was set on high ground across the river, but it was unfinished and would be easy to capture.

Grant pictured the dominoes that might fall if he were able to take the two forts. Beyond them, the Tennessee River was navigable by steampowered gunboats and troop transports all the way to Muscle Shoals, Alabama, where the boats could fire on the Memphis and Charleston Railroad, a vital artery for shuttling Confederate troops and supplies. Moreover, a decent road led twelve miles from Fort Henry to Fort Donelson, on the west bank of the Cumberland River. Grant could march his army over that road and attack Donelson, and once he captured that fort he could move without obstruction up the Cumberland River to Nashville, the center of supply for the entire Confederate line in the West. With his line slashed at the center, Polk would be outflanked in Columbus. He would have no choice but to fall back, and the Confederacy's Gibraltar on the Mississippi would melt away.

Probably no other thread in the fabric of the rebellion would unravel so much with a single tug. Excited, Grant made his own reconnaissance of Fort Henry by steamboat. He concluded that the opportunity was now; the forts must be attacked quickly. Yet when he went to St. Louis to present his plan to Halleck, he got a frosty reception.

Halleck and Grant knew each other only in passing. They hadn't overlapped at West Point, nor had they met during the Mexican War. Both men were posted to California in the 1850s, and they left the army just one day apart. But while Halleck was on his way to earning a fortune, Grant was spiraling downward. Temperamentally, they were opposites: a thinker versus a doer. Halleck's view of war was academic. He was the author of a textbook on military strategy that translated into English the elegant martial science of Antoine-Henri Jomini, a Swiss nobleman who had endeavored to reduce Napoleon's genius to mathematical principles. Grant's principles were not so fancy. "The art of war is simple enough," he once said. "Find out where your enemy is. Get at him as soon as you can. Strike at him as hard as you can and as often as you can, and keep moving on." Where Halleck worried about "too much haste," Grant feared just the opposite. He had a natural appreciation of the fact that the enemy were men no better or worse than he. If he was scared, they must be scared, too; if he was tired, they must be tired, also; and if he was racing to bring new recruits up to readiness and struggling to get guns into their hands, then the enemy was surely unprepared and underequipped as well. Delay, therefore, would gain him nothing.

In St. Louis, Halleck received the eager Grant with such brusque disdain that the visitor could barely stammer out his ideas. As Grant described it in his memoirs, "I had not uttered many sentences before I was cut short as if my plan was preposterous." Grant returned to Cairo dejected but determined—much like his commander in chief in faraway Washington.

The victory at Mill Springs produced few lasting results. Brigadier General Thomas and his men chased the Rebels through the Cumberland Gap almost to Knoxville but, with too few troops to secure a supply line, Thomas had no choice but to pull back, leaving the loyalists of east Tennessee stranded.

In Washington, meanwhile, Lincoln continued to push McClellan. The general reluctantly appeared, as scheduled, for a war council on January 13, but he sat as sullen as a schoolhouse bully in the principal's office. Lincoln asked the division commanders, McDowell and Franklin, to review the options for advancing the Army of the Potomac. McClellan refused to say anything until Meigs pulled a chair up close and whispered to the general in chief that his silence was clearly disrespectful.

Prodded, McClellan launched into a litany of reasons why his army could not move. The first steps should be taken in Kentucky, he said, once again steering the pressure toward Buell and Halleck to divert it from his own army. He dismissed McDowell's idea for a move on Manassas, asserting that the Confederates had 175,000 troops in the area (this was more than three times the actual number). When Chase asked bluntly where and when McClellan would move, the general declined to answer, hinting that Lincoln would leak the information to stir up some favorable press. It was McClellan himself who could not keep a secret: the next day he summoned a reporter from the sympathetic *New York Herald* and laid out his plans in a long interview. This astonishing breach was, in the words of one biographer, "the largest official leak of military secrets in the entire course of the Civil War."

In the days and weeks that followed, Lincoln continued to hear from impatient Republicans urging that McClellan be sacked. For the time being, though, the weather shielded the general in chief from danger. Hardly a day passed without some rain, sleet, or snow—sometimes all three. "The streets and crossings are worse than I have ever seen them," one Washington resident wrote in his diary. The mud was nearly impassable. McClellan's army couldn't have moved on those roads even if the general had suddenly turned vigorous.

Although the war machine was mired, Washington pulsed with energy. "The city was in a fearful condition—swarming not only with troops, but with vagabonds, vampires, and harpies of every description," one visitor noted. Not since the days of the Founders had a Congress gathered with such a crowded and fateful agenda. On January 14 and 15, Chase convened a conference of leading financiers and key congressional committee chairmen to hammer out the details of a modern economy. Within a week, Congress approved the framework for $150 million in new taxes, and bankers agreed to support up to $300 million in new government bonds. Opposition to paper money was quickly eroding.

Given their magnitude, the economic issues alone would have strained an ordinary Congress, but in 1862 they were only the beginning. With the departure of the Southern Democrats, the new Republican majority seized a once-in-a-lifetime chance to reshape the nation to its own vision. Legislation long stalemated by partisanship could finally be passed. Abolitionists introduced a bill to confiscate the property—the slaves—of Southern traitors and set them free; another bill called for the end of slavery in the District of Columbia. Speaker of the House Galusha Grow of Pennsylvania renewed his proposal to give free homesteads in the West to any pioneers willing to live on the land and improve it. Vermont's Justin Morrill proposed to grant large parcels of federal land to the states to fund colleges and universities for the children of farmers and workingmen. The Union faced the flames of destruction, yet Congress was looking beyond the disaster to a future of hardworking homesteaders and an educated middle class.

Perhaps no order of business more clearly captured this optimistic and opportunistic bent than the transcontinental railroad. This massive and forward-looking project had been stalled for years by squabbling between Northern and Southern factions over an acceptable route. Now Congress was more determined than ever to get the railroad started and thus bind the West securely to the Union—a tangible sign, wrought in iron and timber, that the United States had not forgotten its continental ambitions or lost confidence in its industrial might.

The various congressional actions and the prospect of all those millions of dollars and millions of acres drew eager men irresistibly to the capital. The laws passed in 1862 would create fountains of wealth; the only questions were how large the fortunes would be and who would get them. A few words added to one bill or struck from another could make all the difference. As never before, hordes of boosters and bribe spreaders and ballyhoo artists descended on Washington in search of their piece of the future.

The White House bustled as well. Lincoln's oldest son, Bob, was home from Harvard for a holiday. Willie and Tad were the happy owners of a new pony. Lincoln held weekly levees—open house receptions—on Tuesday nights, and Nicolay estimated that more visitors had passed through the city and shaken a president's hand during those January days than ever before in the nation's history. On two clear evenings, the president arranged tests of incendiary artillery shells on the grounds south of the White House. Thousands of spectators watched in awe and delight as the bombs rained fire from midair. Mary Lincoln, meanwhile, was busy with preparations for the grandest party the city had ever seen, a midnight buffet for four hundred invited guests in early February. When the invitations to her gala went out, Mary made the chosen extremely happy and left a much larger group of excluded Washingtonians desperately jealous.

Like many presidential families, the Lincolns never fit comfortably into Washington society. Though Mary very much wanted to make her mark, the president cared not at all about joining the capital's exclusive circles. Some society matrons scorned the Lincolns as frontier rubes, but even those who might have embraced the newcomers were unable to get close to them. To people who saw the Lincolns out on the town, it was obvious that the president and first lady were not eager to engage in casual conversation.

On January 23, for instance, the Lincolns spent an evening at the Washington Theater, watching a performance of Verdi's *Il Trovatore*. But the president found it impossible to relax or forget. Others could thrill to the "Anvil Chorus"; Lincoln could not stop worrying about the navy's failure to finish the flotilla of mortar gunboats that Halleck needed for the western rivers. The city around him seemed to be rushing headlong toward the future, but he felt the loss of every passing day like a lash.

The morning after the opera, across the ocean in Paris, U.S. ambassador William Dayton was ushered into a private meeting with the French foreign minister, Edouard Thouvenel. The situation in Europe, soothed briefly by the settlement of the *Trent* crisis, was sour again. One of Dayton's best sources was reporting that Emperor Louis-Napoleon,

Napoleon III, was preparing a speech for the opening of the French legislature in which he would call for the European powers to intervene on
behalf of the Confederacy. It was now Friday; the emperor's cabinet
would meet on Saturday to discuss this fateful step, and the speech would
be delivered on Monday.

The emperor, a nephew of the great general, was despised by members
of the Lincoln administration. An "unscrupulous adventurer," one confidant of the president called him, who had "no admirers among the garrison of the White House." It was said that Louis-Napoleon rued his
uncle's decision to sell the vast French territory of Louisiana to the shrewd
Thomas Jefferson, and that nothing would please him more than to see
the power created by the Louisiana Purchase split up, with France reestablished in North America. He was, in fact, sending troops to Mexico at that
very moment—ostensibly to collect on old debts, but well-founded rumor
had it that he intended to install a puppet government.

Dayton's mission, daunting for even the most experienced diplomat,
was to persuade the foreign minister that the emperor should defer his
call for intervention. But William Dayton was not an experienced diplomat. He couldn't even speak French. He was a New Jersey lawyer and
politician whose backbone had impressed Lincoln years earlier, an
antislavery man from a state full of Southern sympathizers, a Republican from a Democratic stronghold. Whether this courage and independence would serve him well in high-stakes diplomacy was an open
question.

Dayton began the discussion with a gambit suggested by the secretary
of state. Seward's idea was to play on centuries of hostility between France
and England, in hopes of driving a wedge between the two countries that
would prevent them from taking joint action now. For decades, the
French had grumbled about the unchallenged power of the Royal Navy,
yet in the dispute over the *Trent,* England had defended the right of neutral ships to sail unmolested. For the first time, the bully of the seas had
insisted that navies must honor treaties and respect other nations' vessels.
Wasn't this the moment, Dayton asked Thouvenel, to drive home the
point and call for even more formal restrictions on the use of naval
power? Dayton assured the French minister that the United States would
support its old ally France in any effort to shackle Britain's navy with
tighter international rules.

Thouvenel was quick to respond. What about naval blockades—shouldn't they be restricted as well? The question was hardly academic. Lincoln's blockade of Southern ports was beginning to bite: the French were extremely worried that their textile mills would be idled by lack of cotton, while their luxury exports could not reach the wealthy planters of the South. But Seward had anticipated this question in his last dispatch to Dayton. The quickest way to open the Southern ports, Dayton answered, was to support Lincoln's efforts to put down the rebellion.

But what about Charleston harbor? Thouvenel demanded. In recent weeks, the Union had deliberately sunk a "stone fleet" of weighted ships to obstruct the channel leading to the harbor. The European press was in an uproar over this supposed barbarity, claiming that the port was ruined forever. "One of the principal objects of my visit," Dayton responded smoothly, "is to correct erroneous impressions as to this matter." He proceeded with all his lawyer's skill to explain how easy it would be to remove the sunken hulks when the war was over, if storms and tides didn't move them first. Besides, he added, similar military tactics had been employed around the world since ancient times. Deftly turning the tables, Dayton pointed out that the Confederates were sinking vessels in various river channels to close them to Union gunboats.

Thouvenel seemed impressed. He wondered whether America's ambassador in London had explained all this to the British. And why, he asked, didn't the Americans get these explanations into the press? Dayton could sense that he was gaining ground, so he took out a map of the United States and invited Thouvenel to have a look. Mixing a bit from Seward's dispatches with a dollop from the newspapers, then infusing the whole with his own best guesses, Dayton sketched a broad military campaign to capture ports and force open rivers and cut railroads vital to the Confederacy. He made the task of subduing the rebellion—a task most Europeans considered hopeless—seem plausible. All the United States needed was "a little time," Dayton begged. "Having gotten on our armor, foreign governments must give us a chance."

This subtle performance, running the octaves from classic power politics to earnest pleading, from cool logic to the kindling of ancient grudges, went on for ninety minutes. Dayton left the sumptuous room feeling more confident than he had in months. If he had perhaps promised more than the United States could deliver, well, there had been no choice. With the emperor preparing his incendiary speech, "things had arrived at such a pass . . . that something must be done," he reported to Seward. During his meeting with Thouvenel, the foreign minister had visibly softened, and that was all that mattered.

Dayton waited until the following Monday to complete his dispatch to Washington so that he could include a report on the emperor's speech. Evidently, the administration's arguments had worked; though the emperor briefly lamented the war, he did not call for European intervention. Louis-Napoleon's "reference to our country is all that we could ask or expect," Dayton boasted, but then he added a warning. This victory could not endure without clear progress on the military campaign, progress he had promised to Thouvenel. "If weeks more shall pass away and spring shall open and nothing yet have been done" to win the war, "the impression will, I fear, become fixed in the European mind that our efforts to suppress the insurrection are hopeless."

Abraham Lincoln did not need William Dayton to tell him that. Yet his generals all had reasons why they couldn't start fighting: the roads were too wet, the men were too green, the rebels were too numerous, the armies lacked horses or wagons or muskets or cannon. Each explanation was reasonable in itself; taken together, they were ruinous. The year was already nearly a month old, but Lincoln's difficulty had only become more acute.

And so on January 27, the same day that his ambassador summarized the emperor's speech, Lincoln did some writing of his own. Two weeks earlier, he had toyed with the idea of leading the troops into battle. He would not do that—not yet, anyway—but this would be the next closest thing. "President's General War Order No. 1," he wrote on his official letterhead. "Ordered that the 22nd Day of February 1862"—George Washington's Birthday—"be the day for a general movement of the Land and Naval forces of the United States against the insurgent forces."

As an exercise in military strategy, this order was crude at best. Who knew whether conditions in Washington and Cairo and the Gulf of Mexico would all favor an advance on any given day a few weeks hence? Yet as an assertion of presidential authority over the military, it was both blunt and extraordinary. Once the secret order was issued to all the president's top commanders, no one fighting for the Union could doubt Lincoln's intention to direct the conduct of the war personally.

To one enterprising young general itching to strike a blow, Ulysses Grant, Lincoln's order was precisely what he was looking for. Grant immediately renewed his request for permission to assault the river forts in Tennessee, though he had no intention of waiting for Washington's Birthday.

3

FEBRUARY

In his inaugural address, Abraham Lincoln made a statement that would only later become controversial: "One section of our country believes slavery is *right* and ought to be extended, while the other believes it is *wrong* and ought not to be extended. This is the only substantial dispute." The fact that slavery was the crux and cause of the war did not mean, however, that Northerners were ready to fight and die to end slavery. In early 1862, Lincoln believed that most people in the North cared "comparatively little about the Negro, and [were] anxious only for military successes." As he reminded a visiting abolitionist toward the end of January: "We didn't go into the war to put down slavery. To act differently at this moment would, I have no doubt, not only weaken our cause but smack of bad faith. . . . The first thing you'd see would be a mutiny in the army."

As if in response, *The Atlantic Monthly*, the voice of New England's abolitionist intellectuals, devoted the cover of its February 1862 issue to a new poem of five short stanzas by a Boston writer named Julia Ward Howe. Even by the standards of Boston, hotbed of America's antislavery movement, the poet and her husband held extreme views. Samuel Gridley Howe was an educator and philanthropist whose hatred of slavery and the plantation aristocracy led him to support violent action even before the war broke out. He organized the rescue of fugitive slaves from Northern prisons, funneled guns and ammunition to the antislavery settlers in "Bleeding Kansas," and secretly financed the efforts of John Brown to stir up an armed slave revolt. His wife had a more literary temperament, but her poem demonstrated that her convictions were just as intense.

Howe's verses were an immediate sensation among the strong minority of Northern women and men for whom the Union was not worth saving unless it could be cleansed of the stain of slavery. Her words expressed with coiled power the radical belief that the Union armies must not be wasted on restoring the presecession status quo; no, those thousands of soldiers were God's mighty instrument with which to purge America of its original sin.

> *Mine eyes have seen the glory of the coming of the Lord:*
> *He is trampling out the vintage where the grapes of wrath are stored;*
> *He hath loosed the fateful lightning of His terrible swift sword:*
> > *His truth is marching on.*

In late 1861, Mr. and Mrs. Howe had visited Washington to inspect the camps where troops from Massachusetts were being trained. Because the peacetime U.S. Army had been so small—only about 16,000 soldiers—there was no organization large enough to provide medical care and sanitation for the volunteer armies now numbering in the hundreds of thousands. Private citizens therefore took over the tasks of setting up clean camps, providing healthful foods and medicine, and recruiting surgeons and nurses in ever greater numbers. Women like Dorothea Dix and Clara Barton plunged in, much as Britain's Florence Nightingale had done a few years earlier during the Crimean War. To harness the money and time of Northern citizens who wanted to serve the needs of Federal soldiers, the U.S. Sanitary Commission was created. Little by little, some order was brought to the chaos. Lessons were learned that laid the foundations of America's public health systems and gave birth to the American Red Cross.

What most impressed Julia Ward Howe about those camps of waiting soldiers, though, was not their physical needs so much as their spiritual destiny.

> *I have seen Him in the watch-fires of a hundred circling camps;*
> *They have builded Him an altar in the evening dews and damps;*
> *I can read His righteous sentence by the dim and flaring lamps:*
> > *His day is marching on.*

I have read a fiery gospel writ in burnished rows of steel:
"As ye deal with my contemners, so with you my grace shall deal;
Let the Hero, born of woman, crush the serpent with his heel,
                              Since God is marching on."

The rhythm of the poem, capturing the relentless cadence of marching feet, was no accident. The author had in mind a popular but controversial marching tune sung by abolitionist volunteers as they paraded through the streets of Boston and New York and Washington: "John Brown's body lies a-mouldering in the grave; His soul is marching on."

That song was anathema to men like George McClellan, who worried that zealots would turn a limited war for the Union into a bloodbath over slavery. In the eyes of such citizens, John Brown, the Harpers Ferry raider, was a terrorist who sought the murder of white men, women, and children across the South in a savage uprising of the slaves. Generations of white Americans had grown up hearing stories of the violent revolution of Haitian slaves sixty years earlier, and fear that such scenes would be replayed in the South "hovered over the antislavery debates like a bloodstained ghost," in the words of the historian David Brion Davis. McClellan had idealists like the Howes in mind when he remarked that he despised the reformers of Massachusetts as much as he did the secessionists of South Carolina. "I will not fight for the abolitionists," the general told his wife. "I am fighting to preserve the integrity of the Union & the power of the Government—on no other issue."

Howe's poem took the rhythm of the familiar song and gave it a religious, millennial message; though less vulgar than the song, the poem was every bit as aggressively impatient and intolerant of compromise. There was a message here for McClellan and Buell and Halleck and the other Democratic generals—as well as for Lincoln: God himself was calling the army into holy battle.

He has sounded forth the trumpet that shall never call retreat;
He is sifting out the hearts of men before His judgment-seat:
Oh, be swift, my soul, to answer Him! be jubilant, my feet!
                              Our God is marching on.

Not a day passed without Lincoln hearing from these passionate, idealistic men and women. Abolitionists dominated the congressional joint committee on the war and held chairmanships of many of the major committees in the House and Senate. Their voices rang in pulpits and newspapers across the North. They wrote letters and sent delegations to Washington. Some of them led regiments and brigades of volunteers. And they were fed up with the president's cautious approach to the matter of emancipation. They rejected completely what Lincoln had said in his inaugural address: that the Constitution left the issue of slavery to each state to decide for itself, and that, as president, he was obliged to uphold that Constitution. The abolitionists believed in a higher law, above the Constitution and above the Union itself. As Howe expressed it in her final stanza:

> In the beauty of the lilies Christ was born across the sea,
> With a glory in his bosom that transfigures you and me:
> As he died to make men holy, let us die to make men free,
> While God is marching on.

The North's soldiers would not die for the Union; they would die to set the slaves free. The abolitionists pressed Lincoln relentlessly to adopt this vision of the war, to make Howe's stern, terrifying verses the true Battle Hymn of the Republic.

But the president resisted. In Lincoln's view, the end of slavery was not a matter of if; it was a question of when, and how. Long before he became a national figure, he had predicted that the time would come when all Americans would be forced to choose sides over slavery, and he knew which side he would be on. Slavery was "a great and crying injustice," he said, "an enormous national crime." To one friend he said simply: "Slavery is doomed." On another occasion he said: "I am naturally anti-slavery. If slavery is not wrong, nothing is wrong. I can not remember when I did not so think, and feel." Even so, he perceived a clear impediment: "And yet I have never understood that the Presidency conferred upon me an unrestricted right to act officially upon this judgment and feeling."

Lincoln was constrained by a Constitution that countenanced slavery, by a Supreme Court that defended slavery, by the political need to hold on to the loyal slave states, and by the wide range of opinions among Northern voters. Though the hour for choosing sides seemed to be at hand, Lincoln resisted, offering legalisms and demurrals. He brushed

aside the complaints of antislavery activists—called "ultras" by their critics, on account of their no-compromise approach—or fended them off
with frontier anecdotes. He told one delegation of abolitionists about "a
party of Methodist parsons traveling in Illinois when I was a boy." The
parsons learned that a river up ahead was flooding, "and they got consid-
erin' and discussin' how they should git across it, and they talked about it
for two hours," Lincoln recounted. Finally the oldest one said, "Brethren,
this here talk ain't no use. I never cross a river until I come to it!"

Lincoln urged the ultras to stop pushing him and instead try to build
public support for his idea of a gradual emancipation, phased in over
years or even decades, with the federal government compensating slave
owners for their losses. After all, he noted, the entire country—not just
the South—was complicit in creating the slave economy, and the North
as well as the South had grown rich on it. Everyone should share the cost
of ending slavery. Gradual, compensated emancipation would appeal to
moderate public opinion, Lincoln believed; moreover, such a plan would
cut through constitutional barriers. Chief Justice Taney would never
stand for emancipation by federal order, but he would have no grounds
for objecting to emancipation freely chosen by the states.

Lincoln's careful approach was intended to avoid "a violent and
remorseless revolutionary struggle," as he put it. In fact, Confederate
operatives in Europe were actively using Lincoln's caution *against* him,
assuring French and British opinion leaders that they needn't have
qualms about recognizing the Confederacy, because the alternative—
Lincoln's government—was doing nothing to end slavery, either.

Alarmed, the abolitionists began to fear that the moment chosen by
Providence for the obliteration of slavery would slip away. If Lincoln's
policy was successful and the South rejoined the Union after a Federal
victory or two on the battlefield, the serpent might never be crushed.
Likewise, if Europe decided to tip matters in favor of the Confederates,
slavery would persist in an independent Southern nation. Either way, the
abolition movement would no longer be able to achieve its glorious mission.

So the delegations kept coming. The abolitionist leaders Moncure
Conway and William Ellery Channing called on Lincoln a few days
before Howe's poem was published, and urged him to act more boldly.
Not yet, he answered. "When the hour comes for dealing with slavery, I

trust I will be willing to act, though it costs my life," Lincoln assured them. Then he added ominously, "And gentlemen, lives *will be lost.*"

Among the lives in peril was one cherished by a seafarer from Maine named Nathaniel Gordon, who captained a ship full of whiskey to the Congo River in 1860. There, he traded the liquor for a cargo of about nine hundred human beings. On his return voyage, he was discovered by a U.S. Navy ship that was enforcing the ban on smuggling slaves.

Hundreds of sea captains had violated this ban during the forty years since the United States had outlawed the international slave trade. A fair number had been captured, and some of those were brought to trial. But not one had ever been given the maximum sentence: death. It was Gordon's fate to be the first convicted under a Republican administration. He was sentenced to hang.

Gordon's plea for mercy sat on Lincoln's desk on February 2, and the abolitionists were keen to see what the president would do. As Conway and Channing knew from their visit, Lincoln wasn't deaf to the aspirations of their movement. Indeed, he was cautiously reaching out to them by supporting some of their more modest but symbolically potent ideas, such as diplomatic recognition for the freed-slave nations of Haiti and Liberia, a stronger treaty with Britain to combat the slave trade, and a promise to protect the freedom of slaves liberated by Union expeditions along the Southern coast. The Gordon case had a particular resonance for the ultras. Here, it seemed, was a proper application for God's terrible swift sword. But Lincoln was not eager to pick up that sword, much less wield it. "You do not know how hard it is to have a human being die when you know that a stroke of your pen may save him," Lincoln said of Captain Gordon.

Nevertheless, when the celebrated writer and lecturer Ralph Waldo Emerson paid a call on Lincoln that day, he found the president lit by a "boyish cheerfulness." No doubt Lincoln had heard that the first of some 17,000 troops under Ulysses Grant had been loaded onto passenger steamers that morning, headed toward Fort Henry. In the six days since Lincoln issued his General War Order No. 1, Grant had secured Halleck's permission to attack, organized his troops, distributed rations and ammunition, recruited transportation, and coordinated his strategy with

Andrew Foote, commander of the flotilla of gunboats at Cairo. Finally, an army was moving.

"Oh, Mr. Emerson!" Lincoln said heartily when the philosopher walked in with his tour guide, Senator Charles Sumner of Massachusetts. "I once heard you say in a lecture that a Kentuckian seems to say by his airs and manners, 'Here am I; if you don't like me, the worse for you!'"

Emerson liked the Kentucky-born president more than he had anticipated. Lincoln wasn't the backwoods boor whom he had half expected to meet, but rather "a frank, sincere, well-intentioned man" with the methodical mind of a lawyer and a knack for storytelling. Emerson was charmed by Lincoln's delight in his own jokes: "He looks at you with great satisfaction, and shows all his white teeth, and laughs."

Emerson's views on slavery needed no introduction. Not only was he a founder of the magazine that had printed Julia Ward Howe's battle hymn on its cover, he had spoken at the Smithsonian two nights earlier on the need for forceful government action to resolve once and for all the moral crisis of slavery. Now he and Sumner wanted to discuss the fate of Nathaniel Gordon. Sumner told Lincoln, "I am against capital punishment, yet I am for hanging that slave-trader." He gave three reasons: "(1) to deter slave-traders, (2) to give notice to the world of a change of policy, & (3) to show that the Gov[ernment] can hang a man." When his visitors were finished, the president reviewed the case against the captain point by point, saying at last that he was "not quite satisfied" and would study the evidence once more before deciding. Emerson went away impressed by Lincoln's "fidelity and conscientiousness." Many people assumed that the president, following past policy, would spare Gordon without much thought. Not so: Emerson could see that Lincoln was weighing the matter seriously.

As Lincoln conversed with Emerson, and Grant started up the Tennessee River, Attorney General Bates, nursing a cold, tried to catch up on his diary. His outlook was decidedly bleak. In fact, Bates worried that the administration had no more than a few weeks left to save itself.

The mood in Washington—the plotting, the backstabbing, the double-dealing—was poisonous. Half a billion dollars, enough to run the entire prewar government for seven years, had been spent to raise and equip Union forces, yet there was almost nothing to show for it. Meanwhile, criticism of the administration rolled in from every side. Unionists were reluctant to attack Lincoln openly, so they aimed at his cabinet instead. The navy secretary, Gideon Welles, was under investigation by the Senate Committee on Naval Affairs. The interior secretary, Caleb Smith, was the target of corruption rumors. The most "formidable clique" was arrayed against Seward, whose influence was widely resented and therefore blamed for every failing of the Lincoln government. Anti-Seward schemers were reportedly cultivating Mary Lincoln, preying on her pride in her husband and her anxieties about wily Washingtonians. "They tell her Seward is working to undermine Lincoln and make himself the chief figure in the administration," Bates recorded.

In short, the attorney general concluded, the capital was running out of patience. The government was coming undone, and "a feeling of restless discontent" was spreading quickly. "If we fail to do something effectual in the next 30 days," Bates concluded, "the administration will be shaken to pieces."

In the event, the administration was saved, not in thirty days, but in fourteen. After so many setbacks, Lincoln and his government now experienced their best two weeks since taking office. During this fortnight, Lincoln banked precious political capital, at home and abroad—every penny of which he would desperately need before the year was over.

First, two days after Bates made his gloomy prediction, Lincoln bought some time with the abolitionists by denying Nathaniel Gordon's plea for mercy. Noting the "large number of respectable citizens" who had begged him to spare Gordon's life, the president nevertheless found that "duty" compelled him to allow the execution to proceed. Sending a slave smuggler to the gallows was a small step compared to the giant leap demanded by the abolitionists. Still, Lincoln's decision to enforce the severest sentence for a crime against black victims was a symbolic blow to the doctrine of white supremacy on which slavery rested. By denying Gordon's petition, Lincoln reversed, at least for a moment, the ugly current that had run steady and deep through generations of American history. The power of the government turned fatally against the slave economy.

Gordon had no doubt assumed that he would be treated like all the slave traders before him, and this about-face was so abrupt that Lincoln worried the sea captain might not have time to take it in. The president therefore gave Gordon a brief respite, delaying his execution until later in the month, so that the doomed man could prepare for "the awful change which awaits him."

Lincoln's next bit of good luck arrived in the guise of a successful party. On February 5, after weeks of planning, the day of Mary Lincoln's midnight ball finally arrived. The guest list had grown. Nicolay estimated that "six or seven hundred guests" were invited to this startling break with Washington tradition. Presidents normally entertained at formal dinners, and the invitation list was strictly limited. Or they held open houses, without refreshments, to which almost anyone could come. Mary's idea was to replace the formal dinners with a few grand buffets, which would allow her to entertain more guests for less money. What mattered to the cutthroats of Washington society, of course, was making the guest list for the *first* of these parties.

Determined to show Washington's grandes dames that a woman from the West could entertain in style, Mary hired the finest New York caterer to fill the dining room with huge platters of turkey, duck, ham, and terrapin. Elaborate centerpieces were spun from sugar, fine French wines were uncorked, and punch was served from an enormous bowl delivered from Japan by Commodore Matthew Perry. The new carpets and draperies and furniture Mary had broken the budget to buy were dusted and fluffed for their debut. Multitiered chandeliers illuminated the East Room, above carpets of sea-foam green. The White House staff was dressed in mulberry-colored uniforms to complement the china Mary had chosen for the occasion.

A little after eight P.M., Lincoln knotted his white tie and went into the room where Mary was getting into her elaborate gown with the help of her dressmaker, Elizabeth Keckly. Keckly later recalled the president standing before the fire, lost in thought with his hands behind him, when suddenly the rustle of Mary's long, trailing white skirt—decked with black lace to mark the death of Britain's Prince Albert—called him from his concerns.

"Whew!" Lincoln exclaimed. "Our cat has a long tail tonight." His eye took in the cleavage exposed by her low-cut bodice, and he added: "Mother, it is my opinion, if some of that tail were nearer the head, it would be in better style."

The guests arrived about nine o'clock: generals in full dress uniform; diplomats in regalia; cabinet members; selected congressmen and senators in formal wear. A few firebrands had refused to attend, feeling the times were all wrong for a party. Senator Wade of the joint committee fumed: "Are the President and Mrs. Lincoln aware there is a Civil War?"

With time, such criticisms would grow savage; the abolitionist newspaper *The Liberator* pronounced the ball "not worthy of man or woman with ears open to the wail of the bereaved throughout the country." But as Nicolay acidly observed, Washington has always worshipped the status conveyed by an invitation to an exclusive event, and few could resist the chance to be inside while the rest of the world was stuck outside.

Everyone took note of McClellan, fully recovered from his illness and cutting the figure familiar from the previous autumn: straight-backed, dashing, leaning close to whisper a bit of news or to admire a fellow officer's ornate ceremonial sword. He had spent the previous weekend working diligently on a long letter to Lincoln and Stanton defending his actions as general in chief and explaining in great detail his plans for a spring campaign. As always, he wanted a little bit more time. "If at the expense of 30 days delay we can gain a decisive victory which will probably end the war," he wrote grandly, "it is far cheaper than to gain a battle tomorrow that produces no final results." He made this calculation the same weekend that Edward Bates concluded the administration was down to its last thirty days, absent some pronounced success.

At midnight, the guests crowded down the hallway from the East Room to the dining room, where they found the doors locked and the key missing. During the awkward pause while the key was found, someone made a joke suggesting that the party and the war were alike in being stalled. Even McClellan laughed politely. Then the doors opened, the feast began, and champagne flowed.

The last guests lingered almost until dawn. In the basement, servants worked all night to clean up, drinking leftover wine as they toiled. Hot, tired, and drunk, several of them began arguing, which led to a fistfight in the kitchen. But the guests went home happy; years later, one Washington socialite still remembered the party as "the most splendid . . . ever served at the Presidential mansion, or, perhaps indeed, in Washington at any time." It was Mary's triumph as first lady, and it gave her husband a valuable lift among Washington's elite at a moment when that small but influential world harbored great doubts about his fitness to lead the country out of the wilderness of war.

While the last of the partygoers were making their way home, Brigadier General Grant and his troops awoke in Tennessee, where they were camped just out of range of Fort Henry's artillery. Grant and Andrew Foote had conceived a three-pronged assault. A division of infantry would seize Fort Heiman, across the river, and turn its guns on Henry. Another infantry division would cut the road linking Fort Henry with Fort Donelson, a dozen miles away. Then Foote's flotilla of seven gunboats would steam up to the fort and open fire. Grant ordered the movement to begin at eleven A.M.

Synchronizing these movements proved easier on paper than in reality. Even so, the ironclad gunboats performed brilliantly, pouring shells into the poorly situated Fort Henry and causing the Rebel garrison to flee. "Fort Henry is ours," Grant wired Halleck in midafternoon, adding almost in passing: "I shall take and destroy Fort Donelson"—a major undertaking that had not been part of his orders from St. Louis headquarters.

Grant didn't risk asking Halleck's permission because he worried that his superior might get cold feet. He was right to be concerned: shortly before Grant embarked on his campaign, Halleck had received a report, based on information from a Confederate deserter, that General P. G. T. Beauregard, the Rebel hero of Fort Sumter and Manassas, was on his way west with a large body of reinforcements. (The intelligence was only partly correct: Beauregard was headed west, but he wasn't bringing troops.) The more Halleck thought about that prospect, the more he doubted Grant's ability to hold Fort Henry—to say nothing of taking Donelson—and he sent Grant an order to hunker down and wait for help. But Grant was not much for hunkering. When a correspondent for the *New-York Tribune* told the general that he was leaving for the nearest telegraph to report the capture of Fort Henry, Grant said: "You had better wait a day or two."

"Why?" the man asked.

"Because I am going over to capture Fort Donelson tomorrow," Grant answered.

Grant wasn't sure how well defended the fort was, but he didn't want to delay his advance. In his view, 15,000 men attacking Fort Donelson in early February would have a better chance of succeeding than 50,000 men a month later, after the Confederates had had time to prepare. He drove his men through rain, snow, and sticky mud, and by the time Halleck's order caught up to him, he and his troops had Donelson surrounded.

More good news for the Union effort arrived on February 14, when Stanton strode into a cabinet meeting in Lincoln's office with a fresh report from Ambrose Burnside's amphibious expedition to North Carolina. Reading from the paper in his hands, Stanton pronounced the attack on Roanoke Island a complete success, with four small forts, forty guns, three thousand muskets, and three thousand prisoners taken. The last frightened Rebels had escaped, he said, by plunging into Albemarle Sound and swimming away.

Lincoln was delighted, though his thoughts quickly moved to more distant battlefields. He reminded the cabinet that a Union offensive to capture New Orleans—the "greatest business of all," as he put it—was gathering in the Gulf of Mexico. David Farragut, a seasoned old sailor with the guts of a lion, had set sail earlier in the month to take command of the expedition; he would soon begin dragging his armada over the sandbars at the mouth of the Mississippi to put them in position for an attack. Lincoln also mused that Grant was probably attacking Fort Donelson as they spoke.

The president was right about that, but Donelson proved a formidable nut to crack. The fort commanded the Cumberland River from an intimidating bluff and was manned by a force roughly equal to Grant's. Foote led his flotilla perilously close to the ramparts and opened fire, but this time the Union gunboats were shot to pieces. Denied another easy victory, Grant worried that he might have to mount a siege.

Before he could make his next move, though, the Confederate garrison surprised Grant's right wing on February 15 and broke through the Union line. It was a critical moment: the Rebels were in a position to batter Grant's cordon and perhaps drive him off, thus reopening the road to Nashville. But Grant kept his cool, and his green volunteers fought bravely to fill the hole. Union commanders learned as they fought; some didn't even realize that the men at the front needed a constant supply of ammunition. Fortunately, the Confederate troops were just as raw, and they soon fell back into their fortifications.

Now a siege seemed inevitable—except that Grant had a hunch. He knew the two Rebel generals he was up against, and he held them in contempt. Gideon Pillow had spent the Mexican War scheming for glory rather than winning it on the battlefield; his second in command, John Floyd, had conspired to aid the secessionists while serving as secretary of war in the Buchanan administration. Having just seen their troops retreat, Grant concluded that neither of these generals was much of a warrior and that they would collapse if given a push. Turning to his chief of staff, he declared, "The one who attacks first now will be victorious and the enemy will have to be in a hurry if he gets ahead of me." Audacious as ever, Grant ordered an immediate assault on the Confederate lines. By nightfall, his men had driven the Rebels inside Donelson's walls and were camped in the Confederate trenches.

True to form, Pillow and Floyd abandoned the fort during the night and slipped away on the Cumberland River, leaving a younger general, Simon Bolivar Buckner, to seek terms. Grant knew Buckner from their time together at West Point and in the war with Mexico, but his response to his old friend's overture was cold and unyielding. He would accept nothing less than "an immediate and unconditional surrender," Grant wrote, words that soon made him famous throughout the Union as a general with steel.

Buckner's capitulation completed the most effective and efficient single campaign of the entire war. Never before—and never afterward—was so much accomplished so quickly by so few men. In the space of just two weeks, an army of 17,000 had split the Confederate line in the West and disarmed an entire Rebel army. With their supply lines threatened and their positions flanked, the Confederates had no choice but to retreat from Kentucky, Missouri, and most of Tennessee. Nashville soon fell without a fight, a staggering loss of matériel and transportation for the Rebels. One authority called this "the greatest single supply disaster of the war." The ironworks at Clarksville, Tennessee, second largest in all of Dixie, was dismantled, greatly damaging the Confederacy's ability to produce armor, train rails, and ammunition. Extending the triumph, Foote's gunboats destroyed bridges along the South's main east–west railroad and carried the Stars and Stripes all the way into Alabama.

Lincoln was elated by the news of Grant's success. Such swift and consequential victories seemed to vindicate his six-week effort to push the Union armies forward. Since his visit from Emerson, Lincoln had been reading some of the man's work, and he was particularly taken with Emerson's lecture on the poet Goethe, so much so that he borrowed some of Goethe's works from the Library of Congress. Emerson's idea of the man of genius bravely seeing to the heart of things while others are blinded by "mountainous miscellany" no doubt struck a chord in the president. "Goethe teaches courage," Emerson wrote, in "the darkest and deafest eras."

The president felt like crowing, and when Stanton arrived at his office carrying the necessary papers to promote Grant to major general of volunteers, Lincoln announced: "I cannot speak so confidently about the fighting qualities of the Eastern men, or what are called Yankees . . . but this I know—if the Southerners think that man for man they are better than our Illinois men, or western men generally, they will discover themselves in a grievous mistake." Newly confident, Lincoln fired off a strategy memo to Halleck and Buell, suggesting ways to follow up on the victories. He proposed an amnesty from charges of treason for any Rebels who decided, in light of the news, to rejoin the Union. Now, instead of marking Washington's Birthday with the beginnings of an offensive, he could use the day to celebrate the fruits of one.

This triumph also came at a critical moment for Seward, who had been deeply worried about the political situation in Europe. In early February, Seward had written to Ambassador Adams in London, "We have unmistakeable evidence" that Southern sympathizers in the British Parliament were preparing to move for recognition of the Confederacy. Adams assured Seward that Palmerston's government wasn't ready for that step, but he warned that the South was winning the propaganda war in Britain. Adams begged for solid details of Federal successes: "Our friends want their hands strengthened."

Now Seward had something fresh and encouraging to report. "The great victory at Mill Springs, in Kentucky, has quickly been followed by the capture of Fort Henry . . . and the interruption of the [Confederate] railroad," Seward wrote even before the news from Fort Donelson. When word of that victory reached Washington, Seward composed an additional dispatch to Adams, labeled "Confidential." Now was the time, he suggested, to play up the steps Lincoln was taking against slavery, including the impending execution of Nathaniel Gordon. The British must not be allowed to think that both sides in this war were morally equivalent. He also noted that with each advance of the Union army, more slaves were being liberated: "Although the war has not been waged against slavery, yet the army acts immediately as an emancipating crusade."

It was as if the sun had risen on Northern hopes, and everything looked different in the dawn. A French nobleman visiting Washington in February observed that most foreign diplomats he had met in the capital sympathized with the Rebels and expected the Union to fail. But recent events were causing them to think again, he reported. Ambassador Dayton, writing from Paris, summed up the impact most succinctly. Momentum had been building for intervention, he wrote, but now "the switch had been turned off."

But even as Lincoln experienced his best fortnight as president, he also began a descent into one of the blackest periods of his life. A few of the guests at Mary's midnight ball on February 5 had noticed that the first lady and the president took turns slipping away from the party now and then, only to return with anxious looks on their faces. They were worried about Willie Lincoln, who lay burning with typhoid fever and struggling to breathe. Over the next two weeks, he would seem better for a few hours, then sink deeper. By February 11, the boy was so sick that he "absorbed pretty much all" of the president's attention. A week later, when Willie was still no better, Lincoln began to lose hope.

William Wallace Lincoln was the third of the four Lincoln boys. Their oldest, Robert, was an inward young man who, for reasons that aren't entirely clear, had a distant relationship with his father. Their second son, Edward, had died of tuberculosis in 1850, when he was three. Willie, born in 1850, was the boy most like Lincoln. He was better looking than his father, with light brown hair, blue eyes, and a round, handsome face. But he had his father's common sense and self-control. "He was his father over again both in magnetic personality and in his gifts and tastes," wrote one biographer. Father and son both loved to read and to write poetry; they were both fascinated by trains and arithmetic. Willie was "an amiable, good-hearted boy," in the words of Horatio Taft, the father of Willie's friends Bud and Holly, with "more judgment and foresight than any boy of his age that I have ever known."

Adults were charmed by Willie's quiet self-confidence and early maturity. "He never failed to seek me out in the crowd, shake hands, and make some pleasant remark," the poet Nathaniel Parker Willis remembered, "and this, in a boy ten years of age, was, to say the least, endearing." One day, when Willie was playing on the north lawn of the Executive Mansion, a carriage came up the drive bearing Secretary of State Seward and a prince of France. The two men gave Willie a formal salute, and without a thought the boy straightened his back, removed his hat and bowed as regally as a cavalier, before turning back to his game. As one biographer of the Lincoln family put it, Willie "was the sort of child people imagine their children will be, before they have any."

But he was not the sort of boy who wins over adults while annoying other children. Julia Taft, then a teenager, who often kept an eye on her younger brothers and their playmates, called Willie "the most lovable boy I ever knew, bright, sensible, sweet-tempered and gentle-mannered." (The feeling was mutual; eleven-year-old Willie had a crush on the winsome Julia.) Tad, two years younger than Willie, had none of this polish, and though the two boys were nearly inseparable, he couldn't help resenting, sometimes, Willie's striking self-possession. One morning in church Tad managed to cut his finger with a pocketknife, and when Julia Taft scolded him under her breath, he answered loudly: "Just you keep your eyes on Willie, sitting there good as pie."

On the rack of the war, Lincoln found refuge in his boys. To the astonishment of more traditional parents, the president took delight in nearly everything they did. Lincoln was "the most indulgent parent I ever knew," said one Illinois associate. "His children literally ran over him and he was powerless to withstand their importunities." Mary defended his lax approach, quoting her husband's maxim that "love is the chain whereby to lock a child to its parent." In an age when most adults believed that children were better seen than heard, when paddles and canes were standard classroom accessories, Lincoln's boys had free run of the White House. They shelled a cabinet meeting with a toy cannon, stole the president's reading glasses, and sabotaged the network of bells used to summon servants, so that the whole house jangled at once. No matter how disruptive their pranks, they were rarely scolded.

Recalling the hard labor of his own boyhood, Lincoln seemed determined that his sons would be joyful. He encouraged them to stage musicales and circuses in the White House attic, and he paid a nickel for a ticket to see Willie dancing in his mother's gown and Tad belting out a campaign jingle. The boys dimmed the lights for magic lantern shows, formed their own armies and navies, and brought their pets—including a goat—into the house. When Thomas Stackpole, a White House doorkeeper, complained about the latter, Lincoln answered, "It interests the boys and does them good; let the goat be."

Julia Taft recalled once hearing a commotion in another part of the mansion. Opening a door, she found the president sprawled on the floor with his sons and her brothers, all trying desperately to pin him. He had a determined boy on each leg and one on each arm, and he tossed them at whim as they roared with laughter. Tad saw her in the doorway and cried out, "Julie—come quick and sit on his stomach!"

Of Willie, an Illinois friend declared that Lincoln was "fonder of that boy than he was of anything else." Sometimes, while watching his son, the president felt as if he were seeing himself through the tunnel of time. Lincoln once studied Willie's face as the boy sat at the family table lost in thought, evidently pondering a perplexing matter. Making no move to help, he waited patiently while Willie furrowed his brow and pursed his lips. When his son finally brightened, Lincoln turned to a visitor and said, "I know every step of the process by which that boy arrived at his satisfactory solution." How did he know? "It is by just such slow methods I attain results," the president said.

Willie wasting away from diarrhea and dehydration was a horrible thing to watch, and the family was relieved when he appeared to rally on February 12, his father's fifty-third birthday. But the hopeful moment quickly passed.

Then Tad came down with typhoid as well, and for a time the Lincolns feared they would lose both boys. Tad's condition stabilized, but Willie grew weaker. On February 18, Nicolay recorded in his journal that Willie "is now thought to be in extremis. The President is nearly worn out, with grief and watching."

The scene at the bedside was inexpressibly sad. Willie lay in the elaborately carved rosewood bed his mother had recently purchased in New York, under gold and purple linens. His parents kept a nearly constant vigil. Bud Taft spent hour after hour with his suffering friend, taking his hand when Willie was afraid. Late one night, Lincoln found Bud sitting in the dim room and gently suggested that he go to bed. "If I go he will call for me," the boy answered.

This agony continued for two more days. On February 20, at about five P.M., Nicolay was working silently at his desk when the president staggered in and slumped onto the sofa. He looked drawn and pale. "Well, Nicolay, my boy is gone," Lincoln rasped. "He is actually gone." Then he burst into tears. Sobbing, Lincoln struggled to his feet and lurched back down the corridor.

Mary Lincoln collapsed into her bed and remained there for the next three weeks. Consumed by grief, she banned the Taft boys from the house, saying the sound of their voices was too much for her to bear. Robert Lincoln rushed home from school. Friends pitched in: Senator Browning and his wife alternated with Mary Ellen Welles, wife of the navy secretary, in keeping watch over Tad as he recovered. The celebration that had been planned for Washington's Birthday—every public building and fine home in the capital was to be illuminated with decorative lights—was canceled and the White House was draped in black crepe.

With Mary incapacitated and Tad still very sick, Lincoln was overwhelmed. Dorothea Dix, superintendent of nurses for the army, asked what help she could give him; gratefully, he answered that the family needed an experienced full-time nurse. Dix offered the services of a woman from Chelsea, Massachusetts, named Rebecca Pomroy, who was volunteering at one of Washington's largest military hospitals. Pomroy arrived at the White House to find Willie's body lying in state in the Green Room and Tad in bed weeping over the loss of his brother. She was sitting at Tad's bedside a few hours later when the president walked in and sat across from her. "Are you Miss, or Mrs.?" he asked. "What of your family?" Pomroy answered that she was a widow; she also told Lincoln that two of her three children were dead, while the surviving one was a soldier for the Union. With no one at home to care for, she said, she had come to Washington to serve the war effort.

Despite her many losses, Pomroy must have had a marked tranquility about her, because Lincoln asked her how she had managed to endure so much sorrow. "Did you always feel that you could say, 'Thy will be done'?" The nurse answered no. "It was months after my affliction that God met me," she said, "at a camp-meeting." Ever since that revival experience, she had been comforted by "God's love and care."

Lincoln had been an outspoken religious skeptic in his youth, and William Herndon insisted that he never adopted remotely orthodox Christian views. Yet he was a dedicated reader of the Bible, a "growing man in religion," in the words of his close friend Joshua Speed. "He found difficulty in giving his assent, without mental reservation, to . . . long, complicated statements of Christian doctrine," the Connecticut congressman Henry Deming recalled. But he would quickly join any church whose only membership requirement was to believe one simple statement: "Thou shalt love the Lord thy God with all thy heart, and with all thy soul, and with all thy mind, and thy neighbor as thyself." Especially in times of trial, Lincoln wrestled with the ultimate questions of life and meaning. After his son Eddie died in 1850, Lincoln had begun attending the First Presbyterian Church in Springfield, where he undertook a long exploration of Christian faith guided by the pastor, James Smith.

Now he again found himself in an abyss of sadness, and again he was asking those ultimate questions. "This is the hardest trial of my life," a tearful Lincoln confessed to Pomroy during their first encounter. The following night they had the same discussion. "He would question me upon special points to learn how I obtained my faith in God," the nurse recalled, "and the secret of placing myself in the Divine hands. Again on the third night, he made a similar request, showing the same degree of interest."

Willie's funeral was held on February 24. A fierce storm blew in, with winds so strong they nearly swept Edward Bates off his feet. He had to grab a tree and hang on until his servant could reach him. The rain stopped by early afternoon, but the wind blew harder, toppling a downtown church steeple. Inside the White House, dignitaries gathered quietly as the windows rattled and the gutters whined. Willie's embalmed body, dressed in a fine suit, rested in a rosewood and metal casket in the Green Room. Flowers from the White House conservatory were twined between his fingers. Before the funeral, Mary visited the body with her husband and oldest son for about half an hour, an experience that left her so distraught she refused to attend the service. Instead, just before the casket was closed she sent a messenger to retrieve the flowers as a memento.

The Reverend Phineas Gurley of the New York Avenue Presbyterian Church conducted the funeral in the East Room. It was a simple affair that brought tears to the eyes of many of those attending, including McClellan. Afterward, Lincoln and his oldest son climbed into the presidential carriage, drawn by two black horses. Accompanied by the two senators from Illinois, Orville Browning and Lyman Trumbull, they followed Willie's little casket in a hearse pulled by white horses to the chapel at Oak Hill Cemetery in Georgetown. Behind them rolled carriages bearing a parade of dignitaries half a mile long; following the carriages, on foot, trudged the African-American servants who worked at the White House. Once the procession reached the cemetery, the remains were placed in a crypt, where they would be kept until the family returned home to Springfield.

During the ordeal of Willie's illness, Lincoln tried to keep working, though exhaustion dogged his every step and his temper sometimes frayed. One day shortly after Willie's seeming recovery, an earnest young Treasury agent named Edward Pierce appeared at the president's office, sent there by Salmon Chase. Pierce, an ardent abolitionist, wanted to report on an experiment in which slaves on plantations seized by Union troops along the South Carolina coast were receiving education and religious instruction in hopes of becoming models of emancipation. Perhaps they could even serve in the Union army, Pierce ventured. Lincoln listened briefly, then snapped. Why was he being troubled with such details? "There seems to be a great itching to get Negroes within our lines!" the president exclaimed. He then began complaining bitterly about the radicals in the Senate who were withholding promotions from generals based on their views about slavery. The stunned young man reminded the president that he had been sent by the Treasury secretary. Lincoln composed himself and suggested that Pierce return to Chase's office in the building next door.

Fortunately, the news from the western front continued to be encouraging; under happier circumstances, these would have been the most heartening days of Lincoln's presidency thus far. In the wake of Grant's aggressive strikes in Tennessee, the Confederate line in the West was melting away. With Nashville falling into Union hands, Leonidas Polk began the evacuation of Columbus, the Confederacy's supposed Gibraltar. Seven weeks after Henry Halleck warned Lincoln that at least 50,000 Federal troops would be needed to take the city, the Rebels were forced to give it up without firing a shot, thanks to Grant's brilliant campaign.

Astonishingly, Grant's reward for his victories was to be temporarily relieved of his command. Perhaps Old Brains was wary of Grant's will to action. Or perhaps Halleck was unhappy that Grant sometimes seemed unwilling to wait for orders before taking the fight to the enemy. Whatever the reason, Halleck pointedly snubbed his subordinate after the capture of Fort Donelson. Reporting the victory to his superiors in Washington, Halleck praised a general who had done nothing more than send reinforcements from Kansas, but he had nothing good to say about Grant. In fact, Halleck advised the War Department that all the credit for the colossal success in Tennessee should go to one of Grant's division commanders.

After taking the three forts in Tennessee, Grant did further damage to his relationship with his commanding officer by pressing ahead to exploit the crack in the Rebel line. Eager to get to Nashville before the retreating Confederates could strip the city of supplies, Grant moved east on a path taking him out of Halleck's department and into Buell's. As soon as Halleck learned of the advance, he ordered Grant to stop where he was. But Grant wasn't finished: as resourceful as he was aggressive, he found a kindred spirit among the commanders in General Buell's army and promptly directed that officer to mobilize his division to seize Nashville. When Buell heard that Grant was steering troops from his own command, he was furious. To complete this fiasco, Halleck's increasingly testy telegrams ordering Grant to stop and file a report never reached their destination. Old Brains grew angrier by the day.

This was the Union command at its envious worst. Great as the fruits of his victories had been, Grant believed that much more was possible if the Union kept up the pressure. "We could have marched to Chattanooga, Corinth, Memphis and Vicksburg with the troops we then had," he later wrote. Other military men perceived the same opportunities. One of them, a fiery red-haired warrior named William T. Sherman, was working ferociously in Paducah, organizing troops and supplies and pushing them upriver to Grant as fast as he could. At the time, Sherman outranked Grant, and no protocol in army regulations allowed a junior officer to command a superior. But this meant nothing to Sherman compared with the chance to press the victory. "Every boat that came up with supplies or reinforcements brought a note of encouragement from Sherman," Grant later recalled, "asking me to call on him for any assistance that he could render and saying that if he could be of service at the front I might send for him and he would waive rank." Thus began one of the most important partnerships of the war.

Halleck, however, saw a different opportunity: the chance to add to his own authority. He pleaded with McClellan to combine the two western departments and give him command over Buell. Presented with a choice between a rival (Halleck) and a friend (Buell), McClellan predictably refused. Buell, meanwhile, fretted that Grant's strategic masterstroke was actually a looming disaster. In Buell's view, Grant's victories exposed the Union army to a massive counterattack by Beauregard and his phantom army from the east.

Amid this jockeying for advantage, McClellan weighed in by telegraph with a shocking proposal: the general in chief suggested to Halleck that he place Grant under arrest for failing to file his report. McClellan's recommendation was prompted by a gossipy wire from Halleck suggesting that Grant had "resumed his former bad habits"—that is, the hard drinking that marked his period of depression years earlier while separated from his wife in California. The entire episode appalled Andrew Foote, the gray-haired gunboat commander, who had seen enough of life to recognize immediately what was driving these assaults on Grant: "I was disgusted," he wrote to his wife. "It was jealousy."

Grant wasn't arrested, but he did lose his command for a short time. (It was given to C. F. Smith, a veteran soldier whom Grant greatly admired.) But when word of the strange goings-on in the West reached the White House, Lincoln instructed the War Department to open an investigation. Halleck immediately backpedaled: "You cannot be relieved from your command," he wired Grant. "There is no good reason for it." Grant's authority was soon restored.

As Grant reflected on this bumbling, he was less troubled by the insult than by the squandering of a golden chance amid the pettiness. The more ground his troops secured, the fewer men the Rebels would have available to draft into their armies. The fewer men the Confederates had, the sooner the war would end. Instead, as Grant later wrote, "time was given the enemy to collect armies and fortify his new positions." Over the next two years, this motif—of lost opportunities and unexploited victories—would haunt the Union cause time and again.

While Lincoln remained preoccupied with his son's illness, the thankless task of pushing George McClellan to deploy his ever growing army had fallen to that brusque dynamo Edwin Stanton. The new secretary of war had all of Lincoln's urgency but none of his finesse, and inevitably what had been a friendship between Stanton and McClellan curdled. Stanton quickly lost confidence in the general, and Little Mac added another name to his list of perceived tormentors.

That list was growing very long, and its charter members, the Joint

Committee on the Conduct of the War, still had their sights trained on him. McClellan's excuses for inaction—the muddy roads, the Rebel multitude, the brilliant intricacy of his plans—grew tedious, especially in comparison to Grant's alacrity. On February 19, as Willie Lincoln lay dying, Chairman Wade lit into McClellan during a meeting at the White House, noting correctly that the general had not even managed to clear the Rebel batteries blocking the Potomac River.

This scolding, along with Lincoln's order to move by Washington's Birthday, finally provoked the general in chief to take his first step. Early in the war, Confederate raiders had destroyed the bridge at Harpers Ferry that carried the Baltimore and Ohio Railroad across the Potomac and into the heartland. This key artery needed both a lasting repair and adequate Union forces in the Shenandoah Valley to protect it from future raids. McClellan decided to build a pontoon bridge made of heavy timbers laid across tethered canal boats, and use the bridge to send troops to capture and hold Winchester, Virginia, at the northern end of the valley.

Full of high hopes, McClellan led 8,500 blue-coated soldiers into Virginia on February 26, crossing a lightweight temporary bridge. "It was a magnificent spectacle," he recounted to his wife. "One of the grandest I ever saw." The army's heavy supplies would follow the next day, once the pontoon bridge was completed. Pleased with himself, the general quickly informed Stanton of his splendid progress.

The boats for the pontoon bridge, meanwhile, had been shipped along a canal that paralleled the Potomac. All that remained was to transfer the boats from the canal into the river through a lock connecting the two. There, to his dismay, McClellan discovered that the boats were some six inches wider than the lock. They were stuck in the canal. There would be no pontoon bridge.

The timing of this disaster could not have been worse: just three days had passed since Lincoln watched his son's casket slide into the crypt. McClellan's chief of staff, Randolph Marcy, drew the unpleasant assignment of explaining to the grieving president why the crucial railroad could not be reopened on schedule. Lincoln erupted. "Why in tarnation couldn't the General have known whether a boat would go through that lock before he spent a million of dollars getting them there?" he demanded.

Before Marcy could answer, Lincoln sneered: "I am no engineer"—McClellan was—"but it seems to me that if I wished to know whether a boat would go through a hole, or a lock, common sense would teach me to go and measure it. I am almost despairing. Everything seems to fail! The general impression is growing daily that the General does not intend to do anything. By a failure like this we lose all the prestige we gained by the capture of Fort Donelson."

The president was quiet for a moment and then repeated himself. "I am grievously disappointed and almost in despair."

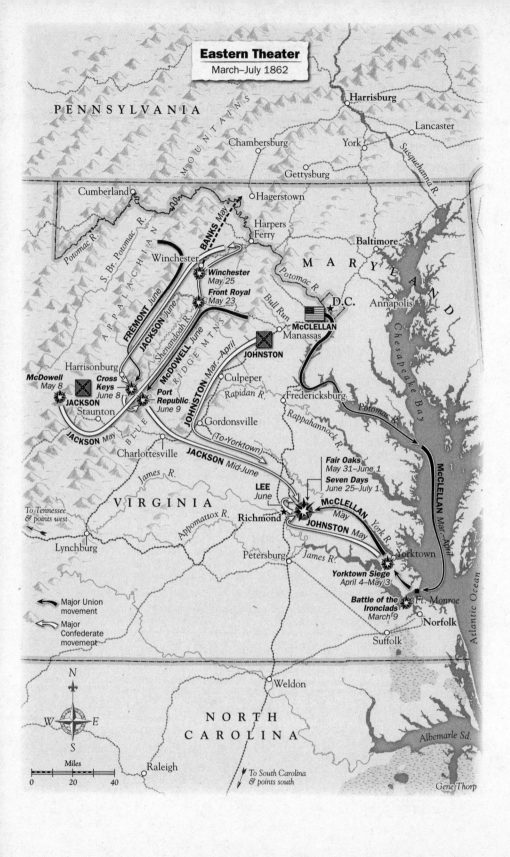

Eastern Theater
March–July 1862

PENNSYLVANIA

Harrisburg

Lancaster

Chambersburg

York

Susquehanna R.

Cumberland

Hagerstown

Gettysburg

Potomac R.

S. Br. Potomac R.

Harpers Ferry

BANKS May

MARYLAND

Baltimore

Winchester

Potomac R.

APPALACHIAN

FREMONT June

JACKSON June

Winchester
May 25

Front Royal
May 23

Bull Run

D.C.

Annapolis

McCLELLAN

Manassas

JOHNSTON

Shenandoah R.

McDOWELL June

Chesapeake Bay

Harrisonburg

Cross
Keys
June 8

McDowell
May 8

JACKSON

Staunton

Port
Republic
June 9

Culpeper

Rapidan R.

Fredericksburg

Rappahannock R.

Potomac R.

JOHNSTON Mar.–April

BLUE RIDGE MTNS

JACKSON May

(To Yorktown)

Gordonsville

JACKSON Mid-June

Charlottesville

James R.

VIRGINIA

To Tennessee
& points west

Appomattox R.

Richmond

Lynchburg

Fair Oaks
May 31–June 1

Seven Days
June 25–July 1

LEE
June

McCLELLAN
May

JOHNSTON May

McCLELLAN Mar.–April

York R.

McCLELLAN Mar.–April

Petersburg

James R.

Yorktown

Yorktown Siege
April 4–May 3

Ft. Monroe

Battle of the
Ironclads
March 9

Norfolk

Atlantic Ocean

Major Union
movement

Major Confederate
movement

Suffolk

N
W E
S

Weldon

NORTH
CAROLINA

Albemarle Sd.

Miles

0   20   40

Raleigh

To South Carolina
& points south

Gene Thorp

— 4 —

MARCH

A year had now passed since William Henry Seward experienced the astounding day when Abraham Lincoln became president instead of him. Any number of men had wanted the job, including at least three others in Lincoln's cabinet. But Seward was the man who was *supposed* to be president. The garrulous and wealthy New Yorker seemed chosen by destiny: his political career had started almost four decades before, when a chance encounter introduced the young Seward to Thurlow Weed, the political kingmaker of the Empire State. With Weed's backing, Seward became governor of New York at age thirty-seven. In the 1850s, he rose to become a dominant figure in the U.S. Senate and a builder of the new Republican Party, and by 1860 he was the most prominent Republican in America. But Seward's apparent strength soon became his weakness, because Republicans—looking for a less controversial candidate for president—chose this moment to select a nominee with a lower profile. Outmaneuvered at the convention by Lincoln and his people, Seward was again trumped by Lincoln when he was steered into the cabinet on the president's terms rather than his own.

Despite this rather stark evidence of Lincoln's superior political skills, Seward attempted to elbow Lincoln aside only weeks after the inauguration. On April 1, 1861, the new secretary of state gave Lincoln a memo asserting that the administration was rudderless; after a month in office, Seward wrote, the president was still "without a policy, either foreign or domestic." Lincoln was too busy handing out patronage jobs, Seward declared, when he ought to be tending to important matters. Seward took it on himself to sketch a few suggestions; notably, he advised Lincoln to stir up a war against a European foe as a way to reunite patriots North and South against a common enemy. "It must be somebody's business to pursue and direct [policy] incessantly," Seward continued. "Either the President must do it himself or . . . some member of his Cabinet." He concluded, disingenuously: "I seek neither to evade nor assume responsibility."

There was some truth in Seward's point about the president's lack of a strategic plan. "I have none," Lincoln once said. "I pass my life in preventing the storm from blowing down the tent, and I drive in the pegs as fast as they are pulled up." To put it more precisely, he had one policy—to preserve the Union—and would adopt no others until he was certain that they advanced him toward his goal. As for Seward's arrogant attempt to seize power, Lincoln simply shrugged it off. He was accustomed to being underestimated; in fact, he made an art of turning low expectations to his own advantage. And his skin was as thick as the hide of a rhinoceros. In response to Seward's memo, he simply batted his secretary of state down—"If this must be done, I must do it," he replied—and went on devoting dozens of hours every week, month after month, to the tedium of doling out federal jobs.

Seward was not the only critic dismayed by the energy that Lincoln appeared to waste on job seekers. "He seems to me to be fonder of details than of principles . . . of patronage, and personal questions than of the weightier matters of empire," complained the writer and attorney Richard Henry Dana. The line of supplicants often ran from the waiting room in the president's second-floor office, out the door, along the corridor, and down the stairs. Nicolay complained of being pestered by people wanting "'to see the President *for only five minutes.*' At present this request meets me from almost every man, woman and child I meet—whether it be by day or night—in the house or on the street."

Lincoln frequently felt overwhelmed by the press of job seekers. Soon after becoming president, he compared himself to "a man so busy in letting rooms in one end of his house that he can't stop to put out the fire that is burning the other." Drowning in minutiae, he seemed not even to know which jobs were truly important. One day early in Lincoln's tenure, Seward escorted the new U.S. ambassador to Great Britain into the president's office. Charles Francis Adams had gold-plated credentials: he was a congressman and a noted antislavery leader, and though he had no formal experience as a diplomat, he was the son and grandson of men who had held the office now occupied by Lincoln. None of this, however, seemed to matter much to Lincoln, who had originally wanted someone else for the job. When Adams entered the president's office, he was dismayed to find Lincoln wearing trousers worn thin at the knees and a pair of slippers on his feet. Sprawled in a chair and distracted, Lincoln only half-listened as Adams offered the customary soliloquy of gratitude for the president's trust and confidence. "Very kind of you to say so Mr. Adams, but you are not my choice," Lincoln answered. "You are Seward's man." Then, turning to Seward, Lincoln brightened and said, "Well, Governor, I've this morning decided the Chicago post-office appointment!"

Adams was appalled, but what he and the other critics failed to see was that Lincoln used patronage as a powerful adhesive, one that went a long way toward holding the fragile Union coalition together. His decision to fight the rebellion required that he ask many competing factions to share a grim and painful ordeal. By shrewdly dispensing the favors at his disposal, he endeavored to give all those factions a stake in the Union's success. Two scholars estimated that in his first year as president Lincoln filled about twelve hundred jobs in "the most sweeping" turnover of the federal workforce the country had ever seen. And as the war fueled further growth of the government, that number grew.

Lincoln often welded political leaders to the Union cause by making them generals—some of them because they had relevant military experience, but many more simply because of their influence with one political group or another. "In regard to the patronage sought with so much eagerness and jealousy, I have prescribed for myself the maxim, 'Fairness to all,'" Lincoln declared. Though Republicans seethed, Lincoln was careful to give stars to a number of prominent Democrats, never forgetting that the opposition carried nearly 45 percent of the Northern vote in 1860. He made generals of John A. Dix, a former Democratic senator from New York; John McClernand, the leading Democrat in southern Illinois; Benjamin Butler, the most prominent Massachusetts Democrat; and, most notably, George McClellan.

Lincoln also catered to ethnic groups. He made the Irish nationalist hero Thomas Meagher a brigadier general, one of a dozen Irish-born Union generals who served in the war. An order to the War Department gives a window into Lincoln's thinking about military patronage: "There has got to be something done unquestionably in the interest of the Dutch, and to that end I want Schimmelfennig appointed." Lincoln knew that the name alone would delight German-Americans. He even learned to be attentive to the religious denominations of his appointees, after being scolded for putting too many Episcopalians in his cabinet. "I must do something for this great Methodist church," he told a visiting congressman. "Seward is an Episcopalian, Chase is an Episcopalian, Bates is an Episcopalian, and Stanton swears enough to be one."

Over the course of his first year in office, Lincoln's painstaking attention to job seekers and favor hunters—which he once compared to "bail[ing] out the Potomac with a spoon"—had come to make more sense to Seward and others as they watched the president struggle to hold the fractured Union together. In the words of Gideon Welles: "Never under any administration were greater care and deliberation required" in dispensing presidential favors, for Lincoln was shoring up "a demoralized government and a crumbling Union."

Despite his initial skepticism about the president's abilities, Seward gradually came to see the discipline and cold calculation behind Lincoln's every decision. Friendship, Seward discovered, rarely clouded the president's view. In early 1862, when Lincoln chose his first Supreme Court justice, he declined to appoint his close friend Orville Browning, whose wife, Eliza, had pleaded with Lincoln on her husband's behalf. He also passed over David Davis, another Illinois friend and the chief engineer of Lincoln's presidential nomination. Instead, he picked an Ohio attorney, Noah H. Swayne—who, not coincidentally, was sponsored by one of Lincoln's most dangerous antagonists, Ben Wade of the congressional joint committee. "He would always give more to his enemies than he would to his friends," a disappointed Davis supporter later wrote. "And the reason was, because he never had anything to spare." Or, as Lincoln himself put it, he "always had more horses than oats." The president trusted that his friends would remain his friends, even when he disappointed them; meanwhile, he took great care to make sure that his enemies were appeased.

In the year since he'd joined the administration, Seward had earned his way into Lincoln's confidence and even his affections, "spen[ding] a considerable portion of every day with the President," according to one cabinet colleague. His adroit handling of the *Trent* affair proved his diplomatic skill, and on a personal level, the two men had much in common. Both were informal, careless about their grooming, and sometimes uncouth. Both liked children and pets. When Seward discovered that the Lincolns had a soft spot for cats, he promptly delivered two kittens to the White House. Both men loved yarns and jokes, including ribald and off-color ones. Lincoln liked to claim that he was the better storyteller: "Mr. Seward is limited to a couple of stories which repeating he believes are true," Lincoln teased. "The two men found it easy to drop into nonsensical and preposterous dialogue," a Seward biographer wrote. Emerson, during his visit in February, caught the flavor of their banter when Seward recounted a typical exchange. "The President said yesterday, when I was going to tell him a story, 'Well, Seward, don't let it be smutty.'"

Where the two men were different, they complemented each other. Lincoln was indifferent to food and took no interest in entertaining guests. Seward, on the other hand, was renowned in Washington as an extravagant and enthusiastic host; his eleven-course dinner parties began with soup and ran through fish, beef, and fowl; then the guests tarried over ice cream and fruit before the evening ended four hours later with port and fine Cuban cigars. As a consequence, he picked up plenty of useful intelligence at his dinner table and other tables around town. More important, Seward's sturdy optimism bolstered the melancholy Lincoln. The secretary of state projected this buoyancy through his frequent letters to U.S. emissaries abroad, so that he became a brash and sunny face of the embattled nation. On March 6, for instance, he visited Lincoln to preview his latest dispatch to Adams in London; his cheerful nature rang from nearly every sentence. "It is now apparent that we are at the beginning of the end of the attempted revolution," Seward wrote. "That end may be indeed delayed by accidents or errors at home, as it may be by aid or sympathy on the part of foreign nations. But it can hardly be deemed uncertain."

Many Confederates might secretly have agreed, for their situation was suddenly beginning to look precarious. On a rainy late February morning in Richmond, Jefferson Davis had been sworn in as president of the Confederacy. In his first message to the Confederate Congress, Davis spoke bluntly of the recent failures of the rebel army. "The Government has attempted more than it had the power successfully to achieve," Davis admitted. The South simply had too many borders and not enough men; it was hopeless to try "to protect by our arms the whole territory of the

Confederate states, seaboard and inland." Davis had summoned General Robert E. Lee to Richmond, asking Lee to suspend his work preparing coastal defenses and advise him on strategy.

The Confederacy's long-term prospects were also being eroded by the North's increasing financial strength. Lincoln had put it simply: "I must have money." Expanding on the theme, he added, "The result of this war is a question of resources. That side will win in the end where the money holds out longest."

Accordingly, the House of Representatives was hard at work on developing a massive system of taxes to pay for a protracted war if necessary. Under their plan, a new commissioner of internal revenue would be appointed, and virtually every money stream in the Union would be tapped—starting with income, which had never been taxed before. Sales taxes were instituted: two cents per pound on sugar, a penny per pound on coffee, ten cents per gallon on coal oil, fifty cents per clock, ten cents per pound on cheap cigars and twenty cents per pound on good ones—on and on went the list, page after page of levies covering rail fares, steamboat tickets, stock transactions, and newspaper advertisements. "Nearly every class will probably find something to complain of," one newspaper allowed.

The North's ability to collect so much revenue from so many new taxes suggested its enormous economic advantage. In 1860, the eleven states that formed the Confederacy had just 10 percent of the nation's industrial capacity. The North, by contrast, had not only a legion of thriving industries, but also nine of the ten largest cities, and two thirds of all railroad tracks. Meanwhile, the manufacturing capacity of many of the Southern states was shrinking. Between 1840 and 1860, Virginia lost one third of its manufacturing jobs; on the eve of the war, it employed approximately the same number of factory workers as the tiny state of Rhode Island.

As spring began arriving across the South, Union forces continued to rally. Troops and gunboats under the command of Brigadier General John Pope raced down the Mississippi and laid siege to the Confederate town of New Madrid, Missouri. A force led by former speaker of the house Nathaniel Banks—one of Lincoln's purely political appointees—started up the Shenandoah Valley from Harpers Ferry toward Winchester, Virginia. Brigadier General Samuel Curtis, a former congressman with West Point training, led some 12,000 bluecoats into northwest

Arkansas, where they confronted a larger Rebel force under Earl Van Dorn at a place called Pea Ridge, near Fayetteville. When the battle commenced on March 7, a cold, wet Friday, the Rebels got the early advantage, but Curtis skillfully divided his army to scatter first one wing of the Confederate force, then the other. It was the biggest battle of the war fought west of the Mississippi, and Curtis's victory effectively ended the danger that the Rebels might peel Missouri away from the Union.

Outside Washington, Joseph E. Johnston weighed the acres of blue spread out around the capital and concluded that he must fall back toward Richmond or risk being cut off by a flanking maneuver. In early March, he very quietly abandoned fortifications that the Rebels had occupied since the battle of Bull Run the previous summer. The Union high command in Washington would not notice his departure for several days, but here, as elsewhere, the South was falling back. Alarmed, the Confederate Congress passed a law requiring military authorities to burn cotton and tobacco rather than let it fall into the hands of advancing Federal troops.

So much had happened so quickly. Now, with the breeze finally at his back, Lincoln concluded that the time had come to raise the stakes against slavery.

He had broached the idea gingerly in his message to Congress in December: the federal government should offer to buy freedom for the slaves. Explaining his reasoning to the abolitionist Moncure Conway, Lincoln said that slavery "was the disease of the entire nation," and that Northerners "should be ready and eager to share largely the pecuniary losses to which the South would be subjected if emancipation should occur. . . . All must share the suffering of its removal."

Having slipped this proposal into public view, he began mentioning it in meetings with various influential visitors. As he told one caller: "American slavery is no small affair, and it cannot be done away with at once. . . . It belongs to our politics, to our industries, to our commerce, and to our religion. Every portion of our territory in some form or other has contributed to the growth and the increase of slavery. . . . It is wrong, a great evil indeed, but the South is no more responsible for the wrong done to the African race than is the North." To another visitor, he put it this way: "Slavery existed . . . by the act of the North as of the South; and in any scheme to get rid of it, the North, as well as the South, was morally bound to do its full and equal share."

The details of such a scheme had been taking shape in Lincoln's mind for years. Once he became president, he enlisted Congressman George Fisher, of Delaware, to help investigate the idea. The results were not entirely encouraging, but by March Lincoln concluded that military successes had made him strong enough to give the plan a big, formal push. He proposed that Congress issue a joint resolution offering to "co-operate with any state which may adopt gradual abolishment of slavery."

Like the hanging of Captain Gordon—who had been executed on February 21—this proposal represented a profound change in the federal government's stance toward slavery. But Lincoln played down that fact; rather than promote emancipation as a moral imperative or a social revolution, he framed it as part of the war effort. Knowing that Confederate leaders nursed hopes of attracting the border states to join their side, he reasoned that he might be able to dash their dreams by persuading those states to give up on slavery. "To deprive them of this hope, substantially ends the rebellion," Lincoln asserted. He also took a moderate position on the pace of this proposed change, writing: "In my judgment, gradual, and not sudden emancipation, is better for all."

His moderate approach led the abolitionist senator Thaddeus Stevens to gripe that Lincoln was serving up "diluted, milk-and-water-gruel," but the president's mild tone did not deceive Stevens's colleague Charles Sumner. Sumner immediately recognized that any vote for emancipation, in the present context, would start a chain of dominoes falling. "The proposition of the Pres[ident] is an epoch," the senator wrote hastily, "& I hope it will commence the end." The antislavery *Daily National Republican* agreed. "The great, transcendent fact is, that for the first time in two generations we have a recommendation from the presidential chair of the *abolition of slavery,*" the newspaper exulted.

Compensated emancipation, freely chosen by the states, was for Lincoln a way around the most difficult problem he faced in regard to slavery: the Supreme Court. With the appointment of Justice Swayne, Lincoln was beginning to remake the panel, but for now it was still Roger Taney's court. On March 17, the Chief Justice marked his eighty-sixth birthday in a glum mood. A week later, when the court adjourned, he asked his fellow justices to pay him a visit before they left town. One by one, they called at his Capitol Hill home and found Taney emotional as he said goodbye until the fall. "He had a presentiment that he should die very soon," Attorney General Bates recorded in his diary. But the author of the *Dred Scott* decision wasn't dead yet.

Lincoln studied the reaction to his proposal very closely. When *The New York Times* fretted that the cost of compensating slave states would be prohibitive in light of "the coming terror of war taxation," he fired off a handwritten letter to the editor, Henry Raymond, marked "private." "Have you noticed the facts that less than one half-day's cost of this war would pay for all the slaves in Delaware, at four hundred dollars per head?" Lincoln asked. "That eighty-seven days' cost of this war would pay for all in Delaware, Maryland, District of Columbia, Kentucky, and Missouri at the same price? Were those states to take the step, do you doubt that it would shorten the war more than eighty-seven days, and thus be an actual saving of expense?" Raymond quickly apologized, praising Lincoln's proposal as "a master-piece of practical wisdom and sound policy."

Following the fiasco with McClellan's canal boats, Lincoln told Sumner, during one of the senator's frequent visits, that he intended "to talk plainly" to his general in chief, who nevertheless managed to avoid the president after returning to Washington from the upper Potomac. (He later complained that Secretary of War Stanton had kept him away from Lincoln.) Instead, the general busied himself with details of a possible mission to clear the Confederate batteries that blocked river traffic into Washington. The long debate over McClellan's plan to assault Richmond via the Chesapeake Bay was bending in McClellan's favor, but the Rebel guns prevented the necessary troopships from reaching his army at the Alexandria docks. McClellan did not yet realize that the Rebels were retreating.

When asked about the failed mission to restore the Harpers Ferry railroad bridge, McClellan overflowed with excuses; he compiled them all into a memo for the War Department in which he pronounced himself "well satisfied with what had been accomplished" on the seemingly feckless expedition. Stanton, however, had already decided that the "damned fizzle" was yet another indication that McClellan "doesn't intend to do anything" to fight the Rebels.

McClellan had greeted Stanton's appointment as "a most unexpected piece of good fortune," but in just two months, their relationship had become poisonous. From his earliest days on the job, Stanton had been hearing "at intervals from a variety of sources" that McClellan was secretly conspiring to lose the war. People whispered that he was a member of a shadowy pro-Confederate group known as the Knights of the Golden Circle. Founded in 1854 by a doctor in Cincinnati, the Knights originally sought to create slave colonies in Mexico and the Caribbean. The colonies would eventually become new states, thus ensuring that proslavery votes would continue to dominate the U.S. Senate. Little came of these half-baked plans, but, with the outbreak of war, the Knights suddenly took on a dark power in the imaginations of suspicious Unionists. They saw the group as a nest of treasonous conspirators at a time when treason and conspiracy were dangerously real. Stanton put enough stock in the rumors about McClellan that, as he confessed to a friend, they "caused great solicitude in my mind." He discussed his concerns with Lincoln, who by now had not spoken with McClellan for more than two weeks, since before the death of his son. The president summoned McClellan to the White House early on March 8, a beautiful spring Saturday.

In the streets of Washington, all signs pointed to some great drama about to unfold. The photographers' shops along Pennsylvania Avenue were packed with men having pictures taken as mementoes for their families and friends; one shop was mounting some two thousand portraits per day. Columns of troops began marching from the hills north of the city and crossing into Virginia over the Long Bridge, their regimental bands playing brightly. Soldiers shouted their farewells to friends they had made and lovers they had wooed during their months in camp, and these sounds mixed with the creaking of wagon wheels and the braying of army mules. Adventurers, journalists, and other thrill seekers from around the world crowded the capital; one diarist described "an immense throng" and went on: "The City seems to be entirely full. The prospect now is that there will be a desperate battle near here soon. McClellan is well-prepared and has an immense army near here all ready and anxious for a fight."

But was that true? The president needed to know.

Behind closed doors with the general, Lincoln launched into the plain talk he had mentioned to Sumner. No matter what McClellan might think, the president was emphatically not "well satisfied" with the results of the canal boat mission. McClellan laid out his excuses; later, he claimed that Lincoln found them persuasive. Perhaps so. But more important was the real reason why Lincoln had called Little Mac to his office: he needed to make sure the young general understood that excuses were no longer enough. McClellan always had excuses. Taken one by one they might each seem persuasive, but compounded over month after month, the litany had severely undermined his credibility. McClellan's enemies no longer trusted his good faith, if they ever had, and this failure of the canal boats now fed suspicions about the general's true intentions. As McClellan later recalled the conversation, Lincoln connected the fiasco at Harpers Ferry to what he called "a very ugly matter," namely, the growing belief that the real motive behind the general's plan to take the Army of the Potomac down the bay was a "traitorous" plot to leave Washington wide open to attack.

When he heard the word "traitor," McClellan exploded, completely missing the fact that Lincoln was trying to help him. He leaped to his feet with tears in his eyes and demanded, in salty terms, a retraction of a charge that Lincoln was merely reporting. Like the president, McClellan—the man who had bragged "I can do it all"—was suffering from exhaustion; as he struggled to keep up with the details of running his own army while supervising the war as a whole, his nerves had become badly frayed. A few days earlier, he had confessed in a private letter that he felt pushed to his limits. "The abolitionists are doing their best to displace me," he wrote. "You have no idea of the undying hate with which they pressure me. . . . I sometimes become quite angry."

Lincoln tried to calm his general in chief, apologizing for the misunderstanding and assuring McClellan that he was only trying to make him aware of the deteriorating political situation. The president explained to McClellan that he needed to be more careful, and he also needed some real success on the battlefield—now. Nothing less would silence his detractors. But with his fine-tuned sense of honor offended, the general would have none of it. He repeated that he could not have his name spoken in the same sentence with that horrible word.

Then McClellan had an idea. He was meeting that morning with the senior generals of the Army of the Potomac. He offered to poll them as to the wisdom of his current strategy. Surely Lincoln would trust them, wouldn't he? So it was that, a short time later, McClellan sent the generals from his headquarters across Lafayette Square to report their conclusions to Lincoln and Stanton.

The people on the sidewalks watching this bustle of braid and brass buttons could hardly have imagined the dysfunction behind it. The secretary of war feared that the general in chief was secretly conspiring with the enemy, so the outraged general in chief was parading his subordinates before the president as character witnesses. The vote of the generals was eight to four in favor of McClellan's proposed plan to sail down the coast and attack Richmond, over Lincoln's preferred approach of attacking the Rebels at Manassas, where they were still believed to be entrenched. A fuming Stanton cross-examined the division commanders, ultimately concluding that they were "afraid to fight." Lincoln professed not to care about which strategy the generals pursued, as long as the army got moving. "All I ask is for you to just pitch in," he exhorted the group.

But he did care. Months later, he was still telling friends "that his opinion always had been that the great fight should have been at Manassas," but that he gave in because the majority of the generals opposed him. After the awkward meeting broke up, Lincoln issued two orders, both of which indicated his continuing lack of trust in McClellan's judgment. The first directed the overworked general to reorganize his army into four corps under the leadership of his four most senior generals. As it happened, all of these men were skeptical to one degree or another of McClellan and his plans. Whether they had earned Lincoln's confidence by their years of experience, or by their independence from McClellan, the effect was the same: the president would not allow Little Mac to promote his friends and favorites. Lincoln's second order was even more pointed. He set a hard deadline: the Army of the Potomac was to begin executing McClellan's plan within the next ten days—but not before the new corps commanders agreed that the capital was completely safe.

No doubt Lincoln believed that by appointing these seasoned generals as auditors of McClellan's movements he was protecting both his general in chief and his administration against suspicions of perfidy or incompetence. But the effect of his two orders was to launch the Union's vast military campaign under a cloud of mistrust and miscommunication.

While the generals were meeting with Lincoln, a strange and fearsome craft was slowly steaming north from Norfolk toward Hampton Roads, looking, in the words of one observer, "like a house submerged to the eaves, borne onward by a flood." It was the Confederate ship *Virginia*, once known as USS *Merrimack*, a 275-foot, forty-gun wooden frigate that had been, for a short time, the U.S. Navy's finest warship.

When Rebel guns fired on Fort Sumter, the *Merrimack* was docked in the navy yard at Norfolk for repairs. Rather than allow the ship to fall into Confederate hands, the officer in charge of the yard ordered her burned and sunk. But soon the Rebels raised the hulk. Great hopes were pinned on the restoration project: scrap iron was salvaged from ships and railroads around the Confederacy and sent to the Tredegar Iron Works in Richmond, where it was recycled into armor plates. The plates were then bolted to pine timbers two feet thick, backed by another four inches of solid oak. Fashioned into a sloping structure with firing ports for four guns on each side and pivot guns fore and aft, the iron cladding and heavy timbers made the formidable craft as unwieldy as it was impervious. A fifteen-hundred-pound iron ram, attached to the prow just below the waterline, completed the rechristened ship's menacing array.

Admirals the world over had known for several years that the long age of wooden warships was coming to an end. The first armored ship in the world, *La Gloire*, was built by the French in 1858, and the British quickly followed with HMS *Warrior* and the recently completed *Ironside*. Those ships had not been battle tested, however, so this was the day and the place that would usher in the modern age of naval warfare.

The *Virginia*'s dark hulk entered the James River under the command of Commodore Franklin Buchanan, who had been the first superintendent of the U.S. Naval Academy at Annapolis. Buchanan drew a bead on the big wooden warships lying at anchor between Norfolk and the Union bastion of Fort Monroe on the opposite shore. At full steam, the ironclad made barely five knots, so the crews of the Federal ships had sufficient time to prepare for the oncoming monster. As she came in range, the fifty-gun USS *Congress* fired first. The cannonballs bounced off the ironclad like hailstones hitting a frying pan. Nearby, the *Cumberland*, carrying thirty guns, opened fire, along with batteries ashore, but equally in vain. Closing the distance, the *Virginia* loosed a volley at the *Congress* and then rammed the *Cumberland*. Water poured through the pierced hull, and the wooden warship sank quickly.

Shaking loose, and losing her ram in the process, the Rebel ironclad began a slow, ponderous turn to fire on the *Congress* again. The Union crew tried to sail away but struck a shoal. Three other Federal ships, steaming upstream toward the fight, also ran aground. Helpless and shot to pieces, the *Congress* surrendered, but by that time the tide was running out and the heavy ironclad, with its twenty-two-foot draft, was in danger of grounding as well. As a parting shot, the Rebels set fire to the *Congress* with a shower of heated cannonballs, eventually producing an immense explosion when the frigate's magazine went up. Then the *Virginia* withdrew for the evening, her crew confident of finishing the Federal flotilla come morning.

Nothing like it had ever occurred before: one ship, carrying a mere ten guns, had achieved a great victory over five wooden vessels bearing more than two hundred guns among them.

The telegraph between Fort Monroe and the War Department happened to be out that night, so news of the disaster did not reach Lincoln until the next morning, March 9. Nicolay was in the office reading aloud from editorials in leading New York newspapers—both Republican and Democratic—that praised the Tycoon's proposal for compensated emancipation. The postmaster general, Montgomery Blair, whose roots in Maryland and Missouri gave him a keen understanding of border state politics, came by, at which point Lincoln asked him why the proposal wasn't generating any discussion where it really counted. "Since I sent in my message [to Congress], about the usual amount of calling by the border state Congressmen has taken place," Lincoln said. "Although they have all been very friendly, not one of them has yet said a word to me about it." He asked Blair whether it would be a good idea to convene a meeting with the border state delegations to "have a frank and direct talk" about his proposal. Perhaps it would be better, Blair replied, to wait for another military victory.

"That is just the reason why I do not wish to wait," Lincoln answered. "If we should have successes, they may feel and say, 'the rebellion is crushed, and it matters not whether we do anything about this matter.' . . . I want to tell them that if they will take hold and do this, the war will cease." Blair agreed to arrange the session.

Shortly after that, Assistant Secretary of War Peter Watson rushed into Lincoln's office with the first report from Hampton Roads. He was soon followed by Stanton, Seward, and Secretary of the Navy Welles. McClellan hurried in, as did Montgomery Meigs. People were talking all at once, each outdoing the others in imagining the calamities that would befall the Union now that the Confederacy had created a new and indestructible war machine. As one of those present reported: "One thought she would go to New York and levy tribute—another to Phila[delphia]—a third to Baltimore, or to Annapolis," where the transport ships for McClellan's army were collected and vulnerable. Another participant in the ad hoc meeting "said that she would come up and burn Washington."

Lincoln listened to this panicky talk for a while, then called for his carriage. He needed some fresh air and decided he would fetch a favorite adviser to join the deliberations at the White House: Captain John Dahlgren, commander of the Washington Navy Yard. Among other skills, Dahlgren was one of the navy's foremost inventors—he specialized in refinements to artillery—and the president was always eager to hear his views about new weapons and technology. When Dahlgren opened his door to the president, the captain was shocked to see how "thin and wasted" Lincoln had become in the fortnight since his son's funeral. On the ride back to the White House, Lincoln asked what would happen if the former *Merrimack* came up the Potomac to Washington. Should the ironclad reach the capital, Dahlgren answered grimly, there would be no defense. The only option, if the ship came north, was to sink obstructions in the river channel to block its path.

Back in his office, Lincoln found Stanton pacing the room "like a caged lion," as one witness put it. He would stalk across the office, drop into a chair, and then leap up again a moment later, all the while listing more and more catastrophic implications. The more agitated he became, the more annoyed he was by the fact that Welles, whose navy had failed to prevent this crisis, was sitting in front of him rather calmly and saying little.

As Welles later described Stanton's tirade: "The *Merrimac,* he said, would destroy every vessel in the service, could lay every city on the coast under contribution, could take Fortress Monroe; McClellan's [plan] to advance by the Peninsula must be abandoned, and Burnside would inevitably be captured" on the North Carolina coast. "Likely the first movement of the *Merrimac* would be to come up the Potomac and disperse Congress, destroy the Capitol and public buildings; or she might go to New York and Boston and destroy those cities, or levy from them contributions sufficient to carry on the War. He asked what vessel or means we had to resist or prevent her from doing whatever she pleased."

Welles replied acidly that the ship couldn't go to Washington and

New York simultaneously. Nor could the heavy ironclad, with its deep draft, get through the Kettle Bottom Shoals downriver from Washington or navigate the shallows that protected Burnside's base on Roanoke Island. Indeed, according to the navy's spies in Norfolk, it was doubtful that the *Virginia* was sufficiently seaworthy to leave Hampton Roads. As for a vessel that would prevent the dreaded ship from "doing whatever she pleased," Welles continued, the Union's own coastal ironclad, the USS *Monitor,* had just arrived at Fort Monroe, having left New York the previous Thursday.

Seward brightened at the news that the Rebel craft had limitations and vulnerabilities; so far, people had discussed only its awesome powers. But Stanton was not mollified. He demanded to know more about the *Monitor.*

Welles described the vessel, an utterly original design by a Swedish-born engineer named John Ericsson. Its 172-foot wooden hull was covered in one-inch iron plates, and the ship rode so low that only eighteen inches showed above the waterline. Topside, the *Monitor* was flat like a raft; mounted at the center was a round turret that was twenty feet across, nine feet high, and encased in iron eight inches thick. The turret rotated to allow its guns to fire in any direction. A board of navy men assigned to consider possible ironclad designs had been skeptical of Ericsson's proposal, but Lincoln, when he saw the plans, thought the idea made sense. Blessing the project, he had said, "I think there is something in it."

Now Stanton homed in on one key detail: How many guns?

Two 11-inch Dahlgren guns, Welles replied.

Stanton's "mingled look of incredulity and contempt cannot be described," Welles wrote afterward, and the tone of his follow-up question—did Welles really mean that the Union should rely on a ship with just two guns?—was "equally indescribable."

But rely on this odd and unproven craft was exactly what the Union did. For even as this tense exchange was taking place, the *Monitor*'s two guns were blazing away at the Rebel ironclad from point-blank range, while the *Virginia*'s guns fired back.

The crew of the *Virginia* had awakened that Sunday morning ready to make short work of the three grounded warships near Fort Monroe, starting with the USS *Minnesota,* sister ship of the ruined *Congress.* To their surprise, they saw, sitting defiantly in their path, a strange vessel that looked "like a pygmy compared with the lofty frigate which she guarded," as one observer described it. The *Monitor* had steamed into place late the night before.

After breakfast, the Rebels started downriver toward a collision that would be, in the words of one Confederate officer, "in some respects the most momentous naval conflict ever witnessed," when "a thousand years of battle and breeze would be forgotten." In a matter of hours, as the London *Times* later put it, almost the entire fleet of Britain's world-dominating navy—147 first-class wooden warships—would be rendered obsolete.

The *Monitor* quickly proved a match for the much bigger *Virginia*. Her light draft and comparatively nimble handling allowed the ship to dance around her sluggish foe, pounding away, and after shots from the rotating guns blew holes in the Rebel craft's smokestack, the *Virginia* was in danger of losing all power. Meanwhile, the Rebel shells fired in response skittered across the low deck of the *Monitor* or left harmless dents in the turret. (Not quite harmless, actually: by the end of the battle the gunners were nearly deaf from the clangor of shells smashing into their iron enclosure, and the *Monitor*'s captain, John Worden, was temporarily blinded by a direct hit on the pilot house.) After a while, one Rebel gun gave up shooting altogether. "Why are you not firing. Mr. Eggleston?" the commander of the *Virginia* demanded. Firing was a waste of powder, the officer replied: "I find I can do her about as much damage by snapping my thumb at her every two minutes and a half."

In an attempt to ram the *Monitor*, the *Virginia* proved "as unwieldy as Noah's ark," in the words of one combatant, and the spry Union ship dodged at the last minute. Frustrated, the Rebel commander ordered his men to prepare to board the enemy for hand-to-hand combat, but the *Monitor* wouldn't remain still long enough. This was fortunate for the Rebels, because the Union sailors were ready to greet the boarders with hand grenades.

After more than four hours of combat, the *Monitor* retreated into shallow water, leaving the battered *Virginia* to sputter its way back to Norfolk. Both crews had discovered flaws in their ships and weaknesses in their strategies, and ultimately the battle was declared a draw. But the draw was in fact a significant Union victory. The Confederates had invested heavily in the construction of their ironclad, only to see it neutralized in

less than a day. They did not have, and never would have, the resources
to build more ships of the same power. In the North, however, additional
Monitor-class gunboats and other ironclads were already under construction. And there would be as many as it took to win.

The battle of Hampton Roads proved the viability and power of
armored warships, but only the North could take advantage of that lesson, especially after the loss of the ironworks in Tennessee to Grant's
campaign. In short, the arrival of the *Monitor* put an end to the South's
hopes of fighting its way through the Union blockade. As one navy man
wrote to another: "Iron will be King, instead of Cotton!"

Back at the White House, none of this was known until about four P.M.,
when a messenger announced that a telegraph connection had been
opened to Fort Monroe. The first message over the wire reassured Lincoln and his impromptu war council that the Rebel ironclad was still at
Hampton Roads—although the news did little to calm Stanton, who had
ordered a fleet of small boats to be sunk at the Potomac shoals to block
the river. Next came a more comprehensive dispatch from Gustavus Fox
of the Navy Department, who had gone south to greet the *Monitor* and
thus became a witness to the great battle. The good news from Fox was
followed by even more: the Confederate retreat from Manassas was at last
confirmed. Brigadier General Joseph Hooker wired a report that the Rebels had abandoned their Potomac batteries without a fight, spiking their
guns and burning their camps. Meanwhile, escaping slaves were entering
Federal camps in northern Virginia with word that the Confederate
army was gone from its trenches. McClellan called for his horse and set
out across the river to see what he could learn.

The emotional span of that single day—from despair to celebration—
left indelible marks on the memories of Lincoln's advisers. Nicolay and
Hay said the activity in the president's office on March 9 was "perhaps the
most excited and impressive of the whole war." And as the calm eye of the
storm, Lincoln may well have taken note of the fact that the news from
Manassas was carried by contrabands—slaves leaving their owners and
seeking a haven with advancing Federal troops. With Union forces on
the march from Virginia to Arkansas, the number of slaves liberated in
this way was rising steeply. In his conversations with conservatives
around this time, the president frequently made the point that this influx

of self-liberated slaves meant that emancipation had already started whether they liked it or not.

Lincoln repeated this point the next day, when Montgomery Blair convened the panel of border state congressmen he had promised. The president told the group that he was afraid his proposal might have been misunderstood as an attack on the citizens of the critically important loyal slave states. That was not his intent, he assured them. He believed slavery "was wrong and should continue to think so," and he would not, in the words of one participant, "pretend to disguise his antislavery feeling." But his proposal was not motivated by his sentiments. The Constitution did not give him or Congress any power over slavery in their states, he said, because "emancipation was a subject exclusively under the control of the states."

Continuing, the president told the congressmen that the unavoidable fact of this war meant that "immense [Union] armies were in the field and must continue in the field as long as the war lasts." Inevitably, the armies would come in contact with slaves, and some of those slaves would seek the army's protection. This was a distraction to Union troops operating in the border states and a source of "continual irritation" for the Federal cause, because he could not order volunteer troops, many of whom ardently opposed slavery, to force these human beings back into bondage. (As Lincoln put it in another conversation about this time, "The Negro who has once touched the hem of the government's garment shall never again be a slave.") His proposal to compensate the border states in exchange for ending slavery, he explained to the group, was his "good faith" answer to the self-emancipation of slaves, and if they would embrace it, they would deal a blow to the rebellion greater than any battle could inflict.

Unfortunately for Lincoln, the border states were still unwilling to change. John Noell of Missouri assured Lincoln that since slavery in his state would soon die out on its own, there was no need to take any action. Maryland's John Crisfield protested that his constituents were ready to end slavery, but that even indirect pressure from outsiders—pressure such as Lincoln's proposal—was unacceptable to them. Stated another way, the citizens of Maryland would be happy to give up slavery provided no one asked them to. Another Missouri representative, William Hall, suggested a national referendum, but this would be exactly the sort of outside pressure that raised the hackles of the Marylanders. Expressing yet another view, Kentucky's Charles Wickliffe argued that Lincoln's idea was unconstitutional.

The meeting broke up without having made any progress. A line of reasoning that seemed obvious and persuasive to Lincoln had failed to break through the emotional responses built up over whole lives accustomed to slavery. Especially in the border states, the default position of elected representatives was to put the divisive question of slavery as far away as possible, whether that required wishful thinking or circular logic, stratagems of delay or appeals to the Constitution.

Lincoln's disappointment must have been apparent to his advisers, because later that week Edward Bates decided that the president needed to be bucked up. In a private visit to the White House, the attorney general—who was from Missouri and well understood the ingrained habits of thought that made slavery so hard to reject—commiserated with Lincoln about the difficulty of steering a course between the extremes of opinion in the Union coalition. He urged the president to "stand firm on his present rock (as to the slavery question) and not yield an inch to either the fierce rush of the northern abolitionists or the timid doubters of the border slave states." Bates added: "You have taken your positions cautiously. Now maintain them bravely, and I will sink or swim with you."

Edwin Stanton was still angry when he arrived for a cabinet meeting in Lincoln's office on March 11. His nasty exchange with Welles two days earlier had festered: Welles had countermanded Stanton's order to prepare obstructions for the Potomac, prompting another furious outburst from Stanton and another acid response from Welles. The Union had spent months trying to open the river and now the Rebel batteries were finally gone, Welles said. Why did Stanton want to block the Potomac again?

Today's unpleasant task for the secretary of war was to report on the state of the Union's military bureaucracy. In two months on the job, Stanton had managed to look under a lot of rocks and throw open plenty of closed doors in his notoriously mismanaged department, and he did not like what he was finding. "Great ignorance, negligence, and lack of order and subordination—and reckless extravagance," summarized one person who heard the secretary's presentation. Cabinet members were shocked when Stanton revealed that the army payroll now numbered nearly 700,000 and that its finances were "shamefully managed."

Stanton said that he routinely received requisitions from the quarter-master general's office that Meigs, the head of the office, knew absolutely nothing about. A bit defensively, Stanton added that he would not take the blame for conditions in his department, which had deteriorated before he arrived.

Indeed, Stanton deserved credit: he was making real progress in cleaning up the mess he had inherited. "Stanton is exceedingly industri-ous, mindful of the interests of his Bureau, never off from his post, works like a trooper and spends day and night at his office when under a strong pressure," wrote one observer. One of the secretary's most effective inno-vations was the institution of "public days," when he personally attended to petitions from would-be contractors while standing at an upright desk in a room where anyone could come and watch his deliberations. He put on quite a show. An individual wanting to do business with the army would wait in a long line until his turn was called. Then, typically, the petitioner would state his case in a low voice, trying to achieve a modicum of privacy, only to have Stanton restate the proposal in booming tones, along with his instant verdict.

One would-be supplier of a hundred thousand surplus French rifles, a man named William Roelofson, recounted his experience of the Stanton style. Roelofson's hopes had soared when Stanton was named secretary of war, because a mutual acquaintance provided an introduction. The con-tractor rushed to Washington to peddle the guns, but Stanton kept him cooling his heels at Willard's Hotel for three weeks. Finally, about a month into Stanton's tenure, Roelofson attended a public day. He handed Stanton a carefully worded proposal, which the secretary snatched, skimmed, and slapped facedown on his desk. He scrawled a few lines, then, peering through his glasses, barked out to everyone assembled what he had written. "The Secretary of War declines to make any contract or arrangement with Mr. Roelofson in respect to the arms mentioned within—because the government has no use for them—and he has no occasion for the services of Mr. Roelofson in his Department of the Gov-ernment." Then, the chastened arms dealer recounted, Stanton returned his proposal "in such a manner that I not only felt chagrined but humili-ated."

No one could accuse the secretary of war of backroom dealing, though many in Washington were coming to think he was a martinet. But if Stanton was beginning to get a grip on his swollen and disordered domain, he had little insight yet into McClellan and his chain of command. He told the president and his fellow cabinet members that the general in chief distrusted the civilian leadership and was using his position to hide information from them. In fact, McClellan had instructed his generals to make all reports directly to him, "and he reports nothing." For more than a month, Stanton informed the group, McClellan had been holding key telegrams at his headquarters, refusing to share them with the War Department. To cure this intolerable situation, Stanton had ordered the main telegraph moved from McClellan's office to his own.

Stanton was correct about the motive behind McClellan's excessive secrecy. He had only the most grudging respect for the constitutional chain of command. On one occasion, the navy's David Dixon Porter was meeting with McClellan to discuss plans to capture New Orleans when an aide announced that Lincoln was outside. "Let him wait. I am busy," McClellan answered. Shocked, Porter protested that Lincoln had a great interest in the New Orleans campaign; and besides, Porter said, "It's not respectful to keep him waiting. Remember that he is our Commander-in-Chief." McClellan replied: "Well, let the Commander-in-Chief wait, he has no business to know what is going on."

Stanton's disturbing report about the telegrams—along with the fact that McClellan and his army had left Washington and advanced through rain and mud to assess the situation in Manassas—moved Lincoln to take an overdue yet fateful step. That evening he instructed John Hay to call Seward, Chase, and Stanton to his office. Seward got there first, and when he arrived Lincoln read aloud his President's Special War Order No. 3, which removed McClellan as general in chief. Seward heartily approved, saying that after the "imbecility" of the canal boat episode, McClellan was lucky to retain command of the Army of the Potomac. Seward suggested publishing the order in Stanton's name, as a way of strengthening the secretary of war, but by then Stanton had entered the room, and he demurred. Feelings were so raw between him and the McClellan faction, he said, that the order would look like a personal insult if it came from him. And indeed it would, because two other items in the order also cut against McClellan's wishes. In the West, Halleck was given command over Buell's department along with his own, while in the mountains of western Virginia a new department was created for the purpose of giving a command to the unreliable but politically powerful John Frémont.

Putting Frémont in charge of an army again was a potentially explosive decision, because he was now engaged in a very public feud with the powerful Blair family, to which the postmaster general belonged and whose active support was an essential part of Lincoln's appeal to Democratic Unionists. Further complicating the situation, the radical general had recently caused great embarrassment to Montgomery Blair by leaking a private letter he'd received from Blair the previous year. Published in the *New-York Tribune* earlier in March, the letter complained of the president's "feeble policy," which Blair considered a vestige of Lincoln's days in the defunct Whig Party. When the letter appeared, Blair immediately went to the White House and offered to "make some amends by resigning." Lincoln answered that he had no intention of reading the letter; he believed it had been published only to stir up trouble. "Forget it," he told Blair, and "never mention or think of it again." This magnanimous gesture no doubt influenced Blair's decision to defend Lincoln's appointment of Frémont in a strongly worded letter to his influential father. The president had no choice but to name Frémont to the post, Blair wrote, to arrest "the spread of factions in the country & prevent divisions at this time."

The consolation for McClellan in all this was that the president did not appoint a new general in chief above him. Instead, he ordered that "all commanders . . . [will] report directly to the Secretary of War," and "prompt, full and frequent reports will be expected of all."

After much tribulation, a key problem facing Lincoln at the beginning of the year—namely, how to assert his authority over McClellan and the army—had at last been addressed. Now, through Stanton, the president would be his own general in chief. Lincoln's confidence in his ability to command the armies had soared after the success of recent campaigns. The simultaneous movements of multiple expeditions had worked just as he predicted, stretching Confederate lines to the breaking point. The armored gunboats he had championed were proving themselves on inland rivers and along the coast.

Public opinion had begun to turn in his favor as well, and the president could find affirmation of his leadership in newspapers throughout the North. The March 12 edition of *The New York Times,* for example, credited Lincoln with the string of victories that surely guaranteed "the end of the rebellion." The paper declared: "With a patience only equaled by that of the people, he awaited the completion of preparations, but the moment these were completed, the word was given which set in motion the immense machinery of destruction, from the Atlantic to the Missouri line. The scheme of the campaign, the discipline of the troops, the elaboration of preliminary details, may be justly credited to others. Action and victory we owe directly to the President."

Lincoln was entitled to feel a new confidence. As he had done so often in his life, he had learned a new subject almost entirely through his own efforts: by reading, by questioning, and through lonely hours of thinking. He was now a competent military commander, having graduated at the top of a class numbering just one. Such rare ability to master a challenge through his own resourcefulness encouraged Lincoln's tendency to rely on himself. Left unchecked, however, this burgeoning confidence threatened to tip into overconfidence.

McClellan took the news of his demotion with surprising good cheer. Getting out of Washington and marching his troops restored some of the exuberance he had shown the previous summer. The newspapers provided reports of meager camps and logs painted to look like cannon in the abandoned Rebel fortifications around Manassas, and Attorney General Bates scoffed that this first mission by the Army of the Potomac was "a fool's errand." But well-trained West Pointers recognized that the positions had been in fact, formidable; McClellan, for one, was delighted to have taken the key railroad junction with hardly any bloodshed. "My movements gave us Manassas with the loss of one life—a gallant cavalry officer—history will, when I am in my grave, record it as the brightest passage of my life that I accomplished so much at so small a cost," he wrote. As for losing the top rank, he professed unconcern. His army was "half glad that I now belong to them alone," while Lincoln, he wrote, "is my strongest friend."

With the Potomac open, McClellan called his transports to Alexandria and prepared to fill them with troops and supplies destined for the peninsula east of Richmond. The Confederate retreat had spoiled his hopes of separating Johnston's army from the Rebel capital, but a campaign on the fine roads between the York and the James rivers still seemed to offer the prospect of a decisive victory, an ambition that had filled his thoughts for months.

Lincoln, by contrast, remained grief-stricken and broken by pain.

Willie's death, he confided to a visitor, "showed me my weakness as I had never felt it before." Mary, "distressed and pale," inconsolable, remained secluded in her room day after day, alternating between silence and loud bursts of tears. Tad's recovery was slow, and many nights he asked his father to sleep with him because he was lonely and afraid. With Mary incapacitated, it fell to the president to handle family crises.

On March 10, for example, he was in the middle of a meeting when John Hay reluctantly interrupted. Stepping into the hall, Lincoln met Rebecca Pomroy, the nurse, who told him that Tad was refusing to take his medicine. After a few minutes alone with the boy, the president emerged from behind the closed sickroom door: "It's all right now. Tad and I have fixed things up," he said. Then he went to his desk, where he wrote out a check, drawn on his Riggs & Company bank account, for five dollars payable "to Tad (when he is well enough to present)."

A few days later marked three weeks since Willie's death; as he had done the previous two Thursdays, Lincoln spent part of the day alone in the room where the boy had died. His quiet there was inviolable. At mid-month, Pomroy returned to her work at the military hospital, but the president often asked her to return to the White House and keep his wife company for a few hours.

As time went on and Mary remained in her room, Pomroy began to weary of the first lady's self-pity: "She suffers from depression of spirits, but I do think if she would only come [to the hospital] and look at the poor soldiers occasionally it would be better for her." Pomroy noted approvingly that Lincoln read the Bible almost daily around lunchtime. One afternoon she found him sprawled on the chaise with the big, worn volume open on his lap. He looked up and asked which book in the Bible was her favorite. The Psalms, Pomroy answered. "Yes, they are the best," he agreed, "for I find in them something for every day of the week."

One of Pomroy's visits fell on March 27—another Thursday, the weekly reminder of the family's unanswerable loss. When it came time to leave, Mary pressed a picture of Willie into Pomroy's hands, along with one of Tad. Then Lincoln offered the nurse a ride home. He was a little sturdier now, no longer asking her the same forlorn questions about God and grief again and again.

A hard rain had turned Fourteenth Street into a bog; the presidential carriage got stuck. Lincoln ordered his driver and footman to hold the nervous horses steady while he got down and found three large stones to make a pathway. Taking Pomroy's hand, he guided her across the stones to the safety of the sidewalk. As he often did, he perceived in this simple scene a principle for living. Standing in his muddy boots, the president counseled the nurse: "All through life, be sure to put your feet in the right place, and then *stand firm*."

In 1862, a transatlantic voyage took two weeks or more, depending on the weather, so news of the war produced a delayed reaction in Europe. The February victories of Grant and Burnside registered in London and Paris only in March, followed a couple of weeks later by news of Lincoln's proposal for a gradual end to slavery. Louis-Napoleon called Ambassador Dayton to the palace at once.

Dayton had been having trouble scheduling a meeting with the foreign minister, Thouvenel, so he was surprised to be summoned on such short notice by the emperor himself. When the New Jersey lawyer was ushered into Louis-Napoleon's presence at two P.M. on March 25, he found the handsome, mustachioed monarch in a very businesslike frame of mind. The emperor wanted to talk about cotton. When the war broke out, French warehouses had been stuffed with raw material for the nation's busy looms, but the stockpiles were gone now and textile workers were jobless. A man with the name Napoleon did not need to be told what might happen when masses of working people found themselves poor and hungry. Having no interest in another French revolution, Louis needed cotton.

Furthermore, the emperor said, his thinking about the American situation had changed in recent weeks. "When the insurrection broke out," Dayton recalled him saying, "he did not suppose the North would succeed; . . . it was the general belief of statesmen in Europe that the two sections would never come together again," because the South "was a large country, and for that reason difficult to subdue." Now Louis was no longer so sure. He had seen the success of the Union war effort and knew that an expedition had been launched to retake the vital port of New Orleans. The monarch seemed favorably impressed by Lincoln's emancipation proposal, which was "almost universally looked upon [in Europe] as the 'beginning of the end'" of the war, Dayton noted.

But the emperor confessed fears "that the war might yet be a long one." And with the Confederates promising to burn cotton rather than let the Yankees capture it and sell it to Europe, he wanted to ask Dayton whether Washington had any strategy for reopening the cotton trade in places liberated by Union troops.

Seeing an opening, Dayton reassured Napoleon that plenty of growers in the South would rather sell their crop than sacrifice it for the Confederate cause; he promised the monarch that once the Union gained control of New Orleans and other Southern ports, the military would find a way to get that cotton to market. However, Dayton added, nothing buoyed the hopes of the Rebels more than the possibility of European intervention. These hopes had been raised when France and Britain declared the Confederacy a lawful belligerent early in the conflict, and they would be crushed if the two countries withdrew that declaration. The rebellion would collapse, the Union blockade would be lifted, the cotton would flow, and the emperor's workers would be back at their spindles.

Louis-Napoleon promised to give Dayton's words careful consideration. Indeed, the monarch had a lot to think about, because by now his grand plan to restore French power in the New World had become exquisitely complex. He badly wanted to conquer Mexico and install the Archduke Maximilian—butterfly-collecting younger brother of the emperor of Austria—as a puppet ruler. But he had to step carefully. He knew that proslavery Southerners had long considered Mexico prime territory for the spread of their peculiar institution, so he was eager to make the Confederacy a friend rather than an enemy. Together, Maximilian of Mexico and Jefferson Davis could more than offset the rising power of the former United States. Still, if the North really was about to throttle the rebellion, Napoleon needed to be on Lincoln's good side, lest the president decide to use his huge new army to enforce the Monroe Doctrine against meddling Europeans. Perhaps the best response, from the emperor's perspective, would be to help the South win its independence while making the North believe that France was still a trusted ally.

Thouvenel took Dayton aside after the meeting with Louis Napoleon to underline the emperor's views: the French government was now confident that the Union would get control of the ports, but lacked faith that the cotton crop could be saved. As for withdrawing the declaration of belligerent rights, Thouvenel felt it was beneath the dignity of a great nation to reverse its position simply because the South appeared beaten. In any event, nothing could be done without the agreement of Great Britain. Thouvenel closed on a hopeful note, according to Dayton. In his report to Seward, the ambassador wrote: "He said, if we took possession of the ports, the war would be altogether internal, and France would have nothing to do with it. . . . He said, furthermore, that we knew very well that all the sympathies of France and her people had been with the north from the beginning."

"The period of inaction has passed," George McClellan announced in a message to his Army of the Potomac, more than 100,000 strong. At last, after all the meetings and intrigues, he was moving. "I will bring you now face to face with the rebels, and only pray that God may defend the right. . . . I am to watch over you as a parent watches over his children, and you know that your General loves you from the depths of his heart."

While newspaper reporters and congressmen prowled through the remains of the Confederate camps around Manassas in late March, McClellan began sending his army south in the largest movement of troops and supplies yet seen in North America. "Numerous steam-tugs were pulling huge sailing vessels here and there, and large transports, loaded with soldiers, horses, bales of hay, and munitions for an army, swept majestically down the river," wrote one awed private. "Every description of water conveyance, from a canal boat to a huge three-decked steamboat, [was] pressed into the service." An English observer termed it "the stride of a giant."

McClellan had revised his plans to account for the consequences of Johnston's retreat. The Rappahannock River was closed now, and the still menacing *Virginia* lurked on the James. He would use the York River on the north side of the peninsula near Richmond as his supply line on the way to the Confederate capital. To accomplish this, he told Stanton, he would need to capture Yorktown in a coordinated attack by infantry and navy gunboats.

But the expedition had scarcely begun when it had to be reined in. To maximize his own force, McClellan left a minimal number of troops behind. Lincoln was dismayed to find the ranks in and around Washington so thin. Though Little Mac's supporters insisted that the capital faced no real risk, Lincoln believed that even a raid by the Rebels could deliver a mortal blow to the Union. "We began to fear the Rebels would take the capital, and once in possession of that, we feared that foreign countries might acknowledge the Confederacy," he later explained. "Nobody could foresee the evil that might come from the destruction of records and property."

Compounding these fears was a fresh barrage of rumors that McClellan was playing a double game. At the very moment when the general steamed away from Washington, a letter arrived on Stanton's desk from Thomas Ewing, an influential former senator and cabinet member. He reported an encounter between his son Philemon and a "reliable" gentleman from New Orleans. In significant detail, the man told Philemon that McClellan had taken the secret oath of the Knights of the Golden Circle in 1860 and that "he is, was, and has been all along a tool of Jeff Davis."

Alarmed, Stanton tucked the letter into his pocket and headed to Lincoln's office, where he found the president meeting with Orville Browning. As it happened, Browning had been asking Lincoln "if he still had confidence in [McClellan's] fidelity." Lincoln answered that "he never had any reason to doubt it." He described the tears in the general's eyes when he confronted him about the rumors of treason. True, Lincoln continued, McClellan was not "sufficiently energetic and aggressive," but that was why he had ordered Little Mac to "move now, and he must do it."

Into this conversation came Stanton. He pulled the letter from his coat, announcing that it was written by "one of the first men of the Nation," someone well known to both Lincoln and Browning, though he was not at liberty to say who it was. He described the explosive charges. Lincoln was skeptical, but to Stanton the conspiracy made sense.

After the meeting, the secretary offered Browning a ride home in his carriage; on the way, Stanton spoke of McClellan's long relationship with Jefferson Davis. When the Mississippi aristocrat served as U.S. secretary of war, Little Mac was one of his favorite officers. Davis had handpicked the young captain to join two more experienced soldiers as American observers of the Crimean War. In doing so, Davis set McClellan apart from the other ambitious veterans of the Mexican War, and Little Mac had been reaping benefits from the military and from private industry ever since. On the basis of these ties, Stanton concluded that McClellan was hard pressed to "emancipate himself from the influence of Jeff Davis." And he feared that the general "wasn't willing to . . . damage the cause of secession." McClellan, Stanton declared, "ought to have been removed long ago."

The secretary struck an even more ominous note in his reply to Ewing. "Private and confidential," Stanton scrawled across a page of War Department stationery. "Movements of the last few days have occasioned greater

anxiety than ever before. The government seems doomed to some fright-
ful calamity. The remedy is in the hands of the Pres[ident], and no effort
of mine can inspire him with any alarm, much less the degree of vigi-
lance and anxiety I think the occasion requires."

Lincoln was not easily rattled, but neither was he willing to risk everything on the enigma that was George McClellan. The general now had an
army on the peninsula roughly four times the size of the force that Grant
took into Tennessee, and that would have to be enough. The president
ordered the last of the four corps earmarked for McClellan's campaign to
remain around Manassas instead, as added security for the capital. A
last-minute alteration, this change was an unsightly crack in the carefully
laid plans of the Young Napoleon.

William Tecumseh Sherman—"Cump" to friends and family—was no
longer behind Ulysses Grant pushing supplies in his direction. He was
now the lead element in Grant's army, having taken a division of fresh
(and untested) troops down the Tennessee River into southern Tennessee.
In late March, near a steamboat dock called Pittsburg Landing not far
from the Mississippi border, Sherman stationed his men around a little
white church and named the position in its honor: Camp Shiloh. A growing army of Rebels gathered just down the road at Corinth, Mississippi,
but Sherman put up no fortifications. He still subscribed to the old-army
idea that "such a course would have made our raw men timid." He waited
to be joined by the rest of Grant's forces and by Buell's Army of the Ohio,
which was marching from Nashville. The plan was to link up and drive
the Confederates into the Mississippi River.

"Indeed all the valley of the Mississippi must be under one Government, otherwise there never can be peace," Sherman wrote as he waited,
"but the task is so gigantic that I am staggered by its cost. To say that the
Southern people are reconciled, or likely to be, may be so, but I cannot
see it. . . . The Southern Leaders know the importance of the Mississippi,
and will fight for every mile of it." Grant's army, he added, was "well fed,
clothed and anxious to do something but *very few appreciate the difficulties and dangers* before us."

Sherman was among the most far-seeing military men in the Union.
The previous fall he had suffered terrible embarrassment, enough to
make him contemplate suicide, when he was denounced as a lunatic for

saying that it would take hundreds of thousands of troops to safeguard Kentucky. Time was vindicating his sanity. But he did not know how quickly the words in his letter would be proven true. The Rebels were indeed going to fight for every mile; in fact, they were marching toward Camp Shiloh even as Sherman folded the paper and addressed the envelope. And they were bringing difficulties and dangers on a scale the North American continent had never seen.

— 5 —

APRIL

"If Albert Sidney Johnston is not a general, then I have no general," said Jefferson Davis, attempting to soothe the outrage in Richmond over Confederate losses in the West. A tall, broad-chested man with blazing eyes, Johnston was a charismatic leader who, by the spring of 1862, was nearly sixty years old and still as tough as a longhorn steak, a veteran of many years' hard marching and fighting against Indians, Mexicans, and ambitious rivals. Winfield Scott once judged him "more than a good officer—he is a God send to the country."

As the war approached, Johnston was promoted to command the Pacific Department of the regular U.S. Army. But when the time came for choosing sides, he went with his adopted state of Texas and joined the Confederacy. Assigned to command the sprawling western theater, Johnston immediately recognized the vulnerability of his long, thin defensive line in Kentucky and Tennessee. Given more time, he might have found a way to strengthen it, but Grant never gave him the chance. Now Johnston had pulled back into a coiled crouch, reconstituting his forces as two clenched fists: one to fend off the Federals on the Mississippi River, the other to deliver a counterpunch intended to send the hero of Fort Donelson reeling.

Johnston's left was clenched at a place called Island No. 10, about halfway between St. Louis and Memphis. The prosaically named island provided an excellent spot for blocking river traffic, for here the Mississippi doubled back on itself to flow north a short distance, then kinked again to resume its southward movement. The guns from the abandoned Rebel fortress at Columbus were transferred to the island and to shore batteries near the town of New Madrid, Missouri, on the western bank of the Big Muddy. Together these guns formed a deadly gantlet, ready to blast unwelcome ships to pieces as they snaked through the bends.

For about a month, Federal forces under Brigadier General John Pope had been working to break this fist. First, Pope captured New Madrid by land; then he cleared a channel through a swamp that allowed a flotilla of small boats to move past Island No. 10 without coming in range of the guns. This put Pope in position to ferry his troops across the river to the eastern shore, where they could cut the line supplying the island. He needed only a couple of Federal gunboats to protect the transports as they crossed. The boats were too large for the improvised channel, but on the night of April 4, after the moon went down and storm clouds darkened the sky, one bold captain slipped his blacked-out steamer past the island batteries. A second boat soon followed, and Pope was ready to finish the job.

Johnston's right fist was located in Corinth, Mississippi, a major intersection in the South's meager network of railroads. During the month of March, Johnston gathered all the Rebel troops he could muster, starting with the army he had led in retreat from Kentucky and Tennessee. To this group he added a large part of the force pulled back from Columbus; he also commandeered reinforcements from the Southern coast, leaving such essential ports as New Orleans and Mobile nearly stripped of infantry. By early April, Johnston had collected some 40,000 men, and he hoped to be joined any day by the army under Earl Van Dorn, summoned from Arkansas after the defeat at Pea Ridge.

As the month began, Johnston and Grant found themselves in almost identical situations. Grant's army, camped at Pittsburg Landing on the Tennessee River about twenty miles northeast of Corinth, was roughly the same size as Johnston's. Both men were waiting for approaching reinforcements; Grant expected Buell to arrive any day. Once strengthened by Buell's army, Grant intended to march down to Corinth and drive the Rebels out of what he later called "the great strategic position at the West between . . . Nashville and Vicksburg."

Johnston decided to strike before that could happen. Stinging from the criticism he had received over the sudden loss of the western line, Johnston determined to reverse the setback and restore his reputation. First, he

would smash Grant in a surprise attack. Then he would cross the Tennessee River and do the same to Buell's approaching army. That accomplished, he would have free range all the way north to the Ohio River.

On April 3, the Texan started his Rebels up the road, hoping Van
Dorn would catch up. Johnston's unseasoned army was so slow and disorderly, however, that the one-day journey turned into a three-day ordeal.
As a consequence, the general assumed that his surprise had been spoiled
by the time he ordered his troops into position in the quiet predawn of
Sunday, April 6. He was wrong: as first light touched the blossoming fruit
trees and lit the pale green of the mixed fields and woodlands, the Yankees were indeed surprised. Although they knew that Rebels were in the
vicinity, they were unprepared for a ferocious frontal assault. When Union
patrols clashed with the lead elements of Johnston's attacking army, the
gray tide rolled over them. One soldier reported that as the Rebels neared
the Union camps, "wild birds in great numbers, rabbits in commotion,
and numerous squirrels came flocking toward the Union lines as though
they were being driven from the woods."

Grant's generation of soldiers grew up in the military church of Napoleon Bonaparte, but the Union commander never imagined he would
face an assault modeled on Napoleon's crashing waves at Waterloo. No
American alive or dead had ever fought a battle like the one that began
that morning. Proud of his recent successes, Grant made the mistake of
underestimating his opponents, believing that the Confederates were
dispirited and would simply wait for him at Corinth. He should have
been better prepared.

Shiloh was, as the historian Shelby Foote put it, "the first great modern battle . . . a cauldron of pure hell." And because it was an unknown
hell, everyone on the battlefield learned as he went, terrible and costly
lessons in a classroom of chaos. "I have been anxious to see a [great bat-
tle]," one young private reflected after the first few minutes of instruction. "I think I have seen enough of it." Multitudes of green troops just
like him, led by inexperienced regimental officers, fought from dawn to
dusk over poorly mapped terrain across a narrow front. Plans that looked
elegant on paper were hopelessly tangled by midmorning. Discipline was
a shambles, as thousands of advancing Rebels broke ranks to plunder
Union camps and thousands of routed Federals fled to the rear. In some
cases, frightened commanders led the way. "I had perhaps a dozen officers arrested for cowardice," Grant later recounted.

Those who stood fast that day fought with a ferocious will. In the center of the field, a Union division under Brigadier General Benjamin Prentiss, an Illinois lawyer and politician, dug in its heels at a sunken wagon road. Ordered by Grant to hold the position at all costs, Prentiss and his troops repulsed one head-on assault after another—eleven charges in all. The buzzing of grapeshot and bullets was so intense that the place was dubbed the Hornet's Nest. For the twelfth try, the Rebels assembled sixty-two artillery pieces on the left flank of Prentiss's position, where one of Lincoln's political friends from Illinois, Brigadier General Stephen Hurlbut, fought with his division in a peach orchard. Under the murderous barrage, Hurlbut fell back, opening a way for Rebel troops to work in behind the Hornet's Nest. When the right flank also gave way a bit later, Prentiss and his stalwart soldiers were surrounded, forced to surrender after ten of the longest hours of the war.

Their valor was not in vain. The hard fighting cost the Confederates valuable hours of daylight. Grant had enough time to collect some fifty guns into a massed battery behind the last ravine separating the Confederate army from his base of supplies, and as the sun went down the first of Buell's reinforcing troops arrived on the battlefield. The stubborn Union stand also cost the Rebels their handsome general. With so much staked on this daring counterpunch, Johnston insisted on driving his troops from the front, and his cool, fearless presence electrified the Rebels wherever he rode among them. But as he encouraged a brigade to follow him on a charge into the peach orchard, Johnston took a bullet through an artery in the back of his leg and bled to death into his boot. Neither the general nor his army watered their horses in the Tennessee River that night, as Johnston had promised at daybreak. Instead, many of them died, and those who survived slept in the Union camps they had captured, as a cold, hard rain drenched the field.

The Confederate attack came within one or two fortunate strokes of breaking Grant's army. Even Sherman, who had three horses shot from under him as his division made the Rebels pay for every inch of ground, was thinking of giving up by day's end. About midnight, with his buckshot-damaged hand wrapped in a bandage, Sherman went looking for Grant to discuss the possibility of falling back behind the river. He found his recently promoted commander huddled beneath a tree, rain streaming from his hat brim.

"Well, Grant, we've had the devil's own day, haven't we?" Sherman began.

"Yes," Grant allowed. But with his army reestablished along a tighter line, a division of fresh troops arriving from his right, and Buell's army coming across the river in ferryboats, Grant was done thinking about today. Ending the exchange, he said simply: "Lick 'em tomorrow, though." Sherman left without mentioning retreat.

Lick 'em they did. Through another day of brutally hard fighting on April 7, the strengthened Union line drove the Rebels back, until finally the Confederates began a ragged retreat after losing more than 10,000 killed, wounded, and missing. Grant's army was too bloodied to follow: it had lost some 13,000 men. Between the two sides, American soldiers suffered more casualties in two days at Shiloh than in all the nation's previous wars combined.

Even before the Rebels were beaten, a new conflict broke out on the Shiloh battleground, one that would rage for decades. The nation was not yet accustomed to carnage, and the bloodletting at Shiloh was so dramatically worse than anything Americans had experienced before that it seemed obvious to many people that some measure of blame must be assigned. Grant's partisans once again painted him as a hero who, despite a stunning blow, had kept his wits and salvaged a hard victory from the chaos of a near catastrophe. But against them rose a legion of bitter critics, who charged that Grant's fatal lassitude at Pittsburg Landing had been redeemed only by the timely arrival of Buell's rescuing army.

There was some truth in both views. Grant's loyalists saw Shiloh from the front, where the Union lines strained terribly but never entirely broke, in part because Grant kept spirits up and communication clear and ammunition flowing. His critics saw the battle from the rear, where thousands of panicked men took shelter under a bluff by the river and told one another exaggerated stories about the failures of their commanders. The frightened stragglers described scenes they never saw because these scenes never happened: Union soldiers surprised in their tents, shot as they slept, bayoneted where they lay. This retreating mob was the first thing Buell's army met on its way to the battlefield, and it was such an alarming spectacle that the commander of Buell's lead column, the imposing William

"Bull" Nelson, asked permission to begin shooting the stragglers because they were upsetting his men. Naturally Buell's version of Shiloh was a tale of incompetent officers and demoralized troops.

A volunteer on Grant's staff, W. C. Carroll, heard some of this wild talk as it circulated through Buell's command. Carroll knew that Buell might be ready to believe it; understandably, the general was more than a little resentful of Grant as he arrived on the Shiloh plain. In a matter of weeks, the respected Ohio soldier had fallen from commanding an entire department to being the third-ranked general of the combined force on the Tennessee. The top officer was General Halleck, formerly Buell's equal, who intended to leave St. Louis and assume field command once the armies of Grant and Buell were combined. More galling was that Grant, the store clerk from Illinois, now outranked Buell thanks to his February exploits. During the week before the battle, a feeling had spread within Grant's army that Buell was taking his sweet time getting to Pittsburg Landing: he and his troops needed twelve days just to cross the Duck River. Carroll, perceiving that Buell would not want his tardy arrival to be blamed for inviting the battle, was convinced that Grant was about to become the target of the "jealousy of Gen. Buell and his officers."

Carroll struck preemptively. After hopping a steamer headed downstream, he disembarked at the Fort Henry telegraph office and cabled a fawning and partly imaginary account of Grant's heroics to the *New York Herald*. This was how most of the public first received news of the battle of Shiloh. Buell's version came later.

But as men fought over credit and blame, the larger meaning of Shiloh was written in the exhausted columns of mauled Confederates retreating through a pounding hailstorm, and in the Union lines too shattered and spent to pursue them. A strong Rebel force, fighting in its own heartland and on its own terms, had hammered a Union army yet failed to break it. And now, even as the Confederates made their way back to Corinth, additional manpower from the North was surging toward Pittsburg Landing: on the same day the Rebels were driven back from Shiloh, Pope's army had finally captured Island No 10. In short, the bluecoats were firmly lodged in Dixie, and they would not be driven out by head-on attacks. Johnston had landed his best punch, but it wasn't enough.

Yet the ferocity of that blow was itself a grim turning point. A line had been crossed; on April 6 the splintered nation had entered an unspeakable realm. Total casualties were more than double the combined losses at Manassas, Wilson's Creek, Fort Donelson, and Pea Ridge—all the major battles in the war thus far. Men saw things at Shiloh that prefigured the horrors of the war to come: entire forests sheared off by cannon fire; brains exposed in crushed foreheads; men holding their own entrails; fields furrowed by shell fragments and littered with muddy haversacks and broken rifles; acres strewn with dead and dying men and horses. One field was so thick with corpses, in Grant's description, "that it would have been possible to walk across the clearing, in any direction, stepping on dead bodies, without a foot touching the ground."

During the battle, a portion of the 55th Illinois Regiment had been trapped in a ravine and surrounded by Rebels who fired down on their heads as fast as they could reload. "It was like shooting into a flock of sheep," said one witness. The blaze of gunpowder and hail of bullets touched off a fire in the ravine's undergrowth, burning dead and wounded together. A young soldier from Buell's army named Ambrose Bierce passed by the ravine the next day and went "down into the valley of death." The bodies lay "half-buried in ashes; some in the unlovely looseness of attitude denoting sudden death by the bullet, but by far the greater number in postures of agony that told of the tormenting flame. Their clothing was half burnt away—their hair and beard entirely; the rain had come too late to save their nails. Some were swollen to double girth; others shriveled to manikins. According to degree of exposure, their faces were bloated and black or yellow and shrunken. The contraction of muscles which had given them claws for hands had cursed each countenance with a hideous grin."

Those who saw and survived Shiloh emerged with a new understanding of the Civil War. In Washington, Attorney General Bates imagined that the paired victories at Island No. 10 and Shiloh "must break the heart of the rebellion." But the heart of the rebellion, as demonstrated in those fields and woodlands on the bank of the Tennessee, was strong and war-ready beyond all expectations. It would be broken only by long, hard fighting; as Sherman wrote to his wife in a letter scrawled with pen in wounded hand, "I still feel the horrid nature of this war, and the piles of dead Gentlemen & wounded & maimed makes me more anxious than ever for some hope of an End but I know such a thing cannot be for a long long time."

Years later, when the whole arc of the Civil War was behind him, Grant pinpointed these two days in April as the moment when he began to realize what the conflict truly would be. "Up to the battle of Shiloh I, as well as thousands of other citizens, believed that the rebellion against the Government would collapse suddenly and soon," he wrote. But when the Rebels answered the defeats at Fort Henry and Fort Donelson by re-forming their lines and "made such a gallant effort to regain what had been lost, then, indeed, I gave up all idea of saving the Union except by complete conquest."

As George McClellan established his headquarters some seventy miles east of Richmond and cast his eye on nearby Yorktown, he was still liv-ing in the pre-Shiloh world. "I think that a [Union victory] here sub-stantially breaks up the rebel cause," he assured the president. But when he learned on April 5 that Lincoln had ordered an entire corps of his army withheld, McClellan was "astonished." The general felt certain that Washington was in no danger because no serious enemy force threatened it. Captured Rebels were telling him that Joseph E. Johnston's army was now arriving at Yorktown to reinforce the garrison. McClellan, who had a bad habit of overestimating the enemy's strength, guessed that he was facing at least 100,000 troops. (In fact, the garrison under John Magruder numbered only about 13,000 when the Federals first approached.) With Confederate guns booming in the distance, McClellan fired off a message to Lincoln begging him to reconsider: "In my deliberate judgment the success of our cause will be imperiled. I am now of the opinion that I shall have to fight all of the available force of the Rebels not far from here. Do not force me to do so with diminished numbers."

Later that night, as his chief of staff snored loudly in one corner of the room, the young general found himself too angry to sleep. By lantern light he poured out his resentment in a letter to his wife, Mary Ellen. "It is the most infamous thing that history has recorded," he wrote. "The idea of depriving a General of 35,000 troops when actually under fire!" Nothing was turning out as McClellan expected. The navy was refusing to send gunboats to support his advance until Confederate shore batter-ies were silenced, but the troops he had assigned to take out the batteries were suddenly detained near Washington. The good sandy roads he had imagined were muddy from rain and snow. Even the maps he relied on proved to be "worthless."

With so much going so badly, McClellan decided that rather than attack Yorktown, he should settle down for a siege. It was Lincoln's turn to be astonished. Responding to the general's plea to have the corps restored to him, Lincoln scolded: "You now have over 100,000 troops with you. I think you better break the enemies' line . . . at once." This infuriated Little Mac even more. Again he expressed his feelings to Mary Ellen. "I was much tempted to reply that he had better come & do it himself," he seethed. Instead, McClellan volleyed back with a telegram disputing Lincoln's math, saying that the force on the peninsula was actually far smaller, only about 85,000 men. "I need all the aid the Government can give me," he begged.

In one short week, the expedition by the Army of the Potomac had gone from the stride of a giant to the slog of a siege. Reading the general's appeal for more troops, the president realized just how far off track things had gone. McClellan had the largest, best-trained, best-supplied army the continent had ever seen, and while most of that army was not yet battle tested, the same was true of the Rebel force. It seemed to Lincoln that his general had changed positions without changing posture: McClellan was still leaning back from the fight, exaggerating obstacles and calling for help. Having pushed him up to the line, Lincoln felt McClellan sliding back into the dangerous zone where his motives could be questioned by his growing legion of enemies. Much of the country was fast concluding that Little Mac was either afraid of the Rebels or in league with them, and Lincoln could do no more to protect him.

In response to McClellan's plea, the president wrote out an argument that he hoped would restore momentum. It was Lincoln at his best: direct, lucid, combining force with sympathy. He explained why he had held back the army corps under the command of Irwin McDowell, asking pointedly: "Do you really think I should permit the line from Richmond . . . to this city to be entirely open, except what resistance could be presented by less than twenty thousand unorganized troops?" That was a question "which the country will not allow me to evade." Lincoln also pronounced McClellan's low troop count "a curious mystery," then once again tried—as he had tried for months—to make the general see that delay gained him nothing while potentially costing him everything. "It is the precise time to strike a blow," the president declared. "It is indispensable to *you*. . . . I beg to assure you that I have never written you, or spoken to you, in greater kindness," he concluded. "*But you must act.*"

Unfortunately, the moment when McClellan could easily have swept over the ramparts at Yorktown was already slipping away. The methodical general set to work dragging heavy siege guns slowly up the muddy roads of the peninsula; at the front, meanwhile, the mighty Army of the Potomac moved forward not another inch. The war had reached its awful maturity in the West, but here in the East it remained bogged down.

Indeed, the most fearful thing McClellan had to report was the "terrible scare" he experienced when his friend Brigadier General Fitz John Porter went floating away in an untethered surveillance balloon. Blown toward the Rebel fortifications, Porter frantically tossed sandbags overboard to gain altitude as the Confederates took potshots. A shift in the wind blew him back toward Union lines, but when he tried to release gas from the balloon, the valve opened wide and he began plunging to earth. With a desperate grab at the last moment, the terrified general latched onto a tree limb, then he nearly suffocated when the vast billows of silk balloon settled over him. Little Mac wrote to Mary Ellen, "You can imagine how I felt!"—but at last Porter came strolling safe and sound into his tent. Balloon flight was added to the list of things that George McClellan would not risk.

Mary Lincoln at last emerged from her private grieving to find that the scandals bubbling around her before Willie's death had worsened. While she was cloistered, Thomas Stackpole of the White House staff had paid a visit to Orville Browning, seeking the senator's help. It seemed that John Watt, the White House gardener, wished to be assigned to a European mission as a special agent of the Interior Department. Stackpole warned Browning that it would be a good idea to get Watt out of town, because he had been coaching Mary Lincoln in the dark art of defrauding the government. Watt "suggested to Mrs. Lincoln the making of false bills so as to get pay for private expenses out of the public treasury." The president already knew about this and thought he had put a stop to it, Stackpole continued; Lincoln "was very indignant, and refunded what had been filched from the government out of his private purse." But the stealing hadn't stopped, and Mary went on filling her wardrobes and cupboards with expensive clothes and jewelry. Now, Stackpole reported, Watt's wife was receiving $100 per month for a nonexistent White House job and kicking the money back to Mary. Stackpole also told of a case in which Mary paid for a new set of silver by having the merchant submit a fraudulent bill to the government for repairs supposedly made to a set of silver already owned by the White House. When Lincoln noticed the new silver, Mary told him it was a gift.

Mrs. Lincoln had once explained her lavish spending thus: "I must dress in costly materials. The people scrutinize every article that I wear with critical curiosity. The very fact of having grown up in the West, subjects me to more searching observation." And she was right. "They say Mrs. L is awfully *Western,* loud & unrefined," harrumphed Harriet Lane, the White House hostess during the administration of the bachelor James Buchanan. Young Julia Taft got closer to the heart of the matter, though, when she said of Mary Lincoln: "She wanted what she wanted when she wanted it, and no substitute." There was an obsessive edge to Mary's spending that went far beyond looking nice. David Davis, a friend of the family who later served as administrator of the president's estate, recalled a bill for three hundred pairs of kid gloves, purchased in the span of about three months.

Following his disturbing meeting with Stackpole, Browning apparently agreed to use his influence to have Watt sent to Europe, thus getting him out of Mrs. Lincoln's orbit. But Watt's departure meant that the gardener's wife would no longer be funneling a paycheck to Mary, and Mary needed that money to help mask her mounting debts. On April 4, dressed head to toe in mourning black, she approached John Hay with a proposal: since Mrs. Watt's departure would create more work for her in running the house, Hay should pay the $100 salary to her. She also asked that Hay put her in charge of the White House stationery budget. The young secretary refused both requests. "I told her to kiss mine," Hay jokingly reported to Nicolay. "Was I right?"

The volatile first lady was furious at being refused, and what had been an uncomfortable tension between her and the young men who shared Lincoln's office now exploded into outright hostility. Mary demanded that Lincoln fire Hay, but Lincoln brushed her off. "The devil is abroad" in the White House, Hay mused. "His daughter, the Hell-Cat . . . is in a 'state of wrath' about the Steward's salary."

At home as well as in his presidential duties, Lincoln thus struggled to moderate between antagonistic factions. He also sought consolation for his continuing grief in a series of sermons written by the Reverend

Francis L. Vinton of New York's Trinity Church. A former West Point soldier from a family of fighting men, the popular priest was characterized by "uncompromising manliness," according to one colleague, and when he called on Lincoln to offer spiritual assurance, he gently scolded the president for despairing over Willie's death. A Christian is hopeful, Vinton preached.

Slowly the Lincolns returned to something like their previous routine. They saw each other mainly at meals. She needled him; he fended off her criticisms with wisecracks. One April day, a guest was amazed to see one of the family cats climb onto a chair beside the president and gobble a morsel of food that Lincoln offered from his golden fork. Half bantering and half scolding, Mary said, "Don't you think it is shameful for Mr. Lincoln to feed tabby with a gold fork?" Lincoln replied with a gibe at his feckless predecessor's expense: "If the gold fork was good enough for Buchanan I think it is good enough for tabby."

Work was a distraction from grief, but it was taking a terrible toll. When a neighbor from Illinois paid a visit in mid-April, Lincoln complained of "the constant pressure," which he found almost unendurable. "You know I am not of a very hopeful temperament," he reminded his friend, though he did have the capacity to "take hold of a thing and hold on for a good while." That was how he managed to get through this "protracted and severe" trial. "I am sometimes astonished at the part I am acting in this terrible drama. I can hardly believe that I am the same man I was a few years ago when I was living in my humble way with you in Springfield. I often ask myself the question, 'When shall I awake and find it all a dream?'"

During her long hours alone in her room, Mary had become fixated on the idea of communicating with Willie in the bourne beyond death. Spiritualism had a strong grip on the public imagination in those days, a grip that grew stronger as the war gathered its terrible harvest. It was therefore not surprising, perhaps, that the first lady's thoughts turned in this direction.

The seed may have been planted, according to Rebecca Pomroy, by an unidentified member of the Senate who told Mrs. Lincoln the story of a mysterious letter. In this strange tale, the senator arrived at his desk one morning to find the letter waiting, tied with a white satin ribbon. He also found instructions to deliver it to a certain Washington clergyman, who in turn would know how to find a particular widow in the capital city—a

nurse whose husband and two children had died. On April 4, this twist-
ing path led to Pomroy, who opened the letter and read it carefully. It was
from a purported spiritualist in the far West, claiming to channel a message from Pomroy's dead son. The boy reported that he had made a new
friend in the spirit world: Willie Lincoln. The spirits of the two boys liked
to hover over their mothers in Mary Lincoln's bedroom, but they hated
that the women were so sad. They wanted their mothers to be happy and
stop grieving. That was the message: Stop grieving.

Mary was electrified by this extraordinary tale and the two women
spoke about the letter whenever Pomroy visited. The nurse quickly
deduced that it must have been sent by a charlatan who once lived across
the street from her family in Massachusetts and thus knew the details of
her life, but Mary wasn't interested in debunking such a reassuring story.
She wanted to pursue it.

As it happened, these two odd events—Mary's appeal to John Hay for
money, and Pomroy's receipt of the message from beyond—both took
place on April 4, a beautiful Friday when the Washington spring made
the world seem fresh and new. Happily, Tad had at last made a full recovery, so Lincoln called for the presidential carriage and the three of them
went for a ride "for the first time since their recent affliction," as *The New
York Times* put it. Two days later, on Sunday morning, the president and
the first lady attended church services together, knowing nothing of the
terrible battle erupting that same moment beside the Tennessee River.

News of the Union victories at Shiloh and Island No. 10 reached Washington on April 9. The fickle springtime was serving up another round of
"rain, sleet and snow," yet citizens poured into the streets to celebrate.
"The City is in wild excitement over the news. A Salute of 100 guns
ordered by the Sec'y of War," Horatio Taft recorded in his diary. "The
great 'Anaconda' is drawing in his coils tighter and tighter around the
rebels," Taft crowed, capturing the full flood of Northern confidence.
"They have behaved most cowardly in every instance where they did not
have the advantage in numbers or position. The proud 'Southerners' had
better strike the word *chivalry* from their vocabulary. I think they are a
race of bombaster cowards and events are proving it every day."

Lincoln proclaimed a national day of thanksgiving "to our Heavenly
Father for these inestimable blessings." Among the blessings, alongside

military successes on land and sea, Lincoln included a suggestion that God was keeping Europe out of the war. Given the deepening cotton shortages, however, the president and his secretary of state weren't content to leave foreign relations entirely in the hands of Providence. Indeed, Lincoln and Seward saw the string of Union victories as a lever they could use to separate the Europeans once and for all from the South. And they needed a lever, because powerful forces in France and England continued to push for intervention.

By April, the French emperor was playing a double game, pleading with Dayton for shipments of cotton while secretly scheming to stir up a joint action with England to break the Federal blockade. Louis-Napoleon needed to get the French textile mills running, and he didn't seem to care which side was helped or hurt in the process. England's position was more complicated. It too needed to feed its looms, but the way the Confederacy boasted of the power of King Cotton to force England's hand offended many British citizens, as did the continuing fact of Southern slavery. For the pragmatic Lord Palmerston, there was also the risk of backing the wrong horse. With Union armies on the move, he had to weigh the danger of recognizing the Confederacy only to have it defeated. That might make an enemy of the United States for generations to come.

The British government could not be blamed for wishing the crisis away. The foreign minister, Lord Russell, summed up the prevailing attitude in a speech in Parliament at about this time. Surely the American territory was big enough for two independent nations, he said, adding that he hoped the Lincoln government would agree to a peaceful separation. Events were moving in exactly the opposite direction, though, for each day Lincoln grew more confident of victory and the Rebels became more ferocious in their resistance. The increasingly bloody war was proof of the vanity of Russell's wishes: there was no longer any chance of the United States becoming two nations by peaceful means.

But while Russell wished and hoped, others in England were taking action. The normally bustling port of Liverpool, quieter now because of the Federal blockade and the Southern cotton embargo, was a hive of Confederate sympathizers. A fund-raising appeal in the city had collected £40,000 to buy arms and ammunition for the Rebels; a second appeal was launched in April, to even greater enthusiasm. Laird Brothers, a major Liverpool shipbuilder, was producing lightning-fast cruisers for Confederate use as blockade-runners or open-sea raiders. The builders pretended

that the ships weren't meant for the Rebels; the first one, recently finished, was already on her way to the West Indies flying a neutral flag and
bearing the name *Oreto*. But that was a charade. As soon as she dropped
anchor, she would be transformed into a Confederate warship. This cyni-
cal violation of Britain's declared neutrality moved Charles Francis
Adams to enter a formal protest, but Lord Russell simply turned a blind
eye. Once again, he saw only what he wished to see.

Reflecting on William Dayton's report of his surprise meeting with
Napoleon in March, Lincoln came to believe that the ambassador had
stumbled onto the perfect answer to the needs of the French and the
wishes of the British. The way to link all these issues—the cotton shortage, the Union victories, and the damage being done by lingering Confederate sympathies—was to strike a deal: Lincoln would begin to reopen
the cotton trade in places where the Union had regained power, and in
exchange France and Britain would withdraw their recognition of the
South as a lawful belligerent. At Seward's request, Adams left London and
crossed the English Channel to hear Dayton's proposal for himself, and on
April 11, he reported to Seward that he "derived great benefit" from meeting with Dayton and would make "a corresponding change of policy" to
conform his approach to his colleague's. As if to give this new strategy a
boost, the Union scored another important victory the same day. Using
modern rifled artillery that fired powerful shells, Federal gunners forced
the surrender of the seemingly impregnable Fort Pulaski, which controlled
access to the port of Savannah, Georgia.

A wild rumor in Washington had Seward embarking on a secret mission to Mississippi to negotiate a peace with the Confederate general P. G.
T. Beauregard, but the secretary of state was in fact in his office that day,
laboring to formalize the delicate proposal. Seward prepared a long
memorandum for Adams to present to the British government, laying
out Lincoln's official version of the bargain. To support his case, Seward
wrote boastfully of "a full month of military successes" and asserted that
the Rebel cause was now "hopeless." He proceeded to explain why in
great detail, and with his letter he enclosed a specially prepared map
illustrating the successes and strategies of the U.S. military. Seward
closed this strong presentation with a characteristically optimistic flourish. The health of the United States, he declared, was "more robust and
vigorous than . . . ever before."

The effort was wasted. As soon as Adams returned from Paris—not

knowing about the message Seward was preparing—he asked for a meeting with Lord Russell, during which he pitched the deal as Dayton had
outlined it, without supporting materials. The two men had a long talk,
candid by diplomatic standards, sparring politely, jabbing each other's
sore spots just hard enough to be noticed but not hard enough to cause
offense. Adams did not trust the British; perhaps no grandson of a colonial revolutionary hero ever could. He believed that they saw a future
rival in the young United States and were not so secretly pulling for its
collapse. Russell, for his part, still believed that the Lincoln administration faced a hopeless task in trying to tame so vast a region. Britain's only
interest in the matter was a quick restoration of normal trade, he said:
cotton headed east, manufactured goods headed west. And the easiest
way to achieve that, from Britain's perspective, would be for the North to
let the South go in peace. Russell also reminded Adams that the Union
had initially asked Europe to remain neutral, and Europe had complied.
Neutrality remained the preferred position.

As the short, dark days began to lengthen in London, Adams worried
that Europe's precarious diplomatic balance would not last long. The
pressure for cotton built daily. The British chancellor of the exchequer,
William Gladstone, a politician with a keen sense of the popular mind,
traveled to the heart of England's mill country to deliver a speech in
Manchester that was more favorable to the Confederates than any he had
given before. "The North fights for supremacy, the South fights for independence," the future prime minister declared. His tone, Adams warned
in a dispatch to Seward, was a dark portent: "As the period approaches
when the end of the existing stock of cotton grows more and more visible, the distress of the [textile workers] appears more aggravated, and
the speculations as to the future are more freely indulged in." Adams
believed that England was watching the French emperor, hoping, "in
secret, that he will have the courage to do what many here wish, but are
ashamed to declare to the world"—that is, deliver victory to the South.

As spelled out in Seward's long memo, the president's proposed grand
bargain appealed to the cold economic calculations of the British government: cotton in exchange for a change of policy. But Lincoln, of all people,
appreciated that the ability to be coldly calculating did not necessarily imply
hardness of heart. The England that cravenly ignored the Confederate

ships under construction in Liverpool was the same England that had led the world in eradicating slavery.

Lincoln was mindful of this nobler aspect of Great Britain; he saw a constant reminder of it on his office wall. Among the military maps, Lincoln had hung only two pictures. One, over the fireplace, was a portrait of Andrew Jackson, hero of the opposition Democrats. Jackson's picture was a reminder to all visitors that preserving the federal Union was not a partisan affair, for Jackson had also faced down a rebellion rooted in South Carolina, over the supposed right of states to nullify federal laws. A smaller portrait hung nearby: a likeness of John Bright, a British abolitionist, reformer, and longtime member of Parliament. Bright was, like Lincoln, a gifted orator steeped in the ideals of an equal-opportunity, free-labor society. He and his colleague Richard Cobden were such devoted proponents of the American system that they were sometimes known as the MPs for the United States. Bright's picture on the president's wall underlined the importance of England's antislavery movement to the success of Lincoln's delicate and perilous foreign policy. And when his eye fell on the large round face and bushy whiskers, he was assured that the Union had strong, true friends in England. His task as president was to help them help him.

With that in mind, Lincoln on April 10 asked the Senate to ratify a treaty long advocated by British abolitionists, guaranteeing American cooperation in shutting down the international slave trade. It was a point of great national pride in England that Her Majesty's navy was the world's leading force against the trafficking of human beings. Over the years, most maritime nations had entered agreements to permit British warships to stop and search suspected slave smugglers at sea. But because the slave states controlled the Senate in the period before the war, the United States was not among them.

Lincoln forwarded the treaty to Charles Sumner at a time when the Senate was busier than it had ever been: major debates raged over bills authorizing confiscation of Rebel property (a way of freeing Confederate-owned slaves) and ending slavery in the District of Columbia. In addition, countless details in the huge tax bill required resolution; long lists of new officials in the fast-growing government needed confirmation; and complex bills involving homesteads, land-grant colleges, and the transcontinental railroad spawned endless committee meetings. Meanwhile, Lincoln wanted to create a new federal department for agriculture, and he continued to argue for diplomatic recognition of Liberia and Haiti. Despite the chamber's heavy workload, Sumner somehow managed to push the treaty to a vote in just two weeks. It passed unanimously.

"*Laus Deo!*"—praise be to God—Sumner wrote after the vote was tallied, for he believed that the treaty would effectively end the slave trade while seeding "good will & friendship between U.S. and England." He rushed from the Capitol to Seward's office to deliver the news. Sumner found the secretary of state napping on his sofa. Startled awake, Seward reacted straight from his deeply political gut: "Good God! The Democrats have disappeared." After a moment's reflection, he added, "This is the greatest act of the Administration." That night, Lord Lyons, the British ambassador, called on Sumner to thank him. "He overflowed with gratitude & delight," the senator reported, "happy that his name was signed to a treaty of such importance—perhaps the last slave-trade treaty which the world will see."

Though never fast enough for abolitionists, the ground was shifting daily under the teetering edifice of slavery. On April 11, the House of Representatives voted overwhelmingly to outlaw slavery in the District of Columbia, the one jurisdiction where Congress had undisputed authority to take this step. The vote came near the close of business that Friday afternoon, too late for action by the Senate. Hundreds of slaves across the city slipped into hiding so that their masters couldn't force them into Maryland or Virginia before the law took effect. Reformers who had worked for a generation to reach this milestone had to wait through another weekend.

When Monday finally came, the Senate passed the bill by a wide margin. Now, surely, the wait was over. After all, Lincoln had offered a similar bill as a young congressman some fourteen years earlier. Unexpectedly, however, the president didn't sign the new bill immediately. Monday ended and Tuesday dragged past, with still no word from the White House. It was well known that Lincoln preferred gradual emancipation on the pragmatic theory that slaves might be unprepared for a freedom that came overnight. Given the prejudice against former slaves, what would become of the suddenly jobless and homeless freed slaves of Washington? Who would provide for helpless children and elderly slaves who could no longer work? Lincoln also supported a public referendum on the question of slavery in the District, not least because it would show border state conservatives that Republicans respected the will of the people.

But these reasons hardly seemed sufficient for Lincoln to withhold his signature. An irritated Sumner went to the White House hoping to speed things along. He tried embarrassing Lincoln, telling the president that as long as he sat on the bill he was "making himself . . . the largest slave-holder in the country." He tried tugging Lincoln's heartstrings, advocating for the "poor slaves" who were "waiting for the day of Freedom to come out from their hiding places."

The president apparently didn't disclose his reason for delaying; indeed, it probably would not have passed the senator's moral muster. Lincoln had promised a seventy-three-year-old Kentucky congressman, Charles Wickliffe, enough time to move two elderly slaves out of the jurisdiction. The three old people had been together a very long time, and while the congressman saw no point in changing their relationship, Lincoln saw no value in upsetting a very important man. Besides, the president owed Wickliffe a favor: the former Kentucky governor had worked with Lincoln's friend Joshua Speed to smuggle thousands of guns into Kentucky in the earliest days of the conflict, thus arming loyal Unionists against a possible secessionist uprising. And Lincoln still hoped to win Wickliffe's support for his compensated emancipation plan.

At last, after the promised interval, the waiting ended on Wednesday, April 16. With a stroke of his pen, Abraham Lincoln became the first U.S. president to give freedom to slaves whom he did not himself own.

Henry Halleck, dressed in a brand-new uniform and wearing his ceremonial sword, arrived at Pittsburg Landing on April 11 to take charge of the combined western armies. It was his first wartime field command, and what he saw must have taken some of the starch out of his shirt. What Grant described as "the most incessant rains . . . ever known" had turned the shallow graves of the Shiloh dead into a slurry of mud and bones. "*Skulls* and *toes* are sticking up from beneath the clay all around and the heavy wagons *crush* the bodies turning up the bones of the buried," one horrified soldier reported. Thousands of wounded men, many of them near death, suffered in the tents and meager farmhouses of the neighborhood, waiting to board transport ships to better facilities in Cincinnati.

Halleck was a wealthy and cultured man, fluent in several languages, and married to the granddaughter of Alexander Hamilton. He was so bookish that he once lashed himself to a bunk during a stormy passage around Cape Horn so that he could safely continue reading by candle-light. He was the sort of general who complained about the way subordinates folded their reports. In other words, Old Brains was completely out of his element on a miserable, corpse-strewn battlefield—a place where Grant was increasingly at home. The short time these mismatched men would spend together very nearly cost the Union its greatest warrior.

For the moment, Grant was the toast of Washington, but Halleck found little to admire. He was appalled by the condition of Grant's bruised army and immediately ordered him to clean up the camps and crack down on discipline. "I never saw a man more deficient in the business of organization," Halleck sniffed. Summoned to Halleck's headquarters aboard a steamer tied to the dock, Grant was forced to stand respectfully as Halleck paced back and forth "scolding him in a loud and haughty manner." Halleck had never commanded a great mass of volunteers, so he didn't understand how they differed from professional soldiers. He was shocked to see that some men sat down on guard duty; worse yet, some of their volunteer officers let them do it. Halleck issued a flurry of orders: to properly train sentinels, to get to work improving the muddy roads around the camps, to close the saloons on board the steamships at the river landings.

Buell did what he could to stoke Halleck's fire. When a complaint crossed Buell's desk about rowdy troops firing their muskets in camp, he added a note blaming Grant's men before he sent it on to Halleck. A week in the same camp with Grant had done nothing to change Buell's belief that Grant's incompetence would have caused the annihilation of his army at Shiloh if Buell had not come to the rescue. By Buell's account, Grant "had no line or order of battle, no defensive works of any sort, no outposts, properly speaking, to give warning" of the attack. When the Rebels struck, Grant was as surprised as his troops: he was caught break-fasting at his headquarters downstream. Worse yet, Buell asserted, Grant had been late to the field and had spent most of the day in retreat until his dwindling and "defeated" force was "driven to refuge in the midst of its magazines, with the triumphant enemy at half-gunshot distance." Only Buell's timely arrival had checked the Rebels, and the next day he had driven them away.

This version of the epic Shiloh battle reached the public on April 14, when a Cincinnati newspaper published a long and scathing description of Grant's failures by Whitelaw Reid, a young journalist from Buell's home state of Ohio. The account was promptly picked up by the *Herald* in New York. Reid's earlier reports from Pittsburg Landing, before the battle, had already caused a stir with their mix of inflammatory charges and hit-or-miss accuracy; this new dispatch landed just as the first lists of Shiloh casualties sowed grief through the towns and farmsteads of the North. Overnight, Grant plunged from his pedestal. No longer was he "Unconditional Surrender" Grant. Now he was an absentee commander who let his men be slaughtered like hogs. After the lieutenant governor of Ohio visited wounded volunteers from his state, he published another version of the same indictment. These shocking reports hit Washington with the power of massed artillery. "All that we hear of our officers at Pittsburg Landing is most painful," wrote Charles Sumner to the governor of Massachusetts, John Andrew. "Some of them ought to be shot."

Grant's first impulse was to ignore the charges. Sherman responded differently: as commander of the division hit first by the Rebels, he was implicated as well, and silence was not his operating style. Despite his bandaged hand, he immediately began scrawling his testimony in letters to his politically powerful relatives: his brother John was a U.S. senator and his foster father was Thomas Ewing, Sr., a confidant of both Stanton's and Lincoln's. "This story of surprise is an afterthought of the Rascals who ran away & had to Excuse their Cowardice," Sherman explained to his brother in the Senate. "Newspapers now rule," he complained to Ewing. "Their representatives the Reporters are to me the most contemptible race of men that exist, cowardly, cringing hanging round and gathering their material out of the most polluted sources." Thus supplied with material to rebut Reid's charges, the Sherman lobby fought back in the press and in Congress.

Sherman understood who was behind many of the stories, and why the attacks were coming out of his home state: the regiments that broke and ran in Sherman's division comprised Ohio volunteers and were led by prominent Ohio citizens. One such officer, Colonel Jesse Appler of the 53rd Ohio, was a young judge whose political ambitions died the moment he called out to his men (who were in fact fighting quite well): "Retreat! Save yourselves!" and began running toward the river. Another, Colonel Rodney Mason of the 71st Ohio, was the son of a well-known lawyer. Like many elected officers of the all-volunteer army, Mason, it was said, "went into the service not from motives of patriotism, but to win a name and fame that would carry him into the Halls of Congress." According to Sherman, Mason not only ran from the battlefield on the first day of fighting but also refused to return on the second day, even after rein-forcements arrived. "Instead of joining with the fragment of his Regi-ment then steadily advancing under fire, he made direct to the Steamboat Landing," Sherman declared, adding: "I will not permit Col. Mason . . . to accuse me [and] shield himself at my expense."

Sherman fought political battles the same way he fought with rifles and cannon, giving no mercy. His testimony won over Halleck while routing his enemies in Washington and Ohio. Thomas Ewing, Jr., in Washington on business, reported on the mood at the highest levels of the army: "Halleck says in a dispatch to [Stanton] that 'Sherman saved the fortunes of the day.'" His father instructed the younger Ewing to report this to the president, "and remind him that I said to him last win-ter Sherman was the best fighting general he had."

Sherman's earlier trial by newspaper—when he was accused of mad-ness for predicting that the Rebels would be very hard to defeat—had left him with a fairly thick skin. This time he was able to take the criticism in stride; he even paused in his letter-writing to hunt up battlefield souve-nirs for his sons, including a box of shells, some of them still live. For Grant, who had grown to enjoy his lionizing coverage, the criticism after Shiloh left him feeling "shockingly abused." Along with the other charges, his enemies exhumed his California drinking problem and used it to bolster the accusation that Grant was drunk during the battle. These charges could not be ignored, much as Lincoln might have wanted to wish them away. The president ordered Stanton to get to the bottom of the matter. On April 23, Stanton wired Halleck, who replied with a luke-warm defense of Grant and the promise of an investigation.

While he waited for the results of this inquiry, the president fended off demands that he cashier the former hero. The story soon spread that he had asked what brand of whiskey Grant preferred because "I'd like to send a barrel to my other generals." (Lincoln later told a questioner that he had not actually said this, but "it would have been very good if [I] had.")

The president badly wanted to believe the version of Shiloh that he was hearing from Sherman's allies, because he needed Grant to be a man possessing, as Lincoln would later put it, "the grit of a bulldog." He had enough failing generals on his hands already; he was willing to overlook many shortcomings in a military leader, including lack of polish on the parade ground and uncertain fealty to the field manual. All that mattered was that his soldiers act according to the simple truth expressed by the Rebel cavalryman Nathan Bedford Forrest: "War means fighting, and fighting means killing." When the Pennsylvania politician Alexander McClure called on Lincoln to say that the outraged citizens of his state were demanding Grant's head, Lincoln answered almost plaintively: "I can't spare this man. He fights."

George McClellan showed little eagerness to fight, but he did take great pleasure in the complex logistics and furious industry required to prepare for battle. He marveled at the projects he himself directed—the digging of elaborate trenches and the placement of enormous siege guns on the road to Richmond—exulting in a letter to his wife that they "may almost be called gigantic."

But the Confederates had been busy, too. By mid-April Joseph E. Johnston had successfully relocated most of his army to positions between McClellan and Richmond—"the best troops of the Confederacy," John Dahlgren fretted, "strongly intrenched and barring the way." McClellan's Peninsula Campaign, designed to swing around Johnston and dash into Richmond, had lost all its swing and dash. On April 22, Senator Ben Wade hosted a dinner party attended by Attorney General Bates where once again conversation turned—as it did everywhere in Washington—to the question of McClellan's true loyalties. A visitor from Ohio claimed to have heard Little Mac say that "the South was right and he would never fight against it." Bates disagreed. "I cannot concur in believing [McClellan] a traitor. With more charity I conclude that he is only a foolish egotist."

In an effort to speed things along, Lincoln took a field trip on April 19 down the Potomac to Aquia Creek, where he hoped to meet Irwin McDowell, commander of his withheld army corps. It was a wet trip, but the president was glad to get out of the White House and free of the capital. Several of Lincoln's advisers were also aboard, including two members of his cabinet, as well as the revered New York attorney David Dudley Fields and Captain Dahlgren with his grown son Ulric. Lincoln chatted with Stanton and Chase as the cutter *Miami* steamed past the stately town houses that climbed the hill behind the Alexandria waterfront, then rounded a bend to find Washington's house at Mount Vernon standing sentinel over its wide green lawn.

When the group arrived at Aquia Landing, McDowell was nowhere to be found. The men bunked for the night aboard ship, "in the little cabin . . . stowed away in a place like a box," Dahlgren recalled. Lincoln spent the evening telling stories and favorite jokes, like the one about a naughty schoolboy who was ordered to hold out his hand to have his knuckles rapped. Shocked at the filthy hand that slowly appeared from behind the boy's back, the schoolmaster declared that he would suspend the punishment if the boy could find anything else so dirty in the entire classroom. "There it is!" cried the boy, presenting his other hand.

Early the next morning, McDowell reported to the president. As rain drummed on the cabin roof, the general said that his troops had chased a detachment of Rebels across the Rappahannock and that now, with his corps scattered between Warrenton and Falmouth, the region south of Washington was well in hand. Lincoln seemed pleased. The Confederate retreat had him feeling more confident about the safety of the capital, and he was thinking about combining McDowell's corps with troops in the Shenandoah Valley under Nathaniel Banks for a march on Richmond from the north.

Stanton took over the discussion, clearly excited by the size and power of the Union forces available to capture the Rebel capital. Generals were beginning to complain about the secretary's tendency to inflate their troop strength; Sherman, for one, warned his brother that "there may be enough on paper, but not enough in fact." True to form, Stanton now spoke of 150,000 men available to McClellan and began imagining how large a force they could gather under McDowell. Why stop with Banks? Stanton asked. Why not add Frémont's army to the thrust?

"There's the political trouble," Lincoln answered: John Frémont was never going to march quietly under the command of Irwin McDowell. But they were both major generals, Stanton countered. "The law authorizes you to give command to any of like commission."

Here it was again, the same old incomprehension. Like Bates telling him at the beginning of the year that he had the authority to fire McClellan, or like the abolitionists who preached to him about his duty to free the slaves, Stanton had an abstract understanding of Lincoln's power but was blind to the political realities constraining that power. It didn't matter what the law authorized Lincoln to do, or what the higher laws of morality called on him to do. It mattered only what he could actually accomplish while keeping his tenuous grip on the fractious Northern coalition. Stanton's grandiose idea was not something he could put into practice, Lincoln said. If he tried to put the radical Republican hero Frémont into a subordinate role under McDowell, in a movement designed to aid the Democrat McClellan, "there would be an outcry."

Still, as he left Aquia that Sunday morning, Lincoln remained intrigued by the idea of combining McDowell and Banks in an overland thrust designed to join McClellan in front of Richmond. He mulled the idea as the week went by—a week marked by anxious waiting for word from Farragut's fleet below New Orleans, and by a troublesome visit to Richmond by the French ambassador Henri Mercier.

The cascade of Confederate losses, along with the emperor's hunger for cotton, inspired Mercier to visit the Rebel capital for a firsthand look at Southern morale. As he rounded the peninsula where McClellan was making his slow way forward, the envoy saw the forest of masts and smokestacks signaling the immense quantities of supplies being ferried daily to the mighty Union army. Mercier's transport, the French warship *Gassendi,* passed the sturdy little *Monitor,* poised at anchor beneath the guns of Fort Monroe. Sailing up the James River and arriving at Richmond, Mercier "expect[ed] to hear talk of surrender," according to the historian Amanda Foreman. Instead, he met unyielding men like the Confederate secretary of state, Judah Benjamin, who deeply impressed the Frenchman with his hatred of the North and his determination to fight to the end. Benjamin and his fellow Rebels were prepared to lose Richmond and New Orleans—indeed, all their ports, if necessary—but they would never submit to Federal authority. Mercier's ears were also filled with warnings of how a Northern victory would spell the end of cotton for years to come: liberated slaves would abandon the fields, and proud Southerners burn their stores.

When Mercier returned to Washington on April 24, Lincoln and Seward welcomed him. The ranking admiral of the French navy, who happened to be in New York, visited Washington for the occasion, and along with the captain of the *Gassendi* he received Lincoln on board "with all the honors paid to a sovereign." There is no record of the president's conversation with Mercier, but Lincoln undoubtedly hoped that the envoy had seen the fatal weakness of the Confederate position and that France would at last accept the grand bargain he was offering. The opposite was the case. Disembarking from the ship, Mercier promptly paid a visit to Lord Lyons, his British counterpart, and argued that the time had come to recognize Confederate independence. The government in Richmond had persuaded him that the Rebels were about to strike back, hard.

That night, Seward hosted Mercier and the French admiral at his mansion across the street from the White House. As the guests consumed an abundant dinner, Mercier was fairly bursting with his knowledge of the Confederacy's secret plans to regain the upper hand. Turning to Dahlgren, he slyly mentioned that he had met Dahlgren's old friend Catesby Jones, the new commander of the dreaded ironclad *Virginia,* during his stay in Richmond. "He sends his respects," Mercier purred, then added, "and said 'not to be *caught napping* at Washington.'" Dahlgren mulled over this cryptic remark, and concluded that Mercier was hinting at something important. He decided to warn the president.

The following day, Lincoln heard not only Dahlgren's warning but also a fresh bit of intelligence picked up by Stanton's assistant Peter Watson. According to Watson's source, the Confederates were preparing a sneak attack on McDowell's scattered army—an attack that, if successful, would open the road to Washington. A few days earlier, Lincoln had been confident enough about the security of the capital to consider sending McDowell on the offensive. Now he was reminded of the enormous risks involved.

When Orville Browning visited the White House that evening, he found the president complaining of a headache. The two old friends began talking, and as he often did when he wanted a distraction, Lincoln steered the conversation around to poetry. He and Browning both had lines by Thomas Hood committed to memory, and after quoting these back and forth, Lincoln asked whether Browning recalled Hood's poem "The Haunted House."

When Browning admitted that he had never read the poem, the president rang for a servant who soon returned with a copy of Hood's works from Lincoln's library. The president proceeded to read aloud the eerie verses—a compendium of broken windows, creaking hinges, scuttling insects, unlit stairs, swarms of bats, a ticking clock, a bloody hand. Lincoln was swept away. When he reached a particularly vivid line or verse, he would pause to talk about why it worked so well. He enjoyed his own performance so much that he rang the bell again and sent for another volume, then performed Hood's low comic poem "The Lost Heir." Lincoln scarcely paused before launching into a third poem, and by the time he finished that one, an hour and half had sped by and both men were in better spirits. But as he said goodbye, Lincoln accurately predicted that when Browning left, there would be "a crowd . . . buzzing about the door like bees, ready to pounce upon him" and return him to "the annoyances and harassments of his position."

From the beginning of the war, New Orleans was the prize Lincoln coveted most. It was the first great city he ever saw as a young man, his destination during the flatboat journey that marked his personal declaration of independence from his father. No other place reflected quite so well the geographical and commercial ties binding North and South, for in happier times the bounty of the continent collected there for shipment around the world. Lincoln had closely monitored months of arduous preparation, first in Washington and then in the Gulf of Mexico, for a Union campaign to take the city. Now, on April 25, the day of Browning's visit to the White House, a fleet of battered warships under David Farragut finally steamed toward the docks of the Crescent City, dodging unmanned barges carrying blazing loads of cotton. The citizens of New Orleans, the largest city and most important port in the Confederacy, had only this futile gesture to make in response to the arrival of Lincoln's conquering armada.

Not long past midnight of the previous day—after sand had been stowed in buckets, ready to be spread across decks that would soon be slick with blood—Farragut had ordered seventeen ships in single file past the two Confederate forts guarding the river below the city. Union mortars had been bombarding the forts for nearly a week, but the passage remained formidable. Farragut's ships first had to steer through a line of sunken hulks. Behind these obstacles the Rebels had prepared bonfires on unmanned rafts, ready to float among the wooden vessels of the Federal fleet. Behind the fire rafts waited the meager Confederate navy, a bold but underweight armada of riverboats mounting a mix of surplus guns. Among them was the half-finished ironclad *Manassas,* a hulking former sidewheel steamboat covered in old railroad tracks so as to be pressed into service as a ram. The Confederate secretary of the navy, Stephen Mallory, had assured Jefferson Davis that the Union's fleet could never get through.

The batteries in the two forts thundered to life at 3:30 A.M. on April

24. "I do not believe there was ever a grander spectacle witnessed before the world than that displayed during the great artillery duel which then followed," a Confederate gunnery captain later recalled. In the hours before dawn, a deafening, firelit struggle played out on the wide, muddy river. The forts were supposed to be invincible; instead, Farragut proved that ships fast enough, sailed by men brave enough, could pass through the terrible barrage. One shell-shot ship at a time, the Union fleet managed to reach safety upstream, beyond the Rebel guns.

While running the terrible gantlet, Farragut's flagship, the *Hartford*—flying a huge Stars and Stripes through the red glare—caught fire when a Confederate tugboat pushed a floating bonfire into her port side. Quickly, the crew pulled out fire hoses and manned the pumps. The admiral's gunners held to their work despite the blistering heat, as Farragut screamed over the roar of the flames, "Don't flinch from that fire, boys! There's hotter fire than that for those who don't do their duty." The burning barge stuck to the *Hartford*, feeding the inferno, until a fast-thinking officer uncapped several shells and shoved them over the side and into the fire. Seconds later, in a huge explosion, the raft of fire disintegrated and sizzled away.

Now, steaming in his wounded craft toward the great prize of New Orleans, Farragut saw black smoke rising from bales of white cotton piled on the wharves, torched by merchants determined not to let the precious crop fall into Yankee hands. Union spies had been correct: the city had no soldiers to speak of. All its guns had been sent north or mounted on the now defeated Rebel riverboats. The last hopes of New Orleans had been pinned on the forts downriver, and on two unfinished ironclads: the *Manassas*, lost in the battle; and the *Mississippi*, scuttled and burning near the shipyard.

Dropping anchor, Farragut allowed the mayor to choose: he could either raise the Union flag or watch his city be turned to rubble by the fleet's guns. When the mayor offered a surly no, the admiral sent marines ashore to raise the red, white, and blue. At last the Crescent City and the mouth of the great river—the strategic endpoint of Winfield Scott's original plan for breaking the Confederacy—once again belonged to the Union.

The capture of New Orleans was a devastating blow to the Confederacy: "the great catastrophe," as Jefferson Davis called it, "the fall of our chief commercial city, and the destruction of the naval vessels on which our hopes most rested for the protection of the lower Mississippi and the harbors of the Gulf." The Rebel diarist Mary Boykin Chesnut wrote: "New Orleans gone—and with it the Confederacy. Are we not cut in two?"

The news astounded European leaders; Charles Frances Adams reported "general incredulity." The French government, which of all institutions should have appreciated the strategic importance of the mouth of North America's greatest river, tried to minimize the significance of Farragut's coup. When Ambassador Dayton mentioned the capture to Foreign Minister Thouvenel, the Frenchman angrily jabbed at a map of the United States, pointing to the empty interior of the Deep South. The Confederates could not be beaten, he scoffed, because "they would retire there"—where he was pointing—and "it was a *vast country.*"

But if the French didn't understand that the South's navigable rivers made it vulnerable to attack, Lincoln and others in Washington did. New Orleans was viewed as the beginning of the end.

— 6 —

MAY

George McClellan's works before Yorktown were just about perfect. As May began, the muddy roads leading to the front were neatly corduroyed with logs for traction, and every rain-swollen creek along the way had been bridged. Behind stout earthen walls reinforced with lumber, the general had installed fixed lines of 13-inch seacoast mortars, fat iron cauldrons that could lob enormous iron balls into the Confederate fortifications. He had 10-inch mortars and 8-inch mortars and 8-inch howitzers, too. He had ordnance guns, Napoleon guns, and Parrott guns of nearly every size—rows and rows of rifled cannon, some capable of firing 200-pound shells at the Rebel batteries. He had many tons of ammunition stockpiled, and an endless train of mule-drawn wagons ready to bring more from his base near Fort Monroe. And he had tens of thousands of infantrymen poised to swarm the Rebel positions once those were softened by the blasting and bombarding.

McClellan looked over all that had been created during the past month and decided that it was . . . not quite enough. He wanted the 30-pound Parrott siege guns that he'd left behind in the forts around Washington. Lincoln, who had been expecting the attack on Yorktown for weeks, was irate.

"Your call for Parrott guns from Washington alarms me—chiefly because it argues indefinite procrastination," the president fumed in a coded telegram. The general responded as he always did, saying in essence that so little was happening because he was doing so much. "All is being done that human labor can accomplish," McClellan declared. No matter how hard Lincoln pushed his general, Little Mac refused to alter his pace; he was like a stubborn child who walks slower when asked to hurry up.

Having watched McClellan for eight months over the quiet ramparts of Manassas and Yorktown, Confederate general Johnston formed a crisp conclusion about his opponent: "McClellan seems not to value time especially." Nevertheless, Johnston believed—as he had in March at Manassas—that the Federals were finally preparing to attack, and on May 5 he ordered another preemptive retreat. Over the past month, the Confederacy had collected some 55,000 troops at Yorktown; flushed from their fortifications, they had to move fast to get safely inside their next line of trenches. In their haste they left behind more than eighty artillery pieces, plus large stores of ammunition, tents, and rations—scarce resources the Rebels could not afford to lose.

The Federals set off after them, catching Johnston's rearguard at the picturesque colonial capital of Williamsburg. There, the Rebel army turned and fought like a hounded stag, tossing the Yankees backward. Hearing this news, McClellan rushed to the battlefield, where he found chaos in the Union ranks. Major General Edwin "Bull Head" Sumner, of the II Corps, was nominally in command. Sumner, who had earned his nickname during a long-ago scrap when a musket ball struck him in the head and supposedly bounced off, had more than forty years' military experience; he was the oldest general to serve in Civil War combat on either side. But he had never led a force remotely as large as the one he commanded at Williamsburg, and he was clearly out of his depth. Quickly surveying the tangled lines of soldiers struggling in the thick Virginia underbrush, McClellan issued a few sharp orders and got the Federals moving forward again to capture Williamsburg's Fort Magruder. "In five minutes after I reached the ground a possible defeat was changed into certain victory," he boasted.

McClellan had never gotten over his annoyance at Lincoln's choice of corps commanders for the Army of the Potomac. He still believed in his own idea of letting the best men rise through the heat of battle, and he insisted that the near disaster at Williamsburg proved his point. In a letter to his wife, he grumbled that the battle was bungled by the "utter stupidity & worthlessness of the Corps Com[manders]," with Sumner the worst offender. Old Bull Head "proved that he was even a greater fool than I had supposed & had come within an ace of having us defeated."

On balance, though, McClellan was delighted with the events of early May. Once again, his careful maneuvering had forced the enemy to give up a fortified position without a fight. "I feel very proud of Yorktown; it and Manassas will be my brightest chaplets in history; for I know that I accomplished everything in both places by pure military skill," he declared. In Washington, the reviews were mixed; by this point everything McClellan did was controversial. John Dahlgren agreed that Yorktown was a masterpiece of military science. "McClellan's strategy seems to be conclusive," he wrote. "He forced the Confederates to leave Manassas without a blow, and now to abandon Yorktown." And yet, Dahlgren reported, "the extreme Republicans are . . . persistent in their attacks on McClellan, as if nothing but a battle would content them."

McClellan's maneuvers on the peninsula had crystallized two irreconcilable views of the proper way to fight the rebellion. One approach emphasized the steady capture of strategic points by the least violent methods available, in hopes that the Confederates would see that their cause was doomed before too much bloodshed made a relatively peaceful resolution impossible. This was McClellan's theory of the war, and it explained why in the midst of a military campaign he insisted that his soldiers protect the property of local Confederate sympathizers. While his letters were full of references to an epic battle ahead, a decisive clash of Blue and Gray, on a deeper level McClellan did not envision a truly decisive moment. Instead, he imagined that his victories would somehow return the United States to its earlier condition, unchanged—except that now levelheaded men like himself would engineer peaceful solutions to the differences between North and South. The war, in his view, was not the bitter fruit of an irrepressible conflict between slavery and freedom. It was an avoidable tragedy wrought by agitators driven by extreme passions and bad motives.

The other school of thought held that the time for coaxing the parties toward peace was long past. The division between North and South had been a long time coming, and nothing short of a fight could resolve it. Especially after Shiloh, the river of blood was running and could not be called back. The Union must press ahead, must crush and conquer the Rebels through relentless battle and waste. Soft war versus hard war: Lincoln, for one, was moving more solidly into the hard-war camp, as evidenced by his growing admiration for Ulysses Grant.

Lincoln was not alone. The hard-war camp was gaining by the day, while the ranks of soft warriors dwindled. McClellan was irritated to discover that even his wife failed to see the brilliance of his relatively bloodless Yorktown campaign. "I really thought that you would appreciate a great result gained by pure skill & at little cost," he sulked after Mary Ellen McClellan greeted the Rebel retreat with the written equivalent of a yawn. "It would have been easy for me to have sacrificed 10,000 lives in taking Yorktown," he added. "I presume the world would have thought it more brilliant." Even in the midst of the most important undertaking of his life, while armored in the manpower and wealth of the North, McClellan saw himself as a lonely hero standing against an uncomprehending and even malicious world.

Despite their differences over politics and military strategy, Lincoln tried to save the vainglorious general from his worst tendencies. When McClellan asked permission to do away with the corps commanders after Williamsburg, the president responded with a frank tutorial in political prudence. McClellan needed to understand how shaky his support was in Congress, Lincoln warned in a private telegram. What was more, he needed to be alert to the fact that many officers in his army were complaining about the cliquishness of McClellan's high command.

"I think it is indispensable for you to know how your struggle against [the corps command structure] is received," Lincoln wrote. "It is looked upon merely as an effort to pamper one or two pets. . . . I am constantly told that you have no consultation or communication with [the corps commanders]; that you consult and communicate with nobody but General Fitz John Porter, and perhaps General [William] Franklin. I do not say these complaints are true or just," he added, "but at all events it is proper you should know of their existence." Coming to his central point, Lincoln cautioned McClellan against overplaying his hand by taking on three corps commanders (and their congressional friends): "Are you strong enough— even with my help—to set your foot upon the necks of Sumner, Heintzelman, and Keyes all at once? This is a practical and very serious question for you."

The general's self-absorption also seemed to blind him to the increasingly obvious fact that the Rebels weren't the least bit mollified by his care for their homes and possessions. They weren't softening; their resistance was intensifying. "There has arisen a desire to see the city [of Richmond] destroyed rather than surrendered," Jefferson Davis proudly informed his wife as McClellan moved up the peninsula. And the Confederates again escalated the violence of the war, this time by planting mines among the supplies they left behind at Yorktown. McClellan was disgusted by this ungentlemanly tactic. "The rebels have been guilty of the most murderous & barbarous conduct in placing torpedoes within the abandoned works, near wells & springs, near flag staffs, magazines, telegraph offices, in carpet bags, barrels of flour, etc.," he wrote. He promised a stern response to these improvised explosives: Rebel prisoners of war would be put to work clearing the mines.

Unlike Grant after Shiloh, McClellan failed to draw the larger lesson from this deeper engagement with the murderous brutality of modern warfare. Month by month, the Confederates were taking the choice between soft war and hard war out of the hands of Northern leaders. Fighting for homes and pride, the insurrectionist army was pushing all its chips onto the table, offering the North no choice but hard war or capitulation.

On Monday, May 5, as his soldiers fought at Williamsburg, Abraham Lincoln boarded the *Miami* at the navy yard, bound for Fort Monroe, near Yorktown, and one of the most remarkable voyages in presidential history. His specific reasons for embarking on the trip are not recorded, but in his role as unofficial general in chief, Lincoln occasionally felt the need to gather his own intelligence, to look men in the eye as they delivered information, and to see for himself certain facts that the telegraph could relay only in hazy outline.

The presidential party, including Stanton and Chase, set off at twilight, cruised almost immediately into a heavy rainstorm, and anchored about fifteen miles below Alexandria when visibility dropped nearly to zero. The storm cleared as the president slept, and the *Miami* was under way again before dawn. She entered the heaving waters of Chesapeake Bay by noon. Lincoln grew wrenchingly seasick. When lunch was served, he couldn't face it; instead, he stretched his long frame across the top of a locker. There he suffered while his cabinet secretaries tried to eat: "The glasses tumbled over and slid and rolled about—and the whole table seemed as topsy-turvy as if some Spiritualist were operating on it," Chase recounted. After lunch, Stanton staggered to another locker and joined Lincoln in prone misery.

When at last the *Miami* reached the harbor at Old Point Comfort, night had settled over the water, but Lincoln wasted no time. He summoned Major General John Wool, the commander of the Fort Monroe garrison, who arrived at the cutter shortly before ten P.M. Wool's independence from McClellan's command—another sore spot for Little Mac—enabled Wool to give Lincoln an unvarnished view of conditions in the wake of the Army of the Potomac's advance. Quickly the president realized that preparations to capitalize on the fall of Yorktown were nonexistent. As McClellan moved up the peninsula toward Richmond, Norfolk and the ironclad in its harbor seemed to have slipped the general's mind. But the *Virginia*'s panic-inducing first voyage was still fresh in Lincoln's memory and he was eager to put the behemoth out of commission. On the spot, he decided to call on the navy's senior man in Hampton Roads, Commander Louis Goldsborough, to see what could be done.

A tugboat ferried Lincoln's party to the commander's flagship. Now it was Chase's turn to grow queasy. The little tug and the much larger *Minnesota* rose and fell on the choppy water, with the only connection between them being the rope ladder dangling from the flagship's bulwark. "The guiding ropes on either hand [were] hardly visible in the darkness," Chase reported in a letter to his daughter. "It seemed to me *very* high and a little fearsome." As the Treasury secretary peered nervously at this arrangement, Lincoln stepped forward confidently and clambered up the side of the frigate. Somehow, Chase managed to follow.

With the president and his party on board, Goldsborough outlined the situation. A Confederate battery at Sewell's Point, across Hampton Roads from Fort Monroe, blocked the mouth of the Elizabeth River leading southward to Norfolk. Behind the battery, in the safe haven of the river, lay the ironclad. Goldsborough's wooden battleships could take out the battery, but they were no match for the *Virginia*. And the *Monitor*, having proven its ability to hold the Rebel ship in check, was too valuable to risk in an all-out assault.

There was, however, a new Federal asset on the scene, a weapon that might tip the stalemate at Hampton Roads in the Union's favor, and Stanton proposed an inspection the following morning. After breakfast on May 7, the group visited a sleek steamship belonging to the Yankee shipping magnate Cornelius Vanderbilt—his personal yacht, perhaps the swiftest and most maneuverable craft afloat, with two masts and twin hundred-ton paddlewheels amidships. By far the wealthiest man in America, Vanderbilt had offered in March to donate the yacht for a specific purpose: after being converted into a U.S. Navy ramming ship, she would hunt down the *Virginia,* punch a hole in her hull, and send her to the bottom. Lincoln had quickly accepted the offer, and now the elegant *Vanderbilt* rode low at anchor in Hampton Roads. The modified ship was virtually solid wood for fifty feet behind her prow, which was heavily plated with rolled iron.

Delighted to find the luxurious ram ready for action, Lincoln's impromptu high command formed a plan of attack. Supported by Wool's big guns at Fort Monroe, Goldsborough's wooden gunships would open fire on the Rebel battery at Sewell's Point. Ideally, this barrage would lure the *Virginia* out of the river and into Hampton Roads to challenge the gunboats, and once the ironclad revealed herself, the speedy *Vanderbilt* would smash her. With the battery silenced and the ironclad out of the way, Wool's troops would land at Sewell's Point and commence the march to Norfolk.

The attack was launched immediately. Lincoln and his entourage went by tugboat to an artificial island in the channel of Hampton Roads to watch the action. Confederate gunners at the shore battery soon abandoned their posts under the hot fire from the gunboats. "The rebel terror," as Chase called the ironclad, came slowly out from her haven. The *Monitor* steamed up to shield the gunboats as they withdrew to safety, while the *Vanderbilt* began maneuvering for position and building steam. But at the critical moment, the *Virginia* declined to take the bait, retreating to safety as the confrontation fizzled. This inconclusive encounter left Chase buzzing with excitement. "The rebel Monster don't *want* to fight and *won't* fight if she can help it," he gloated. But as long as the *Virginia* survived, Wool's army couldn't go ashore at Sewell's Point. Another line of attack would have to be found.

Buoyed by the thrill of observing a small battle from a safe distance, Chase offered to return to the *Miami* and scout for another landing site. Poking along the enemy shoreline proved to be a skittish business, however; at one point, the cutter's captain suddenly veered away from land, having spotted a possible Rebel picket. The nearsighted Chase peered intently at the narrow beach but saw nothing. Then a white flag went up, which the *Miami* crew answered by waving a bedsheet. A group of slaves emerged from the woods; fearing a trap, Chase sent two boatloads of armed men to parley with them and the white woman who soon joined them. She proved to be a Union loyalist ready to point out local paths and roads that led to Norfolk, roughly ten miles away.

Delighted, Chase returned to the fort, only to find that Lincoln was ahead of him. The president was standing over a detailed map of Hampton Roads, a veteran navy ship pilot by his side. Together they were studying every inch of the ragged coast. Soon Lincoln decided that there was a closer landing point than the one Chase had found, and he wanted to have a look at it. Calling for twenty riflemen from Wool's garrison, Lincoln took a boat close enough to the beach to draw the interest of a couple of men on horseback. Satisfied with the lay of the land, the president returned to the fort to finalize preparations for an assault by Wool's infantry.

Though Lincoln enjoyed being away from Washington, he still wore the pall of grief that was his constant garment. Willie was never far from his thoughts, even amid the rumbling guns and tense hours of military planning at Fort Monroe.

During a break one evening, the president turned the conversation to one of his favorite topics, Shakespeare. More than one friend commented that Lincoln seemed to feel a connection to the Bard that erased the centuries between them. His relish for Shakespeare was intimate, not awed; he had strong feelings about the plays that mattered most to him. Of *Hamlet,* for example, he insisted that "To be or not to be" was not as good as its reputation. He much preferred the soliloquy of King Claudius, in which the murderer ponders his guilt and the judgment of eternity. *Macbeth* was perhaps Lincoln's favorite play; he responded powerfully to that harrowing dramatization of the lure and cost of political power (and the challenges of living with a tempestuous, goading wife). More generally, Lincoln was known to say, "I have only one reproach to make of Shakespeare's heroes—that they make long speeches when they are killed."

On this particular evening he turned to a lesser drama, *King John,* and his innermost thoughts bubbled to the surface. In the play's tangled story of rivals for the throne of England, Queen Constance harbors dreams of greatness for her favorite son, Arthur, whose kidnapping and likely murder plunges her into unendurable grief. With the fluency that comes only from repeated careful readings, Lincoln recited the queen's heartbreaking lament for an idealized child:

And, father cardinal, I have heard you say
That we shall see and know our friends in heaven:
If that be true, I shall see my boy again;
For since the birth of Cain, the first male child,
To him that did but yesterday suspire,
There was not such a gracious creature born.
But now will canker-sorrow eat my bud
And chase the native beauty from his cheek
And he will look as hollow as a ghost,
As dim and meagre as an ague's fit,
And so he'll die; and, rising so again,
When I shall meet him in the court of heaven
I shall not know him: therefore never, never
Must I behold my pretty Arthur more.

His eyes were wet when he finished. The passage spoke directly to the demons Lincoln had wrestled since February; he still struggled with the hard fact that he would never see Willie again in this life, and with the rationalist's doubt that he would find his son in a world beyond death. The consolations of hope shared space in his mind with the dread that such comforts were but figments of a yearning imagination. Upon finishing his recitation, Lincoln asked of those keeping him company: "Do you ever dream of some lost friend and feel that you were having a sweet communion with him, and yet have a consciousness that it was not a reality? That is the way I dream of my lost boy Willie."

Such moments of self-revelation were few. Most people saw the hale and laughing Lincoln of fast-growing legend, the man who met the crisis of the Union with an ever-ready arsenal of apt anecdotes and light asides. On this trip, too, Lincoln was often quick with a story or a joke. When Stanton mentioned that he'd received, just before boarding the ship, a confusing telegram from a general in the field, Lincoln launched into a tale of a boy's attempt to answer a question he didn't understand. The lad was assigned to show off a horse up for sale. As he guided the steed through its paces, a man sidled up to him and asked if the animal had "a splint." "Well, mister," the boy replied carefully, "if it's good for him he has got it, but if it isn't good for him he hasn't."

At another point in the trip, Lincoln lightheartedly confessed that his great weakness was his inability to say no—"Thank God for not making me a woman," he said, laughing. At yet another, he eyed a fine hairbrush offered to him by a wealthy volunteer colonel from New York named LaGrand Cannon. "I can't do anything with such a thing as that!" Lincoln scoffed. "It wouldn't go through my hair. Now, if you have anything you comb your horse's mane with, that might do." When visiting with members of the *Miami*'s crew, Lincoln told stories of his days as a flatboat pilot and challenged the strapping young sailors to contests of strength. On deck one morning, he spotted an ax and proceeded to lift it, using just two fingers, straight out from his body, with arm and ax both fully extended. The heavy head of the implement hung in space some six feet from Lincoln's body as he held the ax steady for what seemed like minutes. Lowering his arm, he invited the sailors to try it. No one could match the feat.

On the morning of May 10, three and a half days after arriving on the scene, Lincoln sent his army into battle. Touching Rebel soil on the beach Lincoln had chosen, lead elements of a Union force numbering some 5,000 men moved inland as the president watched offshore. As the blue-coated soldiers approached, the Confederates around Norfolk fell back, offering scant resistance. Wool and Chase followed about three hours behind the lead Federal elements, while the president returned to the fort. There, Lincoln discovered that some of the troops included in his plan of attack had never moved. Flinging his hat in a flash of fury, the president called for Colonel Cannon to take dictation, then spat out an order pushing the regiments into action.

Wool and Chase, meanwhile, advanced through scenes of grim victory: wrecked and abandoned Rebel camps, burning bridges, and captured artillery. Nearing Norfolk, they were met late in the afternoon by a delegation of local officials riding in fine carriages led by the mayor, who announced their desire to surrender the undefended city. Wool and Chase traded their horses for a carriage and then rode in style to city hall, where the formal documents were signed. They promptly returned to the landing in a rig that had been used by the Confederate commander Benjamin Huger that very morning.

It was nearing midnight under a bright moon and sultry sky when Wool and Chase reached Fort Monroe with the surrender in hand. Lincoln was wide awake; the night was hot and he was worried about their safety. "No time for ceremony, Mr. President: Norfolk is ours!" Wool cried. "You can imagine his delight when we told him," Chase reported. Stanton, who had been sleeping, answered the commotion in his night-shirt and "fairly hugged General Wool" when he heard the news. Lincoln guffawed at the sight of his god of war in pajamas embracing the uni-formed general. "Look out, Mars!" he crowed. "If you don't, the General will throw you." The president joked that a painting should be commis-sioned for the new Capitol rotunda, illustrating the capture of Norfolk with a grand tableau of Stanton dressed for bed.

After a few hours' rest, Lincoln was up early and eager to get back to Washington, where even his secretaries were not sure what had become of him. ("I suppose he will be home in a day or two if the rebels don't catch him," Nicolay shrugged.) But as the presidential party gathered in the parlor of Wool's headquarters in advance of their departure, Com-mander Goldsborough arrived with more good news: the *Virginia,* which had stalked so many Union nightmares over the previous two months, was in flames in the Elizabeth River. Rather than let the ironclad fall into Union hands, Confederate officers had ordered her torched and scuttled. Lincoln's urgency about returning to the capital evaporated, for this was a spectacle he could not pass up. He extended his visit a few more hours to take a tour past the smoking hulk of the former *Merrimack* and far enough to see the Stars and Stripes fluttering over the Norfolk shipyard.

Lincoln was proud of what he had accomplished in his week away from the White House, and the success of his Norfolk campaign further increased his confidence as a military strategist and commander. Even Chase was impressed by the president's ability to take the fight to the enemy. Summing up Lincoln's adventures on the battlefield, the Treasury secretary penned a tribute that could not have been easy for a rival to write: "So has ended a brilliant week's campaign of the President, for I think it quite certain that if he had not come down, [Norfolk] would still have been in possession of the enemy and the [*Virginia*] as grim and defi-ant and as much a terror as ever. The whole coast is now virtually ours."

As Jefferson Davis pondered "the drooping cause of our country" and prepared to send his family to safety outside the threatened Confederate capital, Lincoln stepped onto the dock at the Washington Navy Yard on May 12, just in time to catch a grenade unhelpfully lobbed by a friend. In 1860 David Hunter was a hot-tempered army man with a checkered career

when he struck up a correspondence with the soon-to-be president, warning him of the danger of assassination. Lincoln was sufficiently impressed
to invite the aging officer to ride with him from Illinois to the inauguration. Throngs met Lincoln's train at every stop, so Hunter volunteered for
duty as a bodyguard and suffered a dislocated shoulder while holding back
a jostling crowd. When the war soon followed, Hunter's military experience and familiarity with the president earned him a quick commission
as brigadier general and, in the spring of 1862, command of the Department of the South. This undermanned but symbolically important Union
toehold covered coastal regions of South Carolina, Georgia, and Florida.

Hunter's headquarters was at Port Royal, South Carolina, the strategic point controlling the cotton-rich Sea Islands. Located midway
between Savannah and Charleston, Port Royal was originally targeted in
autumn 1861 because the North needed a Southern base for refueling and
repairing ships of the Union blockading fleet. But with the arrival of the
Yankees, the region quickly became a laboratory for testing the future
status of slaves within Union lines. The region's plantation owners had
burned their crops and frightened their slaves by warning them that the
Northerners would sell them into even harsher bondage in Cuba. At first,
the field workers hid in the swamps, but when they finally emerged they
received a grudging welcome into the Union camps. By February there
were some nine thousand plantation workers under the care of the Federal army around Port Royal.

The novel status of the so-called contrabands produced a thicket of
questions. Were they still slaves? How should they be treated? Who was
responsible for them? The answers were political gunpowder. To hard-
war abolitionists, the matter was clear: these were now free men and
women whose skills in cultivating cotton should be put to work immediately to relieve the shortages causing such stress in Europe. For soft-war
conservatives, no step could be more damaging to prospects for peace
than tampering with slavery.

Lincoln wasn't ready to resolve all these questions, so he deferred his
decision about how to respond. In the meantime, he assigned Chase the
job of setting up schools for the workers and organizing them to get a
crop in the ground. Zealous missionaries and Ivy Leaguers flocked to
sign up as Port Royal Treasury agents, but their pure hearts weren't
always matched by good judgment or efficiency. By early May, the administration was ankle deep in a confetti of minutiae concerning the Port

Royal contrabands, ranging from the supposed need for more church-sanctioned marriages among the field workers to the status of an order for "one or two thousand red flannel suits for the blacks, with a view to organization." How, exactly, a legion of farm workers would endure the Hilton Head summer while clad in flannel from head to toe was not on the reformers' agenda.

These halting first steps into the postslavery future were just getting under way when Hunter took command. He was eager to make a splash and afire with the progressive Republican conviction that "rebellion and slavery were intertwined abominations to be struck and conquered simultaneously." Short on troops, the general began to think about training the contrabands and making them soldiers. He also decided that slavery was inconsistent with the Union army's emerging legal values. Officers were under orders not to return contrabands who reached Union lines, which to Hunter meant that the contrabands weren't slaves any longer. If they were not slaves, then they must be free people; therefore, the other roughly 900,000 slaves in his department would likewise be free as soon as the government raised enough troops to push inland from the coast. Wherever the Federal troops went, in other words, the slaves would be liberated. On May 9, Hunter issued a proclamation announcing this policy.

Hunter's order had little practical effect on the lives of the Port Royal contrabands, and even less on the lives of slaves beyond his reach. Red flannel or no, the opportunity for the plantation workers to do anything other than grow cotton was, for the moment anyway, more theory than fact. As a symbol, however, the order was potent indeed. Hunter's reasoning might be plain to abolitionists, but most of the Union army did not share his views. McClellan wanted nothing to do with the slaves on the peninsula; out west, "both Generals Halleck and Grant regarded the slave as still a slave," as Sherman later observed.

Lincoln was caught by surprise when he read about Hunter's proclamation in the Washington newspapers. He didn't object to the theory, but he did object to Hunter's blundering step into the middle of his delicate political dance. "I wanted him to do it, not say it," he told a visiting politician.

Hunter's bomb had a predictable result when it detonated in the capital. As Nicolay and Hay later put it, "the usual acrimonious comments immediately followed: radicals approved it, Democrats and conservatives denounced it; and the President was assailed for inaction on the one hand and for treachery on the other." The influential conservative newspaper *The New York Herald* speculated that Stanton was secretly to blame, having taken over "the nigger business" from Seward and Chase.

Surveying the reaction, Lincoln mused that the upcoming congressional elections would show that he had become a man without a party, too radical for the Democrats, not radical enough for the Republicans. For months, the president had been warning Northern conservatives that war, by its nature, was a radical engine, and that the terms of the slavery debate were changing almost daily. Their chance to have a hand in shaping the future was slipping away.

Everywhere people demanded to know what the president intended to do. Would he support Hunter and risk a conservative revolt? Or would he overrule Hunter as he had overruled Frémont's emancipation order the previous autumn—a step that would further damage his standing with the antislavery voters who had put him into office? McClellan, for one, speculated that Lincoln lacked "the moral courage" to disappoint the abolitionists yet again.

Hunter's order was an indication of the shifting mood, but not the only one. In Congress, Senator Lyman Trumbull, of Illinois, was steadily advancing a revision to the Confiscation Act of 1861 that would effectively transform the Union army into an emancipating force, "confiscating" the slaves in Rebel territory and setting them free. Another bill nearing passage would ban slavery in all Federal territories, obliterating the old Mason-Dixon Line and the Kansas-Nebraska Act of 1854. In the South, slaves themselves were taking action: on May 13, a group led by an enslaved steamboat pilot, Robert Smalls, seized control of the Rebel steamer *Planter* in Charleston, birthplace of the rebellion. Coolly steering the ship past Rebel forts, calling out the secret passwords he had memorized, Smalls reached the Union's blockading ships and surrendered the vessel. Having flawlessly executed a daring and well-laid plan, Smalls and his raiders were immediately hailed in the North as proof that emancipated slaves could make good soldiers.

Lincoln read the currents on this rapidly turning tide, but he was not willing to give up his place at the helm to David Hunter or anyone else. When Chase argued in favor of letting Hunter's order stand, Lincoln replied, "No commanding general shall do such a thing, upon my responsibility, without consulting me."

About this time, Lincoln was reading a treatise by the eminent legal scholar William Whiting on "the war powers of the President." Whiting argued that the law of nations and the Preamble of the Constitution gave the executive extraordinary authority in time of war to take all necessary steps to save the country. While the Constitution did not give Congress or the president power to bypass state slavery laws in times of peace, Whiting explained, emancipation as a war measure was entirely legal. "A handful of slave-masters have broken up [the] Union, have overthrown justice, and have destroyed domestic tranquility," Whiting wrote, echoing the opening phrases of the Constitution. "Taking away [their] slaves from the 'aid and service' of the enemy, and putting them to the aid and service of the United States, is justifiable as an act of war."

Whiting's analysis matched Lincoln's own growing sense of the way forward. He no longer doubted that he could steer around Chief Justice Taney by framing emancipation as a military necessity; the only question now was timing. The public, he feared, still wasn't ready. On May 19, a week after his return from the peninsula, Lincoln rescinded Hunter's order, while at the same time expressly reserving the authority to decide when and whether emancipation was necessary.

Never were the nuances of Lincoln's strategy for dealing with slavery more fully exercised than on that day in Washington. By overruling Hunter, he signaled to conservatives that he would give them one last chance to adjust to the oncoming revolution. Along with his decision, he also renewed his appeal for gradual and compensated emancipation, warning against willfully ignoring the rapid changes afoot. "You can not be blind to the signs of the times," he pleaded. Compared to a sudden military emancipation, his gradual approach "would come as gently as the dews of heaven, not rending or wrecking anything. Will you not embrace it?"

At the same time, by explicitly asserting his own emancipating power, Lincoln took the next big step toward the defining act of his presidency. Even as he did so, however, he sent a contradictory signal. On the very day that he countermanded Hunter's proclamation, he also promised a delegation from the loyal slave state of Maryland that federal authorities in the District of Columbia would not ignore the Fugitive Slave Act, which required the arrest and return of runaways seeking freedom in the capital. This assurance, however heartless it might have seemed, served to underline Lincoln's pledge to conform his actions to the law. Wherever citizens still respected constitutional authority, Lincoln would respect their right to own slaves—though he hoped they would freely choose emancipation. Once again, Lincoln sought to strike an almost impossible balance as he inched his way forward.

By now, Lincoln had come to believe that slavery could not survive the war; whether emancipation came gradually or suddenly, the move toward it had begun and could not be stopped. After overturning Hunter's order, the president put Seward to work explaining this important reality to the European powers. Until this point, he and Seward had put a fence around the subject of slavery, even though doing so weakened the Union cause in Europe by making the effort to put down the rebellion look no more principled than a naked power play. But with Union forces effectively liberating slaves by the thousands from Fort Monroe to New Orleans, the time had come to take down the fence. Lincoln instructed Seward to write another long dispatch to U.S. diplomats laying out the strength of the Northern cause, this time focusing on economic and political matters—that is, on slavery.

Seward's essay, reflecting the president's "strong desire" to communicate "the true condition of the present strife," offered a keen analysis of the inexorable course of the war. With each Federal advance, the South was growing weaker economically through the loss of slave labor and the erosion of its tax base. Its ports were being seized, its cotton and tobacco fields occupied. At least a hundred slaves per day, on average, were leaving their masters and coming into the Federal lines, "and as the army advances the number increases," Seward wrote. Meanwhile, the North's economy was growing stronger every day, thanks to unprecedented spending on ships, trains, guns, and uniforms. The muscle of the North was industry, which the war fed; the muscle of the South was land and slaves, which the war sapped. This process, the secretary of state argued, had become irreversible: the North was winning, the slaves were gaining freedom, and the only question remaining was how long and how bloody the struggle would be. Would Europe continue to encourage the hopes of the Rebels, even at the risk of sparking a violent uprising by impatient slaves?

Lincoln's careful steps toward emancipation were closely observed in the capital. After reflecting on the president's actions, Charles Sumner assured his abolitionist friends that the end of slavery was not far off. Critical, in his view, was the strategy of turning the war into a cause, for

that was the only way to prevent a foreign intervention. "Give us emancipation & the terrible strife will be glorified," he wrote. In another letter,
while praising Lincoln's "calmness, sagacity & firmness," Sumner
reported with emphatic underlining: "*Stanton told me this morning that
a decree of emancipation would be issued within two months.*"

Sumner wasn't alone in feeling hopeful. For this brief moment, buoyed
by the capture of New Orleans and the movement toward Richmond,
something like genuine optimism surged through Washington and the
North. It was not the bravado and false hopes so familiar to Unionists,
but a well-founded confidence that the United States would soon triumph
over the rebellion and embark on a happier future.

Lightheartedness bloomed in the normally sour and quarrelsome
Lincoln cabinet. Jealous, perhaps, of Stanton and Chase after their adven-
ture with Lincoln on the peninsula, Gideon Welles organized his own
reconnaissance, with Seward and Bates in tow. Accompanied by friends
and family, the three men made a jaunty tour of McClellan's army ("Such
visits are always a nuisance," huffed Little Mac) and traveled to Norfolk,
where the citizens "looked sulky and dogged." The secretaries sparred
and poked fun at one another: Welles teased Seward for being afraid to
get too close to the Rebel army, while Seward was delighted when rats
raided Bates's luggage, stealing a tie and a sock. Seward wrote a little
poem celebrating the theft, and doodled pictures to illustrate it. All three
men joined in making fun of the absent Lincoln's eccentricities.

Congress, feeling bullish, looked ahead, not just to the next battle, but
to the distant future of a Union that now seemed likely to endure. West of
the Mississippi lay millions of acres of new and rich frontier—land that
set the fuse on the current conflict. Previous generations of Americans
had been able to live with uneasy compromises over slavery, but those
compromises broke down when the time came to open the West. As early
as 1856, small armies of pro- and antislavery men were waging bloody
battles over the fate of slavery in the Kansas Territory. In a sense, the
Civil War began on the frontier, so it was appropriate that in the midst of
a conflict pitting North against South, Washington never lost sight of the
West.

Three bills before the Congress spoke to the Union's expansive view.
There was the Homestead Act, championed by Speaker of the House

Galusha Grow of Pennsylvania; in May, it cleared the Senate by a wide margin, having sailed through the House in February. There was a bill, introduced by Congressman Justin Morrill of Vermont, to make large grants of land in the West to every loyal state for the purpose of endowing public colleges. Morrill's bill moved smoothly through the committee system, meeting scant resistance. And finally, there was the bill to authorize and fund the transcontinental railroad. Ever since gold was discovered in California in 1848, the idea of building a railroad that would extend all the way to the Pacific had been endlessly debated, but the project had always been stymied by regional strife. As secretary of war under Franklin Pierce, Jefferson Davis tried to site the railroad in the South, while the Republican hero Frémont scouted a more northerly route with the support of his father-in-law, Senator Thomas Hart Benton. Secession had broken the stalemate; a railroad would be built. A multitude of lobbyists descended and a frantic and often underhanded free-for-all broke out over the contracts to build this colossal infrastructure project; in May, the necessary bill passed the House and moved over to the Senate.

So many grand designs were launched in these fateful months that they began to overlap and blur. A case in point: In late April and early May, a forward-thinking businessman named A. J. Isacks, a partner in one of the many ventures aiming to cash in on the transcontinental railroad, got to thinking about how, exactly, his firm would do the work, given that no one in it had ever laid an inch of track. As he pondered, it dawned on him that the matter of slavery, which had seemed entirely separate from his business concerns, was in fact quite relevant. Suppose his putative railroad line employed former slaves to build its tracks, he speculated. Contrabands could be hired for "a small amount of money." And when he said "small," he meant it: he proposed paying the former slaves perhaps as little as "one dollar per month each," along with clothing and provisions, "which it is supposed would amount to four or five dollars per month to each person." Perhaps realizing that $60 a year was not much different from slavery, Isacks added halfheartedly that his company could pay "the remainder in land." But this notion was little short of fantastical, because even in the West, ex-slaves weren't likely to be welcome after the war. As Isacks himself allowed: "The greatest objection to the plan would be in permitting them to settle upon the land."

Lincoln was keenly aware of this problem of the freed slaves; in fact, he had been thinking about it since he was a young man. In his early twenties, as he put down the roots of his political philosophy, he impressed his neighbors in tiny New Salem, Illinois, by reading a biography of Henry Clay written by the famous Kentucky newspaper editor George Prentice. It was 1831, and the impending presidential election would prove to be a catalyst of the American two-party system. Clay's attempt to unseat the Democratic incumbent, Andrew Jackson, fell far short, but it further crystallized the Whig vision of an entrepreneurial American system of free enterprise, robust manufacturing, and equal opportunity. The idea of a society by and for self-made men, bootstrappers like himself, inspired the young Lincoln and convinced him that Clay was "my ideal of a great man."

In his biography, Prentice devoted careful attention to Clay's nuanced views on slavery. The Great Compromiser abhorred the institution, Prentice wrote, considering it "a deadly vampyre draining away the life blood of the republic." But Clay didn't blame slaveholders for an evil that they themselves did not create. Nor did Clay believe that the Constitution gave power to the federal government to end slavery. Time, plus "stream upon stream of philanthropy," would gradually emancipate the slaves, Clay asserted. And when that time came, the next step would be to relocate the freed slaves in distant colonies set up to receive them. Clay was a driving force behind the American Colonization Society, which argued that blacks were better off in Africa, where they could "introduce the blessings of civilization into . . . the darkened moral atmosphere of that ill fated continent." The colony of Liberia was the society's most enduring project.

Lincoln's own gradualist approach to ending slavery was strongly shaped by the views of his political idol. Through the spring of 1862, Lincoln pressed the advantages of voluntary colonization. If necessary, he suggested, Congress should appropriate money to buy territory for a black colony "in a climate congenial to them," because white Americans weren't ready to share their society with large numbers of free blacks. As he explained in a speech long before he became president: "What next? Free them, and make them politically and socially, our equals? My own feelings will not admit of this; and if mine would, we well know that those of the great mass of white people will not." But in that same 1854 speech Lincoln acknowledged the monumental difficulties involved in relocating millions of people to adequate homes in a distant colony. Eight years later the idea remained utterly impractical, and despite Lincoln's appeals, Clay's prescriptions gained little traction with either Congress or the public.

Just as the Union's cause seemed to be surging, the rush of events abruptly slowed to a creep, or so it seemed as McClellan drew up his lines within earshot of Richmond's church bells and Halleck crawled slowly with his massive army toward Beauregard's Rebels at Corinth. Having urged speed for so many months, Lincoln himself turned suddenly cautious, warning Halleck to "be very sure to sustain no reverse in your Department."

Old Brains was very sure indeed, pausing every thousand yards or so to entrench his 100,000 men. His advance was less an attack than "a siege from start to close," in the words of Ulysses Grant. The aggressive Grant chafed miserably in the ceremonial position of second in command; while his conduct at Shiloh was under review, he was, as he later reflected, "little more than an observer" to Halleck's tedious exercise. Ground covered in two days by the raw Rebels attacking Shiloh in early April was a matter of a monthlong journey for the tiptoeing Union forces. John Pope—fresh from his victory at Island No. 10 and advancing on the left wing—couldn't bear the pace and kept sidling forward to skirmish with the enemy. Each time, Halleck hauled him back.

Sherman was more contented. His reputation had survived the Shiloh imbroglio; having been promoted to major general for his stalwart conduct at the great battle, Cump was "in high feather" and felt "fully vindicated," according to his wife; also, he greatly admired Halleck's skills. The slog to Corinth, in fact, revealed enduring personality signatures in both Sherman and Grant. The high-strung Sherman tended to see worst-case scenarios wherever he looked. On the road to Corinth, he fretted over the catastrophic cost of a defeat at this delicate moment, and he therefore praised Halleck for taking every precaution. Sherman was perhaps too intense for any experience short of pitched battle; gunfire seemed to calm his jitters.

Grant, on the other hand, was an optimistic sort, whose motor ran only in forward gears. With every trudging step of Halleck's army, Grant saw the opportunities that might have been: he imagined dashing into Corinth, racing over to Chattanooga, or sweeping down on Vicksburg before the Confederates could fortify the imposing bluffs of that last potential Mississippi River citadel. Grant's misery over the loss of his combat command caused him to overestimate the likely success of these potential initiatives—none was remotely as easy as he suggested—and he fell into such a funk that he considered quitting the army. On May 11, he wrote to Halleck asking to be given a real command or "to be relieved entirely from further duty."

As acting general in chief, Lincoln, too, had perhaps become overconfident about progress in the western theater. After the capture of New Orleans, Farragut had taken his boats unmolested up the Mississippi to demand the surrender of Vicksburg; city officials refused, but many on the Union side considered their defiance a trifling matter. The opening of the great river from top to bottom was generally seen as an accomplished fact, with only a bit of mop-up to do at Memphis and Vicksburg. Lincoln, usually so strategic in his thinking, suffered an unusual lapse of concentration. Instead of pressing his advantage in the West, he put down the whip and left Halleck to his own devices. He continued to pursue his interests in the technology of war, making several trips to the navy yard in May to join Dahlgren in examining the latest artillery innovations. And he enjoyed testing rifles in the company of a young White House secretary, William O. Stoddard. Taking shots at a woodpile south of the mansion one morning, Lincoln remarked: "Our folks are not getting near enough to the enemy to do any good. . . . We've got to get guns that'll carry further."

McClellan and Richmond, not Halleck and Corinth, were the president's prime focus now. After taking Yorktown, Little Mac was free to move troops and supplies along the York River, speeding his progress despite rain and sloppy roads. As he moved, the general continued his urgent calls for reinforcements, for he imagined the Confederate army to be roughly twice its actual size. "My entire force is undoubtedly considerably inferior to that of the Rebels, who still fight well, but I will do all I can with the force at my disposal," he wired Stanton at the War Department. To his friend Ambrose Burnside, he put matters more melodramatically. Should he be forced to fight without more troops, McClellan declared, "If I win, the greater the glory. If I lose they"—he meant Lincoln and Stanton—"will be damned forever, both by God and men."

The president was not deaf to McClellan's pleas. In the days following his return from Fort Monroe, Lincoln completed plans to accommodate Little Mac's pleas, at least partially. The Union now had some 200,000 troops dispersed in a wide arc across Virginia, from Fort Monroe in the east to Franklin in the mountainous west. Roughly half of these men were with McClellan on the peninsula. Another quarter of the force, approximately, was gathering in McDowell's camps between Washington and Richmond. McClellan was desperate to have McDowell's troops sent to him by boat as quickly as possible, but Lincoln was still skittish about leaving the path to Washington unmanned. He was reasonably certain, though, that the Rebel striking power was now all south of McDowell's position, and it seemed that the rumored counterattack of April had evaporated.

Accordingly, Lincoln decided to order McDowell toward Richmond by the overland route. This way, the Union advance would be akin to a stopper being forced deeper into a bottle; even as McDowell's troops moved farther into Rebel territory, they would continue to be a protective barrier for Washington. Then, after a march of fifty or sixty miles, McDowell's left wing would connect with McClellan's right wing on the doorstep of the Confederate capital.

There was only one hitch: the Shenandoah Valley. A seeming paradise of rolling fields and low mountains, the valley was, to men who understood it, a nearly perfect maze in which to operate a light, quick force against a larger, lumbering army. Unfortunately for the Union, none of its generals did understand the valley yet; worse, an army in butternut uniforms was just then marching at the top of the valley toward a little town called Staunton with an audacious plan to prevent the launching of McDowell's men. The lean, tough Rebel troops, many of them barefoot, were led by a lush-bearded man of strange temperament and habits, whose name was Thomas Jonathan Jackson. Ever since he stemmed the Yankee tide at the battle of Manassas, people had called him Stonewall.

The outbreak of war found Stonewall Jackson on the faculty of the Virginia Military Institute in Lexington, where he'd come to appreciate the Shenandoah Valley's strategic advantages through long hours of study in the institute's map library. A distinguished veteran of the Mexican War, Professor Jackson stood out in Lexington as an odd duck, a religious zealot who habitually sucked on lemons and periodically pumped his left hand violently in the air to regulate his blood flow. "He seems to be cut off from his fellow men and to commune with his own spirit only, or with spirits of which we know not," one associate wrote of Jackson. The intense focus that made him a notoriously dull teacher also made him an electrifying combat general, the sort of man who could demand far too much from his troops and yet be unshakably confident that they would deliver. Jackson knew a simple truth about men in armies: even more than shoes or food or sleep, they crave victory.

He also knew, from his map study, that the Shenandoah Valley could be a kind of magic box. Striped north to south by a series of ranges and ridges, the valley allowed an army to be seen one moment and disappear the next, simply by slipping through a gap or pass. It was the perfect place to practice Jackson's philosophy of war: "Always mystify, mislead and surprise the enemy."

Jackson had given the Union its first lesson in valley warfare in March, when he popped up in Kernstown to attack a Union force preparing to leave the vicinity. This led to Lincoln's decision to deploy an army under Nathaniel Banks to pacify the valley, and by the first of May, the former speaker of the house felt confident in his success. Jackson's army, Banks reported, was skedaddling, "bound for Richmond. This is the fact, I have no doubt."

In the wake of this apparent good news, Lincoln ordered one of Banks's divisions, commanded by the Irish politician James Shields, to leave the valley and join McDowell. Jackson promptly reappeared and delivered lesson number two, this time at a railway junction in Staunton, west of Charlottesville. There, he confronted the oncoming army of John Frémont. On May 8, Frémont threw 6,000 men at Jackson's Rebels, who proceeded to push the Federals backward in an afternoon of hot fighting. Then, once again, Jackson's army vanished.

During the following week, as Banks and his army stood guard in the deceptively quiet valley, Lincoln decided it was finally time to order McDowell forward. Communications between McClellan and Stanton had by now broken down almost entirely, but according to intelligence that McClellan sent to Lincoln, "the enemy were concentrating all their available force"—presumably including Jackson's troops—around Richmond. At the same time, Lincoln was being assured that Halleck faced a great mass of Rebels at Corinth. With such large concentrations of Confederate troops reported at both places, the threat of a Rebel offensive down the valley seemed minimal.

On May 17, by secret order, Lincoln directed McDowell to head south and link up with McClellan. But Stonewall Jackson, who was not in Richmond or anywhere near it, had a plan to stop him. The fierce-eyed Jackson put his army in motion—heading north.

If the president felt relatively sanguine about the current progress of the war, he found much to concern him at home. "I feel worried about Mary; her nerves have gone to pieces," Lincoln confided around this time. "She cannot hide from me that the strain she has been under has been too much for her mental as well as her physical health." Adding to her grief over Willie's death and the strain attending her scandalous finances, there came a third blow: Mary received word that her half-brother Samuel Todd had died of wounds suffered while fighting on the Confederate side at Shiloh. Weeks later, she remained so sick with sorrow that she found it impossible to answer a letter of condolence from a Springfield friend.

Mary Lincoln had dreamed from her youth that she would be "Mrs. President" someday; now here she was, and life seemed impossible to bear. When she finally mustered the strength to reply to her friend in Springfield, she wrote: "Our home is very beautiful, the grounds around us are enchanting, the world still smiles & pays homage, yet the charm is dispelled. Everything appears a mockery." The death of her "beloved Willie a being too precious for earth" had left her "completely unnerved. . . . When I can bring myself to realize that he has indeed passed away, my question to myself is, 'can life be endured?'" She had ordered Willie's favorite toys sent away, but she still refused to enter the bedroom where he had died, or the Green Room, where his body had reposed before the funeral.

And she insisted that her sorrow be undisturbed. When the Marine Band prepared for its annual series of public concerts on the White House lawn, a twice-a-week staple of Washington summer evenings, Mary demanded that the programs be canceled. How could she be expected to listen to the brassy tunes that had delighted her cherished son? Citizens protested, leading Navy Secretary Welles to suggest that the concerts be moved to Lafayette Square, but Mary was resolute. "It is our especial desire that the Band does not play in these grounds, this summer," she instructed John Hay. "We expect our wishes to be complied with."

On Sunday, May 19, the first lady agreed to go to church with the

Brownings. The weather was turning warm, and the previous day she had ordered from her favorite milliner a new lightweight mourning bonnet for summer, made of black straw with a long black crepe veil. "I want the crape to be the *finest jet black* English crape—white & black face trimmings—Could you obtain any black & white crape flowers? Small delicate ones—I want it got up, with great taste and gentility."

By this time, Mrs. Lincoln had also ordered a change of scenery. The idea of another hot summer in the White House, where dismal memories crouched around every corner, was so oppressive that she decided to relocate the family to a handsome cottage on the grounds of the Soldiers' Home, a few miles north of Capitol Hill. Formerly the summer home of the Washington banker George W. Riggs, the cottage commanded a hilltop well above the swampy bottomlands occupied by the White House, so it caught fresh breezes instead of the stifling reek of stagnant water. James Buchanan had used the retreat during his term in office, but the Lincolns had been far too busy to move to the cottage during their first summer. Now Mary was counting the days.

After church that Sunday, the president invited Orville Browning to join him on a visit to the hospital where Rebecca Pomroy worked. The dedicated nurse had continued to check in on the grieving Lincoln family, and one day the president—who had come to consider her "one of the best women I ever knew"—had surprised her by saying, "Mrs. Pomroy, I want to do something for you; what shall it be? Be perfectly free to tell me what you want most, and if it is in my power, you shall have it." A few weeks later, she would answer Lincoln's question by seeking his help in getting a regular army commission for her son George, but at first all she could think to ask was that he come meet the wounded soldiers in her care.

When Lincoln and Browning arrived at the hospital, there was a bustle of brass and a banging of drums as officers called for their men to limp into line. "Mr. Lincoln, in his unpretentious way, with his hat off, shook hands with each one, asking his name and the name of his regiment and company," Pomroy recalled. Most of the patients had been wounded in the battle of Williamsburg and belonged to McClellan's devoted Army of the Potomac. Yet Lincoln found that they loved him, too. Several soldiers promised to vote for him when he ran for reelection; one refused to wash his hand for several days after shaking Lincoln's.

As he prepared to leave, Lincoln found Pomroy waiting to say goodbye alongside three black servants who were clearly quite nervous. "And who are these?" Lincoln asked. They were the hospital cooks. Without hesitation, Lincoln shook their hands and greeted them by name. After the presidential carriage rolled away, several officers accused Pomroy of "a mean, contemptible trick": inducing an important white man to touch and speak with lowly black workers. Even her favorite young patient, an orphan from Vermont who had come to love Pomroy like a mother, scolded her. "What could you be thinking of to introduce those niggers to the President?"

Worried, Pomroy later asked Lincoln whether she had done wrong. "No, indeed!" he answered. "It did my soul good." The president had lived in the White House for only a little more than a year, and the servants who kept Washington moving—the cooks, maids, stable hands, and carriage drivers—were a more vital black community than he had known before. His encounters with them were changing his opinions about the capacities of black people; gradually, he was coming to see the despised race as a population and not just as a problem, and to understand that the Union could not afford to keep this significant human resource on the sidelines. As he told Pomroy: "It will not be long before we shall have to use them as soldiers."

May 22 was a relatively quiet Thursday. At the navy yard, Commander Dahlgren was nearing the end of a long day when, to his surprise, Edwin Stanton arrived at about nine P.M. to ask for a ship—immediately. Dahlgren was even more surprised when Lincoln arrived a few minutes later from the White House. "He left so privately that Mrs. Lincoln alone knew of it," Dahlgren said. As a vessel was hastily made ready, the commander served dinner to his unexpected guests. The clocks chimed ten as the three men slipped onto the boat and steamed quietly out of the darkened harbor and down the Potomac.

Near dawn, Lincoln awoke at Aquia Creek, where he had visited McDowell a few weeks before. The general, who had gathered his troops near Fredericksburg, was now preparing to march toward Richmond, and Lincoln wanted to discuss the critical offensive in person while he still had the chance. At the landing, he boarded a rough supply train for the next leg of the journey. Riding in the baggage car, he sat with Stanton and Dahlgren on camp stools. The railroad ended well short of McDow-

ell's headquarters, but the general was waiting for them when the baggage car jerked to a stop.

McDowell quickly assured Lincoln that progress was being made on
extending the southbound rail line to support the Federal advance. As
proof, the general led his visitors to a bridge that Union engineers had
just completed over a wide and deep ravine. An impressive trestle, it rose
perhaps a hundred feet over a winding creek. Beside the rails ran a single
plank for foot traffic, with nothing but open air on either side. "Let us
walk over," Lincoln said eagerly, and strode out onto the plank. McDowell followed. Stanton hesitated before edging his way onto the bridge.
With a doubtful look down at the ribbon of water far below, Dahlgren
brought up the rear. Then Stanton froze. "About half-way, the Secretary
said he was dizzy and feared he would fall," Dahlgren wrote in his diary.
"I managed to step by him, and took his hand." This was itself quite dangerous, because Dahlgren's own head was "somewhat confused by the
giddy height."

Lincoln alit on the other side as if he had strolled down a sidewalk.
Somehow the others made it over, too, at which point they swung into the
saddles of waiting horses for the remaining hour's ride under a cloudy
sky to McDowell's camp. There, the group ate breakfast and talked about
the advance, which promised to close the Union grip on Richmond.
McDowell said that the troops under James Shields had only just arrived
on the Rappahannock, bringing the total Federal strength here to some
45,000 men. Unfortunately, McDowell added, Shields wouldn't be ready
to move again until Sunday. "Take a good ready and start Monday morning," Lincoln answered.

As they talked, various combat commanders dropped by to meet the
president. One of them, the wealthy Pennsylvanian George Meade,
praised Lincoln for revoking Hunter's emancipation order. "I am trying
to do my duty," Lincoln replied, "but no one can imagine what influences
are brought to bear on me." With Brigadier General John Gibbon, the
new commander of the 3rd Brigade, Lincoln preferred to tease. Noting
the surname, he asked: "Is this the man who wrote *The Decline and Fall
of the Roman Empire*?" Gibbon, a regular army man from North Carolina who had chosen his country over his state, stared blankly. "Never
mind, general," Lincoln continued. "If you will write the decline and fall
of this rebellion, I will let you off."

Lincoln was pleased to learn that the French ambassador, Henri

Mercier, was also in camp. Knowing how Mercier's recent visit to Richmond had raised French opinion of Confederate prospects, the president seized the opportunity to show off his own army's strength by inviting Mercier to join him in reviewing the troops. By now "the sun had come out in the morning, and was warm," Dahlgren recorded. "We saw one division after another, all in fine order, the men cheering tremendously. Abe rode along the line with hat off." Eyeing the long ranks of blue stretching in every direction, Dahlgren worried that Lincoln might suffer in the heat. But though "the whole afternoon was consumed, and in one lone ride I thought we traveled ten miles," the president remained energetic and fully engaged. After a pause for a simple dinner, the group made its way, with Mercier still in tow, back to the boat landing. There, Lincoln and the envoy parted company.

On the water again after more than sixteen hours of hard travel, Lincoln ate another meal and read some poetry before dousing the lights. He was up again at five A.M. on May 24, strolling half-dressed into the cabin that Stanton and Dahlgren shared. A conversation the previous day had put him in mind of a joke, the president told his bleary-eyed shipmates. Someone had said that Shields was crazy, and Lincoln recalled that George III was told the same thing about one of his commanders. The king, who admired the man's fighting spirit, replied, "If he's mad, I wish he would bite my other generals."

But the merriment soon ended. Upon returning to the navy yard, Lincoln learned that Stonewall Jackson had materialized the previous day at Front Royal, west of Washington. Falling on a detachment of Banks's army, Jackson's Rebels had already killed or captured about a thousand Union men, and Banks was in peril of losing his entire army and its supplies. After weeks of begging to join the advance on Richmond, Banks was now racing down the Shenandoah Valley in retreat. Lincoln sent an urgent message to McClellan informing the general of this development, which he blamed on the fact that "we have so thinned our line to get troops for other places"—namely McClellan's front. Nevertheless, he assured Little Mac that McDowell was on his way, and urged him to extend his right wing to prepare to meet the reinforcements.

Jackson's attack was exactly what the president had feared: a counterthrust in the vicinity of Washington as McDowell moved south. "Apprehension of something like this," he wrote McClellan, "has always been my reason for withholding McDowell's force from you." Front Royal was just across the Blue Ridge from Manassas, which was just down the road from Washington. When news of Jackson's strike filtered into the capital, people responded with a panic of desperate speculation and hand-wringing. Word went around that there were riots in Baltimore, with secessionists taking up arms to menace Washington from the north. The wild talk at Willard's so upset one woman that she dashed straight from the hotel to the White House, where she buttonholed Nicolay to ask "if she had not better leave the city as soon as possible." *The New York Herald,* which had just published its ruminations on the impending "fall of Richmond," swung to the other extreme, reporting that the whole Rebel army was marching north.

Initially, Lincoln's information was not much better. He knew neither the size of Jackson's force nor which way the Rebels were headed. Eager for news, the president paid a visit to the War Department. As more dispatches arrived in the telegraph office outside Stanton's door, the picture grew bleak. Senator Sumner stopped by to get a fresh report of what had happened, and Lincoln described a disorderly retreat. "Banks's men were running and flinging away their arms, routed and demoralized," Sumner summarized. "Another Bull Run," said Lincoln gloomily. For all he knew, Lincoln told Orville Browning on May 25, the entire Union force in the Shenandoah Valley was lost. The anxious president agreed with Stanton to call on nearby states for spare militia.

But despite the obvious danger, Lincoln that day remained supremely confident in his newfound ability to direct military campaigns. Since the first of the year, his strategic decisions had all proved correct, at least from his vantage point. He had ordered the armies to move, and Grant had quickly broken the Confederate line in the West. The ironclads, mortar boats, and rifled guns he spent hours promoting had revolutionized naval warfare. His philosophy of multiple campaigns pressing the Rebel perimeter from end to end had stretched the Confederacy so thin that New Orleans and Nashville fell without a fight, while Richmond and Corinth teetered on the brink. Even his tactical command skills, on display at Norfolk, proved impressively sharp. Now Lincoln believed that the most controversial of his decisions—to withhold McDowell and the I Corps from McClellan's campaign—had been vindicated. Further, he was convinced that he could discern the motive behind the Rebel counterattack: it was, he told McClellan, "a general and concerted one," not a mere diversionary thrust in the "very desperate defence of Richmond."

And so, after conferring with Stanton, Lincoln took the extraordinary step of ordering McDowell to stop in his tracks, turn around, and head to the valley. He also sent a telegram to Frémont, urging him eastward into the valley from the other direction with "the utmost speed. Do not lose a minute." Informing McClellan that the promised reinforcements weren't coming after all, Lincoln warned the general that his own orders, too, might be about to change. "I think the time is near when you must either attack Richmond or give up the job and come to the defense of Washington."

Trained military men—both the Democrat McClellan and the Republican McDowell—were shocked. "This is a crushing blow," protested McDowell, who felt strongly that his troops were too far from the valley to be of use. McClellan's scorn was withering. "I have this moment received a dispatch from the Pres[ident] who is terribly scared about Washington—& talks about the necessity of my returning in order to save it!" he wrote to his wife. "Heaven save a country governed by such counsels! . . . It is perfectly sickening to deal with such people. . . . I get more sick of them every day—for every day brings with it only additional proofs of their hypocrisy, knavery & folly. . . . A scare will do them good, & may bring them to their senses."

McClellan tried to persuade Lincoln that he was misreading Jackson's intentions: the sudden assault really was nothing more than a desperate bid to distract the Federals at the gates of Richmond. "The object of the enemy's movement is probably to prevent reinforcements being sent to me," he telegraphed. "All the information obtained from balloons, deserters, prisoners & contrabands agrees in the statement that the mass of rebel troops are still in immediate vicinity of Richmond ready to defend it."

McClellan was right in this case and Lincoln was wrong. The move in the valley *was* diversionary, and Lincoln had taken the bait. This became clear once Banks managed to get his army safely across the Potomac after losing so many supply wagons that the Rebels dubbed him "Commissary Banks." But instead of ordering McDowell to resume his advance on Richmond, Lincoln hungrily shifted from defense to offense. He reckoned that if McDowell, moving west, could connect with Frémont, moving east, to trap Jackson as he stood face-to-face with Banks at the bottom of the valley, the Union would have old Stonewall surrounded. Converging Federal troops could then crush the irksome military genius.

Taking the offensive wasn't necessarily bad strategy. Out west, Ulysses Grant—no slouch as a strategist—was looking at Halleck's laborious obsession with Corinth and wondering "how the mere occupation of places" would end the war "while large and effective rebel armies existed." Lincoln weighed the same conceptual alternatives and chose to make the destruction of Jackson's army a priority, ahead of the occupation of Richmond. But the problem with Lincoln's plan was its naïve overconfidence. Imagining a trap on a map, and having the tools to communicate that vision with the blazing speed of electricity, was not the same thing as actually setting the trap and springing it. No less an authority than Napoleon Bonaparte had called the maneuver that Lincoln was attempting—the convergence and combination of large, separate forces in the presence of the enemy—the most difficult of all military movements.

Sure enough, as soon as Lincoln issued his new orders, they began to go awry. Frémont, ordered east, instead marched north. The skies opened, turning roads to muck, then hammered the muck with hail. McDowell's scouts failed for days to find the Rebels. A railroad accident slowed the progress of Shields's division. Banks reported that his troops were "much disabled" by their earlier fighting. At every turn, Lincoln's initiative encountered a catalog of unpredictable, yet somehow inevitable, snares and errors.

Yet Lincoln pursued his trap for most of a week, using the telegraph like a spur to drive the Federal forces into place, even as he struggled to pinpoint the location of his elusive enemy. At one point, the president issued a pass for his friend Ward Hill Lamon to saddle up and look for Jackson himself. By May 29, Lincoln had some 40,000 Union troops converging in what he thought was the vicinity of Jackson's 16,000. But the numerical advantage proved something of a tactical albatross, because the more troops Lincoln drove, the slower they seemed to go. "The game is before you," he pleaded with Frémont on the night of May 30.

By then it was too late. Jackson and his army had already moved southward and slipped between the closing gates of the converging Union forces. The commander in chief's bold gambit had failed.

McClellan seethed. Physically, he was a wreck, suffering a relapse of the malaria he had contracted as a young man in the Mexican War. Emotionally, he was on fire, spinning a dark but undefined plan to deploy in case Lincoln tried to recall his army to Washington. He scarcely tried to hide his delight at Lincoln's miscalculations. "Proves them all to have been a precious lot of fools & that I have been right all the time," he crowed to Mary Ellen.

In Mississippi, the capture of Corinth by Halleck and his army seemed anticlimactic at best. On the night of May 29, Union troops, hunkered in trenches on the outskirts of town, heard one train after another roll in and out of Corinth to the sound of Rebel cheers. Reinforcements, they figured grimly. In fact, Beauregard was evacuating his entire force; the cheers were a ruse. When Halleck resumed his cautious advance the next day, he entered an empty town. The Union gained another place, but the Confederacy kept its army.

The right wing of the Army of the Potomac, meanwhile, lay on the north bank of the rain-swollen Chickahominy River. Just as Lincoln had ordered, it was waiting to connect with General McDowell's left wing. But McDowell's corps was now scattered in Stonewall Jackson's wake and in no condition to advance on Richmond. Instead, this flapping wing of McClellan's caught the attention of Joseph E. Johnston, who had marched backward for the better part of three months until there was no more room to retreat. Now Johnston decided the moment had come to go forward.

7

JUNE

Until spring became summer, no matter how dark his political and military trials or how deep his personal tribulations, Abraham Lincoln always had one consolation: progress. Week by stormy week, he could see that the Union was gaining territory, that fewer people lived as slaves, that McClellan was drawing closer to Richmond, that Europe remained on the sidelines, that more taxes were being collected and more bonds were being sold to put more guns into the hands of more soldiers. But now progress ground to a halt, even as the avalanche of crises continued and then intensified. In the summer of 1862, both Lincoln and the Union were pushed to the brink.

June began with what seemed to be good news. On May 31, Joseph Johnston's Rebels had tried to smash McClellan's army while the Federals awkwardly straddled the flooding Chickahominy. That night, in Washington, initial reports painted a picture of Union disaster. But better tidings arrived the next morning: the Confederate offensive had failed in a welter of driving rains, wrong turns, and snarled communications. Unable to find the proper roads at the proper times, the Rebels marched every which way, spilling plenty of blood—their own and the Yankees'—but never managing to concentrate their force. Ultimately, the battle of Seven Pines, or Fair Oaks, was such a lost opportunity for the Confederates that Rebel generals would be pointing fingers at one another for years to come.

Lincoln, irritable after a night of worry, received this good news by reminding everyone of the exaggerated pessimism of the early accounts.

("That was what I had to sleep on for the night," he groused.) Nevertheless, Nicolay was able to report that optimism prevailed at the White House later that day. "Altogether the events of the week seem to be favorable and encouraging," he wrote to his fiancée back home in Illinois.

June 1 proved to be a portent, however, of harder times ahead. That morning, the Confederate army, newly christened the Army of Northern Virginia, awoke to find itself under the command of a quiet Virginian named Robert E. Lee. In the waning hours of the previous day, Johnston had been badly wounded during the attack on McClellan's right wing. With his top general incapacitated, Jefferson Davis handed the reins to Lee.

In time, Lee's command of the Confederate army would come to seem as inevitable and necessary as the sunrise. He was among the South's most experienced soldiers, and no man better represented the South's ideal image of itself. Lee was the scion of one of America's most distinguished founding families; his father was a Revolutionary War hero, his mother a descendant of a planter so wealthy and powerful in colonial Virginia that he was dubbed Robert "King" Carter. His wife was the great-granddaughter of Martha Washington, and even though he grew up in straitened circumstances after his father squandered a fortune, Lee was as much a part of the plantation aristocracy as anyone could be. He represented virtues esteemed by a culture based on hereditary privilege: good manners, a sense of duty and honor, commitment to land and family. (He also represented a bit of the quirkiness idealized by aristocrats—he kept a pet hen at his army headquarters.)

A majority of Confederate soldiers had never owned a slave, and men in the ranks often grumbled that theirs was "a rich man's war, but a poor man's fight." Lee was an answer to that complaint, because he embodied a version of the rebellion that wasn't about money or slaves. His war was the expression of a proud refusal to have other people—whose forebears had not necessarily settled the continent or fought the British or signed the Declaration of Independence, as his had done—come into Virginia and tell her people what their future would hold. He had a name for his enemies, which spoke volumes about his attitude: "those people." Though he had saluted their flag for most of his life, "those people" were now alien to him. They were trying to dictate to his own people on matters of morals and culture. But the South would not be dictated to.

There is a famous story, perhaps true, about a Union soldier and his

Mary Lincoln was living proof that opposites attract. She was electrifying but insecure; her husband was disciplined and self-possessed. Their son Willie was the president's favorite. One friend said Lincoln was "fonder of that boy than he was of anything else."

George B. McClellan looked every inch the heroic general, but his clashes with Lincoln—which he described in searing letters to his wife, Mary Ellen—made him dangerously unreliable. Ulysses S. Grant, by contrast, moved quickly and uncomplainingly. "I can't spare this man," Lincoln said. "He fights."

William T. Sherman was one of the first generals to realize that this would be a long, hard war. Like others, he expected big things from Henry W. Halleck, the soldier and lawyer known as "Old Brains." But Halleck proved weak as general-in-chief. Lincoln relied on informal advisers for help, including the inventor John Dahlgren, commander of the Washington Navy Yard.

In March, the clash of the ironclads *Monitor* and *Virginia* spelled the end of wooden warships and sent a shock through the administration. It also forced McClellan to advance on Richmond by way of Yorktown, where he spent a month preparing a "gigantic" siege. Lincoln despaired at the delay.

The Battle of Antietam on September 17, 1862, was the bloodiest day in American history, and it left Robert E. Lee's Confederate army decimated. Battlefield photographs by Alexander Gardner gave the public its first raw look at the horror of war. Gardner also turned his camera on Lincoln's fruitless effort to talk McClellan into renewing the attack on Lee.

As 1862 dawned, Attorney General Edward Bates worried that Lincoln lacked the key qualities of a leader. Lincoln's new secretary of war, Edwin Stanton, also lost faith in the president for a time, protesting that Lincoln had given him an impossible job. Through it all, Treasury Secretary Salmon Chase made no secret of his desire to replace Lincoln as president.

Lincoln's close relationship with
William Henry Seward, the
secretary of state, made others in
the cabinet jealous, not least the
odd but effective navy secretary,
Gideon Welles. Seward's
supposed influence also upset
leading abolitionists, including
Senator Charles Sumner of
Massachusetts.

Lincoln's secretaries John Nicolay and John Hay learned from their boss that military success depended on political success. Later, they chronicled the president's arduous path to his defining achievement, the Emancipation Proclamation. The reading of the decree at a September cabinet meeting was memorialized by the painter Francis Carpenter, who spent six months at the White House researching the work.

Rebel prisoner on some battlefield of the long war. "What are you fighting for, anyhow?" asked the man in blue. "I'm fighting because you are down here," the prisoner replied. In the dark gaze of Robert E. Lee, generations of Americans would read that same defiance, that quiet insistence on being left alone, and they would understand a bit better why so many fought so well for so long in a losing and tainted cause.

But for now Lee's reputation was mixed, at best. Originally he had hoped to remain neutral in the conflict between North and South; when Virginia left the Union, however, Lee was forced to choose between the stars offered to him by both armies. In his first command, he failed to keep McClellan out of Virginia's strategically important western mountains. Newspapers howled when he pulled his troops back, dubbing him "Evacuating Lee." After Davis transferred him to South Carolina to bolster the coastal defense, the West Point engineer focused on building trenches and fortifications, earning himself a second derisive nickname: King of Spades. When Davis called Lee to Richmond in early 1862 to serve as his senior military adviser, some junior officers began calling him Granny Lee behind his back, on account of his fussy attention to protocol. No wonder a woman in North Carolina, hearing news of Lee's latest promotion, wrote: "I do not much like him. He 'falls back' too much." The *Richmond Examiner* took the same line, predicting that the Southern army "would never be allowed to fight" with Lee in command.

McClellan made the same mistake. Having bested Lee a year earlier, he welcomed the new arrival across the lines. Assessing his foe in terms that more aptly described himself, McClellan assured Lincoln that Lee was "too cautious & weak under grave responsibility." While he was "personally brave & energetic to a fault," McClellan added, "he is yet wanting in moral firmness when pressed by heavy responsibility & is likely to be timid & irresolute."

It was a season of misjudgments. On matters large and small, Northern leaders suffered a sudden epidemic of foggy thinking. Out west, Henry Halleck completely misread the opportunity that lay before him now that he had possession of the swampy, malarial crossroads of Corinth. Flushed from their fortifications, the southbound Rebels made an enticing target to warriors like Grant, but Halleck, instead of pursuing and fighting the Confederates with his superior numbers, let them go. He was the product of a peacetime army designed for short wars and frontier garrison duty; thus trained, the scholarly Halleck remembered his West

Point lessons too well. "Ever since there had been a United States Army, it had been operated on a constabulary basis, with many isolated posts and forts," wrote the historian Bruce Catton, explaining Halleck's error. "When campaign time arrived, the Army would be assembled from these posts and made into a mobile force; when the campaign ended, it would be redistributed all over the country. . . . This was the system that [Halleck] followed now."

Never mind that Halleck had the enemy off balance; after taking stock of the Yankee-hating citizenry surrounding his army at Corinth, he concluded that he must disperse his troops to pacify the land. "The repair of the railroad is now the great object to be attended to," he advised Washington. Dividing his large army, Halleck restored Grant to field command, but sent him neither toward Tupelo (where the Rebels were reorganizing themselves under a new commander, Braxton Bragg), nor toward Vicksburg (where the Rebels were collecting every available gun to fortify their last stronghold on the Mississippi). Instead, Halleck ordered Grant to the newly captured city of Memphis, where the warrior began to tackle such pressing matters as whether secessionist preachers should be compelled to pray for the Union.

On a larger scale, the fog shrouded the very nature of the war and the Union's path to victory. A great cloud of confidence had billowed up in the period between Grant's victory at Fort Donelson and McClellan's arrival outside Richmond, which now obscured the intensity of the Rebel resistance. While the South instituted a draft to replenish its armies, Stanton had overconfidently shuttered the recruiting offices of the North. Each new Federal victory was heralded as a sign of imminent peace, when in fact the Rebel spine stiffened as Confederate territory shrank.

The setbacks of summer transformed overstated hopes into equally overstated despair. Lincoln would endure many hot and sleepless nights of worry over news that would later prove not quite so bad as it first appeared. When the excess bravado dried up, he was left almost alone to bind himself and the Union to the terrible truth: victory could come only through the slow and wasting destruction of the enemy's capacity to fight. Lincoln would later marvel at how many times he was called upon that summer to shore up the faltering courage of other men—including men who spent their lives in uniform. Melancholy and often fatalistic, he was history's unlikely choice to wield the weapons of steely optimism and dogged determination.

The price of foggy thinking was high. Lincoln's overconfident belief that he could maneuver three armies to trap Stonewall Jackson cost him dearly. He spent most of June cleaning up the mess, because the force he had collected under McDowell was scattered once more and would not be easily reassembled. One exchange of telegrams gives a glimpse of the confusion. On June 3, Lincoln asked McDowell plaintively: "Please tell about where Shields [is]." The general answered: "At Luray, on the road to New Market with an indifferent road which the constant rains are making bad and with the Shenandoah impassable and rising."

Frémont, meanwhile, after being so difficult to get started, proved every bit as difficult to stop. (The Harvard philosopher Josiah Royce once said of Frémont that he "possessed all the qualities of genius except ability.") Blindly pursuing Jackson, and insisting on reinforcements every step of the way, the rogue general stumbled into the Rebels on June 8 and 9 at Cross Keys and Port Republic, in the southern end of the Shenandoah Valley. After a bit of fighting, Jackson disappeared again, while Frémont resumed his fruitless chase.

By now Lincoln had come to see that hounding Jackson was exactly what the Rebels wanted him to do, and he ended the effort in a scorching exchange of telegrams with Frémont a week later. There would be no reinforcements, the president insisted, because the whole point of Jackson's campaign was to siphon Union troops away from the real confrontation: McClellan against Lee. "Jackson's game," as Lincoln put it, "is to magnify the accounts of his numbers and reports of his movements, and thus by constant alarms keep three or four times as many of our troops away from Richmond."

If these words had a familiar ring, it was because McClellan had seen through the game weeks earlier. The fact that Lincoln was slow to embrace the truth about Jackson's strategy further damaged his already threadbare relationship with McClellan. Although Lincoln tried to make amends to the general for diverting McDowell's force—he gave McClellan command of the Fort Monroe garrison and sent him a Pennsylvania division under the elderly professional soldier George McCall—it wasn't enough, for McClellan had lost all respect for the administration. "How glad I will be to get rid of the whole lot," he told his wife. At this point, he believed either that Lincoln and Stanton were incapable of managing the war or that they were secretly plotting his defeat to destroy him as a potential political rival. Inside the White House, meanwhile, Nicolay spoke for others when he complained that McClellan's "extreme caution, or tardiness, or something, [was] utterly exhaustive of all hope and patience."

The president and his top general barely masked their harsh opinions of each other. One back-and-forth paints the picture. On June 3, while catching up on paperwork, Lincoln sent a bit of unsought advice to McClellan: "With these continuous rains, I am very anxious about the Chickahominy so close in your rear, and crossing your line of communication. Please look well to it." Though brief and outwardly friendly, this little missive could hardly have been more insulting. After all, McClellan had regularly been updating the War Department (and thus Lincoln) about his efforts to bridge the river, and he had just finished fighting a sharp battle brought on by the fact that his army was straddling the swollen stream. He didn't need anyone to tell him to pay attention to the river. The general volleyed back: "As the Chickahominy has been almost the only obstacle in my way for several days[,] your Excellency"—never had that title, which Lincoln abhorred, dripped more venom—"may rest assured that it has not been overlooked."

But that was mild compared with the tone of the public debate swirling around Lincoln and McClellan. That very night, in the crowded lobby of Willard's, a drunken Senator Zachariah Chandler—one of a trio of hard-war Republicans dubbed "the Jacobins" by John Hay—was loudly denouncing McClellan as a "liar and coward" when a broad-chested soldier with dark, curly hair pushed through the throng. The stars on his shoulders signaled a man to be reckoned with. He was Samuel D. Sturgis, the soon-to-be commander of the Washington defenses and a West Point classmate of George McClellan. "Sir, I don't know who you are, nor care," Sturgis scolded the swaying senator, "but hearing you talk in this abusive way, against an absent man, I make free to tell you that it is you who are the liar and the coward!"

Men could shout and glower all they wanted; Lincoln had no option but to stay the course with McClellan. Little Mac still enjoyed the trust and support of his fellow Democrats. He was loved by the troops he had trained. Most of all, he was tantalizingly close to the spires of Richmond.

Lincoln understood that he could not change his horse midway across the Chickamoniny. So, as he argued with Frémont via coded wires, the president wrestled with the question of how to restart the southward march he had interrupted, and then push McClellan across the finish line before the Rebels could reinforce Lee. He encouraged Banks in the Shenandoah Valley to watch out for Confederates moving by railroad from the direction of Corinth. He took stock of Shields's troops, concluding sadly that their fruitless marches on the trail of Jackson had put the division "terribly out of shape, out at the elbows and out at the toes . . . it will require a long time to get it in again." And, having recognized the folly of placing three ambitious generals at the heads of three independent armies in a single region, Lincoln concluded that he must reorganize the whole Virginia theater.

He would have to do it quickly, because he was running out of time in the court of public opinion. When McClellan's army in all its glory set sail from Washington, and Farragut muscled his warships up the Mississippi to New Orleans, people all over the North told themselves the end was in sight. "I think of that magnificent 'Army of the Potomac' of 4 months ago and almost weep to think how its powers have been paralyzed," wrote one influential soldier.

Now it was June, yet there was no sign of peace and the Union's momentum was spent. "The current reports from the Peninsula tell of much camping and of comparatively little forward marching," Lincoln's secretary William Stoddard recounted. With patience worn and the blood and red ink rising, the public expressed itself in a blast of criticism. "Never did such wild letters of reproach come pouring through the mails. They come by the hundred," Stoddard wrote. "Your cheeks burn as your eyes glance over the letters." No decision of Lincoln's escaped the lash of the critics. "Halleck is a pedantic fool; Grant is a blundering drunkard; Burnside is a sluggard . . . Buell is a traitor," the secretary summarized. To judge from the president's mail, every general he chose was "a pernicious mistake, and every campaign is a failure."

And that was before news reached the North that a party of some 1,200 Rebel cavalry, led by a flamboyant young general named J. E. B. Stuart, had ridden virtually untouched all the way around McClellan's army. On June 12, Lee sent the bold officer to make a reconnaissance of the Union's right wing, which Stuart did, noting that it was flapping just as loose as it had been three weeks before. But instead of taking this news straight back to headquarters, Stuart kept going, cutting telegraph wires and collecting prisoners and horses as he galloped across the Federal supply lines. Stuart's father-in-law, the Union cavalry commander Philip Cooke, gave chase with his own horsemen, but when the Rebels arrived back in camp on June 15, they had lost only a single rider—and had scored one of the most compelling psychological victories of the war.

Not surprisingly, Lincoln was in a prickly frame of mind the next day when he received several visitors, including the eminent New York physician Horace Green. Green was in Washington after a trip to the peninsula, where he had surveyed conditions in the army's temporary hospitals. Because of the rising temperatures and swampy conditions, the medical service faced a growing problem of infection and disease, Green explained. The doctor's suggestion, shared by a growing number of Republican abolitionists, was to convert a mansion on a verdant hill beside the Pamunkey River into a proper hospital. The U.S. Army had taken possession of this beautiful property on the peninsula, but McClellan's high command resisted the idea of filling it with sick and dying soldiers. Green wanted Lincoln's support.

"Gentlemen, I understand all this matter perfectly well," Lincoln snapped in reply. "It is only a political raid against General McClellan." The president believed that this squabble over a mansion on the peninsula was but a small piece of a larger struggle. The war in Virginia was taking the Union army into a treasure house of American history, and McClellan's conciliatory policy called for preserving its gems, no matter who owned them. The mansion Green had his eye on, called White House, had been the home of Martha Dandridge Custis until her marriage to George Washington. Descendants of the original first lady grew up in that house, including her grandson George Washington Parke Custis, who became the father-in-law of Robert E. Lee. Earlier in the war, Union troops had also seized Lee's own estate, called Arlington, on the heights overlooking Washington, D.C. McClellan was protecting that property as well.

Lee's connection to both estates meant that this dispute, which Dr. Green dropped in Lincoln's lap, was really another version of the hard war–soft war debate. "General McClellan does not choose to give up these grounds, and a political party is determined that he shall be compelled to do it," Lincoln continued, siding with the general. "There is no necessity that this property should be used for this purpose."

But Green was persistent. "Are our brave soldiers to die off like rotten sheep there because General McClellan chooses to protect the grounds of a rebel?" he demanded. As the doctor argued his case, Lincoln's irritation shifted from the Republicans seeking to mortify Lee to the Rebel general himself. If this was to be a hard war—and Lincoln could now see that it was—then the men who chose to wage it must pay the price along with the suffering troops.

Abruptly changing his mind, the president declared: "I will tell you the truth of the case: General McClellan promised Mrs. General Lee that those grounds should be protected from all injury, and that is the reason he doesn't want them used. McClellan has made this promise, but I think it is wrong." It no longer made sense to think that the antebellum world should, or could, be preserved for Rebels to come home to once their project to break up the Union flickered out. Better to snuff the old world forever. Within weeks, the mansion known as White House would be in ruins, and by war's end the rolling grounds of Arlington would become a lasting reminder of the cost of rebellion and the high price of freedom. "He doesn't want to break the promise he has made," Lincoln concluded, "and I will break it for him."

The same unforgiving mood prevailed in Congress, where the Senate was wrestling with a similar question of how to treat the Rebels' property—especially their human property, the slaves. The debate was led by men Lincoln had known for many years. Lyman Trumbull, a thin-faced Yankee schoolteacher turned Illinois politician, occupied the Senate seat that Lincoln had once hoped would be his. A former Democrat, Trumbull was now firmly in the hard-war camp, and his passion during this session of Congress was to promote a bill to confiscate all the slaves in Rebel territory, regardless of their owners' loyalties. Trumbull was steadily gathering support from Republicans tired of Lincoln's cautious approach; among others, he had won over John Sherman of Ohio, who argued that the South's violent resistance made harsh measures unavoidable. How could the North debate property rights when Unionists were being killed in the South? "If we are so forbearing to the Rebels while they are so cruel to loyal citizens, will it not be the interest of every man, even in the Border States, to be a secessionist?" Sherman asked.

Trumbull was trying to accomplish through legislation the emancipation that Lincoln was unwilling to order. The president was skeptical that

Congress actually possessed such power; he was even more doubtful that Trumbull's law, if passed, could survive Roger Taney's Supreme Court. Arguing against the bill was Trumbull's fellow Illinois senator, Orville Browning. In the frantic final weeks of the legislative session, hardly a day went by that Browning didn't visit the president, so when he rose in the Senate to argue that only the chief executive could free the slaves as an act of war, it was reasonable to imagine that he spoke not just for himself but also for the man at the other end of Pennsylvania Avenue. But would Lincoln veto Trumbull's bill if it passed? Not even Browning knew.

Clearly, the slavery issue was coming to its crisis. Congress passed a law that Lincoln happily signed, outlawing slavery in all U.S. territories. The capital city, meanwhile, was filling with runaway slaves from nearby states, seeking freedom. Civilian and military authorities couldn't agree on what to do with them. Under martial law, if the slaves had fled from rebellious owners, they were not to be returned. But under civil law, which applied to slave owners who remained loyal to the Union, returned they must be.

By June 11, some two months after emancipation in the District of Columbia, confusion over how to handle the runaways was so widespread that Lincoln had to haul the city marshal, Ward Hill Lamon, and the commander of the army in Washington, James A. Wadsworth, into his office to hash things out. Lamon, who was being pressed by furious slaveholders from loyal Maryland, argued that it was his duty to enforce the Fugitive Slave Law and return the runaways, while Wadsworth recited his instructions not to return slaves who had reached Union lines. Lincoln asked Browning to arbitrate. Under the president's weary eye, the trio arrived at a laborious process for separating contraband from chattel—a grotesque exercise that served only to show how near the whole rotten slave system was to collapse.

It was increasingly apparent that the problem of slavery and the problem of war were inseparable, not least because slave labor was a significant part of the Confederate war effort. As Jefferson Davis fretted in a letter to his wife dated that same day, a dangerous "prejudice in our Army against Labor" meant that the hard work of running camps and building fortifications was usually being left to slaves. Abolitionist leaders hammered at this idea in their meetings with Lincoln, layering a pragmatic argument for emancipation on top of the moral case they had been making for years.

On June 20, for example, Lincoln received a visit from a delegation of

Progressive Quakers from Chester County, Pennsylvania, outside Philadelphia. Their meetinghouse was an important stop on the Underground
Railroad, and it frequently rang with the voices of the most famous abolitionists in the country. One of them, Thomas Garrett, was credited
with helping to guide some 2,700 runaway slaves to freedom during a
forty-year career as a stationmaster on the secret road. Broad-faced and
white-haired at seventy-two, Garrett now led a group of three men and
three women into Lincoln's office, where they presented the president
with a petition arguing that the war was a "golden opportunity" to end
"the grinding oppression of an unfortunate race." The petition touched on
some of the same ideas Lincoln had been turning over in his own mind,
including the role of Providence in creating the crisis that could end the
iniquity of slavery. The Quakers had no doubt on this point: "Vials of
Divine retribution" were now being "poured out upon the whole land"
because of the nation's offense against the "millions [who] clank their chains
in the house of bondage." Slavery was "the cause, purpose, and combustible
materials" of the bloody rebellion, and must be abolished if the South was
to be tamed.

Characteristically, when the presentation was finished Lincoln
responded with a joke. It was a relief to have visitors who weren't begging
for jobs, he said—office seekers remained his greatest trouble. Pivoting
quickly, he added that slavery was a close second and assured the Quakers that he, too, believed it immoral. But then Lincoln turned defensive.
What good would it do, he asked testily, to issue an emancipation decree
when he couldn't enforce even the Constitution itself in the breakaway
South? Had a decree been enough to free the slaves, John Brown would
have done it already.

His visitors were unmoved. That the Constitution was not respected
in the South did not mean Lincoln should quit trying to enforce it, said a
man named Oliver Johnson. More pragmatically, Johnson argued that
Lincoln couldn't save the Constitution *without* ending slavery: "We are
solemnly convinced the abolition of slavery is indispensable to your success." At this, the president softened his tone, assuring the group that he
"felt the magnitude of the task before him" and hoped for guidance
through "the very trying circumstances by which he was surrounded."

At the mention of the word "guidance," another delegate chimed in.
William Barnard reminded Lincoln of the biblical story of Mordecai and
Queen Esther. In that well-known tale, the queen, at great personal risk,

interceded to save the oppressed people of Israel. Barnard said he hoped
that Lincoln might likewise be led "under divine guidance" to save the
United States from destruction, in which case, generations "yet unborn
would rise up to call him blessed."

This give-and-take seems to have struck a chord with Lincoln, because
it condensed into a brief exchange many of the ideas and tensions he had
been struggling with for months. On one hand, an executive order freeing the slaves would be fraught with dangers in the border states, while
remaining all but meaningless in the Confederacy. On the other hand,
how could he kill the rebellion without striking at its cause and resources?
The idea of being steered by a vast power toward an epic end was compelling to a man who felt himself to be both the main player and a helpless
pawn in a cataclysmic event. Barnard had even touched Lincoln's secret
desire to make a name that would last forever.

Clearly moved, the president confessed to his visitors that he "had
sometime thought that perhaps he might be an instrument in God's
hands" to accomplish the "great work" of ending slavery. The obvious
sincerity in his voice as he said this—so unlike the tone he had struck at
the start of the meeting—left his visitors deeply impressed. But in closing, he added a note of warning. God's way of doing this work, he
reminded the Quakers, might be different from their own.

Lincoln was further along than he let on. Years later, Hannibal Hamlin,
Lincoln's vice president, recalled that he was given a glimpse of Lincoln's
progress toward emancipation two days before the Quakers visited.

Lincoln and Hamlin had a good partnership, as far as it went. They
were nearly the same age, and both were self-schooled and self-made prod-
ucts of wild and nearly empty places. (Hamlin came from Maine.) Though
Lincoln was a disciple of Henry Clay's and Hamlin an Andrew Jackson
man, they followed similar paths through the thicket of midcentury politics, staunchly opposed to the spread of slavery even as they remained
convinced that the Constitution protected slavery where it already existed.
They seem to have liked each other, though Hamlin did not care for the
rather empty job of vice president: he was a fighter stuck on a shelf.

On June 18, Hamlin was preparing to leave Washington for a summer
break back home in Bangor. That afternoon, when he called on Lincoln to
say goodbye, the president invited him to take a ride to the cottage at the

Soldiers' Home. The Lincoln family had finally relocated to the breeze-kissed hills outside of town, where Lincoln enjoyed relief from both the heat and the press of business: "The President comes in every day at ten and goes again at four," Nicolay reported. Of course, work followed Lincoln wherever he went.

Lincoln, as usual, had spent the day on a dizzying variety of tasks. He had settled the question of whether a U.S. marshal in Indiana could lawfully serve as colonel in a volunteer regiment and pushed along the nomination of an assistant quartermaster in Illinois. He had met with a leading supplier of uniforms for the Union army, who took it upon himself to deliver a blistering critique of McClellan and argue that John Pope, the latest darling of zealous Republicans, should take over command of the Army of the Potomac. And he had been in communication with Little Mac himself. In a coded telegram, the president pressed to know "about what day you can attack Richmond," explaining that he could make better plans for sorting out jumbled armies if he knew the general's timetable. McClellan had been reporting that his balloonists could see legions of Rebels arriving daily, sharpening his need for reinforcements. As always, he refused to be pinned down about his intentions; the closest he would come to answering Lincoln was to say he would attack "as soon as Providence will permit."

Now Lincoln and Hamlin were traveling on horseback (or maybe by carriage—Hamlin's account went through several versions over the years) toward the Soldiers' Home. They may well have been entirely by themselves, the president and vice president of the United States making their way alone up the heights from the stifling Potomac lowlands. Lincoln, after all, had continued to resist the idea that he should have a detail of bodyguards. "I see hundreds of strangers every day, and if anybody has the disposition to kill me he will find opportunity," he protested. Stanton suggested a cavalry escort, but Lincoln scoffed that surrounding him with troopers would be like repairing a gap in a fence "when the fence was down all along." Eventually Stanton prevailed, but for now, as Seward noted: "The President . . . goes to and from [the Soldiers' Home] on horseback, night and morning, unguarded. I go there, unattended, at all hours, by daylight and moonlight, by starlight and without any light."

As they were riding, or perhaps at the cottage after they arrived—again, Hamlin's memory is unreliable—Lincoln took out a paper and showed the vice president something he had been working on. Hamlin

was delighted with what he read. It was the first draft of a "military proclamation freeing four millions of slaves." This imperfect account marks
the earliest claimed sighting of what would become the Emancipation
Proclamation; while historians differ over how much credit to assign to
Hamlin's story, other evidence suggests that Lincoln had indeed begun to
put ideas on paper around this time.

The occasion to act was not yet at hand, but Lincoln could see it coming closer and had begun to prepare. When he told the visiting Quakers
two days later that he felt like "an instrument in God's hands," he was
providing a glimpse inside the dynamic process leading him toward the
defining moment of his presidency.

At the American legation in London, Charles Francis Adams received on
June 11 a letter so shocking that his first reaction was the horrified thought
that Britain must be trying to stir up a war. The signature belonged to
Lord Palmerston, but the tone and the obvious haste of the composition
were completely out of character. Written from Palmerston's sprawling
estate outside London, Brocket Hall, the letter was headed "Confidential."
Attached to it was a clipping from the previous day's London *Times*. "My
dear Sir, I cannot refrain from taking the liberty of saying to you that it is
difficult if not impossible to express adequately the Disgust which must be
excited in the mind of every honourable man by the general order of General Butler." Never "in the History of Civilized Nations" had anyone committed "so infamous an act," Palmerston continued, ablaze; he wondered
what sort of government would allow itself to "be served by men capable
of such revolting outrages."

Adams knew very well the outrageous subject of Palmerston's rant:
Benjamin Franklin Butler, the Union commander in New Orleans, five feet
four inches of cross-eyed audacity, with the eyelids of a bloodhound and
the chest of a rooster. If any man in Union blue was going to boil the blood
of a cool and proper Englishman from a distance of some forty-six hundred miles, Butler was the one to do it. A relentless opportunist, the banty
general had been from the beginning an untamed force on the political
front of the war. After a flamboyant career in Massachusetts as a successful attorney and politician, Butler shocked the Bay State in 1860 by steering its Democratic convention delegates to none other than Jefferson
Davis. Then, in early 1861, he shouldered his way to the front of the

Union recruiting effort. Lincoln was so delighted to have a prominent Davis supporter defect to the Federal cause that he made Butler an instant major general.

The president had been mopping up after him ever since. Assigned to keep a rail line open through Maryland, Butler decided to occupy Baltimore instead. Transferred to Fort Monroe—where he temporarily resolved the legal status of runaway slaves by declaring them to be "contraband" property—Butler set off on a disastrous campaign toward Richmond without bothering to tell anyone first; the result was a fiasco near a village called Big Bethel. Once more, Lincoln needed a new place to stash his famous loose cannon. New Orleans seemed ideal. As commander of army troops in what was largely a navy operation, Butler had scant opportunity to cause trouble.

The confinement to safer quarters didn't last. When the navy captured the city and the army moved in to occupy it, Benjamin Butler was again given an important responsibility—and again he proved to be a combustible mixture of competence and catastrophe. Butler rapidly restored order to a city in flames and prevented an incipient epidemic of yellow fever. But the discovery that Rebel passions still ran strong in New Orleans brought out the despot in Butler. He ordered the execution of a gambler named William Mumford, who had ripped the Stars and Stripes from a flagpole and dragged it through the streets. To make his point quite clear, Butler hanged the prisoner from the same pole. When city merchants resisted Butler's efforts to reopen the cotton trade, the general fined them; meanwhile, he installed his brother in a position to profit handsomely from the restored commerce. Even clergymen were ordered to take oaths of allegiance to the Union.

The event that incensed Lord Palmerston had occurred shortly after Butler's arrival in New Orleans on May 1. The general was galled by the open contempt shown by the women of New Orleans for the occupying Yankees. Otherwise well-mannered ladies shouted at the soldiers, even spat on them. In at least one case, a woman dumped a chamber pot on troops passing below her window. In response, Butler issued Order No. 28, warning that henceforth, any woman behaving disrespectfully toward Federal soldiers would "be treated as a woman of the town plying her avocation." Apparently Butler meant that she would be arrested and jailed with ordinary prostitutes, but the prime minister and others took him to be authorizing the wholesale rape of Louisiana women. The letter in Adams's hands practically smoldered as Palmerston pronounced Butler "guilty in cold Blood of so infamous an act as deliberately to hand over the female inhabitants of a conquered city to the unbridled license of an unrestrained soldiery."

This jolt was not what Lincoln's foreign policy needed at yet another delicate moment. The Senate was balking at a secret agreement struck by the U.S. ambassador to Mexico, Thomas Corwin, to pay down Mexico's debts to France and England in exchange for an alliance with the Union. In Europe, the pressure for cotton continued to rise. Any hopes Lincoln still had of dividing the French and the British with respect to the Confederacy were dashed by William Dayton in a brisk message to Seward early in June: "It is vain to hope that France [will] separate her policy from that of England." Meanwhile, another raiding ship for the Rebels, even finer than the *Oreto*, was in the water near Liverpool receiving finishing touches. A three-masted sloop with a copper bottom and powerful steam engines, this sleek new vessel measured 220 feet and promised to outrun almost any ship in the world.

The Palmerston letter, then, would have to be handled with great care. But it dawned on Adams that the rash letter might be a weapon he could throw back at Palmerston. "It strikes me," Adams mused in a report to Seward, "that he has by his precipitation"—that is, his undiplomatic tone—"already put himself in the wrong, and I hope to be able to keep him there." Palmerston's hypocrisy irritated Adams, too; he would have liked to point out to the old man that the women of New Orleans were far safer than the women of Delhi had been four years earlier, when British troops sacked the city and committed hundreds of rapes.

Instead, he took a day to calmly plot his way forward, then answered the prime minister on June 13. Striking a note of consummate diplomacy, Adams said he was reluctant to take official notice of such a provocative message, and frankly was unsure how to proceed. It would help, he added, if Palmerston would explain whether the letter was intended as a statement of the ruling government or simply as the private expression of one gentleman's opinion. This neat response managed to call attention to both the explosive nature of the document and Palmerston's gross violation of diplomatic protocol, while also offering the prime minister a way to back down.

Next, Adams called on the foreign minister, Lord Russell, to ask whether he knew what Palmerston intended. The earl was flummoxed, having heard nothing of Palmerston's letter, and he was annoyed that the prime minister was stirring up diplomatic troubles behind his back.

As for Palmerston, he blustered in reply to Adams's message, but even inside his government it was clear he had gone off half-cocked. Adams, having handled the matter deftly, closed it down. "This anomalous form of proceeding"—namely, emotional letters dashed off in response to newspaper stories—was simply too dangerous, Adams wrote. Therefore, the American ambassador would "decline to entertain any similar correspondence" in the future.

Feeling pleased with himself, Adams traveled to Russell's office on June 19 to keep a four P.M. appointment. The official purpose of the visit was to have the envoy read the lengthy dispatch prepared by Lincoln and Seward explaining the rapidly changing effects of the war on Southern slavery. But when Adams opened his valise and fumbled through his papers, he discovered that he had left the document at home. What might have been a mortifying moment for the straitlaced New Englander instead led to an unusually relaxed and open exchange.

Reporting back to Seward, Adams wrote that he and Russell had a conversation about "the progress of the war," which "his lordship seemed to admit to have the appearance of drawing to a close. We also talked over the action of General Butler. On the whole, I have never known an occasion in which his lordship manifested more good humor and a more kindly spirit." Perhaps Russell had a new feeling about Adams, having seen him outfox Palmerston—a man with whom Russell had been sparring for most of his career. But if the American thought for a moment that this would translate into a political advantage, he would see his mistake soon enough.

The rumor mill in Washington claimed that the president was spending his evenings trying to contact the dead. Rebecca Pomroy's effort to unmask the charlatan who claimed to be speaking with Willie had no effect on Mary; her interest in séances deepened as the days grew longer. She was reportedly a regular at the spiritualist "circles" conducted in Georgetown by a medium named Nettie Colburn Maynard, who later claimed that she held one séance in the Red Room of the White House with the president in attendance.

Lincoln's pastor, Phineas Gurley, had grown increasingly close to the president since Willie's death, and Lincoln had become a fairly regular participant at Gurley's Wednesday evening prayer meetings. As word of Lincoln's attendance began to spread, the meetings swelled with favor seekers hoping to catch the president's attention. Gurley arranged for Lincoln to hide in the pastor's nearby office with the door ajar so that he could join the prayers without being seen. Now, the pastor was worried enough about the rumblings of unorthodoxy to ask Lincoln directly: Was the president dabbling in spiritualism? Lincoln assured the reverend doctor that he was not. "A simple faith in God is good enough for me," he said, "and beyond that I do not concern myself very much."

On Sunday morning, June 22, the president attended the service at Gurley's church. Afterward, he asked Orville Browning to join him for the short carriage ride back to the White House. There, he took the senator to the library, where he showed his friend a collection of "memoranda"—clippings and souvenirs of important recent events. The inauguration of Richard Yates, a Lincoln family friend, as governor of Illinois was documented, along with Lincoln's own inauguration. Major battles from the early days of the war, and the deaths of prominent men, were also memorialized. These treasures had been the makings of Willie Lincoln's first scrapbook; the collection had only recently been discovered, Lincoln said sadly. Perhaps White House servants had turned up the trove as they packed for the move to the summer cottage, or perhaps the president had finally mustered the strength, four months into his grief, to sift through his son's belongings.

Among the fragments was probably a clipping of Willie's first published writing, which appeared in a Washington newspaper after the death of Edward Baker at Ball's Bluff. Baker had called on Lincoln the day before his death, chatting quietly with the president on the White House lawn as the autumn sun blazed, and then lifted Willie for a hug and kiss before riding off to his fate.

> *There was no patriot like Baker,*
> *So noble and so true;*
> *He fell as a soldier on the field,*
> *His face to the sky of blue.*

Four stanzas in all, Willie's poem was a wrenching reminder of what had been and could never be again. These words—"patriot," "noble," "true"—were threaded through the grief of thousands of families across Lincoln's United States; soon there would be tens of thousands more, and unless the war could be redeemed by some high purpose, such words would surely break under the weight of sorrow.

The next day, June 23, Lincoln boarded a private car on a special north-bound train at four P.M. at the Washington station. The train passed through Baltimore, across the Susquehanna River to Philadelphia, and onward in darkness to New York City. Arriving at one thirty A.M., he switched trains for a trip up the Hudson River valley to the hamlet of Garrison, New York, where he boarded a ferry shortly before three A.M. for the river crossing to West Point.

A few hours later, the president left Cozzen's Hotel for breakfast with Winfield Scott, the object of his journey. Nearly eight months had passed since Lincoln had laid eyes on the corpulent old general, and in that time many of Scott's well-planted seeds from the early days of the war had ripened into fruit. The Union controlled the Confederate coast, with only a few major ports still to capture. The Mississippi was nearly open, save for the batteries at Vicksburg. But the South's response to these defeats was not the upwelling of loyal sentiment that Scott had predicted. Consequently, Union armies needed reorganization and Federal strategy needed refreshing. At such a moment, Lincoln required the counsel of a general in chief, but had no one to turn to. His long trip to West Point testified to his belief that Scott—"Old Fat and Feeble," said the wags of Washington—retained a sharp military mind.

Traveling with Lincoln, fresh from the steamy slog to Corinth, was John Pope. The visit to West Point was a homecoming for Pope, who had entered the U.S. Military Academy at age sixteen and had been a soldier ever since, exploring and surveying the western frontier from Minnesota to New Mexico. Now forty years old, Pope was a key to Lincoln's plans for the eastern armies, though much depended on Scott's advice.

Their conference began with a review of the disjointed commands in Virginia. Lincoln described the strength and positions of the forces under McDowell, Banks, and Frémont, as well as McClellan's situation on the peninsula and the force under Sturgis in Washington. Scott absorbed the information, pronounced the capital defenses adequate, and then pointed to the scattered divisions under McDowell as the source of Lincoln's problems. The troops at Fredericksburg were of no use. As Scott put it, they could not "be called up, directly [and] in time, by McClellan, from the want of railroad transportation, or an adequate supply train." The old general proposed the same solution McClellan had been advocating: put McDowell's men on ships and send them by water to the peninsula. The reinforcements would help Little Mac take Richmond, and this, "combined with our previous victories, would be a virtual end of the rebellion, [and] soon restore entire Virginia to the Union."

The meeting continued through the morning and covered the entire conflict. With New Orleans in Union hands, the next objectives were, in Scott's opinion, the ports of Mobile and Charleston and the rail hub at Chattanooga. The president expressed his desire to have a properly trained general in chief in Washington: as he later explained, he "had never professed to be a military man." But he had felt forced to take the reins, owing to "procrastination on the part of commanders, and the pressure from the people . . . and Congress." Who could fill the role now? "All he wanted or had ever wanted was someone who would take the responsibility and act."

Scott had in mind just the man: Henry Halleck. The previous autumn, Scott had done all he could to hold on to the top position until Halleck could arrive from California to replace him, but McClellan had shouldered Scott aside. Nothing since then had altered Scott's opinion that Halleck was the best strategist of his generation. With his Corinth campaign completed, Old Brains was ripe for a new assignment.

The discussion broke up at noon; Lincoln spent the next three hours touring the academy and inspecting the cadets. After a small dinner party back at the hotel, he paid a visit to the nearby foundry where the gunsmith Robert Parker Parrott was casting fearsome rifled cannon for the Union army and navy. By now, news had traveled throughout Dutchess County that the president was in the neighborhood; from nine to eleven P.M., Lincoln received visitors in the parlor of his hotel. At midnight, the West Point band showed up to serenade the exhausted traveler.

By the morning of June 25, a number of newspaper reporters had reached West Point, drawn by the tantalizing intelligence that Lincoln had made an eleven-hour journey just to confer with Scott. "The President's sudden visit set a thousand rumors buzzing," Nicolay noted back in Washington, "as if a beehive had been overturned. There was all sorts of guessing as to what would result—the Cabinet was to break up and be reformed—Generals were to be removed and new war movements were to be organized."

Lincoln invited the newsmen to ride along on his return trip to Washington, so they were on hand for a stop in Jersey City, where he addressed a crowd gathered to meet his no-longer-secret train. "When birds and animals are looked at through a fog they are seen to disadvantage," Lincoln began—precisely the sort of folksy irrelevancy with which he usually signaled his intention to avoid saying anything substantial. "So it might be with you if I were to attempt to tell you why I went to see General Scott. I can only say that my visit to West Point did not have the importance which has been attached to it. . . . It had nothing whatever to do with making or unmaking any General in the country." At this, the audience laughed and applauded, allowing Lincoln to close with a joke. "The Secretary of War, you know, holds a pretty tight rein on the Press," he said, referring to Stanton's control of the telegraph to censor war news. "I'm afraid that if I blab too much he might draw a tight rein on me."

With that, the president was back inside his coach, and in the company of John Pope, who knew that Lincoln had not been entirely truthful: an important new general was in fact being made. When the train reached Washington, Pope would be given command over the combined armies of McDowell, Frémont, and Banks, thus setting up an overnight rival to McClellan's force and authority in Virginia.

How many troops were gathered on the peninsula for the dramatic final week of June? Historians have found it difficult to settle on a number. One prominent authority claimed that the "Army of Northern Virginia counted some 85,000 troops, including Jackson's command," while "McClellan's force on the Chickahominy came to 104,300." Another arrived at quite a different count: "Lee [enjoyed] numerical superiority with 112,220 men present for duty to McClellan's 101,434." Some of these estimates may have been influenced by the writer's feelings, pro or con, about McClellan. In any event, the question can never be resolved, given the imperfections of nineteenth-century record keeping and slippery definitions of what it meant, in armies of independent-minded volunteers and reluctant Rebel conscripts, to be "present for duty."

If we look past the elusive specifics, however, we can see a sharp picture of the general situation: a huge and well-supplied Union army stood at the doorstep of the Confederate capital, opposed by an army of roughly comparable size but more limited resources. The Union held the strategic advantage, according to no less an expert than Robert E. Lee, because little by little McClellan was laying the groundwork for a siege of Richmond, which meant that the Confederates would have to choose between giving up the city to save their army, or risking everything on a bold attack.

A decision to pull back from the Rebel capital might have changed the whole course of the war by committing Lee to a guerrilla operation. From the mountains of Virginia, Lee could, as he put it, "fight those people for years to come," but only "if my soldiers will stand by me." But the man known as "Evacuating Lee" could not be certain that his countrymen would support a decision to leave Richmond. After taking a hard look at that vulnerable right wing of McClellan's mighty host, the Rebel commander resolved to gamble on a desperate attack.

An entirely different picture, painted in lurid lines and vibrant colors, existed inside the mind of George B. McClellan. The general believed that he was outnumbered by at least two to one; that virtually all the Rebels who had been in Corinth had magically relocated to his front and flank; that the administration, up to and including the president, was deliberately undermining him in order to turn the war into a long, remorseless revolution against slavery. On June 20, McClellan's confidant Fitz John Porter put this delusion baldly in a message to a friendly newspaper editor in New York: Stanton and Lincoln, Porter claimed, were ignoring "all calls for aid." Porter asked, "Does the President (controlled by an incompetent [Stanton]) design to cause defeat here for the purpose of prolonging the war?"

McClellan's flatterers assured him that the Republicans were overplaying their treacherous hand and that he would emerge from his troubles as the nation's next president. But McClellan saw only doom. A dysfunction that had begun as an excess of secrecy half a year earlier, when Little Mac was making his plans, then soured into mistrust in March after he set out from the capital with his army, had now become a fever of paranoia. Where it counted—in his own mind—McClellan wasn't the commander of the strongest force the Americas had ever seen. He was a vulnerable underdog menaced on all sides. Suspecting that Lee was about to attack, he narrated his defeat in advance, warning Stanton: "I regret my great inferiority in numbers but feel that I am in no way responsible for it." Having begged for reinforcements and been refused, he wrote: "I will do all that a General can do . . . and if [the army] is destroyed by overwhelming numbers [I] can at least die with it & share its fate. But if the result . . . is a disaster the responsibility cannot be thrown on my shoulders—it must rest where it belongs."

A week of brutal fighting across the peninsula followed that strange telegram. The Army of the Potomac proved itself an extremely tough and well-disciplined force. In the first major clash of the Seven Days battles, McClellan's right wing under Fitz John Porter, amounting to about a fourth of the total Union strength, fought stoutly against roughly two thirds of Lee's army. The tremendous Confederate blow was designed to crumple the Union flank and expose the Federal supply line, but a combination of Porter's grit and Stonewall Jackson's inexplicable lassitude allowed McClellan to execute a daring shift in his base of supplies. Day after day, the Rebels pounded Little Mac's rearguard as he moved his army—with thousands of wagons, tons of supplies, and twenty-five hundred beef cattle—to a new base on the south side of the peninsula, anchored on the James River.

In the final battle, on July 1 at Malvern Hill, Lee threw his nearly spent force in wave after hopeless wave against massed Union artillery. "It was not war," said the Confederate general Daniel Hill of the battle, "it was murder." Another Confederate general, James Longstreet, mournfully summed up the clash as a matter of "losing six thousand men and accomplishing nothing." A mapmaker for the Union army, Robert Sneden, watched the final charge of the day:

About 6 p.m. [after] pushing out about twenty pieces of artillery from their front, followed by four lines of solid infantry colors flying, as if on parade, [the Confederates] advanced at a run with terrifying yells, heard all above the crash of musketry and roar of artillery. We now opened on them with terrible effects. . . . Several times our infantry withheld their fire until the Rebel column, which rushed through the storm of canister and grape, [came] close up to the artillery. Our men then poured a single crashing volley of musketry and charged the enemy with the bayonet with cheers. [We] thus captured many prisoners and colors and drove the remainder in confusion from the field. These would rally under cover of the woods and charge again, but only to be met with the same murderous volleys of shot, shell, and bullets, leaving piles of dead and dying on the plateau along our front. Hundreds of poor maimed wretches were continually crawling on hands and knees across the open, many of whom were killed before they regained shelter in the woods.

The Rebel cavalry were seen driving the remnants of regiments out of the woods into the open ground, and were shooting all those who did not keep in line and "face the music." As the charging columns came up to within 150 yards of our artillery, whole ranks went down at once, battle flags rose and disappeared. Officers on horseback threw their sword arm in the air and [tumbled] to the ground. Riderless horses were running in every direction, while officers on foot were far in advance of their commands, shouting and yelling like madmen.

The week's carnage was hideous: some 20,000 Confederates dead, wounded, or missing, plus 16,000 more from the Union. As at Shiloh, the Rebels gave everything they had, yet failed to break a Union army. But where Grant had beheld disaster and seen through it to victory, McClellan looked on a golden opportunity and saw only defeat. Despite the chaos of battle, he should have been able to discern that Lee had hit the Union right with the majority of his force and thus left only a thin line between the bulk of the Federal army and the streets of Richmond. Now, the Rebels were divided by the river and vulnerable on one wing. With the chance to deliver a devastating blow to the Confederacy directly before him, though, the Young Napoleon lacked the nerve to attack.

The critical moment occurred on June 27, the second day of fighting for Porter's V Corps. A terrible bloodletting at Gaines' Mill left Lee's shock force decimated. Near the end of the day, the Rebels finally broke Porter's line, but the Federals fell back safely south of the Chickahominy and destroyed the bridge. Now the time was ripe for a counterattack: the Union troops all together faced Lee's thin line, while the bulk of the Rebel force was stranded on the opposite bank. McClellan, however, could think only of defensive maneuvers and the nearness of disaster. He would not go forward; he would fall back to a new base of operations.

Even as he made the decision, McClellan knew his critics would call it a retreat. And although he was not a general who led from the front—indeed, he spent most of the Seven Days far from any battlefield—he latched onto the idea that he might die in the next day, leaving his side of this history unrecorded. Shortly after midnight, he took up his pen to defend himself and indict his superiors.

"Had I (20,000) twenty thousand or even (10,000) ten thousand fresh troops to use tomorrow I could take Richmond," he informed Washington. "But I have not a man in reserve." This wasn't true: most of his force was fairly fresh, having seen only jabs and feints by the 25,000 Rebels on the Union left. But McClellan and the rest of the Federal high command were convinced that those 25,000 were actually 100,000, poised to crush the Union army come morning. "I have lost this battle because my force was too small. I again repeat that I am not responsible for this."

The general might have stopped there, but as he wrote he grew angrier and more self-righteous. Letting slip the hatred he had accumulated over six long months, he accused Stanton and Lincoln of "needlessly sacrific[ing]" the brave men of his army. He knew this was grossly insubordinate and tried halfheartedly to excuse himself: "I feel too earnestly tonight—I have seen too many dead & wounded comrades to feel otherwise." But if he was to die with his men in the morning, he would not go out on an apologetic note. "The Government has not sustained this army," he wrote. Then he closed with a paragraph so outrageous that the officer in charge of the telegraph took it on himself to delete it before carrying the message to Stanton. "If I save this Army now I tell you plainly that I owe no thanks to you or to any other persons in Washington—you have done your best to sacrifice this Army."

"They will never forgive me for that," McClellan later told his wife. "I knew it when I wrote it; but as I thought it possible that it might be the last I ever wrote, it seemed better to have it exactly true."

McClellan's salvo landed some one hundred miles to the north in a capital once again nearly mad with speculation, half-truths, and whole lies. "The city here is wild with rumors and suspense," Nicolay wrote on June 29. He described huge crowds, starved for information, gathered on Newspaper Row, across Fourteenth Street from Willard's. There, the papers maintained a large bulletin board on the sidewalk to feed the maw between editions, but the gruel was often thin. "This morning . . . several persons reached the city who left Fortress Monroe yesterday, and of course brought with them all the rumors prevailing there. These have been caught up here and repeated with their usual additions and embellishments," Nicolay explained. "Some enterprising newsgatherer has collated these, sifted an intelligent report out of them as nearly as he could, and posted it up on the bulletin board."

Lincoln, however, was able to draw several clear conclusions about events on the peninsula. First, his commanding general was almost completely unbalanced. Accustomed to hyperbole and melodrama from McClellan, the president now was dealing with something like hysteria. "The evident panic and mental perturbation which pierced through [the telegram's] incoherence filled the President with such dismay that its mutinous insolence was overlooked," Lincoln's secretaries reported. "He could only wonder what terrible catastrophe . . . could have wrung such a terrible outcry as this from the general." Lincoln did his best to calm McClellan. "Save your Army at all events," he wired back. "Will send reinforcements," he added, although of course fresh troops could not arrive in time.

Where McClellan pronounced the battle "lost," Lincoln offered a less dire interpretation: "If you have had a drawn battle, or a repulse, it is the price we pay for the enemy not being in Washington. We protected Washington, and the enemy concentrated on you; had we stripped Washington, he would have been upon us. . . . It is the nature of the case," he concluded, "and neither you or the government is to blame." Sensing that McClellan exaggerated the danger, Lincoln wasn't surprised the next day when a reporter from the *Baltimore American* stopped by the White House with an eyewitness account of Porter's orderly crossing of the Chickahominy. "On the whole," Lincoln said, "I think we had the better of it up to that point."

The second conclusion settled over him as it became apparent that McClellan would decline to advance on Richmond: the end of the war was not at hand. The Rebels in Virginia were just as determined as the troops who had stoked the inferno at Shiloh. In fact, as far as Lincoln and his advisers knew, they might be the very same men. That was a key to the problem: the Confederates still controlled enough of the Southern interior to allow troops to move back and forth from west to east. As long as the Confederacy could shift its limited manpower along compact interior lines, the South would have the means to resist. Furthermore, if McClellan was correct and the Rebels from Corinth had shifted to Richmond, then the Army of the Potomac would have to be reinforced. But this presented a familiar dilemma: Lincoln felt he couldn't send the necessary divisions from Washington, because once the Federals embarked on their boats, Lee's Rebels might well board trains to Manassas and then sack the capital—which would almost certainly invite a foreign intervention to end the conflict.

Another possibility, stripping Union troops from the West to reinforce McClellan, was equally unappealing, since it would give Jefferson

Davis the option of sacrificing Richmond in exchange for the richer prizes
of Tennessee, Kentucky, and Missouri. Lincoln resolved that the proper
strategy was, as Scott had said a few days earlier at West Point, "to hold
what we have in the West, open the Mississippi, and take Chattanooga &
East Tennessee," while at the same time trying to maintain "a reasonable
force" around Washington and reinforce McClellan with new troops.

Executing this strategy would mean reopening the recruiting offices.
But how could he do that? His mail was already full of vitriolic criticism;
the newspapers were crowded with second-guessing. To call now for
fresh troops would be such a sign of weakness and miscalculation that, as
the president confessed to Seward, "I fear a general panic and stampede
would follow."

Lincoln was at a crossroads. His original theory of the war—that it
could be won in short order as the rebellion broke from within—was
wrong. He now faced a stark choice: he could either surrender to the
Southern insurrection or ask the North for a commitment far greater than
he or anyone else could have imagined when the conflict began. And once
enlistment resumed, it wouldn't end until the war was won.

At this critical moment, Lincoln briefly turned away from the crisis
on the peninsula to do a favor for one of Mary's cousins. The cousin's son,
Quintin Campbell, was a first-year student at West Point and hated it.
Lincoln had never met the boy, but Mary asked him to send a letter of
encouragement, which he did on June 28. It was one of the president's
small masterpieces, a fine example of the precision his writing had attained
under the time pressures imposed by the war. And though it was addressed
to the cadet, the message can also be read, under the circumstances, as
Lincoln's attempt to bolster his own resolve:

> Your good mother tells me you are feeling very badly in your new situa-
> tion. Allow me to assure you it is a perfect certainty that you will, very
> soon, feel better—quite happy—if you will only stick to the resolution
> you have taken. . . . I am older than you, have felt badly myself, and *know*,
> what I tell you is true. Adhere to your purpose and you will soon feel as
> well as you ever did. On the contrary, if you falter, and give up, you will
> lose the power of keeping any resolution, and will regret it all your life.

That same day, Lincoln told Seward: "I expect to maintain this contest
until successful, or till I die, or am conquered, or my term expires, or the

Congress or the country forsakes me." Seward in turn carried this message to New York, where he met with Northern governors to arrange the call for troops. All feared the political price Lincoln would pay for requesting more men, and together they hit on the idea of having the governors take the first step by offering to raise new regiments.

This transparently political strategy may not have made many voters feel better. But it's likely that Lincoln felt a bit less lonely when, on July 1, he issued a call for 300,000 men. In a reassuring telegram to McClellan, the president wrote: "We still have strength enough in the country, and will bring it out."

Lincoln's third conclusion in those last days of June followed from the second. If the war was to go on, he must play all the cards in his hand—including military emancipation of the enemy's slaves. During the tense days during and after the week of the Seven Days battles, when communications with the peninsula were spotty and Seward's mission to the governors required careful attention, Lincoln spent long hours in the telegraph office at the War Department, monitoring traffic. One morning, he asked Major Thomas Eckert, chief of the telegraph staff, for some paper and set to work slowly and methodically on what was clearly an important document.

"He would look out of the window a while and then put his pen to paper, but he did not write much at once," Eckert recalled. After a few words, he would pause and stare out the window again, often watching the spiders that worked in a large web beyond the glass. "And when he had made up his mind he would put down a line or two, and then sit quiet for a few minutes." Stopping to read fresh dispatches and trade jokes with the young wire operators, Lincoln never finished so much as one full page on any day. At the end of each day, as he rose to leave, he would ask Eckert to store the papers, which the major could see were speckled with question marks. Come morning, Lincoln resumed his work, painstakingly revising the lines he had written the day before. There was no margin for error.

8

JULY

While his men were preparing to kill and die in the suffocating heat at Malvern Hill, George McClellan took a boat ride down the James River to survey Berkeley Plantation, the ancestral home of the venerable Harrison family of Virginia, which had already given the nation one president and in time would give another. Little Mac's absence on the morning of July 1 was taken in stride: "The Army of the Potomac has fought so many battles without General McClellan's supervision or assistance, that he is not missed when the fighting commences!" one soldier on the headquarters staff remarked.

At the plantation shipyard, known as Harrison's Landing, McClellan found an imposing redbrick mansion rising above the river, and a long pier stretching to meet steamboat traffic. By some accounts the house was the oldest three-story brick residence in Virginia, built in 1726 by slaves belonging to Benjamin Harrison IV on land settled by colonists not long after Jamestown. The house had been standing half a century when Harrison's son signed the Declaration of Independence; the arched interior doorways were a modernizing update designed by a family friend, Thomas Jefferson. McClellan now chose this cradle of the endangered Republic in which to bivouac his army. With the landing as his base, the river as his supply line, and a fleet of Union gunboats to scare away the Rebels, the general felt confident that he could safely await the reinforcements he meant to demand from the scoundrels in Washington. While he waited, he would make preparations to renew his discombobulated campaign.

After surveying the plantation, McClellan ordered his battle captains to fight at Malvern Hill until dark, then give up the bloody ground for a six-mile retreat to Berkeley. That night, the army trudged down the river valley through heavy rain, and the next day Union signalmen waved flags on the rooftop of the mansion while surgeons sawed off limbs on the lawn. Exhausted soldiers pitched their tents—if they still had them after a week of night marches—in the low, muddy fields.

Many of McClellan's men were baffled and frustrated by the experience of winning battles but losing ground, especially when that ground was littered with their wounded comrades, abandoned to the enemy. In a proclamation marking the Fourth of July, the general tried to explain that their retreat was actually a military triumph. "Attacked by vastly superior forces, and without hope of reinforcements, you have succeeded in changing your base of operations by a flank movement, always regarded as the most hazardous of military expedients," he congratulated them. From Washington, Lincoln encouraged this optimistic view, wiring McClellan to let him know that a smuggled copy of a Richmond newspaper praised the Union movement as "a masterpiece of strategy." In truth, however, no one was happy about the loss of so many men and supplies and guns on a grueling march to this place that, however historic, was roughly fifteen miles farther away from Richmond than where the army had begun. Lincoln, for one, felt worse than ever before. "When the Peninsular campaign terminated suddenly at Harrison's Landing, I was as nearly inconsolable as I could be and live," he later recalled.

Judged calmly and soberly, the army's new location was at least as good as the abandoned position on the outskirts of Richmond, and probably better. Harrison's Landing solved the problem of the confounded Chickahominy, and supply lines were simpler. Indeed, McClellan likely would have chosen this as a base of operations at the beginning of his campaign had it not been for the ironclad *Virginia* menacing the waterway. Now clear, the James River allowed the navy to add its guns to McClellan's arsenal; the river also offered the option of trying to strangle Richmond by cutting its railroad link to the deep South.

But it was difficult to remain calm and sober when the violence of the Seven Days battles was so brutally tangible, both in Virginia and in Washington. In the capital, evidence of the bloodshed was everywhere one looked. Nearly every church had been converted into a hospital for wounded troops arriving by boat, and each new train coming into Washington station disgorged more parents and wives and siblings in search of lost soldiers. The city's muggy air reeked of infection and death; routine scenes were tinted with gore. A passenger riding on a train from Washington to New York shared a compartment with three officers from the peninsula: "One shot through the leg below the knee, and one through the arm, and one through the neck." As these bandaged gentlemen loudly described the fighting and criticized the administration, a man boarded at Baltimore whose only son had been killed in the fighting. He had tried to go south for the remains, and was returning home empty-handed and hysterical with grief. As the first passenger described the scene: "He would quote scripture, smite his fists together, roll up his sleeves, cry & laugh a sort of laugh that made me feel worse than his crying."

Faced with such a grim harvest, spirits sank and fear took hold. "I don't think I have ever heard more croaking since the war began," wrote Nicolay. "I am utterly amazed to find so little real faith and courage under difficulties among public leaders and men of intelligence. The average public mind is becoming alarmingly sensational. A single reverse or piece of accidental ill-luck is enough to throw them all into the horrors of despair." Montgomery Meigs panicked one night after reading a pessimistic dispatch from McClellan's new base. He raced from the War Department through the dark night to the Soldiers' Home and rattled the door of the president's cottage. When Lincoln woke, the general urged him to order an immediate retreat. Burn the supplies, slaughter the mules and horses, and pack the army onto boats, he pleaded. Lincoln calmed Meigs and sent him home.

Panic breeds where the unknown meets the unexpected. After the string of triumphs earlier in the year, few in the North had expected anything like the repeated strikes by the elusive Stonewall Jackson, or the violent blow of Lee's Seven Days hammer. The rebellion was supposed to be weak and the end near; now, a victory that had been thought imminent was suddenly feared impossible. Mary Lincoln's handler, Benjamin French, looked back through his journal after the Seven Days to see just "how long we have all been expecting that Richmond would be taken!" The sharp counterthrust of the Rebels had shattered that confidence, he wrote, "and I now almost despair of our ever taking Richmond."

The irresistible impulse, given such a shocking reversal, was to assign blame. What had been whispered was now shouted: Democrats accused the administration of deliberately sabotaging McClellan's plans. Talk of a coup to install McClellan as military dictator reemerged from the Washington shadows. Republicans, for their part, charged McClellan with near treasonous pampering of the enemy and demanded his replacement. While Lincoln stood at the vanishing center and struggled to hold things together, his Union coalition was being ripped apart.

No one was more aware than Lincoln of his precarious position. Around this time, the president received a delegation of prominent New England abolitionists, who admonished him to take a stronger stand against slavery. A long pause followed; then Lincoln surprised his visitors by asking whether they recalled "that a few years ago Blondin walked across a tightrope stretched over the falls of Niagara."

Of course they remembered. Lincoln was referring to a series of dazzling and well-publicized stunts by the tightrope walker Jean-François Gravelet, known as the Great Blondin. In 1859, Gravelet made a series of crossings over the roaring water: he pushed a wheelbarrow, stopped to cook an omelet, even carried his manager on his back. Lincoln had visited Niagara Falls in 1848 and the experience left an indelible impression; now the image of a man making his way along a three-inch rope above that sublime and terrifying force struck home for him.

One of the visitors later recalled the president's words: "Suppose," Lincoln said, "that all the material values in this great country of ours, from the Atlantic to the Pacific—its wealth, its prosperity, its achievements in the present and its hopes for the future—could all have been concentrated, and given to Blondin to carry over that awful crossing and that their preservation should have depended upon his ability to somehow get them across to the other side." And suppose "you had been standing upon the shore as he was going over, as he was carefully feeling his way along and balancing his pole with all his most delicate skill over the thundering cataract. Would you have shouted at him, 'Blondin, a step to the right!' 'Blondin, a step to the left!' Or would you have stood there speechless, and held your breath and prayed to the Almighty to guide and help him safely through the trial?"

But even some who claimed to be the president's friends seemed determined to tip him from his tightrope. The wealthy young governor of Rhode Island, William Sprague, insisted on planning a trip to Mississippi to extend a personal plea to Halleck to rush east with 50,000 men to reinforce McClellan. Could Lincoln give him a letter of introduction to the general? Although the president hoped Halleck might be able to spare McClellan a division, to pull so many of the Union's troops from the West would have been madness. As Lincoln explained to a newsman, "We had better put Richmond off six months than have any backward movement in the West." Given the chance, the Confederates would immediately retake Tennessee and northern Mississippi, and Kentucky and Missouri would unquestionably be at risk. Moreover, "the closing of the [Mississippi] river would have a bad moral effect" on U.S. efforts in England and France. Lincoln therefore had to find a way to indulge the influential Sprague without seeming to offer his stamp of approval; his resulting letter to Halleck was a pretzel of diplomatic contortions.

About the same time, an important associate from Illinois, the congressman-turned-general John McClernand, was cooking up a plan to detach his own large force from the western army to save the day on the peninsula. Lincoln could not afford to alienate McClernand, whose political support he needed in the upcoming congressional elections. Again he was forced to appear to accommodate a friend's ambitions while keeping those ambitions focused in the West.

Lincoln's most pressing task—the next step over the abyss—was to figure out just how bad things were. In this McClellan was no help. Though the general prided himself on his cool rationality, his messages from Harrison's Landing continued to border on the delusional. His calls for reinforcements seemed to pull numbers from thin air. To John Dix at Fort Monroe, Little Mac wrote that "even a thousand fresh men would do much," and the next day he thanked Lincoln in advance for "every thousand men you send." At the same time, however, he was asking the War Department for "fifty thousand," and, two days later, "100,000 men." A scant nine months had passed since McClellan blithely advised Lincoln that the whole state of Tennessee could be cleared of Rebels and kept secure with only 20,000 troops plus local volunteers. Now he was calling for an extra 100,000 to take a single city in Virginia.

Lincoln tried to inject a note of reality: "It is impossible to re-inforce you for your present emergency," he cabled McClellan as the Seven Days battles raged. "If we had a million of men we could not get them to you in time. We have not the men to send." The next day, he tried again: "Allow me to reason with you a moment. When you ask for fifty thousand men to be promptly sent you, you surely labor under some gross mistake of fact. . . . I have not, outside of your Army, seventy-five thousand men East of the mountains. Thus, the idea of sending you fifty thousand, or any other considerable force promptly, is simply absurd."

McClellan, however, was past the point of believing what Lincoln was telling him. Still more troubling were his wild mood swings. Two messages sent just an hour apart on Independence Day must have left the president wondering whether McClellan was losing his sanity. The first, written about noon, was an unnerving description of an army at risk of destruction: "The enemy may attack us in vast numbers and if so our front will be the scene of a desperate battle which if lost will be decisive. Our Army is fearfully weakened. Our communications by the James river are not secure." That was soon followed by another telegram so completely different in tone and attitude that it was as if General Hyde had wakened to find himself General Jekyll: "Bands playing, salutes being fired & all things looking bright," McClellan chirped. Only thirty-six hours later, he was General Hyde again, warning his wife that he expected the next morning to bring a battle that would "determine the fate of the country."

Pressing his case, McClellan sent his chief of staff, Randolph Marcy, to Washington to plead for more men. Marcy infuriated Lincoln by saying that the army might have to "capitulate" unless it received massive reinforcements. Scolded by the president for his defeatist language, Marcy explained he was only speaking of hypothetical possibilities.

With such unreliable sources, Lincoln decided he must see McClellan's army for himself. On July 7, he boarded the steamer *Ariel* at the navy yard, bound for the James River. After setting off, Lincoln realized that he had neglected a promise to send his son some money, so the presidential yacht paused at Fort Monroe the next morning to drop off an urgent wire to Nicolay: "Please borrow and send Bob Two hundred and Eighty (280) dollars." Upriver at Harrison's Landing, the president's ship was met by an exuberant McClellan, who hurried the length of the thousand-foot pier despite the sweltering heat.

The general was disappointed to find that Lincoln was all business. In a series of methodical meetings with McClellan and the corps commanders, the president brusquely read out a series of questions and jotted down each man's answers. Lincoln wanted to know how many troops were in camp and how many had been lost in the fighting. What were the sanitary conditions and where was the enemy? And finally, if a decision was made to evacuate the Army of the Potomac, could the evacuation be done safely?

McClellan had hoped to have a philosophical discussion with Lincoln about grand strategy and national policy. Before the Seven Days battles erupted, he had been preparing a sweeping statement on "the present state of Military affairs throughout the whole country." The congressional debates over Lyman Trumbull's Confiscation Act clearly alarmed McClellan, and he was worried that the president would give in to abolitionist pressure. Now that "this rebellion has assumed the character of a War," McClellan wrote, "it should be conducted upon the highest principles known to Christian Civilization." In the general's view, these principles required strict protection of private property, including slaves. And although he agreed with Lincoln that there would be occasions when the friction of war would likely break the chains binding slaves in one place or another, as a rule "military power should not be allowed to interfere with the relations of servitude."

The letter went on. An emancipation policy, McClellan maintained, would damage foreign relations and, quite possibly, offend the Almighty. Without a doubt, emancipation would cause mass desertions as large numbers of Union soldiers went home in disgust: "A declaration of radical views, especially upon slavery, will rapidly disintegrate our present Armies."

McClellan believed that his letter held the keys to victory, and he presented it to Lincoln during their time together at Harrison's Landing. As McClellan watched expectantly, the president read the missive in silence. Lincoln betrayed no emotion, even when, like Seward the year before, McClellan closed his essay by suggesting that the president find someone else to shoulder his own responsibilities. "You will require a Commander in Chief of the Army," he wrote, as if unaware that this was Lincoln's own constitutional duty. Unpersuasively, he added: "I do not ask that place for myself."

The president finished the letter and put it aside without a word. McClellan was irritated; writing to his wife, he declared that he "did not like the Pres[ident]'s manner—it seemed that of a man about to do something of which he was much ashamed." Lincoln, he groused, "really seems quite incapable of rising to the height of the merits of the question & the magnitude of the crisis."

But Lincoln had not come to Harrison's Landing for more unsolicited advice. He didn't need McClellan shouting from shore, "A step to the right!" Instead, he found what he was seeking during a moonlit ride along robust lines of fit and cheering Union soldiers. His inspection of the troops persuaded him that McClellan's frantic warnings about losing the whole army—and the fevered news accounts spun from such poor material—bore no relation to reality. "He came home in better spirits than he went in," Nicolay reported, "having found the army in better condition and more of it than he expected." Whether the men hailed Lincoln with enthusiasm because they loved him, as some reported, or because McClellan ordered them to, mattered much less than this: they were present for duty and able to shoulder their guns.

The information Lincoln drew from his interviews with the corps commanders confirmed this impression. From them, the president learned that the Army of the Potomac numbered some 80,000 healthy soldiers, and that the Confederates were in no position to attack. The only dispute among the top generals concerned the dangers of leaving the peninsula. Sumner, Heintzelman, and Porter pronounced the idea of pulling out "ruinous." "I think we give up the cause if we do it," said Sumner. "Impossible," said Porter, adding: "Move the Army [and] ruin the country." Erasmus Keyes was less categorical—"It could be done quickly," he allowed—while William Franklin was all for it: "I think we could, and think we better."

McClellan's step backward on the peninsula left Lincoln once again in need of a success, something to check the downward spiral of morale. The man of the western frontier looked for that success in his favorite direction. Ever since the Confederates fell back from Nashville, Senator Andrew Johnson had been working as military governor of Tennessee to reconstruct that gateway to Dixie as a loyal state. A tailor from the Smoky Mountains village of Greeneville, Tennessee, Johnson was one of the true patriots of the Union, an ornery Democrat who refused to join the Confederacy even as all the other senators from rebellious states went with the South. As Tennessee's appointed governor, Johnson had his work cut out for him: despite repeated efforts, the Union still had not established control of large parts of his state. But with the capture of Memphis in the west, he began to hope that the winds might be shifting in his favor.

Halleck had ordered a fresh effort to expel the Rebels from eastern Tennessee. Accordingly, Don Carlos Buell was moving slowly along the torn-up railroad from Corinth toward Chattanooga.

Needing some good news to pull out of his hat, Lincoln immediately thought of Johnson and Tennessee. "My Dear Sir," he cabled the governor on July 3. "You are aware we have called for a big levy of new troops. If we can get a fair share of them in Tennessee I shall value it more highly than a like number from most anywhere else, because of the face of the thing." The sight of loyal men from Tennessee answering the summons to fight for the Union—what Lincoln called "the face of the thing"—would be a clear sign of progress; even better would be an election in which Tennessee voters expressed a desire to return to the fold. "If we could, somehow," Lincoln ventured, "get a vote of the people of Tennessee and have it result properly, it would be worth more to us than a battle gained."

Johnson's answer was only partly encouraging. He could raise the troops, he said confidently, but he could not deliver a pro-Union vote until the loyal population in eastern Tennessee was free to cast their ballots without fear. The next day, as if to prove Johnson's point, Colonel John Hunt Morgan of the Confederate States Army ordered two regiments of cavalrymen into their saddles in Knoxville, the heart of eastern Tennessee, to begin a monthlong raid in Tennessee and Kentucky. Lincoln returned from Harrison's Landing to a depressing telegram from Johnson, who was "in trouble and great anxiety" about Morgan's raid. Union garrisons in Kentucky were calling on Johnson for help, but when the governor tried to send troops, he ran into a stout barricade erected by Buell's staff.

This was a classic clash of military versus civilian. Both claimed superiority; neither would back down. It didn't help that the two men involved despised each other. Johnson had been complaining to Lincoln about Buell for months, and he wouldn't be satisfied until Buell was fired. Well aware of the governor's efforts, Buell's friends tried to undermine the meddlesome tailor. When Lincoln learned that Buell's man in Nashville had actually arrested a fellow Union officer simply for following one of Governor Johnson's orders, the president's mood sank. Confederate raiders were galloping through Kentucky, taking Union prisoners and posting handbills that called for citizens to rise up for Southern freedom, and meanwhile Lincoln's men were squabbling. Where the president had looked for success, he found only another headache.

Nor was there much good news from the recruiting offices. On the theory that a speedy infusion of soldiers on the peninsula might yet embolden McClellan to capture Richmond, Lincoln cajoled the Union governors who had agreed to a new levy: "The quicker you send [troops], the fewer you will have to send." But the governors weren't getting the rousing results they had enjoyed in 1861. Volunteers were no longer springing up in multitudes just because a brass band played in a town square. Men needed time, after Gaines' Mill and Shiloh, to decide whether to join. At the very moment when the president needed an immediate boost, enlistments slowed.

Frustrated, Lincoln began to mull the complicated math of McClellan's army. He had long felt that one reason Little Mac was so hungry for new troops was that the Army of the Potomac leaked deserters like sand through a sieve. He asked the War Department to tell him the total number of men assigned to the general, and when the records were checked the answer came back: more than 160,000. By the end of his visit to Harrison's Landing, Lincoln had determined that McClellan's current strength on the peninsula was 86,500, "leaving 73,500 to be accounted for." Allowing for death by disease and casualties of battle, Lincoln reduced that number to about "45,000 of [the] Army still alive, and not with it." Further, he wrote, "I believe half, or two thirds of them are fit for duty." In other words, between 20,000 and 30,000 men were unaccounted for while their general insisted on reinforcements.

Once again the president chose to challenge McClellan. In a tough cable, he shared his calculations with the general and put two blunt questions to him: "If I am right, and you had these men with you, you could go into Richmond in the next three days. How can they be got to you? And how can they be prevented from getting away in such numbers in the future?" After some introductory bluster, the general grudgingly replied that he was probably short by some 20,000 deserters.

The tightrope was wearing thin. When Charles Sumner suggested that Lincoln make the Fourth of July "more sacred and historic than ever" by issuing "an edict of Emancipation," Lincoln revealed that his old concerns still gnawed at him. "I would do it if I were not afraid that half the officers would fling down their arms and three more states would rise" in rebellion, he said. But the pressure from the abolitionists remained relentless. In a message to Adams in London, Seward wrote that they seemed just as determined as the Rebels to stir up the worst possible result: a murderous insurrection by the slaves.

Searching for the middle, Lincoln decided to try one last time to talk the border states into voluntary, gradual emancipation, with payment for slave owners. On July 12, he again invited the delegations from the loyal slave states to the White House, and this time he read aloud from a carefully written appeal. "I intend no reproach or complaint when I assure you that in my opinion, if you all had voted for the resolution in the gradual emancipation message of last March, the war would now be substantially ended," he began. Once the rebellious states knew for sure that the border states would never join the Confederacy, they would almost certainly give up. Meanwhile, the luxury of wishing change away was over, for "if the war continue long, as it must, [slavery] in your states will be extinguished by mere friction and abrasion—by the mere incident of the war. It will be gone," he warned, "and you will have nothing valuable in lieu of it."

The step would be gradual, Lincoln repeated, and a suitable place in South America would be found for colonizing the freed slaves. His voice was pleading—until he turned to the threat. "I am pressed with a difficulty not yet mentioned," he said. General David Hunter's emancipation proclamation had more support than border staters might realize, and the Union needed Hunter's supporters just as much as the Union needed the conservatives. Lincoln had dared to offend the abolitionists by repudiating Hunter's order because he believed so strongly in the gradual approach. But if this way failed, he hinted, a military order would be the only option left. "The pressure, in this direction, is still upon me, and is increasing."

He closed with a flourish that went past poetry into desperation. He told the congressmen that they had the power to save the nation. Accept his offer, he said, and the country's "form of government is saved to the world; its beloved history, and cherished memories, are vindicated; and its happy future fully assured, and rendered inconceivably grand." To the men before him now, "more than to any others, the privilege is given."

Privilege or no, the offer was refused. Two days after the meeting, by a vote of twenty to eight, the delegations rejected Lincoln's emancipation plan. They gave a host of reasons. The government couldn't afford it; the Rebels would be outraged; loyal slaveholders would resist; the abolitionists would not be appeased. Lincoln tried to answer the first point by asking Congress to authorize bonds to cover the cost of his plan, but it was too late.

One objection from the border state delegations struck Lincoln with force and seemed to provide a narrow opening. Loyal slaveholders rejected the compensated-emancipation plan, he was told, because it would cause them to lose their slaves while Rebels kept theirs. "They felt it would be unjust," Lincoln recalled, because "the blow must fall first and foremost on" the Confederacy. Yet buried in this complaint was the suggestion that public opinion was shifting—that loyal slave owners were becoming reconciled to the idea that "slavery was doomed." They could not be "induced to lead" the way to emancipation, but they might be willing to accept it when it came.

On July 13, the morning after the meeting, while Lincoln was still waiting for a formal reply to his appeal, he recounted his conversation with the border state delegations to Seward and Welles. The men were riding in the presidential carriage on a sad mission to the summer residence of Edwin Stanton, in the wooded uplands north of Georgetown. Stanton's infant son had died after receiving a failed vaccination, and the family was holding a private funeral. The carriage had not gone far when Lincoln stunned his colleagues by announcing that he had "about come to the conclusion" that emancipation "was a military necessity absolutely essential for the salvation of the Union. . . . We must free the slaves or be ourselves subdued."

Up to this point, Lincoln had always been "prompt and emphatic," as Welles put it, in cutting off discussion of compelled emancipation. Now he had clearly changed his mind: "It was forced on him by the rebels themselves," Welles later wrote. "He saw no escape." The enemy had proved surprisingly resilient, but behind one army was another. Slaves were building fortifications, hauling supplies, feeding troops, raising crops—all tasks that freed whites to kill Yankees. The president now believed that only force would return the Rebels to the Union, and that meant stripping them of their war-making resources, slaves included.

The conversation that morning was unleavened by jokes or snatches of poetry. "He dwelt earnestly on the gravity, importance, and delicacy" of this step, Welles reported. Convinced that public opinion in the North was hardening, the president felt that a majority of the people were ready to "strike more vigorous blows," and that they were finally "prepared for" emancipation.

Lincoln asked for reactions from his traveling partners. Seward seemed "startled," Welles thought, and said that such a big step, involving "consequences so vast and momentous," deserved something better than a hasty judgment. Seward wanted to reflect before he gave his answer, but his initial thought was that emancipation was "expedient and necessary." Welles agreed. As the men parted later that day, Lincoln assured them that he was serious: "Something must be done."

But would it work? What if McClellan was correct, and the army "disintegrated" over emancipation? What if Lincoln lost Kentucky, Maryland, and Missouri to the Rebels? The next morning, July 14—the same day the border states representatives formally refused Lincoln's last overture—the Senate passed Trumbull's Confiscation Act. Orville Browning rushed to the White House in distress. The senator minced no words in telling Lincoln that the bill "was a violation of the Constitution and ought to be vetoed." Browning promised that a veto would produce "a storm of enthusiasm in support of the Administration in the border states" and that Democrats everywhere would swarm to Lincoln. But if he signed it, "the [D]emocratic party would again rally, and reorganize an opposition." Lincoln promised to give the matter "his profound consideration."

He apparently slept little that night as he worked through his next step. When Browning called at the cottage after breakfast the next day, the president was busy writing in the library. He had asked not to be interrupted, but made a brief exception for his friend. Browning was alarmed by Lincoln's appearance. "He looked weary, care-worn and troubled. I shook hands with him and asked how he was. He said, 'tolerably well.'" Worried, Browning reminded Lincoln of all that was riding on his shoulders, and urged his friend to take care of himself. Lincoln's huge right hand was still wrapped around Browning's as he replied "in a very tender and touching tone—'Browning, I must die sometime.' . . . He looked very sad, and there was a cadence of deep sadness in his voice. We parted . . . both of us with tears in our eyes."

The British public was appalled by the latest news from the American battlefields. Their own nation's recent bloodlettings in Crimea and India had temporarily fostered an antiwar spirit in the country, so the butchery at Shiloh and on the peninsula filled them with revulsion. The North appeared to be madly pursuing an impossible goal: the South could not be beaten and dragged back into the Union. What lay ahead was nothing but barbaric, fruitless struggle. A large segment of the public believed that it was time for the most powerful nation on earth, Great Britain, to step in and separate the fighters.

This tide of opinion washed into the House of Commons on July 18, when debate began on a proposal to call for intervention by the British government. Sympathy for the South appeared strong. Supporters of the Rebels spoke of states' rights, the need for cotton, and the strength of Southern armies. They charged Lincoln with foot-dragging hypocrisy on the subject of slavery, going so far as to suggest that the institution would die out faster in an independent Confederacy than in a reconstructed Union. William Lindsay, the sponsor of the mediation proposal, boasted to Lord Russell that Parliament would force Her Majesty's government to act within two weeks. The British press was full of sensational and exaggerated reports of the Seven Days battles. "The de facto independence of the Confederate States was regarded by most Englishmen . . . as unchallengeable," according to one historian, and the influential *Times* of London called on the British cabinet to consider formal recognition of the Southern nation if McClellan's army failed to advance.

Ambassador Adams counseled Washington to prepare for a "possible emergency" from the direction of Europe. Disgust at the war and sympathy for the South "is showing itself strongly in private circles here as well as in the newspapers," he wrote, adding that it was "impossible" to counter those sentiments as long as the administration continued its confusing policy on slavery. Unaware that Lincoln had moved so far toward emancipation, Adams warned that Europeans found Lincoln's position baffling, especially since he appeared to be standing on legal niceties. A clear abolition stance would turn the tables by showing that the North was fighting "for the fuller establishment of free principles," not "dominion of one part of the people over the other," Adams argued.

Currents were also running against the Union inside the British cabinet, but they followed a more complicated course. Palmerston and Russell agreed that the North's cause was hopeless and that the sooner the conflict ended, the better for England. But the shocking scale of the war, which incensed the public, had the opposite effect on these experienced statesmen. They understood that armies engaged in such savagery would not be easy to pry apart; how could anyone expect "a successful offer of mediation" in the midst of this extreme conflict? "The Thirty Years' War in Germany was a joke" compared with what was happening in America, the prime minister said. Lincoln and Seward did what they could to encourage this cautious response; in a strongly worded message, Seward urged Adams to explain to Russell that an effort to intercede on the side of the Rebels could turn "this civil war, without our fault [into] a war of continents—a war of the world."

For the time being, the British cabinet's careful approach prevailed, and Parliament adjourned for the summer without passing Lindsay's mediation proposal. But Palmerston's government would not stand idly by; once it found a safe way to take action, it intended to do so. To act alone would be dangerous; to act with the other great powers might be less so. That, however, would mean doing something quite unnatural: England would have to cooperate with France.

As it happened, Louis-Napoleon was thinking along the same lines. On July 16, while the sickly emperor was taking the water cure in the mineral baths of Vichy, he met with the Confederate emissary John Slidell. Since arriving in Paris some six months earlier, Slidell had been angling for such a meeting; McClellan's retreat had at last made it possible. The emperor, who fancied himself a military genius like his uncle, wanted to talk about Lee's triumphs outside Richmond, which had been reported in the French newspapers the previous evening. Slidell knew no more than what he had read in those same papers, but he was delighted to hear Napoleon expound on the French sympathy for underdogs and his own belief that the South could not be conquered. Like Ambassador Dayton, Slidell was struck by the emperor's candor. It was true, Napoleon told him, that France had always seen a strong United States as a necessary counterweight to British power, but now that the Union was breaking up, he preferred to side with the South.

Pressing his advantage, Slidell suggested that France, with its ironclad battleships, could easily break the Union blockade, which would open the flow of money and guns that the Confederacy needed for victory. Napoleon rejected the idea; like Palmerston, he had no interest in a war with the North. What he would like to do, he told Slidell, was join Great Britain in an effort to mediate the conflict. Alas, the emperor added, his overtures to England had thus far been rebuffed.

Slidell had a final card to play. The South was tired of waiting for England and France, with all their ancient grudges and competing interests, to fashion a joint intervention, so Richmond had recently given its emissary an unusual instruction: offer a bribe. Now Slidell smoothly told the emperor that the French determination to install a puppet regime in Mexico—a move stoutly resisted by the Lincoln administration— made this the perfect time for France to ally itself with the Confederacy. A Southern victory would make Mexico safe for France. To encourage Napoleon's active support, the South was prepared to pay France a hundred thousand bales of cotton, worth more than $12 million. What was more, Richmond would provide duty-free access to Southern markets for all the French cargo that could be packed into the ships sent to collect that cotton. By the estimate of Judah Benjamin, the Confederate secretary of state, the bribe could not possibly be worth less than a hundred million French francs.

The emperor registered, but did not react to, this irregular proposal, and after more than an hour of conversation the meeting ended amiably. Napoleon repeated that he hoped to hear from England, yet he also managed to leave Slidell with the feeling that he was moving toward a decision to act alone if necessary.

On July 15, as Congress prepared to adjourn, Lincoln sent messages to the House and Senate asking that the lawmakers delay their departure another day. Word somehow circulated that the president was preparing to veto the Confiscation Act. (Indirect communication was a Lincoln specialty; one irritated congressman complained of his "back-kitchen way of doing this business.") Lincoln's complaint was that the legislation could be construed as punishing a certain class of people without benefit of a trial—making it an unconstitutional "bill of attainder." This was a flaw too obvious for Chief Justice Taney and the Supreme Court to miss.

Congressional leaders quickly drafted a resolution clarifying Trumbull's bill. Lincoln went to the Capitol to be on hand for any last-minute questions or negotiations. When the resolution passed easily, Lincoln signed the bill—"an act to destroy slavery," in the words of Nicolay and

Hay. As a precaution, the president attached his lightly revised veto message, so that his interpretation of the new law would be public record. He also approved changes to the Militia Act of 1795, authorizing the enlistment of blacks in the military. And with those two dramatic actions, the momentous second session of the 37th Congress of the United States came to a close.

In the span of less than eight months, this tempestuous Congress had written the future of the nation. It wrenched American history away from the dead end of slavery and toward the hard, slow course of freedom; it created a modern monetary and fiscal machinery; it established a first-class army and navy; and it opened the frontier to bootstrapping families and supported their toil with a federal Bureau of Agriculture.

The Congress of 1862 also passed legislation that provided the means for establishing a rail link from the Atlantic to the Pacific. The transcontinental railroad's odyssey through Capitol Hill was an unseemly business involving millions of dollars in bribes, for some of the greatest fortunes in American history were at stake. Disputes over the cost and the final route nearly killed the bill in the Senate, but the president had kept the lawmakers moving forward.

As a student of geography and a former railroad lawyer, he was well versed in the subject of possible paths west. Lincoln had arrived in Washington believing that the railroad ought to follow the easy route along the Platte River valley through Nebraska and what became Wyoming. As president, he came to realize that the most plausible proposal for the difficult western end of the line called for crossing the rugged Sierra Nevada at the Donner Pass. With these understandings he became, in the words of one historian, "the greatest friend of the Pacific Railroad . . . exhorting [men of] Congress and business to do their parts." Lincoln signed the law authorizing the immense undertaking on July 1, 1862.

Perhaps most visionary of all, the 37th Congress provided for the world's foremost system of widely available college education. Lincoln believed "that the very best, firmest, and most enduring basis of our republic was education, the thorough and universal education of the American people." In signing Justin Morrill's bill to use federal lands to endow state colleges and universities for the education of the farming and working classes, Lincoln endorsed the transformation of American society and unleashed a mighty engine of economic development. Some of the finest universities in the world—among them Cornell, the University of

California–Berkeley, and the University of Wisconsin–Madison, to say nothing of dozens more—grew out of that bill, with the result that many millions of Americans and students from around the globe would never have to say, as Lincoln did: "That is what I have always regretted—the want of a college education. Those who have it should thank God for it."

After Congress adjourned, Charles Sumner offered an understated assessment: "Our session has been busy." Then he added, with justified pride: "I doubt if any legislative body ever acted on so many important questions." Nicolay, who had been Lincoln's often irritable gatekeeper through the hectic months of congressional activity, sighed with relief. "I am heartily glad that Congress is at last gone," he wrote, "and am sure I shall enjoy the relief from the constant strain of petty cares and troubles which their presence imposes." And yet, he added: "It has done well, and much more than could reasonably have been expected of it—certainly much more than any former Congress has done."

The press of work had forced Lincoln to borrow a third secretary, this one from the Interior Department. William O. Stoddard was an amiable young newspaper editor from Illinois whose chief virtue was his ability to get along with Mary Lincoln. Among the tasks he took on was keeping track of all the inventions and prototypes pushed on the president by would-be arms dealers. "Every proposed vender of condemned European firelocks was possessed by the idea that he might make a sale of them if he could induce the President to overrule the decisions of the Bureau of Ordnance," Stoddard recalled. The various weapons would accumulate in the White House until there was a stack of promising candidates. Then Lincoln and "Stodd" would go test fire them. At that time, the Mall was an overgrown expanse—in Stoddard's words, "badly littered with rubbish"—and "in the middle of it was a huge pile of old building lumber." Placing a target on the woodpile, the men backed up a respectable distance and started shooting.

Lincoln was fascinated by innovation. He loved visiting the navy yard to observe Dahlgren's tests of new artillery, and under the tutelage of Joseph Henry at the Smithsonian Institution he kept abreast of scientific and medical advances. That summer, the president was also personally sponsoring a series of top-secret chemical experiments intended to improve the formula for gunpowder. The year 1862 was a time of tremendous technological progress—of innovations ranging from the mass production of condensed milk in cans to the first underwater ships, called "submarines." The nightmares of generations yet unborn made their first ominous appearances: a schoolteacher in New York, John Doughty, wrote Stanton to explain how artillery shells could be loaded with chlorine gas to force the enemy from their trenches, while an inventor named Richard Gatling opened the first machine-gun factory.

A more welcome breakthrough came at the Gilbert & Bennett factory in Georgetown, Connecticut, begun as a horsehide tannery in the early 1800s. Perplexed by the waste of hair stripped from hides, Benjamin Gilbert soon branched into the business of stuffing horsehair mattresses and seat cushions. Then he began weaving the hair into fine mesh to make sieves. As technology advanced and slender metal wire became widely available, Gilbert's company developed longer-lasting wire-cloth sieves. When the war broke out and Gilbert & Bennett was suddenly unable to sell sieves in the South, the company found itself with piles of surplus metal mesh—until one clever employee thought to paint the stuff, stretch it on frames, and thus create the durable window screen.

This invention had yet to reach Washington in July 1862, where it was sorely needed. "The gas lights over my desk are burning brightly and the windows of the room are open, and all bugdom outside seems to have organized a storming party to take the gas light, in numbers which seem to exceed the contending hosts at Richmond," Nicolay wrote from the White House on the sultry night of July 20. "The air is swarming with them, they are on the ceiling, the walls and the furniture in countless numbers, they are buzzing about the room, and butting their heads against the window panes, they are on my clothes, in my hair, and on the sheet I am writing on."

It was to escape that buggy misery that the Lincolns had moved to the cottage at the Soldiers' Home, where Mary found her new surroundings both therapeutic and depressing. "The drives and walks around here are delightful," she wrote, and "each day brings its visitors." But she couldn't gaze on the lawns and pathways without thinking of "our idolised boy," who would have had so much fun playing with Tad "in this sweet spot." Writing to a friend, she confessed that the memories of Willie and the anguish of knowing that "*he is not with us . . .* oftentimes for days overcomes me."

To make matters worse, Bob, visiting from Harvard, announced that he wanted to join the army. He had been thinking hard about the matter since returning to school after Willie's funeral; in March he had bought a book called *Cadet Life at West Point*. His father's call for more troops undoubtedly fueled his desire, because Lincoln's critics weren't shy about suggesting that the president's own able-bodied son should step to the head of the line. But Mary would not hear of it: "We have lost one son, and his loss is as much as I can bear."

Lincoln had good reason to worry about his wife, for she remained extremely fragile. A newspaper reporter called on her at the cottage that summer and was shocked when she "burst into a passion of tears . . . she could neither think nor talk of anything but Willie." Lincoln approved of his son's soldierly ambitions, but to keep the peace with Mary and bolster her shaky recovery, Lincoln supported her decision to forbid Bob to enlist.

Because this family crisis took place in the midst of the greater calamities, Lincoln had little time to discuss the matter with his son. Young Tad's needs were easy to meet: a hug, a lap, a toy. What Bob required, his father could not give. "Any great intimacy between us became impossible," the younger Lincoln said years later. "I scarcely ever had ten minutes' quiet talk with him during his Presidency, on account of his constant devotion to business."

Early on Monday morning, July 21, Salmon Chase was pursuing one of his favorite hobbies: gossiping about Seward. His first visitor that day was the strange and voluble Adam de Gurowski, a Polish count who wore blue-tinted glasses and, occasionally, a blue veil to match. A man of the world, fluent in several languages, the count spent his days translating foreign newspaper articles for the State Department, his nights flitting from dinner party to salon to hotel lobby, and every free minute recording his thoughts and experiences in a diary written in ink and venom.

Like most abolitionists, Gurowski blamed Seward for Lincoln's cautious policy on slavery, so he was delighted to have some new intelligence for Chase. At dinner the previous night, Gurowski had heard Seward expounding on the virtues of a coup d'état. The other guests, many of them diplomats, "were very much disgusted," reported the count. Chase knew Seward well enough not to take this very seriously: blustering at dinner was one of his trademarks. The secretary of state "loved to talk, was not above monopolizing the conversation," a biographer wrote, "and had many moods, being by turns challenging, pontifical, a cynic, a raconteur, a mimic—altogether something of a show-off, and one whose words could not always be trusted."

Chase had barely said farewell to the count when he received a note from one of Seward's messengers announcing that the president had called a meeting of the cabinet for ten A.M. Chase was surprised; as he put it in his diary, "It has been so long since any consultation has been held that it struck me as a novelty." Upon arriving at the White House, the Treasury secretary found Lincoln in a stern mood, "profoundly concerned" and "determined."

The time had come, the president announced to his cabinet, to harden the administration's policies on the war and the related institution of slavery. He had drafted four orders and wanted to have the reactions of those present. The first would give Union armies permission to confiscate whatever supplies they could find in the Southern regions where they camped and fought. Long supply lines, easily cut by Rebel cavalry raids, were killing the momentum of Federal forces from the Shenandoah to the Mississippi. No longer would hungry men in blue march past crops and livestock being grown to feed the rebellion; they would eat the food themselves. Not a word of dissent came from the cabinet.

Lincoln's second order, which authorized the use of contrabands as army laborers, also met unanimous approval. Order number three attempted to protect whatever pro-Union sentiment might exist in the South: Federal commanders would be instructed to keep records of confiscated supplies and laborers so that Southerners able to prove their loyalty could be compensated for their losses. Chase had serious doubts: How practical would it be to keep scrupulous track of every bushel of corn and every slaughtered hog gathered by armies numbering in the tens of thousands? It seemed an enormous waste of effort "for the benefit of the inhabitants of rebel States," he said. Others in the cabinet agreed.

Lincoln's fourth order was designed to push the colonization project along. But the cabinet had no appetite for this problematic topic; the discussion quickly stalled.

Edwin Stanton got the meeting restarted with his own related agenda item. Several thousand troops had recently been withdrawn from David Hunter's command on the Southern coast and sent to McClellan. Now Hunter was reporting that he was too weak to defend the Sea Island cotton plantations in the event that the Rebels tried to take them back. The

general wanted permission to arm and train 5,000 contrabands to help
him hold his position. Stanton felt the step was necessary, and both
Chase and Seward agreed. This time the president was the lone dissenter.
As Chase put it, Lincoln "was not prepared to decide the question."

Still on that tightrope, Lincoln was acutely aware that tensions were rising
across the country in response to the blizzard of abolitionist activity in
Congress. Some of those who objected responded with violence: recent
days had seen arson in Brooklyn, beatings in Chicago, riots in Indiana and
Ohio. The proslavery congressman Clement Vallandigham, of Ohio,
warned a crowd of white workers in Dayton that the abolitionists, "having
brought on the war, were now trying to bring a horde of negroes into Ohio
to take the bread out of their mouths." In Washington, the *Evening Star*
echoed the alarm: "The real object" of employing black men in the army,
the paper claimed, was "to aid the scheme of forcing negro social and
industrial equality upon the white laborers of the country." Even in Massachusetts, disgruntled Republicans were trying to mount an election challenge to Senator Sumner, whose term was ending. The mayor of Boston
warned Lincoln that the abolitionists of his state, though loud, were small
in number, and did not represent the man on the street.

In the face of such intense resistance, would the president press ahead
or turn back? The cabinet got its answer the next day, July 22, when Lincoln called the council together again. Before the appointed hour, Chase
briefed the president on Union finances. The Treasury was having trouble
selling bonds in the wake of the peninsula retreat, and was now some $10
million behind in paying bills. The markets must be reassured of the
Union's will to win, Chase asserted, and he suggested sending this signal
by firing McClellan and arming black soldiers. "The President came to no
conclusion," Chase noted.

When the cabinet reconvened—meeting in the White House library
rather than in the president's office—Lincoln greeted them with startling
news. In his hand he held two pages, the result of many hours of drafting
over several weeks. The president said he wanted the cabinet's opinion of
what he had written; he let them know, however, that his decision in this
matter was final. There would be no vote. With that, he launched into the
first known reading of his Emancipation Proclamation. Dry, legalistic,

and dispassionate, the style of the document gave little hint of the grandeur or boldness of its purpose. The last few words, however, rang bell-like: As of January 1, 1863, "all persons held as slaves" in places where the rebellion continued "shall then, thenceforward, and forever, be free." Freighted with millions of lives and born from decades of struggle, those final words pointed the war, the Union, and American history in a new direction.

Lincoln would be criticized for the proclamation's failure to address slavery in the loyal border states, but in this he was hemmed in by Taney and by his own sense of constitutional limits. He had no war powers where there was no insurrection. And as the seven men in the room with him well understood, the president was taking a tremendous step by liberating the entire slave population of the South. As the historian Allen Guelzo has put it, Lincoln was speaking "not just of slaves used in Confederate war service or the slaves of disloyal masters but of all the slaves, without exception, in all rebellious areas. And not merely seized as contraband, or vaguely 'free,' but permanently *free,* 'thenceforward, and forever.'"

After Lincoln's reading of the explosive document, Attorney General Bates was the first to find his voice. He offered his endorsement, with one extraordinary reservation: the proclamation ought to be accompanied by an executive order for the immediate forced deportation, not just of former slaves, but of all blacks from the United States. Bates sought the end of slavery, but he could not imagine a multiracial nation, for he was "fully convinced that the two races could not live and thrive" together. Lincoln did not respond to this proposal.

Postmaster General Montgomery Blair spoke next, focusing on the political dangers of emancipation. The proclamation would "cost the Administration the fall elections," he warned. Bates and Blair were on the conservative end of Lincoln's cabinet, but Chase, who sat at the other end of the spectrum, had concerns as well. The Treasury secretary wondered whether the proclamation was too extreme: "Emancipation could be much better and more quietly accomplished by allowing Generals to organize and arm the slaves." That would begin the process of emancipation without stirring up an insurrection by slaves too impatient to await the arrival of liberating Union troops.

But it was Seward who offered the most persuasive objection. Though he didn't say it, Seward believed that a proclamation was unnecessary. As he later explained his thinking, the "death knell" of slavery "was tolled when Abraham Lincoln was elected president"; the passage of time and the friction of war would do the rest. But now he confined his concerns to a single point: he told the president and his fellow cabinet members that the timing was wrong. "The depression of the public mind, consequent upon our repeated reverses, is so great that I fear the effect of so important a step," Seward declared. To issue this extreme statement when the Union had been set on its heels could wreck American foreign policy. Europe would read Lincoln's words as encouraging an uprising of slaves against their masters. England and France would fear the destruction of the cotton industry for years to come. Moreover, Europe would scoff at the notion that the commander in chief of a retreating army could claim dominion over his enemy's slaves. "It may be viewed as the last measure of an exhausted government, a cry for help . . . [a] last *shriek* on the retreat," he predicted, and foreign intervention would likely result. Seward suggested waiting "until you can give it to the country supported by military success."

For all his reflection, Lincoln had not thought of this angle. As he later recalled, "the wisdom of the view of the Secretary of State struck me with very great force." He decided to wait for a battlefield victory, which he hoped to achieve as soon as he straightened out the deployment of forces in Virginia.

Lincoln had all but ignored McClellan since their conversations at Harrison's Landing. As the days passed in silence, the general gradually deduced that an ill wind was blowing. The president's failure to answer his treatise on war policy almost certainly meant that Lincoln's thinking was moving in a very different direction. His paranoia rising, McClellan suspected a new conspiracy to deny him reinforcements and then fire him for failing to advance. "I am confident that [Lincoln] would relieve me tomorrow if he dared to do so," Little Mac wrote to this wife. "His cowardice alone prevents it. I can never regard him with other feelings than those of thorough contempt—for his mind, heart & morality." To his political friend Samuel Barlow, he complained, "I know nothing, absolutely nothing as to the plans and intentions of the Gov[ernmen]t." What he did know, he added, was "that the rascals will get rid of me as soon as they dare—they all know my opinion of them. They are aware that I have seen through their villainous schemes & that if I succeed my foot will be on their necks."

McClellan's belief that the war could be contained and civilized was unshaken by the ordeal of the Seven Days battles. This genteel fantasy led him to send an apologetic letter to the proprietor of the large tobacco plantation where Robert E. Lee's mother had grown up. Located not far from McClellan's Berkeley headquarters, Shirley was the oldest plantation in the country; the current owner, one of Lee's cousins, was complaining that the recent battles had damaged the estate and cost him eighteen runaway slaves. McClellan replied: "I have done my best to secure protection to private property, but I confess that circumstances beyond my control have often defeated my purposes." Though Little Mac opposed the rebellion, he was decidedly in favor of the culture that spawned it. Writing to his wife, he indulged himself in a reverie of a golden age, an era "when abolitionists were not dreamed of [and] . . . psalm singing yankees were animals as rare as camelopards & black swans. I suspect [the Southerners] had a pretty good time, interrupted only by chills & fever, bad luck in gambling [and] the trouble of providing for their woolly headed dependents."

McClellan also took dangerous comfort in "letters from the North urging me to march on Washington" and seize control of the government. Leading antiwar Democrats, including former mayor Fernando Wood of New York, sailed to Harrison's Landing for long talks with the disgruntled general, and a foul climate of conspiracy settled over Berkeley plantation. When Ambrose Burnside, a friend of McClellan's and the hero of Albemarle Sound, went to Harrison's Landing to get a firsthand look at the army, he was shocked at what he heard. A group of division commanders, important men with stars on their shoulders, spoke openly one evening about turning on Washington and toppling the government. "I don't know what you fellows call this talk, but I call it flat Treason, by God!" Burnside scolded.

McClellan seemed to enjoy flirting with the idea of an insurrection of his own. "If they leave me here neglected much longer I shall feel like taking my rather large military family to Wash[ington] to seek an explanation," he wrote his wife. And later: "I do not believe that any nation was ever accursed with such a set of people as those who now rule in Wash[ington]." Mary Ellen McClellan only encouraged him: "I almost wish you *would* march up to Washington & frighten those people a little. I long to have the time come when you can have your revenge."

The general only partly understood his own situation. He was correct that Lincoln had decided to be rid of him, but he was wrong about what was causing the delay. It wasn't cowardice; Lincoln was waiting on the travel plans of Henry Halleck. The day after the president left McClellan at Harrison's Landing, he secretly elevated Halleck to the vacant post of general in chief. Halleck was delayed in reaching Washington, however, by Morgan's cavalry raid in Kentucky. When he finally arrived, on July 23, Lincoln steered him straight to Berkeley plantation, and at the same time made Halleck's promotion public.

McClellan's meeting with the new commander was predictably awkward. Little Mac considered the appointment a "slap in the face" and resented being placed under "a man whom I know by experience to be my inferior." For the moment, Halleck's assignment was merely to size up the situation and decide what to do next. He could restart the campaign with a realistic number of reinforcements, or he could pull the Army of the Potomac back from the peninsula. The president had also told him that he could keep McClellan or fire him, "as he pleased." Lincoln had at long last concluded that this general would never be the man to win a hard war. To Orville Browning, he said: "If by magic [I] could reinforce [McClellan] with 100,000 men today he would be in an ecstasy over it, thank [me] for it, and tell [me] that he would go to Richmond tomorrow," but "when tomorrow came he would telegraph that he had certain information that the enemy had 400,000 men, and that he could not advance without reinforcements."

Halleck was arguably in no position to criticize another general for begging reinforcements, not after his own endless calls for more men as he inched his way to Corinth. But Halleck's mind was set against McClellan for other reasons. The disposition of Union troops in Virginia now violated basic principles of military science as laid out in Halleck's own textbook. McClellan's army was linked to the newly combined force under John Pope by "exterior lines"—military terminology for lines of communication longer and less compact than those of the enemy. Worse, the Confederates, with their "interior lines," were poised between the two Union forces and thus in a strong position to concentrate first against one and then against the other. Given that the Federals still believed that the Rebels outnumbered them, this situation seemed extremely risky. To mitigate the danger, Halleck had already advised Lincoln by telegraph that the Virginia campaign must to be reorganized under a single general.

As the two men talked strategy, McClellan suggested that he make an end run around Lee to cut Richmond's supply line at Petersburg, but Halleck would not approve the idea. Instead, Little Mac promised Halleck that he would march up the north bank of the James and seize Richmond as soon as he received 25,000 fresh troops—but even so, McClellan continued to wring his hands over the superiority of the enemy. Somehow the populous North was unable to spare a man, but in McClellan's mind the much-smaller South could add thousands to its Virginia army day after day.

McClellan's request for yet more reinforcements persuaded Halleck that the president was correct: Little Mac would never feel ready. On August 3, Halleck ordered the evacuation of the army, thus bringing the Peninsula Campaign—launched with such high hopes—to an ignominious end. Predictably, McClellan felt that this disaster was in no way his fault. As he assured his wife: "I cannot feel that I have any intentional error to reproach myself with."

The rise of Henry Halleck and John Pope was a repudiation of George McClellan and the entire eastern command. And in case anyone missed that point, the victor at Island No. 10 ground his boot into the faces of the eastern generals with a pompous introduction to his new Army of Virginia. "I have come to you from the West, where we have always seen the backs of our enemies," Pope declared. "I desire you to dismiss from your minds certain phrases, which I am sorry to find so much in vogue amongst you. I hear constantly of 'taking strong positions and holding them,' of 'lines of retreat,' and 'bases of supplies.' Let us discard such ideas. The strongest position a soldier should desire to occupy is one from which he can most easily advance against the enemy." Pope didn't stop there; he seemed not to want to stop at all. Every line, every word, was an attack: "Let us study the probable lines of retreat of our opponents, and leave our own to take care of themselves. Success and glory are in the advance, disaster and shame lurk in the rear."

Reading these words, McClellan seethed: this "paltry young man who wanted to teach me the art of war . . . [will] be badly whipped." Boastful though he was, however, Pope gave voice to a growing desire in the North for a more aggressive approach to the war. He struck that chord again when he issued orders—following Lincoln's lead—to take what his army needed from enemy territory and arrest disloyal civilians while confiscating their slaves. "The temper of the North has undergone another change," John Dahlgren informed his diary. The Seven Days battles had forged a new "determination to persevere" and the public "will forbear less than before."

Ideas that had seemed far-fetched just weeks earlier were embraced with grim resolution. A week before he officially appointed Halleck general in chief, Lincoln had approved the first military draft in U.S. history, hoping to use the threat of conscription to inspire more voluntary enlistments. He also reopened the question of arming black troops; in particular, he explored the idea of an army of former slaves guarding the shores of the Mississippi, where Rebel snipers were routinely taking potshots at passing boats.

"I shall not surrender this game leaving any available card unplayed," Lincoln advised the former U.S. attorney general Reverdy Johnson. This distinguished statesman had journeyed to New Orleans on a mission to investigate complaints about the treatment of foreign consuls. When Johnson reported back that the leading men of the city were outraged by the Union occupation, he caught the full gale of Lincoln's fresh determination: "It is their own fault, not mine, that they are annoyed by the presence" of Federal troops. To be rid of the troops all the people of New Orleans had to do was rejoin the Union. "If they will not do this, should they not receive harder blows rather than lighter ones?"

Lincoln also let loose a furious blast in a letter to a loyal Louisiana businessman named Cuthbert Bullitt, who passed along complaints from other supposed loyalists. "This class of men," the president seethed, "touch neither a sail nor a pump," but want to be "carried snug and dry, throughout the storm, and safely landed right side up." If they disliked war, Lincoln argued, they should stand tall and throw off the influence of their secessionist neighbors. "What would you do in my position?" he asked Bullitt. "Would you drop the war where it is? Or would you prosecute it in the future with elder-stalk squirts, charged with rose water?" No, he answered himself. He would deliver "heavier [blows]"— though "nothing in malice. What I deal with is too vast for malicious dealing."

Lincoln, it was now plain, had staked everything on victory, and he would force the Confederates to stake everything as well. "Those enemies must understand that they cannot experiment for ten years trying to destroy the government, and if they fail still come back into the Union unhurt."

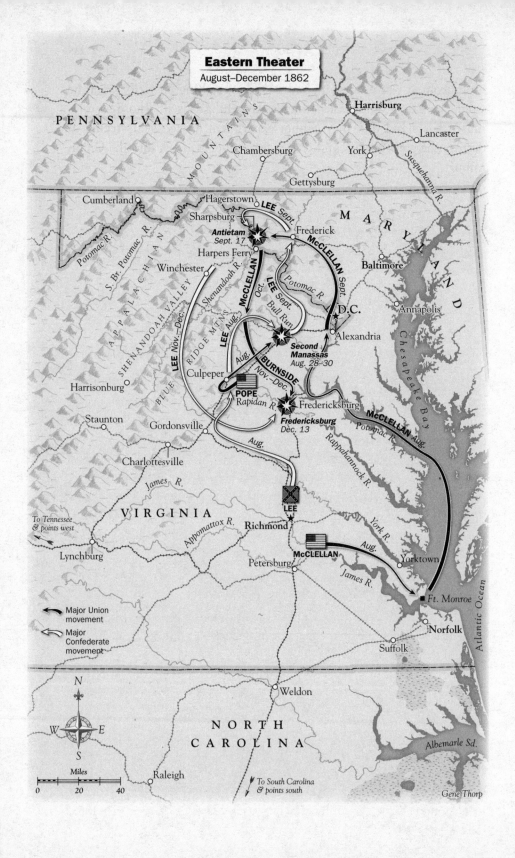

Eastern Theater
August–December 1862

PENNSYLVANIA

Harrisburg

Lancaster

Chambersburg

York

Gettysburg

Cumberland

Hagerstown

LEE Sept.

Sharpsburg

M A R Y L A N D

Antietam
Sept. 17

Frederick

McCLELLAN Sept.

Harpers Ferry

Baltimore

Winchester

McCLELLAN Oct.

LEE Sept.

Potomac R.

D.C.

Annapolis

Chesapeake Bay

S. Br. Potomac R.

Potomac R.

APPALACHIAN

SHENANDOAH VALLEY

Shenandoah R.

LEE Nov.–Dec.

LEE Aug.

BLUE RIDGE MTNS.

Bull Run

Alexandria

Harrisonburg

Culpeper

Aug.

BURNSIDE
Nov.–Dec.

Second
Manassas
Aug. 28–30

POPE

Rapidan R.

Fredericksburg

Fredericksburg
Dec. 13

Staunton

Gordonsville

Aug.

Rappahannock R.

Potomac R.

McCLELLAN Aug.

Charlottesville

James R.

V I R G I N I A

To Tennessee
& points west

Appomattox R.

LEE

Richmond

York R.

Lynchburg

Petersburg

McCLELLAN

Aug.

Yorktown

James R.

■ Ft. Monroe

Atlantic Ocean

⬅ **Major Union**
movement

⬅ **Major**
Confederate
movement

Suffolk

Norfolk

N
W E
S

Weldon

N O R T H
C A R O L I N A

Albemarle Sd.

Miles
0   20   40

Raleigh

To South Carolina
& points south

Gene Thorp

— 9 —

AUGUST

Frequently that summer, a man arrived at the White House whose role in the Civil War was little known at the time and has long since been nearly forgotten. But it mattered enough in those dark months for Lincoln to welcome the man and close the door—always close the door. The president was seen in every mood and variety of transaction in 1862: laughing, crying, raging, despairing, seasick, poetic, calculating, robust, exhausted, pleading, commanding. But these closed-door meetings went unseen and unrecorded because, like the magician who hides the workings of his art, Lincoln preferred to obscure the machinations behind his political victories. His rise from washed-up congressman and frontier lawyer to head of the Republican Party in six short years was a masterpiece of apparent levitation. The work that went into it—the letter writing, the anonymous editorials, the cultivation of powerful men and influential writers, the occasional cunning trick—as much as possible, he kept all these hidden.

Lincoln's visitor was James M. Edmunds, a wealthy lumberyard owner from Michigan and the principal builder of that state's Republican Party. One observer wrote that Edmunds was "said to be one of the best informed and most capable politicians in the country" and among "the shrewdest of long, hawk-nosed, twinkle-eyed, sharp, smiling old men." He bore a passing resemblance to Lincoln—the same high forehead, narrow face, and deep-set eyes capable of flashing from merriment to sorrow in a moment—and, like Lincoln, he was a master organizer. In 1855, when Edmunds was elected chairman of the state Republicans, every member of the Michigan congressional delegation was a Democrat. By 1860, Edmunds's party had captured all six seats. As president, Lincoln chose Edmunds for one of the most politically sensitive jobs in Washington, a job he himself had once dreamed of holding: he named Edmunds commissioner of the General Land Office, a nerve center of patronage and favor trading and feathering of nests. Edmunds, in other words, applied the grease that kept the cogs of government humming.

In most respects during that difficult summer, the president was feeling his way forward one day at a time. As one senator recalled, "Lincoln used to tell us that when he got up in the morning it was his purpose and endeavor to do the very best he could and knew how for that day—not being able to foresee, or devise or determine . . . what was best to be done for the morrow." His meetings with Edmunds were an exception to that rule. The two men were looking ahead to autumn, when Americans would go to the polls for the first time since the war began. Given the sharp drop in Northern morale, Lincoln expected the Democrats to do well, and he needed to prepare for that likelihood. So how could he offset, at least partly, the effect of an opposition victory?

From those meetings with Edmunds came a plan for a new organization, one that seemed to be above politics and independent of the two rival parties. Its purpose was to maintain support for the original, bipartisan cause of the North: saving the Union. A nationwide network of patriotic Unionists, Democrats as well as Republicans, could more effectively rally the public behind Lincoln's war aims than the soon-to-be-diminished Republican Party could do by itself. Lincoln, as one biographer put it, developed an "intelligent political strategy" to make his policies synonymous with "inclusive 'large-tent' patriotism, and [dress] the opponents of the administration in the clothes of narrow, illegitimate faction." And who better to create a network of outwardly nonpartisan Unionist organizations than a couple of master politicians with offices on Pennsylvania Avenue?

For this plan to work, Lincoln's fingerprints must not be visible. Once the strategy was fully hatched, therefore, Edmunds convened a secret meeting away from the White House. One summer evening after working hours, about a dozen handpicked men gathered at his office in the Interior Department building, not far from Willard's Hotel. Among them was William O. Stoddard, the land office clerk currently on loan to the president. From his desk at the White House, Stoddard had watched Edmunds go into Lincoln's office day after day, and it was no great leap to surmise that the two men were cooking up something of a political flavor. Yet when Edmunds invited the young clerk to the after-hours meeting, he ordered Stoddard not to breathe a word to the president. At first Stoddard found this odd: "I half wondered why Mr. Lincoln should send me on an errand which he wished to conceal even from himself." But the clerk soon concluded that this was "something with which he did not wish to appear connected in any way."

The invited men had been chosen to organize the Union League, a "voluntary" association that would, with great efficiency, rally the national spirit while serving to ostracize anyone who dared not to join. As one Union League history explained: "The problem was how to weed out the disloyal element in society with the least friction." The beauty of the Union League was that it neatly classified the North's influential citizens through the simple device of a public invitation. By "declining to join or countenance this movement the stay-aways would be showing their true colors." The idea worked perfectly in Washington, where the founders quickly organized a dozen clubs. Edmunds presided over the first and Stoddard was elected president of the second, holding weekly meetings of "congressmen, senators, Cabinet officers, their assistants, department clerks and army officers." The next phase of the project called for spreading the movement across the country; this required money, and lots of it. Commissioner Edmunds knew where to look. "A number of army contractors became members of our Washington councils, and they speedily became liberal contributors," Stoddard later wrote. After all, the war was making the contractors rich.

Although Lincoln was prepared to cede some ground to the Democrats in the elections, he was also working to minimize the loss. Paradoxically, the new tax law handed him a weapon. A robust tax code requires a multitude of tax collectors, plum jobs that Lincoln could use to strengthen his battered political network in every loyal state. Throughout August, the president spent many hours with Treasury Secretary Chase and key Unionists from across the country, painstakingly distributing these fruits. Chase juggled recommendations from congressmen, governors, and other influential figures. State by state, he forwarded lists of nominees to Lincoln, who vigorously second-guessed them.

Lincoln also canvassed the North for strong candidates to hold the

Union line in the fall elections, and in doing so he took aim at a few of his most prominent critics. One such adversary was Congressman Daniel W. Voorhees of Indiana—"the Sycamore of the Wabash," a towering man at least as big as Lincoln himself—who regularly and vehemently denounced Lincoln's use of his war powers to arrest and jail suspected traitors without regard to their constitutional right of habeas corpus. In one typically bombastic pronouncement, Voorhees declared that history would judge the president and his cabinet harshly, "execrat[ing] the prostitution which they have made of their high offices to the overthrow of the Constitution!" Lincoln had little patience with men like Voorhees, who cherished each brick of the nation's founding document but weren't willing to fight to save the edifice from destruction.

The political wiring of the Union coalition was not the only urgent renovation project; with the Army of the Potomac packing its tents to leave the peninsula near Richmond, almost every aspect of the Northern effort had to be restarted and renewed. Turning his attention overseas, Lincoln engaged in some direct diplomacy. After reassuring the Russian ambassador that plenty of fresh troops were on the way, he dictated a long letter to an influential pro-Union writer in Switzerland. In response to an oft-repeated warning that the North needed to make fresh military progress, Lincoln acknowledged the point, with this reservation: "Yet it seems unreasonable that a series of successes, extending through half-a-year, and clearing more than a hundred thousand square miles of country, should help us so little, while a single half-defeat should hurt us so much. But let us be patient."

Most important, the ranks of fighting men had to be replenished. After a slow start, a combination of carrot and stick had begun to fill the recruiting offices. Cities across the North pooled public funds with private donations to pay bounties for new soldiers. In Philadelphia, for example, the City Bounty Fund was on its way to raising some $700,000. At the same time, the fact of the new conscription law made these incentives doubly attractive: better to enlist and collect a bounty than to be drafted and receive nothing. True, some men skedaddled across the Canadian border to escape the draft, but far more concluded that this was still a war worth fighting. Fifty-three men signed up at a single meeting in the little town of Holton, in the Flint Hills of northeastern Kansas. The surprised recruiter reported that they were "men of the first character and intelligence," lawyers, merchants, ministers, all "going in as privates." Enough volunteered from the villages and cities of the North that Washington was once again thronged with new recruits, as many as eighteen thousand per week. Yet Lincoln pleaded for more troops, and faster.

Many of the fresh soldiers marched off to war singing one or another version of a poem by James Sloan Gibbons that had first appeared in the New York *Evening Post* the previous month. Like Julia Ward Howe's battle hymn six months earlier, this rousing song wrapped the Union cause in a biblical cloak. Now, however, the North's soldiers were trampling the grapes of wrath in service not just of God, but of the president himself. Though his critics were many and loud, these singing legions provided a stirring reply. In the furnace of the war, Lincoln was being transformed into the patriarch of men actually willing to fight and die at the struggle's spear tip.

> *We are coming, Father Abraham, 300,000 more,*
> *From Mississippi's winding stream and from New England's shore.*
> *We leave our plows and workshops, our wives and children dear,*
> *With hearts too full for utterance, with but a silent tear.*
> *We dare not look behind us but steadfastly before.*
> *We are coming, Father Abraham, 300,000 more!*

By now the battle between McClellan and Stanton was painfully public, as Northern newspapers fanned the flame. Lincoln needed to make a fresh start in this regard, too, and he found a novel opportunity on August 6. Union rallies had been organized on short notice in cities across the country, including Washington. Brisk band music summoned the citizenry through the humid evening to the East Lawn of the Capitol, where they gathered in numbers that surprised and delighted the administration. Longtime Washingtonians called it the biggest crowd in the city's history, apart from presidential inaugurations. The rally chairman, Benjamin French, surveyed the throng and felt a surge of hope that he might actually be able to produce the full $300,000 that he had been assigned to raise for bounties. Chase and Bates sat with Lincoln on the dais, where the president gazed, careworn but relieved, at the "immense" congregation. Lincoln listened patiently to one passionate speech after another. At last, during a lull between orators, he turned to Chase and said: "Well! Hadn't I better say a few words and get rid of myself?"

The crowd cheered as Lincoln stepped to the front of the stage. "Fellow citizens!" he began in his high, piercing voice. "I believe there is no precedent for my appearing before you on this occasion." It was true: the idea of a president appearing at a popular rally, let alone delivering a speech, was a clear break from aloof tradition, and Lincoln's audience was delighted by it. They burst into applause, and added laughter when he went on to say: "It is also true that there is no precedent for your being here yourselves."

A voice called out: "Go on: tar and feather the Rebels!" But Lincoln had other ideas; he told the audience that he preferred not to say anything "unless I hope to produce some good by it. The only thing I think of just now," Lincoln continued, his voice turning serious, "is a matter in which we have heard some other people blamed for what I did myself."

Here was a twist no one had expected. Several voices called out, "What is it?"

"There has been a very wide-spread attempt to have a quarrel between General McClellan and the Secretary of War," Lincoln answered. Taking on such a divisive topic at a rally about unity was undeniably risky, but Lincoln could probably have found no more favorable audience for his response to the furor. "Now, I occupy a position that enables me to observe, at least, these two gentlemen are not nearly so deep in the quarrel as some pretending to be their friends." Lincoln assured the crowd that the general and the secretary shared a desire to be successful, which was his only desire as well: "If the military commanders in the field cannot be successful," both Stanton and he himself "would be failures." Under the pressure of battle, he acknowledged disputes sometimes arose over the number of troops available to McClellan; further, he said, "McClellan has sometimes asked for things that the Secretary of War did not give him, and the Secretary of War is not to blame for not giving when he had none to give." This brought a roar of laughter and applause. Then the president declared: "And I say here: as far as I know, *the Secretary of War has withheld no one thing at any time in my power to give him!*"

"Give him enough now!" a voice roared.

But Lincoln had spoken his piece. Closing abruptly, he announced: "I stand here, as justice requires me to do, to take upon myself what has been charged on the Secretary of War." As the audience called for him to speak longer—shouting "No! No! No!"—he finished by saying: "I have talked longer than I expected to do, and now I avail myself of my privilege of saying no more."

The president sat down again to polite applause from an audience that one reporter described as "greatly disappointed."

Salmon Chase, however, was impressed. Perhaps the boisterous crowd had wanted a different sort of speech, but the important thing was the way they responded to Lincoln. "He was received with the most uproarious enthusiasm," the secretary confided to his diary. "His frank, genial, generous face and direct simplicity of bearing, took all hearts." No other politician would have given that speech at that moment, but Lincoln's address succeeded, in the opinion of his rival, because he delivered it with "his usual originality and sagacity."

The new general in chief, Henry Halleck, arrived in Washington to discover that he had a large and rapidly growing mess on his hands—a mess produced by the former Union commander in the West, one Henry Halleck. His decision to disperse his grand army after capturing Corinth had scattered a henhouse's worth of vexatious chickens, and now they were all coming home to roost.

Because Halleck had not pressed on to Vicksburg, the Mississippi was once again blocked. A Rebel ironclad, the *Arkansas*, lurked under the bluff-top guns, and together these obstacles made the river impassable. Moreover, Halleck's decision to let the Confederate army retreat to Tupelo had given the irritable and aggressive Braxton Bragg enough time to organize a leisurely tour of the Deep South for his roughly 60,000 men. As July turned to August, the Rebels rode the railroad down to Mobile, Alabama. They then caught a northbound line to Montgomery, switched trains for the leg to Atlanta, and finally took a ride through the leafy mountains of north Georgia to Chattanooga.

The Federal force under Don Carlos Buell, meanwhile, was biding its time on the west bank of the Tennessee River, waiting for supplies with which to finish a bridge. Buell had no idea how long his army would have to wait, because he was so deep in hostile territory that supplies were arriving only sporadically. Buell's assignment from Halleck—to repair the Memphis & Charleston Railroad and keep it open from Corinth to Chattanooga—proved impossible. Rebel cavalrymen, assisted by local guerrillas, were regularly tearing up tracks and capturing supply wagons, stunting Buell's progress. Nevertheless, the general held stubbornly to a McClellan-like belief that he should protect the private property of Southern civilians. Even when Rebel raiders interrupted his convoys, Buell prohibited foraging for food, so his troops often went hungry. Instead of a strike force into eastern Tennessee, Buell's Army of the Ohio was a stranded, underfed, and tediously overworked gang of tracklayers on a rail line that disappeared almost as quickly as it was replaced.

Ulysses Grant, meanwhile, had command of his old Army of the Tennessee, but he could not do a thing with it. "The remainder of the magnificent army of 120,000 men which entered Corinth on the 30th of May had now become so scattered that I was put entirely on the defensive in a territory whose population was hostile to the Union," Grant lamented. This was, he later recalled, "the most anxious period of the war, to me." Wishing that he could have marched on Vicksburg weeks earlier, Grant was instead reduced to the life of a bureaucrat, albeit a bureaucrat surrounded by armed enemies. Living in a big house outside Corinth with his wife and children, the general went to work each morning trying to implement flawed policies handed down from headquarters.

The worst of these, in early August, was the directive from Washington to reopen the cotton trade. For months, the Lincoln administration had been promising England and France that they would soon get cotton for their mills. When these promises were first made, Lincoln and Seward believed that most people in the South were the victims of rabble-rousers and would welcome the chance to return to normal commerce with their Northern countrymen. Now that idea met its test. Orders came down from Washington to "let trade follow the flag" in large parts of Tennessee, Arkansas, Louisiana, and Mississippi, where the Union had nominal control. Grant was instructed to establish points on the rivers and railroads where plantation owners could exchange baled cotton for gold.

The initiative was an immediate disaster. Grant's soldiers were furious to find themselves standing guard as sharp Northern traders passed bags of precious metal to Southerners who, the soldiers understood, used the money to resupply the enemy. In short order, guns and ammunition were making their way south from Cincinnati, paid for by Confederate agents. Other forbidden commodities also rode the southbound rivers: medicine and shoes and, especially, salt. The Rebels lacked many things, but they were starved for salt, essential for curing bacon, ham, and beef. Without it, meat quickly spoiled in a soldier's knapsack. Braxton Bragg's army, chugging toward Chattanooga, was powered by bacon salted with cotton money.

Grant lodged a respectful protest with Salmon Chase, whose Treasury Department was in charge of renewing trade. He explained that salt, flour, liquor, and other contraband was moving south in amounts too large to be meant for personal use. The only people gaining from this commerce were "greedy traders" and "our enemies south of our lines." And if Chase or anyone in Washington believed that the cotton trade would make friends for the Union in the occupied South, they were deluded, Grant warned.

In fact, the administration was already aware of the folly of the new policy. Lincoln's problem was that he had no good alternative: "England [wants] us to permit her to get $50,000,000 worth of Cotton from the South," he explained to Orville Browning. But "we [can] not let the cotton out without letting its value in."

Worse, this was precisely the wrong time to be letting money into the Confederacy, because the North's economic advantages were starting to pinch, hard. With the Union blockade tightening, Rebel finances were in a tailspin. The enormous wealth of the Southern planters, their land and slaves, could not easily be converted into cash. Cut off from credit markets, Richmond was compelled to pay for its war by printing money, and now inflation had begun to run rampant. In June 1862, a Confederate dollar was buying half as much as it had in January; by the end of the year it would be worth less than 20 cents. Prices were even higher for certain scarce staples. Salt for civilian use, which cost $2 per bag before the war, had rocketed in some parts of the Confederacy to $60 per bag. Spiraling prices weakened the Rebel armies as soldiers deserted in droves to scratch up a living for their families, who would soon be facing winter. Lincoln faced a version of this problem—"Give your paper mill another turn," he once advised a disgusted Chase when money was running short—but the North's gold and silver mines, its abundant harvests, and its generally healthy market for government bonds all helped to ease the bite of inflation.

With so much snarled and snagged, Halleck did what every other Washington official did when things bogged down: he sent urgent telegrams. By August, Buell was fed up, and when Halleck made the mistake of threatening to fire him for failing to reach Chattanooga, Buell answered: Please do. Halleck had no choice but to back off, at least for the moment, because by now Bragg had beaten Buell to the goal, arriving in eastern Tennessee in early August. Suddenly the military situation looked completely different. Opening railroads and guarding cities did not seem so important when a Confederate army stood poised to invade the lightly manned midsection of Tennessee, with the all-important prize of Kentucky just beyond.

The queen of England, still deep in mourning nearly eight months after the death of her husband, Prince Albert, decided to seek consolation among her family and friends on the Continent. To Lord Russell, her foreign minister, fell the tasks of arranging the trip and serving as Her Majesty's companion. This proved a small stroke of luck for Lincoln and his administration, because it meant that nothing would happen to alter British foreign policy until Russell and the queen returned to England. But change was brewing. On August 6, as Russell prepared to embark on the long holiday, he conferred with Palmerston on the situation in America, and the two men found they were both inclining toward a European intervention. They agreed to call a special cabinet meeting in September to move the idea forward.

Apprised of the looming threat, Seward rattled all the swords in his armory. He reminded American envoys that England and France were not dependent only on cotton; they also needed gold from America's western mountains and wheat from its prairies. Would they risk bread for cotton? And would they chance a war with the United States by trying to break the blockade, given that "the construction of iron-clad ships is going on" in American shipyards "on a scale and with a vigor that promises as complete a naval defense as any other nation possesses?" Bluster, however, was not the weapon to stave off Europe. As Charles Francis Adams reminded Seward in a reply, "It is impossible to overestimate the degree of influence that attaches to the operations of the war"—a fancy way of saying that the best diplomacy would be a winning Northern army.

Lincoln pinned his hopes for a decisive victory on the strutting figure of John Pope, who began pushing his new Army of Virginia southward from Manassas along the Orange and Alexandria Railroad, meeting little resistance. By early August, Pope had crossed the Rappahannock and was heading for Gordonsville, where he could cut the east–west rail line running to Richmond. Strengthened by a corps of the Army of the Potomac under Burnside, the slow-moving Union force numbered some 50,000 men. They gathered to the west of Richmond; to the east of the city lay the rest of McClellan's army, still on the peninsula. If combined, Pope's and McClellan's troops would outnumber Lee's army by about 50 percent.

The trick would be just that: combining them. It could not be done directly, because Lee stood between the two forces. Instead, McClellan's troops were to be taken off the peninsula by boat and delivered to points north, including Alexandria, scene of their glorious departure in March. From there, they would make their way overland to join Pope. Many in McClellan's army, especially the senior officers loyal to Little Mac, were unhappy with this plan, for when the linkage was complete George McClellan could wind up a man without an army. Not surprisingly, the general and his men were slow in leaving their base at Harrison's Landing. Ordered off the peninsula on August 3, McClellan did not start boarding troops onto ships until August 14, and he did not set off for Alexandria himself until August 24.

The Federal armies now faced a period of extreme peril. As long as McClellan stood within easy marching distance of Richmond, Lee was limited in the amount of muscle he could throw at Pope. But once the evacuation began, a window of opportunity opened for the Rebels. "Now I am to have a sweat of five or six days," Lincoln fretted as McClellan's move began. "The Confederates will strive to gather on Pope before McClellan can get around." Halleck reported being "so uneasy" during this vulnerable period that he "could hardly sleep."

Anxiety was the appropriate emotion, because Robert E. Lee was not a man to miss such a chance. First he sent Stonewall Jackson and General A. P. Hill to probe the front of Pope's advance, leading to a poorly fought battle at Cedar Mountain near Culpeper on August 9. Then, when he was sure McClellan was leaving, Lee added more troops, under General James Longstreet. By mid-August, two large forces of roughly equal strength faced each other just south of the Rappahannock, not far from a place called Chancellorsville.

But Lee wasn't interested in smashing Pope head-on. His men were in need of food and ammunition, which he knew to be heaped in vast quantities behind Pope's army. He wanted to capture the Manassas supply depot more than he wanted to fight the Army of Virginia. Besides, he had bigger fish to fry beyond Manassas. Like Bragg gazing across Tennessee toward Kentucky, Lee looked north past Pope toward Maryland, another slave state in need of liberation from the tyranny of the Lincoln government. So instead of attacking Pope, Lee directed Longstreet to flex and glare at the Union general long enough to distract him, while Jackson slipped into his beloved Shenandoah Valley and began to move unnoticed behind the mountains and around Pope's right. Then, when Jackson reappeared behind the Union army, Longstreet was to follow Jackson and disappear into the valley as well.

Rarely had tension and torpor kept such close company in the capital. Compared with previous months, August seemed almost sleepy. Congress was gone; the armies were reorganizing. A heat wave settled over Washington like a sweat-soaked quilt: on the north porch of Gideon Welles's house the thermometer registered 100 degrees on Friday, August 8. Two days later, a hint of breeze was worth a diary notation. John Dahlgren devised a bit of relief for the president at the navy yard. After showing Lincoln the latest innovations in rifled cannon and shells, he called for a yacht and took the presidential party for a ride on the Potomac to cool off in the evening air.

Yet underneath the apparent inactivity seethed a volcano. American history was coming to its greatest crisis, the moment when the nation would survive or expire. The Rebels were preparing to enter the border states; the European powers were preparing to throw their weight on the side of the rebellion; and Lincoln was preparing to expand the war into something much larger than he had imagined necessary. A second American Revolution, as the historian James McPherson has rightly put it, would test the unity of the North as it had never been tested before.

As long as this volcano rumbled unseen, Lincoln was forced to live an uncomfortable lie. His mind was made up in favor of emancipation, but he had to pretend otherwise until the moment was right for the announcement. Looking back on this period, the president's secretaries described a leader oscillating between misery and anger as the public badgered him over his seeming fecklessness. Lincoln "grew sensitive and even irritable," wrote Nicolay and Hay. "Could no one exercise patience but himself? . . . Why must they push him to the wall?" The long wait for a victory with which to frame the proclamation was perhaps the most delicate interval of his presidency, the aides wrote: "At no time were political questions so critical." Lincoln "was compelled to keep up an appearance of indecision which only brought upon him a greater flood" of demands for an answer. "During no part of his Administration were his acts and words so persistently misconstrued"—acts and words designed only to "curb and restrain the impatience of zealots from either faction."

No criticism landed more loudly than a letter published on August 20, by the editor of the *New-York Tribune*, Horace Greeley. Claiming to speak on behalf of twenty million Northerners, Greeley denounced Lincoln's failure to take decisive action to free the slaves living within the Confederacy: "The Union cause has suffered and is now suffering immensely, from mistaken deference to Rebel Slavery," Greeley boomed. Lincoln's excessive concern for the opinions of "certain fossil politicians hailing from the border slave states" was "perilous and probably disastrous." Worse, Lincoln was allowing his generals to ignore the Confiscation Act, and as a result, slaves who sought refuge with Federal forces were being turned away to be "butchered or reenslaved." Was Lincoln prepared to bear the blame for this "through future History and at the bar of God?"

Greeley's scathing attack filled two long, densely packed columns of type, with scarcely a word to suggest that Lincoln might face some difficulties. According to Greeley, the path ahead was clear: the president merely needed to stop disregarding his legal obligations. "The triumph of the Union is indispensable not only to the existence of our country, but to the well-being of mankind," Greeley concluded; and addressing the president directly: "I entreat you to render a hearty and unequivocal obedience to the law of the land."

Lincoln may have felt blindsided: only a week earlier, he had given Greeley's second in command, Sidney Howard Gay, a personal interview at the White House. But it was not Greeley's way to be moved by such favors. A mercurial, passionate man given to wild swings of judgment and mood, he divided the world's questions into two categories, simple or hopeless, and nothing was gray but the newsprint. These qualities made for strong admirers and even stronger critics; Greeley was unquestionably among the most widely read writers in America.

Lincoln judged that he should respond somehow to Greeley's charges. He could have brushed them away simply by announcing the administration's decision to enlist and train the former slaves at Port Royal—not just as army laborers, but as armed soldiers ready to defend the cotton plantations under Federal control. This important step would have delighted the abolitionists, but at the moment they were not Lincoln's most irksome constituency, so he preferred to keep silent about it. He instead used Greeley's letter as a chance to appeal to Northern moderates, crafting a calculated reply designed to pave the way for his emancipation proclamation.

Playing off Greeley's bluster, Lincoln struck a cautious and disciplined tone in his response. He explained that his original promise remained: "I would save the Union." This polestar—which had such widespread, bipartisan support at the outset of the war—still guided his decisions, even as he moved closer to grasping the nettle of slavery. But some people, he wrote, wished to preserve only the old "Union as it was," with slavery intact: "I do not agree with them." Other people wished to save the Union only if in the process slavery was abolished. "I do not agree with them. My paramount object in this struggle is to save the Union, and it is not either to save or to destroy slavery." Realizing that readers might interpret this as a statement of moral ambivalence, Lincoln warned that nothing he was saying changed his "oft-expressed personal wish that all men everywhere would be free." His policies, however, were designed to achieve the one goal that bound the North together through this unprecedented turmoil. "If I could save the Union without freeing any slave, I would do it; and if I could save it by freeing all the slaves, I would do it; and if I could save it by freeing some and leaving others alone, I would also do that."

Left unsaid—but well known to his readers—was the fact that many statesmen before him had tried for decades to save the Union without freeing any slaves, and their failures had paved the road to rebellion. Lincoln, for his part, had tried earlier in the year to start the emancipation process by voluntary means; that, too, had failed. Now he had decided to free some three million slaves in order to save the Union, and he had little doubt that his proclamation, when it was enforced by the Union armies, would lead to freedom for all slaves. As before, though, he kept the decision and its implications secret.

On a personal level, the "impatient and dictatorial tone" of Greeley's letter annoyed Lincoln. But the president had a deft answer for that, too. Instead of sending his reply directly to Greeley, to be published under a big headline in the *Tribune*, he sent it to another paper, the *National Intelligencer*. Greeley was forced to reprint it as day-old news.

Another attempt to sugar the pill of emancipation for reluctant Northerners went down less smoothly. On August 14, Lincoln sat down at the White House with a delegation of leaders from Washington's free black community to discuss the idea of moving members of their race to distant colonies. The topic had become a major issue among black residents thanks to that most familiar of devices: money. Twice that year, Congress had appropriated significant sums to get the colonization program moving. The fund now totaled $600,000, enough to attract a number of eager entrepreneurs. As one knowledgeable observer put it, the money was a "carcass over which the turkey buzzards are gathered together!"

Blacks in the capital were split over the idea of leaving America. Some were eager to say goodbye to a country where they were hated and exploited; others rejected the notion that they should have no place in a nation they had helped to build. The great abolitionist Frederick Douglass, himself a former slave, argued that blacks should not even consider the offensive proposal. His son Lewis, by contrast, found it quite appealing. The subject divided even Lincoln's own house. While the president was examining competing colonization proposals, his head servant, William Slade, led an organization that sought to ban recruiters for the colonization schemes from entering the capital.

Liberia, the colony of former slaves in West Africa, was one possible destination. Lincoln, however, was more intrigued with a plan to settle American blacks in what is now Panama, in the supposedly coal-rich region of Chiriqui. The idea was to build a U.S. Navy fueling station where steamers could take on coal. Mining, storing, and loading the coal would keep the immigrants employed. They might also be able to plant cotton.

Eager to explore this prospect, the president sent an emissary to a group of prominent Washington blacks, asking them to choose a delegation to meet with him. Five men were chosen—all of them opposed to colonization. It was a formidable group. One member, John Cook, was educated at Oberlin College before taking over a school for black children founded by his father. Another, Benjamin McCoy, had founded a church and school. The chairman, Edward Thomas, was a messenger in the House of Representatives and a patron of the arts who had "the respect and confidence of every member of Congress."

Lincoln apparently knew little about these men when he welcomed them to his office that afternoon. He asked: "Why should they leave the country?," then answered his own question: "You and we are different races." The antagonism created by this difference was real and deep, he continued. "Your race are suffering, in my judgment, the greatest wrong inflicted on any people," but "I cannot alter it if I would. It is a fact, about which we all think and feel alike, I and you." America was so far from racial harmony that "on this broad continent, not a single man of your race is made the equal of a single man of ours." Indeed, Lincoln went on, it was a mistake ever to bring captive Africans to North America, and now that mistake had led to the calamity of war: "our white men cutting one another's throats . . . [over] the institution of Slavery and the colored race. It is better for us both, therefore, to be separated."

No record has been found to show how the delegates reacted to these words; apparently they sat stoically while Lincoln talked. He went on at length about the need for free and educated blacks like them to embrace colonization as a way of creating opportunity for the "systematically oppressed" former slaves. They could be like George Washington, he said, who endured hardship to make a future for his people. Then he turned to the advantages he saw in the proposed Chiriqui colony: fine harbors and "very rich coal mines," which "will afford an opportunity for the inhabitants for immediate employment." The rest, Lincoln assured them, would come through "self-reliance."

History would vindicate Lincoln's pessimism about the prospects for racial equality after the war was over. Still, his stubborn pursuit of what he once called his "colonization hobby" was a rare case of Lincoln indulging a fantasy. "I am so far behind the Sumner lighthouse," he once admitted—meaning that he could not picture, as the Massachusetts abolitionist could, a future free of racial hatred and discrimination. Unable to see a sensible way forward, he wished the problem away on the implausible wings of a voluntary mass migration. Although he would eventually awaken from this strange (though widely shared) dream, for now he was still in the grip of it.

His visitors clearly were not. As the meeting adjourned, they gave a noncommittal promise to think about the president's proposal. News of the session stirred a storm of protest from abolitionists. But criticism from those quarters was not necessarily a bad thing: Lincoln's colonization hobby cost him little with the radicals who already scorned his efforts, and perhaps gained him some support from the all-important moderate center. Instead, African-Americans—the would-be George Washingtons who ultimately accepted the president's challenge—paid the price for the ill-conceived Chiriqui scheme. Hundreds, if not thousands, eventually signed up for the colony. "Many of us have sold our furniture, have given up our little homes to go on the first voyage," a group of them wrote when it became apparent a few months later that Honduras would not agree to have the colony planted next door. The fantasy of colonization fizzled, and their small savings were squandered for passage on a ship that never sailed.

"Mrs. L . . . is not well," Lincoln wrote on August 21. As a general matter, this was true more often than not, though the specifics of her malady on this particular day are unknown. Mary was perhaps tired after returning from a trip to New York and Boston, where she balanced shopping sprees with earnest efforts to raise donations for Washington's military hospitals. She may also have been privately grieving the death of her favorite half-brother, Alexander Todd, who had died two days earlier of wounds received while fighting the Yankees at Baton Rouge. "Oh Little Aleck, why had you to die?" Mary moaned when she got the news. The first lady usually put on a stony face when talking with others about the Rebels in her family tree. "He made his choice long ago," she once said coldly of Aleck. "He decided against my husband." But there can be little doubt that this sensitive and emotional woman gave in to sorrow when she was alone with her memories.

Mary's interest in spiritualism had deepened over the summer, and now she hosted a séance at the presidential cottage. Her dangerous attraction to flamboyantly shady characters had led her to a medium named Charles J. Colchester, who claimed to be the illegitimate son of an

English aristocrat and called himself "Lord Colchester." Spirits answered his summonses by making various noises in dark rooms, noises only he could translate.

Mary prevailed on her husband to attend Colchester's séance, and Lincoln in turn invited his friend Noah Brooks, a young journalist who later worked as his secretary. By Brooks's account, the circle sat rapt as the lights were doused. Soon, there were sounds of tapping and scratching that Colchester translated as messages from Willie. This may have been the night that Willie first fetched Aleck Todd to accompany him from the afterlife; Mary took special comfort from séances in which her son brought with him his exuberant red-haired uncle. Whatever transpired, it was enough to persuade Lincoln that Colchester was some sort of a fraud; he asked his science expert at the Smithsonian, Dr. Joseph Henry, to investigate.

Dr. Henry invited Colchester to conduct another séance, at which the scientist deduced that the medium must be wearing a device under his clothes that produced noises when he tensed his muscles. But Noah Brooks wanted to be sure, and he subsequently went with a friend to yet another of Colchester's sessions, where Brooks took his seat next to the spirit summoner. When the ghosts stirred up a ruckus of thumps and clanking, Brooks seized Colchester's hand in the dark. Several things happened almost simultaneously: Brooks called for his friend to strike a match; something hard whacked the journalist over the head; and the match flared to reveal a bell in Colchester's hand, poised over a small drum. Caught red-handed, the medium hinted that he had information with which to blackmail Mrs. Lincoln. Brooks, bleeding but delighted, threatened to have him arrested unless he left Washington immediately.

Even Colchester's exposure was not enough to persuade Mary that her fleeting contacts with her lost boy were figments of imagination and deceit. She preferred to feel that Willie—and Eddie, and her brothers Sam and Aleck, and Rebecca Pomroy's family, and the Stanton baby, and all the sons and husbands and fathers in rude graves at Manassas and Pea Ridge and Fort Donelson—were not entirely and forever gone. As she explained to Charles Sumner, she wished to believe that only "a very slight veil separates us from the loved and lost." The deceptions of spiritualism might offend men like her husband and Dr. Henry and Noah Brooks, but "to me there is comfort in the thought that though unseen by us" the dear departed "are very near."

A headline in New York said it baldly: "Mysterious Disappearance of the Rebels." Stonewall Jackson and his army had vanished before John Pope's eyes, and the anonymous reporter who wrote the accompanying story predicted that Jackson "may appear where he is least expected." Sure enough, on August 26, Fitzhugh Lee's cavalry led the way into Manassas Junction with Jackson's hungry Rebels marching behind. The Confederate troops had enjoyed a brisk hike down the Shenandoah Valley from Thoroughfare Gap to Front Royal, screened from view by the Blue Ridge Mountains as they eased past Pope's right flank. Now they moved quickly, plundering Union supply depots. Whooping and hollering, they filled wagons with captured food and ammunition, confiscated herds of horses and mules and beef cattle, and stuffed themselves and their knapsacks.

Like a man stung on the backside by a bee, Pope swung around angrily, not quite sure what had hurt him but determined to find and stomp it. As he wheeled, the Rebels in his front melted into the valley. Confused, Pope began retracing his steps toward Manassas, with enemy troops to his front, flank, and rear. Typically, however, he was brimming with confidence. Pope didn't know what he didn't know, nor did he much care.

The general's confusion spread quickly to Washington, because Jackson's men had cut the telegraph wires linking the army to the capital. Hoping for news of Pope's army, Lincoln went that night to the telegraph room at the War Department. He was prepared to stay until morning if need be, but the room was distressingly quiet. "Do you hear any thing from Pope?" he wired to Ambrose Burnside after a long and fruitless wait. "What news from the front?" he cabled McClellan. "Is the railroad bridge over Bull Run destroyed?" he asked Colonel Herman Haupt, the man in charge of Union trains.

Though he heard almost nothing from nearby sources, Lincoln did receive two urgent telegrams from Minnesota, bringing word of a fresh problem: Sioux warriors had gone to war against white settlers. They struck like lightning from a clear sky, raiding hamlets and farms across the southwestern part of the young state.

These bloody events had been some time coming, with roots that were sadly familiar. People who had once followed abundant game across unmarked prairies were now reduced to paltry lands and routinely cheated by U.S. agents. A week earlier, four hungry young Sioux had dared one another to take some chicken eggs belonging to a white farmer. Their taunts and challenges escalated until the young men had murdered an entire family of five settlers.

Sioux elders faced a decision: hand over the young braves to be punished, or follow their example and make the whites bleed. It wasn't an easy choice, for they knew resistance was futile. More whites would come; they always did. But if the Sioux were ever to fight, now was the ideal moment: as one chieftain put it, "All the white soldiers are in the south fighting other white soldiers." Thorns of grievance and honor spurred Chief Little Crow to war. The next morning, Sioux fighters raided a trading post near New Ulm on the Minnesota River; over the next few days, warriors tortured and killed several dozen men, women, and children, and then slaughtered twenty-four soldiers from the undermanned garrison at Fort Ridgely. On August 23, the settlers of New Ulm waged a day-long battle, holding off a Sioux army in house-to-house fighting. Thirty-four whites and an unknown number of Indians died, while a third of the little town was destroyed.

As the state militia stumbled to respond, Governor Alexander Ramsey appealed to the War Department for help. Could Stanton postpone Minnesota's deadline for delivering its quota of fresh troops for Southern battlefields and send a force of army regulars to Minnesota's rescue? Stanton was leery. He immediately suspected that Confederate agents were stirring up the Indians, and he was reluctant to give an inch to the enemy's designs. Ramsey tried a direct appeal to the president. "The Indian outbreak has come upon us suddenly. Half the population of the State are fugitives," he wired late on August 26. "No one not here can conceive the panic." As it happened, Nicolay was in Minnesota, having just arrived to investigate mistreatment of the Native Americans. He echoed Ramsey's assessment, warning Lincoln that, "a wild panic prevails in nearly one-half of the state."

Lincoln was a practical man; to him, pressing problems demanded workable solutions. A crisis was no time for stickling over rules. Now, while he canvassed for news of Pope's predicament, the president briskly sorted out the conflict between the frightened governor and the War Department. He could not give Minnesota a formal extension on its recruiting deadlines—that would set a terrible precedent; soon, every state would ask for one. But of course the deadline no longer applied. "Attend to the Indians," he advised Ramsey. "If the draft can *not* proceed, of course it *will* not proceed. Necessity knows no law."

Around nightfall on that same August 26, George McClellan stepped onto the wharf at Alexandria. Word of Jackson's raid at Manassas had just arrived. The general wasn't surprised to hear it, nor was he exactly disappointed. "I have a strong idea that Pope will be thrashed during the coming week," he had predicted before leaving the peninsula, and "very badly whipped he will be & ought to be—such a villain as he is ought to bring defeat upon any cause that employs him." Still smoldering during his last days at Berkeley plantation, McClellan had wondered how God allowed "the dolts in Wash[ington] . . . to *live,* much less to occupy the positions they do." But in Pope's troubles he saw fresh hope, for the dolts had grown fearful about their dangerous plan to move his army. After Halleck cabled him on August 21, pleading urgently for him to make haste, McClellan exulted to his wife: "I believe I have triumphed!!" Once again, the nation was calling him to the rescue.

He could not be the hero, though, unless John Pope was made the goat. Accordingly, when McClellan returned to Alexandria, he bubbled with plans for saving Washington but was notably lethargic when asked to send reinforcements to Pope. His first day back from the peninsula, he received orders from Halleck to put Franklin's corps on the road to Manassas. Little Mac answered that he couldn't comply; he had no artillery, and none of his cavalry had arrived. Instead, he peppered the general in chief with advice for protecting the capital. After a year spent poring over maps of Virginia, McClellan knew every fort and trench and road and village between Washington and the Rappahannock. But Halleck—whose short month in Washington had been eaten up with recruiting squabbles, the mess in the West, McClellan's foot-dragging, and Pope's peril—was in no mood just then for Little Mac's counsel, and eventually he snapped. "From your knowledge of the whole country about here, you can best act," he cabled. "I have no time for details."

That night, McClellan went to Washington, where he met with the already overfatigued Halleck until three A.M. After Little Mac's departure, Halleck dropped into bed believing that Franklin's corps would move to Pope's aid within hours, but another hot day dragged past while the Army of the Potomac sat still. Soon the sound of guns booming in the west let Washington know that Pope had stumbled into Jackson. Even now, McClellan found new reasons to decline to send troops. Better to concentrate around Washington and hold the capital, he advised the general in chief repeatedly. Halleck tried hectoring: at three thirty P.M. on August 28, he cabled McClellan, "Not a moment must be lost in pushing as large a force as possible toward Manassas." Four hours later he tried again: "There must be no further delay in moving Franklin's corps toward Manassas. They must go tomorrow morning, ready or not ready."

The next day, believing he had Jackson pinned down near the old Bull Run battlefield, Pope put all he had into breaking the Rebel line. Reinforcements would have been welcome, but Franklin's promised six A.M. departure from the Alexandria neighborhood turned into a one P.M. launch, and his trip to find the enemy quickly halted in peaceful Annandale, more than fifteen miles from the churning battle of Second Bull Run. McClellan explained to a flabbergasted Halleck that "it was not safe" to go any farther. Instead, Little Mac spent the day talking wildly of great hordes of Confederate troops in the vicinity of Washington; doubling reality, as he always seemed to do, he claimed that at least 120,000 Rebels lurked nearby. Rather than move Franklin and then Sumner's corps aggressively to Pope's support, McClellan gave orders to prepare the Chain Bridge over the Potomac for demolition in case Lee tried to cross into the capital.

Finding no help from McClellan, Pope looked to Fitz John Porter, who had fought so well in the Seven Days battles, to join the attack on Jackson's men. But Porter had grown strangely inert after his corps landed at Aquia Creek and was assigned to Pope's army. As the days went by, McClellan's pet managed to give many people the impression that he had no intention of helping the hated John Pope.

Lincoln was beside himself. "What news from the direction of Manassas?" he cabled Haupt, the railroad man. "Any further news?" he asked Burnside. And to McClellan: "What news?"

After more than five weeks of silence, Little Mac decided that now was a good time to resume communications with the president. And what the general chose to say on August 29 shocked Lincoln more deeply than any of McClellan's previous reckless statements. Though armies were clashing within earshot of the White House, McClellan responded to the president with a lecture. Saying that "one of two courses should be adopted," he advised the following: "Concentrate all our available forces to open communication with Pope," or "leave Pope to get out of his scrape" while making "the Capital perfectly safe. No middle course will now answer." In closing, Little Mac chirped: "Tell me what you wish me to do & I will do all in my power to accomplish it."

This was outrageous. For two and a half days, McClellan had been fending off orders precisely to concentrate his forces and open communications with Pope. How could he now claim he was keen to bend his powers in that direction? But if the general's eagerness to pursue the first option was questionable, Lincoln could only conclude that he was entirely serious about the second: McClellan was willing to allow a Union army to fight the enemy unaided while tens of thousands of well-rested, well-equipped reinforcements sat watching nearby.

John Hay rode his horse from the White House to the Soldiers' Home early the next morning and found Lincoln's mount already saddled in the yard. Within moments, the president came down the stone steps and put a big boot in the stirrup. He was eager to give voice to his emotions, and the quiet road into town seemed like a good place to do it. Lincoln was "very outspoken in regard to McClellan's present conduct," Hay noted. That appalling line from the general's telegram—"leave Pope to get out of his own scrape"—was seared in the president's memory and he quoted it perfectly. Nor was that all. He told Hay about McClellan's "dreadful panic" as he prepared to destroy the Chain Bridge (an order that the War Department had immediately reversed), and complained about "his incomprehensible interference with Franklin's corps."

Some thirty miles distant from the two men on horseback, Pope directed his troops on the Manassas plain. He was confident that this day, August 30, would be his glory. After the pounding his men and guns had given Jackson the day before, the Rebels had to be weak. Now Pope's Army of Virginia would stack its muscle on the right and deliver the decisive blow. He did not see the trouble to his left, where Longstreet was quietly emerging from behind the screen of the Blue Ridge Mountains.

Lincoln, suffering a blind spot of his own, was unable to see that his cabinet was on the verge of revolt. McClellan's poisonous return from the peninsula had catalyzed the grievances of these strong, frustrated, overworked men. Stanton was so furious when Little Mac halted Franklin's modest advance that he stormed to Chase's office and told him that McClellan must go. "He has long believed," Chase recorded, "and so have I, that Genl. McClellan ought not to be trusted with the command of any army of the Union; and the events of the last few days have greatly strengthened our judgment." But what could they do? It was pointless to complain to Abraham Lincoln. He listened and then did as he pleased. "Argument was useless," as Chase put it. "It was like throwing water on a duck's back."

But if Lincoln could ignore cabinet members one by one, he could not ignore them all at once. Stanton and Chase hatched a plan to gather signatures on a petition for McClellan's firing. Either the general must go, or the cabinet would collapse.

Even as Pope was throwing his roundhouse right at Jackson's entrenched lines, Stanton and Chase were drafting the petition, with help from Stanton's assistant secretary Peter Watson. When they finished, Chase carried the paper, written in Stanton's unmistakable hand, to the office of Gideon Welles, hoping to collect his signature. Welles was unpredictable. A former Hartford newspaper editor and a Democrat turned abolitionist Republican, he was perhaps the most unusual member of Lincoln's singular cabinet. With his flowing white beard and elaborate wig of curls, Welles was an easy man to ridicule. He also carried a large chip on his shoulder: he believed, not without justification, that his navy accomplished more than the army, and did it with far less, yet never received proper credit. Welles was therefore extremely skeptical of the army's tempestuous boss, Edwin Stanton. This was one reason why he began to smell a rat almost as soon as Chase opened his mouth.

To begin with, Welles said to Chase, the petition he was being asked to sign was intemperate, charging not just dereliction but treason. Welles agreed that McClellan should probably be fired, but he wasn't ready to insist on it. Why couldn't they just talk to Lincoln about this? he asked. Chase responded with surprising vehemence: "The time had arrived when the Cabinet must act with energy," he told Welles, "for either the Government or McClellan must go down." Chase detailed a string of offenses by the general, some of which were new to Welles; still, "this method of getting signatures . . . was repugnant" to the navy man. What about the others in the cabinet? Welles asked. Chase answered that the interior secretary, Caleb Smith, was ready to sign. Welles persisted: How about Attorney General Bates and Postmaster General Blair? "Not yet," Chase replied. "Their turn had not come."

As if on cue, Montgomery Blair walked in. Chase went pale. Noting the Treasury secretary's distress, Welles said nothing about the petition until the cabinet's most conservative member had finished his errand and gone away. Shouldn't we call him back? Welles now asked Chase. After all, Blair was the only member of the group who had military training. "No, not now," Chase blurted as he collected the unsigned letter from Welles. "It is best he should for the present know nothing of it." Chase strode from the room, then stepped back inside. He had a "special request": that the navy secretary tell no one about this meeting.

Lincoln, none the wiser, spent the day foraging for news from the front. Things seemed well enough. Colonel Haupt provided a steady stream of encouraging updates as Union supply trains pushed into Manassas and telegraph lines were repaired. Lincoln was waiting with Hay at Halleck's office when Stanton poked his head in and invited the pair to have lunch at his home. During the meal, the war secretary vented his anger about McClellan—though he never breathed a word about the circulating petition. When this fight was over, he declared, there should be a court-martial, for "nothing but foul play could lose us this battle." Afterward, Lincoln and Hay returned to Halleck's office to find the general in chief quietly confident that "the greatest battle of the Century" was under way and would yield a Union triumph. At about five P.M., hopes for a victory rose still higher when Haupt passed along a premature report that Jackson had surrendered.

Stanton, meanwhile, returned to the War Department, where he was not surprised to receive a visit from a very curious Gideon Welles. Caleb Smith of Interior was already there, and Stanton, still angry, treated his colleagues to a lengthy recitation of McClellan's offenses and his own manifold woes, dating back to his first day in the cabinet. He spoke of the chaos of Simon Cameron's mismanaged department; of $20 million in unpaid bills piled on his desk; and of this secretive, unstable, double-dealing general who "did nothing, but talked always vaguely and indefinitely and of various matters," though never of the matters that really counted. Stanton proceeded through the litany of the canal boats, the confusion over troops left behind to defend Washington, and the squelchy slog up the peninsula, where McClellan had promised the ground was always dry. The secretary retold the whole saga all the way up to the present moment when, "for twenty-four hours [Franklin's] large force remained stationary, hearing the whole time the guns of the battle."

Smith, already convinced, excused himself as soon as Stanton finished. Alone with Welles, Stanton lowered his voice conspiratorially. He had heard from Chase that Welles had "declined to sign the protest." How could Welles "not think we ought to get rid of him?" When Welles answered that the petition was "discourteous and disrespectful to the President," the war secretary almost shouted in reply. What did he, Edwin Stanton, owe the president? "He knew of no particular obligations he was under to" Abraham Lincoln, "who had called him to a difficult position and imposed upon him labors and responsibilities which no man could carry"—burdens made much heavier by the added weight of McClellan, "a commander who was constantly striving to embarrass him." Enough was enough, Stanton spat. "He would not submit to a continuance of this state of things."

That evening, Lincoln still thought victory was at hand—for Pope, and thus for himself. "Everything seemed to be going well and hilarious on Saturday & we went to bed expecting glad tidings at sunrise," Hay reported. In fact, the fight on the Bull Run battlefield was not going well at all: in the gloaming, just as Jackson's line began to crack, Longstreet unleashed his men on Pope's neglected left flank and upended the Union army.

The reversal happened so suddenly, so violently, that word rippled back to Washington in jumbled surges, and a full report came together only the next morning. At eight, as Hay was getting dressed in his tiny room off the president's office, Lincoln called out: "Well, John, we are whipped again, I'm afraid. The enemy reinforced on Pope and drove back his left wing and he has retired to Centerville, where he says he will be able to hold his men. I don't like that expression. I don't like to hear him admit that his men need holding."

As the streets of Washington began to fill with stragglers and runaways from the direction of the battlefield, Stanton's War Department issued orders to prepare all city churches to receive the wounded, and a call went out for government clerks willing to go to the front as nurses. Plans were announced to seize the mansion of the Washington banker and art collector W. W. Corcoran—a Confederate sympathizer—for use as a hospital. ("Malice," sniffed Corcoran's neighbor Gideon Welles. "Vandalism.") McClellan promised his wife he would try to rescue the family silver from their Washington home, lest it fall into the hands of Confederate invaders. Reports of roads jammed with fleeing soldiers brought back memories of the first defeat at Bull Run the previous summer, leading Lincoln to quip mordantly: "I've heard of 'knocking a person into the middle of next week,' but the rebels have knocked us into the middle of last year."

There was a difference, though, between that summer and this: by now Lincoln had seen too much of panic to tolerate any more. With Robert E. Lee's entire army somewhere near the capital, the president spent much of August 31 holed up in his office with Chase, diligently resolving the remaining squabbles over patronage plums under the new tax law. As the day wore on, word arrived from Centerville that Pope had organized a strong defense; emotions subsided a bit and Lincoln adopted, in Hay's words, "a singularly defiant tone of mind." Several times, he said: "We must hurt this enemy before it gets away." Many in the government had difficulty seeing this latest debacle as an opportunity; Hay, for one, thought the Union's situation looked bad, but when he tried to say so, Lincoln scolded him. "No, Mr. Hay. We must whip these people now. Pope must fight them [and] if they are too strong for him he can gradually retire to these fortifications" in Washington. Otherwise, "we may as well stop fighting."

The president still had heard nothing of the brewing cabinet revolt. Chase and Stanton had managed to bring Bates into their scheme by having him write a new version of their petition. They also had a new count to add to their indictment of McClellan: he had refused to send ammunition to the embattled Army of Virginia unless Pope pulled a sufficient force out of action to serve as guards for the supply train. "McClellan ought to be shot," Chase told Welles on September 1, when he went again to plead for the navy secretary's signature.

Despite that sentiment, the Bates draft was more measured and careful than Stanton's original. Welles was surprised that Bates would join the cabal, for his own view of the petition had only darkened since Saturday. "Reflection had more fully satisfied me that this method of conspiring to influence or control the President was repugnant . . . it was unusual, would be disrespectful, and would justly be deemed offensive." Chase's entreaties got him nowhere, for Welles was adamant. Further, as he studied the document and noticed a blank spot where William Seward's signature might go, Welles realized that he had no idea what had become of the secretary of state. He wasn't in Washington. Why? The more he pondered that question, the more Welles suspected that Seward was "purposely absent" precisely to avoid taking sides.

It was indeed an odd time for a vacation, but with Europe relatively quiet as aristocrats took their holidays, the secretary of state had traveled to Auburn, New York, for a brief visit home. The news that rivalries and resentments had poisoned Pope's offensive hit him hard. Before his departure, Seward had gone to Alexandria to see the Army of the Potomac arriving, and he believed that the Union's most perilous hours were past: those Federal legions seemed "invincible." After a lifetime of politics, Seward thought he knew what pettiness men were capable of, but this episode had left him genuinely disillusioned. Encountering John Hay on a Washington sidewalk after his return from New York, Seward asked glumly: "Mr. Hay, what is the use of growing old? You learn something of men and things but never until too late to use it. I have only just now found out what military jealousy is. . . . It never had occurred to me that any jealousy could prevent these generals from acting for their common fame and the welfare of the country."

Hay agreed, saying that it had not seemed possible that one American leader could all but abandon another in the heat of battle. "I don't see why you should have expected it," Seward countered. "You are not old. I should have known it."

Henry Halleck was likewise badly shaken. According to Lincoln, "he broke down—nerve and pluck all gone," reduced almost overnight from a general to "a first-rate clerk." At wit's end, Halleck pleaded with McClellan to come to Washington and tell him what to do. "I beg of you to assist me in this crisis with your ability and experience," he cabled to Alexandria late the night of August 31. "I am utterly tired out." Making matters worse, Halleck was suffering from acutely painful hemorrhoids, inflamed by the stress, and was treating his discomfort with a tincture of opium.

Like his unsteady general in chief, Lincoln saw no alternative but to work with the tools at hand. Reluctantly, he turned to the man who knew more about the defenses of Washington than any other: George McClellan. "Pope should have been sustained, but he was not," Lincoln later explained. "It was humiliating . . . to reward McClellan" by giving him command of the capital. However, "personal considerations must be sacrificed for the public good." On the morning of September 2, Lincoln once again placed McClellan at the head of the army in Washington.

As rumors began to spread that Little Mac was in authority rather than in disgrace, the cabinet uprising reached a dead end. Welles refused to sign the revised petition; Blair was apparently never even asked. Instead, the cabinet gathered at ten A.M. in Lincoln's office. While they were waiting for the president, Stanton hurried in. In a low and trembling voice, he confirmed that McClellan was back on top. Everyone began talking at once, and then into the room walked Lincoln.

Welles later confided to his diary that Lincoln began the meeting by saying he had "done what seemed to him best, and would be responsible for what he had done to the country." Looking at the shocked faces, the president quickly added that the appointment was only temporary. "McClellan knows this whole ground," Lincoln said. "He is a good engineer . . . there is no better organizer; he can be trusted to act on the defensive." True, McClellan suffered from "the slows," but that would not matter in this case.

The reaction was intense. Never, according to Welles, had the fractious cabinet been so "disturbed and desponding." Having given his explanation, Lincoln sat "greatly distressed" as Stanton, Chase, and the others loosed their anger and fears. "Giving the command to [McClellan] was equivalent to giving Washington to the rebels," Chase said finally. Only Blair agreed with Lincoln, and the postmaster general's reasoning was characteristic of his cool political calculation. They had all just seen how venomous army politics had become, and now tens of thousands of armed men—the partisans in that rivalry—were in and around the capital. Unless they believed in the general who led them, they would be an unreliable, even threatening, force. As Blair put it, McClellan "had beyond any [other] officer the confidence of the army."

Lincoln certainly saw it that way. "I must have McClellan to reorganize the army and bring it out of chaos," he said three days later. "There has been been a design, a purpose in breaking down Pope without regard of consequences to the country. It is shocking to see, and I know this, but there is no remedy at present. McClellan has the army with him."

Chase had vowed that either McClellan would go or the cabinet would collapse, but at least for the moment, both went wobbling forward. And then the stakes, higher than they had ever been, were raised again. Lee jabbed at Pope near Chantilly, and without warning anyone Pope pulled his men into the Washington fortifications, having seen the backs of no enemies whatsoever. In a flash, Lee was gone, northbound for Maryland, while in the West the Confederates invaded Kentucky. The Civil War reached its zero hour, and now Lincoln had no choice but to send the infuriating General George McClellan into the field in pursuit of Lee. John Dahlgren's lament spoke for multitudes: "Oh, for our country! Who shall save it?"

SEPTEMBER

Abraham Lincoln was not the sort of man who claimed to know the mind of God. "Probably it is to be my lot to go on in a twilight, feeling and reasoning my way through life," he once said. As a young man, he was "perplexed" by "the debatable wrangles" of religion, and for a time he was a notoriously outspoken skeptic. Over the years, he grew into a fatalist of the most profound sort: one who believes in divine destiny but does not limply surrender to it, who instead seeks to live meaningfully in harmony with the guiding current of history. Walt Whitman, who moved to Washington when his brother was wounded in battle later in 1862, would watch Lincoln riding along Vermont Avenue and come to feel that he knew the man. In his sorrow following the president's death, the great poet got close to an essential truth with his famous image of Lincoln as the captain of a storm-tossed ship. To steer a true course through violent seas, one must understand the wind and tides, despite being powerless to change them. So it was with Providence. "What is to be will be," Lincoln once said. "I have found all my life, as Hamlet says, 'There's a divinity that shapes our ends, rough-hew them how we will.'"

What was to be in that fateful September? The nation's future hung in the balance, as Confederate armies moved into the border states and European leaders shifted forward in their seats, alert to the critical moment at hand. Just as he had struggled in the winter to find the meaning in his son's death, Lincoln now tried to discern a divine purpose behind the string of failures and betrayals that made the summer of 1862 so miserable. At his desk one day in September, "his mind . . . burdened with the weightiest question of his life"—of slavery, the survival of the Union, and the role of each in the war—Lincoln took out a fresh sheet of lightly ruled paper and began writing down his thoughts. "The will of God prevails," he started, slowly and carefully. This was true by definition: if God exists, and God wills a result, then the result must come to pass. That is the nature of infinite power. Lincoln added a second proposition: "In great contests each party claims to act in accordance with the will of God."

From these two ideas, Lincoln began methodically building his analysis, brick by brick, writing more quickly and fluidly as he went. "Both sides *may* be, and one *must* be wrong. God can not be *for*, and *against* the same thing at the same time," he noted. "In the present civil war it is quite possible that God's purpose is something different from the purpose of either party." The Almighty might favor the North or the South—or neither side: Providence chooses its own goals. But the players in this great drama—the generals, whether effective or incompetent; the soldiers, brave or cowardly; the politicians and opinion makers, wise or foolish; indeed, all the "human instrumentalities" of the struggle, as Lincoln put it—must somehow perform the roles they had been given by the directing spirit of God. When John Pope met mutiny rather than triumph on the road to Richmond, it must be because God had something other than immediate Union victory in mind.

All this flowed logically from the first proposition: that the will of God prevails. Now Lincoln inserted a hedge. "I am almost ready to say that this is probably true"—*almost, probably*—"that God wills this contest, and wills that it shall not end yet." If one believed in a divinity shaping history, then it followed that God could have saved or destroyed the Union short of war, or ended the war already, without this painful seesaw struggle. "Yet the contest proceeds."

He put down his pen. Perhaps he was interrupted, or ran out of time, because he seems to have stopped abruptly. The final period at the end of his meditation was jabbed with such velocity that it looked more like a dash. Clearly, he wasn't finished, because the last sentence led so obviously, so irresistibly, to the next question: Why? Toward what end was this uncontrollable force moving? Nicolay and Hay, who discovered this unfinished rumination long after the president had folded it in half, and half again, observed that it had not been intended for others; it was Lincoln's way of ordering his own thoughts.

Yet these few lines suggest a first draft of what would become Lincoln's Second Inaugural Address. In that magnificent speech, delivered two and a half years later, he completed the chain of his logic. The contest proceeds, the president declared then, because "American slavery is one of those offenses which, in the providence of God, must needs come, but which, having continued through His appointed time, He now wills to remove." And because the offense was too large and too grave to be removed without suffering, God "gives to both North and South this terrible war as the woe due to those by whom the offense came." Slavery, Lincoln believed, was like a tumor on the neck of the American nation. Cutting it out might be fatal, but the patient would surely die if the cancer grew unchecked. Thus the president was led to conclude that God was prolonging and inflaming the war so that slavery could not survive the inferno. Providence had chosen to remove the cancer; Lincoln had no choice but to act accordingly.

He was *almost* ready to say this. But how could he be sure? As the Army of the Potomac, under the unreliable George McClellan, prepared to set out from Washington, Robert E. Lee was marching northward through the gentle Maryland countryside, where the first hint of yellow touched the dark green of the trees. Abraham Lincoln made an unspoken accommodation to this power beyond his own. It wasn't a bargain, exactly, because one cannot bargain with the wind. In making his commitment, he was more akin to a captain checking his position by a fixed star: if his calculations were correct, he would know which way to steer. He promised himself, as would later become clear, that if God willed a way for the Union to drive Lee back across the river, Lincoln would interpret the news as confirmation that the Almighty sought freedom for the slaves. And he, Abraham Lincoln, would be the human instrumentality of that divine will, making the war for the Union into an emancipating force unlike any the world had seen. He would follow that path to its end, in the conviction that God would have his way in his good time. And woe to all of them by whom the offense came, the blue as well as the gray.

As September began and stories flew of Confederate columns surging unchecked across Kentucky toward the Ohio River, it was Cincinnati's turn to panic. The governors of Indiana, Ohio, and Pennsylvania called for able-bodied men to grab their shotguns and squirrel rifles and join the home guard militia. Old Thomas Ewing rushed a request to the War Department for proper guns; back came a scrawled note from Henry Halleck: "We have no carbines and cannot get them immediately."

Washington, according to Gideon Welles, was "full of exciting, vague, and absurd rumors." Events were outpacing the capacity of wire and type to communicate them; the large gaps between slivers of fact were filled with fear and recrimination. "There are McClellan parties, and Pope parties and McDowell parties, and after their wranglings come thoughts of the bleeding country requiring every arm and train to save her from ruin and defeat," wrote one prominent Washingtonian. For his part, Lincoln decided that the quality of information in the capital was so poor that he would simply ignore most of it. One September day, his Illinois friend Leonard Swett appeared at his office door. The president asked how long Swett had been in town. When his friend replied that he had arrived the previous day, Lincoln brightened: "Sit down; I want to consult you. If you had been here a week I would not give a cent for your opinions."

When Seward returned from Auburn on September 3, the president spent three hours trading information with him, finally adjourning at midnight. No known account exists of their conversation, but afterward Seward sketched a grim picture for Adams in London. "Our late campaign in Virginia has failed," he wrote. The Rebels "seem to be threatening alike Washington, Baltimore," and Harrisburg, the capital of Pennsylvania. "The insurgents are equally bold" in the West, and "new energies are necessary to save the States of Tennessee and Kentucky for the Union, if not to prevent inroads in Ohio." Seward understood perfectly well that this catalog would incline the Europeans toward intervention, so he reminded Adams to let them know that such action would only drag them into the war. The North, it must be made clear, would not capitulate.

Others with whom Lincoln spoke in early September did record his views. Welles, for example, wrote that although the president was second-guessing himself about the decision to recall McClellan's army from Berkeley plantation, he also accepted that "wise or not . . . these things, right or wrong, had been done." And the plan could have worked, Lincoln added, if not for "military jealousies." Speaking of the second battle of Bull Run, Lincoln said: "We had the enemy in the hollow of our hands on Friday, if our generals, who are vexed with Pope, had done their duty." Instead, "these personal and professional quarrels came in." Now Pope would have to go, and McClellan was in charge again, because he "has the Army with him."

And what about that army? The ranks were in disarray. Soldiers who had signed up expecting a short war were leaking from their units in every direction. Fewer than half of the troops dispatched to Pope were still present and accounted for; McClellan, too, could find only about half of his army. Trying to fill the Federal ranks and keep them filled was "like shoveling fleas across a barnyard," Lincoln complained in his office one day. "There was no doubt that some of our men permitted themselves to be captured," in hopes that they would be paroled by the Rebels and sent home, the president concluded.

McClellan's reappearance in the capital was almost surreal. He "returned to his old Head Quarters, as if the disastrous expedition of near eight months had been only an absence of a few days," Chase wrote disgustedly. "He went out, as of old, to visit the fortifications and the troops," astride his dark steed, twirling his cap, basking in the cheers of his loyal soldiers. A furious John Pope asked for an audience with Lincoln on September 4, during which the scorned general presented a report of his ill-starred campaign that was less a battlefield account than "a manifesto, a narrative, tinged with wounded pride," as Welles described it. Pope asked permission to give his report to the newspapers. Instead, with the cabinet's agreement, Lincoln suppressed the blistering indictment, then reassigned his old friend to lead an army against the warring Sioux in far-off Minnesota. Pope's blundering leadership around Manassas had certainly earned him a demotion; still, this was hard treatment, especially unjust when compared with McClellan's. But in this instance justice was a luxury Lincoln could not afford. For the Union, the way ahead was simply too hazardous.

In Lexington, Kentucky, a mere eighty miles south of Cincinnati, the Rebel raider John Hunt Morgan had by now combined his troops with the army of Edmund Kirby Smith. On September 5, the overall Confederate commander in the West, Braxton Bragg, announced his own entry into the Bluegrass State. "The enemy is in full retreat, with consternation and demoralization devastating his ranks," Bragg boasted. "Kentuckians! The first great blow has been struck for your freedom."

Bragg's mission in Kentucky was both military and political. The military objective was to recover the Confederacy's losses from Grant's campaign on the Southern rivers. With every northbound mile secured by the Rebels, pursuing Union forces were pulled farther away from the territory secured in Alabama and Tennessee. Indeed, Buell was chasing Bragg away from Dixie with far more speed than he ever managed when he was moving south, and his goal was to get all the way to Louisville in time to prevent that crucial prize from falling to the enemy. Just like that, thousands of square miles gained for the Union in late winter were abandoned, along with the freedom of thousands of contrabands left behind. As for the political aspect of Bragg's plan, the general hoped to inspire an uprising of oppressed Kentucky citizens against the "Abolition tyrant" Lincoln. Bragg entered the state with wagons full of precious rifles to arm the legions of volunteers he expected to rally to his banner. Traveling behind him was Richard Hawes, the Confederate provisional governor of Kentucky. Bragg intended to oust the loyalist government when he reached the state capital, Frankfort, and install Hawes instead.

That same day, word reached Lincoln that Lee was crossing the upper Potomac into Maryland. Lee had significant concerns about his troops: the Confederate Army of Northern Virginia, he advised Jefferson Davis, was "not properly equipped for an invasion of an enemy's territory." The spoils of Manassas were all eaten up, and now the Rebels, subsisting on a diet of green corn, were ravenous. In addition, their uniforms were ragged and at least a quarter of them were barefoot. Like Bragg, however, Lee hoped for a warm welcome from the citizens of this slave state, and he counted on their help "in throwing off this foreign yoke" of Federal domination. As Lee's men splashed across the ford, his regimental bands struck up a fiercely anti-Lincoln anthem, "Maryland, My Maryland":

> She is not dead, nor deaf, nor dumb—
> Huzza! She spurns the Northern scum!

But Maryland apparently wanted nothing to do with these lean and battle-hardened men. When Stonewall Jackson led the Confederate columns down a gentle slope into the town of Frederick in the wide Monocacy

Valley, he found the streets empty, the houses closed, and the shops shut-tered. Lee was stoic about this cold-shoulder greeting but he banned enlisted men from the city in hopes of coaxing the locals to soften their resistance. "Overrun" by the Confederate army, "the citizens of Freder-icktown . . . [are] unwilling to open their stores," his order conceded. Therefore, no soldier could enter the town without written permission from his division commander. This gesture accomplished little: the inhabitants continued to spurn their would-be liberators, and Lee was able to scrape up only about fifteen hundred pairs of shoes (roughly a tenth as many as he urgently needed) and as many barrels of flour from western Maryland. "The supply of beef has been very small, and we have been able to procure no bacon." Among farmers and mill operators, there was "reluctance . . . to commit themselves in our favor," he told Davis.

As news of the Rebels' chilly reception spread to Washington and points north, it became a source of pride for the battered Union. Legends of defiance soon wrapped themselves around the simple facts. The poet John Greenleaf Whittier composed a ballad celebrating one such story, and generations of schoolchildren would eventually have to memorize it. Supposedly an elderly Frederick resident named Barbara Frietchie waved the Stars and Stripes defiantly as Jackson passed beneath her attic win-dow: "'Shoot, if you must, this old gray head/But spare your country's flag,' she said."

Jefferson Davis would later explain away the tepid response in the border states by saying that their citizens were cowed, and that they needed to see a victory by the Southern armies before they dared rise up against Lincoln. But the truth was more complex, and far more damag-ing to Southern hopes of independence. As summer had turned to autumn, the loyal slave states, which once wavered between South and North, had become emphatically more loyal than slave. "I may not have made as great a president as some other men," Lincoln said of his success in holding on to this crucial territory, "but I believe I have kept these dis-cordant elements together as well as anyone could."

The people of Kentucky, for example, had elected a loyalist state gov-ernment, and nine of the state's ten congressional seats were filled by Unionists. Kentucky was on its way to sending 100,000 men to the Fed-eral army. In part, this rejection of the Confederate cause reflected the thickly rooted patriotism of the birthplace of Henry Clay and Abraham

Lincoln. It also revealed a clear understanding of Kentucky's future interests. To side with the South would at best leave Kentucky as the eternally tense frontier between two fundamentally incompatible nations. If the South won the war, the planters of deep Dixie could presumably go back to growing their cotton in peace. Kentucky, however, would suffer the friction of inevitable grinding between the two countries as they clashed over such issues as runaway slaves, access to waterways, and ownership of western lands. But if Kentucky aided the successful restoration of the Union, the state could enjoy a prosperous future at the heart of a single, stable nation.

As for Maryland, Lee's reception there might have been friendlier had he taken his troops into the eastern part of the state, where the old aristocratic families still worked slaves on plantations. But geography made it difficult for Lee to head east, because the Army of Northern Virginia depended on the Shenandoah Valley as its lifeline for supplies and communication; a move toward eastern Maryland would have exposed this artery to be cut by Federal troops. Instead, Lee encountered the farmers of western Maryland, who had more in common—culturally, economically, and politically—with their Pennsylvania neighbors than they ever would have with the planters of the South.

The Confederate venture into the border states was a bold effort to win the war then and there. Had Maryland rallied to Lee, Washington, D.C., could have been cut off from the North. Had Kentucky flocked to Bragg, the Ohio River might have been closed. Either one of these outcomes would have been catastrophic for the Union; both together would likely have been fatal. But Lee and Bragg had succumbed to the same mistaken notions that hobbled the thinking of Lincoln and many of his advisers as they planned their southern invasion. Just as many Northerners trusted that a strong vein of Union loyalty ran through the South, so the Rebel generals were convinced that only the harsh hand of Lincoln choked off the border states' true Southern sympathies. On both sides, leaders wrongly believed that their foes were extremists who ruled by oppression and lacked popular support.

For the South, the implications of this error in judgment were profound. The Confederacy lacked the industrial might and the manpower necessary to maintain large armies for long periods in hostile territory. As a consequence, if the Confederacy could not win the contest for hearts and minds in the border states, the Rebels would be destined to fight for their independence primarily on their own territory, ravaging their own cities and their own lands.

Other influential audiences watched the Rebels advance, and their reactions also had the power to decide the war. Northern voters were preparing to choose the governors who would hear future calls for fresh troops, and the congressmen who would debate future war budgets. The first state to go to the polls was Maine, in early September, and the results were ominous for Lincoln: although the Republicans kept their grip on key offices, the party's share of the vote for governor dropped from 62 percent in 1860 to 53 percent now. Because very few states were as solidly Republican as Maine, a similar drop in the remaining Northern states would spell disaster for the president. Were such erosion to occur, it would give the Democratic opposition control of the House of Representatives and a majority of the statehouses.

Lee had these Northern voters in mind when he briefed Jefferson Davis after that disappointing reception in Frederick. Having failed to spark an uprising, he turned to a new strategy: he would "inflict injury" on the North in Pennsylvania, then offer a truce based on Southern independence. With that offer on the table, "the people of the United States [would] determine at their coming elections" whether to keep fighting or bring the war to an end. Lee understood—as his father's friend George Washington had understood—that he didn't have to conquer the enemy to be victorious. He only had to exhaust the enemy's confidence and its appetite for war.

A second attentive audience was, of course, Europe. The Union debacle at Bull Run and the Confederate advance into Kentucky at last persuaded Palmerston that it was time to intervene. He said as much in a letter to Russell, who was still on the Continent with the queen. The foreign minister felt the same; in his reply to Palmerston, he added that if the Union refused a mediated settlement, England should take the next step and recognize the Confederacy as an independent nation. At that point, Britain and France could supply the naval and industrial muscle the Confederates so desperately lacked. When that happened, the project of conquering the South—a project that was already staggering—would become impossible; the North would have to give up. Palmerston and

Russell agreed to put the topic at the top of the cabinet's agenda when they gathered again in October.

The military and political terrain had shifted yet again, and these first two weeks of September determined much of Richmond's strategy for the remainder of the war. The dream of sparking a pro-Confederacy uprising in the border states had fizzled, never to be seriously revived. With it died the South's strategy for winning an outright victory through its own efforts. The Rebels were left to rely on help from outside forces: exhausted Northern voters, emboldened foreign powers, or some combination of the two. That this was a milestone in the course of the conflict was not immediately apparent; as the days went by, the Rebels continued northward and Union armies moved to meet them on fields that would soon be hot with blood and gunfire. But the reconfigured landscape did sharply raise the stakes of these impending battles, because the stars seemed perfectly aligned to bring those outside forces into play. Northern elections were at hand. The Europeans were poised for action. The Rebels would never see a better chance to win foreign support and flay the morale of the North. This was their moment.

On September 6, units of the reorganized Army of the Potomac paraded up Pennsylvania Avenue toward the White House, only to make a sharp right turn before they got there. More than 20,000 troops all made the same ostentatious right face, then took a left onto H Street, which brought them past McClellan's house. The chesty little man in brass and blue basked in the music and salutes.

In a handful of days, the general had done an extraordinary job of putting the army back on its feet. This was, in the words of James McPherson, "perhaps his finest hour." Still, it wasn't clear what McClellan was up to. "There was design" in that detour, fretted Gideon Welles, whose own home was catty-corner from Little Mac's. From his front walk, Welles could look across H Street and over the heads of the marching men to see the proud McClellan in the foreground and—a block away, across Lafayette Square—the Executive Mansion. There was something ominous, something conspiratorial, about that scene. "They cheered the General lustily, instead of passing by the White House and honoring the President," Welles reported. Then, to the west of McClellan's place, the column turned right again to start up the hill toward Tennallytown and onward along the Rockville Pike into Maryland. They were off to hunt the invaders.

If Lincoln noticed the slight, he kept it to himself. What mattered most was that the troops were going after Lee rather than coming for his own head. The army was "becoming reckless and untameable," in the words of one close observer, and word was circulating at high levels in Washington "of a conspiracy on foot among certain generals for a revolution." Similar talk was rampant in New York. Lincoln took such threats in stride, but they strengthened his judgment that McClellan's clique did too much talking and too little fighting. Lee's foray into Union territory provided an opportunity to change that equation. The Rebels were sticking their necks out; where others saw only menace in the Confederate initiative, Lincoln saw an excellent chance to isolate them, cut them off, and crush them.

But for now all was uncertainty, and the pressure of the situation burst the weak seams holding Lincoln's cabinet together. Chase was furious at Welles for refusing to sign the demand for McClellan's ouster, and he blamed the navy secretary for the fact that "everything was going wrong [and] the country was ruined." Welles suspected Stanton of planting stories in the New York press to make the navy look bad whenever the army was in a bind. Caleb Smith of Interior turned on Seward as the source of all "misfortune and mismanagement." Montgomery Blair set on Stanton, spreading accusations that the war secretary was taking bribes. According to Welles, Blair began recruiting colleagues to help him force Stanton from office; it was time, Blair said, to "get this black terrier out of his kennel."

By this point, the bitter feelings had spread well beyond the cabinet itself. Blair, for instance, was the target, along with Seward, of a committee of abolitionists that called on Lincoln on September 10. The committee's spokesman, a distinguished New York lawyer named James Hamilton—a son of Alexander Hamilton—was Chase's houseguest while in Washington. Over breakfast before the meeting with Lincoln, Chase and Hamilton discussed Seward's supposed resistance to emancipation. In Chase's diary entry describing the conversation, he portrayed himself as Seward's stalwart defender. But that wasn't the message Hamilton heard. He left Chase's house so infected with anti-Seward feeling that the president sensed it from the moment the meeting began. As Hamilton launched into his presentation, Lincoln cut him off angrily. "It's plain enough what you want—you want to get Seward out of the Cabinet. There is not one of you who would not see the country ruined if you could turn out Seward."

Stanton, meanwhile, reserved his greatest frustration for Lincoln himself, who continued to display what he called "humiliating submissiveness" to McClellan. The president's latest notion was that he should ride out to the Maryland countryside for a chat with the general, whose army was creeping forward across a wide front in hopes of bumping into the Rebels.

As usual, McClellan was calling for reinforcements as he went. He grossly exaggerated the strength of the enemy, making himself the outnumbered underdog even though he actually led more than twice as many men as Lee. He again gave credence to mistaken reports that multitudes of Rebels were on their way from the West to make the odds against him still longer. In sum, the same calamitous thinking that crippled McClellan on the peninsula set in as soon as he marched away from the fortifications of Washington. The Rebels, he told Henry Halleck, "consist of their oldest regiments, and are commanded by their best Generals . . . their forces are numerically superior to ours by at least twenty-five percent. This, with the prestige of their recent successes, will, without doubt, inspire them with a confidence which will cause them to fight well." Therefore, McClellan continued, "at the risk of being considered slow and overcautious," he was calling for at least 25,000 additional troops. He certainly hoped to win the coming battle, but "if we should be so unfortunate as to meet with defeat, our country is at their mercy."

Stanton was enraged by McClellan's endless predictions of a withering battle against a mighty, if largely imaginary, host. And the president's continued efforts to inspire the general merely led to the fruitless pleading that the war secretary found so demeaning. Even now, Lincoln could pry scarcely a morsel of definitive information from McClellan—and this while being bombarded with frantic pleas for help from Kentucky and Pennsylvania, where authorities were packing up the state archives and Treasury for safekeeping in New York. By the rainy, sleepless night of September 12, the president was desperate for news from the front. "How does it look now?" he cabled Little Mac. The message, written at four A.M., never received an answer.

Later that morning, Salmon Chase began a difficult day by losing a rolled-up sheaf of embarrassing documents—an anti-McClellan memo and several pages of his gossipy journal—while on his way to work. "What if it should fall into the hands of somebody who will make public what is not designed for publication?" he agonized. At his office in the Treasury building, he found a mountain of unpaid bills waiting for him. Funding the war effort was as lonely as it was daunting. "Expenses are enormous, increasing instead of diminishing," he confided to his diary, "but neither the president, his counselors nor his commanding generals seem to care. They rush on from expense to expense and from defeat to defeat, heedless of the abyss of bankruptcy and ruin which yawns before us." Chase's lost papers were soon picked up in the street and returned, much to his relief, but any good feeling was erased by a summons to a cabinet meeting.

The president and his colleagues proved to be in moods as dark as Chase's. Lincoln's irritation, especially with McClellan, was apparent from the start. In the words of one participant, the cabinet engaged in "a long and free discussion of the condition of the army," during which the president lamented the fact that Ambrose Burnside had refused to take command. McClellan, Lincoln complained, "can't go ahead. He can't strike a blow. He got to Rockville, for instance, last Sunday night, and in four days he advanced to Middlebrook—ten miles, in pursuit of an invading enemy. This is rapid movement for him."

Others joined the grumbling. Welles theorized that the Union's problem was too many West Point graduates at the head of the armies. The well-trained engineers excelled at building fortifications, but they just weren't aggressive. This was a stale observation; people had been complaining about West Point generals for months. But Blair took the chance to defend his alma mater and criticize Stanton at the same time. There were plenty of good West Pointers, he said. The problem was a War Department that failed to find and promote them. "There was bluster," Blair asserted, "but not competency."

This sour meeting broke up having accomplished nothing, and Chase went to Stanton's office to commiserate. Why couldn't Lincoln be stronger? they asked each other. Why couldn't he dismiss the conniving Democrats from their field commands; why couldn't he free the slaves and enlist them as soldiers? It was obvious what needed to be done. Chase blamed Lincoln's "negrophobic" friends and advisers for leading him astray.

Seward, of course, was one of the advisers Chase had in mind. Two months ago, Lincoln had been on the cusp of emancipation; now, with McClellan and Buell once again ascendant, it seemed that the conservative Democrats were, if anything, stronger. And the critical voice at the key moment had been Seward's—it was he who had persuaded Lincoln to wait for a victory to issue an emancipation decree. That was the point, Chase felt, when the president seemed to lose his nerve.

The conflict between Chase and Seward was now so open and damaging that Seward's mentor—and Lincoln's frequent sounding board—Thurlow Weed decided to undertake a mission of peace. He called on Chase for "a long talk," during which Chase expressed his frustration that Seward was encouraging "the irresolution and inaction of the President." Weed implored Chase to mend fences with Seward and "agree on a definite line" that the two men could support together. The rumors of Seward's supposed resistance to emancipation were hurting him with his New York political base, Weed revealed. Hoping to play the mediator, Weed promised to relay Chase's complaints to Seward.

Weed's mission was doomed from the start. That Seward and Chase had legitimate differences concerning policy and strategy made the relationship challenging enough; worse, they were opposites in personality while being identical in scope of ambition. Conflict between them was inevitable. Welles summed up their differences nicely: "Seward was supple and dexterous; Chase was clumsy and strong. Seward made constant mistakes, but recovered with a facility that was wonderful and almost always without injury to himself; Chase committed fewer blunders, but persevered in them . . . often to his own serious detriment."

Chase resented Seward's easy relationship with Lincoln. Seward, in turn, took too much pleasure from tweaking the pompous Chase. For example on September 12, after Chase finished commiserating with Stanton, he paid a call on the secretary of state to dispose of a routine matter. Seward, ignoring Chase's businesslike demeanor, chose this moment to make a joke about emancipation. He knew that Chase was not a joking man, especially when it came to issues about which he was passionate, yet Seward quipped that if the Rebels invaded Pennsylvania, "the President should make a Proclamation . . . freeing all the apprentices in the state." Recounting this in his diary, Chase commented icily: "I thought the jest ill-timed."

Backbiting and squabbling were but symptoms of the disease of helplessness: as Little Mac plodded forward in search of the Rebels, there was little to do in Washington but wait. "Alas! Poor country," wrote Charles Sumner, capturing the mood of mid-September. "A vigorous ruler might have saved it."

A young artist for *Harper's Weekly,* Thomas Nast, was traveling with McClellan's staff that same September 12 when the general entered Frederick, Maryland, on his favorite horse, Dan Webster. Later Nast sketched the triumphal scene: American flags decking the buildings; cheering citizens filling the streets and waving from balconies; bouquets raining down on the soldiers; a mother thrusting her baby toward Little Mac, who gave his hat the trademark wave revealing cow-licked hair. The general enjoyed every moment. "I was nearly overwhelmed and pulled to pieces," McClellan reported to his wife, and he enclosed in his letter a "little flag that some enthusiastic lady thrust into or upon Dan's bridle. As to flowers!!— they came in crowds! In truth I was seldom more affected than by the scenes I saw [and] the reception I met with."

The general ordered his men to make camp in the farmlands outside town, which they were happy to do after months of hiking and camping in the hostile environs of Virginia. Tubs of lemonade and fresh-baked pies awaited them at nearly every farmhouse, and the women and children wore smiles on their faces. McClellan was taken with the beauty of the countryside: "one of the most lovely regions I have ever seen—quite broken with lovely valleys in all directions, & some fine mountains in the distance." Lee and his army lay beyond those mountains, gone somewhere to the west. Exactly where was a mystery, and in fact a few reports suggested that the Rebels had recrossed the Potomac to return to Virginia, greatly distressing Lincoln. "Please do not let him get off without being hurt," he telegraphed McClellan.

And how strong was Lee? Governor Andrew Curtin of Pennsylvania deployed a network of spies to find the answer, and his latest estimate was ludicrously high: as many as 190,000 Rebels in Maryland, plus 250,000 south of the river in Virginia, for a total of 440,000 men. The habit of exaggerating enemy forces had finally reached a peak; this was nearly ten times the actual number. Eyes rolled in Washington, but the hyperbole still did damage. This overstatement of Lee's strength by a factor of ten made McClellan's own inflated estimates seem modest. The truth—that

Union forces greatly outnumbered Confederates in the East—could gain little traction.

Saturday, September 13, found the Army of the Potomac resting happily along the Monocacy River outside the welcoming town of Frederick. Its general gazed at the fine, long ridge known as South Mountain and imagined legions of Rebel soldiers—unquestionably more men than McClellan was leading—on the other side, perhaps poised to spring a trap. But his side of the mountain could not be more pleasant, and this was enough to make a man reluctant to cross over. McClellan decided to wait for Lee to make the next move, and he therefore convened a meeting with leading citizens of Frederick to arrange what might be an extended stay for his army. In a wire to Halleck, McClellan promised: "Should the enemy go towards Penn[sylvania] I shall follow him."

As Little Mac was preparing to settle in, however, the strangest thing happened, a twist so unlikely that only history could write it with a straight face. Just outside Frederick, the 27th Indiana Volunteer Infantry Regiment made camp in a meadow that had been home, only days earlier, to Confederate troops under General Daniel H. Hill. Much of the field was still trampled flat, but in a tall patch of grass, a Union corporal named Barton Mitchell noticed a paper package with something inside. He picked it up and was glad, because the package held three fine cigars wrapped in paper. But this was not just any paper—the wrapping was covered in neat script under the heading: "Headquarters, Army of Northern Virginia, Special Orders, No. 191." With his friend Sergeant John Bloss, Corporal Mitchell began reading through various objectives assigned to men with familiar Rebel names: Jackson. Longstreet. Stuart. And at the bottom of the page appeared the most familiar name of all: "By command of Gen. R. E. Lee." The signature purported to be that of Lee's assistant adjutant general, R. H. Chilton.

No doubt the two soldiers understood that this cigar wrap, if genuine, represented an intelligence coup of staggering dimensions. The paper suggested that Lee's forces were widely divided on the other side of the mountains, with Jackson leading a detachment against Harpers Ferry while Lee and Longstreet took the rest of the men toward Hagerstown. They were all to meet up eventually at Boonsboro, but the boom of distant artillery from the direction of Harpers Ferry indicated that the reunion had not yet taken place. If this was true, the Federals now had a golden opportunity to attack the scattered Rebel forces and destroy them piece by piece. But how could anyone possibly know whether the paper was genuine?

The soldiers gave the paper to their captain, who gave it to his colonel, who took it to his general, who showed it to an aide. The aide noticed the signature and announced that he had known R. H. Chilton before the war and would recognize that handwriting anywhere. The document was rushed to McClellan's headquarters, where the general was in the middle of his meeting with town leaders. He studied the paper, then looked up and cried: "Now I know what to do!"

Lincoln was engaged that same day in a lengthy debate with a delegation of Chicago ministers who had come to Washington to plead for an emancipation decree. The president was nursing a sprained wrist after taking a fall; pained, he listened to all the familiar arguments in favor of such action. At points he jousted and parried, poking holes of doubt into the delegation's confidence. He did not think such a measure would be as popular as the ministers seemed to believe. Besides, what power did he have over Southern slaves when the Rebels were at large on Northern territory? "What *good* would a proclamation of emancipation from me do, especially as we are now situated?" he asked. "I do not want to issue a document that the whole world will see must necessarily be inoperative, like the Pope's bull against the comet." (There was a legend, widely known but eventually debunked, that in the fifteenth century Pope Callixtus III had issued an order excommunicating Halley's Comet.)

Back and forth they went until Lincoln ended the meeting on an ambiguous note. "I have not decided against a proclamation of liberty to the slaves," he allowed, "but hold the matter under advisement." The president had already told the delegates that he was accustomed to hearing from religious leaders on the topic of slavery, and he found it strange that while clergymen held every variety of opinion, all of them claimed to know "the Divine will." Why, Lincoln now wondered, didn't God take the forthright approach and reveal his intentions "directly to me, for, unless I am more deceived in myself than I often am, it is my earnest desire to know the will of Providence in this matter. *And if I can learn what it is I will do it!*"

The attending stenographer did not record that a pause followed, but it is reasonable to assume that there was one. Then Lincoln continued on a less declarative note: "These are not, however, the days of miracles, and I suppose it will be granted that I am not to expect a direct revelation. I must study the plain physical facts of the case, ascertain what is possible and learn what appears to be wise and right."

Would the discovery outside Frederick have qualified in Lincoln's ever rational mind as a "miracle," or simply as a "physical fact"? It was a package of cigars, after all, not a voice from a burning bush. Still, in this amalgam of coincidence and fortune, a very important "direct revelation" was received, and a scrap of rubbish in a Maryland meadow became the spark that ignited McClellan at the very moment of Lee's vulnerability.

Little Mac was elated. "Here is a paper with which if I cannot whip 'Bobbie Lee,' I will be willing to go home," the general crowed as the paper worked its electrifying magic. To the president he wired: "I hope for a great success if the plans of the Rebels remain unchanged."

McClellan moved as quickly as he could, which was not as quickly as some other generals might. He began by ordering William B. Franklin to take his corps to Harpers Ferry and rescue the garrison of 12,000 Union troops. With those forces added to his own, Franklin was to mop up Stonewall Jackson's column. It was a perfectly fine plan, but time was of the essence—and McClellan instructed Franklin to get started the next morning. He seemed to have forgotten that soldiers can march at night.

And he, too, stayed overnight in Frederick before setting off on Sunday, September 14, with some 70,000 men, marching in the direction of Hagerstown to snuff out Longstreet and Lee. But the Rebels had made one crucial adjustment in the roughly eighteen hours between the discovery in the meadow and the Union advance. Word of McClellan's good fortune had traveled from a Confederate spy in Frederick to Lee's headquarters, and now Lee was also on the move, embarking on a desperate race to minimize the damage.

He ordered troops into the South Mountain passes, Crampton's Gap and Turner's Gap, to slow the Federals down. Firing downhill at the bluecoats struggling up, the Rebels exacted a high toll for passage over the ridge, chewed up time until darkness fell, and then slipped away. McClellan, watching the fighting from a distance, saw not tactical resistance but bracing confirmation that Lee's army was immense. When Monday dawned and the Federals went through the passes and down into another picturesque valley, Little Mac figured that he was in the presence of more than 100,000 invisible Rebels. Lee, at the same moment, was taking his troops toward a ford in the Potomac where he planned to cross into Virginia, rejoin Jackson, and thus bring his actual strength up to about 43,000. By overestimating the size of the Rebel forces yet again, McClellan erased his substantial advantage over Lee's regrouping army. Instead of attacking, he held back.

Then Lee received word that the Harpers Ferry garrison had surrendered to Jackson before Franklin could reach it, which meant it was no longer necessary to suffer the ignominy of retreating over the river. Jackson could now come to him, here at the farm town of Sharpsburg, behind a winding stream called Antietam Creek. The Rebels spread themselves out and tried to appear numerous while waiting for Jackson to reinforce them. In the meantime, the Federals slowly filled the fields on the other side of the creek and awaited their orders. Night fell.

When Tuesday came up from behind the mountains, a heavy fog lay over the tense fields. Jackson, having left a regiment behind at Harpers Ferry to process prisoners and pack up spoils, crossed the Potomac and formed his men on Lee's left flank. Longstreet arrayed his divisions on the Confederate right. McClellan, meanwhile, polished his plans, which needed to be perfect because he was so badly outnumbered. Only at the end of the day did he finally set his forces in motion: sidling to his right, he accomplished little more than to show Lee where the first blow would fall.

Wednesday, September 17, 1862. The bloodiest day in American history arrived in the middle of a night "so dark, so obscure, so mysterious, so uncertain . . . that there was a half-dreamy sensation about it all," one general wrote. At the presidential cottage, Abraham Lincoln's shallow sleep was troubled by the same "strange dream" that had welled up before Fort Sumter and the first battle of Bull Run. A friend recalled Lincoln's description: "He seemed to be in some singular, indescribable vessel, and . . . he was moving with great rapidity"—where, he did not know. As the president tossed and turned, frightened men pulled on their boots beside the creek and shuffled the stiffness out of their legs and backs. Beneath a dawning sky, the soldiers of I Corps under Major General Joseph Hooker fell in and shouldered their rifles. Led by the black-hatted brigade under the command of John Gibbon—the brigadier general Lincoln had challenged to write the decline and fall of the Confederacy—the three divisions set off down the Hagerstown Turnpike toward the left wing of Lee's army.

There they entered the mouth of hell. "No tongue can tell, no mind conceive, no pen portray the horrible sights I witnessed this morning," a veteran of the battle of Antietam wrote. Yet certain images endure, searing themselves into the imaginations of generation after generation. Of a cornfield stripped bare by storms of gunfire, "cut as closely as with a knife," as one officer described it, the fallen men in rows as neat as the sheared stalks. Of a sunken road gradually filling with Rebel corpses as wave after wave of Union soldiers crashed and broke against it. Of Burnside's IX Corps bottled up at a bridge where one attempt after another to cross ended in a lead hailstorm falling from the bluff overhead.

As the sun rose, flamed, and sank, the awful battle ranged across the entire Confederate front, men dropping by scores, then hundreds, then thousands. If McClellan had managed to feed his troops into the inferno all at once, left, right, and center, he would have crumpled the Army of Northern Virginia once and for all. But such precise coordination is simple only in theory; on actual Civil War battlefields it was virtually nonexistent. Hooker's attack on the Rebel left at dawn was largely spent by the time Sumner and Franklin pushed their men toward the Hagerstown road around nine A.M. The assault on the center consumed the midday, while on the Confederate right, a somewhat sluggish Burnside wasn't over his bridge and charging ahead until late afternoon. Lee, cool and ruthless, shifted his dwindling numbers from point to point along the line. At least twice the Federals actually broke through the butternut wall, and if McClellan had been bold enough to throw his reserves at these cracks, he might have finished matters. But McClellan feared the size of Lee's own reserves, and again he held back. No doubt Little Mac felt vindicated when, at the end of the day, a column of fresh Rebels appeared from the south to halt Burnside's advance just as he was driving Longstreet's weakened line back through the streets of Sharpsburg. Those late-arriving Southern troops weren't reserves or reinforcements, however; this was the regiment Jackson had left behind to wrap up business at Harpers Ferry. They were the last Rebel soldiers for miles and miles, but they were sufficient to bring the horrific day to an end.

Some fourteen hours after it began, the battle was over. Darkness fell,

and the night filled with moans and shouted curses and the screams of
men in field hospitals having their maimed limbs cut off. Dead on the
blasted battlefield lay some 2,100 Union soldiers and as many as 2,700
Confederates. Approximately 18,000 men were wounded, at least 2,000
of them mortally. The total of dead, wounded, and missing men exceeded
25,000.

Two decimated armies now occupied the same side of Antietam Creek,
eyeball to eyeball, with the wide Potomac at Lee's back and just one crossing available for his escape to Virginia. Lee had perhaps 30,000 uninjured soldiers, all of them exhausted. McClellan, reinforced on September
18 by 13,000 new arrivals, had more than 90,000 troops, some 33,000 of
them fresh. With more fresh troops than Lee had troops in all, the Federals now outnumbered their foes by about three to one. A sharp push on
the Confederate right might allow the Union to cut the road to the river
crossing and trap the bloodied, starving Rebels.

Lee, bluff and unyielding, stared at his opponent and did not move.
McClellan, having wired both the War Department and his wife to say
that he planned to renew the battle that day, stared back. Victory lay
before his eyes, but all he saw was disaster. "I am aware of the fact that,
under ordinary circumstances, a general is expected to risk a battle if he
has a reasonable prospect of success," McClellan later explained. "But at
this critical juncture" he needed nothing less than "absolute assurance of
success. At that moment—Virginia lost, Washington menaced, Maryland invaded—the national cause could afford no risk of defeat," he
wrote. "One battle lost, and almost all would have been lost. Lee's army
might then have marched as it pleased on Washington, Baltimore, Philadelphia, or New York . . . and nowhere east of the Alleghanies was there
another organized force able to arrest its march."

It is tempting to second-guess McClellan's decision not to deliver
what could have been a crushing blow. But in fairness to the general and
his circumstances, the fighting of September 17 had left the Union command stunned and partially decapitated; many generals and colonels had
been killed or wounded, and their regiments were scattered and bloody.
George Meade, who took over command of I Corps from a wounded Joe
Hooker, reported that half his force was gone by the morning of September 18, and the half that remained was in no mood to attack. "I do not

think their morale is as good for an offensive as a defensive movement," he warned. Burnside, for his part, was nervously weighing whether to pull back from his position on the Rebel right; pushing forward seemed out of the question.

McClellan, moreover, was whipsawed: the speed with which the military situation had reversed was deeply disorienting. On September 12, Governor Curtin of Pennsylvania had estimated that the Rebel force numbered 440,000; now, a bare six days later, Lee was down to his last 30,000 uninjured men, a single day's hard fighting from destruction. How was such an astounding change of fortune possible? McClellan's inability to recognize and absorb this sudden shift brought on a resurgence of both his natural caution and his fear of failure. So he did nothing on September 18, and he continued to do nothing as Lee marched his army across the ford and into Virginia that night.

Lincoln, too, struggled to understand what was going on, and the seventy miles between Washington and Sharpsburg might as well have been a thousand. "Few and foggy dispatches" made their way from the scene, according to Welles. "The battle of Antietam was fought Wednesday," Lincoln later recalled, "and until Saturday I could not find out whether we had gained a victory or lost a battle." Even then, when the president studied the morning report for Saturday, September 20, he wasn't entirely sure how to think about what had happened. The accounting provided by the Army of the Potomac showed 93,149 men currently present for duty in and around the vicinity of Antietam Creek. As Lincoln's secretaries put it, the president "could not but feel that the result was not commensurate with the efforts made and the resources deployed."

One fact was beyond mistaking, however: Lee was once again on the Virginia side of the Potomac River, less than two weeks after his invasion had begun. Now Lincoln had a promise to keep. As he told one congressman: "When Lee came over the river, I made a resolution that if McClellan drove him back I would send the proclamation after him." The president took his latest draft from his desk and went to work. A visitor to the White House on Sunday evening reported being turned away; Lincoln was too busy writing to see anyone. Referring to the document that so absorbed him, the president later explained that he was "fix[ing] it up a little, and Monday I let them have it."

In Kentucky, Don Carlos Buell spent the early part of September racing neck and neck with Braxton Bragg on parallel paths through the forested hills where Lincoln was born and spent his boyhood. Ulysses Grant, meanwhile, sent Buell all the reinforcements he could gather, and soon he was down to his last 50,000 men, most of them scattered through hostile territory. Sitting in Corinth and becoming ever more vulnerable as Buell's army receded, Grant began to worry. As he feared, the Rebels noticed his predicament. Generals Sterling Price and Earl Van Dorn, fugitives from Missouri and Arkansas, decided to combine the remaining Confederate forces in Mississippi, whip Grant, and launch a third Rebel advance in support of Bragg and Lee.

Rather than wait to be attacked, Grant struck first. As the battle of Antietam was raging in the East, he sent two converging columns toward the little town of Iuka, Mississippi, where Price was camped. Grant planned to bring the columns together like a hammer on an anvil; but, as with McClellan's beautifully synchronized assault near Sharpsburg, Grant's design worked only on paper. The column led by Brigadier General William Rosecrans bogged down on muddy roads and didn't reach Iuka until September 19. There, Rosecrans clashed with Price, but the wind was wrong and the humid air served as a muffler, so the second column never heard the noise of the first column's guns and thus never joined the battle. Price was bloodied, yet Grant's problem remained.

But then the Union got lucky: Bragg decided that he wasn't interested in fighting Buell for possession of Louisville. He halted his army in northern Kentucky and let the Federals have the city and its fortifications. Promptly taking up occupancy, Buell was hailed as the savior of the Ohio River. But he showed little inclination to leave the place, which he would have to do if he was going to push the Rebels back. Lincoln's patience with Buell, already thin, abruptly ran out; he ordered Halleck to fire Buell and replace him with George Thomas, who had proved his mettle by winning in January at Mill Springs.

The order proved premature. Buell was hatching an offensive, and Thomas, informed of his promotion, begged Washington not to swap generals in the middle of a crisis. Politicians in Kentucky and Ohio also peppered Lincoln with protests. Backing down as quickly as he had snapped, the president left Buell in command but living on borrowed time. Buell decided to make the most of the reprieve. At the end of September, he set off in pursuit of Bragg, who was on his way to Frankfort to establish his Rebel-friendly government.

A little after nine A.M. on Monday, September 22, Seward sent messengers to his fellow cabinet members, alerting them that Lincoln wanted to see them all at noon. At the appointed hour, "there was some general talk," Chase reported, as the council collected around the table in the president's office. Lincoln held up a prized possession: his brand-new copy of the latest book by Charles Farrar Browne, his favorite humorist. Browne was better known by his pen name, Artemus Ward, a screwball character who delighted audiences with his misspellings, malapropisms, and daffy adventures as proprietor of a traveling menagerie and wax museum. The president opened the book to page 34 and began to read aloud. "Highhanded Outrage at Utica" was a very short story recounting Ward's "recepshun" in that "trooly grate" upstate New York city. Things went wrong, however, when a "big burly feller" mistook Ward's wax model of Judas Iscariot for the actual betrayer of Jesus Christ. The man dragged the statue from its display and smashed it, whereupon Ward filed a lawsuit. The jury ultimately delivered a verdict "of Arson in the 3d degree."

Lincoln roared. His laugh, in the words of one who knew him, "stood by itself. The 'neigh' of a horse on his native prairie is not more undisguised and hearty." Laughter was "the President's life-preserver," his answer to "the temporary excitement and relief which another man would have found in a glass of wine." The reaction of the cabinet to Lincoln's recitation is a matter of some dispute. Chase reported that they all were amused except for dour Edwin Stanton. According to Stanton, though, no one laughed, not even Seward. By Stanton's account, Lincoln responded to the silence by asking: "Why don't you laugh? With the fearful strain that is on me night and day, if I did not laugh I should die, and you need this medicine as much as I do."

At last the president grew serious. "Gentlemen, I have—as you are aware—thought a great deal about the relation of this war to Slavery," recorded Chase. Everyone in the room recalled that Lincoln had been prepared to use his war powers to order freedom for slaves in Rebel territory; since putting his order aside in July, he continued, "my mind has been much occupied with this subject," even as he watched for the right moment to issue the decree. "I think the time has come now. I wish it were a better time. I wish that we were in better condition. The action of the army against the Rebels has not been quite what I should have best liked. But they have been driven out of Maryland, and Pennsylvania is no longer in danger of invasion."

There was more to the story, and this part he told gingerly, as if he wasn't sure how much to admit. As Welles reported it, Lincoln said he "had made a vow, a covenant, that if God gave us the victory in the approaching battle, he would consider it an indication of Divine will, that it was his duty to move forward in the cause of emancipation."

"I said nothing to anyone," Lincoln explained to his colleagues, "but I made a promise to myself, and"—here, according to Chase, Lincoln hesitated—"to my Maker."

This confession was out of character, and Lincoln worried that some might think it "strange that he had in this way submitted the disposal of matters when the way was not clear to his mind." Strange or not, though, Lincoln said that he was now completely convinced that "God had decided this question in favor of the slaves." And because of his vow and God's answer, Welles wrote later, Lincoln "was satisfied it was right, was confirmed and strengthened in his action. . . . His mind was fixed, his decision made."

He was not, therefore, interested in hearing his colleagues' thoughts "about the main matter." He knew their views already. What he wanted to do was read what he had written and hear their suggestions for improvements. Before he did, however, he wished to make "one other observation." "I know very well," he said, "that many might . . . do better than I can." He acknowledged that his popular support was weakened, but added that "all things considered, [no] other person has more." He had sought this office, and though he could not have imagined what the job would require, only he could execute its duties. As Chase remembered it, Lincoln then said: "I am here. I must do the best I can, and bear the responsibility."

With that, he launched into his reading. This revised version of the Emancipation Proclamation was similar to the one the cabinet had heard in July, but Lincoln was no longer leaning on Congress or the Confiscation Act. The proclamation was entirely a statement of military policy, an exercise of his constitutional power to take all actions necessary to put down an insurrection. Further, the order's key phrase had been moved closer to the beginning: in the proclamation's third paragraph, Lincoln decreed that on January 1, 1863, all slaves held in territory under rebellion "shall be then, thenceforward, and forever free." Ominously for Southerners who lived in fear of a slave uprising, he declared that the government, including the army and navy, would "do no act or acts" to interfere with "any efforts [the slaves] may make for their actual freedom." No one representing the Federal government could return any former slave to bondage in Rebel territory, nor would generals be allowed to ask whether the slave owners were loyalists. Any loyal slaveholders who hoped to avoid emancipation must persuade their neighbors to return to the Union by New Year's Day. As in the previous version of the proclamation, Lincoln's order would not apply to loyal territory.

When the president finished reading, all eyes turned to the secretary of state. "The general question having been decided, nothing can be said further about that," Seward began. He then offered a proposal that may have been surprising, given that he was often accused of being a principal impediment to emancipation. Lincoln had written that the government would "recognize" the freedom of the former slaves; wouldn't it be better, Seward asked, to say, "recognize *and maintain*"? This brief addition, which the president approved, packed a wallop, for it committed the United States not just to proclaim freedom, but to enforce it. Welles was impressed. Having suspected Seward of opposing an emancipation decree, he now saw that "in the final discussion he has . . . cordially supported the measure."

Chase spoke next and gave his own approval, though he couldn't resist pointing out that he would have done a few things differently. Welles also endorsed the decree, although he had no illusions that it would lead to a quick victory. "The subject has, from its magnitude and its consequences, oppressed me," Welles confessed later, for he was sure that it would guarantee a long, terrible conflict, a war of subjugation to destroy a way of life and an economic system. Though "desirable," Welles concluded, Lincoln's proclamation was "an arbitrary and despotic measure in the cause of freedom."

When no one offered criticism of the measure, Lincoln handed the paper to Seward with instructions to publish it the next day. Montgomery Blair now spoke up. He began by asking permission to publish his own written statement against the proclamation, which he had given to Lincoln "some days since." It wasn't that he opposed freedom for slaves, Blair said; on the contrary, he had always been in favor of abolition.

Instead, he was terribly concerned about the impact this proclamation would have in the border states and in the army. "The results," he predicted, "would be to carry over [the loyal slave states] *en masse* to the Secessionists." At the same time, he added, the executive order would hand the Democrats "a club . . . to beat the Administration."

Lincoln was quiet. This wasn't the right moment to reveal just how sharply he felt those same worries. "When I issued that proclamation, I was in great doubt about it myself," he later admitted. "I did not think that the people had been quite educated up to it, and I feared its effects on the Border States. Yet I think it was right. I knew it would help our cause in Europe." In any event, the time for second-guessing was past. Lincoln's capacity for thinking and rethinking was great—but not endless. Determined to go forward, he left Blair's fears hanging there in the room.

Abraham Lincoln's preliminary Emancipation Proclamation was published on September 23 to an immediate storm of protest and praise. Charles Sumner spoke for many abolitionists when he declared that "the skies are brighter and the air is purer, now that slavery has been handed over to judgment." Frederick Douglass was less enthusiastic, remarking that the dry document contained not "one word of regret and shame that this accursed system had remained for long the disgrace and scandal of the Republic." Vice President Hannibal Hamlin was awed: "It will stand as the great act of the age."

Many felt otherwise. In Lincoln's home state of Illinois, the *Macomb Eagle* snorted: "Hoop de-dooden-do! The niggers are free!" Critics of the proclamation attacked it from every direction: The decree was hollow. It was tyrannous. It would unleash a storm of murder and rape across the South. It would flood the North with inferior black refugees. Lincoln did not put much stock in the angry newspaper editorials. When Hay raised the subject after the first round had been published, Lincoln simply replied that he "knew more about it than they did."

Among other things, he knew he was in for a rough ride. "At last we have got our harpoon fairly into the monster," he told a visitor, "but now we must look how we steer, or with one flop of his tail, he will yet send us into eternity." A parade of Washingtonians, celebrating the proclamation with a marching band, paused outside the White House on the day after the decree was released. When they called for a speech, Lincoln said a few

words and then apologized for his brevity: "In my position, I am environed with difficulties." Four days later, replying to Hamlin's note of con-
gratulations, he elaborated. "The stocks have declined, and troops have
come forward more slowly than ever. This, looked soberly in the face, is
not very satisfactory."

Environed with difficulties, but no longer quite so alone. The millions
pleased with Lincoln's decision felt fresh admiration for their president
and a new dedication to the Union cause. The governors of the loyal
states had been planning a meeting to formulate a shared war policy that
might stiffen Lincoln's spine, but now he had shown an oaken backbone
and they threw out their old agenda. Instead, gathering on September 23
and 24 at the big new hotel in Altoona, Pennsylvania, the governors
almost unanimously endorsed Lincoln and his executive order, and then
headed for Washington to tell him so in person.

Emancipation was now front and center as an election issue, so this
sign of solidarity in the Union coalition was a comfort to the president.
But with antiwar agitation on the rise in many Northern states, Lincoln
followed his radical proclamation by issuing a second extraordinary and
dangerous decree: he ordered the military to arrest any persons believed
to be "discouraging volunteer enlistments, resisting militia drafts, or
guilty of any disloyal practice, affording aid and comfort to Rebels." Furthermore, he invoked the power that Congress had granted him to suspend the writ of habeas corpus, the constitutional guarantee that protects
Americans from unlawful imprisonment. (This was not the first time he
had done so: he had issued an executive order suspending the writ at the
beginning of the war, but it had been deemed unconstitutional by Chief
Justice Taney, who ruled that only Congress could grant him that authority.) The message was clear: Lincoln would not fight the battle for public
opinion with words alone.

Lincoln knew that the Emancipation Proclamation marked a critical
moment in the nation's history. By publishing it and announcing his
intention to free all the Confederacy's slaves at the start of the following
year, the president placed a fateful wager on the willingness of the North
to see a hard war through to total victory. He acknowledged what the
Southern secessionists had affirmed when they broke from the Union:
that slavery could no longer be negotiated or compromised away. Either
slavery must go or the Union must go; they could not coexist. What was
more, Lincoln's bet must pay off twice—among the military and at the

ballot box—or it would pay off not at all. With Antietam behind him and
the elections looming, the next several months would tell whether his
wager would succeed.

The military outcome of Lincoln's gamble rested on the banks of the
Potomac, where McClellan's army licked its wounds within a few miles of
Lee and his Rebels. In those quiet camps, McClellan brooded on his
future under a president who had promulgated "such an accursed doctrine." He doubted it was possible to "retain my commission & self respect
at the same time."

His mood dark, the general was cheered by a visit from a delegation of
friendly New York Democrats—the same ones who had met with him on
the peninsula during the slow days of July. Led by the antiwar former
mayor of New York City, Fernando Wood, they had come to Sharpsburg
to persuade McClellan to run for president in 1864. As one of McClellan's
associates later told Lincoln, the delegation proposed that the general run
on a platform promising reconciliation between North and South. But if
that platform was to be viable two years hence, the war had to slow down.
Hostilities must be held in check, hard-war policies somehow softened.
No peaceful settlement between the combatants could be possible where
all common ground was laid waste. Two months earlier, McClellan had
demurred, the general's associate told Lincoln, but at Sharpsburg he
finally accepted the proposal.

This meeting and its outcome may have been the root of a shocking
report that ripped through Washington on September 24. An officer on
McClellan's staff, Major John Key, was quoted as telling the judge advocate, Levi Turner, that Lee's army wasn't "bagged" at Antietam because
"That is not the game." Key allegedly went on to say that "the game"
called for McClellan's army to "tire the rebels out, and ourselves." Why?
Because "that was the only way the Union could be preserved, we come
together fraternally, and slavery be saved."

Lincoln, disgusted by all the loose talk from McClellan's people,
determined that Key should be made an example. He summoned the
young major and demanded to know whether the offending words had
been spoken. Key tried to put a loyal face on his remarks, but the president was not appeased. "If there was a 'game' ever among Union men, to

have our army not take advantage of the enemy when it could," Lincoln said angrily, it was his object "to break up that game." He cashiered Key.

That was all well and good and forceful, but when September ended and Key was gone, McClellan was still resting in the valley of the fresh graves. The enemy was nearby, but no one was making an effort to take advantage of his weakness. For all Lincoln knew, then, the game was still on. And if that was the case, he had no choice but to break it up at a higher level.

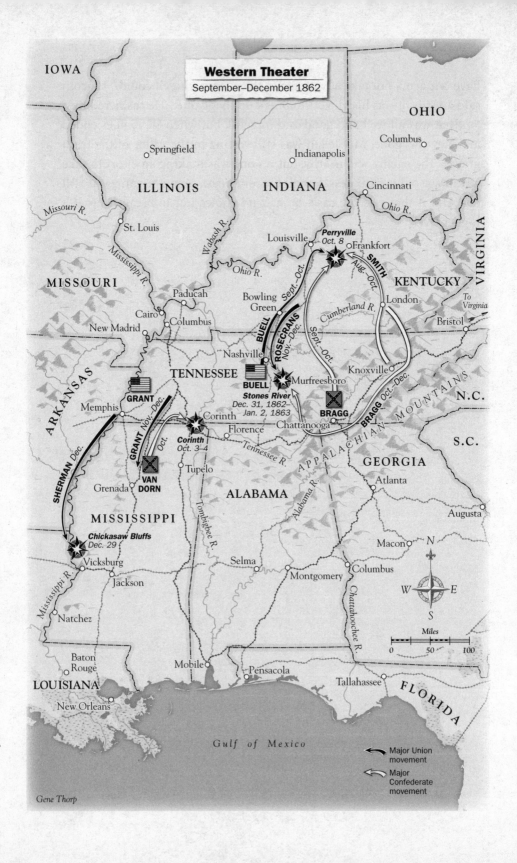

Western Theater
September–December 1862

IOWA

ILLINOIS

INDIANA

OHIO

Springfield

Indianapolis

Columbus

Missouri R.

St. Louis

Cincinnati

Ohio R.

Louisville

Perryville
Oct. 8

Frankfort

MISSOURI

Mississippi R.

Cairo

Paducah

Bowling
Green

Columbus

New Madrid

Nashville

KENTUCKY

London

Cumberland R.

Bristol

To
Virginia

VIRGINIA

BUELL Sept.–Oct.

ROSECRANS Nov.–Dec.

SMITH Aug.–Oct.

Sept.–Oct.

ARKANSAS

Memphis

GRANT

TENNESSEE

BUELL

Stones River
Dec. 31, 1862–
Jan. 2, 1863

Murfreesboro

Knoxville

N.C.

Corinth

Florence

Chattanooga

BRAGG

BRAGG Oct.–Dec.

GRANT Nov.–Dec.

Oct.

Corinth
Oct. 3–4

VAN
DORN

Tennessee R.

Tupelo

Grenada

ALABAMA

GEORGIA

S.C.

Atlanta

Augusta

APPALACHIAN MOUNTAINS

SHERMAN Dec.

MISSISSIPPI

Alabama R.

Macon

N

Chickasaw Bluffs
Dec. 29

Tombigbee R.

Selma

Columbus

W E

Vicksburg

Jackson

Montgomery

Chattahoochee R.

S

Miles
0   50   100

Natchez

Mississippi R.

Baton
Rouge

Mobile

Pensacola

Tallahassee

FLORIDA

LOUISIANA

New Orleans

Gulf of Mexico

Major Union
movement

Major
Confederate
movement

Gene Thorp

II

OCTOBER

In the midst of all his military and political troubles, Abraham Lincoln turned up in the most unexpected role of advertising pitchman. A podiatrist in Manhattan named Isachar Zacharie was papering the metropolis that autumn with testimonials boasting of the famous feet he had tended. Among the endorsements was one from Lincoln, who had placed his aching toes in Zacharie's hands on the advice of Stanton, another satisfied patient. Delighted with the results, Lincoln took time to write a grateful affirmation: "Dr. Zacharie has operated on my feet with great success, and considerable addition to my comfort." The note now featured in Zacharie's advertising campaign.

Little that was embarrassing, scandalous, or sensational got past the *New York Herald*, so naturally this caught the paper's attention. In its October 3 edition, the *Herald* asked archly whether it could be "that many of the haps and mishaps of the nation, during this war, may be traced to a matter no greater than the corns and bunions which have afflicted the feet of our leaders?" Perhaps the Emancipation Proclamation itself could be blamed on Lincoln's tender extremities, for "how could the President put his foot down firmly" with the hectoring abolitionists "when he was troubled with corns?"

The *Herald* was the most widely read newspaper in America, and among its devoted subscribers was Lincoln himself. He might grumble that he had no time to attend to the mewling of the press, but the *Herald* was in a class apart, because of both its reach and its influence among

Democratic Unionists. The loudest voice of the loyal opposition rang out from the *Herald*'s pages; it was the populist soul of a very prickly element of Lincoln's fractious coalition. Not surprisingly, therefore, Lincoln's relationship with the editor and publisher, James Gordon Bennett, was the embodiment of an ancient maxim: Keep your friends close, and your enemies closer.

The brilliant and savage Bennett was one of the most innovative figures in newspaper history, pioneering the coverage of sports, finance, and sensational crimes in the daily penny press. A spine-tingling character with piercing crossed eyes that burned holes in two directions at once, Bennett wrote with the slashing ferocity of a man in a razor fight. He was proudly and crudely racist, and he strongly supported slavery. Yet he also believed in the Union. His fervent views marked the immigrant Scot as a man of New York, which owed much of its rise as a financial center to its role in capitalizing the Southern cotton economy. To save the Union would serve Wall Street's interests, because it would restore easy commerce—but only if it were done with the South's slave system left intact and ready to resume churning out cotton as soon as the war ended.

Bennett was masterly in reading and rallying popular opinion to support this agenda, so Lincoln cultivated him assiduously. He took time to write personal notes thanking Bennett for his "able support"; he gave Bennett's son a plum commission in the navy; he helped to muffle a congressional investigation into the *Herald*'s theft of his annual message to Congress. And he suffered mostly in silence when Bennett portrayed him as a fellow foe of the hated abolitionists, even though the distortions in Bennett's editorials inflamed the impatience of Lincoln's antislavery friends. (The abolitionist William Goodell, in a furious letter warning Lincoln not to be fooled by Bennett's feigned support, referred to the *Herald* as a "pestilent sheet" controlled by "well known Secession-Sympathizers.")

Thus far, Lincoln's handling of Bennett had been mostly a success. The editor trained his lethal fire on other targets and remained ostensibly loyal to the Union cause and to Lincoln himself. "I do very believe that you yourself are the only man in the government that possesses the confidence of the people," Bennett wrote to the president in August (while also asking for a patronage post for a friend). But now Lincoln was at a particularly dangerous point in his relationship with the nation's most powerful and ruthless media baron. The Emancipation Proclamation

landed at a time when Bennett had more than the usual amount of lati-
tude to make trouble. His Democratic pet, McClellan, was surrounded by
voices urging him to overthrow the government, and the influential editor was in a position to amplify those voices. The state of New York,
meanwhile, was in the midst of electing a new governor, and the race
pitted the abolitionist Republican James Wadsworth against the anti-
Lincoln Democrat Horatio Seymour. If he cared to, Bennett could easily
paint Lincoln's face on Wadsworth's lagging candidacy and urge all
Democrats to make Seymour their sign of defiance to the administration's war policy.

Yet more than a week after the announcement of Lincoln's plan to
emancipate the slaves, Bennett still had not publicly criticized the president. Instead, he minimized the importance of what Lincoln had done.
Bennett's archrival Horace Greeley was declaring, GOD BLESS·ABRA-
HAM LINCOLN!, but the *Herald* largely glossed over the revolutionary
implications of the decree. Instead, Bennett latched onto the fact that the
Emancipation Proclamation would not take effect until New Year's Day.
Lincoln, he theorized, was trying to *save* slavery by ending the war
quickly—a notion that mirrored the *Herald*'s agenda. "We accept this
proclamation," the *Herald* announced, "not as that of an armed crusade
against African slavery, but as . . . a liberal warning to our revolted States"
to return to the Union in time to preserve their peculiar institution. The
editor advised his readers to "look through the wretched but transparent
negro" in the proclamation and "see clearly the end of the war."

The president was not the only person at the White House who cultivated Bennett. Mary Lincoln visited, flattered, and gossiped with him
long after his spy, the "Chevalier" Wikoff, had been banished from her
circle. The day after the editorial gently mocking Lincoln's foot problems,
she wrote Bennett a silky letter from the cottage at the Soldiers' Home.
"My Dear Sir," she began, "your kind note . . . has been received." She was
so happy to have it that she intended to ride into town to extend her personal thanks to the gentleman who had hand-delivered it to the Executive
Mansion. "It is so exceedingly dusty, it is quite an undertaking" to make
the trip, she continued, but since the fellow had carried "a note from *you*,
I scarcely feel like having him leave, without seeing him." Shifting from
flattery to gossip, Mary then confided that she agreed with Bennett about
the need for a shakeup of the cabinet, and hinted that many other powerful figures shared his views. She also promised to urge her husband to

take action against the "ambitious fanatics" in his administration, but closed by assuring Bennett that such radicals "have very little control over the P[resident] when his mind is made up, as to what is right." With syrupy apologies for "so long a note"—as if a journalist would ever prefer *less* access to the president's family—she bade farewell to "my dear Mr. Bennett."

In that same letter to Bennett, Mary remarked that her husband was "with the Army of the Potomac." Once again, Lincoln had decided that he needed to see McClellan and his army firsthand. After the unsettling episode with Major Key, he wanted to "satisfy himself personally," in the words of one of his traveling companions, "of the purposes, intentions, and fidelity of McClellan, his officers, and the army." Accordingly, Lincoln set out from Washington on October 1, reaching Harpers Ferry about noon. The Rebels had moved off to the southwest, camping near Winchester in the Shenandoah Valley, and Union troops had retaken possession of the heights surrounding the ferry.

McClellan was in a foul mood that morning. He had resolved to rebuild the railroad bridge at Harpers Ferry—the same bridge he had planned to repair in February, when he was foiled by the canal-boat fiasco. Finally rebuilt that summer, the bridge had been destroyed again by the recently departed Rebels. But Halleck, mindful of Lincoln's hunger for action, rebuked McClellan for dallying over construction projects. "Compel the enemy to fall back or to give you battle," Halleck directed. Little Mac fumed: "I do think that man Halleck is the most stupid idiot I ever heard of—either that or he drinks hard." McClellan was working at his headquarters near Sharpsburg when he learned of Lincoln's arrival. The general was leery: "His ostensible purpose is to see the troops & the battle fields. I incline to think that the real purpose of the visit is to push me into a premature advance," he alerted his wife. The visit was thus steeped in mutual suspicion from the start.

The day was very fine. McClellan met Lincoln at the ferry, and in warm sunshine the two rode south to the Bolivar Heights to review troops from Sumner's corps. Afterward, the general returned to Sharpsburg while Lincoln stayed overnight at Harpers Ferry. The next day, they were together again, and late that afternoon the president took up residence in a big white canvas tent next door to McClellan's own. History would glimpse their meetings and simple accommodations through the lens of the photographer Alexander Gardner, who had arrived at Antietam the previous week to take some of the earliest and most horrifying pictures ever made of the high price of modern war.

In place of the romantic canvases of earlier war artists, Gardner's images offered the public a glimpse of reality: corpses in piles along fencerows and facedown in wheel-worn roads, lined up for burial in a bare field, staring blankly into the unseen sky, twisted at painful angles. It was as if Gardner had "brought bodies and laid them in our dooryards and along the streets," as *The New York Times* put it. This intimacy with the war's ugly face complicated the president's task as he worked to shape public opinion, but Gardner's presence during the visit with McClellan also gave Lincoln a novel opening to show the citizenry that their president was actively encouraging and supporting his general. While in Sharpsburg, Lincoln posed for a series of seemingly casual photos showing him at work with McClellan; in one of the most famous, the viewer glimpses the president and the general conferring at a small table inside a tent, its flap open.

Lincoln was, as always, interested in hard data. He carried a slip of paper on which he wrote the exact number of men in each corps of McClellan's army: 24,130 under Sumner, 14,000 under Burnside, 16,479 under Porter, and so on for a total of more than 88,000 troops. A lot of fleas had been shoveled across the barnyard in the past few months, and now here he was one more time sharing a table with McClellan, hoping to find the magic words that had eluded him all year, words that would persuade Little Mac to use those soldiers fearlessly. "The Pres[ident] was very kind personally," McClellan later wrote of their discussions. He "told me he was convinced I was the best general in the country etc etc. He was very affable & I really think he does feel very kindly towards me personally."

Lincoln, clearly, was wielding more carrot than stick; for his part, McClellan tried to reassure Lincoln of his loyalty. He handed the president at least four letters he had received from friends in the Confederate army urging him to "make himself dictator" and end the conflict. The gesture—which suggested the general's eagerness to let Lincoln know that he was not seriously harboring such thoughts—was slightly wide of the mark, since the president seems never to have doubted McClellan's fundamental loyalty. Instead, Lincoln worried about the passion of the army, particularly because it was led by men so devoted to their general.

McClellan may have been unlikely to lead a coup, but he might allow himself to be carried into one—especially if Lincoln tried to remove him from command. At this point in the war, Lincoln later explained, he "regarded his position . . . as a striking and noteworthy illustration of the dangers to which republican institutions were subjected by wars of such magnitude." Though he was nominally the nation's commander in chief, in truth this was a "season of insubordination, panic, and general demoralization" in which his authority over the troops was far from certain.

That worry lay heavy on Lincoln's mind the next morning, October 3, when he awakened a member of his traveling party, an Illinois politician named Ozias Hatch. Hatch recalled the encounter vividly:

> It was very early, Daylight was just lighting the east—the soldiers were all asleep in their tents. Scarce a sound could be heard except the notes of early birds, and the farm-yard voices from distant farms. Lincoln said to me, "Come, Hatch, I want you to take a walk with me." His tone was serious and impressive. I arose without a word, and as soon as we were dressed we left the tent together. He led me about the camp, and then we walked upon the surrounding hills overlooking the great city of white tents and sleeping soldiers. Very little was spoken between us, beyond a few words as to the pleasantness of the morning. . . . We walked slowly and quietly, meeting here and there a guard . . . looking at the beautiful sunrise and the magnificent scene before us.
>
> Finally, reaching a commanding point where almost that entire camp could be seen—the men were just beginning their morning duties, and evidences of life and activity were becoming apparent . . . the President, waving his hand towards the scene before us, and leaning towards me, said in an almost whispering voice: "Hatch—Hatch, what is all this?"
>
> "Why, Mr. Lincoln," said I, "this is the Army of the Potomac." He hesitated a moment, and then, straightening up, said in a louder tone: "No, Hatch, no. This is General McClellan's body-guard." Nothing more was said. We walked to our tent, and the subject was not alluded to again.

After breakfast, the presidential party toured the site of the great battle, starting at the southern end of the field, where Lincoln and McClellan reviewed Burnside's corps. Little Mac then suggested they hand over their horses to aides and ride to the next camp in the comfort of an ambulance, for it was two or three miles distant. As the wagon lurched along carrying the president and his companions, Lincoln said to Ward Hill Lamon: "Sing one of your sad little songs." Before the war, the two men had been part of a group of lawyers who traveled Illinois's Eighth Judicial Circuit; trying cases by day, the lawyers shared fellowship in the evenings, and Lamon was the singer of the bunch.

Lamon knew immediately which song the president had in mind. The pall of so much death had a depressing effect, and Lincoln was, in Lamon's words, "weary and sad." When such a mood was upon him he liked to hear a "homely tune" called "Twenty Years Ago," about lost friends and unrecoverable youth and true love buried in the grave. No song "touched his great heart" as this one did, Lamon recalled; Lincoln rarely heard it without tears in his eyes.

> I've wandered to the village, Tom,
> I've sat beneath the tree
> Upon the schoolhouse playground,
> That sheltered you and me;
> But none were there to greet me, Tom,
> And few were left to know
> That played with us upon the grass
> Some twenty years ago . . .

The wheels creaked as Lamon's voice drifted down to the low notes of the dirgelike song. His slow words told of the schoolmaster now buried on the hillside where the friends once went sledding, and of the tree where the names of young sweethearts had been carved, now stripped of bark and "dying sure but slow."

> I visited the old churchyard
> And took some flowers to strew
> Upon the graves of those we loved
> Some twenty years ago.

"As I well knew it would, the song only deepened his sadness," Lamon wrote later. He also reported that he then "did what I had done many times before: I startled him from his melancholy." Sometimes Lamon

jolted Lincoln with a ribald joke, sometimes with an outrageous statement. This time, he launched into a comic song made famous in minstrel
shows, one that celebrated the famous banjo player Picayune Butler. It
"broke the spell . . . and restored somewhat his accustomed easy humor."
It also sowed the seeds of a minor scandal: when Lincoln returned to
Washington, he was closely followed by outraged reports that he had
spent his time in Maryland enjoying boisterous songs beside the fresh
graves of the Union dead.

The president left Sharpsburg the next day. As McClellan had expected,
Lincoln warned his general "that he would be a ruined man if he did not
move forward, move rapidly and effectually." But Lincoln was not hopeful. Officially, he had nothing to report at the end of his visit. Passing
through Frederick on the way home, he disappointed a cheering crowd
by saying: "In my present position it is hardly proper for me to make
speeches. Every word is so closely noted that it will not do to make trivial
ones." But to trusted friends he revealed his skepticism. Once again, he
had seen McClellan's forces well-ordered and in good spirits. "For the organization of an army . . . I will back General McClellan against any general
of modern times," he said. "But I begin to believe that he will never get
ready to fight."

While Lamon sang to Lincoln in Maryland, Union forces in faraway
Mississippi were battling fiercely to maintain their foothold in the Deep
South. Sterling Price and Earl Van Dorn had at last managed to combine
their little armies for an attack on Grant at Corinth, and now their troops
pressed through choking smoke in ninety-four-degree heat, driving the
Federals as they came. But as the blue line fell back, it found even stron-
ger positions in the well-built fortifications around the railroad junction.
The first day's combat ended with the Southerners stalled.

The next morning, October 4, the Rebels charged again. Union artillery, firing exploding canisters that sprayed musket balls, blew ragged
holes in the advancing ranks. Grant would have few opportunities in his
long war to enjoy the advantages of fighting while entrenched in a strong
defensive position, but on this day he watched the enemy melt under
murderous fire from his soldiers. After losing nearly a quarter of their
men in the effort to break through, the Rebel generals gave up. Price wept
when he saw what remained of his vanquished army.

The effort to uproot Grant from Dixie died then and there. And with Lee pushed back into Virginia, two of the three Confederate initiatives of September had now been thwarted. Only Bragg's Kentucky invasion remained viable—but not for long. On the day of the battle at Corinth, Bragg was watching his puppet governor Richard Hawes take the oath of office in Frankfort. The general was eager to get on with it, because Union troops under Buell were marching down from Louisville and would arrive at any minute. Sure enough, just as Hawes launched into his inaugural address, the roar of Federal artillery rose from the outskirts of town. The speech was cut short; the Hawes administration did not last much longer.

Bragg decided to avoid a clash at Frankfort and instead attack what he thought was a small detachment of the Union army near Bardstown, to the west. This was just what Buell hoped he would do. In fact, the Federal sortie that broke up the inaugural party in Frankfort was just a feint, while the troops at Bardstown formed Buell's main body. Bragg's confusion led within a few days to the even greater confusion that was the battle of Perryville, fought on October 8. A nightmare of jumbled violence, it was, according to Bragg, "the severest and most desperately contested engagement" ever compressed into a few hours. The chaos on the battlefield was such that at one point the commander of the Confederate right wing, Leonidas Polk, rode straight into the middle of a Union regiment, thinking they were his own troops. The bluecoats responded with equal confusion: when this unknown man with stars on his shoulders (who had quickly realized his mistake) brazenly ordered them to cease firing, the Federals actually put down their rifles. And Polk rode safely away.

Perryville was more than just pointless slaughter, however, for at least two reasons. When the Rebels opened the battle with a sudden attack on what they thought was a small Union force and the surprise threatened to collapse the North's left wing, a young general named Philip Sheridan saw what was happening from a nearby hilltop and swiftly turned his guns on the Confederate flank. He followed this up with a cavalry charge that broke the Rebel momentum. The Confederacy would hear much more from Phil Sheridan, and his response on this day was the sort of quick, decisive, and effective action that was separating the true warrior-generals from the mass of Northern men so hastily pressed into service.

Perryville was also the excuse Bragg needed to bring his deflated project to an end. It was mere vanity to believe that his army could impose Confederate government on a state that didn't want it. When Kentuckians failed to join Bragg's cause, they rendered a clear verdict on his invasion; after that, the only question was how much blood he would spill on his way back to Tennessee. The 7,600 combatants lost on that October afternoon must have been enough, because Bragg mustered his men at midnight and turned them toward the south.

Some in his army disagreed bitterly with this decision, among them General Basil Duke, who still believed the Confederates could crush Buell and then do as they pleased with the singular prize of Kentucky. Whether or not he was right about strategy, Duke was correct when he summed up the effects of Bragg's retreat. "On the 10th of October more than fifty thousand Confederate soldiers were upon the soil of Kentucky," he wrote. "The first of November they were all gone, and with them departed all hope, perhaps, of Southern independence."

Lincoln returned from Sharpsburg to find the White House corridor even more jammed than usual. This was the price he paid for leaving town: after being away for most of a week, he "was perfectly overwhelmed with the crowd on his return." He and his secretaries toiled to catch up on "deferred and delayed business," as Nicolay reported. Lincoln may have been too busy to notice that his monthly paycheck, issued that day, was light by $61. Thanks to the new revenue bill he had signed, an income tax was withheld from the salaries of the nation's highest earners for the first time in American history.

Lincoln departed the Antietam battlefield convinced that a highway to victory lay wide open in front of McClellan. The general could potentially lead his army straight to Richmond, about 150 miles away; with Lee camped to the west of the mountains in the Shenandoah Valley, the path was clear of Rebels. Lincoln would have preferred to see McClellan hit Lee where he stood, but that had not happened. Alternatively, why not set off for Richmond and let Lee try to catch him? If McClellan outmarched the enemy, the Confederate capital would be his prize. If Lee caught up to him, McClellan could choose his ground for the decisive battle that Lincoln desired. Either way, from Lincoln's point of view, the result would be a success. Besides, he felt the clock ticking toward another winter of muddy roads and mired wagon trains and he did not want to lose more time. He instructed Halleck to get Little Mac going.

"The President directs that you cross the Potomac and give battle to the enemy or drive him south," the general in chief wired McClellan. "Your army must move now while the roads are good." By taking the route that kept his army between Lee and Washington, McClellan would provide protection for the capital—a result that, Halleck informed him, would allow the government to send him an additional 30,000 troops.

These orders arrived just as the general was putting the finishing touches on a statement he planned to issue to the entire Army of the Potomac. For two weeks, soldiers had been arguing about the Emancipation Proclamation. Fitz John Porter told the newspaper editor Manton Marble that the camps were rife with "disgust, discontent, and expressions of disloyalty." Not only the soldiers but the whole country wanted to know what McClellan's reaction would be. Everyone understood that this issue was a source of deep division between McClellan's command and the abolitionist Republicans in Washington, and many saw that division as the cause of all the army's woes.

McClellan's initial response to Lincoln's decree was outrage and dismay. He suspected that the order was designed to foment a slave revolt. When Lincoln followed up by suspending habeas corpus protections, the general detected the foul hand of a despot. For days, Little Mac brooded on these twin disasters. At one point he drafted a letter to Lincoln criticizing the policies, but a friend persuaded him to destroy it. He consulted with other generals, including Burnside, who warned him that open defiance of the elected government would be "a fatal error." Even his supporters in New York agreed. One of these advisers, the transportation magnate William Aspinwall, received a letter from McClellan in which the general said he was "very anxious to know how you and men like you regard the recent Proclamations of the Pres[ident]." Aspinwall rushed to Sharpsburg to deliver his answer in person. An open clash between McClellan and Lincoln would only prolong the war, Aspinwall said; the best course was to "submit" and "quietly continue doing [your] duty as a soldier."

Wisely, the general decided to pursue this more conservative course. Released on October 7, his statement to the Army of the Potomac admonished his men to remember that military subordination to civilian government was "a fundamental rule of our political system" and "should be thoroughly understood & observed." Failure to respect this rule in their political conversations could "destroy the discipline & efficiency of troops by substituting the spirit of political faction" for a soldier's "highest duty." This was certainly patriotic and true, but McClellan didn't stop there. Reminding his audience that elections were under way in the North, he added: "The remedy for political error if any are committed is to be found only in the action of the people at the polls." Ostensibly addressed to the men of his army, this sentence had no practical value for them; they were miles from the nearest ballot box. The real audience for this message was the Northern electorate, which McClellan was counting on to boost Democrats into control of Congress, where they could crush Stanton, chasten Lincoln, and implement policies more to the general's liking. Writing to his wife, Little Mac was more candid than he had been in his public statement: "I still hope the indignant people will punish them as they deserve."

But the autumn elections would continue for another month, and meanwhile McClellan had new orders from Washington, along with Halleck's offer of 30,000 new troops. He had been pleading for reinforcements for six months; thanks to renewed recruiting, they were at last available in large numbers. But, as McClellan and other Union generals well understood, all reinforcements are not created equal. The recruits he wanted were fresh soldiers who had not yet been organized into regiments and brigades. Such men could be inserted into existing units to replace fallen troops; in this way the new soldiers would quickly mature by learning from their experienced, battle-hardened comrades.

However, owing to political considerations the reinforcements almost always arrived already formed into new regiments, because new regiments created new positions of honor for their newly elected officers and inspired fresh pride for the communities that sent them marching off to war. This argument—form new regiments or fill old ones—would continue for most of the war, with Lincoln in the middle of it. The military men were correct in military terms, and the politicians were correct in political terms. For Lincoln, politics took priority.

Further complicating matters for McClellan was the difficulty of feeding and clothing the troops already with him. Western Maryland was a remote piece of real estate on which to shelter and supply a force that was growing to number more than 100,000 men. Only a small canal connected Washington to Harpers Ferry, and a single strand of railroad ran from Pennsylvania to Hagerstown, in the rear of McClellan's vast camps. These supply lines were quickly snarled. The Union general John Reynolds complained that many of his men lacked "shoes, tents, blankets, knapsacks, or other clothing." William Franklin's corps was short two thousand tents. George Meade reported that "artillery horses and train animals have been literally starving."

With his seasoned troops still recovering from wounds, his fresh soldiers in need of training, and his entire army poorly supplied, McClellan shrugged off the orders from Halleck and settled down with his wife and year-old daughter in the lovely countryside. "We are having a very quiet & pleasant time," he wrote to a friend.

Across the lines, General J. E. B. Stuart took a less leisurely approach to the business of war, setting out on another bold dash while the Federals sat motionless. Starting in the foggy dawn of October 9, Stuart led some 1,800 cavalry up the Cumberland Valley to Chambersburg, Pennsylvania, where he deepened the Union supply problems by looting a major depot. Then he turned east across the mountains and roared back down through Maryland, gathering livestock as he went. After three days' hard riding, the Rebels recrossed the Potomac to safety, having once again circled the Army of the Potomac.

"It is humiliating, disgraceful," stormed Gideon Welles. "The Rebels have possessed themselves of a good deal of plunder, reclothed their men from our stores, run off a thousand horses, fat cattle, etc. etc. It is not a pleasant fact to know that we are clothing, mounting, and subsisting not only our troops but the Rebels also." Lincoln's reaction was more wry than wrathful: "Three times round and out is the rule," he said, referring to an early version of baseball. "Stuart has been twice around McClellan. The third time, by the rules of the game, he must surrender."

In England, news of the battle of Antietam stunned the public. "The effect upon the popular mind . . . has already been quite considerable," Charles Francis Adams wrote to Seward early in October. Having predicted the fall of Washington, the British newspapers were now reporting Lee's retreat, and the most prevalent reaction, Adams wrote, was "surprise." The invincibility of the Rebels, which had seemed so manifest in mid-September as they advanced on every front, was once again in doubt. Lord Palmerston immediately began to have second thoughts about putting his nose into such a violent quarrel. Prominent lawmakers and members of the cabinet underlined the prime minister's misgivings by warning that Britain would be dragged into the war. When Lincoln's proclamation arrived close behind the unexpected battlefield report, the fine points of the U.S. Constitution confused many people, but the chief implication was obvious: the American conflict had a new aspect. "The whole matter is full of difficulty," Palmerston wrote to Russell, "and can only be cleared up by some more decided events between the contending armies."

Russell disagreed. The foreign minister was now bent on creating a united European front to end the war, and his enthusiasm spread to the chancellor of the exchequer, William Ewart Gladstone. As tribune of Britain's Liberal Party he had no truck with slavery. And he dreaded the mischief that might follow if the United States fractured. But Gladstone was convinced that the South could never be forced back into the Union. Unaware that the prime minister was getting cold feet, Gladstone was delighted to hear that a serious effort was at last being mounted to stop the carnage in North America and prevent riots in cotton-starved England. He was so delighted, in fact, that he couldn't resist hinting at the intervention plan during a speech on October 7 in Newcastle. "We may have our own opinions about slavery," he bellowed, trying to be heard in a hall that swallowed his words. "We may be for or against the South, but there is no doubt that Jefferson Davis and other leaders of the South have made an army; they are making, it appears, a navy; and they have made what is more than either—they have made a nation!" The roar of the crowd testified to the weariness of people who had been waiting in vain for the mills to reopen and for trade to resume with luxury-loving Southern planters.

Adams was angry when he read Gladstone's words in the next day's newspapers, especially the reference to a Confederate navy. He knew very well that Davis and his fellow Rebels weren't making their navy by themselves. The shipwrights of Liverpool were doing it for them, while the British government turned a half-blind eye, secretly pleased by the prospect of sapping U.S. power on the seas. The Confederate cruiser *Alabama,* fresh from the river Mersey, was busy raiding and sinking Union merchant vessels off the Azores, and more ships were in the works.

Adams protested to Russell, but like the other formal complaints the ambassador registered against the flagrant partisanship in the shipyards, this one was stifled in bluster and legalese.

Continuing his push for intervention, Russell filed a strong memo in favor of action. But then the foreign minister's effort stalled. Under pressure from others in his party, Gladstone backpedaled, saying that in Newcastle he had merely been expressing a personal opinion, not an official position. Most important, it became clear that Palmerston had made up his mind. "We must continue merely to be lookers-on," the prime minister said, "till the war shall have taken a more decided turn."

But as Palmerston cooled, across the English Channel the idea of intervention was heating up again. Henri Mercier reported from Washington that the Emancipation Proclamation threatened to bring on a race war that would wipe out the American cotton industry for years to come. This radical initiative was, in his view, driving the border states away from the Union and swelling the popularity of the Democrats. Now was the moment, Mercier urged, for Europe to step in.

The envoy's dispatch arrived in Paris at about the same time as a letter from Leopold I of Belgium, making the case for mediation. Because Leopold was a relative and close adviser of Queen Victoria, Louis-Napoleon took this letter to be a signal of Britain's readiness to step in. He promptly summoned the Confederate emissary, John Slidell, to a meeting.

Slidell was initially elated to find the emperor on the verge of action, but his heart sank when Napoleon announced that he wanted Russia and England to join him. By now the Southerner had come to understand an essential truth about the European powers: they were incapable of forming a true partnership. The Russian czar favored the North as a counterweight to established European powers. The British wanted a quick end to the war, but not one that risked their own safety, and they could not find their way into an effective alliance with France, their eternal foes. Now Slidell tried once again to persuade the emperor to take the plunge alone, to be sole author of Southern independence, in exchange for which the Confederate States would help him build a new Latin American empire.

Slidell's efforts were for naught. Just as the invasion of the border states had been the South's best chance for military victory, so were these busy weeks of October the high tide of Rebel hopes for European support—and the tide quickly receded. As he told Slidell he would do, Napoleon proposed a joint effort, and as Slidell feared would happen, the proposal failed. England backed away, unwilling to risk war with the United States; Russia demurred, not wanting to offend the North; and France, finding itself alone, returned to the sidelines with a Gallic shrug.

A week after Slidell's interview with the emperor, William Dayton met for the first time with the new French foreign minister. The American envoy was pleased to learn that no further initiative was being contemplated. France "wish[ed] that the war could be ended," said Edouard Drouyn de L'Huys mildly, and "reserved to herself the right to express this wish" in some formal way in the future. Dayton considered this enigmatic statement for a moment and then asked: "What will be the consequences" if Washington were to ignore such a wish?

The new minister, a veteran diplomat who had spent years in London, spoke perfect English. "Nothing," he replied.

By now a week had melted away since McClellan was ordered to move, and other than sending cavalry to chase helplessly after J. E. B. Stuart, he had done nothing. On October 13, Lincoln took up pen and paper for one last try to get through to his difficult general. The result was his longest and most closely argued letter to the general, striking in its grasp of military tactics—the fruit of almost a year of close and costly study. Remarkably, despite all McClellan's slights, aspersions, and tantrums, Lincoln still had the patience to make his case respectfully and candidly.

And what was his case? That Northern men were a match for Southern men. That they could march as fast and fight as hard, if only McClellan would have faith in them. Lincoln asked whether the general recalled their conversation at Sharpsburg, when Lincoln had warned him about what he termed "over-cautiousness." Well, this was what he meant by the word: "when you assume that you cannot do what the enemy is constantly doing." Instead of being over-cautious, Lincoln continued, "should you not claim to be at least his equal in prowess, and act upon the claim?"

The president then cited several examples. There was McClellan's recent telegram to Halleck, calling again for railroad improvements before the Army of the Potomac could move south. Lincoln pointed out that Lee had only half as many wagons as McClellan did, and was sending them twice as far to reach the nearest railroad depot. Yet somehow Lee got along without commencing a major construction project that would consume the rest of the year. Why couldn't McClellan do the same?

Lincoln now made the case for launching the footrace mentioned in Halleck's orders a week earlier. Set out toward Richmond on a straight line, he suggested, drawing supplies from Washington. Watch Lee come chasing behind on the longer, curving valley route, and then seize an opportunity to launch an attack through a gap in the Blue Ridge Mountains. "If we never try, we shall never succeed," Lincoln urged.

Next he shifted gears slightly. Suppose that McClellan's worst fear, expressed in his wires to the War Department, came true. What if, instead of racing south to pursue the Army of the Potomac, Lee moved north again toward Pennsylvania? That would be a godsend, Lincoln suggested. "You have nothing to do but to follow, and ruin him!"

This rigorous letter provided a clear window into Lincoln's orderly mind. He reasoned from hard data: specific mileages, waypoints, roads and rivers. He used clear metaphors drawn from mathematics: Lee must march on the arc of the circle while McClellan could march on the chord. He considered possible flaws in his argument and answered each one. Binding it all together was his stoic self-reliance, a faith that fortune smiled on those who shouldered the responsibility and dared to make the attempt, to *try*. Lincoln closed by restating his challenge to Little Mac to have more faith in his army. "It is all easy if our troops march as well as the enemy," he concluded, "and it is unmanly to say they can not do it."

Lincoln showed the letter to Vice President Hamlin before he sent it away. He had scant hope it would do any good—he told a visitor he would fire McClellan now if not for the possible impact on the elections. And indeed, even before the letter could be delivered, McClellan displayed another sign of his deep-seated insecurity. His cavalry was no match for Stuart's, he complained in a message to Halleck. Irritated, Lincoln told Halleck to convey the following response: "If the enemy had more occupation south of the river, his cavalry would not be so likely to make raids north of it."

Bragg, meanwhile, was slipping away in the West, and Buell seemed content to watch him go. "It is rather a good thing to be a Major General and in command of a Department," Nicolay wrote with caustic irony. "One can take things so leisurely!" Halleck conveyed the president's frustration in a message to Buell: "He does not understand why we cannot march as the enemy marches, live as he lives, and fight as he fights. . . .

Your army must enter East Tennessee this fall." Buell's answer, such as it was, rested on the premise that Confederate soldiers were better able to endure hardship than the Federals.

That reply marked the end of Buell's command, this time for good. Lincoln might be stuck with McClellan for the moment, but he wasn't stuck with Buell. He would not tolerate an inferiority complex at the top of the Union armies. Lincoln dismissed the slow-marching general and replaced him with another Ohioan: William Rosecrans, from Grant's command.

"We are all blue here," Nicolay reported on October 14 as election results arrived from Pennsylvania, Ohio, and Indiana. Democrats made large strides in each of these key states, overshadowing more encouraging news from Iowa, where Senator James Grimes exulted in a big Republican victory—"twice our usual majority," he estimated—and predicted a similar landslide in Wisconsin. Grimes gave the credit to the Emancipation Proclamation, but clearly it was an open question whether the public would ultimately support the decree. Lincoln distracted himself from the election returns by commissioning an unusual gift for Tad: he instructed the Bureau of Ordnance to manufacture a miniature, fully functional brass cannon, "a little gun that he can not hurt himself with."

Such pleasures of office were few, even as unwelcome responsibilities multiplied. Among them was the job of reviewing military death sentences. Lincoln felt compelled to undertake this effort: in times of war and revolution, governments often become casual about death, but the president was determined not to let that happen to him. The records of military commissions and courts-martial piled up on his desk with ominous speed. "I must go through these papers and see if I cannot find some excuse to let these poor fellows off," he told one visitor on the eve of what he called a "butcher-day." Such a day came along in late October and after a good deal of reading and creative thinking he managed to find plausible pretexts for sparing three lives. A prisoner from New Mexico, Jose Maria Rivas, spoke only Spanish, so Lincoln reasoned that he might not have known what he was saying when he confessed to being a "spy." A man in Memphis, Sely Lewis, probably was a smuggler, but the president ruled that the military court had no jurisdiction over his case. And Private Conrad Zachringer, who threw his lieutenant to the ground, then beat and throttled him—well, he was drunk and probably didn't know what he was doing.

The authority to grant high offices also came freighted with pain, for Lincoln rarely pleased one man without disappointing at least one other. In October, he took on the excruciating task of deciding which of his friends he would name to the Supreme Court. In late spring he had filled a second vacancy on the court by naming a Kentucky-bred Iowan, Samuel Miller, to the seat left empty after the death of Peter Daniel, one of the *Dred Scott* justices. Now he had a third vacancy to fill, and he at last was at liberty to choose a justice from Illinois. Two men intensely desired the appointment to the court, Orville Browning and David Davis. Davis was arguably Lincoln's most effective political supporter, as close to a campaign manager as Lincoln had. And Browning had been his frequent visitor, adviser, and confidant through the tumultuous first half of 1862. It was Browning who had rushed with his wife, Eliza, to be with the Lincolns when Willie died, and Browning who had taken on the job of arranging the funeral.

Browning had the support of Attorney General Bates and a number of his Republican Senate colleagues. Lincoln agonized over the choice but appeared to have made up his mind when a story circulated that he had remarked: "I do not know what I may do when the time comes, but there has never been a day when if I had to act I should not have appointed Browning." When those words reached Illinois, Davis's supporters had no doubt that they were authentic. "No man but he could have put the situation so quaintly," one recalled. Naturally, they were outraged that the president would turn his back on the Bloomington judge who had done the hard work of organizing Lincoln's campaign for the nomination in 1860.

Leonard Swett announced that he was going immediately to Washington to see his friend Lincoln and straighten him out. "No, you are not," countered Davis, but Swett's mind was made up. Two days later he knocked on the White House door at seven A.M., knowing full well that the light-sleeping president would be at work. Swett settled into an office chair and laid in. Surely, Lincoln had not forgotten "that he had been brought into prominence by the Circuit Court lawyers of the old Eighth Circuit, headed by Judge Davis." In fact, he continued brashly, "if Judge Davis, with his tact and force, had not lived . . . I believe you would not now be sitting where you are."

Lincoln did not disagree. So how, Swett wondered, could Lincoln fail to repay the man who made it possible for him to satisfy his own ambitions? "In justice to yourself," Swett said, "give him this place." The visitor described this conversation as "pleasant," but how pleasant can it have been for Lincoln to know that saying yes to one friend's dream would mean saying no to the other's? As Swett returned to his room at Willard's and replayed the episode in his mind, he put himself in Lincoln's shoes and realized there was something more he could do to tip the excruciating balance. He could promise not to put his friend in another spot like this—in other words, he could surrender his own claims to a presidential favor.

Swett turned around and went back to Lincoln's office, this time to deliver a letter offering to let Davis's fulfillment double as his own. This would "kill 'two birds with one stone,'" Swett wrote. Maybe this offer did the trick, or maybe Browning botched his chances by criticizing Lincoln's Emancipation Proclamation at campaign stops as he battled for reelection across their home state. Maybe Lincoln was swayed by a combination of considerations. However it happened, David Davis was appointed to the U.S. Supreme Court on October 17, and now Chief Justice Taney's proslavery majority was whittled to a single vote. But for Lincoln the price was high: he and Browning were never again as close as they had been in the weeks and months when an old friend from Illinois helped a president survive his grief.

Lincoln's long letter to McClellan reached the general's headquarters on October 16; another day went by before Little Mac offered a reply. A month had now passed since the battle of Antietam, yet McClellan had nothing to report. "I am not wedded to any particular plan of operations," he wrote airily, adding: "I hope to have today reliable information as to the position of the enemy." The president had warned him not to ignore "the question of *time,* which can not, and must not be ignored." But McClellan ignored it with abandon: "Your Excellency may be assured," he wrote, "that I will not adopt a course which differs at all from your views without first fully explaining my reasons & giving you time to issue such instructions as may seem best to you."

Lincoln later said, "I began to fear that he was playing false—that he did not want to hurt the enemy." In his view, the current situation posed a test for McClellan: Lee was in a bind, and if McClellan let him escape, Lincoln would remove him from command.

The long struggle between the president and the general was at last reaching a climax. The "fine dry weather of the autumn [was] daily passing," with "no sign of life in the Army of the Potomac," Nicolay wrote. As the last hours of the test ticked by, both the president and the general grew touchy. McClellan, still suffering from supply problems, complained endlessly of his need for fresh cavalry horses. Lincoln, who knew of only one cavalry in the vicinity that had any reason to be worn out, snapped: "Will you pardon me for asking what the horses of your army have done since the battle of Antietam that fatigue anything?" McClellan complained to his wife about such barbed remarks, which he called Lincoln's "dirty little flings that I can't get used to."

On October 26, nineteen days after Halleck first relayed the order to move, McClellan finally began sending his men across the Potomac. Even then, the tension between the commander in chief and his general did not abate. When Lincoln pronounced himself "so rejoiced" at the news of the army's movement, McClellan perceived his comment as "wretched innuendo." At this critical moment, Little Mac's opinion of Lincoln settled back to the dark depths of his first impressions. Writing to his wife, he said: "There never was a truer epithet applied to a certain individual than that of the 'Gorilla.'"

The river crossing had just begun when Stanton charged through the frosted glass doors leading to the president's office suite, intent on some unrecorded bit of business. Nicolay poked his head into Lincoln's room to announce the secretary of war, and was surprised to see the president surrounded by kneeling Quakers "holding a prayer-meeting around him."

Lincoln "was compelled to bear the infliction until the 'spirit' moved them to stop"; then he offered a brief reply to his fervent visitors. "We are indeed going through a great trial—a fiery trial," he said, adding that he was but "a humble instrument in the hands of our Heavenly Father . . . I have sought his aid." He also acknowledged that he had been unable to control the course of events. "If I had had my way, this war would never have been commenced; if I had been allowed my way this war could have been ended before this, but we find it still continues; and we must believe that He permits it for some wise purpose of his own, mysterious and unknown to us."

Lincoln's view of a Providential destiny working itself out through these strange human instruments was deeply ingrained now, and it would stay with him to the end. But how awful and grinding was the slow machinery of divine will. Lincoln bitterly counted each day as the Army of the Potomac sloshed across the ford, and when the last man stepped onto the Virginia shore, the president did not fail to note that the tally was nine. Later, explaining his reaction to this unforgivable lethargy, Lincoln remarked: "Lee crossed his entire army between one dark night and daylight the next morning. That was the last grain of sand which broke the camel's back."

— 12 —

NOVEMBER

The weather was fair but hinting winter. The first snow of the season was just a few days off. The first family continued to live on the grounds of the Soldiers' Home, and now Lincoln's rides to and from the cottage each day passed through amber fields and woods of thinning yellow, orange, red, and brown. About a mile from the White House, where the city met the woodlots, stood Camp Barker, a hastily constructed village that housed more than four thousand newly freed slaves and contrabands in tents and two-story clapboard dormitories. Lincoln passed the camp twice a day; apparently he stopped at least once for a visit, and according to a witness he wiped tears from his eyes as he listened to a concert of spirituals. He must have noticed that the facility was not designed with winter in mind. The crowded conditions were already unhealthy, and by the end of winter the camp would be losing some twenty-five refugees a week to disease and neglect.

Mary Lincoln was well briefed on conditions among the former slaves. Her dressmaker friend Elizabeth Keckly, herself a freedwoman, was a founder of the Contraband Relief Association of Washington. November found Keckly traveling with Mary and Tad Lincoln to New York and Boston, where she hoped to raise money for relief efforts. But while the free blacks of these cities gave generously, even the reflected glow of the first lady was not enough to open the wallets of white Northerners, and Mrs. Lincoln decided to give Keckly $200 from a discretionary fund donated by a wealthy philanthropist for the president's use. Keckly bought a supply of blankets with the money. In a note to her husband dated November 3, Mary wrote: "She [Keckly] says the immense number of Contrabands in [Washington] are suffering intensely, many without bed covering & having to use any bits of carpeting to cover themselves. I am sure, you will not object to [the money] being used in this way—The cause of humanity requires it."

As this poignant letter suggests, most Americans were completely unprepared for the revolution now under way. Before the guns opened on Fort Sumter, no one could have imagined that the wife of a president would soon be arranging to buy blankets for freed slaves. At the same time, the inadequacy of the gesture is striking; a few hundred blankets, when several thousand former slaves were suffering within a short walk of the White House. And at the same time, the president had recently announced his commitment to add millions more free men, women, and children to a far-flung society that had no place and no plans for them. The fate and future of four million slaves and their descendants loomed large, and that $200 pile of blankets was a minuscule down payment on the enormous moral accounting that would soon come due.

On the battlefield, too, few were prepared to manage the influx of the newly free. In Mississippi and Tennessee, thousands of former bondsmen took refuge in camps commanded by Ulysses Grant. Like Union generals everywhere in the South, he was forced to think about the great upheaval in terms beyond winter blankets. He could put able-bodied young men to work in his army, but what was he to do with the rest? "Orders from the government prohibited the expulsion of the negroes from the protection of the army," he later wrote of this period, and "humanity forbade allowing them to starve." He looked around for work to occupy them, and saw that "the plantations were all deserted; the cotton and corn were ripe." He figured that "men, women and children above ten years of age could be employed saving these crops." In the abstract, this was a fine idea, but to house, nourish, clothe, and educate these workers required a large new bureaucracy inside Grant's Army of the Tennessee, and countless hours of effort. The bureaucracy was created, the effort was spent—and even then, Grant's solution was only a temporary answer to the limited question of how to meet the immediate needs of freedpeople in the vicinity of his troops.

Change was moving so rapidly now and on such a huge scale that America couldn't take it all in. The first lady was caring for refugees from slavery, in a land where the Fugitive Slave Law was still on the books. Black troops were wearing Union blue and carrying rifles in Louisiana and Florida. Louisiana planters were reportedly ready to pay wages to their African-American fieldworkers, news so startling to Lincoln that he wrote in search of confirmation. Any one of these events would have been inconceivable before 1862; now the impossible was happening daily, and racing by in a blur.

Another exchange of letters, later in November, illustrates the same phenomenon in a slightly different light. The prominent Kentucky lawyer George Robertson, a friend of the Todd family and a longtime acquaintance of Lincoln's, raised a complaint with the president: one of his slaves was living in a Union army camp, and the officers were refusing to return Robertson's property. Lincoln was flabbergasted. Here was a learned, observant man who somehow missed the fresh reality taking shape before his eyes. The president drafted a reply comparing Robertson to the farmer in revolutionary times who wandered through the ranks of victorious Americans at Yorktown, demanding the return of two steers that the army had taken from his land. How could anyone be so petty at such a moment? This clever answer evidently went into a file; a few days later, Lincoln sent a milder reply making the same point less colorfully, and offering to compensate the lawyer for his loss. Robertson's experience was "the life of the nation" distilled to a single household, the president noted. The old order was gone, and the slave was not returning. The Union army, Lincoln wrote, was going to "make him free."

This was Lincoln's great worry now: that the American people still were not braced to the scope and scale of the war. Not even Antietam and emancipation had brought the reality home. In early November, as he watched McClellan's inadequate movements and studied the discouraging election returns that had continued to roll in over the past few weeks, the president became convinced that these were two symptoms of the same disease. Both the army and the voters labored under the delusion that there was an easy way to restore the Union. In the ranks, this false hope showed itself in the multitude of soldiers on furlough from the front. Even while standing face-to-face with the enemy, troops by the tens of thousands blithely asked to go home, and their elected officers lacked the backbone to say no. The number of troops away on leave had grown so large that Lincoln could not find precise figures. "At this very moment," he wrote in an undated November memo, "there are between seventy [thousand] and one hundred thousand men absent on furlough from the Army of the Potomac."

Wishful thinking about the war also prevailed among many in the general public, and wherever it did it produced support for Democratic candidates who promised a quick peace and the restoration of the Union "as it was"—the Union with all the old compromises over slavery intact. In a note to himself, the president lamented: "The army, like the nation, has become demoralized by the idea that the war is to be ended, the nation united, and peace restored, by *strategy*, and not by hard desperate fighting."

Lincoln used some of the same words when a delegation of women from the U.S. Sanitary Commission paid him a visit one evening in early November. No civilian organization was more important to the war effort than the Sanitary Commission, which organized volunteers and raised money to meet the medical and morale needs of the troops. The delegation called on the president in hopes of hearing a few words of good news to take home with them, but Lincoln had none to offer. "A deeper gloom rested on his face than on that of any person I had ever seen," the writer and activist Mary Livermore recalled—though, she reported, he did cheer up slightly when he heard that she was from Chicago. Chicago's mud, he joked, was even worse than Washington's.

Then he sagged again. "The military situation is far from bright; and the country knows it as well as I do," he said. The room was silent. "The fact is," Lincoln continued, "the people haven't yet made up their minds that we are at war with the South. They haven't buckled down to the determination to fight this war through; for they have got the idea into their heads that we are going to get out of this fix, somehow, by strategy."

One visitor protested: Surely Mr. Lincoln was not forgetting the fierce fighting at places like Fort Donelson and Shiloh. Yes, he allowed, there had been huge battles—yet the voters were now electing Democrats out of a belief that "there is a royal road to peace, and that General McClellan is to find it." And voters were not the only ones mistaken, he pointed out: "The army has not settled down into the conviction that we are in a terrible war that has got to be fought out—no; and the officers haven't either." Lincoln challenged his visitors to consider their own experiences. "When you came to Washington, ladies . . . very few soldiers came on the trains with you," he ventured. But they should watch carefully on the north-bound return: "You will find the trains and every conveyance crowded with them. You won't find a city on the route, a town, or a village, where soldiers and officers on furlough are not plenty as blackberries."

Pressing his point, Lincoln demanded: "Don't you see? We are engaged in one of the greatest wars the world has ever seen."

Getting this off his chest may have done the president some good, because when Livermore returned on other business the next morning, he was not quite so grim. He still looked "haggard" and "ravage[d]," she noted, but when he heard that his words the previous evening had left his guests feeling "hopeless," he protested earnestly: "Oh, no! Our affairs are by no means hopeless, for we have the right on our side." Hope was exactly what the Union did have, the president insisted—a hope that "the cause of freedom" would prove to be "the cause of God," for "then we may be sure it must ultimately triumph. But between that time and now," he warned, "there is an amount of agony and suffering and trial for the people that they . . . are not prepared for."

Tuesday, November 4, was the last of the autumn election days, and the result did nothing to brighten Lincoln's mood. New Jersey ousted its Republican governor. In Wisconsin, which had seemed so promising to Iowa's Senator Grimes a few weeks earlier, Democrats picked up ground. Lincoln's friend Orville Browning lost his campaign for the Senate, and even the president's home district elected a Democrat to fill the congressional seat he once occupied. Many in his party blamed Lincoln for the defeats, citing his failure to replace slow-moving Democratic generals with hard-fighting Republicans. One congressman from Pittsburgh, J. K. Moorhead, told the president that some Pennsylvania Republicans "would be glad to hear some morning that you had been found hanging from the post of a lamp at the door of the White House." Lincoln glumly answered that "such an event would not surprise me."

By now, however, Lincoln was so accustomed to the depths of gloom that he seemed almost to draw strength from dark hours. He had long since learned that the most effective antidote to a bleak mood is action; by applying this lesson again and again he developed what one writer called an "ability to see clearly and persist sanely in conditions that could have rattled even the strongest minds." Battered by discouraging election results and relentless critics, he responded in ways that were becoming familiar Lincoln signatures.

When attacked by the German-American political leader Carl Schurz, for instance, Lincoln produced a response that could serve as an official statement, much as he had done in answering Horace Greeley's pungent criticisms in August. Schurz, a fellow Republican, framed his party's indictment bluntly in a pair of letters to the president. "Let us indulge in no delusions as to the true causes of our defeat in the elections," he wrote. "The principal management of the war [has] been in the hands of your opponents. . . . It is best that you should see the fact in its true light and appreciate its significance: the result of the elections was a most serious and severe reproof administered to the Administration. Do not refuse to listen to the voice of the people."

Lincoln opened his published response with a flourish of wordplay: "I ought to be blamed, if I could do better. You think I could do better; therefore you blame me already. I think I could not do better; therefore I blame you for blaming me." In a more serious tone, he moved on to reject the idea that the Union's woes could be reduced to simple causes and pinned on particular scapegoats. "I fear we shall at last find out that the difficulty is in our case, rather than in particular generals." This lawyerly phrase—"in our case"—meant that the difficulty was inherent in the facts of the Union's predicament. Progress wasn't slow just because of the listless generals; it was slow because the North faced a gritty and indomitable enemy, because the Union had to build a strong fighting force practically from nothing, and because the army's front lines were spread across the enormous expanse of Southern territory. Then, in a deft gesture to the surging Democrats, Lincoln praised some of the opposition party's fallen war heroes, emphasizing that no Republican gave more for the Union cause than they. What mattered, Lincoln declared, was victory, not party. "I need success more than sympathy," he wrote, and "I have not seen . . . greater evidence of getting success from my sympathizers."

Lincoln also responded privately to the election results. Among the first messages he sent after all the polls closed was a terse summons to Congressman Moses Odell, a prowar Democrat from Brooklyn. "You are re-elected. I wish to see you at once. Will you come?" Odell was the token Democrat among the Republicans who constituted the Congressional Joint Committee on the Conduct of the War. His support had always been valuable to Lincoln, lending a bipartisan veneer to an often partisan project.

That support was now more important than ever, because New York was the scene of the most dramatic of all Democratic victories. Fernando Wood had been elected to Congress and, more ominously for Lincoln, Horatio Seymour was the new governor. The president could never hope to win these men over, but with the help of friendly Democrats like Odell he might soften the impact of their opposition.

As for Seymour, this would be his second term as governor of New York—the first had been ten years earlier—and most of those who enjoyed more than one term as governor of the Empire State cherished thoughts of the presidency. Once Lincoln began taking Seymour's measure, he found a man he could understand, a man of ambitions not unlike his own. Through back channels, he assured the governor's brother that he understood Seymour's next step would be a presidential bid. After all, Lincoln wrote, he himself "was a party man and did not believe in any man who was not." But the new governor should understand that "there could be no next presidency if the country was broken up."

Lincoln sent Thurlow Weed to pay a call in Albany as well, with instructions to remind the governor that the next president would surely be a man who helped to win the war, not one who tipped the balance in favor of the South. "Governor Seymour has greater power just now for good than any other man in the country," the president told Weed. If Seymour would remain loyal—a critic, but loyal—Lincoln would not resist his rise to the White House once his own term was over. The president read Seymour correctly: the New Yorker sought and won the Democratic nomination six years later, in 1868. And whether or not Lincoln's messages swayed Seymour's thinking, the president got the results he wanted. Under Governor Seymour, New York would send more than 150,000 men to the Union army (exceeding its assigned quota) while pouring many millions in tax dollars and war bonds into the Federal Treasury.

In these instances and others, the president reacted to the election returns—but he did not overreact. That made him unusual: most Republicans after the elections of 1862 believed the setback for their party was "a great historical event," as Schurz put it. "The heavens were red as with blood, and our hearts were full of resentment and revenge," one prominent Philadelphia Republican recalled. Charles Sumner pronounced the New York results "worse for our country than the bloodiest disaster on any field of battle."

In reality, though, the results were far from disastrous. Democrats gained thirty-one seats in the House of Representatives, but that was to be expected: the minority party almost always wins seats in a midterm election, and a shift of this magnitude was not uncommon in that era. In the Senate, Republicans actually gained seats. Despite the Democratic victories, then, Lincoln's Republican Party retained a solid congressional majority, the only time in twenty years that an incumbent president had achieved this. At the state level, the same pattern prevailed. Democrats gained ground but did not win control. Despite the opposition's success in mid-Atlantic and midwestern states, Republicans emerged from the polls with majorities in fifteen of the eighteen loyal legislatures (not counting the slaveholding border states). Only two of the eighteen states elected a Democratic governor.

Lincoln had survived a severe political test. He had weathered the carnage of battlefields from Shiloh to Antietam, the humiliating withdrawal from the peninsula, the treacherous defeat at Second Bull Run, the Confederate invasion of the border states, and the announcement of his emancipation plans—not to mention the imposition of unprecedented taxes, the beginnings of a military draft, and the suspension of habeas corpus. His still young party did something unusual even in peacetime: it retained the power to govern. In turn, the president renewed his power to lead.

Which is why, immediately after an election that supposedly left him dangerously weak, Lincoln finally felt strong enough to fire George McClellan.

Lincoln's view of the Union's military leadership had soured considerably during the fall. Henry Halleck was increasingly disregarded; the president's lack of faith in the abilities of his general in chief was especially apparent during a cabinet meeting on November 4, at which McClellan's future was discussed. When Edward Bates suggested putting Halleck in command of the Army of the Potomac, Lincoln scoffed. "Halleck would be an indifferent general in the field," he said. "He shrank from responsibility in his present position; . . . he is a moral coward, worth but little except as a critic."

But it was McClellan who attracted the greatest measure of Lincoln's attention. The general's halfhearted advance in the direction of Richmond stopped almost as soon as it started. Stonewall Jackson had little trouble racing to Culpeper, Virginia, ahead of McClellan and blocking what had been a wide-open road. "The President's patience is at last completely exhausted with McClellan's inaction and never-ending excuses," wrote Nicolay. Lincoln had been "exceedingly reluctant" to relieve the general, the secretary continued, because "in many respects he thinks McClellan a very superior and efficient officer."

Yet the decision to act instantly after the election suggests that the president had been waiting for the moment when he could strike without adding steam to Democratic boilers. One additional factor also influenced his timing: by showing patience with the general and greatly reinforcing his army all through October, Lincoln hoped to demonstrate to the rank-and-file of McClellan's army that their president was not the backstabber of disgruntled camp lore. He wanted success for them, and the failure to outflank Lee belonged to no one but the Young Napoleon.

Lincoln was gradually winning the army's confidence, but the removal of McClellan remained a delicate undertaking. The threat of a mutiny was in some respects more real than ever, because the election results were so widely viewed as a repudiation of the president's leadership and a demand for change at the top. So Lincoln tiptoed. Though he had no qualms about issuing orders under his own signature, he began by arranging for the official order removing McClellan to come from the pen of Halleck, a Democrat. Halleck wasn't good for much, but in this instance his signature provided useful cover.

Equally cautious was Lincoln's choice of a replacement. Ambrose Burnside, the magnificently bewhiskered victor at Roanoke, was well known and liked by McClellan and his clique. "Old Burn," as McClellan called him, had been a year behind Little Mac at West Point; later, they worked together at the Illinois Central Railroad. In 1861, Burnside had done a splendid job of directing the training of the first green troops assigned to the Army of the Potomac, and since then he had marched and fought bravely, honorably, and sometimes successfully. Burnside never claimed to be a better general than he was; his well-founded humility had already led him to rebuff two invitations from Lincoln to take over McClellan's command.

As word began to spread on November 4 that McClellan would be replaced, the general's few remaining supporters in the administration tried to save him. Montgomery Blair rode out to his family's country estate to enlist his father's help, and late that night the patriarch rushed to the presidential cottage nearby. Francis Blair, Sr., was a confidant of presidents going back to Andrew Jackson, and he made as strong a case for McClellan as anyone could. The Blairs interpreted the president's decision to fire McClellan as a fatal display of weakness in the face of the abolitionist "ultras." The old man warned Lincoln that he must stand up to the ultras or they would lead him, the party, and the country to ruin. But Lincoln's mind was made up. He had "tried long enough to bore with an auger too dull to take hold," he told the senior Blair. Rising from his seat, Lincoln "stretched his long arms almost to the ceiling," Blair recounted to his son Montgomery, and explained that he could not back down. "I said I would remove him if he let Lee's army get away from him, and I must do it. He has got the 'slows,' Mr. Blair."

Lincoln could not leave the army without a leader even for an hour, and he needed to be sure that Burnside would accept the promotion before he informed McClellan of the change. No ordinary courier could be entrusted with these responsibilities, so Edwin Stanton assigned Brigadier General Catharinus Buckingham of the War Department staff to carry the orders. He was to go first to Burnside and secure his consent. Only if the general agreed to serve was Buckingham to continue on to McClellan's tent. If Burnside declined, the distinguished messenger was to return to Washington and wait for further instructions.

Buckingham set out from Washington aboard a special train on November 7, as snow fell through darkened skies. At Burnside's tent, some fifty miles west of Washington, he pressed the reluctant general to accept the assignment out of duty—and to prevent it from going to the brash and scheming Joseph Hooker. Successful, Buckingham moved five miles north to Rectortown with McClellan's replacement in tow. Buckingham and Burnside arrived at the general's headquarters around eleven P.M. and were gone again by eleven thirty, at which point McClellan dashed off an account of the meeting to his wife.

"Another interruption—this time more important," he wrote. "It was in the shape of dear good old Burnside accompanied by Genl Buckingham . . . they brought with them the order relieving me from the command of the Army of the Potomac, & assigning Burnside. . . . No cause is given."

He continued: "Poor Burn feels dreadfully, almost crazy—I am sorry for him, & he never showed himself a better man or truer friend than now. Of course I was much surprised—but as I read the order in the presence of

Genl Buckingham, I am sure that not a muscle quivered nor was the slightest expression of feeling visible on my face, which they watched closely. They shall not have that triumph.

"They have made a dreadful mistake," McClellan concluded. "Alas for my poor country." And then, characteristically, the general absolved himself of any responsibility. "If we have failed, it was not our fault."

The public learned of the great change the next day, and if that huge, lumbering Union army was ever inclined to turn on Washington and depose Lincoln, this was the time. There was grumbling in the ranks, and some rifles flung to the ground in protest, but the long-feared military coup never materialized. Some credit for this must go to McClellan, who behaved impeccably. Whatever questions lingered about the general's patriotism were more than answered by his dignified departure from command.

On November 10, George McClellan mounted Dan Webster and rode through the ranks one last time. "Gray-haired men came to me with tears streaming down their cheeks. I never before had to exercise so much self-control," the general wrote. After he passed the last of these straight-backed columns—raw volunteers he had shaped into soldiers—McClellan boarded a railcar as an honor guard fired a final salute. Then the guardsmen crowded around the car and unhooked it from the train. They would not let him go.

At last, the general stepped onto the rear platform and gestured for quiet. "Stand by General Burnside as you have stood by me," he called out in a ringing tone, "and all will be well." At that, the soldiers reconnected the car, the train chuffed slowly away, and with it went, in the words of one soldier, "the romance of war." Robert E. Lee was also sorry to see him go, telling James Longstreet, "we always understood each other so well. I fear they may continue to make these changes until they find someone I don't understand."

Midway across the continent, after his frustrating summer on garrison duty and his successful battles with Price and Van Dorn, Ulysses Grant was finally moving again. He wired Washington to let Halleck know that he intended to gather the troops the general in chief had scattered back in June and try to do something aggressive with them. He got no reply, which he correctly took to mean that he should go ahead.

On November 2, Grant set out from Jackson, Tennessee, heading almost due south down the Tennessee and Ohio Railroad line. He was leading 42,000 men and intended to clear the Rebels as he went: away from the railroad crossing at Grand Junction, Tennessee; out of the supply depot in Holly Springs, Mississippi; away from the crossroads town of Oxford; off the Yalobusha River at Grenada. Patching up the railroad along the way, Grant figured he would eventually reach the Mississippi state capital, Jackson, where he could seize control of the road that led to Vicksburg. Cut off, the Confederates would have no choice but to evacuate their last Mississippi River stronghold and, as Lincoln would later put it, "the Father of Waters" would "again [go] unvexed to the sea."

That was the idea, and Grant's campaign began smartly as he pushed the Rebels out of Grand Junction on November 8. But a cloud quickly formed over the general's advancing army, seeded by Lincoln himself. The president had spent a good deal of time in October with an unhappy general from Grant's command, the Illinois politician John McClernand. McClernand was not just any politician; since the death of his ally Stephen A. Douglas in June 1861, the longtime congressman was arguably the most prominent Democrat in Lincoln's home state. From the opening days of the war, therefore, he was a special case for the president. After Fort Sumter, Lincoln immediately gave the untrained McClernand a generalship and put him in charge of a brigade of soldiers posted to Cairo, in McClernand's own congressional district. Since Grant was the Union commander at Cairo, Lincoln's special case became Grant's special problem. It fell to him to figure out how to get along with a self-aggrandizing second in command whose military experience was limited to sixty days in the state militia, but whose political sway dominated the immediate neighborhood and stretched all the way to the White House.

By the fall of 1862, McClernand was itching to have his own army. When the governor of Illinois invited him along on a trip to Washington in October, McClernand quickly accepted. Washington was a place where he knew how to make things happen. Once there, he pursued Lincoln relentlessly. Whenever he had a moment alone with the president, he pressed his desire to recruit and train a new army of men from Illinois and surrounding states, then take that force down the Mississippi from Memphis to capture Vicksburg. It was a big job for an inexperienced soldier, but considering the moment when McClernand had Lincoln's ear, it's not surprising that the president would listen to such a plan. After all, Lincoln was in search of aggressive generals, Vicksburg was a prize he very much coveted, and during a difficult election season he did not need John McClernand mad at him.

When McClernand left Washington late that month, he carried the orders he coveted. Signed by Stanton, endorsed by Lincoln, and marked "Confidential," the papers authorized McClernand to collect troops from Illinois, Indiana, and Iowa for his mission to open the Mississippi. Within days, however, the newspapers caught wind of McClernand's secret campaign, which is how Grant learned shortly after setting out on his campaign that his special problem was about to get much worse. "Two commanders on the same field are always one too many," Grant later wrote, "and in this case I did not think the general selected had either the experience or the qualifications for so important a position. I feared for the safety of the troops entrusted to him." On November 10, when Grant learned that fresh regiments were being told to report to McClernand, he telegraphed Halleck. "Am I to . . . lay still here while an Expedition is fitted out from Memphis?" he asked. And what about the troops from his army already stationed in Memphis under Sherman: were they to be part of this new "Expedition"?

Grant was relieved when he heard back from the general in chief the next day. "You have command of all troops sent to your Dep[artment]," Halleck wrote, "and have permission to fight the enemy when you please." Thus encouraged, Grant promptly sent his cavalry toward Holly Springs, which they cleared of Rebels and occupied on November 13.

The next few weeks were highly confusing. Halleck continued to reassure Grant that he had sole command, even as Lincoln and Stanton expressed support for McClernand and his expedition. Worried about losing the upper hand, McClernand sought and received help from his political friends. Grant, trying to thwart McClernand, decided the best strategy was to launch his own river-based Vicksburg campaign under Sherman before McClernand arrived in Memphis to claim his command. It was a mystery: was Lincoln playing a double game, allowing an important politician to cherish a little longer his fantasy that he would be entrusted with one of the most important military objectives of the war? When Lincoln authorized the Illinois congressman's mission in October, he didn't know that Grant was about to take the initiative. In urging McClernand forward, he was simply trying to light a fire. Now the pot was boiling, but the president seemed to have little desire to interfere further.

John Pope, once one of Lincoln's favorite generals, had been banished to Minnesota in early September. By the time he arrived, the crisis was over. On October 9, Pope wired the War Department to report: "The Sioux War may be considered at an end." Little Crow, reluctant leader of what had become the deadliest uprising by Native Americans in U.S. history, had predicted the outcome: "The white men are like the locusts," he said; no matter how many settlers the Sioux killed, "ten times ten will come to kill you." But it was not just the white men; it was their rifles and most of all their cannon that scattered the chief and his warriors.

After being routed at the battle of Wood Lake, Little Crow and some of his men fled into the empty plains of Canada. But hundreds of Sioux left behind were taken prisoner, and Pope reported that he was "anxious to execute a number of them." Not a small number, either, but every Indian involved in the fighting. Furthermore, Pope found it difficult to determine which of the Sioux had actually been involved: "I don't know how you can discriminate now between Indians who say they . . . have been friendly, and those who have not." In Minnesota, the press and public, too, wanted revenge on the Sioux.

A military tribunal was established to sort through the prisoners, and Pope admonished its members not to "allow any false sympathy for the Indians to prevent you from acting with the utmost rigor." On November 7, Pope sent Lincoln the names of more than three hundred Sioux prisoners who had been found guilty by the tribunal and sentenced to hang. In all of American history there had never been a mass execution on any comparable scale. Only Lincoln stood in the way.

The president had heard enough from Pope to know that a number of horrific crimes had been committed against innocent men, women, and children, but he strongly suspected that many of those now condemned had been railroaded and did not deserve to die. A plea from Minnesota's governor, Alexander Ramsey, only added to the sense that the state authorities intended to sacrifice the prisoners to satisfy a mob. "I hope the execution of every Sioux Indian condemned by the military court will be at once ordered," Ramsey wrote Lincoln. "It would be wrong upon principle and policy to refuse this. Private revenge would ... take the place of official judgment" if the executions were delayed.

On November 10, as McClellan was bidding farewell to the Army of the Potomac, the president replied that he would take the risk. He was not willing to sanction a massacre masquerading as justice. In a telegram to Pope, Lincoln wrote: "Please forward, as soon as possible, the full and complete record of these convictions. And if the record does not fully indicate the more guilty and influential ... please have a careful statement made on these points and forwarded to me."

No doubt Pope considered this terse rebuke a further humiliation, for his pique showed in his reply. "The only distinction between the culprits is ... which of them murdered most people or violated most young girls," Pope wrote. "All of them are guilty," and "the people ... are exasperated ... and if the guilty are not all executed I think it nearly impossible to prevent the indiscriminate massacre of all the Indians—old men, women, and children." The irritated Pope sent the court records to Washington.

When the documents arrived, Lincoln assigned two lawyers from the attorney general's office to review each case. It was time-consuming work: the names of the Sioux were strange and confusing, and the events described were chaotic. The examination was still under way when Pope again wired Lincoln to warn of possible lynch mobs. "Organizations of Inhabitants are being rapidly made with the purpose of massacring these Indians," he reported.

Still, Lincoln refused to be rushed, so Governor Ramsey tried another tack a few days later. Would Lincoln lift his stay of execution if Ramsey took responsibility for the hangings? "Nothing but the Speedy execution of the tried and convicted Sioux Indians will save us here from Scenes of outrage," he declared. "If you prefer it turn them over to me & I will order their Execution." On November 28, two members of Congress from Minnesota arrived in Washington to plead with Lincoln in person. A bloodbath was about to take place, they urged. He must stop it by allowing the executions to proceed.

Lincoln was hard at work that day on his annual message to Congress, which was due two days later. In Lincoln's time, this report was a vitally important document, a long and detailed accounting of government operations, as well as the president's blueprint for the future. Weeks of preparation went into each one. With the nation in the midst of a devouring civil war, Lincoln's 1862 message had to be perfectly calibrated in every word, phrase, and echo. The president told his visitors he could not put the message aside to deal with the Sioux prisoners—nor would he wash his hands of their fates. The people of Minnesota must wait a bit longer for his answer.

During her trip to New York and Boston earlier that same month, Mary Lincoln became annoyed because her husband had made no effort to communicate with her. "I have waited in vain to hear from you," she wrote on November 2, "yet as you are not given to letter writing, will be charitable enough to impute your silence, to the right cause."

Mary reported that she was doing what she loved to do—shopping, and receiving homage from "all the distinguished in the land." She mentioned that her trip had nearly been spoiled by "one of my severe attacks," but now she was herself again, dragging nine-year-old Tad to the tailor for a fitting, and in search of just the right "fur wrappings for the coachman's carriage trappings." She summarized the political intelligence she had gathered—people wanted action from the army—and passed along the news that Tad had lost a tooth. Most importantly, she could not understand why her husband wouldn't take time to jot a note. Perfect "strangers come up from [Washington] & tell me you are well," but she had heard nothing from the man himself. "One line, to say that we are occasionally remembered will be gratefully received," she wrote, and then closed by passing along a request that the president find a job for a friend of a favorite department store owner.

On November 9, Lincoln finally replied, writing that it had grown so chilly at the cottage that he was once again residing at the White House. The presidential retreat wasn't built for winter. When the season's first cold front had rattled the windows and seeped under the doors, the president's cook suggested it was time to move back to the thick-walled Executive Mansion.

Lincoln's return to the White House brought a change to the friendship he had forged over the previous two months with David Derickson, a volunteer captain from Pennsylvania. In civilian life, Derickson was a businessman from Meadville, near the Ohio border, and when the Union restarted its recruiting efforts in late June, he and his teenage son Charles answered the call. Their unit, Company K of the 150th Pennsylvania Volunteer Regiment, reached Washington in late summer during the panicky days after Pope's defeat at Bull Run. The company was assigned to the grounds of the Soldiers' Home with orders to protect the president and his family. Lincoln had always resisted being surrounded by bodyguards, but with Lee in the vicinity there was no room for debate.

Company K was a godsend for the wounded Lincoln family. Alone and in pain after the death of his brother and the subsequent banishment of the Taft boys, Tad was much in need of friends. During his mother's breakdown, the boy's emotional requirements were met mainly by his overtaxed father, who gave Tad free rein to interrupt meetings, pester official visitors, and roam the White House until he fell asleep on the floor of the president's office or on a nearby sofa. Late at night, Lincoln would hoist the sleeping boy onto his shoulder and carry him to bed.

Once the family moved out to the cottage for the summer, Tad's life brightened. Then, when Company K arrived on the grounds in the early fall, he made the soldiers' camp his own. Several of the young Pennsylvanians welcomed him as a kid brother and mascot. He rode his pony to daily drill, fell in line at chow time for plates of beans, and drafted soldiers to join him on adventures. One day a teamster got in trouble for leaving camp in Tad's company without permission, and the young Lincoln went directly to his father to obtain a permanent pass.

Lincoln sometimes joined Tad with his newfound pals for a game of checkers or a chat about army life. Now and then the president would walk over to a campfire for a cup of strong coffee; one day he watched with delight as two brothers in the company donned a blanket and pretended to be an elephant. At night, he would occasionally pace up and down at the edge of the camp, lost in thought until something caused a swell of rising voices or a burst of laughter. "Whenever he heard loud talking, he would send in and inquire of its cause," one soldier recalled.

Lincoln met David Derickson shortly after Company K's arrival and was immediately drawn to him. Impulsively, he invited the stocky, square-jawed captain to ride with him into Washington on the morning they met, and he stopped along the way to introduce the new recruit to Henry Halleck. As autumn went on, the friendship deepened, especially after Mary and Tad left on their trip to the Northeast. "The Captain and I are getting quite thick," Lincoln joked to Derickson's commanding officer. Another captain assigned to the Soldiers' Home guard, Henry W. Crotzer, often joined the pair for breakfast or dinner, but Crotzer reported that it was Derickson who "advanced . . . [furthest] in the President's confidence and esteem." Derickson earned an invitation to join Lincoln's entourage on the trip to Antietam, and sometimes, the two men stayed up so late talking at the cottage that Lincoln invited Derickson to sleep "in the same bed with him and—it is said—[make] use of His Excellency's nightshirt!"

Some historians have speculated that the relationship was sexually intimate, but the question will likely never be resolved. What is clear is that Orville Browning's departure from Washington in July had left Lincoln in need of a companion with whom he could laugh, read poetry, and give voice to his darkest forebodings. Derickson stepped into the lonely void in Lincoln's late-night lamplight.

Early in November, the army proposed to reassign Company K, but Lincoln intervened to keep Tad's friends and his own nearby. Derickson and his troops were "very agreeable to me," he wrote. Still, the move back to the White House meant that Lincoln and his bodyguards would no longer be as close. By springtime, Captain Derickson would be on to other duties.

John Dahlgren continued to be a friend. On November 15, he arranged for Lincoln to observe the test firing of a new rocket designed by the inventor Joshua Hyde. The notion of killing enemy troops with shrapnel from exploding rockets had originated in Asia; Europeans adopted rocketry during the Napoleonic Wars, and Winfield Scott took rockets to Mexico. What remained to be figured out was how to make a rocket fly straight and explode on cue: that was the riddle Hyde claimed to have solved.

Lincoln, joined by Seward and Chase, drove to the navy yard and down to the water's edge. There they found officers huddled around a cast-iron launching tube, preparing the test.

What the presidential party expected to see and hear was a whoosh, a red glare, a burst in the air, and a rain of shrapnel on the gray surface of the Anacostia River. What they actually saw, after the fuse was set and everyone took a step back from the tube, was "a blast and puff of fire" as the rocket detonated without launching.

When the smoke cleared and Lincoln was still standing with Seward and Chase unbloodied, the relief must have been intense. After all, these were men who could remember clearly what history has largely forgotten: that a failed weapons test in 1844 killed two members of John Tyler's cabinet and, but for luck, might have killed the president as well.

Browning returned to Washington from Illinois late in November and called at the White House on November 29. Lincoln "was apparently very glad to see me, and received me with much cordiality," he recorded. "We had a long familiar talk." But things were different between them now: not only had Browning been passed over for the Supreme Court, he had lost his Senate seat, and he blamed his election defeat on Lincoln's emancipation policy and the suspension of habeas corpus. Browning spoke to his friend at great length about the harmful effect of these decrees. "I told him that his proclamations had been disastrous to us. That prior to issuing them all loyal people were united in support of the war and the administration. That the masses of the democratic party were satisfied with him, and warmly supporting him" until he took those controversial steps.

This was surely not the way Lincoln remembered the dark days of summer, but he didn't interrupt to argue. Browning concluded by telling him that "the proclamations had revived old party issues" and had given the Democrats "a rallying cry." Then, at last, he paused for Lincoln's reaction. "He made no reply," Browning reported.

Lincoln evidently agreed with Browning that the decision on habeas corpus was badly handled—the subsequent widespread abuses of the power to detain people without charge had provoked much anger among the American public. Lincoln had recently responded to the criticism: on November 22, with his consent, Secretary of War Stanton had ordered the release of nearly all the federal prisoners held under the September proclamation.

As to Browning's other charge, had Lincoln chosen to answer he would certainly have pleaded not guilty. He had already said that he "would rather die than take back a word" of his emancipation decree. And although Browning's personal cause may have been hurt by the proclamation, the cause of the Union had survived at the polls.

After Browning aired his complaints, the two friends moved to less divisive topics. Lincoln caught Browning up on the military intrigue he had missed, describing Pope's campaign, the demoralization of the army, and McClellan's brief success and subsequent fatal inertia. When Browning asked about Burnside, the president replied that he had just missed seeing the general, who had earlier met with Lincoln and Halleck to discuss strategy. Then the president brought Browning up to date on Burnside's recent progress.

In the three weeks since assuming command, Burnside had moved the Army of the Potomac off the road blocked by Stonewall Jackson—the same route John Pope had preferred as a pathway to Richmond—and onto the route Irwin McDowell had planned to take back in May. This led the army once again to Fredericksburg, where Burnside camped his men across the Rappahannock from the picturesque town and sent a surrender demand to the mayor. With Lee's army coming to his rescue, the mayor felt emboldened to refuse.

This standoff had prompted Lincoln to cruise down the Potomac to Aquia Creek so that he could discuss alternatives with Burnside. The options were fairly simple: the Federal army could go through Fredericksburg or go around it. As he had shown during his single-minded assault on the bridge at Antietam, Burnside was a straight-ahead sort of thinker. He told Lincoln that he intended to string pontoon boats into a bridge, march across, take the town, and keep going. As the discussion between the two men continued into the next day and then reconvened in Washington, Lincoln showed his own tendency to err in the opposite direction, toward too much complexity. He advocated a complicated maneuver that would require three columns to converge on the Confederate position from three directions. Burnside conceded that his own plan was "somewhat risky." Lincoln acknowledged that his would require a delay for additional preparations.

Further snarling matters, Burnside's pontoon boats, held up by bureaucratic bungling, were late in arriving at the Rappahannock. In the interim, the Rebels had reached Fredericksburg and were taking up strong positions on the formidable ridgeline just behind the city.

Now, Lincoln told Browning, he and Burnside faced a difficult choice between danger and delay. "To cross the Rappahannock . . . in the face of an opposing army was very hazardous," the president said. Perhaps they should "wait a few days" to arrange a diversion along the lines of his own plan. Whatever they concluded, Lincoln said to his friend, "the question would be decided today."

The changed roster of senior commanders had seemed to galvanize Lincoln. "The President is immensely quickened, & the War Department is harder at work than ever," one close observer reported. After dismissing McClellan, Lincoln showed less patience than ever with generals who were slow to fight. On November 22, for instance, he gave Nathaniel Banks a sharp rap on the knuckles. Banks was to replace the lightning rod Benjamin Butler in New Orleans, and his assignment was to take the offensive, moving up the Mississippi Delta. A week past his promised departure date, however, Banks was still in Washington, outfitting his mission in grand McClellanesque style.

When yet another order for equipment arrived at the War Department, Lincoln was shocked. "I have just been overwhelmed and confounded with the sight of a requisition," he wrote Banks, and he was "in some hope that it is not genuine." After pointing out that the order would take at least two months to fill, Lincoln continued, his anger rising: "My dear General, this expanding, this piling up of *impedimenta*, has been, so far, almost our ruin, and will be our final ruin if it is not abandoned." Banks was to pack up whatever men and materials he had managed to collect and get himself out of town. And he was to leave *now*, before a posse of politicians showed up in a sour mood. "You must be off before Congress meets," the president demanded. Banks left.

Mary and Tad having recently returned from their travels, on Sunday, November 30, the first family attended services. Together the Lincolns filed into the New York Avenue Presbyterian Church and took their usual pew. Also in the congregation that morning was Noah Brooks, the young journalist whom the president had brought to his wife's séance earlier in the year. For a time the Maine-born Brooks had lived in Illinois, where he first encountered Lincoln as a speaker on behalf of John Frémont's 1856 presidential campaign. Now, six years later, Brooks was struck by the change in Lincoln's appearance. Reverend Gurley's sermon gave the reporter plenty of time to study and describe the transformation wrought by the nation's ordeal.

"His Excellency has grievously altered from the happy-faced Springfield lawyer of 1856," Brooks wrote. "His hair is grizzled, his gait more stooping, his countenance sallow, and there is a sunken, deathly look about the large, cavernous eyes, which is saddening to those who see there the marks of care and anxiety, such as no President of the United States has ever before known. It is a lesson for human ambition to look upon that anxious and careworn face, prematurely aged by public labors and private griefs, and to remember that with the fleeting glory of his term of office have come responsibilities which make his life one long series of harassing care."

Tomorrow, Lincoln would deliver his annual message to Congress, explaining himself and charting the way forward—not just for Washington, but for the whole country. Today, marked by "the daily scars of mental anxiety and struggle," Lincoln wearily stood at the end of the service and started up the aisle. But as he walked, Brooks reported, his exhausted face was "lighted with a smile" and he gave "a cheerful nod [to] his friends on either side."

DECEMBER

The fateful moment was but a month away: on New Year's Day, Abraham Lincoln was due to sign the Emancipation Proclamation. While no one knew exactly how the consequences of the president's radical decree would unfold, the nation was clearly on the path to yet more violence and upheaval. Naturally, large numbers of Americans found themselves wishing they could reverse course. Lincoln understood this impulse, but he also knew that the brink was already behind them. There was no realistic way back, only forward.

He made this point succinctly in response to a ludicrous proposal from Fernando Wood, the colorful New York City ward boss whose latest public office was a seat in the next Congress. Claiming to have inside information from Confederate sources, Wood told Lincoln that the Rebels were ready to send representatives to rejoin the Federal government, provided they were given blanket amnesty from treason charges. The time was ripe, Wood argued, for the president to declare a cease-fire in the war and explore whether the Southern states might return to the fold. With peace restored, the North and South could send the cream of their two armies to drive the French out of Mexico and annex that country for the purpose of creating nine additional slave states, thus assuring the Southerners that their voices would command respect for years to come in Congress and the electoral college. Wood wanted Lincoln's blessing to open negotiations.

After initially ignoring Wood's insistent demands for a reaction to this scheme, the president finally replied. "I strongly suspect your information will prove to be groundless," Lincoln wrote mildly, "nevertheless I thank you for communicating it to me." To resume their places in the Union, all the Southerners had to do was "cease resistance, and . . . submit to, and maintain the national authority," he explained. Otherwise, there was nothing to negotiate.

Lincoln's second annual message to Congress offered a far more detailed version of his views. After opening the message in traditional style with a general survey of government operations, he turned to the meat of his concerns. At this critical and delicate juncture, he sought to explain again why the nation's ordeal was necessary, and to reassure his nervous countrymen that the future still promised a reign of prosperous peace.

Characteristically, Lincoln went back to first principles to construct a stout ladder of logic. "A nation may be said to consist of its territory, its people, and its laws," he wrote. People and laws could change, but "the territory is the only part which is of certain durability." The physical imperatives of geography were becoming more powerful all the time, Lincoln noted, as technology—"steam, telegraphs, and intelligence"—shrank the distance between far-flung regions.

Looking at the landmass of the United States, Lincoln asserted that it was "well adapted to be the home of one national family," but poorly set up "for two, or more." Why? Because "physically speaking, we cannot separate. There is no line, straight or crooked, suitable for a national boundary." In the East the likeliest border between North and South consisted of rivers, easily crossed and bustling with the commerce of a rapidly growing population. In the western two thirds of the landmass, all possible borders were "merely surveyor's lines, over which people may walk back and forth."

Even if two compatible nations could, in theory, live peacefully within these unnatural boundaries, disputes over slavery made conflict inevitable within the United States, Lincoln continued. Quoting from his own inaugural address, he wrote: "One section of our country believes slavery is *right,* and ought to be extended, while the other believes it is *wrong,* and ought not to be extended." This tension would not disappear simply because the antagonists separated behind borders drawn on a map. Abolitionists in the North would continue to aid and encourage escaping slaves to ford rivers or step across surveyor's lines. Slave catchers from the

South would continue to cross those same weak frontiers in search of their "property," or the South would attempt to harden these borders and thus restrict the free flow of trade from north to south and east to west. A conflict that could not be solved by shared laws within a single nation would be no easier to solve through treaties between two contending nations, Lincoln observed. Strife and violence would be permanent, as they had been on the Kansas prairie in the years before Fort Sumter.

Perhaps it once had been imaginable that New England could go one way and the Deep South another, undoing the great compromise of the Founders. But Lincoln directed attention beyond the original colonies to what he called "the great body of the republic," the nation's muscular midsection. This vast breadbasket, he explained, "is naturally one of the most important [regions] in the world." But it "[has] no sea-coast," and therefore would always depend on routes through adjacent territory to bring its abundant crops and goods to markets around the world. The inhabitants of the American heartland could never be expected to leave their economic destiny hostage to current and future secessionists throwing up new borders and obstacles whenever they pleased. "True to themselves," he wrote, they "will not ask *where* a line of separation shall be, but will vow, rather, that there shall be no such line." Lincoln went on: "There is no possible severing, but would multiply, and not mitigate, evils among us." The land "demands union, and abhors separation."

They were fighting now to avoid fighting later, Lincoln's essay implied. And the sacrifice would be worth it: the slavery question, he predicted, could be "hushed forever with the passing of one generation." With that, the president turned to the prospect of race relations after emancipation, an issue that troubled even the most optimistic Americans. Lincoln renewed his case in favor of colonization, arguing that the seemingly impossible cost of emancipation and colonization would be whittled away by the rapid growth of a peaceful nation. Presciently, he foretold a day when the United States would become more prosperous than all of Europe combined: "And we *will* reach this, too, if we do not ourselves relinquish the chance, by the folly and evils of disunion."

But then Lincoln struck a new note in his presidency. "I strongly favor colonization," he wrote. "And yet—" With those two words, Lincoln turned a corner from past to future, for he then introduced the idea that a harmonious multiracial society was a real possibility. White Americans, he wrote, did not need to fear freedom. Free black workers cannot "displace any more white labor, by being free, than by remaining slaves," he reasoned. "Are they not already in the land? Will liberation make them any more numerous? Equally distributed among the whites of the whole country . . . there would be but one colored to seven whites. Could the one, in any way, greatly disturb the seven?" He pointed his audience to places around the country that already had free black populations as large or larger than one of seven. People there—Maryland and Delaware, for example—lived happily, "without any apparent consciousness of evil from" their diversity.

These words may sound stunted and cautious a century and a half later. But in the context of the time, Lincoln's vision of a diverse new nation was another step on a long road of revolution. Even as he used the annual message to repeat his arguments in favor of distant colonies for the former slaves, he began to prepare the country for the inevitable failure of that unwieldy scheme, and for the task of living together in freedom. No choice remained, Lincoln asserted: the Union must be saved. And when that terrible work was done, Americans would reap untold dividends in a rich and purposeful future. Peaceful emancipation would be ideal, but in any event he would order the army to begin to enforce his proclamation on January 1.

In closing, Lincoln offered a call to action that would ring down through the ages: "Fellow-citizens, *we* cannot escape history. . . . In *giving* freedom to the *slave,* we *assure* freedom to the *free*—honorable alike in what we give, and what we preserve. We shall nobly save, or meanly lose, the last, best hope of earth."

His annual message at last finished, Lincoln turned back to the contentious matter of the condemned Minnesota Sioux. He asked Joseph Holt, the judge advocate general of the army, whether he, Lincoln, could describe a set of standards for choosing which Indians should be hanged and delegate the actual selection to someone else. Holt replied that the president must make the decisions himself. Lincoln dutifully went to work plowing through 303 often confusing files, separating out those warriors who unquestionably participated in massacres (as distinguished from battles) or rapes. Meanwhile, Congress boiled with impatience. The Senate passed a resolution demanding copies of all paperwork relating to the Sioux uprising, while the House debated the feasibility of banning all

Native Americans from Minnesota. On the far-off frontier, a drunken mob marched on the stockade where the prisoners were being held, but a smooth-talking guard managed to dissuade the crowd from rioting.

Lincoln completed his deliberations on December 6 and painstakingly wrote out the names and case numbers of the thirty-nine prisoners whom he had condemned to death. He copied out the unfamiliar names as well as he could; the phonetic renderings made it plain that no one with authority over these lives could speak or understand a word of the Sioux language. Very clear, though, was Lincoln's determination to save as many of the Sioux as he could from unjust punishment. Even after he sent off his list, he continued to worry about the details: he dictated a follow-up message a few days later warning the authorities in Minnesota not to confuse two prisoners who had similar names.

Given the intense political pressure for revenge and the cyclone of war raging around him, Lincoln's care and mercy are impressive. He spared roughly seven out of every eight prisoners, apparently spurred only by his conscience. Lincoln "shrank with evident pain from even the idea of shedding human blood," Army lawyer Joseph Holt later reflected, speaking of the many hours they spent together reviewing the decisions of courts-martial. "These cases came to him by the hundreds, and the carrying out of all these many sentences impressed him as nothing short of 'wholesale butchery.' . . . He always leaned to the side of mercy. His constant desire was to save life."

Lincoln's order was extremely unpopular in Minnesota. But this was one occasion when the president disregarded public opinion. As he later explained, "I could not hang men for votes."

Night after night in the snowy cold on the Rappahannock, the men of the Army of the Potomac could look across the river past the lights of Fredericksburg and see Rebel campfires burning on the yonder hills. Each night, there were more of them to see. By the second week of December, the enemy was so numerous that no one on the Union side had much faith in Burnside's plan for a frontal attack—including Burnside. He was not shy about telling people how little he wanted his job and how inadequate he felt. This fretful talk inevitably led to dissent among his generals, and on the night of December 10 the reluctant commander summoned them to a meeting, during which he told them that he had no use for complaints, only determination. Trained by McClellan to see high-level treachery behind every bad decision, many of those senior officers could only assume that Burnside was being ordered from above to persist in his plans long "after all hope of a surprise had faded away."

They were wrong. Lincoln continued to argue for a more sophisticated plan, but Burnside seemed to have become almost paralyzed as he waited for the arrival of the pontoon boats that would allow his troops to get across the river. On December 11, with the boats at last on hand, he gave the order to link them to form bridges, and soon the blue legions began crossing. Lovely little Fredericksburg was shelled and sacked in the process.

Lee held his fire. He couldn't quite believe his good fortune. He had been assuming that the brunt of the Federal assault would come on his extreme right, as the Union tried to turn his flank. Instead, Burnside appeared intent on attacking across a wide-open field leading to an impregnable position. Longstreet, commanding the Rebel center behind the town, was equally puzzled. Imagining that Burnside might have some ruse in mind, Longstreet asked his superintendent of artillery whether he shouldn't add to the batteries guarding the open plain. "General," came the reply, "a chicken could not live on that field when we open on it."

That was not much of an exaggeration. The field was about a mile wide. It lay just south of town, facing a hill called Marye's Heights, named for the wealthy attorney whose pillared mansion stood on top. The hill was studded with cannon, and at the foot of the hill, facing the field, was a sunken road guarded by a stone wall that provided a perfect shield for regiments of Rebel riflemen. Moreover, the few buildings on the plain made lethal perches for Confederate sharpshooters.

December 13 dawned in a thick fog that covered the approach to the field by the Union's II Corps. When the first brigades charged at noon, the corps commander, Darius Couch, climbed into a church steeple and looked down. As Couch later wrote, he saw "that the whole plain was covered with men, prostrate and dropping, the live men running here and there . . . the wounded coming back. The commands seemed to be mixed up. I had never seen fighting like that, nothing approaching it in terrible uproar and destruction. . . . As they charged the artillery fire would break their formation and they would get mixed; then they would close up, go forward, receive the withering infantry fire, and those who were able would run to the houses and fight as best they could; and then the next brigade coming up in succession would do its duty and melt like snow coming down on warm ground."

Burnside threw seven divisions into this slaughter pen—ordering as many as fourteen hopeless charges—and as the horrible afternoon wore on, the sight of each new brigade appearing in neat formation and marching from the streets of town to meet its dread appointment grew more pathetically moving. Longstreet saw "the Federals come again and again to their death," and thought "that they deserved success if courage and daring could entitle soldiers to victory." It is said that Lee, watching from a nearby hilltop, was moved to speak perhaps his most famous words: "It is well that war is so terrible—we should grow too fond of it."

The green Pennsylvania volunteers who made the last charge into the smoky twilight that day went just as bravely as the combat veterans who made the first. Thousands of dead and wounded lay on the ground before the marching troops. Using the corpses of their comrades as shelter from the Rebel fire, a number of injured soldiers reached up to grab at the legs of the advancing men, trying to hold them back. But the novice bluecoats shook loose and pushed ahead.

After they, too, fell short of the stone barrier, night finally ended the fighting. Bitter cold settled over the field, and wounded men clung to one another for warmth. Burial crews would later find bodies pasted to the earth by frozen gore.

"What will the country say?" Lincoln asked in anguish as the awful dimensions of the Federal debacle at Fredericksburg became clear. Some 13,000 Union troops were dead, wounded, or missing—the equivalent of another Antietam—compared with 5,000 from Lee's army. Also gone were the remnants of morale. Burnside, in an almost suicidal gesture, called for his old IX Corps to form up on December 14 for yet another assault on the murderous heights, promising to lead this one himself. He gave up the idea only after the entire high command of the army told him it was madness. By now the general had completely lost the confidence of his officers; in the ranks, soldiers were stunned and sickened by the waste. Even the government's reliable boosters at *Harper's Weekly* recoiled from the "imbecility, treachery, failure, [and] privation" that seemed to culminate in this battle, warning that the public "cannot be expected to suffer that such massacres as this . . . shall be repeated." As the reactions poured in, Lincoln groaned: "If there is a worse place than Hell, I am in it."

But as the peerless Bruce Catton has noted, this senseless disaster revealed a critical truth about the Union's soldiers and gave an augury of the war's eventual outcome. What was important about Fredericksburg, the historian wrote, "was not, after all, the fact that a stupid general ordered" the assaults, "but the fact that the army which had to make them had never once faltered." In the stirring sight of those seemingly endless ranks of hopeless men bearing polished rifles, Catton saw the "burnished rows of steel" prophesied by Julia Ward Howe, infused with their fiery gospel of freedom and borne by an army that had "lost all its morale but which somehow kept coming on."

Soon after the fighting ended, Lincoln began to see the battle in much the same way. He had spoken of the army's need to engage in "hard desperate fighting," and no battle could ever be harder or more desperate than this one. Now, safely back on the north side of the Rappahannock, the Army of the Potomac still numbered more than 100,000 strong. It would grow even larger, and endure many more losses, before the war was won.

Pondering the lopsided tally at Fredericksburg, Lincoln realized that he had just glimpsed the horrific mathematical essence of the Civil War. As long as the Union armies were willing, somehow, to keep coming on, to keep marching and fighting and dying, they would inevitably prevail. As he put it: "If the same battle were to be fought over again, every day, through a week of days, with the same relative results, the army under Lee would be wiped out to its last man, the Army of the Potomac would still be a mighty host, the war would be over, the Confederacy gone, and peace would be won. . . . No general yet found can face the arithmetic, but the end of the war will be at hand when he shall be discovered."

On December 17, as details from Fredericksburg made headlines across the North, Lincoln was abruptly drawn into a hard, desperate battle of his own. Into his office that day walked Senator Preston King of New York and Assistant Secretary of State Frederick Seward. King handed the president a sheet of paper. Lincoln scanned it in pained confusion: it was a letter of resignation written by Seward's father, the secretary of state. The younger Seward added that he, of course, was also stepping down.

"What does this mean?" the president asked. King painted the background.

The previous day, the Republican caucus of the Senate had gathered for a secret meeting, the purpose of which was to discuss the lack of progress in the war. The latest defeat on the battlefield had come as a bitter blow, and now the senators devised a plan to attack the man they blamed for it: William Seward. In the view of the Senate majority, Seward was soft on slavery, a friend of compromise, the protector of halfhearted warriors like McClellan and Halleck, and, worst of all, Lincoln's closest adviser. Some believed the secretary of state was actually pulling the strings of a puppet president. Supporting evidence for these views was thin, but then as now, truth in Washington was more a matter of belief than fact.

The trouble had started even before Lincoln's inauguration. Two years earlier, Seward had led a failed effort to solve the secession crisis by compromise, and that attempt left him a marked man in a time when compromise was equated with capitulation. When he then worked his way into a closer relationship with Lincoln than the other cabinet secretaries enjoyed, the result was jealousy, especially on the part of Seward's longtime rival Chase. The almost daily meetings between Lincoln and Seward became a convenient explanation for all the president's perceived faults and failures—especially his choice of Democrats to lead armies and what Republican abolitionists saw as his foot-dragging on slavery. Many in Lincoln's party felt that Seward's influence was too great and all wrong, and now it was finally time to stop him.

At the caucus meeting, Morton Wilkinson of Minnesota, still angry over Lincoln's refusal to execute all the Sioux prisoners, led off the attack. As Orville Browning recorded it, Wilkinson "denounced the President and Mr Seward [and] said our cause was lost and the country ruined." Ben Wade went next, with "a long speech in which he declared that the Senate should go in a body and demand of the President the dismissal of Mr Seward." And not only that: Wade also called for a Republican general in chief, who should be given "absolute and despotic powers." William Fessenden of Maine was more temperate, but he too wanted Seward's head. Citing an unnamed member of the cabinet as his source of information, Fessenden claimed that "there was a back stairs & malign influence which controlled the President, and overruled all the decisions of the Cabinet." Pressed to identify his source, Fessenden demurred, but Browning wrote that he recognized that distinctive phrase—"back stairs & malign"—and was convinced that it was pure Chase.

James Grimes of Iowa moved that the caucus make a formal demand. A few senators objected, Browning among them. Given the long hours he had spent with Lincoln urging his own conservative policies, Browning would have been in a good position to knock down the theory that Seward alone poured such ideas into the president's ear. But Browning didn't offer a defense of Lincoln; instead, he protested that the indictment of Seward contained "no evidence the charges were true," and warned that a call for his resignation could provoke a "war between Congress and the President" at a time when unity was essential. The senators decided to adjourn overnight and reflect on the matter, but the next day many of them were even angrier than before. One group proposed that they demand not only Seward's resignation but also Lincoln's.

Ultimately, the majority voted to moderate the wording of their indictment of the secretary, but the result left the meaning clear. Afterward, Preston King took it on himself to warn his friend Seward about the impending crisis. "They may do as they please about me," Seward replied, "but they shall not put the President in a false position on my account." He wrote out his resignation on the spot, instructed his son to do the same, and asked King to join Frederick in delivering the papers to Lincoln.

A year earlier, of course, a similar ill wind had blown down from Capitol Hill. When Congress convened the previous December, all the frustrations over the administration's perceived bungling found expression in the Joint Committee on the Conduct of the War. Now Congress was once again returning from a recess that coincided with dark days for the Republic: the ignominious retreat from the peninsula, the shameful episode at Manassas, McClellan's return to command and subsequent failure to pursue Lee after Antietam. The senators had watched all this from afar, sharing gossip and gripes by mail, but unable to do more than grumble. Much of what they heard came directly or indirectly from inside the cabinet, which had never entirely healed from the failed attempt in August to force Lincoln to fire McClellan. The ringleaders of that effort—Chase, Stanton, and Smith—all faulted Seward for the government's troubles. But among Lincoln's advisers, Chase was believed to be the prime source of the anti-Seward gospel.

This was almost certainly correct. Browning characterized the leaders of the Senate revolt as "the partizans of Mr. Chase," adding, "I had reason to believe that he had set them on." Canny Thomas Ewing "had no doubt Chase was at the bottom of the mischief." One of the disgruntled senators, Charles Sumner, had confided in a letter from Boston that "Chase writes me from Washington," and then delivered a litany of criticisms that could have come almost verbatim from Chase's diary. "A wise, courageous & humane" president would have made the war into an antislavery crusade from the beginning, "[and] have ended it by now," Sumner wrote. "But with Lincoln as Pres[ident] & Seward as Secretary this was impossible." Sumner was convinced that Seward had always opposed emancipation and that the secretary believed "that by some patch-work this great question could be avoided."

What happened a year earlier now happened again: the pent-up recriminations of Congress demanded an outlet. But because this explosion was so destructive and irregular, it was far more dangerous than the creation of the joint committee. Oversight committees are standard features of Congress, and they are charged, at least partly, with finding facts. This demand for Seward's head, by contrast, was little more than a witch hunt. The president knew perfectly well that Seward wasn't secretly running the government. Moreover, he was adamant that Congress should not dictate to him who would serve in the cabinet. In Lincoln's view, the move against Seward was a fatal step beyond the Senate's constitutional duty to advise and consent.

Immediately after receiving Seward's resignation, Lincoln strode across the street to his house, where he found his friend putting a brave face on the situation. It would be a relief to retire to private life, Seward said. "Ah, yes, Governor," Lincoln replied, "that will do very well for you, but I am like the starling in Sterne's story: 'I can't get out.'" (The story of the starling appears in a work by the English writer Laurence Sterne that describes a dawn of conscience as the narrator suddenly realizes the evil of slavery. The plaintive call of a caged bird sounds like someone crying "I can't get out!" Hearing this, the narrator pours out an epiphany in which he compares slavery to "a bitter draught" and cries, "Though thousands in all ages have been made to drink of thee, thou art no less bitter on that account.")

During his conversation with Seward, Lincoln made no promises about how he would respond to the senators' demand. Gideon Welles would later speculate that Seward was disappointed when Lincoln did not reject the resignation out of hand and "refuse to parley with the committee." But the president could not afford to draw battle lines inside the Union coalition. He needed the abolitionist wing as much as he needed the conservatives, so his task was to defuse the Senate challenge, not defy it.

The first step was to understand what was behind it. Needing to hear for himself what the senators from his party were so upset about, Lincoln arranged to host a delegation from the caucus at seven P.M. the next day, December 18. The wait was agony. He had nowhere to turn; as John Hay put it: "He had & could have no adviser" on such a delicate and secret matter, and "must work it out by himself."

When Browning—who would not be part of the Senate delegation— called at the White House shortly before the meeting, he found the president extremely agitated. "What do these men want?" Lincoln demanded.

"I hardly know, Mr. President," Browning answered. "But they are exceedingly violent towards the administration, and what we did yesterday"—issuing the Republican caucus's resolution—"was the gentlest thing that could be done."

Lincoln then answered his own question. "They wish to get rid of me," he said, "and I am sometimes half disposed to gratify them."

"Some of them do," Browning replied. But he urged Lincoln not to give in to them, saying that to lose his steady hand at this point would "bring upon us certain and inevitable ruin."

"We are now on the brink of destruction," the president agreed.

As Lincoln had often said, the key to victory was a united North; now the anti-Seward senators were threatening to sabotage that fragile unity. If they were allowed to blow up the cabinet, they would destroy the tenuous balance between radical and conservative Unionists and make a bad joke of Lincoln's claim to be the man holding the elements together. "It appears to me the Almighty is against us," the president told his friend, "and I can hardly see a ray of hope."

Browning couldn't resist telling Lincoln that he should have "crushed the ultra[s] . . . last summer." But the president did not rise to the bait.

Instead he fumed that the case against Seward was founded on "a lie, an absurd lie." Then he sent Browning away, saying the delegation would be up shortly. "Since I heard last night of the proceedings of the caucus," he added, "I have been more distressed than by any event of my life."

Lincoln may have felt that he was in "a worse place than Hell," but as the nine Republican senators took their seats the president greeted them "with his usual urbanity," one participant noted. The venerable Jacob Collamer of Vermont, the delegation's chairman, stood up again with the caucus resolution in his hands and began to read. The toned-down text was gassy and general, calling for "a vigorous and successful prosecution of the war" by a president working in harness with his cabinet, sharing "combined wisdom and deliberation." It went on like that for four paragraphs. The elder statesman then sat down quietly and invited his fellow senators to speak if they wished.

Ben Wade certainly wished. Fulminating about election losses in the West, he blamed Lincoln for "plac[ing] the direction of our military affairs in the hands of bitter and malignant Democrats." Lincoln had heard this many times from Wade; he made no reply.

Grimes finally got to the point: the senators felt an "entire want of confidence in Secretary Seward." Fessenden concurred. The cabinet, he said, was unable to shape events because Seward "exerted an injurious influence"; this was especially troubling because Seward "was not in accord with the majority." Seward pampered Democrats in high commands, while the administration left abolitionist heroes like John Frémont and David Hunter disgraced and abandoned. And what was the result? McClellan was now busy attacking the government, spreading his lies that the president and his advisers had sabotaged the Peninsula Campaign.

The mention of McClellan and his complaints got Lincoln riled up. Seizing a stack of papers, he began pulling letters from the pile that he had sent to McClellan and then reading them aloud one by one. The recitation went on for thirty minutes until Lincoln felt he had proved his case, which was that "McClellan . . . had been sustained by the government to the utmost of its power." Finally he put the letters back on his desk and was quiet again.

Sumner now turned to the topic of Seward's extensive diplomatic correspondence, which had been published earlier in December. Sumner had been reading the papers closely, and he didn't like what he had found. One short letter was particularly galling. It was a dispatch from Seward to Adams, dated July 5 and marked "Confidential." A vivid example of Seward's love for overstatement and shock, the document seemed designed to sharpen the anger of his enemies. The timing was unfortunate as well: the letter was written just as Washington was filling with wounded veterans of the Seven Days battles and Congress was aflame with passionate debate over Lyman Trumbull's confiscation bill. Seward, the pragmatist, was in a mood to blame the administration's troubles on hard-liners of all stripes. One side pushed secession and the other pushed immediate emancipation; as Seward wrote, "it seems as if the extreme advocates of African slavery and its most vehement opponents were acting in concert together" to ignite violent slave uprisings.

Sumner seethed: to his mind, this official letter placed "the Confederates and the majority of Congress upon the same levels." Nothing could more clearly demonstrate Seward's unacceptable views. Lincoln was at a loss to answer this charge. He explained that he and Seward normally discussed all dispatches before they were sent, but he couldn't recall discussing this one. Pointedly, the president did not defend the decision to write or send the letter, much less to publish it for the world to read.

This colloquy with the senators went on for three long hours, though the tone remained civil throughout. Lincoln struck at least one senator as "cheerful" and "pleased with the interview." Afterward, the president boiled the session down to one pithy remark. As Bates recorded it, Lincoln said that "while they believed in [Lincoln's] honesty, they seemed to think that when he had in him any good purposes, Mr. S[eward] contrived *to suck them out of him unperceived.*"

Overnight, Lincoln sifted through the shards of his situation. He now knew the extent of the complaints against Seward, and he knew most of them weren't true. They were based, as Fessenden had put it, on "common rumor." And the president had a pretty good guess where the rumors were coming from. The difficult question was this: without further inflaming the situation, how could he prove to the senators that the gossip and complaints of Salmon Chase were not to be trusted?

Gideon Welles had barely shrugged off his overcoat at the Navy Department the next morning when a message arrived from John Nicolay announcing an emergency cabinet meeting at half-past ten. Normally, the call to council would come from the office of the secretary of state, but by now the rumor of Seward's resignation was spreading. At the appointed hour, Lincoln convened the group—with Seward conspicuously absent—by admonishing everyone to keep secret what he was about to say. He then recounted the story thus far: the efforts by the Republican caucus to oust the secretary of state; Seward's shock and resignation; the long and "animated" meeting with the Senate delegation the night before. The president told his colleagues that he had explained to the senators how much their resolution "grieved him," particularly because it was based on assumptions that weren't true. The senators had asserted that the cabinet was rife with dissent and division; no, he had told them, the cabinet, which had been carefully chosen to balance the diverse political voices of the Union coalition, had in fact "gone on harmoniously." Of course its members had their differences, but "there had never been serious disagreements." Moreover, Lincoln had assured the senators, the cabinet had "sustained and consoled" him through all his burdens and toils, with "mutual and unselfish confidence and zeal."

This artful opening statement worked on two levels. First, it was an optimistic call to arms at a moment of crisis. Second, it deftly placed Chase, and Seward's other critics, in a tricky spot. No cabinet member was likely to openly disagree with such a glowing tribute to the group's self-sacrificing patriotism. But the alternative to speaking out was to remain silent, and silence could only be interpreted as agreement with Lincoln's summary of the situation. The president had neatly closed off the option of airing and discussing the cabinet's dysfunctions and grievances—by saying at the outset that they didn't exist.

He then asked his colleagues not to do anything rash. Do not undertake "combined movement" to "resist this assault," he begged. He said he was afraid "the rest of [them] might take [this] as a hint to retire also," and "he could not afford to lose" any additional members of his council. They must remain together and be patient. Again, who could disagree?

When Lincoln finished talking, the cabinet chattered awhile over the shocking news, each one telling the others when he first caught wind of Seward's resignation. Blair boasted that he had known since the day before; Stanton said he had heard it from Lincoln during an earlier meeting; Bates reported learning of the news on his way to the White House that morning. Salmon Chase, however, claimed that he had known absolutely nothing of the Senate caucus or of Seward's decision to step down until he had heard it in this room—a statement difficult to believe, when it came from such a gossipy insider. Finally, after some more rambling discussion, Lincoln adjourned the meeting. He asked them all to return at seven thirty P.M.

Lincoln had learned something that morning: neither Chase nor any other unhappy cabinet member was willing to cross him or to level charges against Seward in front of the others. And if they wouldn't do it among themselves, it was unlikely they would do it with the Republican senators in the room. Lincoln sent word to Collamer that he would like to meet with the Senate delegation again. They should come to the White House that evening—at seven thirty.

Elite Washington hummed with the electric excitement of a political crisis. Conversations leapt quickly from the rumor of Seward's resignation to the prospect of a complete upheaval of the cabinet, and from there to the capital's age-old pastime: touting candidates. Who should replace Seward—Sumner? Collamer? If Chase resigned, would Fessenden take his place? Or should Thomas Ewing return to Treasury? Preston King or John Dix would make a fine secretary of war when Stanton went—or should the new secretary be Frémont? Meanwhile, across the aisle, Democrats scoffed at this flurry of Republican names. They were convinced that the crackup of Lincoln's cabinet would force the president to recall McClellan and give him greater powers than ever before. Browning, recording this line of reasoning in his diary, wrote that Little Mac would "*dictate* his own terms," including "the disposal of all the commands in the army!"

When the delegation of senators gathered again that evening in the anteroom of Lincoln's office, they discovered they were not alone. Eyeing the cabinet members with curiosity, they waited briefly until Lincoln welcomed them all into his chamber and announced that he had taken the liberty of inviting the cabinet—minus Seward, of course—"for a free and friendly conversation." Did the senators have any objection? Blindsided, the lawmakers had no opportunity to discuss the proposition; when Collamer acquiesced, the rest of them went along.

Lincoln now had all of them in a room together; it was time to play his hand. The president began with an expanded version of the remarks he had tested with the cabinet that morning. It was true, he admitted, that the cabinet did not meet at regular intervals; the urgent press of the war made that impossible. But "most questions of importance had received a reasonable consideration" by the group. Furthermore, he continued, once decisions were made, the cabinet—including Seward—supported them. The president vouched personally for the secretary of state, saying that Seward was "earnest in the prosecution of the war and had not improperly interfered."

The delegation was deeply skeptical of these claims. Senator Fessenden and Lincoln's old Illinois rival Lyman Trumbull, for instance, later remarked that the president's own words furnished ample evidence that he often failed to keep the cabinet informed. Lincoln acknowledged that he had not consulted his cabinet before choosing McClellan and, later, Halleck, as general in chief. Nor did he come to them prior to reinstating McClellan as head of the army after Pope's loss at Bull Run. Nor did he take a vote on whether he should proclaim emancipation.

Yet, no one in the room was willing to speak up to contradict the president, so it was time for Lincoln to reveal his trump card. As evidence that his cabinet worked together harmoniously, the president declared that Seward sometimes sought advice from Chase about important diplomatic matters. Lincoln then paused, looked at Chase, and asked whether any of the cabinet members disagreed with anything he had said.

Chase was cornered. Everyone in the room knew that he disagreed with Lincoln's description of a collegial cabinet. But would he say so, knowing that the consequences might be dire—for himself, for Lincoln, and for the country? The treasury secretary was visibly angry. As one participant recalled, Chase finally found his voice to protest that "he should not have come here had he known that he was to be arraigned before a committee of the Senate." Grudgingly, however, he agreed with Lincoln that the cabinet had weighed most of the important issues in the war— "though perhaps not as fully as might have been desired," he added weakly. It was also true, he acknowledged, that the cabinet generally concurred with and supported the decisions made by the president.

Stanton, for one, was "disgusted" by this answer. As he told Fessenden the next day, every charge contained in the caucus resolution was true, yet Chase had cut the legs out from under the senators. The war secretary asserted that he "was ashamed of Chase, for he knew better."

But did Stanton speak up? Did any member of the cabinet? Caleb Smith, the interior secretary, was another anti-Seward voice, and he later said that "he had felt strongly tempted to contradict Mr. Chase on the spot." But he had already accepted Lincoln's appointment to the federal bench and would soon be gone, so he too decided to keep quiet.

The senators were stunned. A few days afterward, when Orville Browning heard a description of this meeting, he asked Senator Collamer "how Mr. Chase could venture to make such a statement in the presence" of the very men he had filled with stories of Seward's "back stairs and malign influence."

Collamer's answer was simple: "He lied."

Was Chase lying, or had he exaggerated while telling and retelling all those aggrieved tales he spread around Washington and passed on in his letters—stories in which every Union setback was merely a matter of too much Seward and not enough Chase? None of the senators in the room that evening could be sure.

After the showdown with Chase, the conversation moved on. Various senators detailed their impatience and irritation and fears for the nation's future. Blair and then Bates replied with long speeches about the Constitution and separation of powers and the authority of the executive. Throughout, Lincoln put in comments and anecdotes, most of which the men had heard before.

Chase sat quietly until he abruptly interjected one unexpected piece of information. The conversation had wandered onto the subject of the September 22 cabinet meeting at which Lincoln read his preliminary Emancipation Proclamation. As Lincoln was describing that day's discussion, Chase reminded the president that Seward had actually *strengthened* the decree. Where the president had pledged the government to "recognize" the freedom of former slaves, Seward suggested adding the words "and maintain." Recognize *and maintain*: the senators could unquestionably see the significance of that change. How did this information square with their image of a man skulking on the back stairs of the White House, secretly maneuvering on behalf of slave owners?

It didn't.

After allowing the conversation to go on a bit longer while everyone digested what they had heard, Lincoln asked the senators whether they had changed their minds about the need to force Seward out. Some had, some had not. Fessenden, for one, didn't wish to discuss the subject in front of the president's advisers; provided with this opening, the cabinet departed. By now it was around midnight. Lincoln and the senators kept talking for another hour, as the meeting devolved into a classic late-night airing of long-festering complaints.

Before the session ended, Fessenden made one last stab at Seward. The question was no longer whether to force him out, the senator said; he had resigned. Now the question was whether Lincoln should invite him back in. "Under these circumstances I feel bound to say that as Mr. Seward has seen fit to resign, I should advise that his resignation be accepted," the senator said.

Lincoln, having accomplished over the past several hours precisely what he had intended, said nothing.

"The town is all in a buz," Bates scribbled hastily in his diary on December 20. The scuttlebutt now was that Lincoln's entire cabinet was out, and some people were actually sending lists of possible replacements to the White House in hopes that Lincoln would review them.

But the final act of the drama remained unwritten. To allow the Senate cabal to drive out Seward would have unbalanced the government and pushed it in the radical direction; as Lincoln later put it, "the thing would all have slumped over one way [and] we should have been left with a scanty handful of supporters." On the other hand, Fessenden had correctly pointed out the night before that since everyone in town already knew about Seward's resignation, to coax him back would tilt the administration in the opposite direction. To maintain his precarious balance, Lincoln now needed to resolve the crisis in a way that did not appear to favor one side or the other.

He found the solution when he walked into his office that morning and discovered Chase already there, waiting for him. Welles and Stanton were there, too. The navy secretary was particularly anxious for a word with the president, having just returned from a visit to Seward's house. Undertaken at Lincoln's request, Welles's mission had been to encourage the embattled secretary of state to keep quiet and have faith that "this scheme should be defeated." Careful not to let Chase know where he had been, Welles cryptically assured Lincoln that he "had seen the man . . . and he assented to my views."

Now the president turned to Chase. As Welles recalled it, the Treasury secretary "said he had been painfully affected by the meeting last evening." After a bit of hemming and hawing, Chase came to the point: he was resigning. He had already written the necessary letter. Later that day, Welles recorded in detail what followed:

"'Where is it?' said the President quickly, his eye lighting up in a moment. 'I brought it with me,' said Chase, taking the paper from his pocket; 'I wrote it this morning.' 'Let me have it,' said the President, reaching his long arm and fingers toward C[hase], who held on, seemingly reluctant to part with the letter."

Lincoln managed to get the sealed envelope from Chase and tore it open. "An air of satisfaction spread" over his face as he realized that Chase had given him the perfect way out. The letter, the president declared, "cuts the Gordian knot," and when Stanton took that as a cue to offer his own resignation, Lincoln immediately replied: "I don't want yours. This . . . is all I want—this relieves me—my way is clear—the trouble is ended."

With that, he dismissed the trio, and Chase made his way home to his mansion at Sixth and E streets, slightly baffled. Eventually it dawned on him that the president would now refuse to accept either Seward's resignation or his own. The friends of Seward and the friends of Chase would be equally pleased and equally disappointed; as a consequence, Lincoln would keep his cabinet intact and preserve the delicate balance of his administration.

This was exactly right. Though Chase wrote Lincoln a pleading letter arguing that the president should instead accept both resignations, by the time he delivered it Lincoln had already acted. Seward cheerfully agreed to return to work; Chase followed dyspeptically a day later. The crisis was over.

Somehow, from his lowest point, Lincoln had managed by cool cunning to master a situation that days earlier seemed to threaten disaster. He not only survived what Doris Kearns Goodwin called "the most serious governmental crisis of his presidency," he emerged from it stronger than ever. Reflecting upon his handling of the revolt, Lincoln told John Hay matter-of-factly: "I do not now see how it could have been done better."

More challenges lay ahead, but all of them would end the same way, with Lincoln "more firmly than ever in the saddle," as his secretaries put it. The president liked that equestrian metaphor, and later in December he used a variation of it with Senator Ira Harris of New York to explain what it felt like to have Seward and Chase restored to the cabinet and balance maintained in the government. "Now I can ride," he said. "I have a pumpkin in each end of my bag."

The country shared none of this confidence—not yet, and not for a long time to come. "The war! I have no heart to write about either it or the political aspect of affairs," wrote Mary Lincoln's adviser Benjamin French. "Defeat at Fredericksburg—the Cabinet breaking up—our leading men fighting with each other! Unless something occurs very soon to brighten up affairs, I shall begin to look upon our whole Nation as on its way to destruction." The stalwart Republican proprietor of the *Chicago Tribune*, Joseph Medill, cataloged the woes of the Union: "Failure of the army, weight of taxes, depreciation of money, want of cotton, increasing national debt, deaths in the army"—the list went on. "All combine to produce the existing state of despondency" and lead to the conclusion that "the war is drawing toward a disastrous and disgraceful termination."

John Dahlgren waxed eloquent in his journal. "So we can raise larger armies than any other nation, and make generals as fast as paper money. We can be so rich that a thousand millions may be squandered and not be felt. But we cannot make soldiers or leaders. . . . It is an army of post-masters or other civil placemen with arms in their hands. The nation only wants one man—a General!" Dahlgren was wrong in his lament. The Union was teaching men to be fine soldiers and leaders, but the process took time and the school was harsh and unforgiving.

Even as the gloomy sailor was writing those words, in fact, the one man he pined for—the store clerk on his way to becoming *a General*—was learning a few more lessons the hard way. Ulysses Grant had cleared the Rebels from Oxford, Mississippi, but now his army was sustained by a lifeline of parallel iron rails that grew less reliable with each mile. The Rebel cavalryman Nathan Bedford Forrest looked on that vulnerable railroad like a lion sizing up a limping gazelle. Darting through the Tennessee countryside in the rear of Grant's army, Forrest broke up the railroad at various points along a sixty-mile stretch and slashed Grant's telegraph lines so effectively that the general was unable to communicate with the outside world for two weeks. This taught Grant, in his own words, "the impossibility of maintaining so long a line" to supply "an army moving in any enemy's country."

As the general pondered his next move, he continued to fret over the unsolved problem of shady cotton traders in his zone of occupation. Despite numerous complaints from the field, Washington had done little to help, and Grant was at the end of his patience. His frustration deepened his reflexive anti-Semitism until finally, on December 17, he dashed off his Order No. 11, one of the most regrettable documents of the war. "The Jews, as a class, violating every regulation of trade established by the Treasury Department . . . are hereby expelled," Grant wrote. He directed post commanders throughout his department to find and evict "all of this class of people" within twenty-four hours, and arrest any who remained.

Grant's adjutant, John Rawlins, saw instantly that the order was grossly unjust and would mar the general's reputation, but when he tried to talk his superior out of sending it, Grant reportedly barked, "They can countermand this from Washington if they like."

Lincoln did exactly that. When Grant's order reached Paducah, Jewish merchants there raised a delegation to travel immediately to Washington and protest. As spokesman they chose Cesar Kaskel, the vice president of the recently established Paducah Union League. The men boarded a steamer and started up the Ohio River; within days they were sitting in Lincoln's office. The president heard their complaint and boiled it down to its biblical essence: "And so the children of Israel were driven from the happy land of Canaan?" he asked good-naturedly.

Kaskel was quick on his feet: "Yes," he said, "and that is why we have come unto Father Abraham's bosom, asking protection."

"And this protection you shall have at once," Lincoln promised.

Grant's next lesson was among the most transformative tutorials of the war. Earl Van Dorn, nettlesome as ever, collected what little remained of his Rebel army and marched on the town of Holly Springs, where Grant had stockpiled more than a million dollars' worth of supplies. Colonel R. C. Murphy guarded the cache with 1,500 Union soldiers, which ought to have been sufficient to defend the depot. But to the surprise of the Confederates, and to Grant's eternal fury, Murphy took one look at Van Dorn's motley party and surrendered. What Van Dorn's men could not eat or haul away from the Federal trove, they smashed and burned.

Abruptly Grant found himself far from his Union friends, with no railroad and no supplies. The people around Oxford were delighted by this twist; Grant later remembered that some of them called on him "with broad smiles on their faces, indicating intense joy, to ask what I was going to do now without anything for my soldiers to eat." Grant knew what he was not going to do: he wasn't going to tell his men to starve while they had guns in their hands. Turning the tables, he answered the townspeople by saying that he "had already sent troops and wagons to collect all the food and forage they could find for fifteen miles on each side of the road." The smiles faded as the locals realized that their farms and stores were about to be stripped. "What are *we* to do?" they demanded. Grant advised them to go someplace more than fifteen miles away, and hope they could find some people in a generous mood.

The success of this improvisation startled Grant. Though the raids by Forrest and Van Dorn soon forced him to turn back temporarily from his goal of Vicksburg, he was "amazed at the quantity of supplies the country afforded." He kept his men and mules well fed all the way back to their base. "This taught me a lesson which was taken advantage of later," Grant wrote after the war. That was an understatement: the realization that an army didn't need an umbilical cord, that it was possible to cut loose from the supply line and move quickly while living off the countryside, led to some of the most successful and decisive campaigns of the war. This was the lesson Grant would apply in his brilliant maneuvers to capture Vicksburg the following spring. It was the lesson Sherman would use to gut Georgia and the Carolinas while capturing Savannah in 1864. And it was the lesson Philip Sheridan would apply when he stripped the Shenandoah Valley that same year, thus robbing Lee of his larder.

Grant's retreat from Mississippi in December 1862 was not without cost. It was humiliating and demoralizing, and it left Sherman in the lurch when he attacked the Chickasaw Bluffs near Vicksburg on December 29 in the mistaken belief that Grant's army was still menacing the Rebels from nearby. But that was cheap tuition compared to the value of what Grant learned in Oxford, for arguably no military lesson in the four years of the Civil War did more to decide the outcome.

Mary Lincoln dreaded the approach of Christmas. She enjoyed the shopping, of course; the presidential carriage was a frequent sight around town, Horatio Taft reported, "with its tall driver & footman . . . standing in front of some Merchant's door while Mrs. L[incoln] sits in her seat and examines rich goods which the obsequious Clerk brings out to her." But the holiday season reminded her of the last days of 1861, when the White House rang with the laughter and shouts of four happy boys, two

Lincolns and two Tafts. That was also a time when she had been busy putting the finishing touches on her great redecorating project and dreaming of the social triumph she would engineer in February. Now everything had changed. "From this time until spring each day will be almost a gloomy anniversary," she confided to a friend. To another she wrote: "My precious little Willie is as much mourned over & far more missed (now that we realize he has gone)."

The first lady ended the year with a trip on New Year's Eve "to see a Mrs. Laury, a spiritualist" who lived in Georgetown. Once again, Willie's shade was summoned from the great beyond to console his grieving mother. While in the vicinity, Willie took the opportunity—through the medium—to warn his father that "the Cabinet are all enemies of the President, working for themselves, and that they would have to be dismissed."

Grief was the president's companion as well, though he managed to keep the upper hand. Just before Christmas, Lincoln learned of yet another friend killed in battle. William McCullough had been a court clerk in Bloomington, Illinois. The president knew what he meant to his family. On December 23, in a letter to McCullough's daughter, Lincoln wrote: "In this sad world of ours, sorrow comes to all; and, to the young, it comes with bitterest agony, because it takes them unawares. The older have learned to ever expect it." Endurance, he counseled, was the medicine for grief, and time the therapy. Reassuring her that she was "sure to be happy again," he told the girl: "I have had experience enough to know what I say." Never one to hide from sorrow, Lincoln spent a bittersweet Christmas Day visiting the hospitals of Washington, which were now full with the wounded of Fredericksburg.

The last days of 1862 slipped away. Lincoln salved the hurt feelings of the outfoxed Senate Republicans by agreeing to bend the Constitution to create a new state: West Virginia. Conservatives pleaded with him to block the statehood bill. They dreaded the precedent of dividing a state against its will. After long deliberation, Lincoln signed the legislation, thus rewarding the mountain loyalists while punishing the Rebels in Richmond.

On December 26, a cheer went up in Minnesota when thirty-eight Sioux dropped from a giant scaffold. (One more warrior had been spared at the last minute.) The largest mass execution in American history, it proved to be sufficient vengeance. As Lincoln had calculated, the citizens of the state did not rampage for more blood.

On December 30, the brave little *Monitor* sank in high seas, the victim of bad weather, not Confederate guns. The next day, Lincoln gave his support to an ill-fated project to colonize Ile à Vache, an island off the coast of Haiti. As a consequence, some five hundred black Americans would suffer, and many of them die, at the failed colony, in a tragic fiasco that would finally close the book on Abraham Lincoln's worst idea.

As the old year ticked down, millions of people wondered whether Lincoln would actually go through with his commitment to emancipate the slaves. Would he quail at the last minute from such a momentous step? Was it all a bluff, or was there perhaps some secret compromise in the works to reunite the country and preserve the peculiar institution? Shortly before New Year's Day, Charles Sumner paid a visit to the White House to look the president in the eye and test his resolve. Lincoln assured the senator that once he took a position, he was difficult to move. Questioned again during the last week of December, Lincoln declared that "he could not stop the proclamation if he would, and would not if he could."

Some urged him to reconsider. Browning enlisted a Massachusetts conservative, Benjamin Franklin Thomas, to call on Lincoln "and have a full, frank conversation with him in regard to the threatened proclamation of emancipation," which they both believed to be "fraught with evil, and evil only." After his appeal, Thomas reported back: "The President was fatally bent upon his course, saying that if he should refuse to issue his proclamation there would be a rebellion in the north, and that a dictator would be placed over his head within the week."

As the deadline approached, Lincoln worked with his cabinet to refine every word. His decision to exempt thirteen Louisiana parishes from the proclamation led to some awkward language, and in one cabinet meeting Montgomery Blair argued that such a minor matter should be left out. "As this was destined to be read as a great historical document, it was a pity to have its unity, completeness, and direct simplicity marred by such a trifle of detail," Blair contended. Both Seward and Chase agreed. Pacing by the fireplace, Lincoln said he had promised political leaders in that part of Louisiana that he would count their territory as loyal if they would hold an election for members of Congress. They had done so, and now he was keeping his promise.

Chase objected that Congress was unlikely to recognize those new members. Lincoln stopped his pacing and wheeled on the Treasury secretary. "Then I am to be bullied by Congress am I?" he snapped. Obviously the cabinet crisis had left a sore spot. "I'll be damned if I will."

The day after Christmas, in central Tennessee, General William Rosecrans, Buell's replacement, departed Nashville with some 47,000 men, marching down the road toward Chattanooga. Rosecrans looked like the marble bust of a Greek emperor and hailed from a distinguished military family in Ohio. At West Point, he had rescued a plebe named Grant from hazing. Bred to be a soldier, "Old Rosy" had waited forty-three years to lead a great army. After long preparation, he was ready to try to bring eastern Tennessee back into the Union fold.

At the town of Murfreesboro, on the west fork of the Stones River, Braxton Bragg came out to meet Rosecrans's troops with some 40,000 Rebels. Late in the afternoon of December 30, the two armies settled so close together that their regimental bands staged a fight, blasting "Yankee Doodle" and "Dixie" at each other until they settled on a song they could play in unison: "Home Sweet Home." As the sad tune sounded in the dying light, the rival generals in their headquarters tents bent over their plans, and somehow they settled on precisely the same idea. Rosecrans and Bragg both decided to begin the last day of the year by throwing a hard left hook, thus crashing the enemy's right and cutting his supply line.

Bragg swung first, thundering into the Union lines at daybreak on December 31 and driving the Federals back like a folding knife. But just as the blue wall was about to break, the Confederates came up against a reorganized line fighting under Philip Sheridan. His dark eyes blazing over a slash of mustache, Little Phil refused to let the Rebels through. During four of the hottest hours of the war, the young general lost three brigade commanders and a third of his men, but he and his fighters were unconquerable. When his troops ran out of ammunition, Sheridan ordered them to fix bayonets. And when night fell, his soldiers safely occupied a strong position on favorable high ground.

John Dahlgren had indeed been wrong about the Union's ability to make soldiers and leaders. At the battle of Stones River, Rosecrans lost 31 percent of his army—the highest proportional toll of the war. But the general held his ground, Bragg's exhausted forces turned back, and the terrible confrontation proved to be an important Union victory. For Lincoln, it was a critical success to set against the failure at Fredericksburg, a "check . . . to a dangerous sentiment" of defeat "which was spreading in the North." Two weeks earlier, it seemed that Providence had set its face against the Union, but the news that Bragg's men had been beaten back strengthened Lincoln's confidence that he remained on the right side of history.

In the end, William Rosecrans would not measure up to the president's hopes for him, but Lincoln never lost sight of the service he rendered at Murfreesboro. Months later, after Union victories at Vicksburg and Gettysburg had lifted Northern spirits and put the memory of Stones River behind the scrim of time, the president still felt the debt keenly. In a letter to the general, Lincoln reaffirmed what he owed: "I can never forget, whilst I remember anything, that about the end of last year . . . you gave us a hard earned victory which, had there been a defeat instead, the nation could hardly have lived over."

"A NEW BIRTH OF FREEDOM"

As the White House clocks chimed midnight, 1862 passed into history trailing a ragged tail of loose ends. Abraham Lincoln spent another nearly sleepless night, not least because news of the war's progress remained so bleak. On the Rappahannock, Burnside's tether on the Army of the Potomac had frayed almost to nothing. In the wake of his frontal assault on Fredericksburg, made against the advice of senior officers, the general now faced a mutiny. Though he had given up on another confrontation at Marye's Heights, Burnside remained determined to recross the river and try again to seize the offensive. However, as Lincoln noted, "his Grand Division commanders all oppose[d] the movement," and they made their opposition clear by going over the general's head to Washington. The president wanted Halleck to visit army headquarters at Falmouth and straighten things out by surveying the ground, interviewing the contending generals, and deciding whether Burnside should give the order. But to Lincoln, Halleck seemed to be dodging responsibility. "Your military skill is useless to me, if you will not do this," the president scolded his general in chief in a letter dated January 1, 1863.

Lincoln also had the Army of the Cumberland to worry about that night. He knew that Rosecrans's troops were joined in battle with Bragg's Rebels in Tennessee, but he had no idea how that confrontation would turn out, much less how he could deal with another defeat if one came. Farther west, the military situation was cloaked in perplexing near-silence, for Grant's communications were cut and Sherman's strike force was somewhere in the bayous around Vicksburg. Much had changed in the year since the president wrote his first tentative telegrams asserting his authority over the far-flung Union troops, but one truth was permanent: during these dark vigils, Lincoln was always a lonely commander in chief.

However vague and troubling the news from the battlefield, though, the day had arrived when Lincoln was to sign the Emancipation Proclamation. Despite the president's repeated assurances to Sumner, the cabinet, and various others, many Americans North and South continued to speculate that Lincoln's determination would fail at the last minute, that he would suspend the decree in favor of some final attempt at compromise. Even Mary Lincoln, who knew the enormous pressure her husband was under from conservative supporters to find some excuse to shelve the proclamation, is said to have asked him: "Well, what do you intend doing?" Lincoln answered her by sending a glance heavenward and saying: "I am a man under orders; I cannot do otherwise." The decision was final.

For Lincoln, standing by his commitments was a matter of pride: he once described the "ability to keep my resolves" as "the gem of my character." Yet he understood, more than many of his contemporaries, that his actions on the first day of 1863 would be far more significant than any earlier promise he had pledged and kept. As he would put it later, the Emancipation Proclamation was "the central act of my administration and the great event of the nineteenth century," for it "knocked the bottom out of slavery." Here was the "new birth of freedom" he would speak of so brilliantly at Gettysburg.

Lincoln had come a long way in a year—and a very long way from a New Year's Day twenty-two years earlier, one of the lowest moments of his life. On that occasion, anguish over his muddled future left Lincoln bedridden with depression, so wretched that Joshua Speed feared his friend would try to kill himself. Yet despite—or because of—his torment, this unschooled, unmarried, unpolished man of thirty-one confessed to Speed the true scale of his ambition and the shape of his greatest fear. He wanted to be remembered forever, Lincoln admitted—to engage so impressively with "the events transpiring in his day and generation" as to "link his name with something that would redound to the interest of his fellow man." Only by accomplishing something great could he register his existence on this sad earth beyond his own life span and the lives of those who knew him personally.

Lincoln feared oblivion the way others feared death, and this dread had stalked him from childhood, when, according to one family story, he worked alongside his father fashioning the pegs that would hold his mother's coffin together. They buried his mother in a tiny graveyard on a wild hillside; a dozen years later, they left her behind when they moved away. Revisiting the place as a grown man, Lincoln felt as if the whole world was saturated in death: "Every sound appears a knell/And every spot a grave." Yet no one could name all the anonymous men, women, and children lost to time; it was as if they had never lived. Lincoln's dream was to be the rare individual whose name and story would live on.

Now the moment he sought had come; today he would step across the threshold from mortality to permanence. Later, he would speak in exactly these terms when talking about the Emancipation Proclamation with Joshua Speed. When Lincoln reminded his friend of their long-ago conversation about ambition and fear, Speed remembered it clearly. Lincoln then said he had come to believe that "my fondest hopes will be realized," thanks to his signature on the momentous decree. As Lincoln put it to Charles Sumner on another occasion: "I know very well that the name which is connected with this act will never be forgotten."

As faint light rose in the White House windows, the new year dawned clear and mild—"very smilingly," as one Washingtonian put it. After crossing the second floor from the family quarters to his office, Lincoln inked his pen and began work on the final draft of his decree. At a meeting the previous day, members of the cabinet had suggested a few small changes to the document, and Lincoln decided to incorporate several of them. First, to defend himself against accusations that he was deliberately stirring up a slave insurrection, he added a sentence calling on the freed slaves of the South to "abstain from all violence, unless in necessary self-defense." He also retreated slightly from the promise in his preliminary proclamation that the liberated slaves would be "forever" free. His reasoning, as he deleted that ringing word, was that the order drew its constitutional authority from the president's war powers, and the war would not go on forever. Still, the final proclamation pledged the strength of the U.S. Army and Navy to "maintain" the freedom of the former slaves, and called on the armed forces to enlist freed black troops. These revolutionary commitments would secure lasting freedom far beyond the power of that single missing word.

After filling nearly three pages with his careful handwriting, Lincoln ended the decree with a new flourish. Suggested by Chase and others, it was designed to give this dust-dry document a glow of glory. "And upon this act," Lincoln wrote, "sincerely believed to be an act of justice, warranted by the Constitution, upon military necessity, I invoke the considerate judgment of mankind, and the gracious favor of Almighty God." With that, he summoned a messenger to carry the order to the State Department, where, despite the holiday, a scribe was waiting to make an official copy.

While the proclamation was being prepared for his signature, Lincoln ate his usual Spartan breakfast of egg, toast, and coffee. After the meal, Burnside arrived for a dispiriting meeting to settle on a strategy for ending the standoff at Fredericksburg: the general seemed to want nothing more than to awaken from the bad dream of leading the world's largest army. At midmorning, Seward entered the president's office, carrying what was meant to be the final proclamation. But the historic signing was delayed when Lincoln, proofreading carefully, found that the wrong official boilerplate had been added at the end; it was language appropriate to a treaty, not an executive order. Even the smallest mistake was intolerable in a document that would be so closely scrutinized; the president sent Seward back to the scribe to have it redone. By now there was barely enough time to dress for the annual reception and join the receiving line downstairs.

The morning was another midwinter delight, much like the previous New Year's Day. The streets were jammed and the doors at the homes of Washington's luminaries opened wide. At the Seward mansion, six police officers stood sentinel at the entrance, while an usher loudly announced the name of each visitor who entered the parlor. Stanton's house was a sea of blue jackets and yellow braid. Callers at the Chase mansion greeted not only the Treasury secretary but also his daughter Kate, twenty-two and glorious, with limpid eyes and a slender figure that made her the most celebrated beauty in the capital. As intelligent as she was lovely, Kate was chief counselor and collaborator in her widowed father's barely masked campaign for the next Republican presidential nomination. Somehow, neither father nor daughter—both astute in so many ways—was able to see that in Abraham Lincoln they had met their match.

The Welles home was quiet, the door shut, for it was not yet two months since the death of Hubert Welles, aged nine, a boy with what his father called "a light, bright, cherub face." Of the eight children born to Gideon and Mary Jane Welles, only two were still living, and the navy secretary was glad to have the constant press of crisis to distract him from his grief. Rather than receive callers, he crossed Lafayette Square in the "bright and brilliant" sunshine shortly before eleven A.M. to take his place in the line of dignitaries. Soon thereafter, his hand was swallowed up in the enveloping grip of the Lincoln handshake, and he congratulated the president on the year they had survived together. Welles lingered only a half hour or so, long enough to see the arrival of the costumed diplomatic corps, the Supreme Court justices, the members of Congress, and a legion of preening officers. After heading home again, Welles found himself reflecting on the profound changes wrought by the events and decisions of the past year. "The character of the country is in many respects undergoing a transformation," he wrote.

Mary Lincoln was in a similar mood, a ruminative blend of grief and wonder. She wore black velvet to the reception, signifying mourning, and as she took her place beside Benjamin French in the receiving line, she thought back to their first open house in Washington, precisely one year earlier. "Oh, Mr. French!" she exclaimed. "How much we have passed through since we last stood here."

Her husband towered over her, looking "quite as well as he did a year ago," according to one undoubtedly generous description. If in fact his fatigue wasn't readily apparent, the stream of visitors must have lifted his spirits and lit the dark-ringed hollows of his eyes. After all, the parade of distinguished callers through the Blue Room was, in subtle ways, a measure of his successes. A year ago, when Her Majesty's ambassador, Lord Lyons, electrified the room with his arrival, the United States had narrowly avoided a suicidal war with England. Now, thanks to the skillful diplomacy of the past twelve months, the threat of European intervention in the Civil War had been erased. By holding the North together while mobilizing its latent strength, Lincoln had made the United States too powerful to cross—and thereby opened the door to a new era of cooperation between the United States and Great Britain, an alliance that would eventually become one of the most durable and important in world history.

The previous year, Chief Justice Roger Taney had been an absent yet hovering spirit at the White House reception; this year, the elderly judge decided to pay his respects. Once an openly hostile force at the head of the third branch of government, Taney now shared the Supreme Court with three Lincoln appointees. A fourth was just a few months away. As 1863 began, his once great influence had been largely neutralized. Taney would die in October 1864, and the drafts of opinions already written and tucked into his desk—striking down military conscription, for instance, and invalidating paper money—were destined to remain forever unpublished by the court that Lincoln remade.

A year ago, the military had been a mystery to Lincoln, and Congress was seeking to control his conduct of the war. Now George McClellan, the general who had dominated the Union army, was gone, and with him the threat of a military dictatorship. Pope had been given his chance; he, too, had been relieved of his command. Burnside would soon be cashiered, and though the Union's mortifying loss at Chancellorsville lay ahead, just beyond it was the great victory at Gettysburg. Lincoln was well on his way to solving the managerial riddles posed by the Union's overnight armies, and he had established his clear leadership over his administration, his party, and the government.

And what of the man himself: did the president's visitors know him any better on that New Year's Day than they had a year earlier? Later generations have had the privilege of looking back on Lincoln through hundreds of pairs of eyes and thousands of pages of letters and diaries. But his contemporaries could see him only in glimpses, and they were thus still capable of misjudging him badly even after the extraordinary events of 1862.

An early biographer, J. G. Holland, interviewed dozens of Lincoln's associates and intimates in the months after the president's death and was struck by the fact that "there are not two who agree in their estimate of him." One would say "he was a very ambitious man"; another would assert "that he was without a particle of ambition." People who knew Lincoln, Holland wrote, said that

he was one of the saddest men that ever lived, and that he was one of the jolliest men that ever lived; that he was very religious, but that he was not a Christian; . . . that he was the most cunning man in America, and that he had not a particle of cunning in him; that he had the strongest personal attachments, and that he had no personal attachments at all; . . . that he was a tyrant, and that he was the softest-hearted, most brotherly man that ever lived; . . . that he was a leader of the people, and that he was always led by the people; that he was cool and impassive, and that he was susceptible of the strongest passions.

Ultimately, Holland came to the conclusion that those who knew the president "caught only separate aspects of his character" and that the seemingly contradictory images of Lincoln in fact added up to his essence.

All of these aspects of the president's character had flickered or shone through the ordeal of that year, for Lincoln was very much a work under revision, a man feeling his way among obstacles unlike any navigated by his predecessors. He did not know from one day to the next what would be required of him, nor did he know which tools he would employ to meet each day's challenges. He began the year possessing the raw material of greatness; those who looked into his workshop could see him fashioning one element one day and a different element the next. But when the first day of January came around again, Lincoln's greatness was no longer raw. Even as he had redefined American society, he had invented the modern presidency. He had steered himself and the nation from its darkest New Year's Day to its proudest, and in the process Lincoln had become the towering leader who forever looms over the rebirth of the American experiment.

The White House doors closed and the last of the crowd grasped Lincoln's gloved hand at about two P.M. Exhausted, the president climbed the stairs to his office, where he soon received a visit from William Seward and his son Frederick. They brought with them the perfected Emancipation Proclamation, ready for his signature. The fifth and last page was placed on his desk. Lincoln dipped a pen that he had already promised to Charles Sumner, in recognition of the senator's leadership in the cause of liberty. But when he tightened his fingers to sign, Lincoln felt his hand cramp and begin to tremble. As he later recounted the experience: "I could not for a moment, control my arm, and a superstitious feeling came over me which made me hesitate." In fact his grip was spent after hours of vigorous hand-shaking.

Worried that others might draw the wrong conclusion, the president said to those who witnessed his signature: "I never in my life felt more certain that I was doing right than I do in signing this paper. But I have been receiving calls and shaking hands . . . until my arm is stiff and numb. Now, this signature is one that will be closely examined, and if they find my hand trembled, they will say, 'he had some compunctions.' But, anyway, it is going to be done."

Lincoln took up the pen again and carefully inscribed his name—which emerged a bit shakily at first, but gained strength. Describing the moment later that day, the president said to a guest: "The signature looks a little tremulous, for my hand was tired, but my resolution was firm."

A leaked copy of the proclamation was published that afternoon in the Washington *Evening Star,* and as word of the signing spread by telegraph to mass rallies throughout the North, thousands of Americans erupted in cheers. At Tremont Temple in Boston, the great abolitionist Frederick Douglass thanked God that he had lived to see the death blow dealt to slavery. Cannon thundered salutes from Chicago to Pittsburgh to New York. Lincoln spent the rest of the day fretting over scraps of information from Rosecrans in Tennessee, until, after supper, the White House lawn filled with a cheering throng of citizens, white and black together, calling for a speech. The president went to a window and waved to the crowd, but said nothing. His signature spoke for itself.

News of the proclamation sped to England, where leading citizens across the country convened rallies and town meetings to pass resolutions in favor of Lincoln's leadership; they also called on the British government to refrain from doing anything to help the Confederacy. Charles Francis Adams filled diplomatic pouches with dozens of these expressions of support, documenting a groundswell of public opinion that proved once and for all that the industrial heart of England was now emphatically pro-Union, despite the misery of the unemployed workers at cotton-starved mills. Later that month, the U.S. consul in London, Freeman Morse, reported to Seward that "Emancipation Meetings continue to be held in London every week, sometimes four or five a week at which two and three thousand people have been present and in a majority of cases unanimously with the North." The offices of the American legation noticed a sharp increase in the number of British subjects volunteering for the Union army; the legation secretary, Benjamin Moran, reported that the vicar at his church had begun praying for the North, and that the prayers were always answered by loud amens.

Lincoln was buoyed by this outpouring. "The workingmen of Europe have been subjected to a severe trial," he allowed in a letter replying to a resolution from the factory workers of Manchester. Acknowledging the suffering caused by the Southern cotton embargo and subsequent Northern blockade, Lincoln declared: "I cannot but regard your decisive utterance" against slavery and in favor of the Union "as an instance of sublime Christian heroism which has not been surpassed in any age or in any country. It is, indeed, an energetic and reinspiring assurance of the inherent power of truth and of the ultimate and universal triumph of justice, humanity, and freedom."

The president was also subjected to intense criticism, of course. The new governor of New York, Horatio Seymour, called the proclamation a "bloody, barbarous, revolutionary, and unconstitutional scheme." Negative reaction to the decree invigorated the antiwar Democrats, known derisively as Copperheads. Especially in the West, where farmers and merchants were badly hurt by the loss of Mississippi River commerce, Lincoln's hard line against the South jeopardized his control of the Union. "The people of the West demand peace," roared the Copperhead leader Clement Vallandigham of Ohio. "They begin to more than suspect that New England is in the way." Another Ohio congressman, Samuel Cox, warned that many in the heartland were discussing the possibility of breaking away from abolitionist New England to forge a separate peace with the South. Meanwhile, desertions spiked in some Union army units as conservative soldiers went home in disgust. "It is nothing uncommon for a Capt[ain] to get up in the morning and find half his company gone," wrote one infantryman from Vermont.

But a delicate balance had tilted during 1862 in favor of eradicating what Lincoln would call "the original disturbing cause" that had brought on this terrible war. The nation's center of gravity had shifted, and Horace Greeley correctly described this change when he wrote in his *New-York Tribune* that "the people of 1860 have become, in 1862, a people of a totally different and new intellectual and moral life. Whereas in 1860 we bowed before, while we devoutly believed in, the safety and the wisdom of Human Slavery, in 1862 we know it is our curse and our danger."

Though the road to Union victory remained long and the journey violent, the Federal armies—in spite of frequent complaints and chronic desertion, troubles that also plagued the South—were now pointed clearly and irresistibly toward the end. The army under Grant in the West was one campaign away from opening the Mississippi; the army under Rosecrans, which Grant and Sherman would inherit, was launched on its eventual course to Chattanooga, Atlanta, and Savannah; and the Army of the Potomac had become the hard, unbreakable force that would soon win the greatest battle ever fought in the Americas, and then grind Lee's stubborn host down to a remnant.

Confederate armies, by contrast, had passed their apex and were beginning to erode. Though about a quarter of a million Rebel troops were present for duty on the last day of 1862, the count would never be that high again. They were now outnumbered almost three to one; in two more years it would be five to one. "In all the elements of strength, power, and stability, the Union is stronger . . . today than it was . . . a year ago," Seward aptly informed his envoys in Europe toward the end of 1862. "In all the same elements the insurrection is weaker."

Some critics of the Emancipation Proclamation considered the decree insufficient because it failed to address slavery in loyal territory. As the London political weekly *The Spectator* put it: "The principle is not that a human being cannot justly own another, but that he cannot own him unless he is loyal to the United States." Within a short time, however, and with Lincoln's unflagging support, the decree would lead to a constitutional amendment outlawing slavery altogether, followed by another recognizing freed men and women as equal citizens of the United States. A milestone on the arduous path toward justice and liberty, Lincoln's signature on the proclamation was the crucial step that brought the end of slavery into view. "I can see that time coming," Lincoln declared. "Whoever can wait for it will see it; whoever stands in its way will be run over by it."

Now the outcome of the Civil War was a matter of time—but not *simply* a matter of time, because the passage of each remaining day was costly, and painful to the limits of human endurance. The South's best hopes of victory were behind it. The lever of cotton had failed to move Europe. The huge armies raised by the first and most severe military draft in American history had begun to wither. The high cost of the war was crushing the South's economy even as it galvanized the North's; indeed, at the end of 1862 U.S. government bonds were selling at half the yield they commanded when Lincoln took office, a measure of the confidence investors placed in the credit of the Northern government. The bravery and ferocity of Confederate resistance had not broken the fighting spirit of Union soldiers, nor had the Rebel advance into the border states rallied secession spirit. The morale of the North had proved as resilient as a young tree, bending and sagging under impossible weight, but always springing back.

For Abraham Lincoln, the toll was severe. "He certainly is growing feeble," one associate observed shortly after the president's fifty-fourth birthday in February 1863. "He wrote a note while I was present, and his hand trembled as I never saw it before, and he looked worn & haggard. I remarked that I should think he would feel glad when he could get some rest. He replied that it was a pretty hard life for him." Despite the multitude of challenges, however, Lincoln was sustained not only by his own will and the passion of his supporters, but by the bedrock of American patriotism, which he never failed to trust. Through the darkest days of 1862, when talk of disunion and dictatorship tore through the North like wildfire, no national leader took a meaningful step in those dangerous directions. The catastrophe caused by secession led to neither anarchy nor tyranny, though such disasters had seemed so likely a year before.

This unshakable loyalty to the Union, despite bitter differences of opinion, was not just a triumph of Lincoln's painstaking moderation, nor was it the result of his temporary crackdown on dissent. Credit also belongs to Lincoln's critics. Though numerous and unrelenting, when it counted they were not traitors. Men like McClellan and Seymour broke repeatedly with Lincoln's policies—and with the policies of abolitionist leaders in Congress—but when pressed to the wall they stood by the Constitution. Lincoln was wise enough not to back them into corners, but their patriotism was their own and it played an instrumental role in saving the United States from ruin.

The twelve tumultuous months of 1862 were the hinge of American history, the decisive moment at which the unsustainable compromises of the founding generations were ripped up in favor of a blueprint for a much stronger nation. In the process, millions of lives were transformed: the lives of the slaves who were to be freed, and of the slave owners who would be impoverished; the lives of the soldiers and their families who bore the suffering of the first all-out war of the Industrial Age; the lives of those who would profit from new inventions, longer railroads, and modern finance; the lives of students who would be educated in great public universities. The road taken in 1862 ultimately led to greater prosperity than anyone had ever imagined. For the first time—but certainly not the last—the United States flexed its muscle to turn back an existential threat. Despite the cataclysmic destruction caused by the Civil War, the reunited states, North and South, would be far richer in 1870 than in 1860. During the same period, the nation's population would rise by more than 20 percent, and its gross domestic product would nearly double.

The first day of 1863 did not mark the end of the war, or even the beginning of the end. That would come later in the year, when Grant drove the Rebels out of Vicksburg and Chattanooga on his way to replacing Halleck as general in chief. But the close of 1862—to borrow from Winston Churchill—brought the nation to the end of the beginning. And like the Shakespearean dramas that spoke so powerfully to the genius of Abraham Lincoln, the events of the final scenes were fated by the decisions, actions, omissions, flukes, failures, and successes of the early drama. When that fateful year began, a shattered land looked backward at a dream that seemed forever lost. When a new year arrived, the way forward was perceptible, an upward climb into a challenging but brilliant future.

NOTES

The sheer volume of material, both primary and secondary, related to Abraham Lincoln and the Civil War is so vast that dropping into the subject as a writer is like falling into the sea. As one who has tried to extricate the story of a single stormy year, I've emerged from this inexhaustible reservoir with a deep respect for those who have provided a comprehensive account of either Lincoln's life or the war that remade our nation.

The sources of this work begin with the broad overview of the Civil War rendered in the justly admired general histories by such writers as James McPherson, Bruce Catton, Shelby Foote, Allan Nevins, and the team of Herman Hattaway and Archer Jones, as well as in the invaluable trove collected by the magazine *The Century* and published as *Battles and Leaders of the Civil War*.

I also undertook early in my research to apprehend the evanescent character of Abraham Lincoln. Like many contemporary readers, I was prodded to renew my exploration of this endlessly complex man by David Herbert Donald's 1995 biography, titled *Lincoln*. Indeed, that book planted the seed of this one: after reading the chapters covering 1862, I found myself thinking, "My God, how did he survive that year?" I profited from reading full-dress biographies as diverse as those of William Herndon and Jesse Weik, Albert Beveridge, Carl Sandburg, James G. Randall, Benjamin P. Thomas, William Lee Miller, Richard Carwardine, and Michael Burlingame.

The monumental work of John Nicolay and John Hay, *Abraham Lincoln: A History*, straddles these two categories: it is both a political history of the Civil War and an intellectual biography of President Lincoln. Lincoln never got the chance to write his memoirs, but Nicolay and Hay arguably give us the block of marble from which that treasure would have been carved.

Against this general background, I set out to tell the story of 1862 as much as possible from Lincoln's point of view. But how was I to recover that perspective? I found myself thinking of the old encyclopedia on my parents' bookshelf, which illustrated the human anatomy with a set of clear acetate pages, one printed with the skeleton, the next with the circulatory system, another with the nervous system, and yet another with the digestive system. Layer by layer, they added up to the whole picture. My source material likewise accumulated in layers, beginning with the words actually written, dictated, or signed by Lincoln, as found in *The Collected Works of Abraham Lincoln*, especially the pages in Volumes 5 and 6, which cover 1862.

The richness and authority of this material creates a problem, however, for a writer trying to follow Lincoln through the year, because the written record is strongest when Lincoln was dealing with problems from a distance. Exchanges through the mail and over the telegraph were likely to be preserved, but Lincoln's countless face-to-face meetings in Washington and elsewhere are lost to time, except where someone paused to write them down. Even then, we are at the mercy of the recorder's memory and veracity.

To address these gaps in the historical record, I collated the material in the *Collected Works* with a timeline of known events in Lincoln's life and major events of the war. This was drawn from Earl Schenck Miers's *Lincoln Day by Day*, Vol. 3, and from *The Civil War Day by Day: An Almanac, 1861–1865*, by E. B. Long with Barbara Long. The eminent Lincoln authority Paul Angle once wrote that the Miers collection is "to Lincoln study what the steel frame of a skyscraper is to the finished structure." That is certainly apt in this case.

My next layer of source material was the voluminous correspondence between Secretary of State William H. Seward and American envoys in London, Paris, St. Petersburg, and Madrid. This underexamined material tells us a great deal about Lincoln's evolving military and political thinking, even though the dispatches went out over Seward's signature. Seward consulted extensively with Lincoln in preparing major dispatches, and he read most of these documents to Lincoln before sending them. The amount of time Lincoln spent with Seward was a bone of contention for the rest of the cabinet; for us, it is suggestive of the importance Lincoln placed on foreign policy and the contents of these diplomatic messages.

The next layer comprised diaries, letters, and other firsthand records left by individuals in direct contact with Lincoln, as well as others whose actions, though remote, had significant impact on Lincoln in 1862. These include the diaries and letters of John Hay, John Nicolay, Salmon P. Chase, Edward Bates, Gideon Welles, Orville Hickman Browning, John Dahlgren, Benjamin French, and Horatio Taft; the letters of George McClellan, William T. Sherman, Ulysses Grant, Charles Sumner, Mary Todd Lincoln, Thomas Ewing, Sr., Thomas Ewing, Jr., Gustavus Vasa Fox, and Rebecca Pomroy; the extensive correspondence addressed to Lincoln and preserved in the Lincoln papers; the journalism of Noah Brooks, William Russell, Edward Dicey, and others; and William P. Fessenden's detailed memorandum of the cabinet crisis of December 1862.

Next came a layer of material drawn from the memoirs of figures close to Lincoln or vital to the events of the year, including Ulysses Grant, William T. Sherman, Jefferson Davis, George McClellan, Francis B. Carpenter, Elizabeth Keckly (Keckley), Julia Taft Bayne, David Homer Bates, Winfield Scott, Henry Adams, William O. Stoddard, and Gideon Welles.

I also made extensive use of the *Recollected Words of Abraham Lincoln,* compiled by the great Lincoln scholar Don E. Fehrenbacher and his wife, Virginia Fehrenbacher. Though all of the material in the Fehrenbacher book is available in other firsthand and purportedly firsthand accounts, I have frequently cited *Recollected Words* in my endnotes because doing so allows interested readers to find a number of my sources conveniently in one place and also to read the Fehrenbachers' astute judgments concerning the reliability of various quotations.

I have made sparing use, as indicated in the notes, of the United States War Department's *The War of the Rebellion: A Compilation of the Official Records of the Union and Confederate Armies.* This enormous archive is, of course, the mother lode for military historians of the Civil War. But my purpose has not been to write a military history; I turned to these records primarily to illuminate corners where I found confusion or disagreement among historians on some point.

Finally, beyond these primary sources I relied on a last layer of highly credible secondary sources devoted to particular facets of Lincoln and aspects of the war. These are reflected in the Notes and in the Bibliography.

Certain sources are so frequently cited in the endnotes that I have adopted the following conventions for dealing with them (full citations are found in the bibliography):

Bates diary: *The Diary of Edward Bates, 1859–1866.*
Browning diary: *The Diary of Orville Hickman Browning,* Vol. 1, *1850–1864.*
Chase diary and **Chase to . . . :** *Inside Lincoln's Cabinet: The Civil War Diaries of Salmon P. Chase.*

CW: *The Collected Works of Abraham Lincoln.*

Dahlgren diary: published in Madeleine Vinton Dahlgren, *Memoir of John A. Dahlgren, Rear-Admiral United States Navy,* especially pp. 348–88.

French diary: Benjamin Brown French, *Witness to the Young Republic: A Yankee's Journal, 1828–1870.*

Grant to . . . : *The Papers of Ulysses S. Grant,* Vols. 4–7.

Hay diary: *Inside Lincoln's White House: The Complete Civil War Diary of John Hay.*

Mary Lincoln to . . . : *Mary Todd Lincoln: Her Life and Letters.*

McClellan to . . . : *The Civil War Papers of George B. McClellan: Selected Correspondence, 1860–1865.*

Nicolay diary and **Nicolay to . . . :** *With Lincoln in the White House: Letters, Memoranda, and Other Writings of John G. Nicolay, 1860–1865.*

RW: *Recollected Words of Abraham Lincoln.*

Seward to . . . and **. . . to Seward:** *United States Department of State: Message of the President of the United States to the Two Houses of Congress at the Commencement of the Third Session of the Thirty-Seventh Congress.*

Sherman to . . . : *Sherman's Civil War: Selected Correspondence of William T. Sherman, 1860–1865.*

Sumner to . . . : *The Selected Letters of Charles Sumner,* Vol. 2.

Taft diary: *Washington During the Civil War: The Diary of Horatio Nelson Taft, 1861–1865.*

Welles diary: *Diary of Gideon Welles, Secretary of the Navy Under Lincoln and Johnson,* Vol. 1, *1861–March 30, 1864.* (This idiosyncratic work is partly in the form of undated essays and partly in the form of dated entries. Where I have drawn from dated entries, I cite by date; otherwise by page number.)

PROLOGUE

1 Everyone was out: The scene in Washington, D.C., on January 1, 1862, is based primarily on entries for that date in the diaries of Edward Bates, Horatio Taft, and Orville Hickman Browning. (See Note on Sources, above.) Also, *New York Times,* Jan. 2, 1862. The rapid growth of the city and the army is discussed widely in the literature. A classic account is Leech, *Reveille in Washington: 1860–1865;* also Fergurson, *Freedom Rising: Washington in the Civil War.*

2 everyone was welcome: The pickpocket is mentioned in the Browning diary, Jan. 1, 1862.

2 It was "the greatest jam": *New York Times,* Jan. 2, 1862.

3   The Confederacy was in the process: Hattaway and Jones, *How the North Won: A Military History of the Civil War,* p. 276.

3   "It is in the highest Degree likely": Palmerston to the Foreign Office, Oct. 20, 1861, quoted in Ridley, *Lord Palmerston,* p. 552.

3   Davis was weighing: Nicolay and Hay, *Abraham Lincoln: A History,* Vol. 5, pp. 153–54.

3   The Treasury Department was broke: cf. http://www.usgovernmentspend ing.com/chart_central.php?year=1860.

4   A rebel diplomat crowed: quoted in Owsley, *King Cotton Diplomacy: Foreign Relations of the Confederate States of America,* p. 80.

4   "If there is one division of the states": Andrew Johnson, "Not a Southern or Any Other Confederacy," a speech delivered in the Senate, Dec. 18, 1860, reprinted in Heidler and Heidler, eds., *Encyclopedia of the American Civil War: A Political, Social, and Military History,* pp. 2239–40.

5   "The insurrection is largely: *CW,* Vol. 5, pp. 35–53.

5   Southerners maintained: See, for example, the South Carolina Secession Ordinance of Dec. 24, 1860, at http://avalon.law.yale.edu/19th_century/csa _scarsec.asp.

5   Both experience and history suggested that: See, for example, Dahlgren diary, Oct. 25, 1861.

6   McClellan . . . had toyed: McClellan to Mary Ellen McClellan, July 27, 1861.

6   Frémont's wife . . . had threatened: Nicolay and Hay, *Abraham Lincoln,* Vol. 4, pp. 414–15.

6   "the power of a God": Sumner to Francis Lieber, Sept. 17, 1861.

7   "Never has there been": ibid.

1: NEW YEAR'S DAY

9   proud of his physique: J. Rowan Herndon and Hardin Bale, quoted in *Herndon's Informants,* pp. 7, 13.

9   180 pounds of muscle: Carpenter, *The Inner Life of Abraham Lincoln: Six Months at the White House,* p. 217; *RW,* p. 507.

9   wasting away: Johnson Brigham, quoted in *Herndon's Informants,* pp. 157–58.

9   sketch artist Alfred Waud: see Waud's illustration in *Harper's Weekly* 6, no. 265 (Jan. 25, 1862), pp. 56–57.

10   "remarkably pensive and tender": Carpenter, *The Inner Life of Abraham Lincoln,* p. 218.

10 "never had a confidant": Herndon and Weik, *Abraham Lincoln: The True Story of a Great Life,* Vol. 2, p. 140.

10 "strange, friendless": *CW,* Vol. 1, p. 320. This quote is emended to read "a strange[r]" in *CW,* but I agree with David Herbert Donald that it is more likely that Lincoln wrote it as he meant it. Donald, *"We Are Lincoln Men": Abraham Lincoln and His Friends,* p. 10.

10 Bates had been struck: Bates diary, Dec. 31, 1861.

11 the price tag had doubled: Nicolay and Hay, *Abraham Lincoln,* Vol. 6, pp. 227–30.

12 "The President has lost ground amazingly": quoted in Burlingame, *Abraham Lincoln: A Life,* Vol. 2, p. 203.

12 "I think to lose Kentucky": *CW,* Vol. 4, pp. 531–33.

12 "poor white trash": Wade to Zachariah Chandler, Sept. 23, 1861, quoted in Rafuse, *McClellan's War: The Failure of Moderation in the Struggle for the Union,* p. 135.

12 "murdering your country by inches": quoted in Trefousse, *The Radical Republicans: Lincoln's Vanguard for Racial Justice,* p. 184.

13 "has not the power to command": Bates diary, Dec. 31, 1861.

13 "[He] was charmed with Mary's wit": Elizabeth Todd Edwards, quoted in *Herndon's Informants,* p. 443.

13 "so kindly, so considerate": William O. Stoddard, quoted in Randall, *Mary Lincoln: Biography of a Marriage,* p. 197.

13 Her temper was notorious: Burlingame, "Abraham Lincoln's Emotional Life," pp. 11–13, http://www.lehrmaninstitute.org/lehrman/Hill-school-talk2.pdf.

13 "bring him into disgrace": *RW,* pp. 68–69.

13 "Flub-dubs": French diary, Dec. 14, 1861.

14 "world-renowned whoremonger": quoted in Burlingame, *Abraham Lincoln,* Vol. 2, pp. 274–75.

14 "Some very extraordinary storeys": ibid.

14 Evidently, Wikoff had persuaded: A definitive treatment of Mary Lincoln's scandalous associations is found in Burlingame, *Abraham Lincoln,* Vol. 2, pp. 162–84. See also Berry, *House of Abraham: Lincoln and the Todds, a Family Divided by War,* pp. 100–103.

14 David Todd, an officer: Burlingame, *Abraham Lincoln,* Vol. 1, p. 180.

14 "A case of treasonable action": McClellan to Cameron, Dec. 9, 1861.

15 "While others are asleep": *RW,* pp. 192, 201.

16 "loved him like a brother": Burlingame, *Abraham Lincoln,* Vol. 2, p. 200.

16 "I ain't got any!": McClellan to Mary Ellen McClellan, Nov. 21, 1861.

16   She "looked remarkably well": French diary, Nov. 24, 1861.

16   "eyes of a hyena": Burlingame, *Abraham Lincoln*, Vol. 2, p. 282.

17   "It is not proper": Ibid.

17   "a gawdy show": Bates diary, Jan. 1, 1862.

17   "The most critical point": Nicolay and Hay, *Abraham Lincoln*, Vol. 5, p. 218.

18   "You may stand for this": quoted in Foote, *The Civil War: A Narrative*, Vol. 1, p. 157.

18   His government was already annoyed: Duberman, *Charles Francis Adams, 1807–1886*, p. 43.

19   Europe's "aristocracy [is] bent": Dayton to Seward, Jan. 27, 1862.

19   "They [hope] for our ruin!": quoted by Norman A. Graebner, "Northern Diplomacy and European Neutrality," in Donald, ed., *Why the North Won the Civil War*, p. 57.

19   more room to save face: Crook, *Diplomacy During the American Civil War*, pp. 84–85.

19   Seward devised an artful response: See, for example, Foreman, *A World on Fire: Britain's Crucial Role in the American Civil War*, pp. 194–96.

19   "People are almost frantic": Joseph Gillespie, quoted in Burlingame, *Abraham Lincoln*, Vol. 2, p. 228.

19   keep the foreign powers in check: Adams to Seward, Dec. 27, 1861. Even after the resolution of the *Trent* crisis, Adams pronounced himself "quite doubtful" about England's future course.

20   This was the explanation: *CW*, Vol. 5, pp. 41–42.

20   Taney felt free to spurn: Simon, *Lincoln and Chief Justice Taney: Slavery, Secession, and the President's War Powers*, p. 222.

20   Lincoln's powerful critiques: See, for example, Fehrenbacher, *Prelude to Greatness: Lincoln in the 1850s*, pp. 70–95.

21   priceless propaganda victory: Guelzo, *Lincoln's Emancipation Proclamation: The End of Slavery in America*, pp. 39, 117. This idea is the central thesis of Simon, *Lincoln and Chief Justice Taney*.

21   "I very much doubt": Trollope, *North America*, p. 172.

22   "They knew almost nothing": Williams, *Lincoln and His Generals*, pp. 3–6.

22   none was a true warrior-general: Details of the officers' biographies come from Heidler and Heidler, eds., *Encyclopedia of the American Civil War*, in the articles titled with their respective names.

23   "I can do it all": quoted in Hay diary, undated (describing the evening of Nov. 1, 1861), p. 30.

23 "Draw on me": Ibid.

23 he had a low opinion: McClellan's political philosophy, and its influence over his military strategy, is given a rich and sympathetic treatment by Ethan Rafuse in *McClellan's War.*

24 "By some strange operation": McClellan to Mary Ellen McClellan, July 27, 1861.

24 "letter after letter": McClellan to Mary Ellen McClellan, Aug. 9 [10], 1861.

24 a dangerous blindness: cf. Hay diary, Oct. 26 and Nov. 11, 1861.

24 "The Commander-in-Chief": quoted in Burlingame, *Abraham Lincoln,* Vol. 2, p. 197.

24 "unparalleled insolence": Hay diary, Nov. 13, 1861.

24 Lincoln took the snub: *CW,* Vol. 5, pp. 34–35; McClellan to Lincoln, Dec. 10, 1861.

25 "It is terrible": McClellan to Mary Ellen McClellan, circa Oct. 31, 1861.

25 "his reading was laborious": Stoddard, *Inside the White House in War Times: Memoirs and Reports of Lincoln's Secretary,* pp. 184–85.

26 In his Second Inaugural Address: *CW,* Vol. 8, pp. 333–34.

27 "Help me dodge": McClellan to Samuel Barlow, Nov. 8, 1861.

27 his oft-spoken view: "Emancipation, for Lincoln, was never a question of the end but of how to construct the means in such a way that the end was not put into jeopardy." Guelzo, *Lincoln's Emancipation Proclamation,* p. 26.

27 Lincoln never claimed: *RW,* p. 336.

28 "two of the most truculent": Guelzo, *Lincoln's Emancipation Proclamation,* p. 57.

28 "hitch the whole thing": Ibid., pp. 58–59.

28 "Timid, vacillating, & inefficient": Ibid., p. 67.

28 "the gates were thrown open": *New York Times,* Jan. 3, 1862.

29 Attorney General Bates fretted: Bates diary, Jan. 1, 1862.

29 "He goes at it with both hands": *New York Times,* June 18, 1861.

29 "Anything that kept the people": Hay, quoted in *Herndon's Informants,* p. 331.

29 The foundation of political liberty: This theme recurs in many of Lincoln's speeches. See, for example, *CW,* Vol. 3, pp. 312–15, from the famous 1858 debates: "No matter in what shape it comes, whether from a king who seeks to bestride the people of his own nation and live by the fruit of their labor, or from one race of men as an apology for enslaving another race, it is the same tyrannical principle."

29 "scorned labour": Joseph Gillespie, quoted in *Herndon's Informants,* p. 183.

30 "This is the just": *CW,* Vol. 5, pp. 52–53. Lincoln's economic philosophy is thoroughly examined in Boritt, *Lincoln and the Economics of the American Dream.*

30 "one thing was necessary": Leonard Swett, quoted in *Herndon's Informants,* p. 165.

30 the holiday continued: Taft diary, Jan. 1, 1861.

30 "the bare possibility": Dahlgren diary, Jan. 2, 1862.

30 boys lost joyfully: Taft diary, Jan. 1, 1862.

31 "We have no general": Bates diary, Dec. 31, 1861.

31 "Every war is begun": Nicolay and Hay, *Abraham Lincoln,* Vol. 4, pp. 359–60.

31 "minority president . . . majority general": *RW,* pp. 360–61.

32 "Times are exceedingly dark": Dawes, quoted in Burlingame, *Abraham Lincoln,* Vol. 2, p. 215.

32 "Forty or fifty": Taft diary, Jan. 15, 1862.

32 Measles: Boyden, *Echoes from Hospital and White House: A Record of Mrs. Rebecca R. Pomroy's Experience in War-Times,* pp. 29–35.

32 "almost every Street": Taft diary, Jan. 8, 1862.

33 "General McClellan is sick": *CW,* Vol. 5, p. 84.

33 "There is no arrangement": ibid.

33 "Too much haste": ibid.

33 known as Old Brains: Marszalek, *Commander of All Lincoln's Armies: A Life of Henry W. Halleck,* pp. 42–43.

34 Though only a few sentences long: *CW,* Vol. 5, p. 84.

34 "greatest living soldier": quoted in Peskin, *Winfield Scott and the Profession of Arms,* p. 191.

35 "a real or feigned attack": *CW,* Vol. 5, p. 84.

35 "a perfectly good mood": ibid., p. 88.

2: JANUARY

37 A cold front swept: Taft diary, Jan. 2, 1862.

37 The president was in a low mood: Dahlgren diary, Jan. 2, 1862.

37 "very much better": *CW,* Vol. 5, p. 88.

37 "browsing": McClellan to Mary Ellen McClellan, Oct. 31, 1861.

38 "Not a moment's time": McClellan to Henry Halleck, Jan. 3, 1862.

38 "condemned by every military authority": *CW,* Vol. 5, pp. 87n, 92n, 95n.

38 Buell simply disappeared: ibid., p. 92n.

38 "Delay is ruining us": ibid., p. 94.

38 "It is exceedingly discouraging": ibid., p. 95.

38   an infuriating telegram from Buell: Miers, *Lincoln Day by Day: A Chronology*, Vol. 3, Jan. 6, 1862.

38   A light snow: Taft diary, Jan. 4–7, 1862.

38   Lincoln did much of his best thinking: Joshua Speed, quoted in *Herndon's Informants*, p. 499.

38   "When he walked": Herndon and Weik, *Abraham Lincoln*, Vol. 2, p. 295.

38   "The political consequences": McClellan to Don Carlos Buell, Jan. 6, 1862.

39   "A great deal of discussion": Chase diary, Jan. 6, 1862.

39   "He has got the presidential maggot": "[Nicolay] Conversation with V. P. Wilson . . ." in *An Oral History of Abraham Lincoln: John G. Nicolay's Interviews and Essays*, p. 85.

39   "He would rather be on the bench": John D. Martin to Thomas Ewing, Sr., Jan. 22, 1862, Ewing Family Papers, Box 13, No. 4866, Library of Congress Manuscript Division.

40   the federal debt: Nicolay and Hay, *Abraham Lincoln*, Vol. 6, pp. 227–31.

40   "determined to shut his eyes": *RW*, p. 216.

41   First he defended: Chase diary, Jan. 6, 1862.

41   The committee was sent away: ibid.

41   "they don't give me time": McClellan to Samuel Barlow, Jan. 18, 1862.

41   out for a brisk ride: Taft diary, Jan. 8, 1862.

41   "You better go": *CW*, Vol. 5, p. 94.

42   "Nothing but very marked evidences": Adams to Seward, Dec. 27, 1861.

42   "no general in the army": Nicolay and Hay, *Abraham Lincoln*, Vol. 6, pp. 113–14.

42   Visitors to the White House: Henry C. Whitney, quoted in *Herndon's Informants*, p. 405; Browning diary, June 22, 1862.

42   "unknown in the art of war": Seward to Adams, Jan. 31, 1862.

42   But to a man who could read them: "In charting the movements of armies, the facts of geography stand first." Keegan, *Fields of Battle: The Wars for North America*, p. 8.

42   "My distress": *CW*, Vol. 5, p. 91.

43   "a frontier of rivers": McPherson, *Battle Cry of Freedom: The Civil War Era*, p. 42.

43   received a patent: *CW*, Vol. 2, pp. 32–35.

44   "brown water navy": Joiner, *Mr. Lincoln's Brown Water Navy: The Mississippi Squadron*, pp. 1–21; Stoddard, *Lincoln at Work: Sketches from Life*, pp. 20–25; Hearn, *Ellet's Brigade: The Strangest Outfit of All*.

44   Fog lay thick: Taft diary, Jan. 10, 1862.

44   Lincoln convened the cabinet again: Bates diary, Jan. 10, 1862.

44   Welles echoed the sentiment: Welles diary, p. 61.

44   "The people are impatient": Meigs diary, Jan. 10, 1862, Montgomery C. Meigs Papers, Reel 15, Library of Congress Manuscript Division; see also "Documents: General M. C. Meigs on the Conduct of the Civil War," *American Historical Review* 26 (January 1921), p. 292.

45   the navy implored Lincoln: Welles diary, p. 60.

45   Lincoln had decided to fire Cameron: Barnes, *The Life of Thurlow Weed,* Vol. 2, pp. 330–31.

45   "borrow it": *RW,* p. 332.

46   "Traitors are under me": ibid., pp. 254, 322.

46   Pretending to be sailors: Taft diary, Jan. 11, 1862.

46   an artful pair of letters: *CW,* Vol. 5, pp. 96–97.

47   "a dismissal": Chase diary, Jan. 12, 1862.

47   "bricks in his pocket": *RW,* pp. 135–36.

47   Stanton was not to be trusted: Welles diary, p. 56.

48   "that damned long armed Ape": See, for example, Donald, *Lincoln,* pp. 185–87.

48   His favorite expression: *RW,* p. 221.

48   "Perhaps I have too little": ibid., p. 232.

48   Hay once scoffed: Hay, quoted in *Herndon's Informants,* p. 209.

48   "I know more about it": *RW,* p. 209.

48   The Treasury secretary advised: Chase diary, Jan. 11, 1862.

49   For the first time: Sears, *George B. McClellan: The Young Napoleon,* p. 140.

49   "at least 400,000 Men": Taft diary, Jan. 12, 1862.

49   The lobbies and bars: ibid., Jan. 27, 1862.

50   "shabbier and dirtier": Dicey, *Spectator of America,* pp. 63–64.

50   Lincoln's secretaries appeared at Willard's: Ronald A. Rietveld, "The Lincoln White House Community," *Journal of the Abraham Lincoln Association* 20, no. 2 (Summer 1999), p. 23. Available online at http://quod.lib.unich.edu/j/jala/2629860.0020.204?rgn=main;view-fulltext.

50   "holding court among the belles": Seale, *The President's House: A History,* Vol. 1, p. 381.

50   Orville Hickman Browning: Donald, *"We Are Lincoln Men,"* pp. 101–19; Browning diary, pp. 508–9.

51   he startled Browning: Browning diary, Jan. 12, 1862.

51   he had received a telegram: *CW,* Vol. 5, pp. 98–99.

52   "I would rather like a regiment": Quoted in Sandburg, *Abraham Lincoln: The War Years,* Vol. 1, p. 465.

53   He had not been there long: Grant, *Memoirs and Selected Letters: Personal Memoirs of U.S. Grant, 1839–1865*, p. 188.

53   Using Halleck's feint: ibid.

54   Halleck's view of war: cf. Halleck, *Elements of Military Art and Science,* especially pp. 38–43.

54   "The art of war is simple": This quote, in nearly identical context, can be found in T. Harry Williams, "The Military Leadership of North and South," in Donald, *Why the North Won*, p. 51.

54   "I had not uttered": Grant, *Memoirs and Selected Letters,* pp. 189–90.

55   "the largest official leak": Sears, *George B. McClellan,* pp. 140–42.

55   "The streets and crossings are worse": Taft diary, Jan. 22, 1862.

55   "The city was in a fearful condition": Alexander Williamson, quoted in Seale, *The President's House,* Vol. 1, p. 401.

56   Chase convened a conference: Chase diary, Jan. 14–20, 1862; Taft diary, Jan. 17, 1862.

57   Nicolay estimated: Nicolay to Therena Bates, Jan. 15, 1862.

57   an evening at the Washington Theater: Miers, *Lincoln Day by Day,* Vol. 3, Jan. 23, 1862.

57   across the ocean in Paris: Dayton to Seward, Jan. 27, 1862.

58   An "unscrupulous adventurer": Stoddard, *Lincoln at Work,* pp. 47–53.

59   "Having gotten on our armor": The account of the meeting is from William Dayton's dispatch to Seward, Jan. 27, 1862.

60   "something must be done": ibid.

60   "our efforts . . . are hopeless": ibid.

60   "President's General War Order No. 1: *CW,* Vol. 5, pp. 111–12.

61   precisely what he was looking for: Smith, *Grant,* pp. 139–40.

3: FEBRUARY

62   "One section of our country believes": *CW,* Vol. 4, pp. 268–69.

62   "We didn't go into the war": *RW,* p. 295.

62   a new poem: *The Atlantic Monthly* 9, no. 52 (February 1862), p. 10.

62   Samuel Gridley Howe: Tuchinsky, "Samuel Gridley Howe," in Heidler and Heidler, eds., *Encyclopedia of the American Civil War,* pp. 1011–13.

64   "like a bloodstained ghost": Davis, *Inhuman Bondage: The Rise and Fall of Slavery in the New World,* pp. 157–61.

64   he despised the reformers: Welles diary, Sept. 3, 1862.

64   "I will not fight": McClellan to Mary Ellen McClellan, circa Nov. 14, 1861; see also McClellan to Samuel Barlow, Nov. 8, 1861.

65 he knew which side: John Stuart, quoted in *Herndon's Informants,* p. 64.

65 "a great and crying injustice": *RW,* p. 169.

65 "Slavery is doomed": ibid., p. 303.

65 "I am naturally anti-slavery": *CW,* Vol. 7, pp. 281–83.

66 "a party of Methodist parsons": *RW,* p. 430.

66 the entire country . . . was complicit: ibid., p. 368.

66 Chief Justice Taney: Guelzo, *Lincoln and the Emancipation Proclamation* (for example, pp. 39, 114) provides several lucid insights into the constitutional snares Taney had laid across the path to emancipation. If freeing the slaves could be construed as a punishment imposed on a class of citizens (i.e., slave owners) without benefit of a trial, emancipation could be classed as a bill of attainder, explicitly forbidden by the Constitution. Freeing slaves by presidential order, meanwhile, could run afoul of Taney's 1850 opinion in *Fleming v. Page.*

66 "violent and remorseless": *CW,* Vol. 5, pp. 48–49.

66 Confederate operatives in Europe: Owsley, *King Cotton Diplomacy,* p. 66.

66 abolitionists began to fear: cf. Sumner to Frances Bird, Feb. 19, 1862.

66 "When the hour comes": *RW,* pp. 118–19.

67 Nathaniel Gordon: The story of Gordon's crime, trial, and punishment is told in Soodalter, *Hanging Captain Gordon: The Life and Trial of an American Slave Trader.*

67 "You do not know how hard": *RW,* p. 409.

67 "boyish cheerfulness": Emerson, *Essays and Journals,* p. 667.

68 Finally, an army was moving: Grant, *Memoirs and Selected Letters,* p. 190; Smith, *Grant,* pp. 139–41.

68 "Oh, Mr. Emerson!": Emerson, *Essays and Journals,* p. 667.

68 delight in his own jokes: ibid.

68 he had spoken at the Smithsonian: Richardson, *Emerson: The Mind on Fire,* pp. 563–64.

68 "I am against capital punishment": Sumner to Orestes Brownson, Feb. 2, 1862.

68 "fidelity and conscientiousness": Emerson, *Essays and Journals,* p. 667.

69 "If we fail": Bates diary, Feb. 3, 1862.

69 "duty" compelled him: *CW,* Vol. 5, pp. 128–29.

69 doctrine of white supremacy: See, for example, Alexander Stephens's speech at Savannah, March 21, 1861, excerpted in Stampp, ed., *The Causes of the Civil War,* pp. 116–17: "Our new Government is founded upon . . . its cornerstone rests, upon the great truth that the negro is not equal to the white man."

69   "the awful change": *CW,* Vol. 5, pp. 128–29.

70   Nicolay estimated: Nicolay to Therena Bates, Feb. 2, 1862.

70   Mary's idea was: Keckley, *Behind the Scenes: Thirty Years a Slave and Four Years in the White House,* pp. 95–97.

70   What mattered to the cutthroats: Nicolay to Therena Bates, Feb. 2, 1862.

70   Determined to show: Baker, *Mary Todd Lincoln: A Biography,* pp. 206–7.

70   "Our cat has a long tail": Keckley, *Behind the Scenes,* pp. 101–2. The spelling of Elizabeth Keckly's surname is a matter of dispute. I have chosen to follow the choice of biographer Jennifer Fleischner in Fleischner, *Mrs. Lincoln and Mrs. Keckly: The Remarkable Story of the Friendship Between a First Lady and a Former Slave.*

70   "Are the President and Mrs. Lincoln aware": quoted in Baker, *Mary Todd Lincoln,* p. 206.

71   *The Liberator* pronounced: quoted in Randall, *Mary Lincoln,* pp. 259–60.

71   But as Nicolay acidly observed: Nicolay to Therena Bates, Feb. 6, 1862.

71   McClellan . . . cutting the familiar figure: Dahlgren diary, Feb. 5, 1862.

71   "30 days delay": McClellan to Stanton, Feb. 3, 1862. Stephen W. Sears, editor of *The Civil War Papers of George B. McClellan,* argues persuasively that this document, dated Jan. 31, 1862, is misdated and actually was completed on Feb. 3.

71   During the awkward pause: Poore, *Perley's Reminiscences of Sixty Years in the National Metropolis,* Vol. 2, pp. 119–20.

71   fistfight in the kitchen: Nicolay to Therena Bates, Feb. 6, 1862.

71   "the most splendid": Dahlgren diary, Feb. 5, 1862 (p. 356n).

72   "I shall take and destroy": Grant to Halleck, Feb. 6, 1862.

72   not much for hunkering: Grant, *Memoirs and Selected Letters,* pp. 196–97.

73   Stanton strode into a cabinet meeting: Bates diary, Feb. 14, 1862.

73   Lincoln was delighted: ibid.

73   mount a siege: Grant, *Memoirs and Selected Letters,* p. 204.

73   the Rebels were in position: Hurst, *Men of Fire: Grant, Forrest, and the Campaign That Decided the Civil War,* pp. 262–71.

73   constant supply of ammunition: Grant, *Memoirs and Selected Letters,* p. 205.

73   Grant had a hunch: ibid., p. 196.

74   "The one who attacks first": ibid., p. 205.

74   "greatest single supply disaster": Hattaway and Jones, *How the North Won,* p. 150.

74   Since his visit with Emerson: Miers, *Lincoln Day by Day,* Vol. 3, Feb. 7 and 13, 1862.

75 "Goethe teaches courage": Emerson, "Goethe," in *Representative Men: Seven Lectures,* p. 275.

75 "I cannot speak so confidently": Nicolay journal, Feb. 17, 1862.

75 He proposed an amnesty: *CW,* Vol. 5, p. 135; see also Dahlgren diary, Feb. 16, 1862.

75 "We have unmistakeable evidence": Seward to Adams, Feb. 5, 1862.

75 "Our friends want": Adams to Seward, Feb. 7, 1862.

75 "The great victory at Mill Spring": Seward to Adams, Feb. 17, 1862.

75 A French nobleman: Dahlgren diary, Feb. 21, 1862.

76 "the switch had been turned off": Dayton to Seward, Feb. 27, 1862.

76 They were worried about Willie: Keckley, *Behind the Scenes,* pp. 100–102.

76 "absorbed pretty much all": Nicolay to Therena Bates, Feb. 11, 1862; Nicolay journal, Feb. 18, 1862.

76 "He was his father over again": Randall, *Lincoln's Sons,* p. 51.

76 "an amiable, good-hearted boy": Taft diary, Feb. 20, 1862.

76 "He never failed to seek me out": quoted in Keckley, *Behind the Scenes,* pp. 106–10.

77 removed his hat and bowed: ibid.

77 "before they have any": Randall, *Lincoln's Sons,* p. 127.

77 "the most lovable boy": Bayne, *Tad Lincoln's Father,* p. 3.

77 Willie had a crush: ibid., p. 166.

77 "good as pie": ibid., pp. 31–32.

77 "the most indulgent parent": Joseph Gillespie, quoted in *Herndon's Informants,* p. 181.

77 "love is the chain": *RW,* p. 296.

77 They shelled a cabinet meeting: Bayne, *Tad Lincoln's Father,* pp. 101, 104–5; Stoddard, *Lincoln's Third Secretary: The Memoirs of William O. Stoddard,* pp. 98–99.

77 Recalling the hard labor: John Romine, quoted in *Herndon's Informants,* p. 118.

77 "let the goat be": *RW,* p. 415.

78 "sit on his stomach!": Bayne, *Tad Lincoln's Father,* pp. 109–10.

78 "I know every step": *RW,* p. 185.

78 Willie wasting away: cf. Stoddard, *Inside the White House in War Times,* p. 66.

78 "in extremis": Bates diary, Feb. 18, 1862.

78 carved rosewood bed: Seale, *The President's House,* Vol. 1, pp. 374–86.

78 "If I go he will call for me": quoted in Randall, *Mary Lincoln,* p. 253.

78 "my boy is gone": Nicolay diary, Feb. 20, 1862.

79 Pomroy arrived: Boyden, *Echoes from Hospital and White House,* pp. 52–56.

79 "a growing man in religion": quoted in Carwardine, *Lincoln: A Life of Purpose and Power,* p. 33.

79 "He found difficulty": *RW,* p. 137.

80 "This is the hardest trial": Boyden, *Echoes from Hospital and White House,* pp. 52–56.

80 grab a tree: Bates diary, Feb. 24, 1862.

80 Before the funeral: French diary, March 2, 1862.

80 a simple affair that brought tears: Keckley, *Behind the Scenes,* pp. 106–10.

80 Afterward, Lincoln and his oldest son: French diary, March 2, 1862; Boyden, *Echoes from Hospital and White House,* pp. 56–57.

80 placed in a crypt: Browning diary, Feb. 24, 1862.

81 his temper sometimes frayed: Pierce, "The Freedmen at Port Royal," *The Atlantic Monthly* 12, no. 71 (September 1863), pp. 291–315.

81 "There seems to be a great itching": Edward Pierce, quoted in *Herndon's Informants,* pp. 684–85.

81 credit for the colossal success: Grant, *Memoirs and Selected Letters,* p. 214.

82 this fiasco: ibid., pp. 219–20.

82 "We could have marched": ibid., p. 214.

82 "Every boat that came up": ibid., p. 213.

83 place Grant under arrest: McClellan to Halleck, March 3, 1862.

83 "resumed his former bad habits": Halleck to McClellan, quoted in Foote, *The Civil War,* Vol. 1, p. 317.

83 "I was disgusted": quoted in Smith, *Grant,* pp. 168–69.

83 "You cannot be relieved": Halleck to Grant, March 13, 1862, quoted in Smith, *Grant,* p. 178.

83 "time was given the enemy": Grant, *Memoirs and Selected Letters,* pp. 214–15.

84 This scolding, along with Lincoln's order: Sears, *George B. McClellan,* pp. 156–68.

84 "It was a magnificent spectacle": McClellan to Mary Ellen McClellan, Feb. 27, 1862.

84 "Why in tarnation": Nicolay diary, Feb. 27, 1862.

4: MARCH

87 gave Lincoln a memo: Nicolay and Hay, *Abraham Lincoln: A History,* Vol. 3, pp. 445–49.

88 "I have none": *RW,* p. 269.

88   "fonder of details": Adams, *Richard Henry Dana: A Biography*, Vol. 2, p. 264.

88   "*only five minutes*": Nicolay to Therena Bates, March 24, 1861.

88   "so busy in letting rooms": *RW*, p. 375.

89   "You are Seward's man": Duberman, *Charles Francis Adams*, pp. 256–57.

89   "the Chicago post-office": Adams, *Charles Francis Adams: An American Statesman*, pp. 145–46.

89   Two scholars estimated: Carman and Luthin, *Lincoln and the Patronage*, p. 332; see also Carwardine, *Lincoln*, for an extensive and shrewd discussion of Lincoln's skillful use of political patronage.

89   "'Fairness to all'": Lincoln to Seward, December 1861, quoted in Nicolay, "Lincoln in the Campaign of 1860," in *An Oral History of Abraham Lincoln*, p. 94.

89   a dozen Irish-born Union generals: Carman and Luthin, *Lincoln and the Patronage*, pp. 156-60.

90   "I want Schimmelfennig": *RW*, p. 165.

90   "for this great Methodist church": quoted in "Conversation . . . [with Congressman] Orth of Indiana," in *An Oral History of Abraham Lincoln*, p. 82.

90   "bail[ing] out the Potomac": *RW*, p. 210.

90   "never under any administration": "Two Manuscripts of Gideon Welles," edited by Muriel Burnitt, *The New England Quarterly* 11, no. 3 (September 1938), p. 594.

90   he declined to appoint: Donald, *"We Are Lincoln Men,"* pp. 122–23.

90   "give more to his enemies": Leonard Swett, quoted in Herndon and Weik, *Abraham Lincoln*, Vol. 2, pp. 243–44.

90   "a considerable portion of every day": Welles diary, Sept. 16, 1862.

91   "limited to a couple of stories": *RW*, p. 126.

91   "nonsensical and preposterous dialogue": Van Deusen, *William Henry Seward*, p. 256.

91   "don't let it be smutty": ibid.

91   he visited Lincoln to preview: After Seward's initial reckless steps as secretary of state, Lincoln insisted that major dispatches be edited and approved by him before they were sent. Thus, the diplomatic correspondence between Seward and the American envoys in Europe provides an important window on Lincoln's strategic thinking. Cf. *RW*, p. 156.

91   "at the beginning of the end": Seward to Adams, March 6, 1862.

91   "The Government has attempted more": Davis, quoted in the *New York Times*, March 1, 1862.

92 "a question of resources": *RW*, p. 106.

92 every money stream . . . would be tapped: *New York Times*, March 10, 1862.

92 "something to complain of": ibid., March 4, 1862.

92 enormous economic advantage: National Geographic Society, *Atlas of the Civil War: A Comprehensive Guide to the Tactics and Terrain of Battle*, p. 22.

93 Pea Ridge: Long, *The Civil War Day by Day: An Almanac, 1861–1865*, pp. 179–81; Earl J. Hess, "Battle of Pea Ridge," in Heidler and Heidler, eds., *Encyclopedia of the American Civil War*, pp. 1467–68.

93 "disease of the entire nation": *RW*, p. 119.

93 "slavery is no small affair": ibid., p. 368.

94 "full and equal share": ibid., p. 122.

94 The details . . . had been taking shape: cf. Guelzo, *Lincoln's Emancipation Proclamation*, pp. 60–65, 102–8.

94 He proposed . . . a joint resolution: *CW*, Vol. 5, pp. 144–46.

94 "deprive them of this hope": ibid.

94 "milk-and-water gruel": quoted in Nicolay and Hay, *Abraham Lincoln*, Vol. 6, p. 107.

94 "The proposition . . . is an epoch": Sumner to Frances Bird, March 12, 1862.

94 "The great, transcendent fact": quoted in Guelzo, *Lincoln's Emancipation Proclamation*, p. 107; see also *New York Times*, March 7, 1862.

95 "a presentiment that he should die": Bates diary, March 17, 1862.

95 "Have you noticed the facts": *CW*, Vol. 5, pp. 152–53.

95 "talk plainly": Sumner to John Andrew, March 2, 1862.

95 complained that . . . Stanton kept him away: McClellan, *McClellan's Own Story*, p. 195.

95 bending in McClellan's favor: McClellan to Halleck, March 3, 1862.

95 a memo for the War Department: "To the War Department," in *The Civil War Papers of George B. McClellan: Selected Correspondence, 1860–1865*, pp. 193–94.

95 "damned fizzle": Nicolay diary, Feb. 27, 1862.

95 "unexpected piece of good fortune": McClellan to Samuel Barlow, Jan. 18, 1862.

96 Stanton had been hearing: Stanton to Thomas Ewing, Sr., April 2, 1862, Ewing Family Papers, Box 67, Library of Congress Manuscript Division.

96 "caused great solicitude": ibid.

96 photographers' shops . . . were packed: Taft diary, April 1, 1862.

96 "The City seems to be entirely full": ibid., March 8, 1862.

97   McClellan exploded: McClellan, *McClellan's Own Story*, p. 196.

97   "the undying hate": McClellan to Halleck, March 3, 1862.

98   "just pitch in": Sears, *George B. McClellan*, p. 160.

98   "fight should have been at Manassas": Browning diary, June 18, 1862.

98   "a house submerged": quoted in Greene and Massignani, *Ironclads at War: The Origin and Development of the Armored Warship, 1854–1891*, p. 61.

98   the Confederate ship *Virginia:* Gene A. Smith, "CSS Virginia," in Heidler and Heidler, eds., *Encyclopedia of the Civil War*, pp. 2034–36.

99   this was the day: cf. John T. Wood, "The First Fight of Iron-Clads," in *Battles and Leaders of the Civil War*, Vol. 1, pp. 692–711.

100   "Since I sent in my message": Nicolay diary, March 9, 1862.

101   "One thought she would go": ibid.

101   "thin and wasted": Dahlgren diary, March 9, 1862.

101   "a caged lion": Nicolay diary, March 9, 1862; Welles diary, pp. 61–67.

102   an utterly original design: Gene A. Smith, "Monitor," in Heidler and Heidler, eds., *Encyclopedia of the American Civil War*, pp. 1346–47.

102   "incredulity and contempt": Welles diary, pp. 61–67.

103   "like a pygmy": Wood, "The First Fight of Iron-Clads," p. 701.

103   "a thousand years of battle and breeze": Ibid., p. 692. For further details of the battle, see also S. D. Greene, "In the 'Monitor' Turret," in *Battles and Leaders of the Civil War*, Vol. 1, pp. 719–29.

103   "snapping my thumb": Wood, "The First Fight of Iron-Clads," p. 701.

104   "Iron will be King": L. M. Powell to Gustavus V. Fox, April 4, 1862, in *Confidential Correspondence of Gustavus Vasa Fox, Assistant Secretary of the Navy, 1861–1865*, Vol. 2, p. 287.

104   good news . . . followed by even more: Nicolay diary, March 9, 1862.

104   "most excited and impressive": Nicolay and Hay, *Abraham Lincoln*, Vol. 5, p. 226.

105   emancipation was already started: cf. *RW*, p. 123.

105   panel of border state congressmen: Guelzo, *Lincoln's Emancipation Proclamation*, pp. 105–6.

105   "touched the hem": *RW*, p. 356.

105   "good faith" answer: ibid., pp. 121–22.

106   "sink or swim with you": Bates diary, March 15, 1862.

106   Why . . . block the Potomac again?: Welles diary, pp. 61–67.

106   "Great ignorance": Bates diary, March 11, 1862.

107   "Stanton is exceedingly industrious": *Lincoln Observed: The Civil War Dispatches of Noah Brooks*, p. 47.

107   his experience of the Stanton style: William F. Roelofson to Thomas Ewing,

Sr., Aug. 14, 1862, Ewing Family Papers, Box 14, No. 5100, Library of Congress Manuscript Division.

188 main telegraph moved: Bates, *Lincoln in the Telegraph Office: Recollections of the United States Military Telegraph Corps During the Civil War*, pp. 132–37.

108 "Let him wait": quoted in Burlingame, *Abraham Lincoln*, Vol. 2, p. 197.

108 President's Special War Order No. 3: Hay diary, pp. 35–36.

109 "Forget it": Goodwin, *Team of Rivals: The Political Genius of Abraham Lincoln*, pp. 429–30.

109 "prompt, full, and frequent reports": *CW*, Vol. 5, p. 155.

109 "end of the rebellion": *New York Times*, March 12, 1862.

110 "a fool's errand": Bates diary, March 13, 1862.

110 McClellan . . . was delighted: Rafuse, *McClellan's War*, p. 193.

110 "the brightest passage of my life": McClellan to Samuel Barlow, March 16, 1862.

111 "showed me my weakness": quoted in Goodwin, *Team of Rivals*, pp. 422–23.

111 "distressed and pale": French diary, March 23, 1862.

111 "Tad and I have fixed": Randall, *Lincoln's Sons*, pp. 133–34; *CW*, Vol. 5, p. 154.

111 "depression of spirits": Boyden, *Echoes from Hospital and White House*, pp. 58–62.

111 Mary pressed a picture: ibid.

112 *"stand firm"*: ibid.

112 The emperor wanted to talk: Dayton to Seward, March 25 and 26, 1862.

114 "France would have nothing to do with it": ibid., March 31, 1862.

114 "The period of inaction has passed": "To the Army of the Potomac," in *The Civil War Papers of George B. McClellan*, p. 211.

114 "Numerous steam-tugs": Warren Lee Goss, "Campaigning to No Purpose," in *Battles and Leaders of the Civil War*, Vol. 2, p. 159.

114 "stride of a giant": quoted in Sears, *George B. McClellan*, pp. 168–69.

114 To accomplish this: McClellan to Stanton, March 19, 1862.

114 "We began to fear": *RW*, p. 148.

115 "a tool of Jeff Davis": Ellen Ewing Sherman to Thomas Ewing, Jr., March 20, 1862, Ewing Family Papers, Box 67; Stanton to Thomas Ewing, Sr., April 2, 1862, Ewing Family Papers, Box 67, Library of Congress Manuscript Division.

115 meeting with Orville Browning: Browning diary, April 2, 1862.

115 McClellan's long relationship with . . . Davis: ibid.

116   "The government seems doomed": Stanton to Thomas Ewing, Sr., April 2, 1862, Ewing Family Papers, Box 67, Library of Congress Manuscript Division.

116   "raw men timid": Sherman, *Memoirs of General W. T. Sherman,* p. 249.

116   "the task is so gigantic": Sherman to Thomas Ewing, Jr., April 4, 1862.

5: APRIL

118   "Albert Sidney Johnston": P. Roland Charles, "Albert Sidney Johnston," in Heidler and Heidler, eds., *Encyclopedia of the American Civil War,* pp. 1081–83.

119   "the great strategic position": Grant, *Memoirs and Selected Letters,* p. 222.

119   Johnston decided to strike: Davis, *The Rise and Fall of the Confederate Government,* Vol. 2, p. 50.

120   "wild birds in great numbers": Wheeler, *Voices of the Civil War,* pp. 88–89.

120   believing that the Confederates were dispirited: Grant, *Memoirs and Selected Letters,* p. 223.

120   "the first great modern battle": Foote, *The Civil War,* Vol. 1, p. 338.

120   "I think I have seen enough": Wheeler, *Voices of the Civil War,* p. 89.

120   "perhaps a dozen officers arrested": Grant to Jesse R. Grant, April 26, 1862.

121   Prentiss and his troops repulsed: Hattaway and Jones, *How the North Won,* p. 168.

121   valuable hours of daylight: Wheeler, *Voices of the Civil War,* pp. 95–96.

122   "Lick 'em tomorrow": Smith, *Grant,* pp. 200–201.

122   more casualties in two days at Shiloh: Foote, *The Civil War,* Vol. 1, p. 351.

123   begin shooting the stragglers: ibid., p. 344.

123   the "jealousy of Gen. Buell": cf. Sherman to John Sherman, May 12, 1862: "Grant had been expecting Buell a whole week before he arrived." Also Nicolay and Hay, *Abraham Lincoln,* Vol. 5, p. 318.

123   Carroll struck preemptively: Catton, *Grant Moves South,* pp. 251–52.

123   A line had been crossed: cf. Smith, *Grant,* p. 204 and 204n.

124   "stepping on dead bodies": Grant, *Memoirs and Selected Letters,* pp. 238–39.

124   "like shooting into a flock of sheep": quoted in McDonough, *Shiloh, in Hell Before Night,* p. 156.

124   "valley of death": Ambrose Bierce, "What I Saw of Shiloh," in *Civil War Stories,* pp. 13–14.

124   "break the heart of the rebellion": Bates diary, April 9, 1862.

124 "the horrid nature of this war": Sherman to Ellen Ewing Sherman, April 11, 1862.

125 "except by complete conquest": Grant, *Memoirs and Selected Letters,* p. 246.

125 "breaks up the rebel cause": McClellan to Lincoln, April 20, 1862.

125 McClellan was "astonished": McClellan to Louis M. Goldsborough, April 5, 1862.

125 "In my deliberate judgment": McClellan to Lincoln, April 5, 1862.

125 "the most infamous thing": McClellan to Mary Ellen McClellan, April 6, 1862.

125 Nothing was turning out: Rafuse, *McClellan's War,* pp. 203–5; McClellan to Ambrose Burnside, May 21, 1862.

126 Lincoln scolded: *CW,* Vol. 5, p. 182.

126 "do it himself": McClellan to Mary Ellen McClellan, April 8, 1862.

126 "I need all the aid": McClellan to Lincoln, April 6, 1862.

126 "Do you really think": *CW,* Vol. 5, pp. 184–85.

127 the moment . . . was slipping away: Sears, *George B. McClellan,* p. 179.

127 Porter went floating away: *Eye of the Storm: A Civil War Odyssey Written and Illustrated by Private Robert Knox Sneden,* April 12, 1862.

127 "You can imagine": McClellan to Mary Ellen McClellan, April 11, 1862.

127 defrauding the government: Browning diary, March 3, 1862.

128 "dress in costly materials": quoted in Randall, *Mary Lincoln,* pp. 346–47.

128 "Mrs. L is awfully *Western*": quoted in Seale, *The President's House,* Vol. 1, p. 363.

128 "She wanted what she wanted": Bayne, *Tad Lincoln's Father,* p. 49.

128 three hundred pairs of kid gloves: Browning diary, July 3, 1873.

128 Following his disturbing meeting: Michael Burlingame, "Honest Abe, Dishonest Mary," Historical Bulletin Number 50, Lincoln Fellowship of Wisconsin, 1994, pp. 15–20.

128 White House stationery budget: Miers, *Lincoln Day by Day,* Vol. 3, April 4, 1862.

128 "kiss mine": quoted in Goodwin, *Team of Rivals,* p. 401.

128 "The devil is abroad": ibid.

128 Reverend Francis L. Vinton: Mary Lincoln to Francis L. Vinton, April 13, 1862; Morgan Dix, "Memorial Sermon," in *Francis L. Vinton, Priest and Doctor,* pp. 13–43.

129 "good enough for tabby": Burlingame, *Abraham Lincoln,* Vol. 2, p. 261.

129 "'When shall I awake'": *RW,* p. 330.

129 story of a mysterious letter: Boyden, *Echoes from Hospital and White House,* pp. 67–70.

130   a beautiful Friday: Taft diary, April 4, 1862.

130   went for a ride: *New York Times,* April 5, 1862.

130   "in wild excitement": Taft diary, April 9, 1862.

130   a national day of thanksgiving: *CW,* Vol. 5, pp. 185–86.

131   a double game: Crook, *Diplomacy During the American Civil War,* pp. 64–65.

131   hive of Confederate sympathizers: Seward to Adams, May 2, 1862.

132   formal protest . . . blind eye: Adams to Russell, March 25, 1862; Russell to Adams, March 27, 1862.

132   "change of policy": Adams to Seward, April 11, 1862.

132   A wild rumor: Bates diary, April 11, 1862.

132   a long memorandum for Adams: Seward to Adams, April 14, 1862.

133   The two men had a long talk: Adams to Seward, April 25, 1862.

133   "The North fights for supremacy": Dayton to Seward, May 26, 1862, with attachment from *Le Constitutionnel,* May 23, 1862.

133   "As the period approaches": Adams to Seward, April 25, 1862.

134   a likeness of John Bright: Ronald A. Rietveld, "The Lincoln White House Community," p. 23.

134   ratify a treaty: *CW,* Vol. 5, p. 186.

135   *"Laus Deo!":* Sumner to Francis Lieber, April 25, 1862.

135   Lincoln . . . supported a public referendum: *CW,* Vol. 5, p. 169.

136   "the largest slave-holder": Sumner to John Andrew, April 22, 1862.

136   Lincoln . . . had promised: Browning diary, April 14, 1862.

136   the president owed Wickliffe: Speed, *The Union Cause in Kentucky, 1860–1865,* pp. 99–104.

136   "the most incessant rains": Grant to Julia Dent Grant, April 15, 1862.

136   *"Skulls* and *toes":* quoted in Marszalek, *Commander of All Lincoln's Armies,* pp. 122–23.

136   Thousands of wounded men: *The Papers of Ulysses S. Grant,* Vol. 5, p. 20.

137   lashed himself to a bunk: Sherman to Thomas Ewing, Sr., May 3, 1862.

137   folded their reports: *The Papers of Ulysses S. Grant,* Vol. 5, pp. 48–51.

137   "I never saw a man": Marszalek, *Commander of All Lincoln's Armies,* pp. 122–23.

137   Halleck issued a flurry of orders: *The Papers of Ulysses S. Grant,* Vol. 5, pp. 48–51.

137   When a complaint: ibid., pp. 67–68.

137   Only Buell's timely arrival: Don C. Buell, "Shiloh Reviewed," in *Battles and Leaders of the Civil War,* Vol. 1, pp. 487–536.

138   the same indictment: Flood, *Grant and Sherman: The Friendship That Won the Civil War,* p. 121.

138   "ought to be shot": Sumner to John Andrew, April 22, 1862.

138   "This story of surprise": Sherman to John Sherman, April 22, 1862.

138   "Newspapers now rule": Sherman to Thomas Ewing, Sr., April 27, 1862.

138   "Retreat! Save yourselves!": Daniel, *Shiloh: The Battle That Changed the Civil War*, p. 137.

138   "not from motives of patriotism": from an 1862 editorial in the *Western Standard* of Celina, Ohio; quoted in the Springfield, Ohio, *News-Sun*, Feb. 6, 2011.

139   "I will not permit Col. Mason": Sherman to Philemon B. Ewing, May 16, 1862.

139   "Halleck says . . . 'Sherman saved' ": Thomas Ewing, Jr., to Thomas Ewing, Sr., April 21, 1862, Ewing Family Papers, Box 67, Library of Congress Manuscript Division.

139   "the best fighting general": Thomas Ewing, Sr., to Thomas Ewing, Jr., April 21, 1862, Ewing Family Papers, Box 67, Library of Congress Manuscript Division.

139   "shockingly abused": Grant to Julia Dent Grant, May 11, 1862.

139   an investigation: *The Papers of Ulysses S. Grant,* Vol. 5, pp. 50–51n.

139   The story soon spread: *RW,* pp. 92–93.

139   "grit of a bulldog": ibid., p. 86.

140   "He fights": ibid., p. 315.

140   "almost . . . called gigantic": McClellan to Lincoln, April 23, 1862.

140   "best troops of the Confederacy": Dahlgren diary, April 13, 1862.

140   "only a foolish egotist": Bates diary, April 22, 1862.

140   Lincoln took a field trip: Dahlgren diary, April 19, 1862.

141   "There it is!": *RW,* p. 87; Dahlgren diary, April 19, 1862. It isn't clear from the Dahlgren diary whether this particular joke was told on this occasion, but Lincoln did tell it more than once in slightly varying forms.

141   Early the next morning: Dahlgren diary, April 19, 1862.

141   Generals were beginning to complain: Sherman to John Sherman, May 12, 1862.

141   "There's the political trouble": quoted in Dahlgren diary, April 19, 1862.

142   "an outcry": Ibid.

142   visit to Richmond by . . . Mercier: Foreman, *A World on Fire,* pp. 247–48.

142   Mercier's ears: Owsley, *King Cotton Diplomacy,* pp. 302–3.

142   The ranking admiral: Dahlgren diary, April 24, 1862.

143   the time had come to recognize: Owsley, *King Cotton Diplomacy,* pp. 302–3.

143   " 'caught napping' ": Dahlgren diary, April 24, 1862.

143   He decided to warn: ibid.

143   preparing a sneak attack: *The Civil War Papers of George B. McClellan*, p. 249n.

143   When Orville Browning visited: Browning diary, April 25, 1862.

143   a compendium of broken windows: cf. *The Selected Poems of Thomas Hood*, p. 361.

144   "buzzing . . . like bees": Browning diary, April 25, 1862.

144   Not long past midnight: The story of Farragut's victory at the forts below New Orleans is well told in Hearn, *The Capture of New Orleans, 1862*, pp. 209–36.

145   "a grander spectacle": ibid., pp. 217–18.

145   "Don't flinch!": ibid., pp. 226–27.

145   last hopes of New Orleans: ibid., pp. 239–40.

145   "the great catastrophe": Davis, *The Rise and Fall of the Confederate Government*, Vol. 2, p. 193.

146   "New Orleans gone—": *Mary Chesnut's Civil War*, p. 333.

146   "general incredulity": Adams to Seward, May 15, 1862.

146   Thouvenel . . . angrily jabbed: Dayton to Seward, May 22, 1862.

6: MAY

147   George McClellan's works: McClellan to Lincoln, April 23, 1862; Warren Lee Goss, "Yorktown and Williamsburg," in *Battles and Leaders of the Civil War*, Vol. 2, pp. 193–94.

147   "Your call for Parrott guns": *CW*, Vol. 5, p. 203.

147   "All is being done": Ibid., p. 203n.

148   "seems not to value time": quoted in Nicolay and Hay, *Abraham Lincoln*, Vol. 5, p. 178.

148   "In five minutes": McClellan to Ambrose Burnside, May 21, 1862.

148   "utter stupidity & worthlessness": McClellan to Mary Ellen McClellan, May 6, 1862.

149   "very proud of Yorktown": McClellan to Ambrose Burnside, May 21, 1862.

149   "McClellan's strategy seems": Dahlgren diary, May 5, 1862.

149   McClellan's theory of the war: The origins and substance of McClellan's military strategy are thoroughly examined in Rafuse, *McClellan's War*.

150   "I really thought that you would appreciate": McClellan to Mary Ellen McClellan, May 8, 1862.

150   "pamper one or two pets": *CW*, Vol. 5, pp. 208–9.

150   "There has arisen a desire": Long, *The Civil War Day by Day*, May 16, 1862.

151   "The rebels have been guilty": McClellan to Stanton, May 4, 1862.

151   "The glasses tumbled": Chase to Janet Chase, May 7–8, 1862. Chase is the source of many of the best details of Lincoln and the capture of Norfolk.

152   "The guiding ropes": ibid.

152   By far the wealthiest man: cf. Klepper and Gunther, *The Wealthy 100: From Benjamin Franklin to Bill Gates—A Ranking of the Richest Americans, Past and Present; CW*, Vol. 5, p. 332.

153   The modified ship: Chase to Janet Chase, May 7–8, 1862.

153   "The rebel terror": ibid.

153   The nearsighted Chase: ibid.

154   "I have only one reproach": *RW*, p. 294.

155   *"And, father cardinal"*: Shakespeare, *King John*, Act 3, Scene IV.

155   "Do you ever dream": *RW*, p. 78.

155   "Well, mister": Chase to Janet Chase, May 7–8, 1862.

156   "Thank God": *RW*, pp. 452–53.

156   "wouldn't go through my hair": Ibid., p. 78.

156   he spotted an ax: ibid., pp. 452–53.

156   5,000 men moved inland: *New York Times*, May 12, 1862.

156   Flinging his hat: Joseph B. Carr, "Operations of 1861 About Fort Monroe," in *Battles and Leaders of the Civil War*, Vol. 2, p. 152.

156   Wool and Chase . . . advanced: Chase to Janet Chase, May 11, 1862.

156   It was nearing midnight: *RW*, p. 85.

156   "Norfolk is ours!": quoted in Carpenter, *The Inner Life of Abraham Lincoln*, p. 105.

157   "You can imagine his delight": Chase to Janet Chase, May 11, 1862.

157   "Look out, Mars!": *RW*, p. 78.

157   "I suppose he will be home": Nicolay to Therena Bates, May 9, 1862.

157   Lincoln was proud: Browning diary, May 14, 1862. Lincoln boasted of having "devised and caused to be executed" the entire plan, having "himself . . . explored the Coast and found a landing site for the troops."

157   "a brilliant week's campaign": Chase to Janet Chase, May 11, 1862.

157   "the drooping cause": quoted in Hattaway and Jones, *How the North Won*, p. 178.

158   danger of assassination: David Hunter to Lincoln, Oct. 20, 1860, at http://memory.loc.gov/cgi-bin/ampage.

158   Hunter's military experience: Brad Arnold, "David Hunter," in Heidler and Heidler, eds., *Encyclopedia of the American Civil War*, pp. 1019–20.

158   Port Royal: cf. Pierce, "The Freedmen at Port Royal," p. 299.

159   "red flannel suits": Chase diary, May 1, 1862.

159   "rebellion and slavery were intertwined": Nicolay and Hay, *Abraham Lincoln*, Vol. 6, pp. 90–91.

159 "both ... Halleck and Grant": Sherman, *Memoirs of General W. T. Sherman*, p. 285.

159 "do it, not say it": *RW,* pp. 392–93.

159 "the usual acrimonious comments": Nicolay and Hay, *Abraham Lincoln,* Vol. 6, p. 94.

160 *New York Herald: CW,* Vol. 5, pp. 225–26n.

160 man without a party: Carl Schurz to Lincoln, May 19, 1862: "You told me a week ago in the course of our confidential conversation, that you expected to be left without support at the next congressional elections by the Republican party as well as the democratic; by the latter, because you were too radical and by the former, because you were not radical enough." Abraham Lincoln Papers, Library of Congress Manuscript Division, available online at http://memory.loc.gov/ammem/alhtml/malhome.html.

160 lacked ... "the moral courage": McClellan to Mary Ellen McClellan, May 23, 1862.

160 Robert Smalls: Dorothy L. Drinkard, "Robert Smalls," in Heidler and Heidler, eds., *Encyclopedia of the American Civil War,* pp. 1804–6.

160 "No commanding general": quoted in Warden, *An Account of the Private Life and Public Services of Salmon Portland Chase,* p. 434.

161 Lincoln was reading a treatise: *RW,* p. 88.

161 Whiting argued: Whiting, *The War Powers of the President, and the Legislative Powers of Congress in Relation to Rebellion, Treason and Slavery,* pp. 3, 66–67.

161 Lincoln rescinded Hunter's order: *CW,* Vol. 5, pp. 222–23.

161 "signs of the times": ibid.

161 the Fugitive Slave Act: ibid., p. 224.

162 Seward's essay: Seward to Adams, May 28, 1862.

163 "Give us emancipation": Sumner to Orestes Brownson, May 25, 1862.

163 *"Stanton told me":* Sumner to John Andrew, May 28, 1862.

163 "always a nuisance": McClellan to Mary Ellen McClellan, May 15, 1862; Bates diary, May 13, 1862.

163 The secretaries sparred: Dahlgren diary, May 17, 18, 19, and 21, 1862.

164 a forward-thinking businessman: A. J. Isacks to Thomas Ewing, Jr., April 25 and May 1, 1862, Ewing Family Papers, Box 67, Library of Congress Manuscript Division.

165 "ideal of a great man": cf. *CW,* Vol. 1, pp. 121–32.

165 "a deadly vampyre": Prentice, *Biography of Henry Clay,* p. 266.

165 American Colonization Society: Ibid., p. 267.

165 "What next?": *CW,* Vol. 2, pp. 248–83.

166 "sustain no reverse": ibid., Vol. 5, p. 210.

166   "siege from start to close": Grant, *Memoirs and Selected Letters,* pp. 250–51.

166   "little more than an observer": Sherman, *Memoirs of General W. T. Sherman,* p. 271.

166   "high feather": ibid., pp. 275–76; Sherman to Thomas Ewing, Sr., May 3, 1862; Ellen Ewing Sherman to Hugh Ewing, May 23, 1862, Ewing Family Papers, Box 67, Library of Congress Manuscript Division.

166   Grant saw the opportunities: Sherman to Ewing, Sr., May 3, 1862; Grant, *Memoirs and Selected Letters,* pp. 256–57.

167   "be relieved entirely": Grant to Halleck, May 11, 1862.

167   "guns that'll carry further": *RW,* p. 426.

167   "My entire force": McClellan to Stanton, May 5, 1862.

167   "If I win": McClellan to Ambrose Burnside, May 21, 1862.

168   Stonewall Jackson: James I. Robertson, Jr., "Thomas Jonathan Jackson," in Heidler and Heidler, eds., *Encyclopedia of the American Civil War,* pp. 1058–65.

168   "He seems to be cut off": quoted in Foote, *The Civil War,* Vol. 1, p. 429.

169   "Always mystify": quoted in Robertson, "Thomas Jonathan Jackson," in Heidler and Heidler, eds., *Encyclopedia of the American Civil War,* pp. 1058–65.

169   "bound for Richmond": Foote, *The Civil War,* Vol. 1, p. 427.

169   "the enemy were concentrating": *CW,* Vol. 5, p. 216n.

169   Halleck faced a great mass: ibid., p. 231.

169   secret order: ibid., pp. 219–20.

170   "worried about Mary": *RW,* p. 234.

170   "Our home is very beautiful": Mary Lincoln to Julia Ann Sprigg, May 29, 1862.

170   "our especial desire": quoted in Burlingame, *Abraham Lincoln,* Vol. 2, p. 260.

171   "I want the crape": Mary Lincoln to Ruth Harris, May 17, 1862.

171   counting the days: Mary Lincoln to Julia Ann Sprigg, May 29, 1862.

171   "one of the best": *CW,* Vol. 5, p. 326; Boyden, *Echoes from Hospital and White House,* pp. 93–94.

171   at the hospital: Boyden, *Echoes from Hospital and White House,* pp. 95–98.

172   "It will not be long": ibid.

172   "He left so privately": Dahlgren diary, May 22, 1862.

173   "Let us walk over": ibid.

173   "Take a good ready": *RW,* p. 202.

173   "trying to do my duty": ibid., p. 324.

173 "decline and fall": ibid., p. 167.

174 Mercier . . . also in camp: Dahlgren diary, May 23, 1862.

174 up again at five A.M.: ibid., May 24 and 25, 1862.

174 urgent message to McClellan: *CW*, Vol. 5, pp. 231–32.

174 "Apprehension of something": ibid., pp. 236–37.

175 she buttonholed Nicolay: Nicolay to Therena Bates, May 25, 1862.

175 "fall of Richmond": Foote, *The Civil War*, Vol. 1, p. 437.

175 "Another Bull Run": *RW*, p. 434.

175 For all he knew: Browning diary, May 25, 1862: "President entertained fears that [Banks] was destroyed."

176 "a general and concerted one": *CW*, Vol. 5, pp. 235–36.

176 "the utmost speed": ibid., p. 231.

176 "the time is near": ibid., pp. 235–36.

176 "This is a crushing blow": ibid., p. 233n.

176 McClellan's scorn: McClellan to Mary Ellen McClellan, May 25, 1862.

176 McClellan tried to persuade: McClellan to Lincoln, May 25, 1862.

177 "mere occupation of places": Grant, *Memoirs and Selected Letters*, p. 255.

177 Napoleon Bonaparte had called: Foote, *The Civil War*, Vol. 1, p. 436.

177 Frémont, ordered east: *CW*, Vol. 5, p. 243.

177 The skies opened: Foote, *The Civil War*, Vol. 1, pp. 432–33.

177 McDowell's scouts: *CW*, Vol. 5, pp. 246–48.

177 A railroad accident: ibid., p. 248n.

177 "much disabled": ibid., p. 247n.

177 a pass for . . . Lamon: ibid., p. 247.

177 "The game is before you": ibid., pp. 250–51.

178 "a precious lot of fools": McClellan to Mary Ellen McClellan, May 26, 1862.

7: JUNE

179 fingers at one another: Joseph E. Johnston, "Manassas to Seven Pines," in *Battles and Leaders of the Civil War*, Vol. 2, pp. 202–19; Gustavus W. Smith, "Two Days of Battle at Seven Pines (Fair Oaks)," in *Battle and Leaders of the Civil War*, Vol. 2, pp. 220–63.

180 "what I had to sleep on": Dahlgren diary, June 1, 1862.

180 optimism prevailed: Nicolay to Therena Bates, June 2, 1862.

181 Robert E. Lee: Gary W. Gallagher, "Robert E. Lee," in Heidler and Heidler, eds., *Encyclopedia of the American Civil War*, pp. 1154–55.

181 Lee was "too cautious": McClellan to Lincoln, April 20, 1862.

182 "a constabulary basis": Catton, *Grant Moves South,* pp. 280–81.

182 "repair of the railroad": ibid.

182 ordered Grant . . . to Memphis: Smith, *Grant,* pp. 213–15.

183 One exchange of telegrams: *CW,* Vol. 5, p. 258.

183 "possessed all the qualities": quoted in Richardson, *William James: In the Maelstrom of American Modernism,* p. 385.

183 "Jackson's game": *CW,* Vol. 5, pp. 270–72, 273–74.

183 "How glad I will be": McClellan to Mary Ellen McClellan, June 9, 1862.

184 McClellan's "extreme caution": Nicolay to Therena Bates, June 5, 1862.

184 unsought advice: *CW,* Vol. 5, p. 257.

184 volleyed back: ibid., p. 258n; also Stoddard, *Inside the White House,* p. 163: "I have inadvertently spoken of the President as 'his Excellency' . . . the use of which Mr. Lincoln always disapproved."

184 the crowded lobby of Willard's: Bates diary, June 4, 1862.

185 He encouraged Banks: *CW,* Vol. 5, p. 280.

185 "terribly out of shape": ibid., p. 272.

185 "I . . . almost weep": J. G. Barnard to Gustavus V. Fox, July 24, 1862, in *Confidential Correspondence of Gustavus Vasa Fox,* pp. 330–31.

185 "The current reports": Stoddard, *Inside the White House,* pp. 79–80.

185 J. E. B. Stuart, had ridden: cf. W. T. Robins, "Stuart's Ride Around McClellan," in *Battles and Leaders of the Civil War,* Vol. 2, pp. 271–75.

186 "only a political raid": *RW,* p. 183.

187 "I will break it for him": ibid.; also Donald, *Lincoln,* p. 359.

187 "If we are so forbearing": John Sherman to Thomas Ewing, Sr., June 5, 1862, Ewing Family Papers, Box 14, No. 5036, Library of Congress Manuscript Division.

188 confusion over . . . runaways: Browning diary, June 11, 1862.

188 "prejudice . . . against Labor": quoted in Long, *The Civil War Day by Day,* June 11, 1862.

189 Progressive Quakers: A brief history of the meeting is found at http://undergroundrr.kennett.net/lincolnvisit.html.

189 "We are solemnly convinced": *CW,* Vol. 5, pp. 278–79.

189 softened his tone: ibid.

190 "under divine guidance": ibid.

190 The obvious sincerity: *New-York Tribune,* June 21, 1862.

191 "comes in every day at ten": Nicolay to Therena Bates, June 15, 1862.

191 In a coded telegram: *CW,* Vol. 5, p. 276.

191 legions of Rebels: McClellan to Stanton, June 14, 1862.

191 refused to be pinned down: McClellan to Lincoln, June 18, 1862.

191 "I see hundreds": *RW*, pp. 171, 349.

191 "by daylight and moonlight": quoted in Pinsker, *Lincoln's Sanctuary: Abraham Lincoln and the Soldiers' Home*, p. 50.

191 Hamlin was delighted: Hamlin, *The Life and Times of Hannibal Hamlin*, Vol. 2, pp. 428–29.

192 put ideas on paper: Guelzo, *Lincoln's Emancipation Proclamation*, pp. 140–45.

192 "My dear Sir": Ridley, *Lord Palmerston*, p. 556.

192 Benjamin Franklin Butler: Kathleen R. Zebley, "Benjamin Franklin Butler," in Heidler and Heidler, eds., *Encyclopedia of the American Civil War*, pp. 329–31.

194 "guilty in cold Blood": Ridley, *Lord Palmerston*, p. 556.

194 pay down Mexico's debts: Seward to Adams, June 7, 1862; *CW*, Vol. 5, p. 281.

194 "It is vain to hope": Dayton to Seward, June 2, 1862.

194 finer than the *Oreto*: Spencer C. Tucker, "CSS Alabama," in Heidler and Heidler, eds., *Encyclopedia of the American Civil War*, pp. 22–23.

194 "It strikes me": quoted in Adams, *Charles Francis Adams: An American Statesman*, p. 257.

194 the women of Delhi: Ridley, *Lord Palmerston*, p. 556; Dalrymple, *The Last Mughal: The Fall of a Dynasty: Delhi, 1857*, p. 427.

194 It would help: Adams, *Charles Francis Adams*, p. 257.

195 "anomalous form of proceeding": ibid., p. 258.

195 "the progress of the war": Adams to Seward, June 20, 1862.

195 séance in the Red Room: Randall, *Mary Lincoln*, pp. 261–63.

196 participant at . . . prayer meetings: Johnson, *Abraham Lincoln the Christian*, pp. 13–15.

196 "A simple faith in God": *RW*, p. 191.

196 a collection of "memoranda": Browning diary, June 22, 1862.

196 riding off to his fate: Randall, *Lincoln's Sons*, pp. 120–21.

197 a private car: Miers, *Lincoln Day by Day*, Vol. 3, June 23, 1862.

197 John Pope: John C. Fredriksen, "John Pope," in Heidler and Heidler, eds., *Encyclopedia of the American Civil War*, pp. 1541–42.

198 As Scott put it: *CW*, Vol. 5, p. 284n.

198 the next objectives: ibid.

198 "All he wanted": *RW*, p. 179.

198 in mind just the man: Eisenhower, *Agent of Destiny: The Life and Times of General Winfield Scott*, pp. 396–97, 403.

198 broke up at noon: Miers, *Lincoln Day by Day*, Vol. 3, June 24, 1862.

198 "a thousand rumors buzzing": Nicolay to Therena Bates, June 27, 1862.

199 "When birds and animals": *CW*, Vol. 5, p. 284.

199 One . . . claimed . . . 104,300: Sears, *George B. McClellan*, p. 207.

199 quite a different count: Rafuse, *McClellan's War*, p. 221.

200 "fight those people for years": quoted in Foote, *The Civil War*, Vol. 1, p. 469.

200 Porter put this delusion: quoted in Sears, *George B. McClellan*, p. 203.

200 McClellan's flatterers: cf. Samuel Barlow to McClellan, June 17, 1862.

200 "I regret my great inferiority": McClellan to Stanton, June 25, 1862.

201 A week of brutal fighting: Sears, *George B. McClellan*, p. 217.

201 "It was not war": quoted in Rafuse, *McClellan's War*, p. 229.

201 watched the final charge: *Eye of the Storm*, July 1, 1862.

202 "Had I (20,000)": McClellan to Stanton, June 28, 1862; also Bates, *Lincoln in the Telegraph Office*, pp. 108–9.

203 "They will never forgive": quoted in Foote, *The Civil War*, Vol. 1, p. 493.

203 "Some enterprising newsgatherer": Nicolay to Therena Bates, June 29, 1862.

204 "The evident panic": Nicolay and Hay, *Abraham Lincoln: A History*, Vol. 5, p. 443.

204 "Save your Army": *CW*, Vol. 5, pp. 289–91.

204 "On the whole": ibid., pp. 292–93.

205 the proper strategy: ibid., p. 284n.

205 recruiting offices: ibid., pp. 291–92.

205 "a general panic": ibid.

205 "Your good mother": ibid., p. 288.

205 "maintain this contest": ibid., pp. 291–92.

206 issued a call for 300,000: ibid., pp. 295–97.

206 "We still have strength enough": ibid., p. 298.

206 "He would look out of the window": Bates, *Lincoln in the Telegraph Office*, pp. 138–41.

8: JULY

207 "he is not missed": *Eye of the Storm*, July 1, 1862.

208 signalmen waved flags: ibid., July 4, 1862.

208 "Attacked by . . . superior forces": Sears, *George B. McClellan*, pp. 224–25.

208 "a masterpiece of strategy": *CW*, Vol. 5, p. 308.

208 "inconsolable as I could be": *RW*, pp. 136–37.

208 Judged calmly and soberly: Ethan Rafuse makes a strong case for Harrison's

Landing as an ideal base for fresh operations in *McClellan's War*, for example on p. 231.

209 three officers from the peninsula: French diary, July 7, 1862.

209 "so little real faith": Nicolay to Therena Bates, July 6 and 13, 1862.

209 pessimistic dispatch: McClellan to Lorenzo Thomas, July 1, 1862; McClellan to Lincoln, July 4, 1862.

209 "how long we have . . . been expecting": French diary, July 4, 1862.

210 "Blondin walked across a tightrope": "Conversation with Hon. T. Lyle Dickey (of Chicago Ill) Washington Oct 20, 1876" in *An Oral History of Abraham Lincoln*, p. 49; see also http://www.tourniagara.com/history/daredevils/jean-francois-gravelet/.

211 "put Richmond off": *RW*, pp. 198–99.

211 pretzel of diplomatic contortions: *CW*, Vol. 5, p. 308.

211 John McClernand: Browning diary, July 16, 1862.

211 "even a thousand fresh men": McClellan to John Dix, July 1, 1862; McClellan to Lincoln, July 2, 1862.

211 A scant nine months: McClellan, *Report of Major-General George B. McClellan upon the Organization of the Army of the Potomac, and Its Campaigns in Virginia and Maryland, July 26, 1861, to November 7, 1862*, p. 4.

211 "impossible to re-inforce": *CW*, Vol. 5, p. 298.

211 "Allow me to reason": ibid., p. 301.

212 Two messages . . . an hour apart: McClellan to Lincoln, July 4, 1862 [noon]; McClellan to Lincoln, July 4, 1862, 1 P.M.

212 thirty-six hours later: McClellan to Mary Ellen McClellan, July 6, 1862.

212 Pressing his case: Browning diary, July 14, 1862; Sears, *George B. McClellan*, p. 226.

212 "borrow and send Bob": *CW*, Vol. 5, p. 309.

212 Upriver at Harrison's Landing: Rafuse, *McClellan's War*, p. 233; McClellan to Mary Ellen McClellan, July 8, 1862.

212 Lincoln wanted to know: *CW*, Vol. 5, pp. 309–12.

213 "present state of Military affairs": McClellan to Lincoln, June 20, 1862.

213 "the character of a War": McClellan to Lincoln, July 7, 1862.

213 "A declaration of radical views": ibid.

213 Lincoln's own constitutional duty: The Constitution of the United States of America, Article II, Section 2.

213 "the Pres[ident]'s manner": McClellan to Mary Ellen McClellan, July 9 and 10, 1862.

214 "came home in better spirits": Nicolay to Therena Bates, July 13, 1862.

214   information Lincoln drew: *CW*, Vol. 5, pp. 309–12.

215   "big levy of new troops": ibid., pp. 302–3.

215   Johnson's answer: ibid., p. 303n.

215   a depressing telegram: ibid., p. 313.

216   Lincoln cajoled the . . . governors: ibid., p. 304.

216   "If I am right": ibid., p. 322.

216   the general grudgingly replied: McClellan to Lincoln, July 15, 1862.

216   When Charles Sumner suggested: Sumner to John Bright, Aug. 5, 1862.

217   worst possible result: Seward to Adams, July 5, 1862.

217   to talk the border states: *CW*, Vol. 5, pp. 317–19.

217   "The pressure . . . is increasing": ibid.

217   closed with a flourish: ibid.

217   the offer was refused: ibid., p. 319n.

218   Lincoln tried to answer: ibid., p. 324.

218   "it would be unjust": Gideon Welles, "The History of Emancipation," *The Galaxy* 14, no. 6 (1872), pp. 842–43, available online at http://www.archive .org/stream/historyofemancip00well#page/n1/mode/2up.

218   Lincoln stunned his colleagues: Welles diary, July 13, 1862.

218   "He saw no escape": Welles, "The History of Emancipation," p. 843.

218   stripping . . . their war-making resources: ibid.

218   "He dwelt earnestly": ibid.

219   Seward seemed "startled": Welles, *Lincoln and Seward. Remarks upon the Memorial Address of Chas. Francis Adams, on the Late William H. Seward, with Incidents and Comments Illustrative of the Measure and Policy of the Administration of Abraham Lincoln. And Views as to the Relative Positions of the Late President and Secretary of State*, p. 210.

219   "ought to be vetoed": Browning diary, July 14, 1862.

219   "He looked weary": ibid., July 15, 1862.

220   William Lindsay . . . boasted: Crook, *Diplomacy During the American Civil War*, pp. 82–84.

220   "de facto independence": Anonymous, *The History of The Times: The Tradition Established, 1841–1884*, p. 380.

220   a "possible emergency": Adams to Seward, July 17, 1862.

221   "The Thirty Years' War": Crook, *The North, the South, and the Powers, 1861–1865*, pp. 216–17.

221   "a war of the world": Seward to Adams, July 28, 1862.

221   Napoleon . . . was thinking: Owsley, *King Cotton Diplomacy*, pp. 310–13; Nicolay and Hay, *Abraham Lincoln*, Vol. 6, pp. 76–79.

222   "back-kitchen way": quoted in Guelzo, *Lincoln's Emancipation Proclamation*, p. 115.

222   Lincoln's complaint: *CW,* Vol. 5, pp. 328–31.

222   "act to destroy slavery": Nicolay and Hay, *Abraham Lincoln,* Vol. 6, p. 101.

223   As a precaution: *CW,* Vol. 5, pp. 328–31.

223   "greatest friend of the . . . Railroad": Bain, *Empire Express: Building the First Transcontinental Railroad,* p. 218.

223   "thorough and universal education": *RW,* p. 244.

224   "what I have always regretted": ibid., p. 160.

224   "Our session has been busy": Sumner to John Bright, Aug. 5, 1862.

224   "I am heartily glad": Nicolay to Therena Bates, July 13 and 18, 1862.

224   "condemned European firelocks": Stoddard, *Lincoln's Third Secretary,* pp. 137–40.

224   top-secret chemical experiments: *CW,* Vol. 5, pp. 354 and 385.

225   nightmares of generations . . . unborn: Henig and Niderost, *Civil War Firsts: The Legacies of America's Bloodiest Conflict,* pp. 76–83.

225   Gilbert & Bennett: A brief history of the firm that claims to have invented a mass-produced woven wire window screen can be found online at http://historyofredding.net/HGgilbertbennett.htm.

225   "The gas lights": Nicolay to Therena Bates, July 20, 1862.

225   "The drives and walks": Mary Lincoln to Mrs. Charles Eames, July 26, 1862.

225   Bob . . . wanted to join the army: Randall, *Lincoln's Sons,* p. 145.

226   critics weren't shy: ibid., p. 144.

226   "We have lost one son": ibid., p. 145.

226   "a passion of tears": Randall, *Mary Lincoln,* pp. 264–65.

226   "I scarcely ever had ten minutes": ibid., p. 144.

226   His first visitor was . . . Gurowski: Chase diary, July 21, 1862.

226   "loved to talk": Van Deusen, *William Henry Seward,* pp. 258–59.

227   "struck me as a novelty": Chase diary, June 21, 1862.

227   Chase had serious doubts: ibid.

228   responded with violence: Guelzo, *Lincoln's Emancipation Proclamation,* pp. 124–25.

228   trouble selling bonds: Chase diary, July 22, 1862.

228   first known reading of the Emancipation Proclamation: ibid.

228   "all the slaves, without exception": Guelzo, *Lincoln's Emancipation Proclamation,* p. 121.

229   Lincoln did not respond: Welles, "The History of Emancipation," p. 844.

229   "more quietly accomplished": Chase diary, July 22, 1862.

230   "death knell" of slavery: Carpenter, *The Inner Life of Abraham Lincoln,* pp. 72–73.

230   "last *shriek*": Nicolay and Hay, *Abraham Lincoln,* Vol. 6, pp. 127–30.

230 "wisdom . . . struck me": Carpenter, *The Inner Life of Abraham Lincoln*, p. 22.

230 "[Lincoln] would relieve me": McClellan to Mary Ellen McClellan, July 27, 1862.

230 "I know nothing": McClellan to Samuel Barlow, July 30, 1862.

231 "I have done my best": McClellan to Hill Carter, July 11, 1862.

231 "psalm singing yankees": McClellan to Mary Ellen McClellan, July 22, 1862.

231 "I call it flat Treason": quoted in Sears, *George B. McClellan*, p. 241.

231 "rather large military family": McClellan to Mary Ellen McClellan, July 29 and 31, 1862.

231 Mary Ellen . . . encouraged him: Sears, *George B. McClellan*, p. 236.

232 "slap in the face": McClellan to Samuel Barlow, July 23, 1862; Sears, *George B. McClellan*, p. 240.

232 "If by magic": Browning diary, July 25, 1862.

232 To mitigate the danger: *CW*, Vol. 5, p. 308.

233 in no way his fault: McClellan to Mary Ellen McClellan, July 31, 1862.

233 "I have come to you from the West": *Battles and Leaders of the Civil War*, Vol. 2, p. 530n.

233 "paltry young man": McClellan to Mary Ellen McClellan, July 22, 1862.

234 "The temper of the North": Dahlgren diary, June 21, 1862.

234 arming black troops: Chase diary, July 25, 1862.

234 "I shall not surrender": *CW*, Vol. 5, pp. 342–43.

234 "This class of men": ibid., pp. 344–46.

235 "enemies must understand": ibid., pp. 350–51.

9: AUGUST

237 always close the door: Stoddard, *Lincoln's Third Secretary*, pp. 100–101.

237 rise from washed-up congressman: See, for example, Beveridge, *Abraham Lincoln*, Vol. 2, *1809–1858*, pp. 362–442; Carwardine, *Lincoln*; Fehrenbacher, *Prelude to Greatness*; Harris, *Lincoln's Rise to the Presidency*; Holzer, *Lincoln at Cooper Union: The Speech That Made Abraham Lincoln President*.

237 "shrewdest of long, hawk-nosed": Stoddard, *Lincoln's Third Secretary*, pp. 100–101.

238 "Lincoln used to tell us": quoted in *An Oral History of Abraham Lincoln*, p. 61.

238 "intelligent political strategy": Carwardine, *Lincoln*, pp. 272–74.

239 "I half wondered why": Stoddard, *Lincoln's Third Secretary,* pp. 101–2.

239 "The problem was": Anonymous, *Chronicle of the Union League of Philadelphia: 1862–1902,* p. 35.

239 "A number of army contractors": Stoddard, *Lincoln's Third Secretary,* pp. 101–2.

239 painstakingly distributing these fruits: Chase diary, August 1862. The extensive work by Lincoln and Chase devoted to choosing new officeholders under the 1862 internal revenue bill is a recurring theme of Chase's diary during this period.

240 one typically bombastic pronouncement: "The Liberty of the Citizen," in *Speeches of Daniel W. Voorhees, of Indiana, Embracing His Most Prominent Forensic, Political, Occasional and Literary Addresses,* p. 94.

240 "Yet it seems unreasonable": *CW,* Vol. 5, pp. 355–56.

240 Philadelphia . . . City Bounty Fund: Gallman, *Mastering Wartime: A Social History of Philadelphia During the Civil War,* p. 18.

240 Fifty-three men . . . in the Flint Hills: Thomas Ewing, Jr. to Ellen Ewing, Aug. 17, 1862, Ewing Family Papers, Box 67, Library of Congress Manuscript Division.

240 "men of the first character": Thomas Ewing, Jr., to Thomas Ewing, Sr., Aug. 23, 1862, Ewing Family Papers, Box 14, No. 5111, Library of Congress Manuscript Division.

241 eighteen thousand per week: Dahlgren diary, Aug. 17, 1862; Welles diary, Aug. 22, 1862.

241 Lincoln pleaded for more troops: *CW,* Vol. 5, pp. 368 (to Andrew G. Curtin) and 393 (to Richard Yates).

241 French, surveyed the throng: French diary, Aug. 6, 1862.

241 "Hadn't I better say a few words": Chase diary, Aug. 6, 1862.

242 "Fellow citizens!": *CW,* Vol. 5, pp. 358–59.

243 "greatly disappointed": *New-York Daily Tribune,* Aug. 7, 1862, p. 4.

243 Chase, however, was impressed: Chase diary, Aug. 6, 1862.

243 waiting for supplies: Foote, *The Civil War,* Vol. 1, pp. 564–65.

244 Instead of a strike force: Hattaway and Jones, *How the North Won,* pp. 214–18.

244 "The remainder of the magnificent army": Grant, *Memoirs and Selected Letters,* pp. 263–65.

244 the life of a bureaucrat: Grant to Elihu Washburne, July 22, 1862.

244 Grant's soldiers were furious: Grant, *Memoirs and Selected Letters,* p. 267.

245 if Chase . . . believed: Grant to Chase, July 31, 1862.

245 "England [wants] . . . cotton": quoted in Browning diary, July 25, 1862.

245   Spiraling prices: McPherson, *Battle Cry of Freedom,* pp. 437–42.

245   "Give your paper mill": Nicolay, quoted in *An Oral History of Abraham Lincoln,* p. 90.

246   Seward rattled . . . the swords: Seward to Adams, Aug. 13, 1862.

246   "construction of iron-clad ships": ibid.

246   "impossible to overestimate": Adams to Seward, July 31, 1862.

247   McClellan did not start: Sears, *George B. McClellan,* pp. 242–48.

247   "I am to have a sweat": Dahlgren diary, Aug. 19, 1862.

247   "so uneasy": quoted in Hattaway and Jones, *How the North Won,* pp. 223–24.

248   A heat wave: Welles diary, Aug. 8 and 10, 1862.

248   a bit of relief: Dahlgren diary, Aug. 7, 1862.

248   A second American Revolution: McPherson, *Abraham Lincoln and the Second American Revolution,* pp. 3–22.

249   "sensitive and even irritable": Nicolay and Hay, *Abraham Lincoln,* Vol. 6, pp. 147–58.

249   a letter published on August 20 . . . Greeley: *New-York Daily Tribune,* Aug. 20, 1862.

250   "I would save the Union": *CW,* Vol. 5, pp. 388–89.

251   "the turkey buzzards": quoted in Kate Masur, "The African American Delegation to Abraham Lincoln: A Reappraisal," *Civil War History* 45, no. 2 (June 2010), pp. 117–44.

251   Frederick Douglass . . . argued: ibid.

251   head servant, William Slade: ibid.

252   a formidable group: ibid.

252   "Why should they leave": *CW,* Vol. 5, pp. 370–75.

252   "better for us both": ibid.

252   "behind the Sumner lighthouse": quoted in Brodie, *Thaddeus Stevens, Scourge of the South,* p. 161.

253   "Many of us have sold": Masur, "The African American Delegation," p. 121.

253   "Mrs. L . . . is not well": *CW,* Vol. 5, p. 386.

253   "Oh Little Aleck": quoted in Baker, *Mary Todd Lincoln,* p. 223.

254   Colchester's séance: ibid., pp. 220–22; Pinsker, *Lincoln's Sanctuary,* pp. 30–32; Randall, *Mary Lincoln,* pp. 261–65.

254   "a very slight veil": quoted in Baker, *Mary Todd Lincoln,* p. 220.

255   A headline in New York: *New-York Tribune,* Aug. 19, 1862.

255   Lincoln went . . . to the telegraph room: Bates, *Lincoln in the Telegraph Office,* p. 118.

255   "Do you hear any thing?": *CW,* Vol. 5, pp. 395–96.

256   four hungry young Sioux: Cox, *Lincoln and the Sioux Uprising of 1862*, pp. 15–20.

256   "All the white soldiers": ibid., pp. 20–26.

256   Thorns of grievance and honor: ibid., pp. 50–52, 67–69.

256   "panic" . . . "a wild panic": *CW*, Vol. 5, pp. 396–67n.

257   "Necessity knows no law": ibid., pp. 396–67.

257   "Pope will be thrashed": McClellan to Mary Ellen McClellan, Aug. 10, 1862.

257   "I believe I have triumphed!!": ibid., Aug. 21, 1862.

257   Little Mac . . . couldn't comply: McClellan to Halleck, Aug. 27, 1862, 1:15 P.M.

257   "no time for details": Halleck to McClellan, Aug. 27, 1862, 4 P.M.

257   with . . . Halleck until three A.M.: McClellan to Mary Ellen McClellan, Aug. 28, 1862.

258   Better to concentrate: McClellan to Halleck, multiple telegrams, Aug. 28, 1862.

258   "Not a moment must be lost": Halleck to McClellan, Aug. 28, 1862, 3:30 P.M.

258   "no further delay": ibid., 7:40 P.M.

258   explained to a flabbergasted Halleck: McClellan to Halleck, Aug. 29, 1862, 8 P.M.

258   Fitz John Porter: United States War Department, *The War of the Rebellion: A Compilation of the Official Records of the Union and Confederate Armies*, Series 1, Vol. 12, Supplement.

258   "What news" . . . "What news?": *CW*, Vol. 5, pp. 398–402.

258   "one of two courses": McClellan to Lincoln, Aug. 29, 1862, 2:45 P.M.

259   Lincoln was "very outspoken": Hay diary, Sept. 1, 1862.

259   Stanton was so furious: Chase diary, Aug. 29, 1862.

260   "Argument was useless": Welles diary, Sept. 1, 1862.

260   the petition . . . was intemperate: ibid., Aug. 31, 1862.

261   "No, not now": ibid.

261   "nothing but foul play": Hay diary, Sept. 1, 1862.

261   hopes for a victory rose: *CW*, Vol. 5, pp. 400–401.

261   Stanton, still angry: Welles diary, Aug. 31, 1862.

261   lowered his voice conspiratorially: ibid.

262   "well and hilarious": Hay diary, Sept. 1, 1862.

262   "we are whipped again": ibid.

262   "Malice . . . Vandalism": Welles diary, Aug. 31, 1862.

262   rescue the family silver: McClellan to Mary Ellen McClellan, Aug. 31, 1862.

263 "middle of last year": *RW,* p. 256.

263 remaining squabbles over patronage: Chase diary, Aug. 31, 1862.

263 "singularly defiant tone": Hay diary, Sept. 1, 1862.

263 "McClellan ought to be shot": Welles diary, Sept. 1, 1862.

263 Welles was surprised: ibid.

264 "Mr. Hay, what is the use": Hay diary, undated.

264 "he broke down": *RW,* p. 224.

264 "I beg of you": Halleck to McClellan, Aug. 31, 1862, 10:07 P.M.

264 Making matters worse: Marszalek, *Commander of All Lincoln's Armies,* pp. 146–53.

264 "Pope should have been sustained": *RW,* p. 472.

265 Lincoln began the meeting: Welles diary, Sept. 2, 1862.

265 "a good engineer": ibid.; also Chase diary, Sept. 2, 1862.

265 Never . . . so "disturbed": Welles diary, Sept. 2, 1862.

265 "giving Washington to the rebels": Chase diary, Sept. 2, 1862.

265 "the confidence of the army": Welles diary, Sept. 2, 1862.

265 "There has been a design": ibid., Sept. 7, 1862.

265 "Who shall save it?": Dahlgren diary, Sept. 2, 1862.

10: SEPTEMBER

266 "it is to be my lot": *RW,* p. 373.

266 "What is to be": quoted in Carwardine, *Lincoln,* p. 39.

267 "the weightiest question of his life": Nicolay and Hay, *Abraham Lincoln,* Vol. 6, pp. 341–42.

267 "The will of God prevails": *CW,* Vol. 5, pp. 403–4.

267 jabbed with such velocity: An image of the document was examined at http://dl.lib.brown.edu/catalog/.

268 Second Inaugural Address: *CW,* Vol. 8, pp. 333–34.

268 Slavery . . . was like a tumor: *CW,* Vol. 5, p. 327.

269 "We have no carbines": Halleck to Thomas Ewing, Sr., Aug. 14, 1862, Ewing Family Papers, Box 14, No. 5098, Library of Congress Manuscript Division.

269 "exciting, vague, and absurd": Welles diary, Sept. 3, 1862.

269 "There are McClellan parties": Gustavus V. Fox to James Grimes, Sept. 6, 1862, in *Confidential Correspondence of Gustavus Vasa Fox,* Vol. 2, p. 369.

269 "I want to consult you": *RW,* p. 440.

269 "Our late campaign . . . has failed": Seward to Adams, Sept. 8, 1862.

269 "wise or not": Welles diary, Sept. 5, 1862.

270 "like shoveling fleas": Nicolay and Hay, *Abraham Lincoln,* Vol. 6, p. 142.

270 "permitted themselves to be captured": Welles diary, Sept. 5, 1862.

270 "He went out, as of old": Chase diary, Sept. 3, 1862.

270 "a manifesto, a narrative": Welles diary, Sept. 4, 1862.

271 "Kentuckians!": Quoted in McPherson, *Crossroads of Freedom: Antietam, the Battle That Changed the Course of the Civil War,* p. 77.

271 Bragg entered the state: Foote, *The Civil War,* Vol. 1, p. 584; Nicolay and Hay, *Abraham Lincoln,* Vol. 6, pp. 273–76.

271 Lee had significant concerns: Lee to Jefferson Davis, Sept. 3, 1862, Papers of Jefferson Davis, Rice University, available online at http://jeffersondavis .rice.edu/Content.aspx?id=111.

271 "throwing off . . . yoke": McPherson, *Battle Cry of Freedom,* p. 536.

272 Lee . . . banned enlisted men: *The War of the Rebellion,* Series 1, Vol. 19, Part 2, pp. 603–4.

272 Lee was able to scrape up: ibid., pp. 605, 602.

272 Whittier composed a ballad: Whittier, *The Complete Poetical Works of Whittier,* pp. 342–43.

272 Davis would later explain: Davis, *The Rise and Fall of the Confederate Government,* Vol. 2, pp. 276–77.

272 "these discordant elements": *RW,* p. 441.

274 he would "inflict injury": Lee to Davis, Sept. 8, 1862, in *The Wartime Papers of Robert E. Lee,* p. 301.

274 Palmerston and Russell agreed: Crook, *Diplomacy During the American Civil War,* pp. 86–88.

275 "perhaps his finest hour": McPherson, *Crossroads of Freedom,* pp. 87–88.

275 "There was design": Welles diary, Sept. 6, 1862.

276 "reckless and untameable": ibid., Sept. 8 and 10, 1862.

276 Chase was furious at Welles: ibid., Sept. 7, 1862.

276 Welles suspected Stanton: ibid., Sept. 11, 1862.

276 Smith . . . turned on Seward: ibid., Sept. 10, 1862.

276 Blair set on Stanton: ibid., Sept. 12, 1862.

277 "you want . . . Seward out": Chase diary, Sept. 10, 1862.

277 "humiliating submissiveness": ibid., Sept. 12, 1862.

277 As usual: Sears, *George B. McClellan,* pp. 273–78.

277 credence to mistaken reports: *CW,* Vol. 5, p. 409.

277 "consist of their oldest regiments": McClellan to Halleck, Sept. 11 [Sept. 10], 1862.

277 "How does it look now?": *CW,* Vol. 5, p. 418.

278 "fall into the hands": Chase diary, Sept. 12, 1862.

278 "a long and free discussion": Welles diary, Sept. 12, 1862.

278 "There was bluster": ibid.

279 Weed . . . called on Chase: Chase diary, Sept. 15, 1862.

279   "Seward was supple": Welles diary, Sept. 17, 1862.

279   "freeing all the apprentices": Chase diary, Sept. 12, 1862.

280   "Alas, poor country": Sumner to Francis Lieber, Sept. 16, 1862.

280   Nast sketched the . . . scene: *Harper's Weekly* 6, no. 301 (Oct. 4, 1862), p. 1.

280   "I was nearly overwhelmed": McClellan to Mary Ellen McClellan, Sept. 14, 1862.

280   Tubs of lemonade: Sears, *Landscape Turned Red: The Battle of Antietam*, pp. 108–11.

280   beauty of the countryside: McClellan to Mary Ellen McClellan, Sept. 12, 1862.

280   "Please do not let him get off": *CW*, Vol. 5, p. 418.

280   latest estimate was ludicrously high: Chase diary, Sept. 13, 1862.

281   "I shall follow": McClellan to Halleck, Sept. 12, 1862, 5:30 P.M.

281   a twist so unlikely: Sears, *Landscape Turned Red*, pp. 112–13.

282   "Now I know": ibid.

282   debate with . . . Chicago ministers: *CW*, Vol. 5, pp. 420–25.

282   eventually debunked: William P. Rigge, "The Pope and the Comet," *Popular Astronomy* 16 (October 1908), pp. 481–83.

282   "I have not decided": *CW*, Vol. 5, pp. 420–25.

282   *"I will do it"*: ibid.

283   "study the plain physical facts": ibid.

283   "Here is a paper": Gibbon, *Personal Recollections of the Civil War*, p. 73.

283   "hope for a great success": McClellan to Lincoln, Sept. 13, 1862.

284   "so dark, so obscure": quoted in McPherson, *Crossroads of Freedom*, p. 117.

284   the same "strange dream": *RW*, p. 486.

285   "No tongue can tell": quoted in Hattaway and Jones, *How the North Won*, p. 243.

286   planned to renew the battle: McClellan to Halleck, Sept. 18, 1862, 8 A.M.; McClellan to Mary Ellen McClellan, Sept. 18, 1862, 8 A.M.

286   "I am aware of the fact": McClellan, *Report of Major-General George B. McClellan*, pp. 149–50.

286   stunned and partially decapitated: ibid.

287   "Few and foggy dispatches": Welles diary, Sept. 18, 1862.

287   "Antietam was fought Wednesday": Nicolay and Hay, *Abraham Lincoln*, Vol. 6, pp. 164–65.

287   president "could not but feel": ibid., p. 146.

287   "When Lee came over": *RW*, p. 38.

287   too busy writing: Chase diary, Sept. 21, 1862.

287   "I let them have it": Nicolay and Hay, *Abraham Lincoln*, Vol. 6, pp. 164–65.

289 "there was some general talk": Chase diary, Sept. 22, 1862.

289 "High-handed Outrage": *Artemus Ward: His Book,* pp. 34–35.

289 "The 'neigh' of a horse": Carpenter, *The Inner Life of Abraham Lincoln,* pp. 150–51.

289 "Why don't you laugh?": *RW,* p. 417.

289 the president grew serious: Chase diary, Sept. 22, 1862.

290 he "had made a vow": Welles diary, Sept. 22, 1862.

290 Lincoln hesitated: Chase diary, Sept. 22, 1862.

290 "God had decided this question": Welles diary, Sept. 22, 1862.

290 "I am here": Chase diary, Sept. 22, 1862.

290 This revised version: Guelzo, *Lincoln's Emancipation Proclamation,* pp. 172–73.

291 Seward . . . offered a proposal: Chase diary, Sept. 22, 1862.

291 Welles was impressed: Welles diary, Sept. 22, 1862.

291 Chase spoke next: Chase diary, Sept. 22, 1862.

291 Welles also endorsed: Welles diary, Sept. 22, 1862.

291 Blair now spoke up: Chase diary, Sept. 22, 1862.

292 hand the Democrats "a club": Welles diary, Sept. 22, 1862.

292 "in great doubt myself": *RW,* p. 314.

292 Sumner . . . Douglass . . . Hamlin: quoted in Guelzo, *Lincoln's Emancipation Proclamation,* pp. 157–62.

292 "Hoop de-dooden-do": ibid.

292 he "knew more": Hay diary, Sept. 24, 1862.

292 "our harpoon": Carpenter, *The Inner Life of Abraham Lincoln,* p. 75.

293 "environed with difficulties": *CW,* Vol. 5, p. 438.

293 "The stocks have declined": ibid., p. 444.

293 a second . . . dangerous decree: ibid., pp. 436–37.

294 "such an accursed doctrine": McClellan to Mary Ellen McClellan, Sept. 25, 1862.

294 later told Lincoln: Hay diary, Sept. 25, 1864.

294 "That is not the game": Welles diary, Sept. 24, 1862.

295 He cashiered Key: *CW,* Vol. 5, pp. 442–43.

11: OCTOBER

297 "Dr. Zacharie has operated": *CW,* Vol. 5, p. 436.

297 "put his foot down firmly": ibid., p. 436n.

298 helped to muffle: ibid., p. 225.

298 "pestilent sheet": William Goodell to Lincoln, July 9, 1862, Abraham Lincoln Papers, Library of Congress Manuscript Division.

298 "I do very believe": James Gordon Bennett to Lincoln, Aug. 11, 1862, Abraham Lincoln Papers, Library of Congress Manuscript Division.

299 "accept this proclamation": Fermer, *James Gordon Bennett and the New York Herald: A Study of Editorial Opinion in the Civil War Era, 1854–1867*, pp. 221–25.

299 "your kind note": Mary Lincoln to James Gordon Bennett, Oct. 4, 1862.

300 "satisfy himself personally": "Conversation with Hon. O. M. Hatch, Springfield, June 1875," in *An Oral History of Abraham Lincoln*, p. 16.

300 "Compel the enemy": McClellan to Halleck, Oct. 1, 1862; McClellan to Mary Ellen McClellan, Oct. 2, 1862.

300 "His ostensible purpose": McClellan to Mary Ellen McClellan, Oct. 2, 1862.

301 Gardner . . . "brought bodies": *New York Times*, Oct. 20, 1862.

301 "very kind personally": McClellan to Mary Ellen McClellan, Oct. 5, 1862.

301 at least four letters: "Conversation with Hon. O. M. Hatch, Springfield, June 1875," p. 16.

302 Lincoln . . . "regarded his position": *RW*, pp. 275–76.

302 Hatch recalled the encounter: quoted in Browne, *The Every-Day Life of Abraham Lincoln: A Narrative and Descriptive Biography with Pen-Pictures and Personal Recollections by Those Who Knew Him*, pp. 529–30.

303 "Sing one of your sad . . . songs": Lamon, *Recollections of Abraham Lincoln, 1847–1865*, pp. 145–48.

304 "he would be a ruined man": *RW*, p. 132.

304 disappointed a cheering crowd: *CW*, Vol. 5, p. 450.

304 "I will back General McClellan": *RW*, p. 425.

305 "most desperately contested": Foote, *The Civil War*, Vol. 1, pp. 726–38.

306 the effects of Bragg's retreat: Duke, *Reminiscences of General Basil W. Duke*, p. 333.

306 "overwhelmed with the crowd": Nicolay to Therena Bates, Oct. 9, 1862.

306 his monthly paycheck: Miers, *Lincoln Day by Day*, Vol. 3, Oct. 6, 1862.

307 "The President directs": *CW*, Vol. 5, p. 452n.

307 "disgust, discontent . . . disloyalty": Sears, *George B. McClellan*, p. 325.

307 "a fatal error": ibid., pp. 326–27.

307 transportation magnate William Aspinwall: McClellan to Mary Ellen McClellan, Oct. 5, 1862.

308 "remedy for political error": Williams, *Lincoln and His Generals*, p. 171.

308 "hope the indignant people": McClellan to Mary Ellen McClellan, Sept. 29, 1862; see also McClellan to Mary Ellen McClellan, Sept. 25, 1862.

309 lacked "shoes, tents, blankets": Rafuse, *McClellan's War*, pp. 353, 358.

309 "quiet & pleasant time": McClellan to Samuel Barlow, Oct. 17, 1862.

309 "It is humiliating": Welles diary, Oct. 13, 1862.

309 "Three times round and out": *RW*, p. 256.

309 "effect upon the popular mind": Adams to Seward, Oct. 3, 1862.

310 "full of difficulty": Foreman, *A World on Fire*, pp. 319–20.

310 "they have made a nation!": Crook, *Diplomacy During the American Civil War*, pp. 87–92.

310 Adams was angry: Adams to Seward, Oct. 10, 1862.

311 "merely . . . lookers-on": Crook, *Diplomacy During the American Civil War*, p. 98.

311 Now was the moment: Owsley, *King Cotton Diplomacy*, pp. 331–33.

311 Napoleon took this letter: ibid.

311 take the plunge: ibid.

312 "Nothing," he replied: Dayton to Seward, Nov. 5, 1862.

312 Lincoln took up pen: *CW*, Vol. 5, pp. 460–61.

313 he would fire McClellan now: Sears, *George B. McClellan*, p. 335.

313 cavalry was no match: McClellan to Halleck, Oct. 14, 1862; Lincoln's reaction is found in Halleck to McClellan, *The War of the Rebellion*, Series 1, Vol. 19, Part 2, p. 421.

313 "take things so leisurely!": Nicolay to Therena Bates, Oct. 16, 1862.

313 "He does not understand": Nicolay and Hay, *Abraham Lincoln*, Vol. 6, p. 280.

314 "all blue here": Nicolay to Therena Bates, Oct. 16, 1862.

314 "twice our usual majority": J. W. Grimes to G. V. Fox, Oct. 24, 1862, in *Confidential Correspondence of Gustavus Vasa Fox*, Vol. 2, pp. 410–11.

314 "a little gun": *CW*, Vol. 5, p. 463.

314 "butcher-day": Herndon and Weik, *Abraham Lincoln*, Vol. 2, p. 245.

314 sparing three lives: *CW*, Vol. 5, pp. 475–76.

315 "No man but he": Herndon and Weik, *Abraham Lincoln*, Vol. 2, pp. 212–15.

316 a combination of considerations: Donald, *"We Are Lincoln Men,"* pp. 122–27.

316 "I am not wedded": McClellan to Lincoln, Oct. 17, 1862.

316 "the question of *time*": *CW*, Vol. 5, p. 460.

316 "Your Excellency": McClellan to Lincoln, Oct. 17, 1862.

316 "fear that he was playing false": Hay diary, Sept. 25, 1864.

317 "fine dry weather": Nicolay to Therena Bates, Oct. 20, 1862.

317 "pardon me for asking": *CW*, Vol. 5, p. 474.

317 "dirty little flings": McClellan to Mary Ellen McClellan, Oct. 26, 1862.

317 "so rejoiced" . . . "wretched innuendo": *CW,* Vol. 5, p. 477; McClellan to Mary Ellen McClellan, Oct. 29, 1862.

317 "never was a truer epithet": McClellan to Mary Ellen McClellan, Oct. 29, 1862.

317 "holding a prayer-meeting": Nicolay to Therena Bates, Oct. 26, 1862.

317 "a fiery trial": *CW,* Vol. 5, p. 478.

318 "last grain of sand": *RW,* pp. 380–81.

12: NOVEMBER

319 first snow: Bates diary, Nov. 7, 1862.

319 passed the camp twice a day: Pinsker, *Lincoln's Sanctuary,* pp. 66–68.

319 twenty-five refugees a week: Joseph P. Reidy, " 'Coming from the Shadow of the Past': The Transition from Slavery to Freedom at Freedmen's Village, 1863–1900," *The Virginia Magazine of History and Biography* 95, no. 4 (October 1987), pp. 403–28.

320 "The cause of humanity": Mary Todd Lincoln to Abraham Lincoln, Nov. 3, 1862.

320 Grant . . . was forced to think: Grant, *Memoirs and Selected Letters,* pp. 284–85.

321 news so startling: *CW,* Vol. 5, p. 487.

321 The president drafted a reply: ibid., pp. 502–3.

321 "the life of the nation": ibid., pp. 512–13.

322 "men absent on furlough": ibid., p. 484.

322 "hard desperate fighting": ibid.

322 "A deeper gloom": Livermore, *My Story of the War: Four Years Personal Experience in The Sanitary Service of the Rebellion,* pp. 555–61.

323 "hanging from the post": Donald, *Lincoln,* p. 384.

323 "see clearly and persist": Shenk, *Lincoln's Melancholy: How Depression Challenged a President and Fueled His Greatness,* p. 189.

324 "indulge in no delusions": Schurz to Lincoln, Nov. 20, 1862, in Schurz, *Speeches, Correspondence and Political Papers of Carl Schurz,* pp. 213–19.

324 "I ought to be blamed": *CW,* Vol. 5, pp. 509–11.

324 "You are re-elected": ibid., p. 487.

325 "no next presidency": *RW,* p. 400.

325 Lincoln would not resist: Barnes, *The Life of Thurlow Weed,* Vol. 2, p. 428.

325 Under Governor Seymour: Mitchell, *Horatio Seymour of New York,* pp. 318–19.

325 "The heavens were red": Anonymous, *Chronicle of the Union League of Philadelphia: 1862–1902,* pp. 45–50.

325 "worse . . . than the bloodiest": Sumner to Lincoln, Nov. 8, 1862.

326 far from disastrous: McPherson, *Crossroads of Freedom*, pp. 153–54.

326 shift of this magnitude: For purposes of comparison, the party composition of each U.S. Congress can be accessed at http://artandhistory.house .gov/house_history/index.aspx.

326 "Halleck would be an indifferent": Welles diary, Nov. 4, 1862.

327 "The President's patience": Nicolay to Therena Bates, Nov. 5, 1862.

327 Montgomery Blair rode out: Pinsker, *Lincoln's Sanctuary*, pp. 87–88.

328 No ordinary courier: Sears, *George B. McClellan*, p. 340.

328 Rectortown with McClellan's replacement: Rafuse, *McClellan's War*, p. 376.

328 "Another interruption": McClellan to Mary Ellen McClellan, Nov. 7, 1862.

329 "a dreadful mistake": ibid.

329 "Gray-haired men": McClellan to Mary Ellen McClellan, Nov. 10, 1862.

329 "the romance of war": quoted in Catton, *Mr. Lincoln's Army*, pp. 329–30.

329 "we always understood each other": James Longstreet, "The Battle of Fredericksburg," in *Battles and Leaders of the Civil War*, Vol. 3, p. 70.

329 Grant . . . let Halleck know: *The Papers of Ulysses S. Grant*, Vol. 6, pp. 199–201.

330 intended to clear the Rebels: ibid., p. 243.

330 "unvexed to the sea": *CW*, Vol. 6, p. 410.

330 out of Grand Junction: Grant, *Memoirs and Selected Letters*, p. 284.

330 John McClernand: Christopher C. Meyers, "John Alexander McClernand," in Heidler and Heidler, eds., *Encyclopedia of the American Civil War*, pp. 1277–79.

331 the orders he coveted: *CW*, Vol. 5, pp. 468–69.

331 "Two commanders": Grant, *Memoirs and Selected Letters*, p. 285.

331 "Am I to . . . lay still": *The Papers of Ulysses S. Grant*, Vol. 6, p. 288.

331 "You have command": ibid.

331 Grant promptly sent his cavalry: Grant, *Memoirs and Selected Letters*, p. 286.

331 trying to thwart McClernand: ibid., p. 288.

332 "The Sioux War": Cox, *Lincoln and the Sioux Uprising of 1862*, p. 152.

332 "like the locusts": ibid., p. 26.

332 "anxious to execute": ibid., pp. 152–53.

332 A plea from . . . Ramsey: *CW*, Vol. 5, p. 493n.

333 "Please forward": ibid., p. 493.

333 "The only distinction": ibid., p. 493n.

333 possible lynch mobs: Pope to Lincoln, Nov. 24, 1862, Abraham Lincoln Papers, Library of Congress Manuscript Division.

333 "turn them over to me": Ramsey to Lincoln, Nov. 28, 1862, Abraham Lincoln Papers, Library of Congress Manuscript Division.

334 The president told his visitors: *CW,* Vol. 5, p. 493n.

334 "I have waited in vain": Mary Lincoln to Abraham Lincoln, Nov. 2, 1862.

334 Lincoln finally replied: *CW,* Vol. 5, p. 494.

335 Company K: Pinsker, *Lincoln's Sanctuary,* pp. 79–81.

335 "loud talking": ibid., p. 83.

335 "getting quite thick": ibid., p. 84.

336 "in the same bed": Chamberlin, *History of the One Hundred and Fiftieth Regiment, Pennsylvania Volunteers, Second Regiment, Bucktail Brigade,* p. 38.

336 Some historians have speculated: cf. Tripp, *The Intimate World of Abraham Lincoln.*

336 "very agreeable to me": *CW,* Vol. 5, pp. 484–85.

336 test firing of a new rocket: Bruce, *Lincoln and the Tools of War,* pp. 217–19.

337 "a long familiar talk": Browning diary, Nov. 29, 1862.

337 ordered the release: Long, *The Civil War Day by Day,* p. 289.

337 "would rather die": *CW,* Vol. 5, pp. 503–4.

338 Browning asked about Burnside: Browning diary, Nov. 29, 1862.

338 "somewhat risky": *CW,* Vol. 5, pp. 514–15.

338 "To cross the Rappahannock": Browning diary, Nov. 29, 1862.

339 "The President is . . . quickened": Sumner to John Bright, Nov. 18, 1862.

339 Lincoln was shocked: *CW,* Vol. 5, pp. 505–6.

339 "His hair is grizzled": *Lincoln Observed,* pp. 13–14.

13: DECEMBER

342 "I strongly suspect": *CW,* Vol. 5, pp. 553–54.

342 second annual message to Congress: ibid., pp. 518–37.

344 make the decisions himself: ibid., pp. 537–38.

344 303 often confusing files: Cox, *Lincoln and the Sioux Uprising of 1862,* p. 182.

345 a drunken mob marched: ibid., pp. 189–90.

345 a follow-up message: Nicolay to Henry H. Sibley, Dec. 9, 1862.

345 "shrank with evident pain": "Conversation with Hon. J. Holt Washington Oct 25 1875," in *An Oral History of Abraham Lincoln,* p. 69.

345 "hang men for votes": quoted in Cox, *Lincoln and the Sioux Uprising of 1862,* p. 184.

346 "after all hope": William B. Franklin, "Franklin's Left Grand Division," in *Battles and Leaders of the Civil War,* Vol. 3, p. 133.

346 "a chicken could not live": James Longstreet, "The Battle of Fredericksburg," in *Battles and Leaders of the Civil War,* Vol. 3, p. 79.

346 "men, prostrate and dropping": Darius Couch, "Sumner's 'Right Grand Division,'" in *Battles and Leaders of the Civil War,* Vol. 3, p. 113.

347 Longstreet saw "the Federals": James Longstreet, "The Battle of Fredericksburg," p. 82.

347 grab at the legs: Lang, *The Forgotten Charge: The 123rd Pennsylvania at Marye's Heights,* p. 74.

347 "imbecility, treachery, failure": quoted in McPherson, *Battle Cry of Freedom,* pp. 573–74.

348 "never once faltered": Catton, *Glory Road,* p. 62.

348 "If the same battle": *RW,* p. 426.

349 Wilkinson . . . Wade . . . Fessenden: Browning diary, Dec. 16, 1862.

350 Browning . . . protested: ibid., Dec. 22, 1862.

350 "no evidence": Goodwin, *Team of Rivals,* 487–88.

350 demand . . . Seward's resignation: Browning diary, Dec. 17, 1862.

350 "do as they please about me": quoted in Goodwin, *Team of Rivals,* p. 488.

351 "partizans of Mr. Chase": Browning diary, Dec. 22, 1862.

351 Ewing "had no doubt": ibid., Dec. 19, 1862.

351 "Chase writes me": Sumner to John Bright, Nov. 18, 1862.

351 "like the starling": *RW,* p. 397.

351 "a bitter draught": Sterne, *A Sentimental Journey Through France and Italy,* p. 242.

352 "refuse to parley": Welles diary, Dec. 20, 1862.

352 Needing to hear exactly: ibid., Dec. 19, 1862.

352 "He had . . . no adviser": Hay diary, Oct. 30, 1863.

352 When Browning . . . called: Browning diary, Dec. 18, 1862.

353 Republican senators took their seats: Fessenden, *The Life and Public Services of William Pitt Fessenden,* Vol. 1, pp. 239–43.

354 "contrived *to suck them out*": Bates diary, Dec. 19, 1862.

354 "common rumor": Fessenden, *The Life and Public Services of William Pitt Fessenden,* Vol. 1, p. 241.

354 The difficult question: Hay diary, Oct. 30, 1863.

355 emergency cabinet meeting: Welles diary, Dec. 19, 1862.

355 Do not . . . "resist this assault": ibid.

355 "could not afford to lose": Bates diary, Dec. 19, 1862.

355 the cabinet chattered: ibid.; Welles diary, Dec. 19, 1862.

356 touting candidates: Browning diary, Dec. 19, 1862; Bates diary, Dec. 20, 1862.

356   they were not alone: Fessenden, *The Life and Public Services of William Pitt Fessenden,* Vol. 1, p. 243.

357   Lincoln then paused, looked at Chase: ibid., pp. 243–44.

357   "arraigned before a committee": ibid., pp. 244–46.

357   Stanton . . . was "disgusted": ibid., pp. 248–49.

358   Smith . . . "felt strongly tempted": ibid.

358   "He lied": Browning diary, Dec. 22, 1862.

358   Lincoln put in comments: Fessenden, *The Life and Public Services of William Pitt Fessenden,* Vol. 1, pp. 244–46.

358   Recognize *and maintain:* ibid.

359   "Seward has seen fit to resign": ibid., p. 248.

359   "all in a buz": Bates diary, Dec. 20, 1862.

359   "slumped over one way": Hay diary, Oct. 30, 1863.

359   to coax him back would tilt: Fessenden, *The Life and Public Services of William Pitt Fessenden,* Vol. 1, pp. 247–48.

359   Welles's mission: Welles diary, Dec. 20, 1862.

360   " 'Where is it?' ": ibid.

360   "the most serious governmental crisis": Goodwin, *Team of Rivals,* p. 495.

360   "I do not now see": Hay diary, Oct. 30, 1863.

360   "more firmly . . . in the saddle": Nicolay and Hay, *Abraham Lincoln,* Vol. 6, p. 271.

361   "Now I can ride": *RW,* p. 200.

361   "The war!": French diary, Dec. 21, 1862.

361   Medill . . . cataloged the woes: quoted in Donald, *Lincoln,* p. 399.

361   Dahlgren waxed eloquent: Dahlgren diary, Dec. 16, 1862.

361   "impossibility of . . . so long a line": Grant, *Memoirs and Selected Letters,* p. 289.

362   Order No. 11: Smith, *Grant,* pp. 224–26.

362   "the children of Israel": Korn, *American Jewry and the Civil War,* p. 125.

362   Grant's next lesson: Grant, *Memoirs and Selected Letters,* pp. 290–91.

363   "amazed at the . . . supplies": ibid.

363   She enjoyed the shopping: Taft diary, Jan. 2, 1863.

364   "From this time until spring": Mary Lincoln to William A. Newell, Dec. 16, 1862.

364   "Mrs. Laury, a spiritualist": Browning diary, Jan. 1, 1863.

364   a letter to McCullough's daughter: *CW,* Vol. 6, pp. 16–17.

364   West Virginia: ibid., pp. 26–28.

364   a cheer . . . in Minnesota: Cox, *Lincoln and the Sioux Uprising of 1862,* p. 192.

365   Ile à Vache: Guelzo, *Lincoln's Emancipation Proclamation,* pp. 223–24.

365 "he could not stop": *RW,* p. 435.

365 "fraught with evil": Browning diary, Dec. 31, 1862.

365 worked with his cabinet to refine: "Conversation with Hon. J. P. Usher, Wash[ingto]n Oct 8, 1878," in *An Oral History of Abraham Lincoln,* pp. 66–67.

366 At the town of Murfreesboro: G. C. Kniffin, "The Battle of Stone's River," in *Battles and Leaders of the Civil War,* Vol. 3, pp. 613–32.

366 highest proportional toll: McPherson, *Battle Cry of Freedom,* p. 582.

367 "check . . . to a dangerous sentiment": *CW,* Vol. 6, pp. 424–25.

367 "I can never forget": ibid.

EPILOGUE

368 "Your military skill is useless": *CW,* Vol. 6, pp. 31–33.

369 "what do you intend doing?": Guelzo, *Lincoln's Emancipation Proclamation,* p. 181.

369 "gem of my character": quoted in Donald, *Lincoln,* pp. 87–88.

369 "the central act . . . knocked": *RW,* pp. 90, 120.

369 be remembered forever: ibid., p. 413.

370 "Every sound appears a knell": *CW,* Vol. 1, p. 379.

370 "my fondest hopes": *RW,* p. 413.

370 "never be forgotten": quoted in Guelzo, *Lincoln's Emancipation Proclamation,* p. 186.

370 "very smilingly": Taft diary, Jan. 1, 1863.

370 a few small changes: Guelzo, *Lincoln's Emancipation Proclamation,* pp. 178–81.

371 a new flourish: *CW,* Vol. 6, p. 30.

371 Lincoln, proofreading carefully: Guelzo, *Lincoln's Emancipation Proclamation,* p. 181.

371 At the Seward mansion: Taft diary, Jan. 2, 1863.

372 The Welles home was quiet: Welles diary, Jan. 1, 1863.

372 "bright, cherub face": ibid., Dec. 3, 1862.

372 "The character of the country": ibid., Jan. 1, 1863.

372 "Oh, Mr. French!": Randall, *Mary Lincoln,* p. 320.

372 looking "quite as well": Taft diary, Jan. 1, 1863.

373 opinions already written: Simon, *Lincoln and Chief Justice Taney,* pp. 222, 245.

373 An early biographer, J. G. Holland: quoted in Herndon and Weik, *Abraham Lincoln,* Vol. 2, pp. 292–93.

374   Emancipation Proclamation, ready for his signature: Guelzo, *Lincoln's Emancipation Proclamation*, pp. 182–83.

375   "I never . . . felt more certain": *RW*, p. 397.

375   carefully inscribed his name: An image of the signature was viewed at http://www.archives.gov/exhibits/featured_documents/emancipation_ proclamation/images/emancipation_05.jpg.

375   "The signature looks": *RW*, p. 112.

375   Americans erupted in cheers: Guelzo, *Lincoln's Emancipation Proclamation*, pp. 183–86.

375   "Emancipation Meetings" . . . amens: Foreman, *A World on Fire*, pp. 395–97.

376   "The workingmen of Europe": *CW*, Vol. 6, pp. 63–65.

376   "bloody, barbarous . . . scheme": quoted in Guelzo, *Lincoln's Emancipation Proclamation*, pp. 187–88.

376   Vallandigham . . . Cox: McPherson, *Battle Cry of Freedom*, pp. 592–94.

376   "half his company gone": Guelzo, *Lincoln's Emancipation Proclamation*, pp. 187–88.

376   "the people of . . . 1862": *New-York Tribune*, Sept. 24, 1862.

377   a quarter of a million Rebel troops: Long, *The Civil War Day by Day*, p. 706.

377   "the Union is stronger": Seward to Dayton, Dec. 1, 1862; Seward to Adams, Nov. 30, 1862.

377   the London *Spectator*: Foreman, *A World on Fire*, pp. 318–19.

377   "I can see that time coming": *RW*, pp. 440–41.

378   bonds were selling at half: Nicolay and Hay, *Abraham Lincoln*, Vol. 10, p. 340.

378   "certainly is growing feeble": French diary, Feb. 18, 1863.

379   richer in 1870: Nicolay and Hay, *Abraham Lincoln*, Vol. 10, p. 340.

BIBLIOGRAPHY

Adams, Brooks. *Charles Francis Adams: An American Statesman*. Boston: Massachusetts Historical Society, 1912.

Adams, Charles Francis, Jr. *American Statesmen: Charles Francis Adams*. Boston: Houghton Mifflin Company, 1900.

———. *Richard Henry Dana: A Biography*. 2 volumes. Boston: Houghton Mifflin and Company, 1890.

Adams, Henry. *The Education of Henry Adams: An Autobiography*. Boston: Houghton Mifflin Company, 1961.

Adams, James Truslow. *The Adams Family*. New York: Literary Guild, 1930.

Aimone, Alan C., and Barbara A. Aimone. *A User's Guide to the Official Records of the American Civil War*. Shippensburg, PA: White Mane Publishing, 1993.

Alexander, Bevin. *How the South Could Have Won the Civil War: The Fatal Errors That Led to Confederate Defeat*. New York: Crown, 2007.

All for the Union: The Civil War Diary and Letters of Elisha Hunt Rhodes. Edited by Robert Hunt Rhodes. New York: Orion Books, 1985.

America's War: Talking About the Civil War and Emancipation on Their 150th Anniversaries. Edited by Edward L. Ayers. Chicago: American Library Association and the National Endowment for the Humanities, 2011.

Andrews, J. Cutler. *The North Reports the Civil War*. Pittsburgh: University of Pittsburgh Press, 1955.

———. *The South Reports the Civil War*. Princeton, NJ: Princeton University Press, 1970.

Anonymous. *Chronicle of the Union League of Philadelphia: 1862–1902*. Philadelphia: Union League Board of Directors, 1902.

Anonymous. *General H. W. Halleck's Report Reviewed in the Light of the Facts.* New York: Anson D. F. Randolph, 1862.

Anonymous. *The History of The Times: The Tradition Established, 1841–1884.* London: Office of The Times, 1939.

Artemus Ward, His Book. New York: Carleton, 1862 (facsimile edition, Santa Barbara, CA: Wallace Hebberd, 1964).

Bain, David Haward. *Empire Express: Building the First Transcontinental Railroad.* New York: Viking, 1999.

Baker, Jean H. *Mary Todd Lincoln: A Biography.* New York: W. W. Norton, 1987.

Ball, Edward. *Slaves in the Family.* New York: Ballantine Books, 1999.

Barnes, Thurlow Weed. *The Life of Thurlow Weed.* Vol. 2, *Memoir of Thurlow Weed.* New York: Da Capo Press, 1970.

Bates, David Homer. *Lincoln in the Telegraph Office: Recollections of the United States Military Telegraph Corps During the Civil War.* New York: Century, 1907.

Battles and Leaders of the Civil War. 4 volumes. Edited by Robert Underwood Johnson and Clarence Clough Buel. New York: Thomas Yoseloff, 1956.

Bayne, Julia Taft. *Tad Lincoln's Father.* Boston: Little, Brown, 1931.

Bearss, Edwin C. *Fields of Honor: Pivotal Battles of the Civil War.* Washington, DC: National Geographic, 2006.

Beckett, Ian F. W. *The War Correspondents: The American Civil War.* London: Grange Books, 1993.

Benjamin Brown French, Witness to the Young Republic: A Yankee's Journal, 1828–1870. Edited by Donald B. Cole and John J. McDonough. Hanover, NH: University Press of New England, 1989.

Berlin, Ida, Barbara J. Fields, Steven F. Miller, Joseph P. Reidy, and Leslie S. Rowland, eds. *Free at Last: A Documentary History of Slavery, Freedom, and the Civil War.* New York: New Press, 1992.

Berry, Stephen William. *House of Abraham: Lincoln and the Todds, a Family Divided by War.* Boston: Houghton Mifflin, 2007.

Beveridge, Albert J. *Abraham Lincoln, 1809–1858.* 2 volumes. Boston: Houghton Mifflin, 1928.

Bierce, Ambrose. *Civil War Stories.* New York: Dover Publications, 1994.

Bishop, Jim. *The Day Lincoln Was Shot.* New York: Harper & Brothers, 1955.

The Blue and the Gray: The Story of the Civil War as Told by Participants. Edited by Henry Steele Commager. New York: Fairfax Press, 1982.

Boritt, Gabor S. *Lincoln and the Economics of the American Dream.* Urbana: University of Illinois Press, 1994.

Boyden, Anna L. *Echoes from Hospital and White House: A Record of Mrs. Rebecca R. Pomroy's Experience in War-Times*. Boston: D. Lothrop, 1884.

Brodie, Fawn M. *Thaddeus Stevens, Scourge of the South*. New York: W. W. Norton, 1959.

Brooks, Noah. *Washington DC in Lincoln's Time*. Edited by Herbert Mitgang. Chicago: Quadrangle Books, 1971.

Browne, Frances Fisher. *The Every-Day Life of Abraham Lincoln: A Narrative and Descriptive Biography with Pen-Pictures and Personal Recollections by Those Who Knew Him*. Chicago: Browne & Howell, 1913.

Bruce, Robert V. *Lincoln and the Tools of War*. Champaign: University of Illinois Press, 1989.

Buell, Thomas B. *The Warrior Generals: Combat Leadership in the Civil War*. New York: Three Rivers Press, 1997.

Burkhimer, Michael. *100 Essential Lincoln Books*. Nashville, TN: Cumberland House, 2003.

Burlingame, Michael. *Abraham Lincoln: A Life*. 2 volumes. Baltimore: Johns Hopkins Press, 2008.

———. "Honest Abe, Dishonest Mary." Historical Bulletin Number 50, Lincoln Fellowship of Wisconsin, 1994.

Carman, Harry J., and Reinhard H. Luthin. *Lincoln and the Patronage*. Gloucester, MA: Peter Smith, 1964.

Carpenter, F. B. *The Inner Life of Abraham Lincoln: Six Months at the White House*. Lincoln: University of Nebraska Press, 1995.

Carwardine, Richard. *Lincoln: A Life of Purpose and Power*. New York: Alfred A. Knopf, 2006.

Catton, Bruce. *The Coming Fury*. New York: Doubleday, 1961.

———. *Glory Road*. New York: Doubleday, 1952.

———. *Grant Moves South*. Boston: Little, Brown, 1960.

———. *Mr. Lincoln's Army*. New York: Doubleday, 1951.

———. *Never Call Retreat*. New York: Doubleday, 1965.

———. *A Stillness at Appomattox*. New York: Doubleday, 1953.

———. *Terrible Swift Sword*. New York: Doubleday, 1963.

Chadwick, Bruce. *The Two American Presidents: A Dual Biography of Abraham Lincoln and Jefferson Davis*. Secaucus, NJ: Birch Lane Press, 1990.

Chamberlin, Thomas. *History of the One Hundred and Fiftieth Regiment, Pennsylvania Volunteers, Second Regiment, Bucktail Brigade*. Rev. ed. Philadelphia: F. McManus, Jr., 1905.

Chandler, David G. *Atlas of Military Strategy: The Art, Theory and Practice of War, 1618–1878*. London: Arms & Armour Press, 1980.

The Civil War Papers of George B. McClellan: Selected Correspondence, 1860–1865. Edited by Stephen W. Sears. New York: Ticknor & Fields, 1989.

The Collected Works of Abraham Lincoln. 8 volumes (plus Index). Edited by Roy P. Basler. New Brunswick, NJ: Rutgers University Press, 1953.

Confidential Correspondence of Gustavus Vasa Fox, Assistant Secretary of the Navy, 1861–1865. 2 volumes. Edited by Robert Means Thompson and Richard Wainwright. Freeport, NY: Books for Libraries Press, 1972.

Coopersmith, Andrew S. *Fighting Words: An Illustrated History of Newspaper Accounts of the Civil War*. New York: New Press, 2004.

Cowley, Robert, ed. *With My Face to the Enemy: Perspectives on the Civil War*. New York: G. P. Putnam's Sons, 2001.

Cox, Hank. *Lincoln and the Sioux Uprising of 1862*. Nashville, TN: Cumberland House Publishing, 2005.

Craighill, William P. *The Army Officer's Pocket Companion*. New York: D. Van Nostrand, 1862 (facsimile edition, Mechanicsville, PA: Stackpole Books, 2002).

Crete and James: Personal Letters of Lucretia and James Garfield. Edited by John Shaw. East Lansing: Michigan State University Press, 1994.

Crook, David P. *Diplomacy During the American Civil War*. New York: Wiley & Sons, 1975.

———. *The North, the South, and the Powers, 1861–1865*. New York: John Wiley & Sons, 1974.

Cuomo, Mario, and Harold Holzer. *Lincoln on Democracy: His Own Words, with Essays by America's Foremost Historians*. New York: HarperCollins, 1990.

Dahlgren, Madeleine Vinton. *Memoir of John A. Dahlgren, Rear-Admiral United States Navy*. Boston: J. R. Osgood, 1882.

Dalrymple, William. *The Last Mughal: The Fall of a Dynasty: Delhi, 1857*. New York: Alfred A. Knopf, 2006.

Daniel, John M. *The Richmond Examiner During the War*. New York: Arno & The New York Times, 1970.

Daniel, Larry J. *Shiloh: The Battle That Changed the Civil War*. New York: Simon & Schuster, 1998.

Davis, David Brion. *Inhuman Bondage: The Rise and Fall of Slavery in the New World*. New York: Oxford University Press, 2006.

Davis, Jefferson. *The Rise and Fall of the Confederate Government*. Vols. 1 and 2. New York: Da Capo Press, 1990.

Denney, Robert E. *The Civil War Years: A Day-by-Day Chronicle of the Life of a Nation*. New York: Sterling Publishing, 1992.

The Diary of Edward Bates, 1859–1866. Edited by Howard K. Beale. New York: Da Capo Press, 1971.

Diary of Gideon Welles, Secretary of the Navy Under Lincoln and Johnson. Vol. 1, *1861–March 30, 1864.* Edited by John T. Morse. Boston: Houghton Mifflin, 1911.

The Diary of Orville Hickman Browning. Vol. 1, *1850–1864.* Edited by Theodore Calvin Pease and James G. Randall. Springfield, IL: Trustees of the Illinois State Historical Library, 1925.

Dicey, Edward. *Spectator of America.* Athens: University of Georgia Press, 1971.

Dix, Morgan. "Memorial Sermon." In *Francis L. Vinton, Priest and Doctor.* New York: William Moore, Church Printer, 1873.

Donald, David Herbert, ed. *Inside Lincoln's Cabinet: The Civil War Diaries of Salmon P. Chase.* New York: Longmans, Green, 1954.

———. *Lincoln.* New York: Simon & Schuster, 1995.

———. *Lincoln at Home: Two Glimpses of Abraham Lincoln's Family Life.* New York: Simon & Schuster, 2000.

———. *Lincoln's Herndon: A Biography.* New York: Da Capo Press, 1988.

———. *"We Are Lincoln Men": Abraham Lincoln and His Friends.* New York: Simon & Schuster, 2003.

———. *Why the North Won the Civil War.* New York: Collier, 1962.

D'Orléans, François-Ferdinand-Philippe-Louis-Marie ("Prince du Joinville"). *The Army of the Potomac: Its Organization, Its Commander, and Its Campaign.* Translated by William Henry Hurlbert. New York: Anson D. F. Randolph, 1862.

Duberman, Martin. *Charles Francis Adams, 1807–1886.* Boston: Houghton Mifflin, 1960.

Dufwa, Thamar Emelia. *Transcontinental Railroad Legislation, 1835–1862.* New York: Arno Press, 1981.

Duke, Basil Wilson. *Reminiscences of General Basil W. Duke.* Garden City, NY: Doubleday, Page, 1911.

Earle, Jonathan. *John Brown's Raid on Harper's Ferry: A Brief History with Documents.* Boston: Bedford/St. Martin's, 2008.

1862 Class Report, 1912: Class of 1862 Harvard University. Norwood, MA: Plimpton Press, 1912.

1862 Manual for Army Cooking, a Reproduction with Essay by Elizabeth Stroud Kory. Norristown, PA: Norristown Press, 1993.

Eisenhower, John S. D. *Agent of Destiny: The Life and Times of General Winfield Scott.* New York: Free Press, 1997.

Eisenschiml, Otto. *The Celebrated Case of Fitz John Porter: An American Dreyfus Affair.* New York: Bobbs-Merrill Company, 1950.

Ellet, Charles, Jr. *The Mississippi and Ohio Rivers.* New York: Arno and The New York Times, 1970.

Emerson, Ralph Waldo. *Essays and Journals.* Edited by Lewis Mumford. New York: Doubleday, 1968.

———. *Representative Men: Seven Lectures.* Boston: Houghton Mifflin, 1883.

Eye of the Storm: A Civil War Odyssey Written and Illustrated by Private Robert Knox Sneden. Edited by Charles F. Bryan and Nelson D. Lankford. New York: Free Press, 2000.

Fehrenbacher, Don C. *Prelude to Greatness: Lincoln in the 1850s.* Stanford, CA: Stanford University Press, 1962.

Fenster, Julie M. *The Case of Abraham Lincoln: A Story of Adultery, Murder, and the Making of a Great President.* New York: Palgrave Macmillan, 2007.

Fermer, Douglas. *James Gordon Bennett and the New York Herald: A Study of Editorial Opinion in the Civil War Era, 1854–1867.* New York: St. Martin's Press, 1986.

Fessenden, Francis. *The Life and Public Services of William Pitt Fessenden.* 2 volumes. Boston: Houghton Mifflin, 1907.

Fleischner, Jennifer. *Mrs. Lincoln and Mrs. Keckly: The Remarkable Story of the Friendship Between a First Lady and a Former Slave.* New York: Broadway Books, 2003.

Flood, Charles Bracelen. *1864: Lincoln at the Gates of History.* New York: Simon & Schuster, 2009.

———. *Grant and Sherman: The Friendship That Won the Civil War.* New York: Farrar, Straus and Giroux, 2005.

Foner, Eric. *The Fiery Trial: Abraham Lincoln and American Slavery.* New York: W. W. Norton, 2010.

Foote, Shelby. *The Civil War: A Narrative.* 3 volumes. New York: Vintage Books, 1986.

Foreman, Amanda. *A World on Fire: Britain's Crucial Role in the American Civil War.* New York: Random House, 2010.

Franklin, John H. *The Emancipation Proclamation.* Garden City, NY: Doubleday, 1963.

Furgurson, Ernest B. *Freedom Rising: Washington in the Civil War.* New York: Vintage Books, 2005.

Gallagher, Gary W. *Causes Won, Lost & Forgotten: How Hollywood and Popular Art Shape What We Know About the Civil War.* Chapel Hill: University of North Carolina Press, 2008.

Gallman, J. Matthew. *Mastering Wartime: A Social History of Philadelphia During the Civil War.* Philadelphia: University of Pennsylvania Press, 2000.

Garfield-Hinsdale Letters: Correspondence Between James Abram Garfield and Burke Aaron Hinsdale. Edited by Mary L. Hinsdale. Ann Arbor: University of Michigan Press, 1949.

Gates, Paul Wallace. *Fifty Million Acres: Conflicts over Kansas Land Policy, 1854–1890.* Norman: University of Oklahoma Press, 1997.

Gibbon, John. *Personal Recollections of the Civil War.* New York: G. P. Putnam's Sons, 1928.

Goodrich, Thomas. *War to the Knife: Bleeding Kansas, 1854–1861.* Lincoln: University of Nebraska Press, 2004.

Goodwin, Doris Kearns. *Team of Rivals: The Political Genius of Abraham Lincoln.* New York: Simon & Schuster, 2005.

Grant, Ulysses S. *Memoirs and Selected Letters: Personal Memoirs of U. S. Grant, Selected Letters, 1839–1865.* New York: The Library of America, 1990.

Greene, Jack, and Alessandro Massignani. *Ironclads at War: The Origin and Development of the Armored Warship, 1854–1891.* New York: Da Capo Press, 1998.

Griess, Thomas E., ed. *Atlas for the American Civil War.* New York: Square One, 2002.

———. ed. *The West Point Military History Series: The American Civil War.* New York: Square One, 2002.

Guelzo, Allen. *Lincoln and Douglas: The Debates That Defined America.* New York: Simon & Schuster, 2008.

———. *Lincoln's Emancipation Proclamation: The End of Slavery in America.* New York: Simon & Schuster, 2004.

Halleck, Henry W. *Elements of Military Art and Science.* New York: D. Appleton, 1846.

Hamlin, Charles E. *The Life and Times of Hannibal Hamlin.* Volume 2. Port Washington, NY: Kennikat Press, 1971.

Harris, William C. *Lincoln's Rise to the Presidency.* Lawrence: University Press of Kansas, 2007.

Hattaway, Herman, and Archer Jones. *How the North Won: A Military History of the Civil War.* Urbana: University of Illinois Press, 1991.

Hearn, Chester G. *The Capture of New Orleans, 1862.* Baton Rouge: Louisiana State University Press, 1995.

———. *Ellet's Brigade: The Strangest Outfit of All.* Baton Rouge: Louisiana State University Press, 2000.

Heidler, David Stephen, and Jeanne T. Heidler, eds., *Encyclopedia of the American Civil War: A Political, Social, and Military History.* Santa Barbara, CA: ABC-CLIO, 2000.

Henig, Gerald S., and Eric Niderost. *Civil War Firsts: The Legacies of America's Bloodiest Conflict*. Mechanicsburg, PA: Stackpole Books, 2001.

Herndon, William, and Jesse Weik. *Abraham Lincoln: The True Story of a Great Life*. Volumes 1 and 2. New York: D. Appleton, 1895.

Herndon's Informants: Letters, Interviews, and Statements About Abraham Lincoln. Edited by Douglas L. Wilson and Rodney O. Davis. Urbana: University of Illinois Press, 1998.

Herndon's Life of Lincoln: The History and Personal Recollections of Abraham Lincoln as Originally Written by William H. Herndon and Jesse W. Weik. Edited by Paul M. Angle. New York: Da Capo Press, 1983.

Holzer, Harold. *Lincoln at Cooper Union: The Speech That Made Abraham Lincoln President*. New York: Simon & Schuster, 2004.

———. *Lincoln President-Elect: Abraham Lincoln and the Great Secession Winter, 1860–1861*. New York: Simon & Schuster, 2008.

Hood, Thomas. *The Selected Poems of Thomas Hood*. Edited by John Clubbe. Cambridge, MA: Harvard University Press, 1970.

Horwitz, Tony. *Midnight Rising: John Brown and the Raid That Sparked the Civil War*. New York: Henry Holt and Company, 2011.

Hurst, Jack. *Men of Fire: Grant, Forrest, and the Campaign That Decided the Civil War*. New York: Basic Books, 2007.

Ilisevich, Robert D. *Galusha A. Grow: The People's Candidate*. Pittsburgh: University of Pittsburgh Press, 1968.

Inside Lincoln's Cabinet: The Civil War Diaries of Salmon P. Chase. Edited by David Donald. New York: Longmans, Green, 1954.

Inside Lincoln's White House: The Complete Civil War Diary of John Hay. Edited by Michael Burlingame and John R. T. Ettlinger. Carbondale: Southern Illinois University Press, 1999.

Jenkins, Sally, and John Stauffer. *The State of Jones: The Small Southern County That Seceded from the Confederacy*. New York: Anchor Books, 2010.

Johnson, William J. *Abraham Lincoln the Christian*. Fenton, MI: Mott Media, 1976.

Joiner, Gary D. *Mr. Lincoln's Brown Water Navy: The Mississippi Squadron*. Lanham, MD: Rowman & Littlefield, 2007.

Keckley [Keckly], Elizabeth. *Behind the Scenes: Thirty Years a Slave and Four Years in the White House*. New York: Arno Press and the *New York Times*, 1968.

Keegan, John. *The American Civil War: A Military History*. New York: Alfred A. Knopf, 2009.

———. *The Face of Battle*. New York: Viking Press, 1976.

———. *Fields of Battle: The Wars for North America*. New York: Alfred A. Knopf, 1996.

———. *The Mask of Command*. New York: Penguin Books, 1988.

Kelley, William D. *Lincoln and Stanton: A Study of the War Administration of 1861 and 1862, with Special Consideration of Some Recent Statements of Gen. Geo. B. McClellan*. New York: G. P. Putnam's Sons, 1885.

Klepper, Michael M., and Robert Gunther. *The Wealthy 100: From Benjamin Franklin to Bill Gates—A Ranking of the Richest Americans, Past and Present*. New York: Citadel Press, 1996.

Konstam, Angus. *Duel of the Ironclads: USS Monitor & CSS Virginia at Hampton Roads, 1862*. Oxford, UK: Osprey Publishing, 2003.

Korn, Bertram Wallace. *American Jewry and the Civil War*. Philadelphia: Jewish Publication Society of America, 1951.

Kunhardt, Philip B., III, Peter W. Kunhardt, and Peter W. Kunhardt, Jr. *Lincoln, Life-Size*. New York: Alfred A. Knopf, 2009.

———. *Looking for Lincoln: The Making of an American Icon*. New York: Alfred A. Knopf, 2008.

Lamon, Ward Hill. *Recollections of Abraham Lincoln, 1847–1865*. Edited by Dorothy Lamon Teillard. Washington, DC: Published by the Editor, 1911.

Lang, Scott B. *The Forgotten Charge: The 123rd Pennsylvania at Marye's Heights, Fredericksburg, Virginia*. Shippensburg, PA: White Mane Books, 2002.

Leech, Margaret. *Reveille in Washington: 1860–1865*. New York: Harper & Brothers, 1941.

Lincoln Observed: The Civil War Dispatches of Noah Brooks. Edited by Michael Burlingame. Baltimore: Johns Hopkins University Press, 1998.

Livermore, Mary A. *My Story of the War: Four Years Personal Experience in the Sanitary Service of the Rebellion*. Hartford, CT: A. D. Worthington, 1889.

Long, E. B., with Barbara Long. *The Civil War Day by Day: An Almanac, 1861–1865*. New York: Da Capo Press, 1971.

Marszalek, John F. *Commander of All Lincoln's Armies: A Life of Henry W. Halleck*. Cambridge, MA: Belknap Press of Harvard University Press, 2004.

Marvel, William. *Lincoln's Darkest Year: The War in 1862*. Boston: Houghton Mifflin, 2008.

Mary Chesnut's Civil War. Edited by C. Vann Woodward. New Haven, CT: Yale University Press, 1981.

Mary Todd Lincoln: Her Life and Letters. Edited by Justin G. Turner and Linda Turner. New York: Fromm International, 1987.

Masur, Kate. "The African American Delegation to Abraham Lincoln: A Reappraisal," *Civil War History* 45, no. 2 (June 2010).

——. *An Example for All the Land: Emancipation and the Struggle over Equality in Washington, D.C.* Chapel Hill: University of North Carolina Press, 2010.

Matloff, Maurice, general ed. *American Military History.* Washington, DC: Office of the Chief of Military History, United States Army, 1969.

McClellan, George B. *McClellan's Own Story.* Scituate, MA: Digital Scanning, 1998.

——. *Report of Major-General George B. McClellan upon the Organization of the Army of the Potomac, and Its Campaigns in Virginia and Maryland, July 26, 1861, to November 7, 1862.* Boston: Office of the Boston Courier, 1864.

McDonough, James L. *Shiloh, in Hell Before Night.* Knoxville: University of Tennessee Press, 1977.

McFeely, William S. *Frederick Douglass.* New York: W. W. Norton, 1991.

McPherson, James M. *Abraham Lincoln and the Second American Revolution.* New York: Oxford University Press, 1991.

——. *Battle Cry of Freedom: The Civil War Era.* New York: Oxford University Press, 1988.

——. *Crossroads of Freedom: Antietam, the Battle That Changed the Course of the Civil War.* New York: Oxford University Press, 2002.

——. *Drawn with the Sword: Reflections on the American Civil War.* New York: Oxford University Press, 1996.

——. *Tried by War: Abraham Lincoln as Commander-in-Chief.* New York: Penguin Press, 2008.

Miers, Earl Schenck, ed. *Lincoln Day by Day: A Chronology.* Volumes 1–3. Washington, DC: Lincoln Sesquicentennial Commission, 1960.

Miller, William Lee. *Lincoln's Virtues: An Ethical Biography.* New York: Alfred A. Knopf, 2002.

——. *President Lincoln: The Duty of a Statesman.* New York: Alfred A. Knopf, 2008.

Mitchell, Stewart. *Horatio Seymour of New York.* Cambridge, MA: Harvard University Press, 1938.

National Geographic Society. *Atlas of the Civil War: A Comprehensive Guide to the Tactics and Terrain of Battle.* Edited by Neil Kagan. Washington, DC: National Geographic Society, 2009.

Neely, Mark E., Jr. *The Fate of Liberty: Abraham Lincoln and Civil Liberties.* New York: Oxford University Press, 1992.

——. *The Last Best Hope of Earth: Abraham Lincoln and the Promise of America.* Cambridge, MA: Harvard University Press, 1995.

Nicolay, John G., and John Hay. *Abraham Lincoln: A History.* 10 volumes. New York: Century, 1917.

Niven, John. *Salmon P. Chase: A Biography.* New York: Oxford University Press, 1995.

An Oral History of Abraham Lincoln: John G. Nicolay's Interviews and Essays. Edited by Michael Burlingame. Carbondale: Southern Illinois University Press, 1996.

Owsley, Frank Lawrence. *King Cotton Diplomacy: Foreign Relations of the Confederate States of America.* 2nd ed., rev. Chicago: University of Chicago Press, 1959.

Packard, Jerrold M. *The Lincolns in the White House: Four Years That Shattered a Family.* New York: St. Martin's Press, 2005.

Papers Relating to Foreign Affairs, Communicated to Congress Dec. 1, 1862. Volumes 1 and 2. Washington, DC: Government Printing Office, 1862.

Papers Relating to Foreign Affairs, Communicated to Congress Dec. 1, 1863. Volumes 1 and 2. Washington, DC: Government Printing Office, 1863.

The Papers of Ulysses S. Grant. Volumes 4–7. Edited by John Y. Simon. Carbondale: University of Southern Illinois Press, 1972–1979.

Parker, William Belmont. *The Life and Public Services of Justin Smith Morrill.* Boston: Houghton Mifflin, 1924.

Perret, Geoffrey. *Lincoln's War: The Untold Story of America's Greatest President as Commander in Chief.* New York: Random House, 2004.

Peskin, Allan. *Winfield Scott and the Profession of Arms.* Kent, OH: Kent State University Press, 2003.

Petrowski, William Robinson. *The Kansas Pacific: A Study in Railroad Promotion.* New York: Arno Press, 1981.

Pinsker, Matthew. *Lincoln's Sanctuary: Abraham Lincoln and the Soldiers' Home.* New York: Oxford University Press, 2003.

Poore, Ben Perley. *Perley's Reminiscences of Sixty Years in the National Metropolis.* Volumes 1 and 2. New York: AMS Press, 1971.

Prentice, George D. *Biography of Henry Clay.* Hartford, CT: Samuel Hanmer, Jr. and John Jay Phelps, 1831.

Rafuse, Ethan S. *McClellan's War: The Failure of Moderation in the Struggle for the Union.* Bloomington: Indiana University Press, 2005.

Randall, James G. *Lincoln, the President.* 4 volumes. New York: Dodd, Mead, 1945–1955.

Randall, Ruth Painter. *Lincoln's Sons.* Boston: Little, Brown, 1955.

———. *Mary Lincoln: Biography of a Marriage.* Boston: Little, Brown, 1953.

Recollected Words of Abraham Lincoln. Edited by Don E. Fehrenbacher and Virginia Fehrenbacher. Stanford, CA: Stanford University Press, 1996.

Reed, William B. *A Review of Mr. Seward's Diplomacy by a Northern Man.* N.p.: 1862.

Reidy, Joseph P. "Coming from the Shadow of the Past: The Transition from Slavery to Freedom at Freedmen's Village, 1863–1869," *The Virginia Magazine of History and Biography* 95, no. 4 (October 1987).

Richardson, Robert D. *Emerson: The Mind on Fire.* Berkeley: University of California Press, 1995.

———. *William James: In the Maelstrom of American Modernism.* Boston: Houghton Mifflin Harcourt, 2007.

Ridley, Jasper. *Lord Palmerston.* New York: E. P. Dutton, 1970.

Sandburg, Carl. *Abraham Lincoln: The War Years.* 4 volumes. New York: Harcourt, Brace, 1939.

Sanderson, James M. *Camp Fire and Camp Cooking; or, Culinary Hints for the Soldier.* Washington, DC: Government Printing Office, 1862.

Schurz, Carl. *Speeches, Correspondence and Political Papers of Carl Schurz.* Volume 1. Edited by Frederic Bancroft. New York: Negro Universities Press, 1969.

Scott, Winfield. *Memoirs of Lieut-General Scott, LLD; Written by Himself.* 2 volumes. New York: Sheldon, 1864.

Seale, William. *The President's House: A History.* Volume 1. Washington, DC: White House Historical Association, 1986.

Sears, Stephen W. *George B. McClellan: The Young Napoleon.* New York: Da Capo Press, 1988.

———. *Landscape Turned Red: The Battle of Antietam.* New Haven, CT: Ticknor & Fields, 1983.

The Selected Letters of Charles Sumner. Volume 2. Edited by Beverly Wilson Palmer. Boston: Northeastern University Press, 1990.

Shenk, Joshua Wolf. *Lincoln's Melancholy: How Depression Challenged a President and Fueled His Greatness.* Boston: Houghton Mifflin, 2005.

Sherman, William Tecumseh. *Memoirs of General W. T. Sherman.* New York: Library of America, 1990.

Sherman's Civil War: Selected Correspondence of William T. Sherman, 1860–1865. Edited by Brooks D. Simpson and Jean V. Berlin. Chapel Hill: University of North Carolina Press, 1999.

Simon, James F. *Lincoln and Chief Justice Taney: Slavery, Secession, and the President's War Powers.* New York: Simon & Schuster, 2006.

Simon, John Y. *Grant and Halleck: Contrasts in Command, the Frank L. Klement Lectures.* Milwaukee, WI: Marquette University Press, 1996.

Smith, Jean Edward. *Grant.* New York: Simon & Schuster, 2001.

Soodalter, Ron. *Hanging Captain Gordon: The Life and Trial of an American Slave Trader.* New York: Atria, 2006.

Speed, Thomas. *The Union Cause in Kentucky, 1860–1865.* New York: G. P. Putnam's Sons, 1907.

Stampp, Kenneth M., ed. *The Causes of the Civil War.* Englewood Cliffs, NJ: Prentice Hall, 1974.

Stauffer, John. *The Black Hearts of Men: Radical Abolitionists and the Transformation of Race.* Cambridge, MA: Harvard University Press, 2002.

Sterne, Laurence. *A Sentimental Journey Through France and Italy.* New York: J. F. Taylor, 1904.

Stevens, Joseph E. *1863: The Rebirth of a Nation.* New York: Bantam Books, 1999.

Stille, Charles J. *How a Free People Conduct a Long War: A Chapter from English History.* Philadelphia: Collins, Printer, 1862.

Stoddard, William O. *Inside the White House in War Times: Memoirs and Reports of Lincoln's Secretary.* Edited by Michael Burlingame. Lincoln: University of Nebraska Press, 2000.

———. *Lincoln at Work: Sketches from Life.* Boston: United Society of Christian Endeavor, 1900.

———. *Lincoln's Third Secretary: The Memoirs of William O. Stoddard.* Edited by William O. Stoddard, Jr. New York: Exposition Press, 1955.

———. *Lincoln's White House Secretary: The Adventurous Life of William O. Stoddard.* Edited by Harold Holzer. Carbondale: Southern Illinois University, 2007.

Sutherland, Daniel E. *Fredericksburg & Chancellorsville: The Dare Mark Campaign.* Lincoln: University of Nebraska Press, 1998.

Swanson, James L. *Manhunt: The 12-Day Chase for Lincoln's Killer.* New York: William Morrow, 2006.

Tap, Bruce. *Over Lincoln's Shoulder: The Committee on the Conduct of the War.* Lawrence: University Press of Kansas, 1998.

Thomas, Benjamin P. *Abraham Lincoln: A Biography.* New York: Modern Library, 1968.

Thomas, William G. *The Iron Way: Railroads, the Civil War, and the Making of Modern America.* New Haven, CT: Yale University Press, 2011.

Trefousse, Hans L. *The Radical Republicans: Lincoln's Vanguard for Racial Justice.* New York: Alfred A. Knopf, 1968.

Tripp, C. A. *The Intimate World of Abraham Lincoln.* New York: Free Press, 2005.

Trollope, Anthony. *An Autobiography.* New York: Harper & Brothers, 1883.

———. *North America.* Volumes 1 and 2. New York: Harper & Brothers, 1863.

United States Department of State: Message of the President of the United States to the Two Houses of Congress at the Commencement of the Third Session of the Thirty-Seventh Congress. Washington, DC: U.S. Government Printing Office, 1862. Available at http://digital.library.wisc.edu/1711.dl/FRUS.

United States War Department. *The War of the Rebellion: A Compilation of the Official Records of the Union and Confederate Armies.* Washington, DC: Government Printing Office, 1880–1901.

Van Deusen, Glyndon G. *William Henry Seward.* New York: Oxford University Press, 1967.

Voorhees, Daniel W. "The Liberty of the Citizen." In *Speeches of Daniel W. Voorhees, of Indiana, Embracing His Most Prominent Forensic, Political, Occasional, and Literary Addresses . . . with a Short Biographical Sketch.* Edited by Charles S. Voorhees. Cincinnati: Robert Clarke, 1875.

Warden, Robert B. *An Account of the Private Life and Public Services of Salmon Portland Chase.* Cincinnati: Wilsatch, Baldwin, 1874.

Wartime in Washington: The Civil War Letters of Elizabeth Blair Lee. Edited by Virginia Jeans Laas. Chicago: University of Illinois Press, 1991.

The Wartime Papers of Robert E. Lee. Edited by Clifford Dowdey and Louis H. Manarin. New York: Da Capo Press, 1987.

Washington During the Civil War: The Diary of Horatio Nelson Taft, 1861–1865, accessed online at the Library of Congress website: http://memory.loc.gov/ammem/tafthtml/tafthome.html.

Weed, Thurlow. *The Life of Thurlow Weed.* Vol. 1, *Autobiography of Thurlow Weed.* Edited by Harriet A. Weed. New York: Da Capo Press, 1970.

Welles, Gideon. *Lincoln and Seward. Remarks upon the Memorial Address of Chas. Francis Adams, on the Late William H. Seward, with Incidents and Comments Illustrative of the Measure and Policy of the Administration of Abraham Lincoln. And Views as to the Relative Positions of the Late President and Secretary of State.* New York: Sheldon, 1874.

Wheeler, Richard. *Voices of the Civil War.* New York: Meridian, 1990.

White, Ronald C., Jr. *A. Lincoln: A Biography.* New York: Random House, 2009.

Whiting, William. *The War Powers of the President, and the Legislative Powers of Congress in Relation to Rebellion, Treason and Slavery.* Boston: John L. Shorey, 1862.

Whitman, Walt. *Leaves of Grass.* Philadelphia: David McKay, 1900.

———. *Walt Whitman: The Correspondence.* Vol. 1, *1842–1867.* Edited by Edwin Haviland Miller. New York: New York University Press, 1961.

Whittier, John Greenleaf. *The Complete Poetical Works of Whittier.* Edited by Horace E. Scudder. Boston: Houghton Mifflin, 1894.

Williams, Kenneth P. *Lincoln Finds a General: A Military History of the Civil War.* Bloomington: Indiana University Press, 1985.

Williams, T. Harry. *Lincoln and His Generals.* New York: Alfred A. Knopf, 1952.

Wilson, Douglas L. *Lincoln's Sword: The Presidency and the Power of Words.* New York: Alfred A. Knopf, 2006.

With Lincoln in the White House: Letters, Memoranda, and Other Writings of John G. Nicolay, 1860–1865. Edited by Michael Burlingame. Carbondale: Southern Illinois University Press, 2000.

Woodworth, Steven E., and Kenneth J. Winkle. *Atlas of the Civil War.* New York: Oxford University Press, 2004.

ACKNOWLEDGMENTS

In 1968, when I was in second or third grade, my parents joined the Book-of-the-Month Club and allowed me to choose a few of the promotional books they received for a penny. I chose Bruce Catton's magnificent three-volume history of the Army of the Potomac—books far, far beyond my capacity to read or comprehend at the time. But when I look at them on my shelf today, they remind me how enduring my interest has been in Abraham Lincoln and the Civil War. My desire to indulge this fascination was the motivation behind this book.

Although this was a labor of love, at many points along the way the emphasis was on "labor." I would never have finished without the generous support of my patrons at *Time* magazine (Rick Stengel, John Huey, Nancy Gibbs, and Michael Duffy) and, earlier, at *The Washington Post* (Don Graham, Leonard Downie, and Phil Bennett).

It is widely said that books no longer get edited, but it is my great fortune to know that this is not always true. At Henry Holt, George Hodgman helped me launch this project. Then John Sterling—perhaps the world's most patient man—passed his careful eye over every sentence. Even then, Jolanta Benal dug into the pages and found so much that we missed. At every stage, my publisher's devotion to this project was a gift and an honor. Thanks, Esther Newberg, for matching me with them.

I further imposed on a number of others to read the manuscript, and all of them came through with sharp-eyed advice. They made this book better than it would have been otherwise: Joel Achenbach, Trent Jones,

Kate Masur, Bob Richardson, Tom Shroder, John Stauffer, Mike Stradinger, and Gene Weingarten. Where imperfections remain, the fault is mine.

The helpful staff of the Library of Congress not only guided me through that incomparable resource, they also provided me with an office where I wrote one failed opening after another.

A number of historians listened to my ideas and offered encouragement. Some may not remember ever crossing my path, and none can be blamed for anything here. But I am mindful of their kindness: David Blight, Gabor Borritt, Diane Burke, Orville Burton, Jonathan Earle, Adam Green, Mark Grimsley, Harold Holzer, Michael Musick, and Thomas Schwartz.

As always, I have been borne up by my friends, whose support took many forms. They gave me quiet havens to work, listened patiently to my droning lectures, bolstered my confidence, covered for my absences as a parent. This book took so long, and there were so many that I can't name them all, but my thanks to: Henry Allen, Kevin Baker, Beverly and Bucky Brooks, Carl Cannon, Peter Carlson, Doug and Madelyn Dalgleish, Annie Dillard, Gus and Elinor Eisemann, Tom Frail, Michael Grunwald, Lisa and Randy Hendricks, Roscoe Hill, Brad and Colleen Honnold, Tony Horwitz, Steve Jennings, Steve Kraske, Josh and Tess Lewis, Larka and Hatch McCray, Eileen Mackevich, Scott and Cindy Padon, John Pancake, Jason Pottenger, Adam Sachs, Maralee Schwartz, Al Simmons, Peter Slevin, Jim and Christy Somerville, Mit Spears and Kyle Gibson, Carrie and Tom Wagstaff, the Scribblers (Rick Atkinson, David Maraniss, and Rafe Sagalyn), the Von Drehles and the Balls, the guys in the book club, John Goldberg, who caught the cancer, and Dan Holmes, who killed it.

To Sally Jenkins: "thank you" falls so far short.

To Karen and the kids: *we* did it.

INDEX

Page numbers in *italics* refer to maps.